Sumatran Sultanate and Colonial State

Jambi and the Rise of Dutch Imperialism, 1830-1907

And on the deck of the drumming liner
Watching the furrow that widens behind you,
You shall not think "the past is finished"
Or "the future is before us."

T. S. Eliot, *Dry Salvages*

Elsbeth Locher-Scholten

Sumatran Sultanate and Colonial State

Jambi and the Rise of Dutch Imperialism, 1830-1907

Translated from the Dutch by Beverley Jackson

SOUTHEAST ASIA PROGRAM PUBLICATIONS
Southeast Asia Program
Cornell University
Ithaca, New York
2003

Cornell Southeast Asia Program Publications
640 Stewart Avenue, Ithaca, NY 14850-3857

Studies on Southeast Asia No. 37

Printed in the United States of America

ISBN 0-87727-736-2

TABLE OF CONTENTS

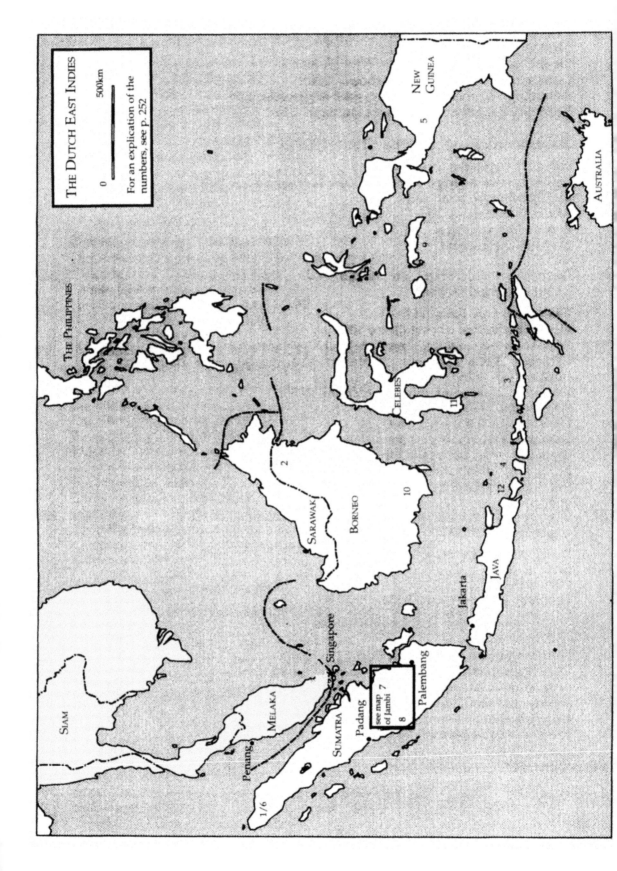

THE DUTCH EAST INDIES

0   500km

For an explication of the
numbers, see p. 252

NEW GUINEA

AUSTRALIA

THE PHILIPPINES

CELEBES

SARAWAK

BORNEO

SIAM

MELAKA

Penang

SUMATRA

Singapore

Padang

see map
of Jambi

Palembang

Jakarta

JAVA

1/6

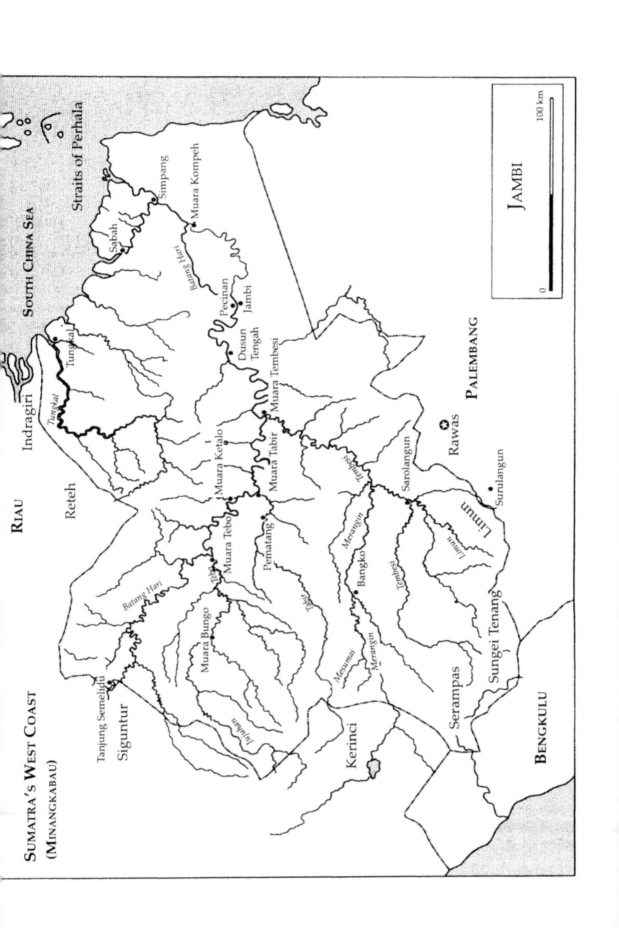

FOREWORD TO THE ENGLISH EDITION

On Thanksgiving Day 2000 I had reason to be especially thankful. It was on that evening that I met Dr. Audrey Kahin in Amsterdam. She suggested bringing my study of Jambi, published in Dutch in 1994, to the attention of Cornell University Southeast Asia Program Publications. The result of her initiative lies before you.

The Netherlands Organization for Scientific Research (NWO) financed this English translation. Beverley Jackson did the real work—she translated my book. She had been recommended to me by the most critical native speaker of English at KITLV Press, and it proved an excellent piece of advice. Thanks to Beverley, the process of seeing the translation unfold was more than a feast—or a frown—of recognition, it became a new intellectual exercise. Her critical questions about ambiguous points, elliptical sentences, and abrupt conclusions led to a more sharply focused narrative. Her feeling for language and her enthusiastic response to the sometimes dramatic and sometimes amusing developments in the relations between the Jambian sultan's administration and the Dutch colonial authorities could not but enhance the text. I should like to thank Beverley Jackson, Audrey Kahin, and the NWO for their key role in making this book a reality. I also want to express my gratitude to my Dutch-American friend and colleague Frances Gouda, who hosted the auspicious Thanksgiving dinner in 2000. Her intellectual fire and moral support were a great help when I was wrestling with the final chapters of the book.

This English text is substantially the same as the Dutch publication of 1994. New literature is cited only in the case of manuscripts that have since been published and English translations of works consulted in Dutch for the original text.

PREFACE

In the Indonesian archipelago, Dutch imperialism—if it can be defined as such, for precisely this controversy will be addressed in these pages—has been discussed from many angles, including economic theories, economic history, and foreign policy. One approach that was previously lacking, however, was that of a case study of the relations between the colonial government of the East Indies and a specific region, followed over an extended period of time. The present book sets out to fill that gap by exploring the relations between Batavia and the South Sumatran sultanate of Jambi in the period 1830–1907, with an epilogue on the years 1907–49.

My interest in this sultanate dates from 1980, when I taught a course on the abolition of the sultan's administration in Jambi in 1901. Since then, the colonial relations with the region have continued to fascinate me. It is a multifaceted field embracing theories of modern imperialism, foreign intervention, the piratical exploits of the American adventurer Walter Murray Gibson, the avoidance behavior that Sultan Taha managed to sustain for decades, the role played by oil, war, and guerrilla activities, and finally, between 1945 and 1949, the development of a pro-Dutch and anti-Republican separatism. This subject, which continually turns established assumptions on their head, offered a fine cross-section of more than a century of Dutch colonialism in the region.

This book begins with a theoretical chapter on themes, theories, and issues bearing on modern imperialism and the precolonial state, raising questions to which the conclusion, after the eight narrative chapters in between, suggests answers. The book finishes, in the epilogue, with a brief sequel, an account of Jambi's history in the years after the Jambi War.

Two chapters have appeared in a slightly different form elsewhere: chapter 7 in *Modern Asian Studies* 27 (1993), and part of the conclusion in the *Journal of Southeast Asian Studies* 25 (1994) (reprinted in *South East Asia: Colonial History*, vol. 2, *Empire-Building during the Nineteenth Century*, ed. Paul H. Kratoska [2001]). The conferences for which these chapters were written as papers (the Tenth Kota Conference in Amsterdam, 1990, and a seminar held at the Woodrow Wilson Center in Washington, D.C., 1991) sharpened my insight into the processes described. Classes on Dutch imperialism that I taught in Leiden and Utrecht in 1980, 1987, and 1991 provided an added impetus to explore the subject in greater depth. Students made their own contribution to this work with their critical questions and observations.

Although research is a solitary activity, it always relies on the cooperation of others. I should like to thank Sierk Plantenga and his colleagues at the reading room at the National Archives (NA) in the Hague for their help in making available what were sometimes cartloads of indexes and archives. I am also very grateful to Rini Hogewoning and her staff at the reading room of the KITLV for providing assistance and giving me the benefit of their expertise.

Dr. Sander Adelaar and Mr. Husni Rahiem helped me to read some of the texts in Jawi, for which I should like to express my gratitude. Partly thanks to a grant from the Ministry of Education and Science and with the cooperation of the Indonesian Institute of Sciences (LIPI), I was able to spend a brief period of time in Jakarta in 1985 to conduct research at the National Archives of Indonesia (Arsip Nasional Republik Indonesia, ANRI). Besides providing useful additions to my Dutch archival material, that visit led to enjoyable exchanges with my Indonesian counterpart Dr. Adri Lapian and inspiring debates with Professor Han Resink. My visit to Jambi that year gave me a keen physical sense of the region's history, which was enhanced by the tour of the province with Mr. M. Nazif, director of the Museum Negeri Jambi. Without this Indonesian context, for which I am very grateful to all those concerned, I would have written an entirely different book.

By commenting on earlier versions of the text, a number of fellow historians—Petra Groen, Maarten Kuitenbrouwer, Luc Nagtegaal, Tessel Pollmann, and Barbara Watson Andaya—prevented me from becoming too entrenched in my own habitual mode of thought. I am truly grateful to all of them. For the end result, of course, I bear sole responsibility; nor would I wish it otherwise.

CHAPTER ONE

THEMES AND THEORIES

Was there a Dutch imperialism? Did the Netherlands take part in the historical process of "modern imperialism," by which we denote the dividing up of the Afro-Asian world by the Western powers between 1870 and 1914? Does the expansion of Dutch sovereignty in the Indonesian archipelago after 1870—and at an accelerated pace after 1890—deserve to be ranked under this heading? Or should "the pacification of the Outer Islands," as the old historiography euphemistically called it, be viewed as a unique, quintessentially Dutch phenomenon?

These are the central questions addressed in this book. The scholarly debate on Dutch imperialism did not get under way until the 1970s. And only since 1985 has the Netherlands been seen by some—not all—as a fully fledged participant in this historical arena.[1] The debate has led to conflicting conclusions and renewed interest in the many specific examples of Dutch expansion in the Outer Islands, as they are called (i.e., the archipelago excluding Java) between 1890 and 1914. The following study of the relationship between the East Indies government at Batavia and the Sumatran sultanate of Jambi should be seen in this context. The relationship is illustrative of Dutch imperialism, as I shall call it straight away for brevity's sake, and of reactions to it on the part of the indigenous population.

This book covers the period from 1830 to 1949. It starts with the events leading to the conclusion of the first contract in 1833 and includes the ousting of the sultan from power (1901), the Jambi War (1901–07) and the introduction of direct rule (1906), with an epilogue defining key events up to 1949. In the conclusion, developments in Jambi are compared to those in other parts of the archipelago around 1900 and viewed in the light of recent research findings. An examination of this context is highly relevant, since a concrete example of Dutch expansion—Jambi in this case—can be used as a touchstone for theories of Dutch imperialism only if it is demonstrably characteristic of relations between Batavia and local princes, and hence is illustrative of the Netherlands' brand of modern imperialism.

[1] M. Kuitenbrouwer, The Netherlands and the Rise of Modern Imperialism: Colonies and Foreign Policy, 1870–1902 (New York: Berg, 1991); J. van Goor, ed., Imperialisme in de marge: De afronding van Nederlands-Indië (Utrecht: HES, 1986); H. L. Wesseling "Bestond er een Nederlands imperialisme?" Tijdschrift voor Geschiedenis 99 (1986): 214–25; H. L. Wesseling, Indië verloren, rampspoed geboren en andere opstellen over de geschiedenis van de Europese expansie (Amsterdam: Bert Bakker, 1988); H. L. Wesseling, "The Giant That Was a Dwarf, or the Strange History of Dutch Imperialism," in Theory and Practice in the History of European Expansion: Essays in Honour of Ronald Robinson, ed. A. Porter and R. Holland, special issue of Journal of Imperial and Commonwealth History 16 (1987–88): 58–70; H. L. Wesseling, "Colonial Wars: An Introduction," in Imperialism and War: Essays on Colonial Wars in Asia and Africa, ed. J. A. de Moor and H. L. Wesseling (Leiden: Brill/Leiden University Press, 1989), pp. 1–11.

Why the little-known Jambi and not a larger Sumatran sultanate such as Siak or Aceh? Jambi, today a province of the Republic of Indonesia, was a relatively small and insignificant *kerajaan,* or sultanate, in the nineteenth century. Early colonial historians give the impression that it was almost by chance that the Dutch established an administrative presence there in the early 1830s. But events in the marginal possessions are particularly illuminating; the "neglected islands of history" can enhance our understanding of historical processes.[2] The history of Dutch relations with this sultanate illustrates the entire gamut of motives cited by theories of modern imperialism to explain the expansionist drive: economic factors, fear of competition from other countries, administrative aspirations, scholarly interest, and ideological arguments. Furthermore, the relations were consolidated as early as 1833, fulfilling the criterion of extended periodization that is emphasized in the recent historiography of modern imperialism.[3] The protracted period makes it possible to make an in-depth historical analysis of the history of colonial relations with a local sultanate, an analysis that brings out the separate layers with their different colors and illustrates colonial practice.

One final reason for focusing on Jambi is the fact that Sultan Ratu Taha Safiuddin (1855–1904) was proclaimed a national hero of Indonesia in 1977 for his enduring opposition to colonial rule.[4] When Dutch troops ousted him from his throne in 1858, he continued to act as sultan from his new upstream capital. His policy vis-à-vis his powerful opponent, Batavia, is therefore a rewarding object of study.

A regional study in the true sense of the term proved not to be feasible. This historical genre, which has enjoyed a vogue since the 1960s in response to calls for an Indonesia-centered historiography,[5] can only be practiced when the sources supply more detailed material on the local situation than those available for Jambi. Since the latter, almost exclusively, are derivatives of the ties between Batavia and Jambi, what these pages describe is first and foremost the history of a relationship. Critical perusal of these sources, however, does shed light on the other side of the colonial story, the Jambian vantage point.

SOURCES

Anyone wanting to study this area is primarily reliant on colonial records. The most important source material derives from the records of the Ministry of Colonies in the National Archives (NA) in The Hague. These records are fairly informative concerning the years 1840-70, and even more so for the period after 1870. The absence of any information on the years before 1840 made other sets of records

---

[2] Marshall Sahlins, *Islands of History* (Chicago: University of Chicago Press 1985), p. 2.

[3] See below and J. Gallagher and R. Robinson, "The Imperialism of Free Trade," *Economic History Review,* 2nd ser., 6,1 (1953): 1–15; R. F. Betts, *The False Dawn: European Imperialism in the Nineteenth Century* (Minneapolis: University of Minnesota Press, 1975); D. K. Fieldhouse, *Economics and Empire 1830–1914,* 2nd ed. (London: Macmillan, 1984).

[4] Kamajaya, *Delapan Raja-Raja Pahlawan Nasional, Buku I.* (Yogya: U. P. Indonesia, 1981), pp. 33–40; *Album 86 Pahlawan Nasional* (Jakarta: Bahtera Jaya, 1985), p. 18.

[5] J. R. W. Smail, "On the Possibility of an Autonomous History of Modern Southeast Asia," *Journal of Southeast Asian History* 2,2 (1961): 72–102; H. A. J. Klooster, *Indonesiërs schrijven hun geschiedenis: De ontwikkeling van de Indonesische geschiedbeoefening in theorie en praktijk, 1900–1980* (Dordrecht: Foris, 1986).

indispensable: those of the General Secretariat (*Algemene secretarie*, the governor-general's office) and the Residency of Palembang in Indonesia's own national archives (ANRI). [rephrased] As for the local records of the Residency of Jambi, some were burned before the arrival of the Japanese occupying force and the rest by the Japanese themselves, so that none of them, unfortunately, have been preserved.[6]

In his 1987 study *Orientalism*, Edward Said gave a clear analysis of the distortions built into this colonial source material. Europeans, in this case the Dutch, assessed the local population by their own standards and generally wrote their reports and accounts in justification of their own policy.[7] What is more, colonial records are rather like newspapers, in that they focus on subjects that they view as problems. The bulk of the material in the colonial archives relates to questions that troubled the colonial authorities' minds. Little was written about Jambi in uneventful times—the 1840s and early 1850s, the years 1860–78, and the 1880s. The most important material dates from the 1830s, the time of the first confrontations and the first contracts; from the late 1850s, when a second military expedition ousted Sultan Taha; from the years 1878–80, when the scientific expedition of the Royal Dutch Geographical Society focused attention on this area again, and from the years of the "final reckoning," the Jambi War from 1901 to 1907.

Unfortunately, the other parts in the colonial chorus are missing. Malay sources on the region are extremely rare. Whatever documents existed in Jambi about the earlier forms of government and previous borders were burned by Dutch troops during the storming of the *kraton* (palace) in 1858.[8] Very little remains: two statute books, or *undang-undang*,[9] some legends and genealogies of the sultan's line and its history, two stories about internal wars in the first two decades of the previous century, and a few accounts of Dutch journeys to Jambi dating from 1852, 1861, and 1878. All these sources appear to have been prepared in response to Dutch requests seeking to gain a better grasp of the internal situation in Jambi. Some date from 1837-38, when the local envoy who had maintained contact with Jambi in 1832–33 recorded what he knew. Others come from the estate of Resident J. A. W. van Ophuijsen (1861–62 and 1867–70), who visited Jambi on several occasions while

---

[6] Report issued by Assistant Resident Lieutenant-Colonel C. Monod de Froideville to the governor of Sumatra, October 20, 1945, National Archives (NA), The Hague, Col., Algemene Secretarie (General Secretariat) 3133.

[7] Edward Said, *Orientalism*, 3rd ed. (London: Penguin, 1987).

[8] Travel account by Resident of Palembang to governor-general, *Reisverslag* 1861, NA, Col., *verbaal* (file, hereafter "vb."), November 2, 1878, no. 7.

[9] L. W. C. van den Berg, "Rechtsbronnen van Zuid-Sumatra, uitgegeven, vertaald en toegelicht door L. W. C. van den Berg," *Bijdragen tot de Taal-, Land- en Volkenkunde* 43 (1894): 123–96; C. A. Van Ophuijsen, "Eenige opmerkingen naar aanleiding van de door Prof. Mr. L. W. C. van den Berg bezorgde uitgave van de Oendang-Oendang Djambi," *Bijdragen tot de Taal-, Land- en Volkenkunde* 46 (1896): 153–213.

serving in Palembang, and from the records of the expedition to Central Sumatra of 1877–78. With one exception, they all appear to have been written after 1833.[10]

Little has been written on the history of Jambi.[11] E. B. Kielstra, the Netherlands' imperial historian, wrote briefly on the overthrow of the sultanate of Jambi, which he had supported as early as 1887.[12] Hendrik Colijn devoted a few words to Jambi in his voluminous report of 1907–09 concerning policy on the Outer Islands.[13] The most important general study on Jambi from before the Second World War, by Tideman and Sigar, however, contains only a few pages on its history, which are, unfortunately, rich in errors and misrepresentations.[14] What is more, all these works are written from the same perspective and pursue the same goal—to justify the expansion of Dutch rule over Jambi.

However, the age in which Europeans could describe their expansionist drive as a natural and justifiable exercise of power over an empty and amorphous region, or even assert that the colonial presence was welcomed by the local population, is long past. Traditional colonial studies have had their day; they can only serve as a source for critical historians and as illustrations of the colonial mentality. Recent studies of Jambi, embracing more modern principles of scholarship and written from a more Indonesian-centered perspective, are few and far between. *To Live as Brothers: Southeast Sumatra in the Seventeenth and Eighteenth Centuries* by the Australian historian Barbara Watson Andaya, which deals with Palembang and Jambi, appeared roughly at the same time as the Dutch version of this book.[15] Watson Andaya's research has also yielded several fascinating articles.[16] Yang Aisyah Muttalib's dissertation on the Jambi War of 1901–07 and the revolt of 1916 was published earlier, but only in abbreviated form.[17]

---

[10] H. H. Juynboll, *Catalogus van de Maleische en Soendaneesche handschriften der Leidsche Universiteits Bibliotheek* (Leiden: Brill, 1899); P. S. van Ronkel, *Supplement-catalogus der Maleische en Minangkabausche handschriften in de Leidsche Universiteitsbibliotheek* (Leiden: Brill, 1921); Van den Berg, "Rechtsbronnen van Zuid-Sumatra"; Van Ophuyzen, "Eenige Opmerkingen."

[11] Whatever exists by way of older unpublished material may be ascertained from J. W. J. Wellan and O. L. Helfrich, *Zuid-Sumatra: Overzicht van de literatuur der gewesten Bengkoelen, Djambi, de Lampongsche Districten en Palembang*, 2 vols. (The Hague: Smits, 1923, 1938).

[12] E. B. Kielstra, "De uitbreiding van het Nederlandsch gezag op Sumatra," *De Gids* 51,4 (1887): 256–96; E. B. Kielstra, *Indisch Nederland* (Haarlem: Bohn, 1910), pp. 242–83; E. B. Kielstra, *De vestiging van het Nederlandsche gezag in den Indischen archipel* (Haarlem: Bohn, 1920), pp. 136–41.

[13] *Politiek beleid en bestuurszorg in de buitenbezittingen*, 4 vols. (Batavia: Landsdrukkerij, 1907–09), 2: 1–17.

[14] J. Tideman and P. L. F. Sigar, *Djambi* (Amsterdam: Koloniaal Instituut, 1938), pp. 28–42.

[15] B. Watson Andaya, *To Live as Brothers: Southeast Sumatra in the Seventeenth and Eighteenth Centuries* (Honolulu: University of Hawaii Press, 1993).

[16] B. Watson Andaya, "The Cloth Trade in Jambi and Palembang Society during the Seventeenth and Eighteenth Centuries," *Indonesia* 48 (1989): 26–46; B. Watson Andaya, "Cash Cropping and Upstream-Downstream Tensions: The Case of Jambi in the Seventeenth and Eighteenth Centuries," in *Southeast Asia in the Early Modern Era: Trade, Power and Belief*, ed. A. Reid (Ithaca, N.Y.: Cornell University Press, 1993), pp. 91–122.

[17] Jang Aisjah Muttalib, "Jambi 1900–1916: From War to Rebellion" (PhD diss., Columbia University, 1977); Jang Aisjah Muttalib, "Suatu Tinjauan Mengenai Beberapa Gerakan Sosial Di Jambi Pada Perempatan Pertama Abad Ke 20," *Prisma* 8 (1980): 26–37.

The structure and sources of the present study will provide a constant shift of viewpoint. One moment we shall be discussing the sultan's policies vis-à-vis the government; then the stage shifts to colonial politics in Batavia or to foreign policy in The Hague, when the latter was influenced by developments in Jambi. These three levels—the micro-level of the region itself, the meso-level of Batavia, and the macro-level of The Hague—determined the history of the relationship in mutual interaction.[18] But before drawing the curtain to reveal this three-tiered action, we should first look at some of the questions and theoretical considerations underlying this dramatization of the Jambi-Dutch-Indonesian past.

THEORIES OF MODERN IMPERIALISM

Modern imperialism is a term used in historiography to describe the period from about 1870 or 1880 to 1914, in which Western powers seized power over non-Western territories, in particular the Afro-Asian world. "Imperialism" is a term with a long history and multiple meanings. Besides its primary denotation of various types of dominance and asymmetrical power relations, it is sometimes used simply as a term of abuse for exploitation.[19] What is more, political scientists and historians use the term in different ways. The following discussion will confine itself to the usage within the field of history, which itself yields ample material for discussion.

Although the phenomenon of imperialism has been consigned to the past, the academic battle over its causes and background factors, over motives and results, has been raging for almost a hundred years, and no end is in sight. An overview of all the international theories of imperialism raised in this long debate would go beyond the scope of this book. Several fine surveys already exist.[20] But it is useful to single out a few contrasts in schools of thought:

- the distinction between "economists" and "political generalists"—between those who insist on the primacy of economic explanatory models and those who base their explanations on international diplomatic rivalries or domestic affairs;
- the distinction between those who identify 1870 or 1880 as a clear turning point and those who believe that developments followed a longer and more continuous line;
- the distinction between Eurocentrists and "peripherists," that is, between those who seek causes in the mother countries and those who seek them in the "periphery," the colonies themselves.

---

[18] C. Fasseur, "Een koloniale paradox: De Nederlandse expansie in de Indonesische archipel in het midden van de negentiende eeuw (1830–1870)," *Tijdschrift voor Geschiedenis* 92 (1979): 162–87.

[19] R. Koebner and H. D. Schmid, *Imperialism: The Story and Significance of a Political Word, 1840–1960* (Cambridge: Cambridge University Press, 1960).

[20] W. Baumgart, *Der Imperialismus: Idee und Wirklichkeit der englischen und französischen Kolonialexpansion 1880–1914* (Wiesbaden: Steiner, 1975); Betts, *False Dawn*; W. J. Mommsen, *Der europäische Imperialismus: Aufsätze und Abhandlungen* (Göttingen: Vandenhoeck und Ruprecht, 1979); W. J. Mommsen, *Imperialismustheorien: Ein Überblick über die neueren Imperialismusinterpretationen*, 2nd ed. (Göttingen: Vandenhoeck und Ruprecht, 1980); M. Kuitenbrouwer, *The Netherlands and Imperialism*.

The initial efforts to define, explain, and periodize imperialism were formulated in terms of economic arguments. The earliest theories stressed the interests of capital. In 1902 the British historian John Hobson launched the debate with his *Imperialism: A Study,* which examined the Boer War. His thesis was that Britain's expansionist drive in South Africa was fueled by the interests of British capital. But whether it was British capital exports, as Hobson maintained,[21] or the interests of monopoly capital, according to Rudolf Hilferding,[22] or a combination of the two, as in Lenin's model,[23] capital always preceded the flag. Other explanations were based on commercial economics, positing that growing international competition boosted the domestic demand for raw materials and markets.[24] It should be borne in mind that these early explanations of imperialism did not spring from any concern for the victims of expansion. Both Hobson and Lenin were highly Eurocentric in their approach. According to Hobson, investment in the colonies caused underconsumption in Britain, with all the adverse consequences for British workers this entailed. Lenin regarded this imperialism with its investments in colonial territories (including Russian expansion in Central Asia) as the epitome of capitalism. This complicated the debate: imperialism was seen not as a race for the colonies but as a phase in the development of monopoly capital within a particular—Western—economic order.[25]

The economic or Marxist gauntlet was taken up by historians with a pragmatic bent, who analyzed concrete cases and found that the alleged link between capital and expansion did not always withstand scrutiny. There was no connection, for instance, between the countries targeted by British capital, which were in Latin America, and expansion. These scholars also noted that colonies often made a loss, although investors may of course have had high expectations to begin with.[26] In any case, the link between economics and imperialism turned out to be less direct than the frequently rather simplistic analyses had suggested. More recent studies confirm this. In their book published in 1986, L. Davis and R. Huttenback used computerized calculations to demonstrate something that had been shown before, though in a less statistical fashion: that the colonies were not the main recipients of British capital, and that after 1880 the profits made on colonial investments lagged behind those made on investments in the United Kingdom or the dominions. Their mammoth calculations also revealed, however, that British imperialism resulted in a transfer of income from the British middle classes, who paid for the expansion, to the upper class (the landed gentry in southern England and the

---

[21] J. A. Hobson, *Imperialism: A Study* (London: Allen and Unwin, 1902).

[22] Rudolf Hilferding, *Finance Capital: A Study of the Latest Phase of Capitalist Development,* ed. Tom Bottomore, trans. Morris Watnick and Sam Gordon (London: Routledge and Kegan Paul, 1981).

[23] V. I. Lenin, *Imperialism: The Highest Stage of Capitalism* (New York: International Publishers, 1977).

[24] *Studies in the Theory of Imperialism,* ed. R. Owen and B. Sutcliffe (London: Longman, 1972), pp. 15–35.

[25] T. Kemp, "The Marxist Theory of Imperialism," in *Studies in the Theory of Imperialism,* ed. R. Owen and B. Sutcliffe (London: Longman, 1972), pp. 15–35.

[26] D. K. Fieldhouse, "'Imperialism': An Historiographical Revision," *Economic History Review,* 2nd ser., 14,2 (1961): 187–209.

economic elite of the City of London), who plucked the economic fruits of it.[27] It may well have been the profits made by the "cream" of British society that inspired Hobson and others to develop their theories.

The "political generalists" rejected this stress on economic motives, postulating instead the primacy of foreign policy.[28] In their view, the political rivalries between Europe's two major industrial powers, Britain and France, and between France and the new German Reich, were the decisive factors in the race for the colonies. This view was developed by several scholars after the Second World War, both in Britain and in France.[29] In the words of D. K. Fieldhouse's terse summary, "Imperialism may best be seen as the extension into the periphery of the political struggle in Europe."[30] Studies with a narrower, national focus incorporated the riposte to the economic theorists, demonstrating that each country had its own mix of decisive motives.[31] Marxists too revised their theories on the basis of national examples. In his book on Bismarck in 1969, H. U. Wehler remarked that the chancellor thought joining the race for the colonies a crucial distraction from domestic tensions, which had been generated by uneven industrial growth and the associated unequal distribution of incomes in Germany.[32] Wehler was not the only proponent of a model based on "social imperialism." British and American writers too had emphasized domestic political factors.[33]

Exponents and opponents of the economic model agreed on the date when the race began. The large-scale carving up of the world started in 1880, with some anticipatory movements in the 1870s. This implies that Europe changed its orientation toward the non-Western world around this time. Having previously focused largely on regions of white settlement such as Canada, Australia, and Latin America, it shifted its attention to Africa and Asia in the 1880s. Writing in 1953, the British historians R. Robinson and J. Gallagher pointed out, that Britain's relations with overseas territories displayed a large measure of continuity. While trade remained the prime objective, the methods adopted to achieve it gradually changed from "informal" to "formal" imperialism.[34] Far from uncontroversial, this view is still being criticized today.[35] Yet the attention it draws to certain

---

[27] See L. Davis and R. Huttenback, *Mammon and the Pursuit of Empire: The Political Economy of British Imperialism, 1860–1917* (Cambridge: Cambridge University Press, 1986); see also P. J. Cain and A. G. Hopkins, "Gentlemanly Capitalism and British Expansion Overseas, I: The Old Colonial System, 1688–1850," *Economic History Review*, 2nd ser., 39,4 (1986): 501–25; P. J. Cain and A. G. Hopkins, "Gentlemanly Capitalism and British Expansion Overseas, II: New Imperialism, 1850–1945," *Economic History Review*, 2nd ser., 40,1 (1987): 1–26.

[28] See, for example , W. L. Langer, *The Diplomacy of Imperialism, 1890–1902*, 2nd ed. (New York: Knopf, 1972).

[29] H. Brunschwig, *Mythes et réalités de l'impérialisme colonial français, 1870–1914* (Paris: Colin, 1960); Fieldhouse, "Imperialism."

[30] Fieldhouse, "Imperialism," quoted in Betts, *False Dawn*, p. 249.

[31] For Britain this argument was the need to defend its interests in India, for France it was nationalism in the form of revenge after its defeat in the Franco-Prussian War, while Germany's ambitions tend to be discussed in terms of social imperialism.

[32] H. U. Wehler, *Bismarck und der Imperialismus* (Cologne: Kiepenhauer und Witsch, 1969).

[33] See, for example, B. Semmel, *Imperialism and Social Reform: English Social-Imperialist Thought 1895–1914* (London: Allen and Unwin, 1960).

[34] Gallagher and Robinson, "Imperialism of Free Trade."

[35] Cain and Hopkins, "Gentlemanly Capitalism," pts. 1 and 2.

continuities in the nineteenth-century process of expansion presents distinct heuristic advantages.

The above paragraphs have shown that theories of modern imperialism tend to fall into three rival lines, according to an emphasis on economic factors, international politics, and the domestic social and political balance of power. The three schools of thought have one thing in common, however: they are all Eurocentric. The conquest of the world was a European venture, and it was explained in terms of European causes and factors.

However, with decolonization came a parallel trend in scholarly views of imperialism. In the 1960s the gaze shifted away from Europe to the "Third World," placing the colonial past in a new light. Researchers turned their attention to local élites and their roles in the process of European expansion. The old Eurocentric views prompted enquiries into the influence of the white colonists and of colonial societies as such. Certain pressure groups, such as soldiers, traders and administrative officials, were found to have displayed forms of sub-imperialist behavior in the colonies, especially around the "turbulent frontier." The power vacuum along the borders of colonial territories and the resulting unrest were identified as causes of imperialism. Europeans, it was now maintained, had been "sucked" into new areas in order to protect existing conquests, often against the wishes of the government of the non-expansionist mother country.[36]

Like the colonial élites, the local élites were also "decolonized." Back in 1960 J. D. Hargreaves had already pointed to this missing link in the history of the carving up of Africa.[37] Robinson elaborated this issue further in an analysis of the expansion of British rule in Egypt in the 1880s. He regarded imperialism as "a political function of the process of integrating some countries at some times into the international economy."[38] Whether or not this integration took place through political control depended, in his view, on the nature of the cooperation (or collaboration) by the native elite. The less European the latter's political and economic institutions, the less likely they were to steer clear of direct European control. Whether and when European control was introduced was thus determined not by Europe but by the Afro-Asian context. Imperialism, states Robinson, "was as much and often more a function of Afro-Asian politics than of European politics and economics."[39] From this viewpoint, it was often not even the product of European influences but of autonomous changes in domestic politics in parts of Africa and Asia.

This "collaboration theory" was the first to focus squarely on the Afro-Asian world. It also explained why so few Europeans—often a mere handful—were able to continue ruling over the non-European world: under pressure, and with a shift in the balance of power, the native elite proved willing to cooperate. It also explained why colonial rule came to an end when a new, nationalist elite

---

[36] J. S. Galbraith, "The 'Turbulent Frontier' as a Factor in British Expansion," *Comparative Studies in Society and History* 2 (1960): 150–68.

[37] Betts, *False Dawn*, p. 250; J. D. Hargreaves, "Towards a History of the Partition of Africa," *Journal of African History* 1 (1960): 96–109.

[38] R. Robinson, "Non-European Foundations of European Imperialism: Sketch for a Theory of Collaboration," in *Studies in the Theory of Imperialism*, ed. R. Owen and B. Sutcliffe (London: Longman, 1972), p. 117.

[39] Robinson, "Non-European Foundations," p. 139.

withdrew their cooperation. Furthermore, the shift of attention to the colonies themselves put an end to the fruitless tug-of-war between the economic and political explanations within the development of Eurocentric theories.[40]

The most recent surveys summarize and integrate these topics.[41] Here too, the monocausal school of thought has given way to the new academic paradigm of "configurations" or "networks," the pattern of interdependent factors underlying any new phenomenon. R. F. Betts emphasizes European motives, but without disregarding the periphery. He too stresses continuity. More central to his work, however, are two other concepts: contiguity and preemption. "Contiguity" alludes to geographical context: the new expansion was generally directed from older settlements, and local factors could be crucial. Betts's second key concept, "preemption," is purely Eurocentric. The goal of expansion was often to be one step ahead of other European powers; it was "imperialism as a precautionary measure," with fear playing a key role. Betts emphasizes this psychological factor more than others; he even refers to an "imperialism of anxiety," a term that encapsulates the international competition between the European powers.[42] Given this focus on Europe, it is not surprising that Maarten Kuitenbrouwer drew on Betts in his study of Dutch foreign and colonial politics between 1870 and 1901. For a case study of this kind, however, which focuses on the periphery, the British historian Fieldhouse presents a better point of departure.

In his *Economics and Empire, 1830–1914*, a voluminous book on modern imperialism, Fieldhouse adopts a firm position on the three topics mentioned above. He too inclines toward continuity, and he too sees modern imperialism as a product of earlier trade and colonial relations. However, unlike Gallagher and Robinson, he does not reduce empire simply to an imperialism of free trade, but sketches a more complex pattern. European countries or companies had substantial interests, whether economic, political, or religious, almost everywhere—even in the "empty" continent of Africa. Hence European expansion was "the end of an old story, not the start of a new one."[43] Only "the speed and universality of the European advance" were new, not "the mere fact that it happened."

Secondly, and this is not without relevance to the present study, Fieldhouse distances himself from a strictly Eurocentric explanation and highlights the role of the periphery. He denies that European statesmen had "a clear vision of universal empire" before 1880; an imperialist ideology was developed later, either during or after the event. He consequently rejects any suggestion of an imperialist master plan in the mother country or of a calculated imperialist policy, and sees the shift in the continuity of relations as the result of crises in the periphery. He defines the cause of this change, which he situates around 1880, as the disturbed balance of power between Europe and what is now known as the developing world—"a profound change in the pathology of international relations." The Afro-Asian structures could no longer meet Europe's growing need for economic and political ties. The colonial empires arose as a result of impromptu responses to rapidly spiraling crises in the periphery: European statesmen could think of no other reaction than formal occupation. Fieldhouse comments almost *en passant* that the expansion of

---

[40] Kuitenbrouwer, *The Netherlands and Imperialism*, p. 11.

[41] Betts, *False Dawn*; Fieldhouse, *Economics and Empire*.

[42] Betts, *False Dawn*, pp. 81–83; Kuitenbrouwer, *The Netherlands and Imperialism*, pp. 16–17.

[43] Fieldhouse, *Economics and Empire*, p. 460.

European activities in the periphery was partly responsible for these crises, implying that it was Europe, after all, that determined the imperialist agenda. Still, in his analysis imperialism was primarily a consequence of "crisis and coincidence in the periphery . . . . Europe was pulled into imperialism by the magnetic force of the periphery."[44]

In his third conclusion, Fieldhouse reassesses the role of the economy. Revising his earlier views,[45] he accords it a definite place. Almost every act of expansion has economic facets, he maintains. However, European governments were prepared to solve *economic* problems in the periphery by empire building only when they gave rise to *political* problems. Economic factors would first have to be politicized, or believed to jeopardize the national interest, before they triggered expansion. Before 1880, the European powers preferred to solve such problems through negotiation, limited military action, and—loose—territorial control. After 1880 they increasingly favored the last. This was partly because of the growing number of conflicts in the periphery. As existing trends and rivalries intensified, it became more common for economic activities to generate political problems. Increasingly, government leaders saw expansion as the most efficient remedy.[46]

Thus Fieldhouse's model accommodates all the traditional Eurocentric motives: economic, international, and national. Still, the importance he accords to the role of the periphery should not be overemphasized. It was Europe, with its industrial revolution, that caused the disturbance in the balance of power, and Europe that determined whether and when the Afro-Asian context made expansion necessary. What is more, Fieldhouse himself measures the Afro-Asian world by European standards, namely, the degree to which it was able and willing to cooperate with the European powers. On the one hand his "periphery" approach provides insight into the role played by the "frontier" and the indigenous society in the process of European expansion, and into the effects of growing ties between different cultures. On the other hand, however, it has the considerable disadvantage of obscuring the fact that the balance of power was heavily weighted on the European side.

One particular merit of these new models is that they broke down the linear link between economic factors and Europe's actions. What emerges is a far more subtle causality than was customary in traditional exegeses. Imperialism is no longer viewed as a deliberate policy of expansion devised by the mother country, specifically arising from the economic interests of a small group in that country. Instead, it is seen as a complex and nuanced interplay between West and non-West, between the center and periphery, and among the Western powers. This vision divests imperialism of both its monocausal and its monolithic character. As national studies of the subject have shown, the hierarchy of the determining factors and their interrelationship differed from one country to the next. From this vantage point, the colorful historical reality is shown to better advantage. With his choice of time span, his emphasis on the periphery, and his nuanced view of the economic motives, Fieldhouse's comprehensive approach provides a valuable heuristic model for a study of the expansion of Dutch rule in the Indonesian

---

[44] Ibid., pp. 460–63.

[45] Fieldhouse, "Imperialism."

[46] Fieldhouse, *Economics and Empire*, p. 476.

archipelago in general, and in Jambi in particular. For here too, it is the dynamic of the periphery that is the central issue.

MODERN IMPERIALISM AND THE NETHERLANDS

How does the Dutch expansion of around 1900 fit into this imperialism debate, and to what extent can the "completion of the Dutch East Indies"[47] be regarded as the Dutch variant of modern imperialism? The debate on these issues—characteristically for the Netherlands—started relatively late. The general theories tend to gloss over the Netherlands. It was not one of the great powers traditionally highlighted as the authors of imperialism. Nor did it participate in the carving up of Africa, in relation to which modern imperialism was first conceptualized; on the contrary, it ceded its last African colony (Elmina on the Gold Coast) to Great Britain in 1871. Moreover, its expansion was one to two decades later than that of the other powers: its expansionist drive in Asia did not come until the 1890s—and then it operated within its own nominally recognized frontiers of the Indonesian archipelago. Finally, it claimed to be motivated by a desire to promote the welfare and edification of the population; driven by this "ethical policy," it was supposedly "pacifying," not conquering. For a long time, this ideological stalking horse obfuscated the similarities and differences between the general process of Western expansion and its Dutch variant.[48] So the Netherlands was a special case for three reasons: its late start, its expansion within its own frontiers, and its ethical pretensions. However, there is also a more practical explanation for the exclusion of the Netherlands from international studies of imperialism. The relevant literature has tended to be written in Dutch, rendering the history of the Dutch East Indies inaccessible to most historians and theorists.

There was a clear need for a Dutch initiative to open up this field for academic debate. Yet it was not until 1970, at a conference of the Dutch Historical Society, that the first efforts were made to place Dutch expansion in a wider international theoretical framework.[49] The ensuing debate was just as lively as the earlier one on international imperialism. In 1980, Joep à Campo wrote a cogent article demonstrating that the traditional theories of economic imperialism could not account for Dutch expansion in the East Indies. Because of the Netherlands' late industrial revolution (after 1890), none of the conditions posited in these theories (a need for new markets for industrial products, a demand for new raw materials, trade monopolies, accumulation of capital in search of new investment) was present in a sufficient degree to explain a policy of colonial expansion. In fact, the dynamics of the process were rather the other way around: the colonial possessions initially retarded economic development, while later on, the economic expansion overseas stimulated Dutch industry.[50] À Campo therefore places Dutch

---

[47] The subtitle of Van Goor's book *Imperialisme in de marge*.

[48] Elsbeth Locher-Scholten, *Ethiek in fragmenten: Vijf studies over koloniaal denken en doen van Nederlanders in de Indonesische archipel 1877–1942* (Utrecht: HES, 1981), pp. 194–200; Kuitenbrouwer, *The Netherlands and Imperialism*, pp. 17–27.

[49] See the conference reports on "De Nederlandse expansie in Indonesië in de tijd van het moderne imperialisme," *Bijdragen en Mededelingen betreffende de Geschiedenis der Nederlanden* 86 (1971): 1–89.

[50] J. à Campo, "Orde, rust en welvaart: Over de Nederlandse expansie in de Indische Archipel omstreeks 1900," *Acta Politica* 15 (1980): 145–89, esp. 179.

imperialism in a wider, international framework. It was not the relations between the mother country and the colony that accounted for Dutch expansion after 1895, in his view, but those between the world market and the Dutch East Indies, with the Netherlands acting as a channel or intermediary. "In that sense, Dutch imperialism in the East Indies was a function of the development of the world market rather than of Dutch economic development."[51] He therefore regards Dutch imperialism in two respects as a reaction: the Netherlands reacted economically to the development of the world market, and politically to the imperialist race for the colonies. This proposition reconciles the apparent discrepancies between economic theories of imperialism and the historical development of Dutch imperialism.

With his Netherlands-centered study, à Campo implicitly authenticates Dutch expansion as a product of modern imperialism. Maarten Kuitenbrouwer does so more explicitly. On the basis of research into the Netherlands' foreign and colonial policies between 1870 and 1901, he concludes that there was, indeed, a Dutch imperialism. He acknowledges the applicability of Betts's concepts of "preemption" and "contiguity," while adding that this small-power imperialism had certain distinctive characteristics. It was based on a long tradition of colonial possession and was supported by nationalistically tinted "ethical" convictions. Still, with the exception of the 1880s, the same factors were relevant here as those identified elsewhere: international diplomatic competition, economic interests (especially anticipated profits), and activities in the periphery.[52]

Kuitenbrouwer's "authentication" was challenged within a year of its publication, however.[53] Clearly, whether or not the Netherlands was an imperialist country in the period in question is primarily a matter of definitions. According to the Leiden historian Henk Wesseling, Kuitenbrouwer misuses the terms "preemption" and "contiguity." The former Wesseling dismisses altogether as being inapplicable to the East Indies. In his view, "preemption" meant more than just occupying territories in order to be one step ahead of other powers. "Imperialism as a precautionary measure," he feels, should be interpreted as "an indiscriminate staking of claims out of a vague fear of being left out in the cold, of finding the world has already been divided up."[54] Wesseling considers this behavior typical of late arrivals or newcomers such as Germany, Italy, and Japan, but inapplicable to the Netherlands, which already possessed more than it felt it could govern and operated only within internationally recognized borders. Betts himself does refer to these newcomers but also gives examples of expansion that strongly recall the Dutch actions in the Indonesian archipelago.[55]

As for "contiguity," Wesseling does not consider this a true characteristic of modern imperialism, a stance that places him indirectly at odds with Betts. He argues that the primary feature of imperialism was obtaining power over areas

---

[51] Ibid., p. 178.

[52] Kuitenbrouwer, *The Netherlands and Imperialism*, pp. 204–05.

[53] Wesseling, "Bestond er een Nederlands imperialisme?" Wesseling, *Indië verloren;* Wesseling, "The Giant"; Wesseling, "Colonial Wars."

[54] Wesseling, *Indië verloren*, p. 188.

[55] We do find panic reactions caused by a fear of finding the door shut in the form of paper conquests in the Dutch East Indies, but these were earlier, in the 1840s and 1850s; see chapters 3 and 4.

with which countries had no common borders. The Netherlands, with its "contiguity," its expansion from a colonial center, was atypical in this respect.

What is more, Wesseling follows his colleague Ivo Schöffer in emphasizing continuity in policy on the East Indies.[56] He takes issue with Kuitenbrouwer's assertion that the Dutch embarked on a new policy of systematic expansion from about 1894–96 onward. In his view, imperialism means more than simply pushing back the frontiers of colonial rule. The point is not whether a country truly exercised power over Afro-Asian territory, but whether its claims were recognized by the great powers. From an international vantage point, nothing new happened in the archipelago: the borders of the East Indies were already recognized. The Netherlands was not making inroads into new territories. It did not evince a new imperialist mentality, nor did it have any autonomous motives for changing its policy. It did not so much act as react. Dutch expansion appears to have been "nothing more than a function of international politics. The only motive for Dutch imperialism was the imperialism of others." It was "secondary imperialism," a view that Wesseling shares with the early work of à Campo and others.[57]

Thus Wesseling is exclusively concerned with the new trend of an international scramble for territories, with the great powers undertaking new action and, fired by fresh fervor, claiming blank areas in the map of the world. In later versions of his first review, he pays more attention to recent nuances and acknowledges what he calls the "strange history of Dutch imperialism," with a gap in the 1890s.[58] But he persists in his objections to the terms used by Kuitenbrouwer and Betts.

It is certainly hard to fit the Netherlands into Wesseling's consistent but traditionally Eurocentric approach. But his views can be reassessed on the basis of the recent literature. Modern imperialism was not only about "annexation on paper" or "pegging out claims for the future" so as to be one step ahead of everyone else. After the Berlin Conference of 1884–85, it was also about the international requirement of "effective occupation."[59] Wesseling himself makes this point in his fine narrative on the dividing up of Africa: there was "paper partition" in the 1880s and "partition on the ground" afterward.[60] This appears to resolve the earlier disagreements. The expansion of Dutch rule over what had previously been nominally administered regions corresponds completely to this description, including its chronology.

Furthermore, Kuitenbrouwer is concerned not with expansion pure and simple but with the *systematic* nature of the expansion of colonial rule after 1894. Incidental punitive campaigns were a thing of the past: every flash point of unrest was immediately extinguished. After 1900, autonomous or independent rulers were no longer permitted to act on their own initiative. Recent research also reveals a

---

[56] Schöffer. I., "Dutch 'Expansion' and Indonesian Reactions: Some Dilemmas of Modern Colonial Rule (1900–1942)," in *Expansion and Reaction: Essays on European Expansion and Reaction in Asia and Africa*, ed. H. L. Wesseling (Leiden: Leiden University Press, 1978), pp. 78–99.

[57] Wesseling, *Indië verloren*, pp. 189–90; À Campo, "Orde, rust en welvaart," p. 180.

[58] Wesseling, "The Giant," p. 58.

[59] H. L. Wesseling, "Nederland en de Conferentie van Berlijn, 1884–1885," *Tijdschrift voor Geschiedenis* 93 (1980): 559–77.

[60] H. L. Wesseling, *Verdeel en heers: De deling van Afrika 1880–1914* (Amsterdam: Bert Bakker, 1991), p. 450.

shift in public opinion in the Netherlands in 1894. Here, too, a new national consciousness was emerging, that did not call in question the legitimacy of Dutch rule over the East Indies, particularly when it was justified by invoking motives of development and "ethical policies."[61] So for the Netherlands too we can identify autonomous motives, in particular a new national zeal, although these were certainly inspired in part by the imperialism of other nations.

Perhaps insisting on "autonomous motives," as Wesseling does, is in itself a questionable criterion; surely it is not just the motives that count, but the action of systematic expansion itself. A reaction to others' actions can lead to an identical action: a child straying out of bounds to copy her friends, or a thief stealing in emulation of those around him, is still straying or stealing, "autonomous motives" or not. To those responsible for judging them—parents or courts—the actions remain the same. Similarly, the Netherlands joined in—partly in reaction to other countries' behavior and partly for reasons of its own—the general pattern of "straying" or "stealing" in blank areas on the Indonesian map.[62]

Thomas Lindblad has also discussed Dutch policy in the East Indies as an instance of modern imperialism.[63] What is more, with his definition of imperialism as an "intensification of actual control" within a framework of "formal political domination," he bridges the gap between Wesseling (continuity) and Kuitenbrouwer (shift to a systematic expansion of control). In periodization too he adopts an intermediate position. While Cees Fasseur regards 1898 as the watershed year,[64] and Kuitenbrouwer inclines to 1894, Lindblad sees the years 1870–90 as a transitional period that witnessed the gradual abandonment of the traditional policy of abstention from interference in the Outer Islands without any radical change of policy. His analysis of the microeconomic and macroeconomic changes in the Indonesian archipelago around 1900 leads him to conclude that Dutch imperialism is the right name for what took place.

The debate has not changed Kuitenbrouwer's views, as a recent article makes clear.[65] Reiterating that there was no certainty about the borders internationally, he cites domestic Dutch factors such as administrative interests, nationalism, and private investment, and holds firm to the terms "preemption" and "contiguity," pointing out that Betts used these terms to allude not solely to geographical frontiers but to a wider formulation of interests.

---

[61] J. van Goor, "De Lombok expeditie en het Nederlands nationalisme," in *Imperialisme in de marge,* ed. van Goor, pp. 19–70.

[62] In his work on Africa, Wesseling presents a far subtler picture of imperialism than when he discusses the Netherlands in the Indonesian archipelago. There he gives a non-monocausal interpretation of imperialism, and for each separate case he identifies different "hierarchies" of factors and varying features of the role of the periphery (Wesseling, *Verdeel en heers,* pp. 447–61).

[63] J. T. Lindblad, "Economic Aspects of the Dutch Expansion in Indonesia, 1870–1914," *Modern Asian Studies* 23 (1989): 1–23.

[64] Fasseur, "Een koloniale paradox."

[65] M. Kuitenbrouwer, "Het imperialisme van een kleine mogendheid: De overzeese expansie van Nederland 1870–1914," in *De kracht van Nederland: Internationale positie en buitenlands beleid,* ed. N. C. F. van Sas (Haarlem: Becht, 1991), pp. 42–71.

In his impressive doctoral dissertation, à Campo reaches similar conclusions, though from an entirely different vantage point.[66] His book on the Dutch Royal Mail Steam Packet Company (KPM) and its relations with the colonial state between 1888 and 1914 widens the debate on modern imperialism by treating it as colonial state formation, an approach that is also adopted in the present case study. Imperialism and state formation are both about "the establishment and reinforcement of true sovereignty over, and the actual administration of, a clearly defined territory by a foreign power," on which colonial state formation builds further in an effort to achieve more independence from the mother country and to narrow the gap between the different sections of the population.[67] In this context à Campo identifies two simultaneous and analogous processes, calculated to reinforce one another: the growth of the colonial state and the commercial development of packet shipping, accompanied in both cases by a desire to achieve a national monopoly in the area concerned.

Looking through the lens of packet services brings several matters into sharper focus. À Campo's work also confirms the transitional status of the two decades from 1870 to 1890: it was a period that witnessed the gradual evolution of a national consciousness, against the backdrop of an international economic crisis, growing industrialization elsewhere, and the Aceh War in the East Indies. This culminated in the launching of a national shipping company in 1888, run from the mother country but operational in, and exerting its influence from, the periphery. Although à Campo does not say so explicitly, the history of the KPM again emphasizes the interplay between initiatives originating from Europe (the "center") and the interests of Europeans in the colonies (the "periphery").

Furthermore, à Campo's work confirms that the 1890s constituted a gap in the process of expanding Dutch rule in the archipelago. Where the Dutch were tightening their grip, the KPM often did preparatory administrative work as well as providing maritime support: as an "internal maritime administrative authority," its ships called at new ports as emblems of Dutch authority. It was both factor and actor in the process of expansion, enabling and profiting at the same time. À Campo's analysis of a few specific instances of Dutch expansion also demonstrates the diversity of factors at play, as a result of which he further nuances the emphasis in his earlier work on economic factors at the international level.[68]

The academic controversies that have been described above determine the theoretical parameters of this book. As these contentions frequently come down to matters of terminology and the use of language, it is important to start off with clear definitions. I shall use the historical term "imperialism" to refer to the process of acceleration and further concentration of the expansion of Western rule between 1870 and 1914, which culminated in the political dominion of Western states over most of the non-Western world and in colonial state formation. The analytical framework of the theories outlined in this chapter makes it possible to elucidate both the general and the unique qualities of Dutch expansion. Every country introduced its own accents into the overall pattern or the configuration of

---

[66] J. à Campo, *Koninklijke Paketvaart Maatschappij: Stoomvaart en staatsvorming in de Indonesische archipel 1888–1914* (Hilversum: Verloren, 1992).

[67] Ibid., p. 27.

[68] Ibid., p. 214.

factors, and the Netherlands was no exception. The most important questions can therefore be reduced, following Fieldhouse, Fasseur, and the other authors discussed above, to an enquiry into continuity and discontinuity; into the key protagonists in the process of the expansion of Dutch rule in Jambi (in the center, The Hague, in the periphery, Batavia, and in the "periphery of the periphery," Palembang and the Jambian elite); and into the priority of motives at the various key times of expansion (economic factors, whether politicized or not, fear of other countries, the ideology of power, and so-called ethical factors).

These questions are all relevant to the matter at hand, since with the exception of à Campo's work, other studies have not explored in depth the background and motives, over a relatively long period of time, underlying the many expeditions into different parts of the Indonesian archipelago that embodied this Dutch imperialism.[69] À Campo was still focusing on economic developments in 1980, applying Eurocentric theories of economic imperialism. Lindblad wrote as an economic historian, while Wesseling wrote from his wide-ranging knowledge of modern imperialism as a theoretical concept and an international phenomenon. Kuitenbrouwer took domestic and foreign policy relations in the Netherlands as the framework for his research. It is therefore worth looking at whether their conclusions are confirmed or refuted by the findings of a case study.

THE PRECOLONIAL STATE IN SOUTHEAST ASIA

Answering these questions, however, will not tell us anything about the nature of the precolonial state in Southeast Asia, which is well worth studying, particularly from the vantage point of the periphery. This subject too has attracted the sharp scrutiny of academic theory formation—and like other issues it has been "decolonized." Only in the past few decades have Western political thinkers, molded as they are by Western political institutions, come to appreciate the fact that power may be exercised in unfamiliar ways.[70] Where the states of Southeast Asia are concerned, we can broadly distinguish two schools of thought.

The first analyzes forms of government on the basis of ideas on the state and the place of the ruler as recorded in local texts; exponents of this approach may be called "idealists." The second analyzes precolonial power structures on the basis of their functionality; I would therefore call their exponents "functionalists."[71]

---

[69] Short-term motives have in fact been analyzed. See, for example, P. Jobse, *De tin-expedities naar Flores 1887–1891: Een episode uit de geschiedenis van Nederlands-Indië in het tijdperk van het moderne imperialisme*, Utrechtse Historische Cahiers 3 (Utrecht: Department of History, Utrecht University, 1980,; P. M. H. Groen, "'Soldaat' en 'bestuursman': Het Indische leger en de Nederlandse gezagsvestiging op Ceram: Een case study," *Mededelingen van de Sectie Militaire Geschiedenis Landmachtstaf* 5 (1982): 203–44; J. van Goor, *Imperialisme in de marge*; H. J. van der Tholen, "De expeditie naar Korintji in 1902–1903: Imperialisme of ethische politiek," *Mededelingen van de Sectie Militaire Geschiedenis Landmachtstaf* 10 (1987): 70–89.

[70] C. Geertz, "Introduction," in *Centers, Symbols and Hierarchies: Essays on the Classical States of Southeast Asia*, ed. L. Gesick (New Haven: Yale University Press, 1983), pp. viii-x, esp. viii.

[71] See Luc Nagtegaal, *Riding the Dutch Tiger*, trans. Beverley Jackson (Leiden: KITLV Press, 1996). Alternative classifications are of course perfectly possible. For instance, the British archeologist J. Wisseman Christie divides theories about the Southeast Asian state into a "sociological" and an "oriental despotism" school, influenced by economic, structural, and symbolic anthropology, and by Karl Marx and K. Wittfogel, respectively (J. Wisseman Christie,

The first group has deepened our understanding of the expectations, ideas, and self-images that characterized the native rulers and their immediate surroundings and helped determine their actions.[72] Westerners found themselves confronted with completely unfamiliar ideas about power, ideas more reminiscent of European antiquity or the Middle Ages than their own times.[73] The ruler's magical or religious significance, his intermediate position between microcosm and macrocosm, and the often circular symbolic order of the power structure contrasted sharply with the secularized and uncompromisingly hierarchical view of power in the West. Blurring fact and fiction, the chronicles, *babad* and *syair*, which originated from courtly circles, praised the great deeds of the ruler and his ancestors. They invested the ruler's power with legitimacy by placing it in a historical tradition and tracing his supposedly illustrious lineage. In this way they functioned as "Mirrors of Princes," providing moral instruction and giving the ruler implicit guidelines on how to behave. They also placed great emphasis on harmony within the Southeast Asian state.[74]

The "functionalists," on the other hand, who include older authors such as D. H. Burger, but also more recent researchers such as Michael Adas and Jan Breman, have consistently emphasized the universal human characteristics of the exercise of power, and decline to treat Southeast Asia as a special case.[75] In contrast to the "idealists," they pay far more attention to specific instances of historical behavior, to actual institutions and their *modi operandi*. This has given them a keener eye for the constant struggle and discord in Southeast Asian states, a struggle and discord that were entirely at odds with the ruler's role, which was supposedly that of creating and maintaining harmony and of preserving order between microcosm and microcosm. Adas has therefore coined the phrase "contest states" for such kingdoms, since the proliferation of claimants to the throne generated a permanent struggle between elites about the succession, controls on labor, and the economic surplus.[76]

This debate too has developed by way of thesis and antithesis into a synthesis, partly thanks to sociological studies of patron-client relations as the most characteristic and permanent element of non-Western societies. On the basis of his

---

Theatre States and Oriental Despotisms: Early Southeast Asia in the Eyes of the West, Occasional Papers 10 (Hull: Centre for South-East Asian Studies, University of Hull, 1985).

[72] This group includes Soemarsaid Moertono, *State and Statecraft in Old Java: A Study of the Later Mataram Period, 16th to 19th Century* (Ithaca, N.Y.: Cornell SEAP Publications, 1972); Benedict Anderson, "The Idea of Power in Javanese Culture," in *Culture and Politics in Indonesia*, ed. C. Holt (Ithaca, N.Y.: Cornell University Press, 1972), pp. 1–69; and Clifford Geertz, *Negara: The Theater State in Nineteenth-Century Bali* (Princeton, N.J.: Princeton University Press, 1980).

[73] See, for example, Versnel's article about the cult surrounding the Roman emperor: H. S. Versnel, "Geef de Keizer wat des Keizers is en Gode wat Gods is: Een essay over een utopisch conflict," *Lampas* 21 (1988): 233–56.

[74] Nagtegaal, *Riding the Dutch Tiger*, pp. 1–14; Henk Schulte Nordholt, *The Spell of Power: A History of Balinese Politics 1650–1940* (Leiden: KITLV Press, 1996), pp. 1–17.

[75] D. H. Burger, *Sociologische-economische geschiedenis van Indonesië met een historiografische introductie van J. S. Wigboldus* (Wageningen: Landbouwhogeschool, 1975); Michael Adas, "From Avoidance to Confrontation: Peasant Protest in Colonial and Precolonial Southeast Asia," *Comparative Studies in Society and History* 32 (1981): 217–47; Jan Breman, *The Shattered Image: Construction and Deconstruction of the Village in Colonial Asia* (Dordrecht: Foris, 1988).

[76] Adas, "From Avoidance to Confrontation."

study of the Thai state, the American anthropologist Stanley J. Tambiah combined the contrasting elements of a harmonizing center and a constant power struggle in his model of "galactic polity": the Southeast Asian system of government as a pulsating galaxy.[77] Around the central cosmological figure of the ruler, his followers revolved like satellites in separate orbits, each one often serving as a center for others. And these galactic systems influenced one another, expanding or shrinking as a result; the balance of power was never static. Thus "divine kingship" was dialectically linked to permanent rebellion. The stronger the state, the more detail and more differentiation this pattern displayed in the structure connecting the ruler and his followers within the state, and in the relationships between the center (the capital) and the peripheral regions.

Tambiah discusses the Malay state as a weak form of this model. In this field the contrast between functionalism and idealism is reflected in the writings of J. M. Gullick (functionalist) and A. C. Milner (idealist). Their studies of the Malay sovereign, the *raja*, underline different aspects, partly on the basis of their sources. Malay epic poems taught Milner that the *raja*'s religious role entitled him to call upon local chieftains for support. A sultan derived his power primarily from his religious title. By serving him, followers could acquire fame and glory, in this world and the next. Gullick, on the other hand, basing himself on the British colonial archives, emphasizes the economic power of the Malay ruler, obtained through commerce or by levying taxes.[78] The ruler's only real supporters, whose allegiance he forged with these riches, were those in his own retinue. Gullick posits a wider gap between the sovereign and his subjects than Milner. But he too acknowledges the sovereign's ideological power, reaffirming this point in response to Milner's polemic against him.[79]

It is impossible to adopt any position in this debate on the basis of Jambian sources. There is simply no material indicating how local people viewed the sultanate. All we can do is distill certain conclusions about the sultan's religious significance and economic power from people's actions. So I shall necessarily be treating the subject as a "functionalist," although my personal preference is for the recent integration of the two approaches.[80] Still, the debate described above and the concepts derived from it provide an indispensable context for anyone wishing to study the Malay form of government.

NATIVE OR DUTCH SOVEREIGNTY

One final point concerning the native state that should be addressed in this context is that of its sovereign rights in the nineteenth century. Here too the issue of

[77] S. J. Tambiah, *Culture, Thought and Social Action: An Anthropological Perspective* (Cambridge: Harvard University Press, 1985), pp. 252–81, 316–38.

[78] A. C. Milner, *Kerajaan: Malay Political Culture on the Eve of Colonial Rule* (Tucson: University of Arizona Press, 1982). J. M. Gullick, *Indigenous Political Systems of Western Malaya*, 2nd ed. (London: London School of Economics, 1965); J. M. Gullick "The Condition of Having a Raja: A Review of *Kerajaan*, by A. C. Milner," *Review of Indonesian and Malayan Affairs* 16,2 (1982): 109–29.

[79] Gullick, "Condition of Having a Raja."

[80] See M. C. Ricklefs, *Jogyakarta under Sultan Mangkubumi 1749–1792: A History of the Division of Java* (London: Oxford University Press, 1974); Schulte Nordholt, *Spell of Power*; Nagtegaal, *Riding the Dutch Tiger*.

continuity versus discontinuity has been raised, by G. J. Resink, a scholar of Indonesian law. The numerous articles he produced in the 1950s and 1960s, collected in a single volume in 1968, demonstrate—on the basis of the texts of official memoranda, ordinances, and legal sources—that under international law the self-governing territories outside Java retained their full sovereignty.[81] It was not until around the turn of the century that the colonial administrators tightened their grip, putting an end to this independence. Before this, the Netherlands possessed only suzerain power over autonomous regions—its sovereignty was confined to territories in which it exercised direct rule. Thus autonomous rulers retained rights in relation to nationality and jurisdiction over their territorial waters. They were empowered to conclude treaties among themselves and were not automatically at war with the enemies of the colonial government. The officials who administered the Dutch East Indies were stationed at the native rulers' courts as foreign envoys. The treaties themselves provide conclusive evidence for the sovereignty of these territories under international law, since they were concluded by sovereign rulers and possessed legal force in respect of third parties.[82] In his final article of 1968, Resink compares this "sovereignty and independence of the vassal and allied realms"—ostensibly a contradiction in terms—to a "dust cloud of sovereignties" like those, for instance, in nineteenth-century Germany, Switzerland, and Italy prior to their unification.[83] His characterization of different forms of sovereignty also implies that there was no such thing as complete equality between the different forms of sovereignty. The relationship between the government of the Dutch East Indies and the native rulers of autonomous territories resembled that between major powers and their weaker allies or satellites. They constituted an "unequal alliance" that did not stop the Dutch from making "rather drastic inroads" into that sovereignty.[84]

Resink's views have certainly not gone unchallenged. Justus van der Kroef finds ample evidence of indisputable Dutch sovereignty: the explicit recognition of Dutch sovereignty in contracts, the powers of the Dutch authorities to intervene in internal affairs, the contractual assertion that the ruler's realm belonged to the territory of the Dutch East Indies, and most important of all, the simple fact that Dutch sovereignty was never questioned by foreign states. A crucial element of sovereignty, after all, is the control of one's own foreign relations. It was sheer necessity, in the form of limited administrative and financial resources, that caused the government to opt for a gradual transition to a uniform sovereign policy. Acquiring sovereign rights was a constant objective of colonial policy.[85]

Van der Kroef is more of a pragmatic historian than the legal expert Resink. He bases his analysis of the past not on texts and pronouncements but on the actual balance of power and actual views of power. Here too we find the "functionalist" opposed to the "idealist." The discourse of international law evidently has

---

[81] G. J. Resink, *Indonesia's History between the Myths: Essays in Legal History and Historical Theory* (The Hague: Van Hoeve, 1968).

[82] Ibid., p. 329.

[83] Ibid., pp. 334–35.

[84] Ibid., p. 340.

[85] J. M. van der Kroef, "On the Writing of Indonesian History," *Pacific Affairs* 31 (1958): 352–71. J. M. van der Kroef "On the Sovereignty of Indonesian States: A Rejoinder," *Bijdragen tot de Taal-, Land- en Volkenkunde* 117 (1961): 238–66.

different foci than political history. The latter is also concerned with the question of how much Indonesian rulers allowed themselves to be influenced by the international law aspects of treaties. Recent regional studies have shown that it was not the letter of the contract but the way in which power was actually exercised that determined the value of an agreement for the native ruler.[86]

Perhaps the contrast is ultimately less sharp than I have depicted it here. Resink's 1968 article reviewing this subject is far more nuanced than his earlier work, which prompted Van der Kroef's riposte. This is clear from subtleties of language such as some already quoted ("the sovereignty and independence of the vassal"). There is an implicit acknowledgment here that the vassal's foreign relations were of a limited nature. Vassals enjoyed sovereignty beneath the glass dome of Dutch authority.[87] In general, both "sovereignty" and "independence" convey more than Resink appears to have intended. The adat specialist Cornelis van Vollenhoven, in whose tradition Resink was trained at the Batavian Law Faculty, distinguished between international treaties and political contracts with native rulers.[88] Treaties were concluded with powerful states that led international lives; contracts were concluded with states that had lost their separate international identities and had been subsumed by Dutch suzerainty. After 1855, treaties fell outside the competence of the governor-general and could only be concluded through the offices of the Ministry of Foreign Affairs, while contraacts remained under the governor-general's competence. International relations, it seems, came in many shapes and sizes.

The main value of Resink's approach, then, is that it has sharpened our awareness of the varicolored exercise of power within the archipelago in the nineteenth century. The Dutch East Indies was not a single entity but a multiplicity of entities: one territory under direct Dutch rule alongside innumerable local states. There was not a single flag but many flags; not a single tariff system but many different tariffs; not a single kind of nationality but many different forms.[89] Resink's approach induces researchers to analyze the relationship between the colonial government and the self-governing territories in more detail, in relation to the political reality underlying the contracts as well as the contracts themselves. The history of Jambi supplies plenty of material with which to make this analysis.

---

[86] L. Y. Andaya, "Treaty Conceptions and Misconceptions: A Case Study from South Sulawesi," *Bijdragen tot de Taal-, Land- en Volkenkunde* 134 (1978): 275–95; Schulte Nordholt, *Spell of Power.*

[87] Resink used this metaphor in a personal communication to the author in 1985.

[88] C. van Vollenhoven, *Mr. C. van Vollenhoven's Verspreide Geschriften*, 3 vols. (Haarlem: Tjeenk Willink; The Hague: Nijhoff, 1935), 3: 200–02.

[89] Resink, *Indonesia's History between the Myths*, pp. 336–37

CHAPTER TWO

JAMBI AND BATAVIA BEFORE 1830

In 1833 the government and the Sultan of Jambi concluded their first, provisional contract, followed in 1834 by a second, more permanent one. Before discussing these beginnings of the nineteenth-century relationship between Jambi and "Batavia,"[1] we should look at each of these powers in turn and briefly review their history. We know far more about Jambi's past and the Jambi/Malay system of government today than Batavia's officials knew at the time.

THE GEOGRAPHY OF JAMBI

Although Jambi was one of the smallest sultanates on Sumatra, it was still (certainly as a Dutch Residency in the twentieth century[2]) one and a half times as big as the Netherlands. According to records dating from 1932, it stretched 350 km from east to west and 220 km from north to south.[3] At the beginning of the nineteenth century it bordered to the south on the Residency of Palembang, constituted as such since 1819, with which it had direct contact through Bengkulu and the Rawas (a district of Palembang). To the north of Jambi lay the sultanate of Indragiri and a number of independent Minangkabau principalities such as Siguntur and Lima Kota. In the west, in the Bukit Barisan mountains, it bordered on the Minangkabau region of the Padang Uplands, a Residency since 1816. The sultanate's geographical location between Palembang and Minangkabau would determine its political future.

In the seventeenth and part of the eighteenth century, Jambi had still controlled the fertile region of Kerinci in the southeast, a valley in the Bukit Barisan measuring some 40 km long and 12 km wide. But since the mid-eighteenth century the region had paid little heed to nominal Jambian sovereignty. Nor could the Sultan of Jambi impose his authority on other regions in the southeast such as Serampas and Sungai Tenang.

Like other Malay principalities along the Straits of Melaka and the southern part of the South China Sea, Jambi had developed in the basin of a river and its many tributaries. The Batang Hari, Sumatra's longest river, which rose in the Bukit Barisan and meandered a full 800 km, was the backbone of the realm. Its tributaries, the Tembesi (with its tributary the Merangin) and, further upstream, the Tabir, the Tebo (with its tributary the Pelepat) and the Jujuhan, were scarcely

---

[1] "Batavia" will be used to denote the colonial administration of the Dutch East Indies.

[2] The Residency embraced the original sultanate with outlying territories such as Serampas and Sungei Tenang.

[3] J. Tideman and P. L. F. Sigar, *Djambi* (Amsterdam: Koloniaal Instituut, 1938), p. 1.

less important. Only the northeast had its own catchment basin in the Tungkal on the border with Indragiri.

These rivers constituted the main arteries for transport; it was along their banks that the population of Jambi had settled in hamlets, or *dusun,* their size varying from five to eight hundred dwellings. The capital, also called Jambi, lay on the Batang Hari, about ninety kilometers from the river estuary. But the waterways were not always navigable. Even between the capital and Muara Tembesi, a *dusun* located where the Tembesi joined the Batang Hari, water levels sometimes fell to one meter in the dry season between April and October.[4] In this period low water levels also severed links between Upper and Lower Jambi. In the rainy season, on the other hand, the rivers sometimes overflowed their banks by several kilometers. Even when boats could navigate the rivers, they had to proceed very slowly. Until the 1920s, it took a paddle steamer forty-eight hours to travel the approximately one hundred kilometers between Jambi and Muara Tembesi.[5]

Although the rivers charted Jambi's most visible communication patterns, there were also a number of land links. Crossing the forests were networks of narrow footpaths between the *dusun,* connecting Palembang to Minangkabau and Indragiri.[6] Jambi was a well-watered and verdant region, its rolling land gradually rising toward the Bukit Barisan mountains in the west, with their peaks of 1,600 to 3,000 meters. For the rest this undulating territory was broken only by two ranges of hills between the Tembesi and the Tabir and on the border with Indragiri: the Duabelas and Tigapuluh (rising to about 500–700 meters).

It was a largely empty realm. In 1852 the population was estimated at approximately 60,000. Jambi would remain an empty land well into the twentieth century; the 1930 census identified it as one of the most sparsely populated parts of Sumatra.[7] Eastern Jambi, the low-lying, marshy coastal region that stretched deep into the interior in places, was almost completely uninhabited.[8]

Although Jambi's soil is not very fertile, agriculture was the second most important means of subsistence, after fisheries. In lowland areas rice was cultivated in *ladang*s or dry-land plantations cleared with slash-and-burn techniques; in the more fertile Tembesi and Tebo regions it was grown in *sawah*s (flooded paddy fields), which sometimes actually yielded surpluses for transport to lowland areas. The Tebo region, flat and situated at a relatively high altitude,

---

[4] Its location close to the equator, at latitudes from 0°47' to 2°47' south caused—and still causes—only minor variations between the east and west monsoons, although the months from October through April have the most rainfall.

[5] When a highway was finally constructed here in 1931, the journey took two and a half hours. *Memorie van overgave* (Memorandum on leaving office) from Resident J. R. F. Verschoor van Nisse 1931, p. 138, National Archives (NA), The Hague, Col., MvO 223.

[6] Report appended to letter from the army commander to the governor-general, December 6, 1881, NA, Col., *mailrapport* (postal report; hereafter "mr.") 1882/27.

[7] Resident of Palembang to governor-general, December 16, 1852, M24, NA, Col., *verbaal* (file, hereafter "vb.") February 15, 1853, no. 26. In 1930, population density stood at 5.46 persons per square kilometer. Only the Gayo, Alas, and Bengkalis districts had even lower population densities (Tideman and Sigar, *Djambi,* p. 45).

[8] John Anderson, *Mission to the East Coast of Sumatra in 1823* (1826; repr., Kuala Lumpur: Oxford University Press, 1971), pp. 397–98; Soerat banyaknya sekalian marga doesoen, National Archives of Indonesia (Arsip Nasional Republik Indonesia, hereafter ANRI) Palembang Residency Records 66.12; Resident of Palembang to governor-general, December 16, 1852, M24, NA, Col., vb. February 15, 1853, no. 26.

was one of the most prosperous and densely populated parts of Jambi. Here and in the equally prosperous Upper Tembesi, a substantial quantity of livestock was kept.[9]

As elsewhere in the Malay region, trade generated a measure of prosperity. Forest products, beeswax, resin, gum, cane, and timber were collected in the jungle and transported by river to markets outside Jambi on the Melaka Straits (mainly to Singapore after 1819), where they were exchanged for goods such as cotton, salt, earthenware, and ironware.[10] Some people panned for gold in the upper reaches of the rivers. Like many states in the Malay world, Jambi was divided geographically into an upstream *(ulu)* and downstream *(ilir)* region.[11] The uplands, deemed to begin at Muara Tembesi, were economically essential for the lowlands, supplying exports (mainly forest products, pepper, and gold in the seventeenth and eighteenth centuries) and labor.

Jambi's population, though small, was nonetheless heterogeneous. The original Kubu population had withdrawn to the jungle, where they led a nomadic existence. Ethnic Malays had settled on the banks of the Batang Hari and the Tembesi. Upper Jambi was inhabited by *batin*, to whom the adat literature incorrectly ascribes Minangkabau origins.[12] All these groups had preserved many of their legal institutions and enjoyed a large measure of autonomy. Some Minangkabau, who had migrated south in the seventeenth century or later because of a lack of land in the mountains and rivalries between princes and chiefs, had accepted subjection to this *batin* population as *penghulu*.[13] A second, migrant *batin* group lived in the Rawas on the border between Jambi and Palembang.[14] The Sultan of Jambi ruled, nominally at least, over all these groups.

JAMBI BEFORE 1600

The Jambi line of sultans did not boast an age-old tradition; it had not consolidated its position until the sixteenth century.[15] Its power grew in tandem

---

[9] Report appended to letter from army commander to governor-general, December 6, 1881, no. 915x, NA, Col., mr. 1882/27; B. Watson Andaya, "Cash Cropping and Upstream-Downstream Tensions: The Case of Jambi in the Seventeenth and Eighteenth Centuries," in *Southeast Asia in the Early Modern Era: Trade, Power and Belief*, ed. A. Reid (Ithaca, N.Y.: Cornell University Press, 1993), p. 91.

[10] Statistical report on trade, industry and agriculture, 1822, NA, Col., no. 3075; ANRI, Algemeene Secretarie, *gouvernementsbesluit* (resolution adopted by the colonial authorities), September 20, 1834, no. 4.

[11] Watson Andaya, "Cash Cropping."

[12] Watson Andaya, communicated personally. Only the population of the regions known as the "VII Kota" and "IX Kota" were said to be of Minangkabau origin (Watson Andaya, "Cash Cropping," pp. 99–100).

[13] The terms *batin* and *penghulu*, though denoting separate ethnic groups, etymologically express hierarchical relations. *Batin* means supreme chief, while *penghulu* expresses a subordinate role. *Batin* rulers appointed *penghulu* as local chiefs . K. R. Hall, "The Coming of Islam to the Archipelago: A Reassessment," in *Economic Exchange and Social Interaction in Southeast Asia: Perspectives from Prehistory, History and Ethnography*, ed. K. L. Hutterer, Michigan Papers on South and Southeast Asia 13 (Ann Arbor: Center for South and Southeast Asian Studies, University of Michigan 1977), p. 224.

[14] These were the *suku-pindah* (lit.: migrating *suku*).

[15] *Memorie van overgave* from Resident H. C. L. Petrie 1923, NA, Col., MvO 878.

with processes of state formation, Islamization, and economic growth that took place in various parts of the Indonesian archipelago, from west to east, in the same period. All the information we have on Jambi's early history derives from archeological finds and Chinese sources. Its reconstruction provokes numerous questions.[16] We know that the seventh-century realm of Malayu was in Jambi,[17] and that it was subsequently absorbed, either as an independent trading community or as a subject region, into the Srivijaya empire in southern Sumatra. Srivijaya's power derived from its special political and economic ties with China, from its geographical location at the intersection of trading routes between India, China, and Java, and from its own commercial products from the jungle. In the thirteenth century, Srivijaya had to contend not only with an attack by the Javanese Majapahit, whose sovereignty it was compelled to recognize, but with expansion from Thailand as well.[18] At the end of the fourteenth century, Jambi became a vassal region of Majapahit, though it managed to wrench itself free again after the fall of this empire at the beginning of the sixteenth century. Javanese influences continued to color Jambi's sultanate throughout the seventeenth and eighteenth centuries.

The early history of the sultanate of Jambi roughly coincided with the advent of Islam, though precise dates are impossible to pinpoint. The Islamization of Sumatra is generally believed to have begun in the fifteenth century. Around then Malay princes became more receptive to merchants from southern India, who were spreading Persian-bred beliefs about princely authority that corresponded to Southeast Asian views of the ruler's unique position as God's representative on earth.[19] Southeast Asian princes gravitated to these Hindu and Buddhist adaptations of the new political thinking as an idiom in which they could express their claims to sovereignty, both at home and to the outside world.

Islam clothed the rule of the Jambian princes in legitimacy. According to legends that the Dutch collected in the nineteenth and early twentieth centuries, the forefather of the sultan's family had been a foreigner, originally from Turkey.[20] Throughout this period, Turkey was seen as the embodiment of the Jambian ideal of near-divine strength and succor, and as a savior in times of emergency. What is more, the motif of a dynasty founded by an outsider provided Jambian folklore with its own version of the regional "stranger-king" theme that is commonplace throughout Austronesian cultures.[21]

---

[16] See B. Watson Andaya, *To Live as Brothers: Southeast Sumatra in the Seventeenth and Eighteenth Centuries* (Honolulu: University of Hawaii Press, 1993).

[17] B. Watson Andaya and L. Y. Andaya, *A History of Malaysia* (London: Macmillan, 1982), p. 20.

[18] See Watson Andaya and Andaya, *A History of Malaysia*, pp. 19–31.

[19] A. C. Milner, "Islam and the Muslim State," in *Islam in South-East Asia*, ed. M. B. Hooker (Leiden: Brill, 1983), pp. 23–49.

[20] J. W. Boers, "Oud volksgebruik in het Rijk van Jambi," *Tijdschrift van Neêrland's Indië* 3,1 (1840): 372–84; "Legenden van Djambi," *Tijdschrift Voor Neêrland's Indië* 8,4 (1846): 33–56; H. M. M. Mennes, "Eenige aanteekeningen omtrent Djambi," *Koloniaal Tijdschrift* 21 (1932): 26–30; Tideman and Sigar, *Djambi*, p. 63.

[21] Hall, "Coming of Islam," p. 213; J. W. Schoorl, "Power, Ideology and Change in the Early State of Buton" (paper given at the Fifth Netherlands-Indonesia Historical Conference, Lage Vuursche, 1986).

THE SEVENTEENTH AND EIGHTEENTH CENTURIES

Jambi's new rulers capitalized on the growth of trade in the Malay waters in the sixteenth century.[22] Their development was intrinsically bound up with the advent of new products and new partners in commerce. From the mid-1550s to the end of the seventeenth century, the sultanate did a roaring trade in pepper, initially with the Portuguese and from 1615 with the English and Dutch East Indies companies, a trade in which the Chinese, Malay, Makassarese, and Javanese were also involved. Local princes were dependent on the income generated either by a trading monopoly or by export duties. This certainly applied to the sultans of Jambi, who prospered greatly with the passage of time.

In 1616, the capital of Jambi was already seen as Sumatra's second-richest port, after Aceh. According to estimates from this period made by of the Dutch East India Company (*Vereenigde Oost-Indische Compagnie*, or VOC), the sultan made a profit of 30–35 percent on the pepper it sold.[23] Jambi took an active part in the international politics of the region, and in the 1670s its might was on a par with that of powerful neighbors such as Palembang and Johore.

This golden age would not endure. In the 1680s, Jambi lost its position as the major pepper port on Sumatra's east coast through conflict with Johore, followed by internal unrest. Problems associated with trade, such as debts and contraband, generated tension between producers and middlemen, that is to say between upstream and downstream regions, *ulu* and *ilir*. The sultan's family, representative of the downstream peoples and related to foreigners, came off worst. The English gave up their trading post in Jambi in 1679; the VOC stayed somewhat longer, although its office brought in very little after 1680.[24]

As the economic problems worsened, the VOC intervened more actively. In 1688, the Dutch arrested the Sultan when he came to the trading post in response to an invitation, and banished him to Batavia. These actions had the effect of splitting Jambi into two sultanates: upstream and downstream.[25] Gone was the former prosperity; it did not return even after the reunification of the kingdom in the 1720s. In the uplands, people switched to cultivating rice and cotton, since imported Indian cotton had risen in price, while pepper prices had fallen.[26] Meanwhile, gold was replacing pepper as the main export. The court reaped little revenue from the gold trade, however, since the Minangkabau gold diggers exported their wares wherever profits would be highest, not necessarily from the

---

[22] Jambi's development in the seventeenth and eighteenth centuries is discussed only in brief here, as it is the subject of Barbara Watson Andaya, "Cash Cropping."

[23] Watson Andaya, "Cash Cropping," p. 99.

[24] See Els M. Jacobs, *Koopman in Azië: De handel van de Verenigde Oost-Indische Compagnie tijdens de 18de eeuw* (Zutphen: Walburg Pers, 2000).

[25] His treacherous arrest would be etched into Jambi's collective memory well into the nineteenth century. A temporary split between upstream and downstream groups was a common enough pattern in the Malay world; it was seen in Perak (1743) and Selangor (1784), for instance (see R. C. Vos, *Gentle Janus, Merchant Prince: The VOC and the Tightrope of Diplomacy in the Malay World, 1740–1800*, trans. Beverley Jackson (Leiden: KITLV Press, 1993), pp. 56, 165.

[26] B. Watson Andaya, "The Cloth Trade in Jambi and Palembang Society during the Seventeenth and Eighteenth Centuries," *Indonesia* 47 (1989): 26–46.

Jambian capital; the sultan had no effective authority over them.[27] So from about 1700 onward the sultan's coffers were chronically empty, and even the regalia, the *pusaka*, had to be pledged as collateral.[28]

Growing Minangkabau influence also ensued from immigration, which had started around the mid-seventeenth century and was part of a major emigration thrust that had taken the Minangkabau as far as the coasts of the Malay peninsula. A hundred years later, this trend had assumed such proportions that the entire upland region of Jambi was said to have been "Minangkabaued."[29] Gold was a strong attraction. By the end of the eighteenth century, in fact, gold mining in Jambi was entirely under the control of these foreigners.[30] Upper Jambi—the *ulu*—had become a Minangkabau region, whose inhabitants expressed their cultural affinity with the homeland in many ways, including economically, through exports. This sealed the fate of the *ilir*; from then on, the primacy of the *ulu* was absolute. By the end of the eighteenth century, the impoverished Jambian sultanate was a vassal state under the Minangkabau prince of Pagaruyung,[31] whose approval had to be obtained, for instance, for Jambi's choice of sultan.

The VOC was increasingly concerned about its products and about security, and in 1768, after Jambians attacked its trading post there, it decided to close the post. Like the British East India Company before it, the VOC turned its attention to the west coast instead. The ports there, Bengkulu (British since 1658) and Padang, proved to be more accessible to sailing vessels than those in the swampy eastern part of the island. These ports attracted the growing exports of pepper and coffee from central Sumatra.[32] They proved valuable footholds, now that the trade route from Java to Melaka had moved from Sumatra's east to its west coast.

A POOR REGION AND A POOR PRINCE

Civil war further eroded the sultan's power after 1800. In 1811, the population of the capital, led by Arab merchants and the *suku* Raja Empat Puluh ("*suku* of the

---

[27] B. Watson Andaya, "Cash Cropping," p. 100. In 1710, Jambi's exports still consisted entirely of pepper. By 1730, more than half consisted of gold, and by 1750 over 80 percent. The total amounts of money involved were minor, however, compared to the VOC's overall turnover: 5,000 guilders (1710), 7,500 guilders (1730) and 16,000 guilders (1750). In 1710 exports were still being dispatched to Melaka, but in the subsequent reference years they went only to Batavia (see Jacobs, *Koopman in Azië*, p. 234).

[28] Watson Andaya, communicated personally. She gives seventeenth- and eighteenth-century examples of Milner's concept of an ideal sultan who attracted followers without offering material rewards alongside examples of followers who abandoned sultans unable to reward them for services rendered.

[29] Watson Andaya, "Cash Cropping," p. 115.

[30] W. Marsden, *The History of Sumatra, containing an Account of the Government, Laws, Customs and Manners of the Native Inhabitants with a Description of the Natural Productions and a Relation of the Ancient Political State of that Island*, 3rd ed. (1811; repr. Kuala Lumpur: Longman, 1966).

[31] Watson Andaya, "Cash Cropping," p. 119. For instance, approval was given for the choice of Sultan Mohildin in 1811 and for that of Facharuddin, who was installed between 1821 and 1829; see the report issued by Darpa Wiguna, n.d., NA, De Kock collection, VROA 1891, 11.2.

[32] C. Dobbin, *Islamic Revivalism in a Changing Peasant Economy in Central Sumatra 1784–1847* (London: Curzon Press, 1983).

forty rajas"), rose up against the reigning Sultan Mohildin, because of his wife's alleged treatment of several daughters from well-to-do families.[33] Mohildin asked his brother, who had once claimed the throne himself, to offer his family protection. Mohildin's brother agreed, but only on condition that his own son, Raden Tabun, would be pronounced *pangeran ratu* (crown prince and heir) after the sultan's death. Mohildin gave his word, but eventually declined the proffered assistance; his opponents having put down their arms, he could return to the capital.

The unrest remained, however. There was some fighting in 1817 or 1818, this time between Mohildin and another cousin. The conflict was waged in the customary Malay way, as irregular skirmishes in which the parties fired at each other from behind fortifications and did little damage. Out of hundreds of supporters, a mere handful of people were killed. Mohildin was defeated and would not settle in Jambi again for some time, although the cousin was killed shortly afterward.[34] In 1820, the sultan controlled the upper reaches of the Tembesi, while the *pangeran ratu* controlled the upper reaches of the Batang Hari. However, the pangeran ratu spent a large part of his time in neighboring Palembang in this period, making his authority in the upland areas fairly ineffectual.[35]

Internal tensions remained, as Mohildin's son, Facharuddin, when pronounced sultan (some time between 1821 and 1829) named his brother pangeran ratu. By thus reneging on his father's promise to make Raden Tabun crown prince, Facharuddin made a formidable enemy. The passed-over Raden Tabun was a wealthy merchant and could count on the support of the people of the prosperous northern region of Jambi, even though his selection was unlawful according to adat, as he was not the son of a former sultan. A political marriage, a common solution throughout the Indonesian archipelago, seemly briefly to hold out a solution. Marriages were scarcely emotional bonds between individuals at this time; they could forge political alliances between families and were therefore ideal vehicles for cementing power. Relations between relatives and in-laws (*bhisan*) were seldom neutral. Accordingly, the two rivals married each other's sisters, with Raden Tabun's sister acquiring the highest title of *ratu agung*. But the attitude of the rivals' previous wives torpedoed this peacemaking effort.[36] Mohildin's broken

---

[33] Report of Darpa Wiguna, n.d., NA, De Kock collection. Sultan Mohildin's wife was alleged to have enslaved or even murdered girls from the city out of jealousy of her husband's infidelities. The political machinations underlying such events are unclear. According to another source ("Dit is hetgeen onderzocht . . . ," ANRI, Palembang Residency records 5.2), the sultana had one girl put to death for "communing with evil spirits."

[34] Anderson, *Mission to the East Coast*, p. 404; A. Reid, *Europe and Southeast Asia: The Military Balance*, Occasional Papers 16 (Townsville, Queensland: Centre for Southeast Asian Studies, 1982), p. 1.

[35] Commander of Palembang expedition to governor-general, July 22, 1821, no. 26, ANRI, Algemeene Secretarie, *gouvernementsbesluit* August 21, 1821, no. 16. The second son, Pangeran Surio, controlled the downstream areas. However, he was heavily influenced by his brother-in-law, Pangeran Petra, and had also joined forces with an adventurer, the pirate chieftain Tengku Long, who had been adopted by the sultan, and who was Pangeran Petra's rival (Anderson, *Mission to the East Coast*, p. 403).

[36] Report from Darpa Wiguna, NA, De Kock collection. Tabun leaned heavily on the support of the VII and IX Kota, districts in the upland areas of northern Jambi. A. V. Michiels to

promise continued to fuel open or latent tension in and around the Jambian court well into the 1840s.

Sultan Facharuddin would not be installed in accordance with adat, and it was not until 1833 that he settled in the kraton of Jambi. He resided in the populous upland regions, sometimes at Muara Tebo and sometimes at Sarolangun on the Upper Tembesi,[37] leaving the less important lowland areas to his kinsmen. But this meant that significant revenue from trade passed him by. Duties on trade in forest products had been relinquished to the *anak raja* (Jambian nobility) by then.[38] In 1834, the sultan's relatives in Jambi were more powerful than the sultan himself.[39] They controlled the salt trade; Facharuddin had lost the monopoly on this trade by then, although he continued to receive some revenue from it. The same applied to the trade in opium, which was popular among gold miners and panners in the Limun region.[40]

Jambian trade did not in fact amount to very much. By the end of the eighteenth century, its pepper was deemed to be of inferior quality.[41] Seafaring merchants from the Archipelago (Javanese, Makassarese, Chinese, and Europeans) no longer called at Jambi in the early nineteenth century.[42] Commercial ties with neighboring Palembang were negligible. Jambi accounted for less than 0.5 percent of Palembang's imports and exports. Jambi's main trading partner was Singapore. The only appreciable part of this trade was in gold, but most gold was still being exported via the west coast and Palembang.[43]

---

lieutenant governor-general, August 22, 1833, no. 428, ANRI, Algemeene Secretarie, *gouvernementbesluit*, September 20, 1834, no. 4.

[37] Resident of Palembang to governor-general, February 10, 1835, no. 43, ANRI, Algemeene Secretarie, *gouvernementsbesluit*, August 25, 1835, no. 9; Resident of Palembang to governor-general, October 10, 1837, no. 76, ANRI, Palembang Residency records 70.15; report Darpa Wiguna, NA, De Kock collection. The same applied, it may be added, to his successor, Sultan Abdulrachman Nazaruddin (1841–55), see Resident of Palembang to governor-general, December 16, 1852, M24, NA, Col., vb. February 15, 1853, no. 26. The colonial authorities would carry on trying to settle the sultans in the capital until the end of the nineteenth century, the aim being to strengthen their grip on the realm through them.

[38] Resident of Palembang to governor-general, December 16, 1852, M24, NA, Col., vb. February 15, 1853, no. 26. Whether they paid the promised percentages depended on the prevailing balance of power. Under Mohildin, the *jajah* (a form of tax) was also not collected everywhere. Kerinci, though liable to pay taxes, did not pay anything by then (Anderson, *Mission to the East Coast*, p. 403).

[39] For example, Mohamad Kassim, a relative of Facharuddin and the son of a former sultan; Pangeran Surio; his Arab kinsman Said Mohamad (J. W. Boers, "Bezoek ter Hoofdplaatse van het Djambische Rijk op Sumatra in 1834, door den toenmaligen Resident van Palembang," *Tijdschrift van Nederlandsch Indië* 12,2 [1850]: 463–70); see chapter three.

[40] That the sultan nonetheless acquired revenue from trade in opium and salt is clear from data for the 1860s (then 3,600 and 2,000 guilders respectively). See Resident of Palembang to governor-general, January 4, 1868, and December 3, 1869, NA, Col., vb. November 2, 1878, no. 7.

[41] Marsden, *History of Sumatra*, p. 144.

[42] Michiels to commissioner-general, January 8, 1834, no. 11, ANRI, Algemeene Secretarie, *gouvernementsbesluit*, September 20, 1834, no. 4.

[43] Figures for 1833 show that gold exports (valued at 320,000 guilders) accounted for virtually the whole of Jambi's economic value (estimated at 375,900 guilders). Jambi probably benefited here from the effects of the Padri War in the Minangkabau, which temporarily impeded exports from the west coast; Memorandum on Jambi trade ("Nota handelsgegevens

THE EUROPEAN VIEW

In short, the sultanate amounted to very little, whether economically or administratively, in the late eighteenth and early nineteenth centuries. The British writer William Marsden published his *History of Sumatra* in 1783, after having spent nine years working in Bengkulu as an official of the East India Company, and he was fairly dismissive when he came to Jambi:

> Although of considerable size it is inferior to Siak and Indragiri. At an early stage of European commerce in these parts it was of some importance. . . . The trade consists chiefly in gold dust, pepper, and canes [rattan] but the most of what is collected of the first article proceeds across the country to the western coast, and the quality of the second is not held in high esteem. The port is therefore but little frequented by any other than native merchants.[44]

To Marsden, Jambi contrasted sharply with Palembang, which he deemed to be "of considerable importance."[45] However, he had not visited Jambi himself and relied on hearsay, citing matters "of common notoriety to every person residing on the island."[46]

Another Briton, S. C. Crooke, who did visit Jambi himself, was similarly disparaging. Having been dispatched together with R. Ibbetson "on a mission of a highly confidential and important nature,"[47] the aim being to explore the scope for Britain's pepper trade with Sumatra, Crooke sailed up the Batang Hari on June 25, 1820. It was more than a week later, on July 3, when he arrived at the capital, where the dry monsoon forced him to moor two miles south of Jambi. From that unpropitious vantage point, and exacerbated by "the general ignorance of all classes,"[48] he spent the next ten days trying to gather as much information as possible. But Ibbetson fell ill and the journey was a failure. Jambi was deemed unworthy of another visit when a second journey was undertaken in 1823.[49] However, the journey has given us an interesting report on Jambi, including a crushing verdict on its polity. In the words of rapporteur Crooke:

Jambi"); Michiels to commissioner-general, January 8, 1834, no. 11, both in ANRI, Algemeene Secretarie, *gouvernementsbesluit*, September 20, 1833, no. 4. In 1822, after the unrest in Palembang, imports from Jambi to Palembang, consisting of Bali textiles, *jernang* or dragon's blood, cane, rice, gums, resins, and elephant tusks accounted for a mere 0.1 percent of Palembang's total imports; exports from Palembang to Jambi, primarily earthenware and textiles, accounted for 0.3 percent of its total exports. Statistical survey of trade, industry and agriculture ("Statistieke opgave omtrent handel, nijverheid en landbouw"), Palembang Residency, 1822, NA, Col., no. 3075.

[44] Marsden, *History of Sumatra*, p. 358.

[45] Ibid.

[46] John Bastin, "Introduction," in Marsden, *History of Sumatra*, pp. v–vi.

[47] Anderson, *Mission to the East Coast*, p. 361.

[48] Ibid., p. 387.

[49] John Anderson, *Acheen and the Ports on the North and East Coast of Sumatra* (London: Allen, 1840), pp. 169–70.

They have no regular forms of law, police or government, in any of its modifications; but the sultan is nominally supreme and arbitrary. Ignorant and weak however, in reality, his authority is slighted and usurped by every ambitious chieftain and the kingdom is throughout in a state of confusion and misrule.[50]

A Dutch official expressed a similar verdict in 1838, after several years' experience with Jambian administration: "It goes without saying that in a Kingdom in which the ruler concerns himself solely with fishing, hunting and so forth, leaving the affairs [of government] to others, that many irregularities go unpunished."[51] Clearly, Jambi held few attractions for Europeans wanting to acquire influence for trade or some other purpose.

Even so, this negative assessment deserves to be qualified. From the early nineteenth century, Europeans were in general increasingly disparaging about native kingdoms.[52] Malay states were measured in terms of their usefulness to the colonizers, their visible power, based on wealth and commercial products. As long as the states had presented themselves as powerful trading partners, the VOC had continued to value them highly. The damning nineteenth-century assessments arose in part from self-interest and in part from a change in colonial attitudes. Weak rulers had proven tricky partners (at least as tricky as strong ones, but for different reasons) in colonial constructions. They had no control over their territory and were unwilling or unable to live up to their political promises; they promoted their own goals and were as elusive as they were inscrutable. The impossibility of constructing a colonial realm with indirect rule, based on weak local rulers and fluid Malay structures, determined European views. Moreover, the Europeans' need to prove their own supremacy or to invest a takeover with legitimacy curtailed their ability to comprehend other forms of government. Colonial actions had to be justified. A sincere belief in their own European power and a condemnation of the other party's weakness both served this end.

That Jambi was impoverished and divided at the beginning of the nineteenth century is beyond dispute, but the Europeans' contemptuous views of it were reinforced by ignorance of Sumatra in general and native structures of government in particular. According to W. Marsden, "Sumatra [was] of all accessible places of the world, that which was the least known."[53] Our knowledge of it today derives largely from twentieth-century adat literature and historical studies of states in the region; the archives contain little detailed information on Jambi. Ignorance, a sense of superiority, and an inability to mold and manipulate the native state at will determined the Europeans' opinions. That local polities had arisen from

---

[50] Anderson, *Mission to the East Coast*, pp. 402–03.

[51] "Dan spreekt het vanzelve, dat in een Rijk, alwaar het hoofd zich slechts met visschen, jagen enz. ophoudt en de zaken aan anderen overlaat, vele ongeregeldheden ongestraft blijven," naval commander to governor-general, October 25, 1838, ANRI, Algemeene Secretarie, *gouvernementsbesluit*, January 13, 1839, no. 16.

[52] J. S. Galbraith, "The 'Turbulent Frontier' as a Factor in British Expansion," *Comparative Studies in Society and History* 2 (1960): 157; H. Sutherland, "The Taming of the Trengganu Elite," in *Southeast Asian Transitions: Approaches through Social History*, ed. Ruth T. McVey (New Haven: Yale University Press, 1978), p. 32

[53] Bastin, "Introduction," p. v.

specific geographical and demographic conditions and answered local needs was simply not understood.

THE MALAY STATE

In mitigation it should be said that Malay states were hard to compare with European states as these had developed since the end of the Middle Ages. Like the other states of Southeast Asia, they did not have precise borders or a powerful central authority, their central government had no monopoly on the use of force, their rulers had no well-defined constitutional powers, and there was not a trace of popular sovereignty. In other words, they had none of the characteristics of the modern Western state.[54] The power of the Malay state and ruler was more fluid in terms of territory and structure, and sacral and symbolic in nature.[55]

The *raja* (prince) was above all a symbol of the unity and prosperity of the state. To his subjects, a *kerajaan*, or principality, was nothing more or less than life under a *raja*. This meant that these subjects were assured of protection, since the ruler constituted the link between microcosm and macrocosm, the earthly and the divine, and preserved the balance between the two worlds. The mark of his success was the degree of prosperity in the country, whether or not disasters and crop failures could be held at bay. What is more, his power guaranteed his immediate followers a place in the afterlife; heroic deeds performed for him would be rewarded, if not on earth then certainly with an honorable position in the life to come. According to Milner, this explains how rulers without riches were able to attract followers.[56]

The raja's supernatural status meant that he had few specific responsibilities; this was indeed a sign of his dignity. His everyday occupations were hunting and fishing. He left government to the *pangeran ratu*, who, like the sultan, was chosen by members of noble families from the sultan's family. He ruled in cooperation with frequently powerful ministers and an advisory council. The only functions fulfilled by the sultan himself were those that expressed the unity of the state: he was at the fore in foreign relations, he acted as supreme commander in times of war, arbitrated internal conflicts, and assumed the highest judicial power. His role was to represent the state to the outside world, and to mediate within. This meant that he was the symbol of the state's unity, and in these roles his symbolic power acquired political substance.[57]

Thus in spite of what was theoretically a pivotal role, he had fairly little authority. Appanage holders and "officials" circled around their sovereign and had patron-client relations of their own, which conferred power and influence. The sultan's strength was derived from the size and power of his retinue, not the size of

---

[54] C. Tilly, "Reflections on the History of Western State Making," in *The Formation of National States in Western Europe*, ed. C. Tilly (Princeton, N.J.: Princeton University Press, 1975), pp. 3–83, esp. 27.

[55] J. M. Gullick, "The Condition of Having a Raja: A Review of *Kerajaan*, by A. C. Milner," *Review of Indonesian and Malayan Affairs* 16,2 (1982): 109–29; J. M. Gullick, *Indigenous Political Systems of Western Malaya*, 2nd ed. (London: London School of Economics, 1965); A. C. Milner, *Kerajaan: Malay Political Culture on the Eve of Colonial Rule* (Tucson: University of Arizona Press, 1982).

[56] Milner, *Kerajaan*.

[57] Gullick, *Indigenous Political Systems*.

his territory. People, the scarcest "commodity" in a part of the world with an abundance of land, were the primary measure of his power.

To acquire this reservoir of power, sacred status was not enough; rulers also needed financial resources with which to secure their followers' loyalty. These resources came not from taxes on crop yields, as in the agriculture-based realms of Java, but from duties on imports and exports at the mouth of the river and from trade monopolies. Monopolies existed in varying degrees of legality, in Western eyes, and sometimes amounted to sheer piracy. This meant that the sultan's financial resources, and hence his power, fluctuated wildly from one year to the next.

Poor communications, problems caused for the sultan by a small population and a relatively large territory, and constant fluctuations in revenue combined to produce a process of state formation that was specific to Southeast Asia. Furthermore, friction within the elite, partly caused and exacerbated by polygamy and consequent rival claims to the throne, attenuated the ruler's power. He was dependent on this elite, not only because they had chosen him, but also because of their vital role in the country's administration. "Contest states" were characteristic of Southeast Asia.[58] It was this ever-shifting power structure surrounding a central nucleus of authority, duplicated in a pattern of highly placed followers with their own supporters, that led to the "pulsating galactic polity" described by Tambiah.[59]

THE STRUCTURE OF THE JAMBIAN STATE

In many ways Jambi fitted this stereotype of the classic Malay state. Here too the raja's power was invested with mythical qualities, and he was held responsible for preserving the cosmic balance between heaven and earth.[60] As in other Malay states, he led his people in foreign relations and served internally as arbitrator and highest judicial authority, at least for his Jambian subjects. The Jambian sultan and *pangeran ratu* were both elected by representatives of Jambi's four noble families or *suku*: the Kraton, Kedipan, Perban, and Raja Empat Puluh.[61] The candidates for the throne all came from the largest of the four and the one with most voters, the *suku* Kraton, which had the status of a royal family.[62] Jambi

---

[58] M. Adas, "From Avoidance to Confrontation: Peasant Protest in Precolonial and Colonial Southeast Asia," *Comparative Studies in Society and History* 32 (1981): 217–47.

[59] S. J. Tambiah, *Culture, Thought and Social Action: An Anthropological Perspective* (Cambridge: Harvard University Press, 1985).

[60] This may be inferred from a comment made by the last "contract" sultan, Zainuddin, who attributed disasters such as crop failures and diseases, which had afflicted Jambi in the 1890s, to the sultan's flawed descent (see Resident of Palembang to governor-general, December 14, 1900, NA, Col., vb. August 19, 1901, no. 46).

[61] Haga distinguishes five *suku*, the four named here and the *suku* Permas. In the genealogical lists and nineteenth-century reports studied for this book, however, the *suku* Permas is not mentioned. In the adat literature, too, its function and position are unclear (B. J. Haga, "Eenige opmerkingen over het Adatstaatsrecht van Djambi," in *Feestbundel uitgegeven door het Koninklijk Bataviaasch Genootschap van Kunsten en Wetenschappen bij gelegenheid van zijn 150 jarig bestaan 1778–1928*, 2 vols. (Weltevreden: Kolff, 1929), 1: 233–50.

[62] In 1901, nineteen of the thirty-three men eligible to vote belonged to the *suku* Kraton. Possibly this represents some distortion that arose with time, however. Sultan Taha had consolidated his position by the end of the nineteenth century, and this list may not reflect

did not have a system of direct succession, although its genealogy shows that only the son of a former sultan could ascend to the throne.[63] Hence, as elsewhere in the Archipelago, the Jambian contest for the throne was always within the *suku* Kraton, with the mother's social status determining the hierarchy among the candidates.

As we have seen, the sultan was almost wholly dependent for his income on commerce and export duties. He possessed nominal monopolies of salt and opium, but farmed them out in lean times. Duties imposed by way of corporate tax yielded very little, but the sultan enjoyed a monopoly on certain objects and products with ritualistic value.[64] Like other leading nobles, he could also rely on the labor of debt slaves and their families.[65]

Jambi also corresponded to the Southeast Asian model in terms of its sparse population and poor communication channels. And as in other parts of the Malay region, the sultan passed his days fishing and hunting, leaving the *pangeran ratu* to get on with the business of government. The Twelve-strong Council, the Rapat XII, was the crown prince's advisory and administrative arm. Its members were prominent *anak raja*, including the heads of the four leading noble families.[66] If he wished, the sultan could appoint a specific councillor as ambassador, to represent him in relations with foreign powers such as the colonial authorities.[67]

---

those traditionally eligible to vote (Resident of Palembang to governor-general, May 15, 1901, no. 64, top secret, appendix, NA, Col., vb. August 19, 1901, no. 46).

[63] See the genealogy of Darpa Wiguna, NA, De Kock collection and appendix 1.

[64] E. Gobée and C. Adriaanse, eds., *Ambtelijke adviezen van C. Snouck Hurgronje 1889–1936*, 3 vols. (The Hague: Nijhoff, 1957–65), 3: 2059. For instance, he had a monopoly on ivory, wax, and rhinoceros horn, as well as on certain magical items: gold objects found in the ground (which were regarded as the supernatural gold of the Sultan of Pagaruyung), elephant teeth (the royal gifts that accompanied every consignment sent to the governor-general), the *cunding* (an unspecified) part of the female elephant's abdomen, the *bezoar* (an unspecified part) of three animals, the porcupine, the elephant, and the snake, as well as the genitals of the male squirrel, which was believed to shed them. These were always to be surrendered to the sultan without payment (notes, n.d., documents relating to Jambi 1839–40, 5.2, ANRI, Palembang Residency records 60.12; R. C. van de Bor, "Aanteekeningen betreffende het grondbezit in de Boven-Tembesi," *Tijdschrift voor het Binnenlandsch Bestuur* 30 [1906] 189).

[65] Gobée and Adriaanse, *Ambtelijke Adviezen*, 3: 2055; A. Reid, "Introduction," in *Slavery, Bondage and Dependency in Southeast Asia*, ed. A. Reid and J. Brewster (St. Lucia: University of Queensland Press, 1983), p. 11.

[66] According to a report dating from 1852, some dignitaries fulfilled specific functions: the *pepati dalam*, for instance, supervised the palace household and was authorized to make decisions in the sultan's absence (Resident of Palembang to governor-general, December 16, 1852, M24, NA, Col., vb. February 15, 1853, no. 26). A report from 1878 notes that Pangeran Mangku Negara, head of the *suku* Perban, was always head of the *Rapat XII* (Political officer to Resident of Palembang, April 13, 1878, NA, Col., vb. November 2, 1878, no. 7). Opinions are divided, however, concerning the powers of the *Rapat XII*: in their book *Djambi*, Tideman and Sigar write conflicting things about them. The *Rapat XII* is mentioned only once in the historical sources, and it is impossible to gain a clear picture of its work and influence. Nor are there any references to it in material from the seventeenth or eighteenth centuries (Watson Andaya, communicated personally). It is not impossible that Dutch officials were actually inventing tradition when they drew up detailed reports on this Council in 1929 and 1931 (see Haga, "Eenige opmerkingen"; *Memorie van overgave* by Resident J. F. Verschoor van Nisse, 1931, pp. 61–62, NA, Col., MvO 223).

[67] This happened after 1858; see below.

GOVERNING A DIVERSE POPULATION

In one key respect, however, Jambi departed from the Malay pattern. The sultan ruled, not over a homogeneous Malay population that derived its identity from shared Malay origins, but over many different ethnic groups (the *batin*, Minangkabau, *penghulu, suku-pindah,* and Kubu). The court itself was more Javanese than Malay, as reflected in its Javanese titles.

The heterogeneity of the Jambian population made it extremely difficult to exercise consistent centralized authority. Jambians (i.e., those of Malay origin) living along the Batang Hari and part of the Tembesi enjoyed special ties with the sultan, which popular myths expressed in metaphors of kinship. The Bangsa XII (Twelve Tribes) were said to be the descendants of twelve of the thirteen sons of a former sultan. They did not pay taxes but contributed services instead: they were responsible for maintaining law and order and served as the sultan's bodyguard; they supplied timber, worked as oarsmen, and carried the royal parasol.[68] Only for them did the Sultan serve as the highest judicial power. He renounced his power over the Minangkabau in the upper reaches of the Tebo, Tabir, and Tembesi to the original ruler, the prince of Pagaruyung. In fact, some communities along tributaries of the Tembesi and the Tebo never recognized the sultan's sovereignty at all; even in the twentieth century traces of the resulting dual sovereignty were still to be found in the titles of local chiefs.[69]

The chiefs of the original *batin* population, organized in *dusun* or federations of *dusun,* possessed a large measure of autonomy. They were elected by their own people; their letter of appointment from the sultan was a mere formality.[70] They determined who could use what land; not even the sultan could interfere in such matters.[71] They had jurisdiction over their own affairs, and for them the Bangsa XII, not the sultan, was the highest court of appeal.[72] Their only obligations to the sultan consisted of border controls and taxation *(jajah).* The taxes were collected once every two or three years in money and goods by the *jenang,*[73] and differed from

---

[68] Gobée and Adriaanse, *Ambtelijke adviezen,* 3:2052–53; Mennes, "Eenige aanteekeningen omtrent Djambi," pp. 29–33; Tideman and Sigar, *Djambi,* p. 66.

[69] "Adatrechtgegevens uit Sarolangoen (1905)," in *Adatrechtbundel* 30 (1932): 264, 267; W. C. van der Meulen, "Aantekeningen betreffende de bestuursinrichting in de onderafdeeling Tebo en de daarmede samenhangende volksinstellingen en gebruiken," *Tijdschrift voor het Binnenlandsch Bestuur* 36 (1911): 4; R. C. van der Bor, "Een en ander betreffende het ressort van den controlleur te Sarolangoen, onderafdeeling Boven-Tembesi, der afdeling Djambi," *Tijdschrift voor het Binnenlandsch Bestuur* 30 (1906): 6; R. C. van den Bor, "Aanteekeningen betreffende bestuursvorm en rechtspraak in de Boven-Tembesi tijdens het sultanaat van Djambi," *Tijdschrift voor het Binnenlandsch Bestuur* 30 (1906): 446.

[70] They had a variety of titles *(penghulu, batin, rio, depati),* some originating from the Minangkabau and some acquired from the sultans of Jambi in the seventeenth and eighteenth centuries (Tideman and Sigar, *Djambi,* p. 129; B. Watson Andaya, "Cloth Trade and Palembang Society," p. 22).

[71] Van de Bor, "Aanteekeningen betreffende het grondbezit," p. 183.

[72] Haga, "Eenige opmerkingen."

[73] The *jenang* had originally (around 1500) been no more than an envoy of the sultan, who disseminated the tidings of the end of Javanese supremacy. In the course of time he had become a tax collector, and in some regions he had also acquired the power to administer justice. Besides varying from one region to the next, the *jenang's* influence also depended on the person concerned (Van den Bor, "Aanteekeningen betreffende bestuursvorm en rechtspraak,"

one district to the next. So here too, there was a complete lack of uniformity. Taxation was more important as a formal recognition of the sultan's authority than as an appreciable source of state revenue, especially since every family first received a *serah*, a gift signifying liability to pay taxes, in the form of a machete, clothing, or salt.[74] There was no additional taxation on the yield from crops or the proceeds of forestry. The *batin* groups did have certain obligations, however, in connection with the sultan's visits and in the defense of border areas.

The *penghulu* and *suku-pindah* were even less subject to the sultan's central authority. They had no obligation to pay tribute or to do military service, but were merely required to pay certain sums to the *batin* chieftains for the use of land and forest. The nomadic Kubu lived outside the sultan's authority by virtue of their isolation in the jungle, as did settlements of foreigners, the *orang laut* or *orang timur*, around the Batang Hari estuary.[75] On the other hand, the mixed population on the river Tungkal, largely Minangkabau, Johorese, and Javanese, did come under the sultan's authority and were required to pay taxes and render services such as defending border areas.[76] The few Arab families in the capital—totaling twenty people out of the town's total population of six hundred in 1830—were also nominally subject to the sultan's authority.[77] But as an economically powerful and highly respected group, they were closely associated with the Kraton, an association that helped them assert their independence. Some of them would play important roles in nineteenth-century Jambian history. As for the Chinese communities that had once been so important as middlemen in the pepper trade,[78]

---

p. 430; see also "Aanteekening hofdiensten sultan," n.d., ANRI, Palembang Residency records, 5.2).

[74] There are two conflicting explanations of *serah*. According to one, it was presented as a token that the ruler demanded taxes due to him, and sometimes as an allowance and a means of making an income. If the ruler expected his subjects to give him money or goods, he had to make it possible for them to acquire them (Van den Bor, "Aanteekeningen betreffende bestuursvorm en rechtspraak," p. 439). According to an alternative explanation, however, it was not every family but only the tax collector who received *serah*, in the form of a suit of clothes presented after he had given his superiors the proceeds. Levies imposed in the uplands in the early nineteenth century consisted of textiles, mats, salt, and gold, and some regions were also expected to contribute slaves and rice. The value of these levies varied enormously. A percentage went to officials (see "Aanteekening hofdiensten sultan," n.d., ANRI, Palembang Residency records 5.2.). In 1835 the estimate from Tungkal came to 80 *reals* or 2.5 *koyang* of rice, plus services, ivory, wax, dragon's blood, and gum benzoin. In 1878, five guilders were demanded every other year from each family living on the banks of the Tembesi (see P. J. Veth, ed., *Midden-Sumatra: Reizen en onderzoekingen der Sumatra-Expeditie, uitgerust door het Aardrijkskundig Genootschap 1877–1879*, 4 vols. [Leiden: Brill, 1881–92], 4 part 1: 200). Around 1900 the sum mentioned is *Dfl.* 3.50. In the Upper Batang Hari, rice was offered once every three years; village heads, villagers, and *jenang* presented it to the sultan in festive processions (see the memorandum "Nota aangaande de Batang Hari van Moeara Tebo tot Tanjoeng," KITLV, Wellan collection, 590a).

[75] This group, whose people lived from fishing, remained under the authority of its own chieftains (Anderson, *Mission to the East*, p. 405).

[76] Piagem, "Aanstellingsbrief van Orang Kaija Wira Sentika" 1190, ANRI, Algemeene Secretarie, *gouvernementsbesluit*, August 25, 1934, no. 9; Haga, "Eenige opmerkingen."

[77] Resident of Palembang to governor-general, January 17, 1831, no. 24, NA, Col., file "Zeeroverij in Nederlandsch-Oost-Indië 1831–1835" ("Piracy in the Dutch East Indies 1831–1835"): 4168.

[78] B. Watson Andaya, "Cash Cropping," pp. 103–04, 108.

they were no longer found in the capital in the early nineteenth century. Their presence was not reported there again until the 1860s.[79]

To sum up, the sultan had only nominal authority over the *penghulu* and *suku-pindah* population, the Kubu, and *orang laut* and greater power over the more populous *batin* groups in the upland territories. But only the largest group, the Jambians themselves, were directly subject to the sultan's authority.[80]

To govern this mixed population, the sultan was dependent on local *batin* chieftains and on members of the elite, the *anak raja*, who served as appanage holders and tax collectors. Like the political marriages mentioned above, appanages were significant factors in political rivalries; they could help to bolster support and strengthen positions. Members of the three other important noble families were eligible for them, but here too the sultan's family took precedence. Some fifteen appanages are known to have existed around 1900, and almost all belonged to the sultan's family.[81] Most were temporary ones that had to be returned to the sultan upon the holder's decease, following the choice of a new sultan, or in the event of a conflict with him.[82] They therefore remained marketable; the sultan handed out his political capital in measured quantities. Only the district around the Merangin, a tributary of the Tembesi, was traditionally in the hands of another noble family, the Kedipan. The Perban held smaller areas on the banks of the Tebo and the Pelepat (a tributary of the Tebo).[83]

The power of appanage holders was derived from the sultan's, and it therefore included similar privileges: appanage holders could impose taxes and issue judgments in appeal cases, and they were entitled to set maximum prices and to mediate in conflicts.[84] Appanage holders and other *anak raja* generally lived together with their followers and debt slaves in a separate *dusun* in their own region.[85] The sultan himself did not reside permanently in the kraton in the Jambian capital. Like other Malay princes, but unlike those on Java, every sultan certainly had his permanent residence after 1858, though each was in a different village. Sultan Facharuddin, as we have already seen, had not settled in the capital before 1833. This custom reflected the realm's peripatetic central power. Since power was divided among several bodies, and many sections of the population had varying degrees of autonomy, the Jambian ruler exerted little central authority, and the Jambian form of government deviated even more from the European ideal than the classic Malay model.

---

[79] Anderson, *Mission to the East Coast*, p. 396; see chapter 6.

[80] According to a census held in 1930, 58 percent of the population was Jambian as compared to 25 percent Minangkabau that year, the latter being divided into 16 percent *batin*, 6 percent *penghulu*, and 3 percent others. Kubu accounted for less than 1 percent, and those of Palembang origin almost 2 percent (Tideman and Sigar, *Djambi*, p. 46).

[81] See chapter 8.

[82] Haga, "Eenige opmerkingen"; "Nota over de Batang Hari van Moeara Tebo tot Tanjoeng," KITLV, Wellan collection, 590a.

[83] Gobée and Adriaanse, *Ambtelijke adviezen*, 3: 2046.

[84] O. L. Helfrich, "Nota omtrent het stroomgebied der Boelian Djeba en Djangga," *Tijdschrift van het Bataviaasch Genootschap* 45 (1902): 530–40, 536, 538; Van der Meulen, "Aantekeningen betreffende de bestuursinrichting in de onderafdeeling Tebo," p. 10; "De adel van Benkoelen en Djambi," in *Adatrechtbundel* 22 (1923): 309–40, esp. 330.

[85] See "Nota inheemse bestuursstructuur," April 13, 1878, NA, Col., vb. November 2, 1878, no. 7.

EUROPEAN IMAGES AND COLONIAL REALITY

Whenever Europeans compared this form of government with their own, they found it wanting. Nonetheless, in retrospect it becomes clear that the colonial power structure at the beginning of the nineteenth century displayed similarities to the precolonial state, simply because the geopolitical circumstances were the same. The emerging colonial state of the Dutch East Indies was constrained by the geographical parameters of the region: the colonial government too had to contend with the vastness and inaccessibility of the territory, for until the end of the 1840s it too was dependent on sailing vessels and hence on monsoons and winds. The colonial authorities too had undergone a gradual development that had only started in the seventeenth century, similarly under the influence of, and in concert with, trade and commercial interests in the region. The colonial borders too were still fluid, since the long process of solidifying them did not start until the 1820s. The colonial state too continued to manifest significant local differences in the exercise of power in the nineteenth century, so much so that we usually discuss the colonial state in the East Indies as a twentieth-century construction. The colonial authorities too ruled over very different groups, each with their own customs, judiciary, and tax systems. And the colonial state too was still, by necessity, a decentralized structure in the early nineteenth century, and had very limited power in the various regions. In other words, its authority was largely nominal.

Until 1830 the problem of finances also complicated life for the colonial state. Without the army, which was technologically superior to native military capabilities, the colonial authorities would have been weaker still. For Dutch government lacked the sacred qualities that gave the sultan his influence. However, considerations of this kind played no role for the officials of the Dutch East Indies. They took the lawfulness of their authority for granted, and Britain's return of these territories in 1816 strengthened this conviction. It is time to look more closely at the authority exercised by the Dutch in the early nineteenth century and at the first contacts between Batavia and Jambi.

BATAVIA AND THE OUTER ISLANDS FROM 1816 ONWARD

The power that the Netherlands wielded in the archipelago in the early nineteenth century extended over a limited area. What the great Dutch novelist Multatuli would later call its "girdle of emerald" then consisted of a few precious fragments rather than a chain of gems. The VOC's trading interests had clashed with expansionist aspirations and the related administrative costs. Before Britain's takeover in 1811, the territory over which the Netherlands exercised direct rule was limited to Java, small parts of the Moluccas, and North Celebes and South Celebes. On Sumatra, the only place under Dutch control was Padang, on the west coast. Elsewhere the Dutch and local rulers had formed trade agreements, many of which had political implications.

In 1816, the British started returning the former Dutch possessions, which they had held for five years, to the control of the East Indies government. Anglo-Dutch relations and rivalries would remain a major factor in shaping Dutch expansionist aspirations until around 1871, and to a lesser degree thereafter. The economic competition between the two countries in the Malay region had already become fiercer toward the close of the eighteenth century, and in 1786, after the Fourth Anglo-Dutch War (1780–84), it led to the establishment of the British settlement at Penang, on the coast of the Malay peninsula. During its period of control (1811–16), Britain had used Penang as a center for strengthening its trading interests in the Archipelago with coffee exports and cotton imports. Britain was apprehensive of any challenge to its trading routes to China, and Th. S. Raffles did his best to create a permanent British influence in the Archipelago. He feared the imposition of a Dutch trading monopoly, as had been customary under the VOC. So the actual transfer of power by British officials in 1816 and subsequent years was a rather nervous business, and friction was most apparent on Sumatra.[86] As governor of Bengkulu, Raffles tried to retain influence there and concluded numerous friendship contracts with local princes, one being with the Sultan of Aceh in 1819. That same year, he also secured from the Sultan of Riau the rights to a trading post in Singapore. In 1824, after four years of negotiations, the British and Dutch governments finally signed an agreement full of compromises, which, among other things, fixed the borders in the western parts of the Archipelago under international law. In the Treaty of London of March 1824, the British withdrew to the Malay peninsula, where they controlled the Melaka Straits from the ports of Penang and Singapore. In exchange for Bengkulu, the Netherlands relinquished its claims to Melaka and Singapore, which gave them a free hand over Sumatra up to the border with Aceh. The independence of this northern region of Sumatra, a strategically important area at the beginning of the Melaka Straits, was guaranteed. To safeguard British commercial interests, Articles 3 and 4 laid down that neither country should impede the other's trade with native rulers, with whom new contracts would be concluded; The Hague promised to notify London of any such new agreements.[87]

The Treaty of London had been drafted primarily with a view to resolving the problems in Sumatra and on the Malay peninsula. Britain, a far more influential power internationally, agreed to it because it wanted a strong Netherlands in Europe and was anxious to ward off interference in the Archipelago on the part of other powers; it kept a weather eye on the American and French pepper trade in Sumatra, for instance.[88] The treaty safeguarded Britain's trade with China—an important criterion for the British. What is more, Article 3 safeguarded the trading interests of Penang and Singapore in the Archipelago.

The treaty also suited the Dutch, who had an interest in freedom of trade and activity on Sumatra, but for whom territorial control held little appeal. They continued the VOC's old policy of refraining from intervention: rights were claimed over territories only in the event of some threat, whether internal or external;

---

[86] N. Tarling, *Anglo-Dutch Rivalry in the Malay World 1780–1824* (Cambridge: Cambridge University Press; Sydney: University of Queensland Press, 1962), pp. 81–93.

[87] C. M. Smulders, *Geschiedenis en verklaring van het Tractaat van 17 maart 1824 te Londen gesloten tusschen Nederland en Groot-Brittannië ter regeling van wederzijdsche belangen en rechten in Oost-Indië* (Utrecht: Siddré, 1856); P. H. van der Kemp, *Handboek tot de kennis van 's Lands zoutmiddel in Nederlandsch-Indië: Eene economisch-historische studie* (Batavia: Kolff, 1894); N. Tarling, "British Policy in the Malay Peninsula and Archipelago 1824–1871," *Journal of the Malayan Branch of the Royal Asiatic Society* 30,3 (1957): 123–32; Tarling, *Anglo-Dutch Rivalry*, pp. 81–177; N. Tarling, *Imperial Britain in South-East Asia* (Kuala Lumpur: Oxford University Press, 1975), pp. 19–22.

[88] Tarling, "British Policy in the Malay Peninsula."

otherwise the colonial government contented itself with nominal authority at most. The Netherlands, with a population of two million, simply did not have the staff or financial resources to exercise direct rule over a territory of almost two million square kilometers and twenty million inhabitants on the other side of the world.[89] Since the country's period under French rule (1806–13), the public debt had put pressure on Dutch government spending and until the 1830s the deficit in the East Indies budget continued to grow, reaching 50 percent of total government expenditure at the time of the Java War (1825–30).[90]

Besides the lack of people and resources, transport and communications were not far enough advanced to enable the Dutch to take firmer control of Sumatra and the rest of the Archipelago. Steamships did not arrive on the scene until the mid-1840s. Given their reliance on wind and water conditions, connections between the center of the Archipelago and the periphery by sailing vessel were incidental and irregular before then (and afterward too, as it turned out). Around 1830, for instance, Palembang went three months without hearing anything from Batavia. Even when the wind was favorable, it took more than three weeks for an urgent message from Palembang to reach Batavia in 1833.[91] This time lag meant that the Residents (heads of district administration) had a large measure of freedom in their activity. Quite often, their policies had to be authorized retroactively.

The same applied, at the time, to the governors-general. Batavia too enjoyed considerable autonomy because of the poor connections between the Netherlands and the colony. Letters to and from the East Indies were transported by sailing vessel until the mid-1830s. As a result, answers to questions took eight to ten months to reach their destination. Moreover, the number of senior colonial officials in The Hague was very small. In 1842, when the Ministry of Colonies was detached from the Naval Ministry, a total of only twenty-three officials were responsible for the administration of the East and West Indies together.[92] All this gave Batavia ample room to maneuver; King William I and his ministers had little opportunity to influence colonial policy directly. They did map out the broad contours of policy, especially in finances, but for the details they were dependent on the "King's Representative" in Batavia. This explains why the governor-general and the Minister of Colonies were constantly changing places in the nineteenth century. This job swapping guaranteed good cooperation, continuity, and expertise,

---

[89] As late as 1865, no more than 175 European officials worked for the administrative authorities of Java, the most intensively governed island in the archipelago and the one with the busiest commerce, an island with a population of 12–13 million (C. Fasseur, *The Politics of Colonial Exploitation: Java, the Dutch and the Cultivation System*, trans. R. E. Elson and Ary Kraal [Ithaca, N.Y.: Cornell Southeast Asia Program Publications, 1992], p. 22).

[90] Creutzberg, P., ed., *Public Finance 1816–1939; Changing Economy in Indonesia: A Selection of Statistical Source Material from the Early Nineteenth Century up to 1940*, vol. 2 (The Hague: Nijhoff, 1976), pp. 49–50.

[91] Resident of Palembang to Commissioner-General van den Bosch, December 30, 1829, ANRI, Palembang Residency records 45.10; Resident of Palembang to commissioner-general, July 1, 1833, ANRI, Algemeene Secretarie, *gouvernementsbesluit*, September 19, 1833, no. 1.

[92] *De semi-officiële particuliere briefwisseling tussen J. C. Baud en J. J. Rochussen 1845–1851 en enige daarop betrekking hebbende andere stukken*, ed. W. A. Baud, 3 vols. (Assen: Van Gorcum, 1983), 1: 7.

especially when the minister's post was filled first and the king had already gotten to know his governor-general in that position beforehand.[93]

Notwithstanding structural problems of control, the Netherlands' traditional policy in the region of ruling from a distance, and the diplomatic talks in preparation for the Treaty of London, the East Indies colonial authorities soon focused their attention on Sumatra. It was here that they ran into difficulties straight away, and Raffles initially exploited the situation to his advantage. Both in Palembang and in Minangkabau, two regions that bounded parts of Jambi, the advent of Dutch control had exacerbated internal divisions, culminating in resistance to the colonizers. In Minangkabau, the rapid expansion of coffee-growing and the coffee trade at the end of the eighteenth century had generated hostility between the new commercial elite and the traditional ruling classes, whose power was based on rice cultivation and gold mining. Islamic fundamentalism, imported from the Middle East, had given the former the new trading ethic they had sought, which explains the subsequent Islamic revival. A movement intent on the purification of Islam had provoked a civil war, in which the colonial authorities had become embroiled after their arrival in 1818. Indeed, they were in the midst of the fray. For political and economic reasons, they had chosen the side of the traditional elite, despite their interest in the coffee trade, and a Minangkabau civil war had grown into a revolt against the colonial *kafir* authorities. Thus began the Padri War, the first Dutch colonial war in the nineteenth century, which would last from 1818 until 1838.[94]

The unrest in Palembang was even more strongly a legacy of British rule, as it had been caused by an internal factional struggle at court, which Raffles had encouraged. When the Dutch returned in 1818 they replaced Najamuddin, whom Raffles had installed, by the former sultan, Badaruddin. But while Raffles continued to support Najamuddin, Badaruddin proved understandably reluctant to give up his independence as required by the East Indies colonial authorities.[95] In June 1819, the conflict escalated into open battle in Palembang, and after a few days H. W. Muntinghe, the Dutch commissioner of Palembang and Bangka, was forced to retreat. When a punitive expedition conducted in August that year also ended in failure, the colonial authorities set up a blockade on the river Musi. For eighteen months they had no contact at all with Palembang, and both sides prepared for the coming battle. Finally, in May 1821, the Dutch were able to launch a new expedition, one involving the unprecedented number of 4,500 troops in land and naval forces. The jubilation with which the Netherlands responded to the ensuing

---

[93] Examples of this exchange of roles abound: J. van den Bosch was governor-general from 1828 to 1833, commissioner-general from June 1833 to February 1834, minister from 1834 to 1840; J. C. Baud was interim governor-general from 1833 to 1836 and minister from 1840 to 1848; C. F. Pahud was minister from 1849 to 1856 and governor-general from 1856 to 1860; J. J. Rochussen was governor-general from 1845 to 1851 and minister from 1858 to 1861; P. Mijer was minister from 1856 to 1858 and for a few months in 1866, and governor-general from 1866 to 1872; J. Loudon was minister from 1861 to 1862 and governor-general from 1872 to 1875; see J. J. Westendorp Boerma and appendixes 4 and 5 of this volume. J. J. Westendorp Boerma, ed., *Briefwisseling tussen J. van den Bosch en J. C. Baud, 1829–1832 en 1834–1836*, 2 vols. (Utrecht: Kemink & Son, 1956), 1: 7–8.

[94] Dobbin, *Islamic Revivalism*, pp. 4, 125, 143.

[95] M. O. Woelders, *Het sultanaat Palembang 1811–1925*, KITLV verhandelingen 72 (The Hague: Nijhoff, 1975), pp. 1–27.

victory is a measure of the importance that the Dutch attached to the conquest. Badaruddin was sent to Batavia, like many native princes before and after him, with a kinsman being installed in his place. In 1823, a permanent contract was signed with this new sultan, in which he officially relinquished sovereignty over Palembang in exchange for a fixed income. In the autumn of 1824, a desperate attack by Palembang insurgents on the kraton, which by then was occupied by the Resident, prompted the abolition of the sultan's power altogether, and the Residency came under direct Dutch rule. Unrest persisted, however, particularly in the Rawas areas bordering on Jambi. These two flash points, Palembang and Minangkabau, which were both partly influenced by the proximity of the British, formed the context for the first meetings between representatives of Jambi and Batavia in 1819.

BATAVIA AND JAMBI: INITIAL CONTACT

In 1818, an envoy had visited the Sultan of Jambi in connection with the conflict in Palembang and the Rawas. Commissioner H. W. Muntinghe was hoping to forge alliances in the region, and rumors that the Pangeran Ratu Anom Keumo Judo planned to join the rebels with at least a thousand troops had sowed alarm.[96] After the defeat of 1819, the colonial government informed the Sultan of Jambi of its decision to blockade not only the river Musi (in Palembang) but the Batang Hari as well. This notification—which was accompanied by assurances of friendship toward Jambi—was a diplomatic courtesy and prompted an equally diplomatic reply. The sultan professed his friendship and declared that neither he nor any of his subjects would ever support the Sultan of Palembang.[97]

The colonial government first considered strengthening ties with Jambi in July 1820, with a view to the planned expedition against Palembang. But given reports of internal divisions there, it started by sending a reliable Arab with gifts to assess the situation. The outcome of this mission is unclear.

Shortly before the expedition of May 1821, however, the *pangeran ratu* of Jambi, later the Sultan Facharuddin, displayed his good will. He had already been living in Palembang for two or three years, and was willing to sign a contract. Furthermore, he offered help against Badaruddin in exchange for a quantity of silver coins equivalent to 4,400 guilders to pay off debts or, as he conveyed confidentially, to win over followers. He was given the money in token of friendship.[98] For the government this was the first sign of the indigence of the Jambian sultan's family (later to become notorious) and the first in a long series of Jambian requests for financial assistance.

It is improbable that the Pangeran Ratu Anom Keumo Judo, acting as commander of the Palembang batteries during the siege, actually provided the promised assistance. H. M. de Kock, the leader of the expedition and the highest army officer in the East Indies at the time, certainly doubted it. After his victory, he was approached several times by the Pangeran Ratu Anom Keumo Judo, whose

---

[96] P. H. van der Kemp, "Palembang en Banka in 1816–1920," *Bijdragen tot de Taal-, Land- en Volkenkunde* 51 (1900): 458, 479.

[97] Besluit, November 11, 1819, A; May 9, 1820, A; July 6, 1820, C, all secret Council decisions (decisions *in Rade*), in NA, Col., 4526.

[98] *Gouvernementsbesluit*, July 14, 1821, no. 6, ANRI, Algemeene Secretarie.

father had instructed him to ask the Dutch "to plant their flag in that realm too" in exchange for monopolies on opium and salt.[99] He said he hoped for help in fighting the pirates of Lingga and Riau. So the crown prince was basically interested in securing political and financial support from what was evidently now the strongest power in the region, an understandable goal given the weakness of the Jambian sultanate. It was perfectly common in the eighteenth century for Malay states to request help from influential neighbors in their internal power struggles, and these requests did not originate—as later on—from suggestions by Dutch officials.[100] These were internal political maneuvers, which were prompted solely by the local leaders' own estimates of the balance of power.

There was a second motive underlying Jambi's request, according to the Dutch. The sultan probably feared that after Palembang, Jambi would be next; by taking the initiative he hoped to secure favorable terms. But the colonial authorities were not yet interested and decided "to review the matter should the occasion arise."[101] Jambi was no longer needed to stabilize the situation in Palembang, and contact between Jambi and Batavia petered out. It was not until 1829 that talks resumed, prompted by the scourge of piracy.

PIRACY

Piracy was an old and honorable profession in the Indonesian archipelago, closely connected with trade—the distinction between these two forms of "business at sea" was indeed rather blurred. Merchants sometimes had recourse to what Westerners saw as simple robbery. As long as they returned richly laden, no one seemed very concerned about where the goods had come from. Concepts of "mine and thine" did not apply here, any more than they did in the English Channel, where similar practices were common well into the nineteenth century. In the East Indies, piracy was a means of survival for ousted scions of royal families unable to make a livelihood on land in their own region, and a last resort for down-and-out shipowners and captains. Local princes were always willing to offer protection in exchange for a percentage of the booty. And nature itself provided additional protection in the form of swampy coastal regions full of inlets and coves, which sheltered the pirates and hid them from view.[102]

Piracy had greatly increased in the late eighteenth century, partly because of the destruction of the Johore sultanate at Riau. In 1794, the Resident of Palembang reported that pirates had besieged the tin island of Bangka virtually the whole year. Within a decade, they had decimated the island's population and virtually ruined the tin trade.[103] In the early nineteenth century, the political and military

---

[99] Commander-in-chief of Palembang expedition to governor-general, July 22, 1821, no. 26, ANRI, Algemeene Secretarie, *gouvernementsbesluit*, August 21, 1821, no. 16.

[100] J. van Goor, "Seapower, Trade and State-Formation: Pontianak and the Dutch," in *Trading Companies in Asia 1600–1830*, ed. J. van Goor (Utrecht: HES, 1986), pp. 83–106; Vos, *Gentle Janus, Merchant Prince*.

[101] *Gouvernementsbesluit*, August 21, 1821, no. 16, ANRI, Algemeene Secretarie.

[102] L. A. Mills, "British Malaya, 1824–1867," *Journal of the Malaysian Branch of the Royal Asiatic Society* 33,3 (1960): 225; Milner, *Kerajaan*, p. 20; R. C. Vos, *Gentle Janus, Merchant Prince*, pp. 191–97.

[103] Vos, *Gentle Janus, Merchant Prince*, p. 197.

handovers of power between the Dutch and the British presented new opportunities. What is more, after 1819 the new trading center of Singapore in the west of the Archipelago enticed pirates with its promise of easy spoils. Piracy was fueled by the Malay sultans' growing need for money. Privateers needed a measure of protection to market their goods; besides taking a share of the booty, local rulers obtained protection for their own trade in exchange for licenses. But piracy posed a direct threat to small merchants, to local prosperity and hence indirectly to European sources of revenue.[104] The relatively larger European ships were less vulnerable to attack. Pirates wanted to obtain booty and slaves at low cost, and therefore tended to victimize local proas. Piracy became a major threat to local trade.

The VOC had already embarked on a campaign against piracy, and the colonial government renewed its efforts in 1816. The Treaty of London of 1824 included a clause about joint measures, but it had remained a dead letter. Each power would eventually have to clean up its own backyard, or rather patrol its own seas. The Dutch authorities in the East Indies, more willing to exert themselves than the British, used a wide range of tactics.[105] Proas patrolled the coasts, and government regulations were adopted banning the construction and use of the types of vessels favored by the pirates. In addition, efforts were made at an early stage to persuade local rulers to conclude contracts agreeing to help in the fight against piracy. If none of these measures availed, military expeditions were a last resort.[106] Under the predecessor of Johannes van den Bosch, however, patrols had dwindled and there had been no expeditions at all. Budgetary cuts took their toll, and patrol proas that were not lying in disrepair at the ports were being used for regular transport.[107] Piracy reached its peak in the Straits of Melaka in the period 1828–35.[108] In July 1829, the Resident of Palembang had notified Batavia that not a single merchant proa had called there for months because traders were afraid of the pirates that scoured the coasts.[109] In May of that year, pirates from the settlement of Saba on the Batang Hari had even attacked a ship belonging to the

---

[104] J. P. Cornets de Groot van Kraaijenburg, "Notices historiques sur les pirateries commises dans l'Archipel Indien-Oriental, et sur les mesures prises pour les réprimer par le gouvernement Néerlandais, dans les trente dernières années," *Le Moniteur des Indes-Orientales et Occidentales* 1 (1847): 267.

[105] For an overview of Dutch anti-piracy efforts, see ibid., pp. 158–63, 194–204, 230–41, 267–76, 319–30. The author, a former member of the Council of the Dutch East Indies, wrote his memorandum while serving as secretary-general at the Ministry of Colonies, his aim being to persuade the British that the Dutch were making a serious effort to suppress piracy. He undoubtedly availed himself of the collection of texts "Zeeroverij in Nederlandsch Oost-Indië," which can still be found intact in the records of the Ministry of Colonies (NA, Col., 4168). See also (although less reliable) J. H. P. E. Kniphorst, "Historische schets van den zeeroof in den Oost-Indischen Archipel," *Tijdschrift voor het Zeewezen*, 1875–81 (with sequels in *Tijdschrift voor Nederlandsch-Indië*, 1882, and *Indische Gids*, 1883), p. 45.

[106] Mills, "British Malaya, 1824–1867," p. 261; Cornets de Groot van Kraaijenburg, "Notices historiques sur les pirateries," pp. 241, 267.

[107] Cornets de Groot van Kraaijenburg, "Notices historiques sur les pirateries," pp. 240, 330.

[108] Mills, "British Malaya, 1824–1867," p. 272.

[109] Resident of Palembang to commissioner-general, July 7, 1829, no. 15, ANRI, Algemeene Secretarie, *gouvernementsbesluit*, November 13, 1829, no. 18.

Dutch colonial authorities. This audacious action prompted the authorities to renew their overtures to the Sultan of Jambi.[110]

RENEWED CONTACT WITH JAMBI

In August and October 1829, the ambitious Resident of Palembang F. C. E. Praetorius, who had only just taken office, sent an envoy related to the Jambian royal house on a mission to Sultan Facharuddin. The sultan was asked to help trace the seized Dutch ship, and later on he was given to understand, in guarded terms, that he should expel all pirates from his territory.[111] Its location and geographical conditions made Jambi a pirates' haven: the marshy and cove-filled estuary of the Batang Hari created a natural and inaccessible refuge. Around 1800, pirates, originating from the islands to the west of Borneo, succeeded in establishing a base here and ensconced themselves in a stronghold, Muara Saba. Their leader, Tengku Long, had acquired considerable political influence in the capital in 1820.[112] Two years later, however, he had been driven out of Jambi and had sought refuge in the vicinity of Siak.[113] This did not diminish the pirates' influence, however. They were estimated to number some 1,000 to 1,500 men in 1831, one-third of whom were slaves. According to the Residents of Palembang and Bangka, the booty was sold at the marketplace in Jambi.[114] Resident Praetorius placed very little reliance in the authority of Sultan Facharuddin; the Sultan did not even live in the capital, as the first mission made plain, but was away at the Minangkabau border fighting the Padri for the Sultan of Pagarujung. Meanwhile, a power struggle had developed in the capital between Arab merchants, the sultan's representative (his son-in-law, Pangeran Nata di Raja), and Pangeran Kassim (a rich merchant and a member of the *suku* Kraton). Without waiting for the sultan's reply, Praetorius suggested to his superiors that he himself should undertake an expedition against the pirates. But this went too far for Batavia, if only because of the expense. In November 1829, however, Batavia instructed Praetorius to renew contact with the Sultan of Jambi, "with the aim of concluding a contract including explicit clauses about combating piracy."[115] Early in 1830, the East Indies Advisory Council asserted that the colonial authorities would eventually be compelled to seek some measure

---

[110] Resident of Palembang to Resident of Bangka, June 6, 1829, no. 91, ANRI, Palembang Residency records 45.3.

[111] Resident of Palembang to commissioner-general, October 4, 1829, no. 97; Resident of Palembang to Resident of Bangka, November 19, 1829, no. 123, ANRI, Palembang Residency records 45.4.

[112] See note 37 above.

[113] He was rehabilitated by the colonial authorities in 1828, and the sultan of Lingga placed him in charge of Reteh. In 1857 he refused to recognize the sultan newly approved by the Dutch administration, and the following year he was killed in a punitive expedition (E. de Waal, *Onze Indische financiën: Nieuwe reeks aanteekeningen*, 10 vols. [The Hague: Nijhoff, 1876–1907], 3: 31).

[114] Resident of Palembang to commissioner-general, January 17, 1831, no. 24, secret; Resident van Banka to governor-general, January 19, 1831, no. 115, NA, Col., file "Zeeroverij," 4168.

[115] "... met derzelven een kontrakt te sluiten waarbij expresselijk worde gestipuleerd het tegengaan der zeeroverij"; Resident of Palembang to commissioner-general, August 12, 1829, no. 57, ANRI, Algemeene Secretarie, *gouvernementsbesluit*, November 13, 1829, no. 18.

of involvement with Jambi.[116] Johannes van den Bosch, the new governor-general (1830–34) who had arrived in Batavia at the beginning of January 1830, entirely agreed.[117] We should view the events that took place between 1830 and 1934 and the conclusion of a "permanent" contract with Jambi against the backdrop of his policy on Sumatra.

JOHANNES VAN DEN BOSCH AND SUMATRA

Van den Bosch set out his policy on Sumatra at the end of 1830, in response to the Padri War on the west coast of the island. In July 1829, he had set sail for the East Indies with clear instructions from King William I. He was to reverse the losses being suffered by the Dutch possessions in the East Indies as quickly as possible. These had fluctuated between 5 and 16.5 million guilders annually since 1824, partly because of the Java War that had broken out in 1825; the budget was being exceeded by 25-50 percent.[118] How Van den Bosch carried out these instructions is amply documented. On Java, his Cultivation System (Cultuurstelsel) would lead to a surplus amounting to several million guilders in the 1830s and subsequent decades. But we know little about his plans for the development of Sumatra's resources. No glorious profits here; the success story of his years in the East Indies lay elsewhere.

Van den Bosch in fact knew little about Sumatra, as he himself was well aware. In December 1830, when he first formulated his ideas and presented his policy to C. P. J. Elout, the new Resident of Riau, he confessed to being "very poorly acquainted" with the island's local affairs. He could indeed write, in all innocence, that Sumatra appeared, like Java, "to be divided in two by a mountain range."[119] This ignorance would often show through in his plans.

These plans belonged in his wider conception of a relationship in which colonies, he felt, should fill the mother country's coffers. "Colonies are there to serve the mother country, not the other way around," the government regulations of 1802 stated baldly, in spite of enlightened influences. The same adage continued to

---

[116] Van Sevenhoven to commander-in-chief, January 6, 1830, ANRI, Algemeene Secretarie, app. February 2, 1830, XIV. Before this could happen, the council also asserted, negotiations would be held, not only with Jambi but with other east coast realms too, Siak in particular. A naval vessel would sail along the coast and gather information about the geographical situation.

[117] Van den Bosch had been posted for three years, but in October 1830, afflicted by poor health, he was already pressing The Hague to send a successor or replacement. For this position William I chose J. C. Baud, a senior colonial official at the Ministry of Navy and Colonies, who arrived in Batavia in January 1833; the two worked closely together until Van den Bosch's departure in February 1834. In June 1833, Van den Bosch became commissioner-general while Baud was appointed interim governor-general. On his return to the Netherlands in May 1834, Van den Bosch was immediately appointed Minister of Colonies. Baud remained in the East Indies after D. J. de Eerens took over as governor-general in September 1834 to acclimatize him to the job. He did not return to the Netherlands until 1836, and he remained involved in all important colonial matters after this in an advisory capacity. In December 1839, he succeeded Van den Bosch as Minister of Colonies (a post he held until 1848). In all, Van den Bosch and Baud together determined policy on Sumatra for almost twenty years (Westendorp Boerma, *Briefwisseling*, 1: 6–9).

[118] Creutzberg, *Public Finance 1816–1939*, pp. 49–50.

[119] Governor-general to Resident of Riau, December 26, 1830, secret, NA, Col., exh. September 26, 1830, no. 28.

apply unabated in the post-Napoleonic era. The soaring national debt was in itself sufficient justification for such pragmatism in the colonizers' eyes. Trade was the way to increase revenue. It has often been pointed out—and Van den Bosch commented on it himself—that the Cultivation System, with its emphasis on indigenous commercial goods, linked up seamlessly with the traditional commercial policies of the VOC. The principle was that money should flow to the Netherlands not through direct taxation, but through trade. Fitting the proceeds from the colonies into the national and international trading circuit would maximize the yield harvested from the tropical soil. These ideas, inspired by the enlightened mercantilism of William I, provided the foundations for the Cultivation System that was introduced into Java in 1830. Regulating local labor by making it compulsory was seen as the cheapest way of procuring Java's agricultural produce for export.[120]

Outside Java, in the absence of direct colonial rule—and hence of controls on local labor—Van den Bosch sought other ways of accomplishing his aims, namely, by gaining control of local trade flows. The colonial authorities would protect and regulate trade by setting up safe marketplaces, where local merchants could supply their wares to the Dutch of their own free will, out of enlightened self-interest and at fair prices. Another way in which the Dutch could control trade was by monitoring key imports. "Whoever is in the possession of opium, linen, salt, and rice, and can supply these goods for the lowest prices, is master of trade in the archipelago," Van den Bosch told his minister in July 1831.[121] At this point, he was not yet clear about exactly how the authorities would obtain this merchandise, and he did not submit a definite proposal. High taxes were at odds with this objective; the population should be enabled to market their wares for as favorable a price as possible. At most, the colonial authorities could decide to collect any duties still accruing to the local rulers themselves to help pay for the small fortresses that needed to be built.

As a political realist, Van den Bosch was aware that only harmony could yield the economic relations and profits that the Dutch envisaged. He therefore warned against expanding Dutch authority by military means. Territorial possessions were anathema to him. As he wrote in January 1831, "Territorial possessions in most of those countries yield no benefits, require costly administration, plunge us into wars, and alienate the population."[122] Although he wanted to bring the entire Archipelago "under the influence of Dutch rule," this implied only recognition of sovereignty,[123] an objective he hoped to accomplish through voluntary contracts, cooperation with native leaders, and indirect administration. Direct rule should

---

[120] Benjamin White, *'Agricultural Involution' and Its Critics: Twenty Years after Clifford Geertz*, Working Papers Series 6 (The Hague: Institute of Social Studies, 1983); Leonard Blussé, "Labour Takes Root: Mobilization and Immobilization of Javanese Rural Society under the Cultivation System," *Itinerario* 8,1 (1984): 77–117.

[121] "Die in het bezit is van amfioen [opium], lijnwaden, zout en rijst en deze artikelen tot de minste prijs kan leveren is meester van den handel in den archipel"; Westendorp Boerma, *Briefwisseling*, 1: 97.

[122] "Het territoriaal bezit in de meeste dier landen leidt tot geen resultaat, vordert een kostbare administratie, wikkelt ons in oorlogen en verwijdert de bevolking van ons"; ibid., p. 76.

[123] Governor-general to Resident of Riau, December 26, 1830, secret, NA, Col., exh. September 26, 1830, no. 28.

not extend beyond "the range of our artillery." Furthermore, the Dutch administration should refrain from all interference, even with what were objectionable abuses in Western eyes. After all, did not everyone wish to be "master of his own country"? Such noninterference did not reflect a purely academic interest in the inherent qualities of the islanders but, as before, a pragmatic approach to administration. Combating abuses would be impossible without "making the native into a different, more civilized person," and that would take time.[124] The most important thing, he stressed, was gaining the people's confidence and guaranteeing the safety of individuals and goods. This would please the native population so much that they would voluntarily agree to subordination. The economic interests of the peoples themselves should be the foundations on which the system was built.

For his objective—controlling native trade—Van den Bosch could not manage entirely without military support, however. But all that was needed, in his view, was a single marketplace on the coast and a number of small strongholds near trading centers along the borders of the territory under direct rule.[125] He also wanted a chain of ten to twelve strongholds built along both the west and east coasts of Sumatra, each manned by fifteen soldiers.

In his letter to Resident Elout in Riau, Van den Bosch ascribed a special role to Sumatra's east coast. Here he was concerned not only with trade but more particularly with the struggle against the Padri. If the policy of reconciliation and confidence building were to misfire and the opposition proved intransigent, the solution was to isolate the Padri territory and surround it with one's allies—a remedy that brought Jambi to mind.[126] Just as Jambi had once been given a role in the conflict in Palembang, it came to the foreground again in connection with the Minangkabau troubles.

Van den Bosch decided against occupying Aceh, although he was convinced, as early as in 1830, that the piracy based in Aceh justified seizing the pirates' haunts.[127] In 1831, he wrote that the Treaty of London was "a vexatious impediment," and that he would gladly revoke it. It was not until he served as Minister of Colonies (1834–40) that he acquired a more mature insight into international affairs and hence into the importance to the Netherlands' overseas territories of preserving good relations with Britain. This led him to drop his protests.[128]

Thus Van den Bosch was already proposing the occupation of Sumatra in 1830, albeit a loosely structured, peaceful occupation. In January 1833, nine months before the actions against Jambi, he made it clear that he wanted the west coast brought under Dutch sovereignty. All the lands of Sumatra from the Sunda Straits to the kingdom of Aceh should be subject to Dutch rule: communications between the west coast and Siak or "other eastern realms" should be broken off with the aid of small fortresses to prevent smuggling.[129] But he was more ambitious still: he wanted not just the west coast but the subjection of "that entire. . . part of Sumatra which was

---

[124] Ibid.

[125] The small strongholds he envisaged were three-storey towers surrounded by an earthen parapet with bamboo cane, such as could be built by one hundred men in a month (ibid.).

[126] Ibid.

[127] Ibid.

[128] Westendorp Boerma, *Briefwisseling*, 1: 97.

[129] Ibid.,1: 97, 205.

not removed from our rule upon the conclusion of the Treaty of London of 17 March 1824."[130] He looked on Sumatra as equal in importance to Java: its location was just as favorable for trade, it had good harbors and fertile soil, and it was rich in minerals. "Without Sumatra, our position is weak and too confined to control the East Indies archipelago," he asserted in 1836. He predicted that it would take a mere twenty-five years to subject the entire region by peaceful means.[131]

Van den Bosch held faithfully to his views. In 1838 he summarized them again, toward the end of the Padri War, in the instructions he drew up together with William I for Pieter Merkus, the new commissioner on Sumatra. These instructions again defined the primary objective of the Dutch on the island as "the expansion of trade achieved by means proportionate to the benefits it can yield." To promote trade, what was needed was to build up friendly ties with the chieftains, to set up marketplaces, to foster cordial commercial relations, to ensure safety for merchants and to build good connecting roads that could serve strategic military goals as well as accommodating trade. The importance of trade, especially with Sumatra's west coast, made it essential to keep a close watch on the east coast states to the north of Palembang, while avoiding any unpleasantness with "other European powers" (i.e. Britain). The best way to keep watch was with contracts and fortresses. The commissioner had to forge as many friendly ties as possible with the chieftains in North Sumatra and beware of doing anything that could jeopardize merchants' safety, for instance by exposing them to piracy.[132] So trade was crucial, but protecting it was not allowed to cost anything.

These plans for Sumatra deviated from the policy for the other "outer islands," defined tersely by Van den Bosch as "maintaining a firm distance." Officials should never launch any offensive against local princes or peoples, on penalty of losing their position, without the prior approval of Batavia.[133] From The Hague, too, Van den Bosch would continue to reiterate his dictum of preserving the peace and refraining from interference. Only then could the proceeds from Java (and secondarily from Sumatra) be exploited to full advantage. All expenditure that did not produce rapid returns should be avoided. For this reason he was less interested in the other outer islands than in Sumatra.[134]

In retrospect, this policy plan that Van den Bosch devised for peaceful expansion on Sumatra through contracts seems to reflect a utopian vision of reality.

---

[130] "... eene geheele onderwerping ... van dat gedeelte van Sumatra, hetwelk bij het sluiten van het Traktaat van London (March 17, 1824) niet aan onze heerschappij onttrokken is geworden"; *Laporan Politik Tahun 1837/Staatkundig overzicht van Nederlandsch-Indië* (Jakarta: Arsip Nasional Republik Indonesia, 1971), p. 96; Westendorp Boerma, *Briefwisseling*, 1: 205.

[131] "Zonder Sumatra is onze positie gebrekkig en te beperkt om den Indische archipel te beheerschen"; F. C. Gerretson and W. P. Coolhaas, eds., *Particuliere briefwisseling tussen J. van den Bosch en D. J. de Eerens 1830–1840 en eenige daarop betrekking hebbende andere stukken* (Groningen: Wolters, 1960), p. 158; Van den Bosch to De Eerens, April 30, 1836, no. 2 and March 23, 1838, no. 1, NA, Baud collection.

[132] "De denkbeelden van den Generaal van den Bosch over het Nederlandsch gezag op Sumatra," *Tijdschrift voor Nederlandsch Indië*, 3rd ser., 1 (1867): 408–13.

[133] *Gouvernementsbesluit*, November 30, 1833, no. 1, NA, Col., 2849, quoted in Cornelis Fasseur, "Een koloniale paradox: De Nederlandse expansie in de Indonesische archipel in het midden van de negentiende eeuw (1830–1870)," *Tijdschrift voor Geschiedenis* 92 (1979): 166.

[134] "De denkbeelden van den Generaal van den Bosch," p. 385.

Untroubled by much knowledge of other cultures, he based his ideas on the respect that he expected the local population to have for the colonial authorities. He recognized the independent and democratic nature of the Malay peoples and their active impulse to engage in trade.[135] And he was realistic enough to take account of bare facts such as a lack of money and staff. But he overestimated the advantages and the appeal to the Malay or Sumatran population of the trade links with the colonial government. Essentially, he tried to reconcile irreconcilables: to achieve control through the cheap route of indirect rule and voluntary trade relations. Only on paper did it look like a sound plan.

This policy, aimed at controlling local commerce, called for a renewed onslaught on piracy. He went about this straight away by commissioning twenty new patrol proas and gathering information about hotbeds of piracy in the Archipelago.[136] Expeditions could not be launched until 1834, when the cease-fire in the Belgian dispute afforded the navy more scope for action. But D. H. Kolff, Van den Bosch's lieutenant, had already been put in charge of the actions in 1831. He would emerge as the key figure and prime connoisseur of piracy in the Indonesian archipelago and the fight against it.[137] In this capacity, he also became embroiled in the affairs of Jambi.[138]

Regional conflict in Palembang and Minangkabau, efforts to eradicate piracy, and the policy on Sumatra pursued by Governor-General Johannes van den Bosch were the ingredients that fired the colonial authorities' interest in the small, obscure, and insignificant Malay sultanate of Jambi. It was incorporated into the colonial government's larger plans for Sumatra as a whole. Sultan Facharuddin would soon discover this for himself, to his regret.

---

[135] *Minuut,* December 29, 1838, R10, NA, Col., vb. December 29, 1838, R10.

[136] Cornets de Groot van Kraaijenburg, "Notices historiques sur les pirateries," p. 267.

[137] J. P. Cornets de Groot van Kraaijenburg, "Dirk Hendrik Kolff Jr., Kapitein ter Zee," *Handelingen en Geschriften van het Indisch Genootschap* 5 (1858): 180–200; "Kolff, Dirk H. Jr.," in *Biographisch Woordenboek der Nederlanden,* ed. A. J. van der Aa, 7 vols. (Haarlem: van Brederode, 1852–78), 4: 93–94.

[138] It was not until about 1860, however, that piracy really declined, partly because of the advent of small steamships that could sail against the wind to track down pirates—who were initially terrified by the sight of what they took to be magical ships bearing down on them (Mills, "British Malaya, 1824–1867," p. 276).

Confluence of the rivers Tembesi and Batang Hari
KITLV photograph collection 7145

CHAPTER THREE

CONTRACT AND SOVEREIGNTY (1830–1839)

In 1833 the king of Jambi made bold to invade the Kingdom of Palembang, without there being the least occasion to do so; indeed, the colonial administration was on very good terms with that Sovereign and had helped him drive the pirates from his coast, as he had requested, only the year before. As a result, negotiations were entered into with Mohammad Facharuddin, the king of Jambi, leading to the conclusion of the provisional treaty of November 14, 1833, in which he placed himself and his country under the protection and supreme authority of the colonial government.[1]

This passage from a government report of 1838, presenting the sultan of Jambi as a treacherous and ungrateful king who invaded Palembang in exchange for help and surrendered his sovereignty after an expedition, determined the Dutch historiography and political assessments of relations between Jambi and Batavia for more than a century and a half. The historian and civil servant E. B. Kielstra presented the same views in an article in the authoritative monthly *De Gids* in 1887, and they were regurgitated uncritically for another fifty years.[2]

As usual, however, the reality was more complex. In fact the contract represented the culmination of several years' diplomacy, starting in 1830; no expedition against the pirates ever took place, and the putative surrender of sovereignty is open to a variety of interpretations.

NEGOTIATIONS

The colonial authorities prepared meticulously for the signing of the contract. In 1830 Sultan Facharuddin and Resident Praetorius exchanged envoys and gifts. The Resident evidently wanted to start by building confidence and good relations. He asked the sultan's advice on how to go about defeating the pirates, if he himself lacked the necessary resources. Meanwhile, he urged his counterpart in Bangka to prevent any rumors about an expedition, which might disrupt this

---

[1] *Laporan Politik Tahun 1837/Staatkundig Overzicht van Nederlandsch-Indië 1837* (Jakarta: Arsip Nasional Republik Indonesia, 1971), pp. 95–96.

[2] E. B. Kielstra, "De uitbreiding van het Nederlandsch gezag op Sumatra," *De Gids* 51, 4 (1887): 256–96; J. Tideman and P. L. F. Sigar, *Djambi* (Amsterdam: Koloniaal Instituut, 1938), p. 30; A. J. N. Engelenberg, "Opmerkingen over en naar aanleiding van ons bestuur in Djambi," *Verslagen der Algemeene Vergaderingen van het Indisch Genootschap 1911–1912* (1912): 81–112.

diplomatic offensive.[3] Facharuddin stated in April and again in October 1830 that the pirates had settled in his realm without his approval. He said that he was not strong enough to stop them alone and made an official request for help.[4] This prompted Van den Bosch to request further information about the pirates from the Residents of Palembang, Bangka, and Bantam, and to ask whether Riau had any rights of sovereignty over Jambi. The reply reached him early in 1831, but for some reason nothing was done with the information that year.[5] When it came to assessing situations and making decisions, East Indies officialdom was not known for its speed.

It was not until 1832 that the relief expedition and the mooted contract were raised again. In January 1832, Facharuddin again requested assistance to root out the pirates, and the colonial authorities decided in response to dispatch an expedition to the coast of Sumatra at the beginning of March. Van den Bosch rightly remarked that compliance with Jambi's request was entirely in line with his policy on Sumatra, geared toward expanding Dutch influence.[6]

Yet this expedition never put to sea. Plans were certainly drafted and preparations made from May to July 1832. Ten ships of different sizes and a landing force of two to three hundred infantrymen were assembled to destroy the pirates' hideouts in Reteh, Jambi, and Indragiri, all on Sumatra's east coast. When the sultan arrived in Jambi, he would be offered a contract to sign. It might be necessary to send fifty troops and an officer to occupy the pirates' stronghold at Muara Saba. But all these plans came to naught. Van den Bosch first postponed the expedition, and then in August he called it off altogether because of the approaching monsoon season, which began as early as September on the east coast. As there was still a lack of information, he dispatched only a corvette and two gunboats to reconnoiter the Batang Hari.[7]

This reconnaissance mission, which took in only a small part of the river up to the old VOC fortress at Muara Kompeh, was actually carried out in October and November 1832.[8] But it was not these Dutch ships that ousted the pirates. The people of Jambi did it themselves, and they were able to do so because an internal

---

[3] Resident of Palembang to commissioner-general, April 3, 1830, no. 72 and April 29, 1830, no. 89; Resident of Palembang to Resident of Bangka, April 23, 1830, no. 77, all in ANRI, Palembang Residency records, 45.5.

[4] Resident of Palembang to commissioner-general, January 17, 1831, no. 24, secret; "Extract uit report nopens den staat der zeeroverijen in den Nederlandsch-Indischen archipel voor Z. E. de commissaris-generaal door den majoor-adjudant Kolff," November 1, 1831 (National Archives (NA), The Hague, Col., volume "Zeeroverij in Nederlandsch Oost-Indië 1831–1835," no. 4168).

[5] See reports in NA, Col., vol. "Zeeroverij in Nederlandsch Oost-Indië 1831–1835," no. 4168.

[6] *Gouvernementsbesluit* (Resolution adopted by the colonial authorities) March 5, 1832, no. 3, ANRI, Algemeene Secretarie.

[7] Van den Bosch to naval commander, August 17, 1832, no. 1418, NA, Van den Bosch collection, 246.

[8] Resident of Palembang to commissioner-general, July 1, 1833, no. 201, ANRI, Algemeene Secretarie, *gouvernementsbesluit*, September 20, 1834, no. 4. That this river reconnaissance mission could not be equated with an expedition is clear from Resident Praetorius's communication urging a swift decision on an expedition in July 1833 (see Resident of Palembang to commissioner-general, July 1, 1833, no. 201, ANRI, Algemeene Secretarie, *gouvernementsbesluit*, September 20, 1834, no. 4).

conflict had erupted in Muara Saba, according to a detailed report written in 1835.[9] The sultan therefore had no reason whatsoever to thank the colonial authorities for their support.

In May 1832, shortly after the initial decision was made to send an expedition against the pirates, Resident Praetorius received renewed official orders from Batavia to conclude a contract. It was to be signed after the expedition arrived.[10] This time the Resident took the initiative himself. In his letter to Sultan Facharuddin, which the experienced envoy Intje Heydar handed over in June,[11] Praetorius explicitly broached the subject of a contract for the first time. To discuss the matter, he proposed a meeting between himself and Facharuddin in the Rawas, where Jambi bordered on Palembang. Facharuddin immediately replied in a very positive vein: opening the Resident's letter, he had been struck by the "sweet fragrance" emanating from it.[12] He was happy to leave the pirates to the colonial authorities, whom he regarded as better qualified to do battle with them, but he was fully prepared to journey to the Rawas to sign the contract, which he too wanted to conclude. He did, however, request clear arrangements and a definite date, as he was extremely busy settling disputes in the uplands.

Curiously, the Resident failed to reply, an omission for which he claimed to have good reason. With a view to the forthcoming expedition against the pirates, he could not, or rather would not, leave Palembang. Furthermore, the Dutch would have a far stronger negotiating position after the expedition than before it, as he put to his superiors at the beginning of August.[13] It remains puzzling that Praetorius should have requested a meeting in June and forgone it a month later. He had probably hoped that the action against the pirates would take place sooner, and in this respect his invitation had been rather premature.

Facharuddin did not let the matter rest. In the autumn of 1832, he repeated his request (or offer) to meet the Resident. But Praetorius declined the invitation. He was a vain man, who craved promotion and hoped to distinguish himself with a successful military action. What is more, since the expedition had been suspended, he did not know on what terms he should negotiate with the sultan.[14] He therefore

---

[9] The report was written by Kolff, the Dutch expert on pirates; "Nadere aanteekeningen betrekkelijk de zeeroverijen in Nederlandsch-Indië 1835," NA, Col., vol. "Zeeroverij in Nederlandsch Oost-Indië 1831–1835" (4168); cf. also "Expeditie naar Jambi en Muara Kompeh in 1833, overgenomen uit den boedel van D. H. Kolff jr.," NA, Col., 4135.

[10] Commissioner-general to Resident of Palembang, May 18, 1832, no. 902, secret, NA, Van den Bosch collection, 234.

[11] Intje Heydar left Palembang on June 16, 1832 (see P. S. van Ronkel, "De Maleische handschriften van Nederlandsch-Indië van het Koninklijk Instituut voor Taal-, Land- en Volkenkunde," *Bijdragen tot de Taal-, Land- en Volkenkunde* 60 (1908): 181–248; here pp. 210–12).

[12] Facharuddin to Resident of Palembang, 13 safar 1248 (=July 12, 1832), translation, ANRI, Algemeene Secretarie, agenda September 11, 1832, no. 651.

[13] Resident of Palembang to lieutenant governor-general, August 2, 1832, no. 250, ANRI, Algemeene Secretarie, agenda September 11, 1832, no. 651.

[14] Official report, June 30, 1833, ANRI, Algemeene Secretarie, *gouvernementsbesluit*, September 20, 1834, no. 4; see also Van den Bosch to Resident of Palembang, May 18, 1832, no. 902 and August 17, 1832, no. 1419, NA, Van den Bosch collection, 246.

informed Facharuddin that business prevented him "from coming to see him" for the time being.[15]

So this is how matters stood in 1833. The colonial authorities were interested in a contract with Facharuddin because it suited their policy, which was aimed at expanding Dutch authority on Sumatra, isolating Minangkabau, and trying to root out piracy. Facharuddin was aware of this interest, and some of his aims coincided with those of the Dutch. He was not in a strong position in his own realm: his power was challenged in the capital, there were disputes to be dealt with in the upland areas, and his coffers were empty. Meanwhile, the Resident kept the pot boiling because he wanted to strengthen his own position first by conducting an expedition against the pirates. The sultan continued to urge an agreement, or at least a meeting. In all probability the reconnaissance of the river that was conducted instead of the promised expedition, undertaken with little respect for the local people (the crew failed to ask permission for their mission, which was contrary to adat),[16] aroused Facharuddin's mistrust, a mistrust that was only exacerbated by the Resident's prevarication. The sultan obviously felt threatened. Was the powerful colonial administration planning to take over his realm behind his back, instead of providing the help and support that he needed and had hoped for? He dreaded an attack, and the people of Jambi evidently anticipated one.[17]

In 1833, Facharuddin took matters into his own hands and tried to arrange a meeting with the Dutch authorities. In April, he again requested a meeting with the Resident. In response, he was told that the Resident would meet him at the border. In June, Facharuddin informed the Resident that he was coming to the Rawas. Without waiting for a reply, he soon arrived there with a retinue of two hundred people, including a large number of women and children and several Palembang dignitaries. The Rawas was a rugged border territory in which the sovereignty of the two sultanates, Palembang and Jambi, had always been poorly defined.[18] It had a tradition of rebellion against the authority of both the sultan of Palembang and the Dutch authorities.

When reports of the sultan's presence reached Palembang at the end of June 1833, they therefore caused considerable alarm. On June 30, the Resident decided on countermeasures of his own: he sent a Palembang dignitary accompanied by an armed guard of local men to ascertain the sultan's intentions. Meanwhile, he asked the Resident of Bangka for reinforcements and sent the same request to Batavia, asking whether the expedition planned earlier should still be carried out. The

---

[15] Resident of Palembang to commissioner-general, July 1, 1833, no, 201, ANRI, Algemeene Secretarie, *gouvernementsbesluit*, September 20, 1834, no. 4. On October 6, 1832, Intje Heydar left for Jambi once again, this time heading for Sarolangun, closer to Palembang (Van Ronkel, "De Maleische handschriften van Nederlandsch-Indië," pp. 210–12).

[16] "Expeditie naar Jambi en Muara Kompeh in 1833, overgenomen uit den boedel van D. H. Kolff jr.," NA, Col., 4135.

[17] Michiels to lieutenant governor-general, August 22, 1833, no. 4; Resident of Palembang to commissioner-general, July 1, 1833, no. 201, ANRI, Algemeene Secretarie, *gouvernementsbesluit*, September 20, 1834, no. 4.

[18] Resident of Palembang to commissioner-general, April 30, 1830, no. 89, ANRI, Palembang Residency records, 45.5. Thus a single district contained *dusun* subject to Jambian rule and others subject to Palembang rule, which was also the case in the Javanese realms (see also report from mil. commander of December 2, 1881, NA, Col., *mailrapport* (postal report; hereafter "mr.") 1882/27).

Resident was particularly nervous because he had not heard any news from Java for six weeks, in particular about the Belgian dispute—he did not know whether there was war or peace in Europe.[19]

At the beginning of July he received notification that the vanguard of the Jambian troops had advanced to one and a half day's rowing distance from the capital. Palembang's defenses were placed on the alert, and the Resident called upon the population, a few thousand people including at most ten Europeans, to take up arms.[20] He also issued an ultimatum. Facharuddin could come to Palembang with one hundred of his followers but should send the rest back to Jambi. If he failed to comply, he would be driven out by force.[21]

Facharuddin continued to insist that he had come with peaceful intentions. However, certain events had taken place in the interim that the Dutch saw as proof of the contrary. Jambian subjects, enemies of the sultan who feared that he would indeed come to an agreement with the colonial authorities, attacked some Palembang merchants, settling old scores.[22] Meanwhile, the sultan's retinue had now grown to a thousand, or even two thousand according to some rumors, including Minangkabau and people from the Rawas and other parts of Palembang.[23] Since Pangeran Surio was advancing on Palembang, and Facharuddin had ensconced himself in a *dusun*, Praetorius had little reason to believe in the sultan's peaceful intentions, even if he had been inclined to give him the benefit of the doubt. Furthermore, a letter from Facharuddin was intercepted, dated July 10, addressed to a kinsman of the former sultan of Palembang, who was now working for the colonial administration. It contained an offer to restore the sultan's rule and to avenge the insult that had been perpetrated upon Islam.[24]

We can infer from this that Facharuddin had decided to make an initial move in July 1833, possibly motivated by fear of the colonial authorities, and that the Jambian opposition had probably responded by bringing pressure to bear on him and causing the situation to escalate. The time seemed propitious, since rumors were circulating in the archipelago that war was brewing between France and Britain, on the one hand, and Holland, on the other. Perhaps Facharuddin also viewed action against the colonial authorities as a useful means of expanding his host of

---

[19] Resident of Palembang to commissioner-general, July 1, 1833, no. 201, ANRI, Algemeene Secretarie, *gouvernementsbesluit*, September 20, 1834, no. 4.

[20] *Besluit* (resolution) by Resident of Palembang, July 4, 1833, nos. 21 and 22, ANRI, Algemeene Secretarie, *gouvernementsbesluit*, September 20, 1834, no. 4.

[21] *Besluit* by Resident of Palembang, July 4, 1833, nos. 21 and 22, ANRI, Algemeene Secretarie, *gouvernementsbesluit*, September 20, 1834, no. 4.

[22] Neither Raden Tabun nor Pangeran Mohamad Kassim (a kinsman of Facharuddin and a man of influence in the capital) had followed him. Others did accompany him, however: his brother, Pangeran Surio, an appanage holder in the lowlands, and Said Mohamad, his sister's son and one of the most influential merchants in Jambi (see Assistant Resident to Resident of Palembang, July 25, 1833, no. 11, ANRI, Algemeene Secretarie, *gouvernementsbesluit*, September 19, 1833, no. 1).

[23] Resident of Palembang to commissioner-general, July 19, 1833, no. 231, ANRI, Algemeene Secretarie, *gouvernementsbesluit*, September 19, 1833, no. 1.

[24] Sultan to Perdana Mantri, 21 safar 1249 (=July 10, 1833), translation; Resident of Palembang to commissioner-general, July 19, 1833, no. 231, both in ANRI, Algemeene Secretarie, *gouvernementsbesluit*, September 19, 1833, no. 1.

followers and increasing his power. If the reports about his growing retinue were correct, this aim, in any case, was proving successful.

Yet Facharuddin's missives continued to stress his desire for peace and friendship. In a letter sent at the end of July, he distanced himself from his unruly followers, who had run amok. He repeatedly rejected the Resident's ultimatum. He wanted to meet "my friend the Resident" in the Rawas, as agreed before.[25] In the circumstances, and given his distrust of the colonial authorities, a journey to Palembang was probably just as unacceptable to him as a journey in the other direction was to the Resident. Praetorius regarded himself as superior, and for that reason alone he would not deign to consider undertaking a journey. The sultan's unauthorized presence in territory under Dutch rule was unacceptable, and armed conflict was now inevitable. The hostilities began in mid-July and lasted a month. The last Jambian troops were driven from Palembang on August 16, and Facharuddin himself had to dive into the river and brave its currents to save his life.[26]

RESPONSE IN BATAVIA

This was not the end of the matter. Batavia's plans for Sumatra in general and Jambi in particular were already far advanced, and there was no question of abandoning them. But the report of the incident took a full three weeks to reach Batavia. Van den Bosch immediately placed his own interpretation on the events: he blamed the international situation, "troublemaking" from Singapore, and the rumors about a European war. The sultan, stirred up by Palembang dignitaries, had seized the day by exploiting a temporary lapse in Dutch might. Van den Bosch dismissed the idea that the reconnaissance mission had sown mistrust and that this explained Facharuddin's journey to Palembang. He thought the sultan had too little power to have mounted an attack for that reason.[27] No blame at all was attached to the colonial authorities.

It was certainly true that a chronic lack of information in the East Indies in 1833 had heightened apprehension about a possible war in Europe. Reports had been received of the besieged Antwerp Citadel falling to the French at the end of December 1832, and the colonials had also heard of the French-British embargo on Dutch ships at the end of 1832. But the news about the provisional agreement of May 1833 had not yet reached the East Indies in July. So Van den Bosch saw the outbreak of war in Europe as a serious possibility, and only a few days before receiving the reports of the clash in Palembang he had drawn up a memorandum detailing the policy to be pursued in this eventuality.[28] This explanation for Facharuddin's actions was therefore not entirely unfounded, although it was neither affirmed nor denied in the later reports submitted by the commander of the

---

[25] Sultan to Assistant Resident, 6 rabil-awal 1249 (=July 24, 1833) and 7 rabil-awal 1249 (=July 25, 1833), ANRI, Algemeene Secretarie, *gouvernementsbesluit*, September 19, 1833, no. 1.

[26] Assistant Resident to Resident of Palembang, August 17, 1833, no. 20, ANRI, Algemeene Secretarie, *gouvernementsbesluit*, September 20, 1834, no. 4.

[27] Commissioner-General J. Van den Bosch to Acting Governor-General J. C. Baud, July 26, 1833, ANRI. Algemeene Secretarie, *gouvernementsbesluit*, September 20, 1834, no. 4.

[28] Cf. "Memorie opgesteld in geval van oorlogshandelingen in Europa," July 26, 1833, NA, Baud collection, file 377.

Dutch forces. Rumors, expectations, or hopes revolving around war in Europe certainly formed the backdrop for the events in Palembang.

Since Van den Bosch was due to leave in early August for the west coast of Sumatra, where war had broken out again in January 1833 with the revolt of Padri leader Imam Bonjol, speed was of the essence. The governor-general unhesitatingly seized the opportunity to implement his policy on Sumatra. The very day on which he received the letters from Palembang, he decided to dispatch a naval expedition under Kolff and an expedition of land forces under Colonel A. V. Michiels.[29] The latter's orders were carefully attuned to Van den Bosch's plans for the island. The primary goal was to drive the enemy from Palembang. Michiels was instructed to subdue Jambi—as well as Indragiri, further north, if it was shown to have collaborated—and then to take possession of the great rivers, the Batang Hari and the Indragiri, building strongholds or devising other means to achieve permanent control. The second objective was to build a road through the inland region between Palembang and the Batang Hari. Third and last, Michiels had to investigate the scope for setting up a Residency in the hinterland between Palembang and Sumatra's west coast. In the words of the orders, "good communication lines between Padang and Palembang remain a primary interest and must not be neglected."[30] This ambitious program encapsulated the Dutch battle plan against Palembang, the Padri, and Jambi in one fell swoop, but took little account of Sumatra's geography and the vast distances to be covered in remote and hostile territory. Once again, Van den Bosch was untroubled by too much knowledge of the region he governed. A map of Jambi would have been a boon, but no such thing existed.[31]

Of the two expeditions, by land and by sea, the latter was therefore the more successful. In mid-September, Kolff, who had overall command of the fleet, occupied the old VOC fortress at Muara Kompeh. And there he waited, complaining of a lack of men and concerned that he had not yet heard from Michiels. Meanwhile, Michiels, who had an impressive military record,[32] was sending to Batavia balanced and carefully worded reports providing cogent analyses of the situation in Jambi. His military actions, however, were less opportune. He was constantly complaining of a lack of troops. It was not until November that he had enough coolies to permit another three days' march. The last part of his orders, the formation of a new Residency, proved a completely fanciful idea; the first, the sultan's expulsion from Palembang, was accomplished before he arrived.

The second order, the subjection of Jambi, proved impossible to achieve with an army; the task called for a combination of naval, economic, and diplomatic

---

[29] Commissioner-general to Resident of Palembang, July 29, 1833, no. 131, ANRI, Algemeene Secretarie, *gouvernementsbesluit*, September 20, 1834, no. 4. The fleet consisted of a schooner and four patrol proas with crews totalling a hundred men, while the land force consisted of soldiers garrisoned in Palembang, plus eighty from Bangka and three hundred Madurese from Surabaya.

[30] Official instructions given to Michiels, July 29, 1833, no. 133, ANRI, Algemeene Secretarie, *gouvernementsbesluit*, September 20, 1834, no. 4.

[31] Commander-in-chief of army to commissioner-general, October 1, 1833, no. 1/10, ANRI, Algemeene Secretarie, *gouvernementsbesluit*, September 20, 1834, no. 4.

[32] "Michiels (Andreas Victor)," in *Encyclopaedie van Nederlandsch-Indië* (The Hague: M. Nijhoff, Leiden: Brill, 1917–40), 2: 724.

pressure. Kolff's blockade of the Batang Hari led to a salt shortage and growing resentment in Jambi. This was shrewdly exploited by Facharuddin's opponents in the capital (including Raden Tabun) who had not joined the expedition to Palembang. Because the upland regions under the influence of Raden Tabun refused to supply rice to Facharuddin's troops, his following rapidly shrank. And when Michiels proved willing to negotiate with the opposition, Facharuddin gave in. The internal divisions had eroded his power beyond remedy.[33]

In November 1833, a provisional contract was signed at Sungai Bawang, a small *dusun* in the Rawas. After first acknowledging responsibility for the attack, the sultan and the *pangeran ratu* placed themselves and their realm "under the benevolent rule of the Dutch administration" (art. 1, Malay version). In exchange, the sultan would receive a regular sum of money, the amount yet to be determined, toward his living expenses (art. 2). This "generosity" on the part of the colonial authorities was offset by several benefits: the Dutch retained the fortress at Muara Kompeh (art. 3) and were empowered to levy import and export duties on trade with Jambi (art. 5). In the event of conflict with the uplands in Padang, the Dutch could count on the sultan's auxiliaries (art. 6). Any rebels against Dutch rule would be handed over. A permanent contract was finally concluded in 1834.[34]

VICTORS' JUSTICE

The above paragraphs demonstrate the difference between the brief account in the historiography and the actual sequence of events as revealed by the records. The picture of a treacherous ruler who accepted help against the pirates and then responded by attacking Palembang for no reason is completely false. The sultan had been corresponding with the colonial authorities about the piracy problem since 1829. He had certainly requested assistance, and in 1832 he had been promised help; but the planned expedition had never taken place. On the contrary, reconnaissance maneuvers around the coast and mouth of the Batang Hari River had strengthened fears of an imminent Dutch assault. Furthermore, Batavia had held out the prospect of a contract in 1832, even proposing a meeting with the Resident. These friendly overtures had probably encouraged Facharuddin to hope for favorable terms. Then, when the Resident postponed the negotiations pending the expedition, the sultan grew suspicious and decided to take the initiative. He went to meet the Resident in the Rawas, and the ensuing tension escalated into a military conflict that ultimately curtailed his sovereignty.

Clearly, the Dutch actions did not tally with the picture of blamelessness presented in the literature. Van den Bosch had definite plans for Sumatra. The sultan's incursion into his territory provided a welcome opportunity to pursue more general objectives, such as expanding Dutch authority and rooting out piracy. And Praetorius himself had aroused certain expectations.

Where did the simplistic account of Jambi's past, which remained unquestioned for so long, come from? It originated with Van den Bosch himself. On August 1, he

---

[33] Michiels to Interim governor-general, November 8, 1833, no. 9 and November 23, 1833, no. 10, ANRI, Algemeene Secretarie, *gouvernementsbesluit*, September 20, 1834, no. 4.

[34] The Dutch text of these treaties is in ANRI, Algemeene Secretarie, *gouvernementsbesluit*, September 20, 1834, no. 4; Malay and Dutch versions of both may be found in NA, Col., vb. October 17, 1903, D 16.

notified the Minister of Colonies of the recent events. He already had a rebellion in Bonjol to contend with, and now the sultan of Jambi had made bold to invade Palembang, "without there being the least occasion to do so. Indeed, we had been on the most cordial of terms with that ruler and provided assistance last year to drive the pirates from his shores as he had requested."[35] The General Secretariat's annual report for 1837 repeated this brief communication.

It was probably this material that Kielstra used for his article in *De Gids* in 1887, given that he had access to the Ministry's records. Thus the highly abridged account that Batavia sent to the Netherlands in the 1830s generated enduring misconceptions. It was not for another forty years that a rule was adopted requiring colonial authorities to send all noteworthy documents to the Ministry of Colonies.[36] Did Van den Bosch deliberately distort the facts or was it a case of unwitting misrepresentation? Were the errors caused by carelessness, undue haste, or calculated self-interest? He surely must have known the facts about the assistance promised against the pirates. Did he equate his reconnaissance mission with the planned expedition? Or was he guilty of no more than a slip of the pen, writing "provided assistance" when he meant "promised assistance"? It is impossible to say. As we have seen, Van den Bosch shrugged off the Resident's suggestion that Facharuddin may have felt threatened. That even a hawk such as Colonel Michiels would later accept this explanation after conducting a local investigation was something Van den Bosch did not know when he reported to The Hague. The preamble to the provisional contract, it may be added, made no mention of Dutch help against the pirates. As so often is the case, it was the victors who wrote the history. The views of those who were in power determined the enduring picture of the events surrounding the Jambian sultanate in 1833.

SOVEREIGNTY SURRENDERED

Part of this picture was the notion that the sultan of Jambi had signed a contract surrendering his sovereignty to Batavia. About this the Dutch were in no doubt. Had the sultan not placed himself "under the protection and supreme authority" of the colonial government, as stated in the report of 1838?[37] More than ten years later this phrase was summarized as "recognition of sovereignty,"[38] and the term would stick.

To see how things looked from the Jambian point of view, we should review the permanent contract of 1834 and then the way in which it was implemented in the 1830s. The contract was signed in Jambi in December 1834 by the sultan and *pangeran ratu*, on the one hand, and by J. W. Boers, the new Resident of Palembang, on the other.[39]

---

[35] Commissioner-general to Minister of National Industry and Colonies, August 1, 1833, NA, Col., vb. December 23, 1833, no. 156k, secret.

[36] See Foreword to the index of mr. for 1869, NA, Col.

[37] *Laporan Politik Tahun 1837*, p. 96.

[38] *Ikhtisar Keadaan Politik Hindia-Belanda Tahun 1839–1848* (Jakarta: Arsip Nasional Republik Indonesia, 1973), p. 110.

[39] J. W. Boers, "Bezoek ter hoofdplaatse van het Djambische Rijk op Sumatra in 1834, door den toenmaligen Resident of Palembang," *Tijdschrift van Nederlandsch Indië* 12,2 (1850): 463–70. Praetorius (1799–1846) was "rewarded" with the Residency of Pekalongan, and subsequently that of Japara, where he exploited the population and deliberately inflated the price of sugar.

According to the contract of 1833, Sultan Facharuddin had placed himself and his realm permanently "under the immediate protection and supreme authority of the colonial government" (art. 1). This phrase was repeated in the Dutch version of the 1834 contract (the differences between the Dutch and Malay versions will be dealt with below). The colonial authorities gained possession of the fortress of Muara Kompeh; they could relocate to another part of Jambi later, following proper consultations. At the same time they acquired a monopoly on the imposition of import and export duties on commerce with Jambi at the tariff set in Palembang. Six guilders per picul would be imposed on imports of "foreign" (i.e., non-Javanese) salt,[40] which amounted to a ban on imports of foreign salt.[41] Meanwhile, plans under consideration in Batavia to introduce a salt monopoly in the East Indies were put on hold, as far as Jambi was concerned. The sultan also promised not to enter into any friendly relations with the enemies of the colonial authorities and to provide assistance against the Padri if necessary. He would promote agriculture in his realm, in particular the cultivation of the once so lucrative cash crop of pepper. Importing slaves was outlawed, but the sultan was not required to free the slaves he already had.

In exchange, Facharuddin was given assurances that the colonial authorities would uphold and protect his rights. He would receive an annuity of eight thousand guilders, payable on a quarterly basis, and the contract allowed for this amount to be raised to fifteen thousand guilders or more. The sultan retained the right to administer and impose taxes in his own territory without any interference from Batavia. Jambi's trade with Java and other territories under Dutch rule would be treated in the same way as that of subjects and allies of the colonial authorities.

SATISFACTION IN BATAVIA

This was quite enough to please Van den Bosch. His goal had been achieved: the sultan had pledged himself to the colonial authorities, and his territory could now be controlled from a small fortress at Muara Kompeh at the Batang Hari estuary. This would be a better vantage point from which to assail the pirates than a settlement in Jambi, the capital. And it would also be a good base from which to gather more knowledge about Jambi's internal situation. One snag was the alarmingly high incidence of disease at Muara Kompeh. In the first eighteen months the mortality rate among the soldiers encamped there was 32 percent, more than three times the average of 10 percent[42] The remoteness of the fortress was an added disadvantage; amid jungle and swamps, Muara Kompeh was almost

---

His career peaked in 1840 when he was appointed Director of Cultures, but two years later he returned to the Netherlands for health reasons. In the Netherlands too he was good at promoting his own interests: in 1843, he procured a sugar contract, but did not enjoy the profits from it for very long, as he died in Besuki in 1846 (see NA, Col., Stamboek Indische ambtenaren A 259; R. Reinsma, "De cultuurprocenten in de praktijk en in de ogen der tijdgenoten," in *Geld en geweten: Een bundel opstellen over anderhalve eeuw Nederlands bestuur in de Indonesische Archipel*, ed. C. Fasseur, 2 vols. (The Hague: M. Nijhoff, 1980), 1: 69.

[40] A picul is about 61 kg.

[41] P. H. van der Kemp, *Handboek tot de kennis van 's lands zoutmiddel in Nederlandsch-Indië: Eene economisch-historische studie* (Batavia/The Hague: Kolff, 1894), p. 210.

[42] Commander-in-chief of army to governor-general, July 15, 1835, no. 38, ANRI, Algemeene Secretarie, *gouvernementsbesluit*, August 15, 1835, no. 2.

inaccessible to sailing vessels in the monsoon season. But relocating to Jambi did not seem a viable option, as it would provoke more resistance and therefore involve higher security expenses.

After all, the first short-term objective was still to gain a better understanding of the Jambian context and to improve relations with the court. For the present, the imposition of import and export duties was of lesser importance. So Van den Bosch did not grind his teeth about reports of smuggling in other parts of the Batang Hari estuary. He was content to move one step at a time, confident that he had established a Dutch presence. It was not until the Dutch fully understood the economy and the internal politics of Jambi that they could start manipulating it and taking real control of trade. This is why the contract made only a passing reference to a salt monopoly (and none whatsoever to an opium monopoly) and mentioned the fight against piracy only in oblique terms.

Van den Bosch had now accomplished his primary objective. Dutch authority on Sumatra had expanded toward the north, although it had been a far more troublesome enterprise than he had anticipated. As part of his overall Sumatra policy, this was a satisfactory outcome.

SATISFACTION IN JAMBI?

Sultan Facharuddin too had reason to be pleased. He had been promised an annuity with the prospect of a substantial rise in pay—no trivial matter given his chronic indigence. Resident Boers had been struck by this poverty immediately when he arrived in Jambi in 1834: the guest rooms were completely bare. Facharuddin had requested an advance of two hundred guilders straightaway, "as he was entirely lacking in the finances that were so indispensable to the exercise of his authority."[43] And even if the sultan were to share his new income with other dignitaries such as the *pangeran ratu* and Raden Tabun, it was still a significant sum of money.[44] Furthermore, from now on he could count on political and military protection against his opponents.

True, he had relinquished what was in the Malay world a preeminently regal privilege: the imposition of import and export duties. But we have already seen how little that privilege was worth in Jambi around 1830. The appanage holders, who were also merchants in the lowlands, had therefore been hit harder by the contract than the sultan, politically as well as economically. Understandably, they were its most vociferous opponents, with Mohamad Kassim and Pangeran Surio their most conspicuous representatives.[45]

Facharuddin had in fact secured quite favorable terms, more so than his neighbors the sultans of Palembang, Riau, and Minangkabau. He had not been removed from office like the former sultan of Palembang, nor had he become a

---

[43] Boers, "Bezoek ter hoofdplaatse van het Djambische Rijk," p. 465.

[44] Administrative officer to Resident of Palembang, December 15, 1839, no. 200, ANRI, Residency records Palembang 66.12.

[45] Boers, "Bezoek ter hoofdplaatse van het Djambische Rijk."

vassal of the colonial authorities like the former sultan of Riau.[46] He did not have to relinquish his own sources of income, except for those from trade: the colonial authorities would not impose any further taxes in his realm, in contrast to the surtax introduced in Palembang, on Sumatra's west coast, and in Riau. True, the sultan of Riau received the princely sum of 48,000 guilders annually, but in exchange he had been obliged to give up many of his own tax collections in 1830, and he was not permitted to impose any new ones without first consulting the colonial authorities.

Another difference was the absence of a clause forbidding Facharuddin to maintain foreign relations. He was merely asked not to ally himself with the enemies of the colonial authorities, such as the Padri. The contract of October 20, 1830, with Riau, in contrast, forbade agreements with "any power." Nor did the Jambian contract contain any provisions about succession, hereditary or otherwise, a popular Dutch instrument for refashioning the balance of power. It said nothing about the appointment of a new sultan being subject to the approval of the Dutch East Indies administration, or about a new oath of allegiance or the renewal of the contract when a new sultan took office, terms explicitly dictated in the contract of 1830 with Riau.

In many ways, then, Facharuddin had good reason to feel satisfied. The contract he had signed was a relatively mild one. It is not entirely clear to what extent he was aware of this. He may have been well aware, given the presence of Arab merchants, who were good sources of regional news. Arabs from the capital were not among his most loyal supporters, but he certainly maintained ties with them. One of his wives was of Arab descent. And for the archipelago's rulers generally, Arab traders functioned as a diplomatic intelligence service working through family relations and trade networks.[47]

Facharuddin had another reason to be pleased. The terms of the 1834 contract were more favorable (in the Malay version, at any rate) than those of 1833. The differences were relatively minor: in both cases the sultan relinquished Muara Kompeh and the right to impose import and export duties. In 1833, however, Facharuddin had promised to place himself and his territory under the permanent authority of the colonial administration.[48] In 1834, there was no such clause. Under the terms of article 3, the sultan and *pangeran ratu*—both of whom signed this time—solemnly acknowledged the proof of the colonial authorities' goodwill, affection, and generosity toward their realm. In consequence, they promised that they and all their descendants would remain loyal *(aken tinggal setia)* to the Dutch administration and refrain from concluding any friendship with its

---

[46] For a comparison of the contracts, see *Surat-surat Perdjandjian antara Kesultanan Riau dengan Pemerintahan-Pemerintahan VOC dan Hindia-Belanda, 1784–1909* (Jakarta: Arsip Nasional Republik Indonesia, 1970), pp. 69–89; E. de Waal, *Onze Indische financiën: Nieuwe reeks aanteekeningen,* 10 vols. (The Hague: M. Nijhoff, 1876–1907), 7: 76–82.

[47] The Residency administration of Palembang also made grateful use of their services (Resident of Palembang to commissioner-general, October 4, 1829, no. 97, ANRI, Residency records Palembang 45.4).

[48] In Malay this was worded as follows: "Sri padoeka Sulthan Jambi Mohamad Phaharoedin serta dirinja dan negrinja selamanja di atas kabadjikan en printahan Gouvernement Nederland"; art. 1, contract of 1833, NA, Col., vb. October 17, 1903, D 16.

enemies.[49] Other articles of the contract, in Malay, exuded a similar air of peace and friendship. If the sultan wished to send a mission to Batavia, for instance, the Resident would ask the colonial authorities to grant permission (art. 6). The contract's heading, indeed, calls the document a *soerat perdjandjian dan sahabat bersahabat*, that is, a letter of agreement and friendship. Numerous articles (e.g., 1, 2, 5, and 7) include explicit or implicit references to the word *sahabat* (friend).

If he was so inclined, Facharuddin could therefore look on this contract of 1834 as a treaty of peace and friendship, concluded on the basis of equality between a now contrite ruler and a forgiving colonial administration. Sovereignty was surrendered in two areas only: Muarah Kompeh and the levying of tolls. The ban on slavery and the promotion of agriculture could more properly be classified as joint agreements. It was only if the contract of 1833 had been deemed to constitute the basis for that of 1834 (which, according to the Dutch version, was the correct interpretation by law)[50] that the sultan had accepted subjection. The word "sovereignty" did not occur in the contract; there was indeed no Malay equivalent for it.[51] When the sultan of Jambi explicitly surrendered his independence in 1858, the Malay text used the word *perdirian* (standing alone, independence).[52]

The Dutch version of the contracts was far more explicit than the Malay and differed from it in essential details. Such discrepancies between the Dutch and local versions of contracts were not uncommon in the nineteenth century.[53] The Dutch text used the same translation for a variety of terms in Malay. For instance, both article 1 of the contract of 1833 and article 3 of the contract of 1834 stated that the sultan had "placed himself permanently under the immediate protection and supreme authority of the Dutch East Indies Government," a significant departure from the Malay text of 1834, which contained only a promise of allegiance.

The Dutch version adopted an altogether cooler tone. Regarding the possibility of a Jambian mission to Batavia, for instance, the Malay text referred to the Resident's willingness to pass on Jambi's request to those concerned. The Dutch version, however, stated that the sultan and *pangeran ratu* could send a mission to Batavia if the colonial authorities considered it necessary. Thus in Malay the

---

[49] In Malay, "Bahoewa Padoeka sri Sulthan serta padoeka Pangeran Ratoe ada mengakoe dengan soengoeh sekali dari pada hal karadjahannja itoe kerna kasihan dan kemoerahan Gouvernement maka oleh sebab itoe jang Padoeka sri Sulthan serta Padoeka Pangeran Ratoe mengakoe dengan sekalian toeroen-toeroenoen aken tinggal setia kapada Gouvernement dengan berdjandji apa jang mendjadi satroe kapada Gouvernement, jang Padoeka sri Sulthan tida memboeat sahabat"; art. 3, contract of 1834, NA, Col., vb. October 17, 1903, D 16.

[50] The Dutch version included a lengthy account of the contract's history. It then proclaimed "eternal ties of friendship," adopted the provisional treaty of 1833, and concluded a permanent contract based on this earlier version. The Malay version also referred to the previous history, before stating that the colonial authorities had received the treaty of 1833 ("ada terima'") and that both partners now wanted to exchange this contract for a new one (see contract 1834, NA, Col., vb. October 17, 1903, D 16).

[51] The Indonesian word *kedaulatan* is a neologism, derived from *daulat*, which means salvation or happiness, generally as a felicitation in connection with the sultan. This is how it was used in Asahan in 1933 when the new sultan was installed. See G. J. Resink, *Indonesia's History between the Myths: Essays in Legal History and Historical Theory* (The Hague: Van Hoeve, 1968), p. 344.

[52] *Besluit* of December 22, 1858, no. 25, NA, Col.

[53] J. van Goor, "De Lombokexpeditie en het Nederlands nationalisme," in *Imperialisme in de marge: De afronding van Nederlands-Indië*, ed. J. van Goor (Utrecht: HES, 1986), p. 23.

reference was to an initiative on the sultan's part, whereas in Dutch it was to an order issued by the colonial authorities.

How such differences could have arisen is impossible to say. In general, contracts were drafted in the region, on the basis of guidelines issued by Batavia. It was not until 1875 that a standard contract was introduced. The guidelines were produced by the "historical department" of the General Secretariat at Buitenzorg, which was responsible for contractual relations with the Outer Islands. The initial version drafted on the basis of these guidelines would then be submitted for approval to the Council of the Dutch East Indies, after which it would be translated into Malay. The Resident would then be authorized to conclude the contract with the local ruler and dignitaries, and the process concluded with the formal adoption of the contract by resolution of the colonial administration.[54] Bound in yellow silk—the color and material of royalty—and fitted with gold clasps, the final contract would then be presented to the local ruler.[55]

So the Dutch version served as the point of departure. Given the uneven balance of power, the initiative lay almost exclusively with the colonial authorities. Although some commentators have asserted that the Malay version took precedence under law,[56] sheer power carried more weight than legal arguments in the nineteenth century. When the differences were pointed out, first in 1858 and then again in 1903, both the colonial administration and the Dutch government consistently invoked the provisions of the 1833 contract as the basis for those of 1834 and made light of the other discrepancies.[57]

Was this "speaking with a forked tongue" a question of malice, shrewd diplomacy, or simple carelessness? A case could be made for all three. Resident Boers was well aware of the opposition to the contract in Jambi. During his visit there a large crowd of armed Jambians had burst into the *pendoppo* (reception hall), disrupting his first meeting with the sultan. His retinue had been unable to buy food at the market. Mohamad Kassim, fearing that he would be handed over to the Dutch for salt smuggling, had even suggested to the sultan that he might run amok in the *pendoppo*, an offer that the sultan declined.[58] The first draft contract had not been accepted immediately, and a new version was presented a few days later. That the Dutch wanted to sweeten the pill as much as possible is understandable. Moreover, Boers had the customary European contempt for the "Malay," whom he saw as uncivilized and unreliable.[59] So why should he be concerned about an accurate translation of the contract, even assuming that he had sufficient command of the language to perceive the differences?

Whatever the case may be, Facharuddin proved willing to sign a contract on relatively favorable terms, which demanded little and promised more. That he

---

[54] Cf. the account of the preparations for and conclusion of the contract of 1858 in chapter 6.

[55] Explanatory memorandum accompanying the model standard contract, NA, Col., vb. January 17, 1876, E1; NA, Col., *gouvernementsbesluit*, February 16, 1881, no. 67 and September 16, 1885, no. 13.

[56] *Politiek beleid en bestuurszorg in de buitenbezittingen*, 4 vols. (Batavia: Landsdrukkerij, 1907–09), vol. 2b; Resink, *Indonesia's History between the Myths*, p. 341.

[57] Council of the Dutch East Indies, January 29, 1858, no. 10, NA, Col., vb. June 3, 1858, no. 222/Q, secret, and vb. October 17, 1903, D 16.

[58] Statement made by Anjong, January 9, 1835, ANRI, Palembang Residency records 72.4.

[59] Boers, "Bezoek ter hoofdplaatse van het Djambische Rijk."

strengthened his own position by doing so was soon apparent when he established his seat in the capital. Now, finally, he could celebrate his official inauguration.[60]

SOVEREIGNTY IN PRACTICE

The rights and obligations of the two parties have been spelled out in detail to illustrate that it was possible from the outset to see the relationship between the Jambian sultanate and the colonial authorities from different perspectives. No clashes ensued in the 1830s or 1840s, partly because of the circumspect way in which the colonial authorities exercised their rights and took advantage of the sultan's expectations.

The Dutch were not concerned to maximize their advantage in Jambi straightaway. Nor did they have the capability. The sole representative of European authority in Jambi was the administrative officer (*civiel gezaghebber*) at Muara Kompeh, who was supported by a local official and a garrison of eighty men, half of whom were European. In practice, maintaining ties with the Jambian court was left to the local official. In 1834 the Palembang envoy Intje Heydar was appointed to this position. As the brother of the sultan's authorized representative (*tiku*), he had excellent credentials and would perform admirably.[61] Five years later he was replaced by his brother, Tumenggung Astro Wiguno, the former *tiku*, who was even better informed about the Jambian court.[62] In 1847 he was indeed described as impossible to replace and therefore ineligible for transfer.[63] Resident Boers, who continued in office until 1840, had no further contact with the sultan. In 1836 he made one isolated attempt at a meeting, which was unsuccessful for reasons that remain unclear. After 1836 the Residents of Palembang did not even visit Muara Kompeh any more, because of the expense involved. It was not until 1852, almost twenty years after the conclusion of the permanent contract, that another Dutch mission appeared at the court of Jambi. Until then, the administrative officer at Muara Kompeh was the only representative of Dutch authority and the only physical sign of the European presence in the sultanate.

The prime objective of the Dutch in relation to Jambi was to restore relations with the court. Even before the new contract had been concluded, Sultan Facharuddin was given an advance of two thousand guilders. Both advocates and opponents of the Dutch presence, including Mohamad Kassim, Pangeran Surio, Said Mohamad, and Raden Tabun, were showered with gifts.[64] Import duties were kept extremely low, to prevent the sultan breaking the contract without the colonial

---

[60] He had still not done so by 1837. After so many revolutions, the custom had evidently fallen into disuse, as the Resident of Palembang reported; only a few chiefs at court were still acquainted with it (Resident of Palembang to governor-general, October 10, 1837, no. 76, ANRI, Residency records Palembang 70.15).

[61] Orders given to the administrative officer at Muara Kompeh, ANRI, Algemeene Secretarie, *gouvernementsbesluit*, February 8, 1836, no. 22. In 1837, he was authorized to bear a *pajong* and to assume the title of Demang Darpa Wiguna, ANRI, Algemeene Secretarie, *gouvernementsbesluit*, June 30, 1837, no. 9.

[62] *Besluit* of February 9, 1839, no. 8, ANRI, Algemeene Secretarie.

[63] *Besluit* of October 19, 1847, no. 8, ANRI, Algemeene Secretarie.

[64] Resident of Palembang to governor-general, October 31, 1834, no. 298, ANRI, Algemeene Secretarie, *gouvernementsbesluit*, January 23, 1835, no. 8.

authorities being able to do much about it.[65] In 1839 Pieter Merkus, commissioner for Sumatra, ordered the continuation of this policy once again during a visit to Palembang.[66]

The administrative officer at Muara Kompeh also received orders in 1836 to avoid taking any action that might lead to disturbances. In accordance with the terms of the contract, he was reminded that he should refrain from any interference with Jambi's internal affairs. All correspondence with the court should be conducted in the friendliest of terms. The officer was urged in particular to gain the confidence of the influential *pangeran ratu* and to respond positively to any suggestion he might make. Any mistrust of Raden Tabun must be concealed. If he became aware of any unrest in the vicinity of the stronghold, he should notify the *pangeran ratu* and the Resident of Palembang. The only actions he was permitted to undertake were against salt smugglers.[67] Clearly, in practice the colonial authorities exercised their sovereign rights with considerable caution.

The same applied to the surveillance of Muara Saba on the Batang Hari estuary. The people of this former pirates' colony were now suspected of salt smuggling. The "native investigative officer" stationed there could not do much about it if he wanted to avoid provoking unrest. For this reason, the colonial authorities soon asked Facharuddin to relinquish control of this settlement. The sultan consented quite readily, partly, we may assume, because the inhabitants were *orang timur*, a non-Jambian group, and partly because he had already experienced friction with the colonial authorities on this score in the past.[68] But here too, the colonial authorities remained cautious and exercised their sovereign rights sparingly: showing political acumen, Resident Boers allowed the people of Muara Saba to become accustomed to their new rulers very gradually, and refrained from bringing the *dusun* under Dutch control immediately.[69]

SALT AND COINS

Only in relation to salt did the colonial authorities insist on their sovereign rights. Jambi's salt came from Siam via Singapore and cost three guilders a picul. For both parties, it was an important product. As we have seen, the salt trade was largely controlled by oppositional kinsmen of the sultan. Public resentment of the obstruction of the salt supply meant that this opposition had lost its power base, however—a weakness that made it bow to the inevitability of the contract in 1833.[70] Salt was an important source of income for the Dutch. The salt monopoly had been introduced on Sumatra's west coast in 1832, and its introduction in

---

[65] Resident of Palembang to governor-general, February 10, 1835, no. 43, ANRI, Algemeene Secretarie, *gouvernementsbesluit*, August 25, 1835, no. 9.

[66] Resident of Palembang to governor-general, February 15, 1843, no. 362, NA, Col., vb. August 14, 1844, no. 377, secret.

[67] Orders given to the administrative officer, ANRI, Algemeene Secretarie, *gouvernementsbesluit*, February 8, 1836, no. 22.

[68] Appendix of letter from Resident of Palembang to governor-general, October 23, 1836, no. 78a, ANRI, Algemeene Secretarie, *gouvernementsbesluit*, April 26, 1837, no. 26.

[69] Appendix of letter from Resident of Palembang to governor-general, October 23, 1836, no. 78a, ANRI, Algemeene Secretarie, *gouvernementsbesluit*, April 26, 1837, no. 26.

[70] Michiels to interim governor-general, November 8, 1833, no. 9, ANRI, Algemeene Secretarie, *gouvernementsbesluit*, September 20, 1834, no. 4.

Palembang was being debated.[71] To stimulate Dutch salt imports from Java, the contract had imposed duties of six guilders a picul on imports of salt from Siam. This would raise the price of Siamese salt by 200 percent, making Javanese salt competitive, at five guilders a picul.[72]

In this area, the Dutch held fast to the contract. Boers had demanded compensation from Mohamad Kassim before signing the contract of 1834.[73] Furthermore, the administrative officer's main responsibility was to curb salt smuggling. When the official who held this position in 1837 proved "too reticent" in this regard, he was replaced.[74] One year earlier Boers had called Facharuddin to account about salt imports, which had fallen dramatically.[75] The sources do not reveal whether he received a satisfactory response.

Salt continued to cause problems, however. Facharuddin displayed some willingness to oblige the colonial authorities, but only if he could benefit in some way. In 1836 he requested two hundred *kojang* of salt on credit in order to market it himself, but the Council of the Dutch East Indies was initially unresponsive. It was not until 1837, when salt imports for some reason became a critical problem in the uplands, that the Resident allowed him one hundred *kojang* of salt on credit.[76] The repayment of the advance did not go smoothly. One year later, two-thirds of it was still outstanding; after that it was deducted from Facharuddin's annuity.[77] So the Dutch efforts to use the sultan to strengthen their hand on the salt market were unsuccessful. In 1840 all the salt in Jambi still came from Siam.[78] By then, the Dutch had been obliged to drop their plan of securing a salt monopoly; no such monopoly materialized in Jambi until 1931.[79] The Dutch did not even have the resources to curb salt smuggling. Basically, the entire salt policy in Jambi was a failure, reflecting Batavia's weak administrative influence there. Powerlessness and caution went hand in hand, and Batavia had enough self-knowledge to acknowledge as much, internally at least.

The same set of factors determined the debate on the agreements concerning copper coinage. In April 1836, Boers received orders from Batavia to pressure Facharuddin to prohibit imports of copper coins from Singapore. The sultan had reportedly purchased pennies valued at 120 pennies to the guilder at the exchange rate of 180 pennies to the guilder—using money derived from his contract with the

---

[71] Van der Kemp, *Handboek tot de kennis van 's lands zoutmiddel.*

[72] Resident of Palembang to governor-general, October 23, 1836, no. 78a, ANRI, Algemeene Secretarie, *besluit* of April 26, 1837, no. 26.

[73] Boers, "Bezoek ter hoofdplaatse van het Djambische Rijk."

[74] Palembang Residency, general report for 1836, 1837, and 1838, KITLV, De Kock collection, 289.

[75] Resident of Palembang to governor-general, October 23, 1836, no. 78a, ANRI, Algemeene Secretarie, *besluit* of April 26, 1837, no. 26, Algemeene Secretarie. In 1835, they totaled 196 Malay *kojang* (equal to 40 piculs); in the first nine months of 1836, there were only 25.

[76] *Besluit* of April 26, 1837, no. 26 and March 8, 1838, no. 13, ANRI, Algemeene Secretarie.

[77] *Besluit* of January 14, 1839, no. 26, ANRI, Algemeene Secretarie.

[78] Rough note, n.d., vol. 1839–40, ANRI, Palembang Residency records 66.12.

[79] Van der Kemp, *Handboek tot de kennis van's lands zoutmiddel*, p. 211. The introduction of a monopoly was justified by invoking the high salt prices, which were disadvantageous for the population, and by urging the need to market the Dutch salt surplus from Madura; *Memorie van Overgave* (Memorandum on leaving office), Resident J. R. F. Verschoor van Nisse 1931, p. 110, NA, Col., MvO 223.

Dutch.[80] Facharuddin's response was prompt and positive. He was willing to halt the imports of coins from Singapore, to admit only Dutch currency to Muara Kompeh, and to promote its circulation in other parts of his realm. The colonial authorities heaved a sigh of relief. Once again, they were painfully aware of the ban on intervention, according to the letter of the contract, and they had no intention of trying to enforce their will by military might.[81] The issue appeared to have been resolved amicably, on paper at least, since Singapore coinage continued to be common in Jambi. In return for his cooperation, Facharuddin asked for half of his annuity to be paid in copper at the rate of 130 pennies to the guilder, so that he could still make a modest profit out of the situation. Unfortunately for him, Batavia declined the request.[82]

All things considered, Batavia was very prudent in its exercise of sovereignty. Concerning what were in principle sovereign monopolies—salt imports, the collection of import and export duties, the control of Muara Saba, and the regulation of the unit of currency—sovereign rights were exercised with moderation. Facharuddin scarcely appeared bowed down by Dutch pressure; he acted like someone obliging a powerful ally in the hope that the favor would be returned. By various means he sought to profit from the Dutch presence. His primary aspiration was to strengthen his financial and political position, the two being inextricably linked in the Malay world. His request for an annual income and the measures he took in the salt trade were not the only signs of this objective. In the fall of 1833, shortly after signing the provisional contract, he had sought to acquire twenty chests of opium from the colonial authorities, which he wanted to barter for gold from the uplands. It would strengthen his hold on both the gold and opium trades in his realm.[83] His request was denied.

In 1836 he made another stab at the gold trade. In exchange for one-third of the proceeds, he offered the colonial authorities the right to work the gold mines in his territory. As he had no influence whatsoever over the gold mines at the time, this would have presented him with distinct benefits. The Council of the Dutch East Indies considered the risks associated with a state-run mining operation too high to take him up on the offer, however.[84]

Facharuddin also tried to set himself up in the salt trade, in which he was equally unsuccessful. And in 1837 he requested a free-trade agreement, which would have given him a monopoly on trade in Jambi. Batavia dismissed this request out of hand, as it would have meant a further reduction in the already meager import and export duties.[85] Whatever expectations Facharuddin may have had of the Dutch presence, he certainly did not achieve any overall improvement in his trading position. The colonial authorities do not even appear to have noticed that he was

---

[80] *Gouvernementsbesluit*, April 5, 1836, no. 20, ANRI, Algemeene Secretarie.

[81] Director of Finance to governor-general, March 7, 1836, no. 137, ANRI, Algemeene Secretarie, *gouvernementsbesluit*, April 5, 1836, no. 20.

[82] *Besluit*, May 31, 1837, no. 9, ANRI, Algemeene Secretarie.

[83] Michiels to interim governor-general, January 8, 1834, no. 11, ANRI, Algemeene Secretarie, *gouvernementsbesluit*, September 20, 1834, no. 4.

[84] Council of the Dutch East Indies, January 24, 1837, no. 91, ANRI, Algemeene Secretarie, *besluit*, February 28, 1837, no. 1; Council of the Dutch East Indies, January 24, 1837, no. 91, ANRI, Algemeene Secretarie, *besluit*, mgs. April 14, 1837, no. 356.

[85] *Besluit*, October 11, 1837, no. 28, ANRI, Algemeene Secretarie.

systematically attempting to make such an improvement; in any case, the documents do not mention any connections between his various overtures. For the time being, his behavior was seen only as reflecting his obliging, affable nature.

UNREST IN JAMBI

By 1838 it must have been clear to Facharuddin that he could expect little support from the Dutch. All his requests for economic favors had been rejected. Could it have been a coincidence that the colonial authorities found themselves facing unrest and polarization that year in Jambi? Did Facharuddin have anything to do with it, or was he simply too weak to restrain his nobles?

In June 1838, Said Mohamad, "a brave and enterprising man,"[86] attacked Muara Kompeh. The action was an expression of his outrage at having been arrested on a charge of murder by the young Dutch official J. D. K. Lammleth, the newly appointed administrative officer.[87] In arresting him, Lammleth not only had breached the contract, which left the administration of justice to Jambi's local administrators, but had also violated adat, according to which the punishment of a member of the *suku* Kraton for murder was the prerogative of the sultan himself. Worse still, Said Mohamad proved to be innocent, and was released shortly afterward. That an overly zealous European upstart should have imprisoned Said Mohamad, one of the most prominent members of the Jambian elite, ignited smoldering resentment.[88] It was only with the greatest of difficulty that the retaliatory strike by the aggrieved noble was repulsed.[89] Batavia sent reinforcements in August 1838 and again in January 1839, but the sense of insecurity among the Dutch at Muara Kompeh persisted in 1839.[90] These feelings were exacerbated by Said Mohamad's constant efforts to recruit more followers and by his ties with the equally hostile Pangeran Surio, who was himself busy trying to

---

[86] This epithet was bestowed upon him by the commander of the fleet at Palembang in a letter to the governor-general of October 25, 1838, ANRI, Algemeene Secretarie, *besluit*, January 13, 1839, no. 16.

[87] Johannes Karel Daniël Lammleth, then "honorair 1e luitenant van het op te richten korps mariniers," had been appointed commander of one of the first steamships in the Indonesian archipelago in 1837. In that capacity he was responsible, later that year, for allowing the ship carrying the acting governor of the Moluccas to his new post to run aground. He and 140 other men, women, and children spent five weeks on a reef in the Banda Sea. He was later absolved from blame, but his appointment as civil administrator at the insalubrious stronghold of Muara Kompeh can scarcely have been a promotion (see "Stoomvaart," in *Encyclopaedie van Nederlandsch-Indië* [The Hague: M. Nijhoff, Leiden: Brill, 1917–40], 4: 114). In 1847, after eight years' loyal service, he was appointed Assistant Resident on Sumatra's west coast, where he died prematurely only two years later. Muara Kompeh had probably taken its toll.

[88] Pangeran ratu to civil administrator, 10 Rabil-awal 1254 (=June 3, 1838), translation, ANRI, Algemeene Secretarie, *gouvernementsbesluit*, October 17, 1838, no. 7.

[89] Some people were robbed of their possessions, including the *nyai* (housewife, concubine) of Keyner, the retired civil administrator; twenty-three people were killed, wounded, or missing (Resident of Palembang to governor-general, September 22, 1838, no. 67, ANRI, Algemeene Secretarie, *gouvernementsbesluit*, January 13, 1839, no. 16; G. B. Hooyer, *De krijgsgeschiedenis van Nederlandsch-Indië van 1811 tot 1894*, 3 vols. with atlas (The Hague: van Cleef, Batavia: Kolff, 1895–97), 2: 200.

[90] *Gouvernementsbesluit*, October 17, 1838, no. 7, and January 13, 1839, no. 16, ANRI, Algemeene Secretarie.

gain Jambi's support to bolster riots in the Rawas, which had broken out at the same time.[91]

Facharuddin immediately tried to prove that he had nothing to do with the matter. Had he not recently admonished Said Mohamad for neglecting his villages? As evidence of good faith, he dispatched twelve hundred troops under the *pangeran ratu* and Raden Tabun—recently elevated to Pangeran Adipati—to provide assistance. Unfortunately they arrived too late to make much of an impact.[92]

By the end of 1839 the internal divisions at court had deepened. Raden Tabun offered, as Pangeran Adipati, to place himself under the immediate authority of Batavia. Resentful at the fact that he did not receive any part of the annuity paid by the Dutch and at the lack of respect with which Sultan Facharuddin treated his wife, Tabun's sister, he had withdrawn to his territory in the upper reaches of the Batang Hari and broken all ties with Jambi. He wielded power there more or less openly until 1845.[93]

All this agitation made it clear that the honeymoon was over. By 1838, disillusionment had set in on both sides. The colonial authorities claimed sovereign rights, but while initially disinclined to press their claims heavily, they subsequently found they could not do so. The sultan had hoped to strengthen his position, but he had been disappointed. Insurgency was rumbling through his realm once again, and it was unclear whether or not he was involved in it. Frustrated, the Dutch turned away from him and pinned their faith on the *pangeran ratu* instead. Boers, who suspected Facharuddin of conspiring with Said Mohamad, would have preferred to place the latter, whom he saw as a more powerful dignitary, on the throne, and to support him from a Dutch post in Jambi's capital. Jambian affairs, about which he had first been so sanguine, had become complicated now that prominent members of the Jambian elite were supporting the revolt in the Rawas, and some were even leading it.[94]

Nonetheless, for Batavia this was a very inconvenient moment to replace the sultan of Jambi, as it had just entered into negotiations with the ruler of Indragiri, not far to the north. It would make a very bad impression on him to see his Jambian counterpart being replaced.[95] The Dutch did want to strengthen the *pangeran ratu's* hand as much as possible, however. So he was given an advance of two thousand guilders at his request in 1840; it was a small concession, however, since he had asked for five times that amount. The authorities also declined Raden Tabun's offer to accept subjection to the Dutch, suggesting that it would be better for him to

---

[91] See letters from Resident of Palembang to governor-general in *gouvernementsbesluit*, January 13, 1839, no. 16, ANRI, Algemeene Secretarie.

[92] Resident of Palembang to governor-general, August 1, 1838, no. 58, and August 7, 1838, G, ANRI, Algemeene Secretarie, *gouvernementsbesluit*, October 17, 1838, no. 7.

[93] The areas over which he wielded power were the VII and IX Kota in northern Jambi (Resident of Palembang to governor-general, December 24, 1839, no. 315, ANRI, Algemeene Secretarie, Cl. January 21, 1840, no. 132).

[94] Commander-in-chief of the army to governor-general, September 6, 1838, no. 6, ANRI, Algemeene Secretarie, *gouvernementsbesluit*, October 17, 1838, no. 7; Resident Palembang to governor-general, October 18, 1838, no. 69, ANRI, Algemeene Secretarie, *gouvernementsbesluit*, January 13, 1839, no. 16.

[95] Commander-in-chief of the army to governor-general, September 6, 1838, no. 6, ANRI, Algemeene Secretarie, *gouvernementsbesluit*, October 17, 1838, no. 7.

support the pangeran ratu in Jambi. Batavia was therefore relieved that he did not repeat his offer.[96]

REVIEW AND CONCLUSIONS

The events related in this chapter lead to two main conclusions. First, it appears that the expansion of authority in Jambi was an expression of *Batavian* imperialism rather than a policy dictated by The Hague. The policy on Jambi was an initiative taken in Batavia, and the Minister of Colonies was not informed about it until afterward. The report dealing with the proposed expansion did not reach the Netherlands until December 1833, when the provisional contract had been signed in the Rawas and the expedition was already on its way back to Java. The Minister obviously knew the main outlines of Van den Bosch's policy on Sumatra, so the context was clear. But both these outlines and their details were drafted in Batavia.

This imperialist drive certainly had an economic component. Not that the Dutch were expecting Jambi to be the goose that laid the golden egg; on the contrary. Merkus, at the time a member of the Council of the Dutch East Indies, had written as early as January 1834, in his advisory opinion on the contract, "that all these possessions [on the east coast] will be and remain millstones."[97] Still, he expected them to yield some benefits, as they could make it easier to conduct trade to the west coast. And Baud's pragmatic verdict was "No immediate financial benefit; on the contrary, an increase in expenditure."[98] The Dutch had no illusions about Jambi's poverty. They valued the territory not for itself but as part of Sumatra, and as a factor in their economic plans for the island. International politics had little to do with it. Van den Bosch did have fears in the international sphere, as we have seen, but his aim in taking military action was not to be one step ahead of other colonial powers.

The second conclusion that can be drawn is that the exercise of sovereign rights was an ill-defined subject in this decade. Facharuddin had signed a relatively mild contract that was enforced more mildly still. As a weak ruler, he had been able to assert very few sovereign rights beforehand, even by Malay standards. The contract did not compel him to relinquish many more, however: the largest single loss was Muara Kompeh. His other concession, the surrender of import and export duties, was not enforced strictly; in this area his commercial rivals in Jambi were the real losers rather than himself. But if Facharuddin did not lose much, he did not gain much either: his hopes of strengthening his position with the help of the colonial authorities came to naught.

In theory (that is, according to the contract of 1834) and in practice, Facharuddin could consider himself a sovereign ruler, albeit a weak one, ruling over a territory with a Dutch enclave and allied through a treaty of friendship to

---

[96] Brief report by the Residency of Palembang for 1840, KITLV, De Kock collection, 290.

[97] "... dat alle deeze bezittingen [op de oostkust] lastposten zullen zijn en blijven"; Merkus to commissioner-general, January 25, 1834, Memorandum no. 2, ANRI, Algemeene Secretarie, *gouvernementsbesluit*, September 20, 1834, no. 4.

[98] "Geene dadelijke geldelijke voordeelen maar integendeel eene vermeerdering van uitgaven"; governor-general to Minister of Colonies, April 12, 1835, no. 79, NA, Col., exh. October 26, 1835, no. 33

a powerful neighbor, to whom he had relinquished a major source of income in exchange for a guaranteed annuity. He had retained the internal administration of his territory. The contract did not explicitly forbid him to pursue an independent foreign policy. In that sense too, he had not lost his sovereignty. He had been left with so much independence that he could continue to see himself as an autonomous ruler and to view his ties with Batavia as a relationship under international law, were he to have taken any interest in such legal niceties. Unfortunately, however, no trace has survived of any interaction between the sultan and the outside world that could help us understand just what sovereignty meant to him, as a Malay ruler. The sources do not refer to ties with independent Sumatran rulers, with Singapore, or with other foreign powers, nor do they document any true exercise of his rights of sovereignty.

The colonial authorities, on the other hand, took it for granted that they had acquired sovereign rights over Jambi, though their ability to exercise them was limited by a lack of resources. The Hague had decided that no money should be spent on Sumatra. They did not want a new drain on the economy, now that the Cultivation System was bearing fruit for the Dutch for the first time, and the expensive Padri War was over (in 1838). So Batavia sought to expand its influence on Sumatra by following the cheap route of diplomacy; witness the contract that was concluded with Indragiri in 1838—just after the contract with Jambi and cast in the same mold.

In the following decades, the Netherlands would often have to contest claims that Jambi was a sovereign nation and to defend its own rights vigorously. Thus our focus shifts from the relations between the colonial administration and the Jambian sultanate in Jambi itself to the ideology underlying those relations and to international political repercussions in the 1840s and 1850s.

CHAPTER FOUR

INTERNATIONAL INTEREST IN JAMBI (1840–1858)

Up to now, the only Western interest in Jambi—aside from Crooke and Ibbetson's lightning visit in 1821—was expressed by the Dutch East Indies authorities in Batavia. Even the Ministry in The Hague had never responded officially to the 1834 report about the signing of a contract. All this would change in the 1840s and 1850s, however, as the British and American governments started showing an interest in Sumatra in general and Jambi in particular. In response, the Netherlands' foreign and colonial policies were closely attuned, as has often been noted in relation to the nineteenth and twentieth centuries.[1] In both areas it defended its actions by invoking the contract of 1834 with the Sultan of Jambi and arguing that the sultan had relinquished his sovereignty.

BRITAIN'S DIPLOMATIC OFFENSIVE

Until 1871, the fate of Sumatra's principalities was a direct derivative of the relationship between the Netherlands and Britain, the "exclusive lords of the East" well into the nineteenth century.[2] This political entwinement, expressed on paper in the 1824 Treaty of London, was underpinned by economic interests.[3] The Indonesian Archipelago was an important market for the British cloth trade. From 1834 to 1839 the ratio between British and Dutch imports to Java stood at 6:7, "a share . . . which, if the matter was reversed, would be considered by the British merchants as rather a large one for a foreign nation to enjoy," as a British report of 1841 keenly observed.[4] As transit ports, Singapore and Penang, which belonged to the British crown colony of the Straits Settlements, were among the main beneficiaries. Almost 20 percent of Singapore's trade had been with the

---

[1] C. B. Wels, *Aloofness and Neutrality: Studies on Dutch Foreign Relations and Policy-Making Institutions* (Utrecht: HES, 1982); M. Kuitenbrouwer, *The Netherlands and the Rise of Modern Imperialism: Colonies and Foreign Policy* (Cambridge: Berg, 1985).

[2] This comment by George Canning dates from January 15, 1824, and is quoted by N. Tarling, "British Policy in the Malay Peninsula and Archipelago 1824–1871," *Journal of the Malayan Branch of the Royal Asiatic Society* 30,3 (1957): 5–228, esp. 128.

[3] See text in *Recueil international des traité's du XIXe siècle contenant l'ensemble du droit conventionnel entre les états et les sentences arbitrales (textes originaux avec traduction francaises)*, ed. Baron Descamps, Louis Renault and Jules Basdevant (Paris: Rousseau, 1914), pp. 931–43.

[4] Wong Lin Ken, "The Trade of Singapore 1819–69," *Journal of the Malaysian Branch of the Royal Asiatic Society* 33, 4 (1960): 46.

archipelago in the mid-1830s. For Penang, Sumatra in particular was significant,[5] as competition with the new Singapore had led its merchants to turn their attention to the region; in 1828–29 one-fifth of Penang's trade relations depended on Sumatra. For Singapore, trade with Sumatra—at only 6 percent that same year—was of less consequence. But it too was indirectly involved in the British trade with the island, as a transit port to Penang.[6]

Given these trading interests, it was hardly surprising that the British government viewed the Netherlands' activities in the archipelago with suspicion. Complaints about Dutch import duties and port restrictions had been the order of the day in the diplomatic exchanges between the two governments from 1825 onward. The Belgian question had aggravated this tariff war, and import restrictions were further tightened to ward off Belgian cloth.[7] New provisions introduced in 1837 clarified the situation.[8] They set import duties at 12.5 percent for cloth of Dutch origin, imposing the higher rate of 25 percent for British cloth. Goods transported from the place of origin on Dutch ships were taxed at half the rate applicable to non-Dutch ships.[9] The new provisions clarified; they did not gratify. Singapore feared that favoring direct transport from place of origin to final destination would harm its entrepôt function. Furthermore, there was an uneasiness about the possible impact on British trade if the East Indies government expanded its authority over Sumatra and started concluding treaties with

---

[5] Ibid., p. 255.

[6] L. A. Mills, "British Malaya, 1824–1867," *Journal of the Malaysian Branch of the Royal Asiatic Society* 33,3 (1960): 5–424, esp. 58; Wong, "Trade of Singapore," p. 55.

[7] The British complaints focused on the following provisions:

a. In connection with the Belgian Revolt, it had been determined in 1834 (gouvernementsbesluit [resolution adopted by the colonial authorities] of June 1, 1834, no. 4) to tax imports of cotton and woolen fabrics from non-friendly countries at 50 percent to 70 percent of their value, regardless of whether they were imported on foreign or Dutch ships.

b. It had been determined that same year (gouvernementsbesluit of November 14, 1834, no. 4), also in relation to Belgium, that woolen and cotton fabrics made to the west of the Cape of Good Hope could only be imported through three ports on Java (Batavia, Semarang and Surabaya), where certificates asserting their country of origin would be issued. Padang had been added to the list of ports in 1837. The restriction obviously formed a serious impediment to direct transport, which Straits merchants contended was incompatible with the principle of free trade with indigenous peoples in the Archipelago (art. 3, Treaty of London). The Dutch government defended the measure as a wartime necessity and argued a shortage of customs facilities (Tarling, "British Policy," pp. 142, 145).

These measures were revoked in the course of 1839, as a result of the Treaty of Belgium of April 1839, but appear to have been applied de facto for longer. See A. J. M. Goedemans, Indië in de branding: Een diplomatiek steekspel 1840–1843 (Utrecht: Oosthoek, 1953); Tarling, "British Policy," p. 145. After their revocation British trade could focus on ports that had been opened up for "major trade," trade with European rigged sailing vessels and steamships (for Sumatra: Palembang, Bengkulu, Padang, and Tapanuli). The "small ports" remained closed to international trade (Minister of Colonies to British ambassador, March 21, 1841, National Archives [NA] The Hague, Col., vb. March 21, 1841, no. 21).

c. The provisions of 1837, also mentioned in the text above, which Straits merchants feared would give an unfair advantage to Dutch trade and boost direct transport, adversely affecting its position as an entrepôt (Wong, "Trade of Singapore," p. 45).

[8] Wong, "Trade of Singapore," pp. 45–49; E. S. De Klerck, *History of the Netherlands East Indies*, 2 vols. (Rotterdam: Brusse, 1938), 2: 254–56.

[9] Wong, "Trade of Singapore," p. 45.

individual sultans. Would its trade with local ports on the island, guaranteed by articles 3 and 4 of the Treaty of London, be able to continue unimpeded?[10] The British had been well aware since 1820 that Dutch supremacy was based not on "general supremacy and exclusive rights of commerce" but on "a multiplicity of single rights of possession and exclusion," depending on "occupation, cession, or treaty with sovereign native princes," as the India Board described it that year.[11]

Despite these concerns, the expansion of Dutch authority over Jambi had not provoked any British protests, partly because Singapore's trading interests with Jambi did not amount to much.[12] In July 1838 the governor of the Straits Settlements wrote to his superiors in Calcutta about the dangers posed by Van den Bosch's expansionist policy:

> It is generally believed, that the Dutch intend to subjugate the entire interior lying between Padang on the West Coast and Siak and Indragiri on the East Coast. If they succeed . . ., they will doubtless according to their national custom do all in their power to injure and ruin the commerce at present existing between the Native Ports on the East Coast of Sumatra with Singapore. This they can do easily by forming small Establishments at the mouths of the various rivers whereby they will be enabled to prevent the Natives from bringing as heretofore produce from the interior of their valuable Island and thus entirely annihilate the existing commerce or direct its stream to the Western Coast where they are paramount.[13]

Accordingly, Britain viewed the preservation of the independence of the principalities on Sumatra as providing the best guarantee of its interests.

Britain's suspicions were soon confirmed. In 1838, with the Padri War virtually settled, the East Indies government had occupied the ports of Panei and Bila on Sumatra's east coast. In 1839 and 1840, by way of a punitive measure, followed the

---

[10] Article 3 of the Treaty of London:

The High Contracting Parties engage that no Treaty hereafter made by either, with any native Power in the Eastern Seas, shall contain any Article tending, either expressly, or by the imposition of unequal duties, to exclude the trade of the other party from the ports of such native Power: and that if, in any Treaty now existing on either part, any Article to that effect has been admitted, such Article shall be abrogated upon the conclusion of the present Treaty. It is understood that, before the conclusion of the present Treaty, communication has been made by each of the Contracting Parties to the other, of all Treaties or Engagements subsisting between each of them, respectively, and any native Power in the Eastern Seas; and that the like communication shall be made of all such Treaties concluded by them, respectively, hereafter.

Article 4:

Their Britannic and Netherland Majesties engage to give strict orders, as well to their civil and military authorities, as to their ships of war, to respect the freedom of trade, established by Articles 1, 2, and 3; and, in no case, to impede a free communication of the natives in the Eastern Archipelago, with the ports of the two Governments, respectively, or of the subjects of the two Governments with the ports belonging to native Powers.

(Descamps, Renault, and Basdevant, *Recueil international*, pp. 933–34).

[11] Tarling, "British Policy," p. 127.

[12] Singapore was more important to Jambi than vice versa. Almost all Jambi's exports were to this free port; Wong, "Trade of Singapore," p. 55.

[13] Ibid.

occupation of Baros, Tapos, and Singkel, west coast ports under Acehnese sovereignty, and the Sultan of Singkel asked the governor of Melaka for assistance. What is more, September 1838 saw the conclusion of a contract with the Sultan of Indragiri that was analogous to the one with Jambi. And in May 1840 followed the first official overtures to the Sultan of Siak, one of the last independent sultans on the east coast, who had concluded a treaty of friendship with the British authorities in the Straits Settlements back in 1818.[14] True, this treaty had been nullified by the Treaty of London, but it was nonetheless suggestive of an emotional tie.

It was not really until January 1841 that Britain's Whig government became receptive to the concerns of the Straits Settlements authorities. In 1839 it had merely asked The Hague whether the expansion of the Netherlands' authority on Sumatra had been authorized by the Supreme Government, as article 6 of the 1824 Treaty required. The affirmative answer to this question had satisfied London for the time being. This seemed to have settled matters; but two years later began a more serious diplomatic sparring match.

The British government's concern in this diplomatic debate was to defend its commercial interests, not to stake territorial claims. It launched an initial offensive in January 1841 with a complaint on the restrictive tariffs of 1834, followed in March by a protest against the threatened expansion of Dutch authority over Siak.

MINISTER BAUD'S RESPONSE

With the death of Johannes van den Bosch, Minister of Colonies, in 1840 and the abdication of King William I that same year, ended ten years of cooperation in colonial affairs between the enterprising pair who had shaped the policy on Sumatra and devised the Cultivation System. It was up to their respective successors—both of them more cautious, more conservative, and more diplomatic men—to consolidate their pioneering work. William II and his Minister of Colonies J. C. Baud (1840–48) did not follow unquestioningly in their predecessors' footsteps. Britain's protestations prompted them to devise a policy of their own.

It was Baud who determined the Netherlands' part in this diplomatic skirmish; since colonial issues were at stake, he scripted the responses of both the foreign minister and the king. Since the early nineteenth century, the Belgian question had created a distinct chill in relations between Britain and the Netherlands. Furthermore, William II leaned more toward France and displayed a more guarded attitude to the Netherlands' one-time "natural ally."

Jambi became entangled in the international intrigues right away. In March 1841 Baud sent the 1834 contract with Jambi through the Dutch Ministry of Foreign Affairs to London, the aim being to demonstrate the good intentions of the Dutch government. To his mind the contract provided conclusive evidence that there was free trade on Sumatra and that the occupation of Jambi had been a matter of pure necessity, not about promoting commercial interests: "self-preservation was the sole basis for these conquests."[15] A few weeks later he reiterated that "our conquests on

---

[14] *Ikhtisar Keadaan Politik Hindia-Belanda Tahun 1839–1848* (Jakarta: Arsip Nasional Republik Indonesia, 1979), p. 111; Tarling, "British Policy," pp. 124–25.

[15] Minuut, March 14, 1841, no. 21, NA, Col., vb. March 12, 1841, no. 21.

Sumatra are motivated by the principle of self-preservation."[16] This accounted for the taking of Palembang in 1821 and Jambi in 1833, and for the contract with Indragiri in 1838 (the latter in a bid to root out piracy). Self-defense, he explained, was the cornerstone of his policy.

Sending the contract to the British government was not in fact such a wise move, as it handed its rival counterarguments on a plate. For article 8 of the contract made it permissible to levy import duties, while article 9 raised the prospect of a monopoly on salt. According to Lord Palmerston, the British prime minister, these provisions were in direct contravention of article 3 of the Treaty of London, which laid down that the two countries should be free from trade restrictions in each other's territories. The subsequent debate therefore hinged on the question of whether article 3 of the Treaty of London applied to rulers who had relinquished their sovereignty. This question had already been discussed internally at the Foreign Office in May 1841. If Jambi was still independent, the Netherlands was not entitled to impose differential duties. "If, on the other hand, we consider the territory of Jambi as having become an integral portion of the Dutch dominions in the Eastern Archipelago, it will be impossible to deny the right of Holland of introducing into a conquered state the institutions and regulations already established in other portions of her dominions."[17] Ultimately, therefore the issue revolved around the question of whether the Treaty of London excluded conquest, which the writer of the memorandum thought improbable.

The possibility of opening new trading posts had indeed already been broached before, during the talks held in 1824, and article 6 explicitly allowed it, provided it was authorized by the government in Europe.[18] Thus the expansion of Dutch authority in Sumatra had not been ruled out in advance, any more than British expansion on the Malay Peninsula.

Baud repeated this argument in a memorandum of October 26, 1841. The provision related solely to contracts with independent states, not to rulers who had placed themselves under Dutch authority and whose territory was a dominion of the Netherlands. It therefore did not apply to contracts with Jambi and Indragiri, whose rulers had been left in charge of internal administration only "as vassals of the Dutch colonial government."[19] Baud was fully aware that the British protest could effectively impede any expansion of Dutch authority,[20] something he was not prepared to countenance without a struggle. He therefore claimed the right of free trade on Sumatra for the Netherlands, on the same basis that he consented to the British rights over Melaka. The argument would be raised repeatedly in the

---

[16] Minuut, April 6, 1841, no. 142 secret, NA, Col., vb. April 6, 1841, no. 142 secret.

[17] Memorandum May 20,1841, Foreign Office records, quoted in Tarling, "British Policy," p. 143.

[18] P. H. van der Kemp, "De geschiedenis van het Londensch Tractaat van 17 Maart 1824," *Bijdragen tot de Taal-, Land- en Volkenkunde* 56 (1904): 1–245, esp. 162; C. M. Smulders, *Geschiedenis en verklaring van het tractaat van 17 maart 1824 te Londen gesloten tusschen Nederland en Groot-Brittannië ter regeling van wederzijdsche belangen en rechten in Oost-Indie* (Utrecht: Siddré, 1856), p. 67.

[19] Minuut, October 26, 1841, no. 459 secret, NA, Col., vb. October 26, 1841, no. 459 secret.

[20] Unless this were to be combined with free trade. Whether Baud realized this is unclear. In any case, free trade was still quite an uncommon practice. Britain did not introduce it for Europe until 1842, and the Dutch government did not introduce it for the Dutch East Indies until 1873.

British-Dutch controversy about the archipelago in the 1840s. And as Lord Palmerston himself acknowledged in a letter to the British ambassador to the Netherlands in 1846, "If the right of conquest is mutually retained, I do not see any ground upon which either party can pretend to prescribe to the other what regulations shall be established in regard to trade in the conquest so made."[21] After all, logic dictated that taking a different view would rule out any conquest for Britain as well. And although the British government held fast to a policy of complete abstention from interference on the Malay Peninsula until 1867,[22] Palmerston too was loath to cut off the option of expansion in 1846.

The British government did not raise the Jambi question again after the spring of 1841, but shifted its attention to the archipelago as a whole. While the Straits Settlements government was mainly concerned about Dutch expansion on Sumatra, which it saw as a threat to its entrepôt trade, the Foreign Office in London, under pressure from the domestic textile lobby, wanted a comprehensive trade agreement. Britain should seek to acquire the free import of textiles in the archipelago in exchange for allowing free imports of Javanese sugar into Britain.[23] From December 1841 onward, the new Tory government therefore took issue with the Treaty of London itself, since its provisions had proved ambiguous. Minister of Colonies Baud, who saw no advantage in being allowed free sugar imports or indeed in renegotiating the treaty, stuck to his policy of denial and trivializing the problems. The British ambassador made little headway. In 1843, the exchange of diplomatic notes came to an end, although London continued to keep a close watch on the Netherlands' policy in the archipelago for the rest of the decade, including its expeditions to Bali, and monitored it at the diplomatic level. In 1850, however, growing economic interests in Australia and America diverted Britain's attention from the archipelago.[24]

BAUD'S POLICY ON SUMATRA

In the meantime, Baud had done more than simply defend the contract with Jambi. The main outcome of the diplomatic consultations was the decision of September 1, 1841, to pursue a strict *onthoudingspolitiek*, a policy of abstention from interference in the Outer Islands, and to vacate all the civil and military posts on Sumatra's east coast. This decision impinged directly on Jambi. It formally revised old regulations that had gradually been disregarded—certainly where Sumatra was concerned—and ushered in an official policy of abstention in the Outer Islands that would be maintained until the 1890s, although its lax implementation made it, as Fasseur has commented, "a paradox."[25] It was Baud's most controversial move, and later historians of imperialism such as E. B. Kielstra

---

[21] Tarling, "British Policy," p. 147.

[22] Britain saw this as the only way of safeguarding its trade interests: the Malay states were thought to be too bogged down in war and anarchy for involvement there to bear any fruit (Mills, "British Malaya," p. 203).

[23] De Klerck, *History*, 2: 266–67.

[24] Goedemans, *Indie in de branding*; Tarling, "British Policy," pp. 140–51.

[25] C. Fasseur, "Een koloniale paradox: De Nederlandse expansie in de Indonesische archipel in het midden van de negentiende eeuw (1830–1870)," *Tijdschrift voor Geschiedenis* 92 (1979): 162–87.

and J. Somer thought it wholly incomprehensible.[26] Yet it was completely in line with Baud's view that expansion on Sumatra should not go too fast and should never be allowed to prejudice the Netherlands' interests on Java or the Dutch Treasury. In fact he might well have made the same decision even without the British complaints.

In his exchanges with Britain, Baud had always explained Dutch expansion on Sumatra as a consequence of the war in the Minangkabau and the Netherlands' right to defend itself. He did not oppose the action undertaken in Siak, where Dutch officials had made overtures to the sultan in 1840, as this was part and parcel of Van den Bosch's policy. But any such action must be subordinate to higher interests, he insisted in a letter of April 1841. Britain must not be given any excuse for frustrating the plans for expansion. Was Siak, in particular, really worth an acrimonious controversy with London? "The sparsely populated east coast is of no immediate territorial interest to us," he wrote.[27] He therefore advised William II, as early as April 1841, to postpone taking possession of Siak and of any other east-coast ports. At the beginning of May 1841, the Crown made this into an official order to the governor-general: the occupation of Siak was to be delayed as long as possible, as it was hard to justify on the grounds of self-defense that had been invoked by the British. However, the East Indies government was free to spread its power and influence to the interior.[28]

This ambivalent order was one of the first signs of a new policy on Sumatra dictated by The Hague. Six months earlier, Baud had told his governor-general—also in connection with British complaints—to slow down on Sumatra. In May he added, to make the decision less bitter to swallow, that expansion on Sumatra's east coast was not really necessary at that time. Now that exports had been shifted almost completely to the west coast, the Dutch already had sufficient control over trade on Sumatra.[29] After these preparatory steps, he gave strict orders on September 1, 1841, to abandon all fortresses on the east coast.

This was not merely a response to British demands; in that case it would have been done before. At least as important was the reported revolt of the Minangkabau leader Batipo in the uplands of Padang. The revolt had taken place in February 1841 and had in fact been subdued within a month. However, the distance between the Netherlands and its colony meant that the events were reported, as usual, with a substantial delay. At the beginning of June 1841 an informal message reached the king by way of London. It was not until August 12 that the official report of Acting Governor-General Merkus arrived at the Ministry, including the information that troops had been sent from Java to Padang to put down the uprising.[30]

---

[26] Goedemans, *Indie in de branding*, p. 3.

[27] "De zeer schaars bevolkte Oostkust heeft voor ons geen onmiddellijk territoriaal belang"; Minuut, April 6, 1841, no. 142 secret, NA, Col., vb. April 6, 1841, no. 142 secret.

[28] Minuut, May 6, 1841, no. 184 secret, NA, Col., vb. May 6, 1841, no. 184 secret.

[29] Ibid. That the colonial government still did not have total control of trade is clear from Baud's instructions to Governor-General J. J. Rochussen in 1845 to spread the east coast trade more towards the west. See W. A. Baud, ed., *De semi-officiële particuliere briefwisseling tussen J. C. Baud en J .J. Rochussen 1845–1851 en enige daarop betrekking hebbende andere stukken*, 3 vols. (Assen: Van Gorcum, 1983), 2: 317, 3: 56.

[30] Goedemans, *Indie in de branding*, pp. 64–65.

Before receiving the official news, however, William II had already ordered a radical revision of the policy on Sumatra. "His Majesty regards the existing system of a full and rapid conquest of that Island as unproductive," Baud wrote in his diary on August 10, 1841,[31] which made William II decide on a more cautious approach. Although Baud allowed the king to take the credit for the new initiative, it is fair to assume that he himself was the prime mover, since the decision reflected his own views as expressed in the past. Back in 1835 he had already told Van den Bosch that while endorsing the objectives of the latter's policy on Sumatra, he disagreed with the proposed time scale: "I believe that one should not be impatient and desire to see something accomplished within a year that requires a longer period of time."[32] Now he was clearer still: "The idea of subjugating Sumatra need not, therefore, be abandoned, but it should be done in the course of one hundred years rather than twenty-five."[33]

Baud wanted a change of pace, not a change of policy. His "abstention" applied only to the physical presence of Dutch soldiers and officials. This is clear from his warnings that Britain should not be allowed to impede the plans for expansion and that it was acceptable to influence Siak from within in spite of the official withdrawal of the Dutch presence. It is also clear from his instructions to the governor-general to make sure to obtain, before pulling out, "full recognition of our sovereignty and our right to build strongholds, and administer ingoing and outgoing duties in exchange for financial compensation."[34] Encouraging local rulers to send regular missions to Batavia was a useful way of maintaining good relations. Furthermore, they should be given to understand that provided they adhered to the rules of good conduct, the Netherlands would not insist on its sovereign rights. Ever the shrewd tactician, Baud therefore wanted merely to remove the unmistakable signs of the Dutch presence: the manning of the fortresses. Through treaties, however, Batavia would keep all its rights intact. Baud indeed insisted, in the years that followed, on a list being made of all the territories that belonged to the Dutch East Indies. Where rights of sovereignty were unclear, they should be exercised and thus made secure. But it should all be done discreetly—with

---

[31] "Het bestaande stelsel eener algehele en spoedige verovering van dat Eiland beschouwt Z. M. als ondoelmatig"; Baud's journal, manuscript August 10, 1841, which its editor, W. R. Hugenholtz, kindly allowed me to inspect. The criticism that the former General H. J. J. L. De Stuers expressed of the policy pursued by his successor A. V. Michiels (the colonel from Jambi, 1833) in the Minangkabau had strengthened him in his conviction, although he disagreed with De Stuers' "solution"—slowing down expansion with the exception of the ports (minuut, August 27, 1841, A1 and September 17, 1841, no. 396 secret, NA, Col., vb. August 27, 1841, A1 and vb. September 17, 1841, no. 396 secret).

[32] "Ik geloof, dat men niet ongeduldig moet zijn en in een jaar willen tot stand gebracht zien, wat eene veel langere tijdsruimte vereischt"; J. J. Westendorp Boerma, ed., *Briefwisseling tussen J. van den Bosch en J. C.Baud, 1829–1832 en 1834–1836*, 2 vols. (Utrecht: Kemink, 1956), 2: 171.

[33] "Het denkbeeld van onderwerping van Sumatra hoeft daarom niet opgegeven te worden, maar men moet er een eeuw in plaats van 25 jaar aan besteeden"; draft proposal for the amendment of the policy on Sumatra, NA, Col., vb. August 27, 1841, no. 358 secret, sent to the Dutch East Indies on September 1, 1841, NA, Col., vb. September 1, 1841, no. 383 secret.

[34] "Volledige erkenning van onze souvereiniteit te verkrijgen en van onze bevoegdheid om forten te bouwen, de in- en uitgaande rechten tegen schadeloosstelling onder beheer te nemen"; draft proposal for an amendment of the policy on Sumatra, NA, Col., vb. August 27, 1841, no. 358 secret, sent to the Dutch East Indies on September 1, 1841, NA, Col., vb. September 1, 1841, no. 383 secret.

"scientific expeditions, administrative measures, the quelling of minor disturbances and the settlement of minor disputes."[35]

Cutting costs in the Outer Islands was a decisive factor in this decision, as it had been the prime factor underlying Baud's criticism of Van den Bosch's plans. For Baud, it was Java, where the Cultivation System had finally yielded the long-awaited profits, that had the highest priority. Sumatra would therefore have to pay for itself, as Baud stated; the island must be conquered "at the pace Sumatra's own resources will permit."[36] A memorandum of 1843 from the General Secretariat put it more bluntly still: "No action taken on Sumatra must put in jeopardy either the political balance on Java or the financial position of the Treasury."[37]

These comments confirm that it must have been Baud who decided on the policy of abstention. In fact the British government had not requested withdrawal, it merely wanted to retain its former freedoms. Baud could therefore say to the lower house of Parliament in all sincerity in 1857 that he had not succumbed to British pressure but had merely acted "in accordance with our own firm beliefs as to what is in our own best interests."[38] Nor did he communicate his decision straightaway; he broached it six months later, in a resumption of diplomatic correspondence with London. There is no evidence whatsoever to support the view of the later Minister of Colonies I. D. Fransen van de Putte that he feared a British attack on the Dutch fortresses in the archipelago in this period.[39] In fact the records suggest that the diplomatic skirmish with Britain had chiefly furnished him with a reason for imposing his own policy on Sumatra.

Baud's decision was also in tune with Dutch foreign policy, that of a small country that had decided after the Belgian uprising in 1839 to embrace a policy of abstention and neutrality in Europe and not to give any offense to its neighbors and rivals. In the Dutch East Indies, however, it was an equivocal policy. Indeed, "abstention" hardly seems an apt word for it, given the degree to which diplomatic ties with the local rulers were strengthened under the cloak of withdrawal. The term is only serviceable in the idiosyncratic sense in which Baud used it. For not only was his new policy paradoxical in that it could never be fully adhered to—it created a discrepancy between theory and practice that would endure throughout

---

[35] "Natuurkundige nasporingen, administratieve maatregelen, het dempen van kleine onlusten en het regelen van kleine geschillen"; NA, Col., vb. November 4, 1843, no. 459; Fasseur, "Een koloniale paradox," p. 169.

[36] "Sumatra moet worden veroverd met den spoed dien de eigen geldmiddelen van Sumatra gedoogen"; NA, Col., vb. November 4, 1843, no. 459; Fasseur, "Een koloniale paradox," p. 169.

[37] "Handelingen op Sumatra mogen noch staatkundig ten opzichte van Java noch geldelijk ten aanzien van 's lands financiën bedenkelijk wezen"; note sent from Buitenzorg, March 20, 1843, no. 77, NA, Col., vb. May 18, 1844, no. 226 secret.

[38] "Voor onze eigen overtuiging, omtrent hetgeen wij oordeelden in ons belang te zijn." Handelingen der Staten-Generaal: Tweede Kamer 1856–57, p. 723. See also Fasseur, "Een koloniale paradox," p. 167.

[39] See Maarseveen, J. G. S. J. van, ed., *Briefwisseling van Nicolaas Gerard Pierson 1839–1909 vol. 1, 1851–1884* (Amsterdam: Nederlandsche Bank, 1990), p. 309: "Het is mij gebleken . . . dat hij [Baud] van 1840–1847 . . . toen Engeland nog niet was teruggekomen op zijne koloniale uitbreidingspolitiek nog altijd vreesde dat een of ander conflict zou ontstaan en men ons het rijke Java zou afnemen. Daarop motiveerde hij . . . ook ons schandelijk terugtrekken in 1842 van de O.kust van Sumatra, onze houding tegenover Brookes encroachements enz. . . . dit was inderdaad een *idée fixe* bij hem geworden."

the nineteenth century[40]—but the decision itself was paradoxical. It prescribed physical abstention alongside political and contractual intervention. The Dutch claims to exercise sovereignty over the archipelago were never questioned. On the contrary, although they were not yet defined or delimited on paper, they proved to be deeply embedded in Dutch politicians' minds. Thus all that was at issue was a diplomatic measure of outward show, aimed at forestalling problems with Britain for the time being. At the same time, diplomatic overtures to local rulers and the firm belief of the Dutch in their rights over what they saw as colonial possessions sowed the seeds of fresh conflict.

With his new course Baud also ushered in the strategy of "preemption": warding off rivals in the colonial sphere by formalizing contractual rights and obligations on paper so that Batavia could later base its claims to sovereignty on them. It was a very popular strategy among powers such as Britain and France, which availed themselves of it freely in the 1880s, the early phase of modern imperialism[41] Even a small power such as the Netherlands, however, was no stranger to it.

As the most important power in the region, Batavia wanted to leave local rulers in no doubt about its rights. Yet the decision had something in it for everyone: it assuaged the British, who saw it as a splendid concession; it boosted the flow of cash to the treasury of the East Indies—that is to say, of the Netherlands—and it was even of some advantage to the local rulers themselves, who regained some of their autonomy with the strengthening of diplomatic ties.

THE CONSEQUENCES FOR JAMBI

The decision to scale down the Dutch presence understandably met with dismay in Batavia and aroused profound resentment and frustration. Not for a moment did the Dutch officials doubt the Netherlands' right to expand its power in the archipelago, and men from the highest to the lowest rank felt as if they had put in years of work for nothing. Acting Governor-General Merkus, who had come to the East Indies aged eighteen and had quickly made a career there,[42] had little insight into the subtleties of foreign policy in Europe. As a member of the Council of the Dutch East Indies, he had initially railed against Van den Bosch's plans for the Cultivation System. He had always been a warm advocate of his Sumatra policy, however. In 1839–40, while Commissioner of Sumatra, he had visited the island and made his plans. True, Minister Van den Bosch had already warned him that the policy of territorial expansion must not give rise to any unpleasant encounters with European powers,[43] but he had not realized what this might mean. He was therefore bitterly offended that the plan "to add Sumatra to the King's crown as a new pearl" had to be relinquished "for a fear which, having regard to

---

[40] Fasseur, "Een koloniale paradox."

[41] D. K. Fieldhouse, "'Imperialism': An Historiographical Revision," *Economic History Review*, 2d ser., 14 (1961): 187–209; R. F. Betts, *The False Dawn: European Imperialism in the Nineteenth Century* (Minneapolis: University of Minnesota Press, 1975).

[42] "Merkus," in *Encyclopaedie van Nederlandsch-Indië* (The Hague: M. Nijhoff; Leiden: Brill, 1917-40), 2: 713–14.

[43] *Ikhtisar*, p. 117.

our just rights, need not exist."[44] Interestingly, his fiery protestations were not against the true rationale for the decision: sacrificing the Outer Islands to the needs of the Dutch treasury. Perhaps he failed to take this in.

Reluctantly and dragging his feet, Merkus eventually implemented the Dutch orders, but not until the fall of 1842.[45] The fortress at Bila was vacated on the last day of 1842, followed by those at the other ports. In January 1843, Batavia and the sultanate of Indragiri concluded a new contract giving the sultan more autonomy and the Dutch the guarantees they wanted of their sovereignty.[46]

Jambi seemed set to suffer the same fate: in the fall of 1842, Batavia ordered the beginning of negotiations with the sultan with a view to giving up Muara Kompeh. There were scarcely any economic counterarguments to be advanced. According to the Resident of Palembang, A. H. W. de Kock, this occupation cost the government more than 16,000 guilders in administrative and 24,000 guilders in military expenses in 1842, while the revenue amounted to a meager 3,400 guilders— less than 10 percent of expenditure.[47] The policy dictated from Palembang to practice leniency in collecting duties made it hard to do any better. The volume of trade was in any case minimal,[48] and Dutch officials had accordingly paid little attention to Jambi. The Residents of Palembang had missed Muara Kompeh out altogether on their inspection trips of 1839, 1840, 1841, and 1842.[49] Basically, the only grounds for objecting to abandoning the fortresses had to do with Palembang's interests and the fight against piracy. These objections were duly raised.

Batavia no longer had Facharuddin to deal with. After his death in January 1841 he had been succeeded by his brother, the *pangeran ratu*, Abdulrachman Nazaruddin.[50] In accordance with the terms of the contract he had merely notified the Dutch authorities of his succession. It was not until early 1843—two years

---

[44] Merkus failed to understand why the plan of adding Sumatra "als eene nieuwe paarl aan 's Konings kroon te hechten" had to be given up "voor een vrees, welke, lettende op ons goed regt, niet behoeft te bestaan"; *Ikhtisar*, p. 118.

[45] De Klerck, *History*, 2: 268.

[46] Dutch authority was recognized explicitly on paper, combined with the promise of mutual friendship. The colonial authorities reserved for the future all the rights they had claimed before, without immediately exercising them. Wherever it was thought desirable they would build fortresses and found settlements, appoint officials, and tax trade. The sultan promised again to take action against piracy and the slave trade, to extradite criminals, to protect shipping and trade, and to provide transport for the Dutch authorities. With an annuity of 3,300 guilders, half that of 1838, the sultan and his deputy were tied to Batavia. They were to fetch this sum annually from Riau and would receive it on the express condition that they lived in harmony. In line with Baud's instructions, the change in the relationship was explained to the sultan as constituting proof of Batavia's confidence in him and its recognition of the cooperative attitude of the sultan's administration (*Ikhtisar*, p. 118).

[47] Resident of Palembang to governor-general, December 18, 1842, NA, Col., vb. May 18, 1844, no. 226 secret.

[48] Resident of Palembang to governor-general, February 15, 1843, NA, Col., vb. July 29, 1844, no. 345 secret. It had therefore been deemed impossible for the provisions of the gouvernementsbesluit of July 30, 1842, no. 19, doubling the import duties on linen from the British East Indies and China, even to be proclaimed in Jambi.

[49] See Algemeen Verslag der Residentie Palembang over de Jaren 1839–1840 en 1841, and Algemeen Jaarlijksch Verslag der Residentie Palembang over den Jare 1843, KITLV, De Kock collection, H 291, 293.

[50] Administrative officer to the Resident of Palembang, February 18, 1841, ANRI, Algemeene Secretarie, comm. April 20, 1841.

later—that the new sultan received a letter of congratulation from Batavia. The letter also informed him that a new contract in his favor would be concluded with him later on to confirm their friendship.[51] The slow response was partly attributable to Merkus's plans. As former Commissioner of Sumatra, who had become thoroughly acquainted with the affairs of Jambi during his journey through Palembang in 1839–40, he would have liked to seize the opportunity to improve the colonial government's position. Furthermore, in 1840 the then Resident of Palembang had urged that a military presence was needed in Jambi's capital to improve the grip of the Dutch on the upland regions bordering on Palembang.[52] The subject was clearly in the air, as is apparent from a letter written by the Resident of Palembang in February 1841 asking for instructions concerning the accession of the new sultan in Jambi and concerning proposed changes to the contract that had been debated in the Council of the Dutch East Indies. These had not yet been settled when Baud's instructions of September 1, 1841, reached the East Indies in the fall—instructions that were at odds with Batavia's policy.

Raden Tabun had once again been passed over for the sultanate, even though the title had been promised to him.[53] Nazaruddin must have known this would produce a backlash, especially since tensions were already running high. In 1842, one region of Jambi revolted against Nazaruddin. By 1845 the menace of civil war loomed so clearly that the Resident of Palembang requested advance instructions from Batavia on how to respond if Nazaruddin were to ask him for assistance. However, the crisis passed and at the beginning of 1846 the parties were reconciled.[54]

Nazaruddin was acutely aware of his dependence on the Dutch. His previous position as *pangeran ratu* had made him more astute about his political partners than the other *anak raja*. Resident De Kock described him as "the only person in the entire kingdom" who inclined to the Dutch, and said he was certain to be ousted or assassinated if the fortress at Muara Kompeh were abandoned.[55] He would be losing his annuity and, above all, the political support of the Dutch at a time when he was facing serious internal opposition. Indeed, in the fall of 1843, when he finally heard from a Palembang *demang* (an official) that the Dutch planned to vacate Muara Kompeh, Nazaruddin reacted with dismay. He considered any change to the existing situation to be highly undesirable. Had he not always adhered strictly to the terms of the contract? He would not ask for the sultan's former position of power to be restored unless compelled to do so.[56] With alacrity Nazaruddin therefore seized the only escape clause that the Dutch authorities had left the Resident in the negotiations. If the sultan asked "explicitly and in writing" for the abandonment of the fortress at Muara Kompeh to be delayed, the

---

[51] *Ikhtisar*, p. 119.

[52] Concise report of the Residency of Palembang for 1840, KITLV, De Kock collection, H 290.

[53] *Ikhtisar*, p. 120.

[54] Ibid., p. 122.

[55] Resident of Palembang to governor-general, October 13, 1843; governor-general to Minister of Colonies, February 11, 1844, NA, Col., vb. July 29, 1844, no. 345.

[56] Resident of Palembang to governor-general, October 13, 1843, NA, Col., vb. July 29, 1844, no. 345.

Resident was to inform Batavia forthwith.[57] Nazaruddin instantly requested a delay. And to demonstrate his good will, he took action against the pirates at the same time, in the fall of 1843, for which Batavia expressed its sincere gratitude. Internally the Dutch East Indies authorities remained convinced that Nazaruddin could not curb piracy without Dutch support.[58]

Batavia's interests now coincided with those of the local rulers. What ensued was a well-orchestrated effort by the three authorities involved: the local ruler, the Residency, and the colonial government. Nazaruddin's request gave Resident De Kock and Governor-General Merkus a welcome excuse to justify the continuation of at least a limited Dutch presence in east Sumatra. Like many other Dutch colonial administrators, De Kock had spoken out against any scaling down of this presence back in 1842, especially the abandonment of Muara Kompeh. It would undermine the security of Palembang's borders, especially in the Rawas, and make it harder to take action against the pirates.[59] As for Merkus, his disgruntlement with the orders from The Hague has already been discussed. In February 1844 he therefore proposed to Baud that the fortress at Muara Kompeh be retained. He backed up his proposal with new arguments to resist Britain's pressure, arguments more illustrative of his resourceful imagination than of a sound grasp of history.

Merkus maintained, first, that as an old VOC fortress, Muara Kompeh fell outside the scope of the Treaty of London, which prohibited the imposition of duties only in the areas occupied after 1824. He wisely passed over the fact that the VOC had abandoned Muara Kompeh in the mid-eighteenth century and that the company had never imposed duties on trade there, but only on consignments of goods such as pepper. It was an argument that had not even been raised in 1833, when the Dutch first made contact with Jambi. Second, Merkus repeated Baud's own argument of self-preservation. And third, he said that making Muara Kompeh a free port would suffice to accommodate Britain's desire for a trading advantage. That would scarcely damage Dutch interests: trade with Jambi was negligible, yielding a trivial revenue, and duties were already imposed with the utmost leniency.

In August 1844, when the diplomatic clash with Britain was abating, William II agreed. He was undoubtedly swayed by the actions of the Englishman James Brooke in Borneo, whom the Sultan of Brunei had recognized as the ruler of Sarawak in 1841. The Hague had learned of this only in 1842. In response, Baud had toned down the policy of abstention and again asked Batavia to ensure that the Dutch rights of sovereignty were formalized contractually.[60]

In January 1845 Nazaruddin received the reassuring news that the Dutch presence at Muara Kompeh was to be retained.[61] The introduction of free trade there proceeded slowly, however, and was not accomplished until April 1847. The small port was opened up for "major commerce": ships sailing under all flags could

---

[57] Governor-general to Minister of Colonies, February 11, 1844, NA, Col., vb. August 14, 1844, no. 377 secret.

[58] General secretary to Resident of Palembang, November 30, 1843, B5, NA, Col., vb. August 14, 1844, no. 377 secrèt.

[59] Resident of Palembang to governor-general, December 18, 1842, NA, Col., vb. May 18, 1844, no. 226.

[60] De Klerck, *History*, vol. II, p. 297.

[61] *Ikhtisar*, p. 121.

call there, and their trade would be taxed at only 6 percent.[62] The British government, which had already thanked the Netherlands officially for its withdrawal from Sumatra's east coast in 1846, and had asked at the same time for all ports in the Dutch East Indies to be opened up for trade, hence saw its wishes granted only at Muara Kompeh. The decision of 1847 was added as a late dessert, as it were, to the negotiation menu, that could be of only symbolic significance to British trade in the Straits Settlements. The *Overland Singapore Free Press* of December 7, 1847, described Muara Kompeh as "a most miserable village with little or no commerce," and its opening up as "a barefaced attempt at imposition."[63]

Thus ended one of the stormier patches of nineteenth-century Anglo-Dutch relations on colonial affairs, a period that gave William II and Baud an opportunity to formulate their own policy on Sumatra, from which Jambi was excepted. It was an exception born of weakness, not of strength: Jambi's administrative "anarchy" made Batavia fearful of renewed piracy and raids in the ever-restive Palembang. To protect their own "backyard," the Dutch needed to maintain their presence. The interests at stake now (piracy, the security of Palembang) were the same as those that had played a role in 1833: the power vacuum in the "periphery" was a magnet to a power-hungry colonial administration. More explicitly than in the 1830s, it was a presence maintained at the request of local rulers, one that served the sultan's interests and did not totally subjugate him, if only because the communication channels were so poor. Nazaruddin knew he had plenty of room to maneuver independently. Again, we may inquire what he had relinquished, in his own eyes, in exchange for the Dutch presence: overall sovereignty or only Muara Kompeh and trade. The latter is the most probable answer. In consequence of The Hague's intervention in the policy on Sumatra, Batavia had not, in any case, laid down its rights in a new contract. What is more, the fact that the accession of a new sultan had been communicated to the Dutch in the form of a simple message would prove an important precedent in the later relations between the Dutch authorities and the sultan's court.

Finally, to the outside world, the Netherlands had now officially claimed sovereignty over Jambi, reinforcing its right to expand Dutch authority on Sumatra. Not that this fired Dutch enthusiasm. For the time being, Jambi remained an obscure region that officials omitted from their itineraries. A lack of substitute staff made inspections quite impossible at this time.[64] The authorities in Palembang had to content themselves with reading the reports of the administrative officer *(civiel gezaghebber)* at Muara Kompeh.

In 1852, the escapades of an American adventurer, Walter Murray Gibson, reawakened the interest of the colonial authorities in this sultanate. His actions, which were characteristic of individual initiatives in the pre-imperial age, ushered in a fresh assault on Dutch rights of sovereignty over Jambi and drove home the imprecision with which these rights were formulated.

---

[62] Gouvernementsbesluit, April 23, 1847, no. 4, NA, Col., exh. June 26, 1847, no. 5.

[63] Tarling, "British Policy," p. 146.

[64] See reports of the Residency of Palembang for the years 1840–47, KITLV, De Kock collection, 290–97, esp. 295.

PIRATES ON THE COAST

The nineteenth century was the century of private enterprise, both domestic and international. American adventurers journeyed to distant parts of the world in search of self-advancement. More than romantic travelers, they became enmeshed in local politics and tried to acquire positions of power, sometimes through commerce, sometimes by securing positions as local leaders or colonial rulers. Around 1850, Americans were chiefly interested in Latin America, where they wove their own political intrigues.[65] The British were more interested in the Indonesian archipelago. The finest monument to these adventurers is a literary one, in the form of Joseph Conrad's novels, and their best-known model the Englishman James Brooke. In 1839–40 Brooke helped the Sultan of Brunei put down Dayak insurgents, in exchange for which he was given Sarawak in 1841.[66] His fellow countryman Murray was less successful in his own efforts to make good in Borneo and, in 1843, met his death in a battle with local tribesmen in Kutai. If, like Brooke, he had sought to bolster a small piece of the British empire, his actions were wholly counterproductive. A Dutch investigation of his death culminated in a treaty with the Sultan of Kutai, who subsequently recognized Dutch authority.[67] In 1856 another British adventurer, a certain Wilson, intervened in the civil war in the independent realm of Siak. He was driven out by a Dutch expedition, at the request of one of the claimants to the throne. Similarly, in 1852, the American filibuster Walter Murray Gibson achieved little or nothing, either for himself or for Jambi.

THE AMERICAN ADVENTURER GIBSON

Gibson set foot on Sumatran soil on January 17, 1852. He could not have chosen a worse time. Since James Brooke's interference, all foreigners were viewed with suspicion. What is more, Gibson's arrival coincided with a critical point in Palembang's history. There had been unrest in the Residency since 1849. Though an uprising in the south had been quelled, trouble had broken out in other parts of the Residency, including the Palembang uplands bordering on Jambi. To crush the rebellion it had been decided in 1850 to vest civil and military authority alike in the hands of one man, Colonel G. A. de Brauw. Palembang's local administrator, whom the Dutch authorities believed was masterminding the insurgency, was coaxed aboard a ship in September 1851 and sent to Batavia. Even these measures did not produce the desired pacification, however; in 1852, Dutch authority was effectively limited to the capital, Palembang. January of that year saw De Brauw waiting in desperation for reinforcements from Java. They would not arrive until April; Gibson got there first.[68]

The authorities in Palembang gave Gibson a frosty reception, much like the one he had previously received in Bangka. His defense of the United States' recent

---

[65] J. W. Gould, "The Filibuster of Walter Murray Gibson," *Report for the Hawaiian Historical Society* (1960): 7–32, esp. 7–8.

[66] G. Irwin, *Nineteenth-Century Borneo: A Study in Diplomatic Rivalry* (The Hague: M. Nijhoff, 1955).

[67] De Klerck, *History*, 2: 274.

[68] Ibid., pp. 277–78.

attempt to annex Cuba and his admiration for the decisive way in which James Brooke had tackled piracy in Borneo had not gone down well here. Immediately following his arrival in Palembang, he was welcomed by the head of the Arab community, while other local rulers too courted his favor.

Early on February 5, 1852, he dispatched his twenty-six-year-old first officer, Charles Graham, to northern Palembang to visit the Sultan of Jambi and other parts of Sumatra. However, Graham's ship was detained only a few hours out of port. A permit from the district authorities was required for all journeys within the territory, and no such permit had been applied for, let alone obtained. More incriminating, however, was the discovery of a letter in one of Graham's stockings offering Sultan Nazaruddin quite concrete American help against the Dutch. The Dutch translation of this letter, preserved at the National Archives in The Hague, may be rendered as follows in English:

> I am now in a position, oh Sultan, to help you acquire all that you desire, while the American Government has no shortage of gunpowder, bullets, cannons, rifles and lilahs [a kind of cannon]. I can help create prosperity for all the Malay peoples, since I bear no love for the Dutch, as you, oh Sultan, may assure all the Malays; and you and I will be able to strike an agreement. I also wish to know how to travel from Jambi to Palembang and how many days this will require. I can help to make everything splendid and I wish the Malays to be governed as of old. . . . I can be at the mouth of the river Jambi in one month's time; you may agree the best course of action with this man, my officer, since the American government has no shortage of steamships and warships. . . . in the whole of the uplands of Jambi and Palembang I wish everything to be in good order, and if possible I wish to destroy all the Dutch; I shall arrive in a few days' time and can take over this realm at that time.
>
> Sultan, please accept the gracious greetings of myself and all my officers.[69]

A few hours later that day, February 5, 1852, Gibson was arrested on a charge of high treason and sent to Batavia. Twelve months and five trials later he was finally convicted; at the beginning of May 1853 he was sentenced to twelve years in a house of correction, half an hour of being displayed to the public beneath the gallows, and subsequent perpetual exile. He would never undergo any of this, however, since he had escaped from custody in April 1853.

---

[69] "Ik ben nu in staat om U, Sulthan, te helpen aan alles wat U verlangt, dewijl het Amerikaansch Gouvernement geen gebrek heeft aan kruid, kogels, kanonnen, geweren en lilah's. Ik kan helpen om het aan alle Maleijers goed te maken, omdat ik niet veel van al de Hollanders houd, kunnende Gij, Sulthan hiervan de verzekering geven aan al de Maleijers; en Gij zult het met mij eens kunnen worden; ook wensch ik te kennen den weg van Jambie naar Palembang, in hoeveel tijds men die reis kan afleggen; ik kan helpen om alles fraai te maken en wensch ik, dat de Maleijers bestuurd worden zoals in vroegere tijden. Over eene maand kan ik aan de monding der Jambierivier zijn; met dezen mijnen officier kunt gij, Sultan, overeenkomen, dat het beste is, aangezien het Amerikaanse gouvernement geen gebrek heeft aan stoom- en oorlogsschepen . . .; geheel de bovenlanden van Jambie en die van Palembang wil ik alles in goede orde brengen, en indien het mogelijk is, wil ik alle Hollanders vernietigen; binnen weinige dagen zal ik komen en kan ik alsdan dit rijk overnemen. Ik en alle officieren zenden vele groeten aan U, Sulthan." Dutch East Indies Supreme Court judgment of May 3, 1853, NA, Col., exh. June 25, 1855, no. 330 secret.

GUILTY OR NOT GUILTY

Gibson saw the whole episode as an elaborate intrigue staged by a paranoid government. His fascinating *The Prison of Weltevreden and a Glance at the East Indian Archipelago* (1856) gives an eloquent—and almost persuasive—account of the events. Let us start by looking at them through his eyes, a view full of romanticism and outraged innocence. On his arrival Gibson was almost thirty years old.[70] Married at seventeen, he had led the life of an adventurer and hunter exploring the forests and rivers of South Carolina. When he was twenty his wife had died, after which he spent several years in business, earning enough money to embark on fresh adventures. A Guatemalan potentate had commissioned him to equip a warship, but New York's neutrality laws proved an insurmountable obstacle. Having bought the *Flirt*, Gibson found he could not buy guns for it. He decided to make a virtue of necessity and kept the vessel himself to sail the seas.[71]

His arrival in the Indonesian archipelago was the fulfillment of a childhood dream inspired by stories his uncle had told him about Sumatra. He had ended up in Palembang almost by chance, having been invited to join a voyage by the captain of a Dutch ship. He soon discovered that the local chiefs saw America as an ally that could free Palembang from the exploitation and deception of the Dutch (the "Wolanda), who had recently abducted their highest-ranking official. This charge they substantiated in ornate prose, and Gibson replied in kind, promising to relay their message to his countrymen.[72] Meanwhile, he held fast, by his own account, to scholarly objectives. His interest in the Kubu people, timid forest-dwellers who were the region's original inhabitants, aroused his curiosity about Sultan Abdul Nazaruddin of Jambi, who was rumored to have large numbers of Kubu slaves. He sought out a Palembang *pangeran* to find out more about him.[73] His informant explained that the sultan was independent, and that anyone who was not afraid of the Dutch at Muara Kompeh could visit him. The previous sultan had concluded a contract with the VOC granting it a monopoly on salt and a trading post at Muara Kompeh.[74] But Abdul Nazaruddin hated the Dutch and wanted neither to trade with them nor to court their friendship. The country abounded in precious raw materials including gold, pepper, camphor, cinnamon, nutmeg, and benzoin (a gum-like resin). The sultan and other merchants would have been happy to exchange such goods in free trade with the British or Americans, but the Dutch, those "ravenous beasts," stopped them from doing so.[75]

The official Dutch version is rather different. According to their account the sultans of Jambi were not independent at all, Nazaruddin was a friend, Jambi extremely poor, and trade with Muara Kompeh unrestricted. True, disputes had arisen about import and export duties at the end of 1851 between several prominent merchants in Jambi, supported by the sultan, and the administrative officer at

---

[70] He himself shrouded his biography in secrecy, as a result of which historians disagree on matters such as his date of birth and early childhood (see Gould, "Filibuster," p. 7).

[71] W. M. Gibson, *The Prison of Weltevreden and a Glance at the East Indian Archipelago: Illustrated from Original Sketches* (London: Sampson Low, Son, and Co; New York: Riker, 1856), pp. 23–45.

[72] Ibid., pp. 124–94.

[73] Ibid., pp. 182–84.

[74] As we know, the latter was true, but the former was not.

[75] Gibson, *Prison of Weltevreden*, p. 183.

Etching of the ship *Flirt*
from W. M. Gibson, *The Prison of Weltevreden and a Glance at the East Indian Archipelago:*
Illustrated from Original Sketches (London: Sampson Low, Son, and Co.;
New York: Riker, 1856)

Etching of W. M. Gibson's prison,
from the title page of *The Prison of Weltevreden*

Muara Kompeh. The new official did not share his predecessor's flexible attitude to collecting duties.[76] Such disputes were probably a well-known source of trouble in Palembang. To Gibson, however, this explanation spoke volumes. "I wanted to go and see a Prince, who was not surrounded by the trammels of European power. I wanted to see the Malay, the ruling race of the archipelago in his highest state of independence."[77]

But he had changed his plans when he became aware of the Dutch mistrust. He had decided to sail to Singapore and to organize his travels through the archipelago from there. Meanwhile, his first officer, Graham, wanted to travel through the hinterland of Sumatra to the north, after which they would meet up again in Singapore. Graham had been given several letters of introduction to local rulers, written on Gibson's instructions by a new secretary taken on in Palembang. Gibson himself knew neither the language nor Jawi, the form of the Arabic language in which they were written,[78] but he stated that the original text of the disputed letter had read as follows:

> I ——, residing in the great land of America, send greetings to the lord Sultan who rules over the empire of Jambee. This writing will be brought into your presence, by the chief officer commanding my vessel; a man of truth and skill, in whose words and knowledge I have great confidence. He will speak of the great land from whence I come; of the wealth and power of America, and of the friendly dispositions of the American people towards his Highness of Jambee. He will inform my lord Sultan of my wish to visit the kraton at Jambee, that I may present some gifts, and sentiments of friendship to his Highness. Therefore my lord Sultan will be pleased to give orders to his officers, that the bearer of this may be allowed to dwell for a time with peace and comfort in the territory of Jambee; and afterwards, when he shall have accomplished his desire, to be permitted to go his way without molestation.[79]

According to Gibson, the letter found in Graham's stocking was a forgery written by a Dutch spy. Witnesses who could prove as much had been silenced, and lawyers had been pressured by the Dutch authorities.[80]

It is debatable whose paranoia was greater. It can certainly not be ruled out that the Dutch colonial administration used spies.[81] And the incumbent governor-general, A. J. Duymaer van Twist undeniably took a keen interest in the Gibson affair. He immediately sent the case file to the attorney-general in February, asked to be informed about the progress in the case on a weekly basis, and reported the events to the Minister through the more confidential medium of semiofficial correspondence.[82] Nor did he follow the advice that he received in March from the

---

[76] Resident of Palembang to governor-general, January 7, 1852, ANRI, Algemene Secretarie, Comm. January 13, 1852, no. 625.

[77] Gibson, *Prison of Weltevreden*, p. 183.

[78] Ibid., pp. 201–2, 214.

[79] Ibid., p. 204.

[80] Ibid., pp. 403, 431–39.

[81] S. K. Andriessen, "De affaire-Gibson," *Spiegel Historiael* 15 (1980): 42–48, esp. 46–47.

[82] Governor-general to Minister of Colonies, February 25, 1852, NA, Col., exh. June 19, 1855, no. 27; governor-general to Minister of Colonies, February 16, 1952, no. 114, NA, Col.,

Dutch East Indies Council, which took a more laconic view of the case and saw the documents "as evidence of indeterminate foolishness rather than malice or crime" and thought the best solution would be to drop the charges. Even if it had been "a prank," he again urged Minister C. F. Pahud in a semiofficial letter, "it is a prank affecting what are for us major interests, and it is time to set an example, if possible, that will inspire any similar instigators to be more circumspect."[83] But as for tampering with the administration of justice, of which Gibson suspected him, for this there is no evidence. On the contrary, there are numerous signs in the semiofficial correspondence of his belief that the independent courts must have their say: "However the Gentlemen of the judiciary may rule, that we must respect."[84]

Indeed, Batavia's Court of Justice acquitted Gibson four times. The first judgment of February 21, 1852, which cited procedural errors, reveals more about the power struggle between the higher and lower court than about any attitude toward Gibson. After an appeal to the Supreme Court, the Court of Justice had to consider the case again. Gibson was subsequently acquitted three times (in August 1852, December 1852, and March 1853), not because he was believed innocent of having written the letter, but because so little of his plan had been carried out that his actions did not correspond to any offense under the law of the Dutch East Indies.[85] A conviction for "high treason," as requested by the public prosecutor, would only have been possible if the letter had reached its destination. Although the Court deemed Gibson's intentions and his writing of the letter to have been proven, it concluded that these facts constituted neither an indictable crime nor a misdemeanor."[86] Following each separate verdict the public prosecutor appealed to the Supreme Court on the attorney-general's instructions; this was hence the court that ultimately had to rule on the case, which it did in May 1853. So one cannot disavow a certain obstinacy on the part of the attorney-general, the most senior civil servant of the Dutch authorities. Still, that appointments to this position were manipulated in order to secure Gibson's conviction, as the American believed, is not true; Duymaer van Twist established as much in his later reaction of March 1854. The Supreme Court had undeniably acted with remarkable consistency throughout the eighteen-month period. However, Duymaer saw the fact that the courts regularly found against the colonial authorities as proof of the independence

semiofficial correspondence. The governor-general had the power to drop charges before judicial proceedings were instituted and to grant clemency after a final and conclusive judgment had been handed down.

[83] Governor-general to Minister of Colonies, March 22, 1852, no. 115, NA, Col., semiofficial correspondence.

[84] Governor-general to Minister of Colonies, February 16, 1852, no. 114, see also governor-general to Minister of Colonies, October 20, 1852, no. 122 and May 16, 1853, no. 129, all in NA, Col., semiofficial correspondence.

[85] Minister of Colonies to Minister of Foreign Affairs, December 2, 1853, NA, Col., vb. December 2, 1853, no. 455 secret.

[86] Governor-general to Minister of Colonies, March 9, 1854, NA, Col., exh. June 19, 1855, no. 27. In this statement of defense, Duymaer responded to the various complaints enumerated in a detailed Note from A. Belmont, the U.S. ambassador to The Hague; its appendices show the meticulousness with which each separate element had been investigated in Batavia. Gould ("Filibuster"), who considered that Duymaer's share in the case had been proven, does not refer to this material, and probably did not see it.

of the judiciary. He too regretted that the proceedings had taken so long. But this was not the fault of the authorities, which had responded to every request by sending steamships, the newest and fastest mode of transport at the time, to fetch witnesses from Sumatra. The delay was attributable to the legal proceedings in the East Indies, the difference of opinion between the higher and lower courts, the distance between Batavia and the scene of the crime—that is to say, the witnesses' place of residence of—and the unrest in Palembang that had made it impossible to bring the witnesses (including the Resident) to court straightaway.[87]

Furthermore, Gibson's own confessions, his character, and the surrounding events were greatly incriminating. Gibson confessed his guilt both to Duymaer and to the American Secretary of State. Requesting clemency in February 1852, he wrote to Duymaer that he had often been carried away "by some high colored romantic idea"; he conceded that he had made mistakes such as associating too freely with the local people, sending his first officer into the hinterland without permission, and signing a letter the content of which he had not checked adequately. He also confessed to having "indulged in bravadoes that I would become a potentate in the East," "a vainglorious boasting" after imbibing plentiful quantities of wine.[88] Then, in April 1853—two weeks before his escape from Batavia—he confessed to the Secretary of State "admitting . . . entire culpability," though failing to specify wherein this culpability lay.[89] His request for the Secretary of State's support concerned the charge of high treason. Later on (in 1856) he dismissed the first of these confessions as "a false and garbled statement of a memorial addressed to the Governor."[90] His book too presents him as a wholly innocent victim of a miscarriage of justice.

Gibson's character, as described by those who had dealings with him, was scarcely suggestive of solidity. He generally made a good first impression: "A gentleman of refined manners, handsome figure and remarkable intellectual aspect. . . . he had so quiet a deportment . . . that you would have fancied him moving always along some peaceful and secluded way of life. . . . frank, kind hearted, intelligent, upright, and gentlemanly" was the verdict of some Americans who met him after 1853.[91] He was a wonderful storyteller—in March 1854 a meeting of the venerable American Geographical and Statistical Society hung on his every word as he told them the most astonishing tales of the hairy Kubu and the beauties of Nias.[92] In the words of another writer, "He [has] the facility of narrating his adventures with wonderful eloquence— . . . in fact, they were so admirably done that I could never more than half believe them . . . . There was an Oriental

---

[87] Governor-general to Minister of Colonies, March 9, 1854, NA, Col., exh. June 19, 1855, no. 27.

[88] Gibson to governor-general, February 25, 1852, appendix to governor-general to Minister of Colonies, February 25, 1852, NA, Col., exh. May 6, 1855, no. 10.

[89] Gibson to Secretary of State, April 10, 1853, National Archives, State Department, Consular Reports Batavia, vol. 3.

[90] NA, Col., exh. March 8, 1855, no. 8 secret.

[91] J. Adler and G. Barrett, eds., *The Diaries of Walter Murray Gibson 1886, 1887* (Honolulu: University of Hawaii Press, 1973), pp. xii–xiii.

[92] Report of American Geographical and Statistical Society, Regular Monthly Meeting, March 1854. National Archives, State Department, Consular Reports Batavia, vol. 3.

fragrance breathing through his talk and an odor of the Spice Islands still lingering in his garments."[93]

At the hearings, he described himself as someone who was "rather garrulous and thinks highly of [himself]; I am also very vain and always like to lead the conversation in company."[94] Articulate and argumentative, he was a raconteur who seemed to believe his own stories.

There was certainly an opposing—American—view of Gibson: "totally unworthy of the protection of his government . . . unprincipled villain . . . pirate [who] swindled."[95] On the journey through Europe that he undertook in 1854 to defend his interests, these qualities became visible to those he met,[96] costing him a lot of goodwill. When it transpired that he had gained access to his file shortly before the U.S. government published an official report on it, in which his confession was conspicuous by its absence, the government withdrew its support altogether; the Dutch envoy J. C. Gevers was then able to use the omitted document to discredit Gibson to the U.S. government.[97] The Dutch officials in Batavia were already acquainted with this side of Gibson. In his "jail," a plainly furnished room with a veranda, he had lived the good life, consuming his fill of Dutch gin, wine, and beer. His account totaling 1,745 guilders remained unpaid at his escape, along with two others of 2,000 guilders each. Since a bottle of wine cost 1 to 1.50 guilders, clearly his jail term was not entirely without its pleasant side, though his book does not mention it.[98]

Furthermore, this was not Gibson's first political escapade; he had once planned to assemble a fleet to sail for Guatemala. Nor was it his last. After 1853 he continued to dream of a kingdom in the east. He became a Mormon and used the church's influence to found a colony on one of the islands near Hawaii. Turned out of the church after a dispute in 1864, he openly embraced politics. In 1878, he became the president of Hawaii's parliament and served as prime minister from 1882 to 1887, until ousted in a revolution. The dream he had first conceived in Jambi was thus realized for a short period in Hawaii—not a bad bargain in geographical terms.[99]

Returning to Gibson's plans for Jambi, to what extent was he indeed guilty of "vainglorious boasting"? Did he really ever have any chance of mobilizing the U.S. government for his plans? The claims made in the letter to the sultan were in fact flagrant exaggerations. Gibson could never have procured his government's support or assembled a fleet within the space of a month. Furthermore, the United States seemed little interested in territorial possessions. American policy at this time was based on the primacy of trade. Still, change was in the air. In 1848, the Pacific coast had been reached overland, and the frontier had been pushed back to

---

[93] Adler and Barrett, *Diaries of Walter Murray Gibson*, p. xii.

[94] Gibson said he was "eenigszins babbelachtig van aard en veel met mijzelve ophebbende, daarbij ben ik zeer ijdel en wanneer ik in gezelschap ben wil ik altijd het hoogste woord voeren"; hearing of February 28, 1852, NA, Col., exh. June 19, 1855, no. 27.

[95] Gould, "Filibuster," p. 15.

[96] Ibid., pp. 18, 21–22.

[97] Ibid., p. 23.

[98] Consular agent A. A. Reed to Secretary of State, November 22, 1853, National Archives, State Department, Consular Reports Batavia, vol. 3.

[99] Gould, "Filibuster," pp. 25–26.

the ocean. After this, overseas trade with California rapidly expanded. And in 1853, American warships would force Japan to open its ports. To Washington, the navy's protection of trade and negotiations on commercial treaties were of paramount importance. Precisely for this reason, the United States took exception to the attitude of the Dutch in the East Indies.[100] Thus although Gibson's plan was rather a pipe dream, Dutch fears of American interference were not wholly groundless. More important than the question of guilt or innocence, however, are the consequences of Gibson's actions.

CONSEQUENCES: RELATIONS WITH THE UNITED STATES

The Gibson affair produced ripples that were felt on the far shores of the Pacific. The case led to an exchange of diplomatic notes between the Dutch government and A. Belmont, the American ambassador to The Hague, an exchange that was every bit as fierce as the one that had taken place with Britain ten years earlier.

Gibson had succeeded in arousing the interest of the U.S. Navy in the region in 1852, but only temporarily, and to little effect.[101] In April 1853 he had written a long letter urging the U.S. government to help him.[102] Belmont, the new American ambassador to The Hague, was assigned to his defense. After his escape Gibson became his own advocate, pressing a substantial claim for compensation. For the loss of his ship, time, and health, he claimed $100,000, or 250,000 guilders,[103] scarcely a modest claim given that Batavia estimated the value of the "completely unseaworthy" *Flirt* at 5,000 guilders and his outstanding debts at almost 6,000 guilders.[104] In 1854, Gibson personally came to the "assistance" of Belmont in The Hague. All he accomplished was the return of his personal papers, in which some of the trial documents had inadvertently become mixed up.[105] He refused to send these documents back when asked to do so, instead claiming that he now possessed ample evidence of the interference of the Dutch authorities in his case.[106]

In June 1854, Ambassador Belmont received a firm rejection of Gibson's compensation claim. He had already written about the case to his friend, Commodore M. C. Perry, who was in the Pacific waiting for Japan to respond to his

[100] T. Eltink, "Wat doet Amerika? Een onderzoek naar Amerikaans imperialisme in de Indische archipel in de negentiende eeuw, de vrees daarvoor bij Nederlandse bestuurders en waar die toe leidde" (MA thesis, University Nymegen, 1985).

[101] Gould, "Filibuster," pp. 12–13.

[102] Gibson to Secretary of State, April 10, 1853, National Archives, State Department, Consular Reports Batavia, vol. 3.

[103] Dutch ambassador to Washington to Minister of Foreign Affairs, August 27, 1956, NA, Col., vb. September 23, 1856, no. 553 secret.

[104] G. L. J. van der Hucht to general secretary, March 3, 1854, appendix to letter from governor-general to Minister of Colonies, March 9, 1854, NA, Col., June 19, 1855, no. 27.

[105] The documents he acquired were those relating to the hearings and sentences in several judgments handed down by the Court of Justice in Batavia, viz. those of August 25, 1852, of December 22, 1852, and March 5, 1853. The documents relating to the judgment of February 21, 1852 (Court of Justice) and May 3, 1853 (Supreme Court) are present in the records, however, see NA, Col., exh. June 19, 1855, no. 27.

[106] Gould, "Filibuster," p. 18.

demands. The two men agreed that the United States had the same rights to negotiate with local rulers in the Indonesian archipelago as the Netherlands. Belmont indeed believed that "the unfettered trade . . . would be at least fully worth as much for our countrymen, as what we may reap from the opening of Japanese ports."[107]

Belmont protested against the rejection of Gibson's claim, and when another reply came in the same vein, he responded with an ultimatum. Further correspondence was clearly pointless, he wrote, since the last reply was "quite as inadmissible" as the notes that had preceded it. He concluded with the words "It now only remains for my government to take such measures for the enforcement of Mr. Gibson's claim, as it may deem fit and proper in the premises."[108] In the diplomatic language of the time, this suggested war. Foreign Minister F. A. van Hall decided to call his bluff. He had received no indication from the Dutch ambassador in Washington that matters had reached a critical point. So he politely asked for clarification; because of his poor knowledge of English (French was the main language of diplomacy in the nineteenth century) he had not entirely understood Belmont's remarks. Given the long-standing friendship between the two countries, he assumed that the words did not amount to a threat. It proved a successful stratagem: the ambassador backed down and wrote at the end of September that he was at a loss to understand how his letter could have caused offense.

Van Hall now hastened to meet this appeasement with a concession from the Dutch side: he opened up the Dutch East Indies for foreign consuls. The Netherlands had always refused to do so in the past. Since 1840, American interests had been represented by A. A. Reed, the head of a trading company in Batavia. Reed's experience had been that the Dutch authorities had always been willing "to grant all aid possible . . . while at all times scrupulously avoiding any action that could be construed into the acknowledgement of a Consul."[109] It is certainly true that Governor-General J. J. Rochussen had refused to recognize the officially appointed consul C. Wells in 1850, prompting the indignant man to return home, where he submitted a claim for compensation to the State Department.[110] Reed had also advocated change in 1851, partly because the emergence of trade with California had led to his receiving more and more requests for assistance from fellow Americans.[111] But in 1852, the foreign minister had again refused to open up the East Indies for foreign consuls. His decision was frowned upon by Duymaer van Twist, who pointed out that consuls were admitted everywhere "except in our territories, which places us, in this respect, at about the same level as Japan," as

---

[107] Ibid., pp. 16–17.

[108] Ibid., p. 20.

[109] Commercial agent Reed to Secretary of State, January 5, 1854, National Archives, State Department, Consular Reports Batavia, vol. 3.

[110] Governor-general to C. Wells, August 14, 1850, no. 164; C. Wells to Secretary of State, January 21, 1851, National Archives, State Department, Consular Reports Batavia. vol. 3.

[111] Acting consul Reed to Secretary of State, October 16, 1851, National Archives, State Department, Consular Reports Batavia, vol. 3.

he wrote in 1852, a year before Japan itself was forced to open up to the outside world.[112]

Gibson had stepped up the pressure even more. In his letter asking the Secretary of State for support in April 1853, he blamed his poor treatment in part on the absence of anyone who could officially represent his interests. He therefore urged "the great necessity that the government of Holland should be induced to recognize consuls in their East India possessions."[113] Belmont first broached this American desire in 1853 when discussing the case of Gibson. In 1854 initial negotiations were opened on the subject, and in 1855, to the satisfaction of U.S. Secretary of State W. L. Marcy, statutory provision was made for the admission of foreign consuls to the Dutch East Indies as commercial agents.[114] The Dutch foreign minister took this first step on the path toward the liberalization of economic affairs because he believed it to be in the interest of international diplomatic relations, and won the grudging acquiescence of the Ministry of Colonies.[115] Without the Gibson case, it would probably have taken many more years for the Dutch to admit consuls. The United States had essentially opened up the East Indies. After this, the Netherlands concluded consular agreements with a number of countries for the colony.

Furthermore, the Gibson affair had made the United States look more closely at the archipelago. Gibson himself would continue his efforts to interest the U.S. government and Congress in his cause and in the East Indies until 1857. Though he was initially unsuccessful, his second attempt bore fruit. In 1856 a motion was put before Congress to intervene in the Gibson case and to conduct a local investigation of the Netherlands' rights of sovereignty in the Indonesian archipelago. If insufficient evidence of these rights were to be found, the U.S. government should conclude friendship and trade treaties with the local rulers and peoples. A resolution to this effect was put to the Senate in January 1857.[116] To the relief of The Hague and the Dutch ambassador to Washington, it was never actually discussed.[117] The United States confined itself to its traditional policy of protecting the lawful interests of its citizens and its trade. Even so, because of Gibson, the U.S. public took a greater interest in the Indonesian archipelago in the 1850s than at any other time in the nineteenth century.[118]

---

[112] Governor-general to Minister of Colonies, April 19, 1852, no. 116, NA, Col., semiofficial correspondence.

[113] His relationship with Reed was anything but cordial. Reed had departed for the United States shortly after his arrival in Batavia and stayed there until June 1852, putting an associate in charge of defending Gibson's interests. In a New York Times article of August 10, 1853, Gibson heaped abuse on Reed, after which a conflict ensued about the dispatch of objects given to him for safekeeping (see Reed to Secretary of State, November 22, 1853, January 1, 1854, June 5, 1854, National Archives, State Department, Consular Reports Batavia, vol. 3).

[114] Dutch ambassador in Washington to Minister of Foreign Affairs, March 5, 1855, NA, Col., exh. March 26, 1855, no. 27; Bulletin of Acts and Orders (Staatsblad) 1855, no. 63.

[115] Relations between the Ministries of Colonies and Foreign Affairs often displayed this pattern, for instance, when the Japanese were given the same rights as Europeans in 1899 and at the end of the decolonization struggle in 1949.

[116] See NA, Col., minuut vb. March 7, 1857, no. 122 secret.

[117] Gould, "Filibuster," p. 24.

[118] Ibid., p. 26.

CONSEQUENCES: JAMBI AND THE EAST INDIES

The affair also had repercussions for Jambi and the Dutch East Indies as a whole. In April 1853 Governor-General Duymaer van Twist received instructions from Minister C. F. Pahud (1849–56) to conclude contracts with independent ("free") local rulers as soon as possible, especially on Sumatra, and to take measures "to prevent other powers from establishing a presence there."[119] It was a repeat of the earlier instructions from Baud. By this time Jambi had received an official visit from a senior representative of the Dutch government for the first time in fourteen years. The purpose of this visit by the Assistant Resident of Palembang, F. J. R. Storm van 's Gravesande—a grand event that took place in November 1852—was to enforce the terms of the contract more firmly, to procure information, and to assess the damage that new provisions had allegedly inflicted on Jambian merchants; for at the end of July 1852, the colonial government had banned the import and trade of firearms in Muara Kompeh and Palembang because of the rebellion in Palembang.[120] The consequent blockade just off the coast of Sumatra had created bad blood, especially in trading circles surrounding the sultan.

Once again—in what was by now a familiar pattern—the visiting Dutch official was struck by the poverty of Jambi, the absence of proprieties, and the sultan's weakness, although the dispute with Raden Tabun had been resolved by then and he was in the party that received the Dutchman. The key issue in the talks was the stricter enforcement of the terms of the contract, especially in relation to import and export duties. In the future, every ship had to be unloaded in the presence of the administrative officer, since the administrative officer's instructions now read: "Our relations with Jambi are regulated primarily by the manner in which we impose duties."[121] He was required to travel to Jambi each year, preferably by steamship. To speed up the journey, a pilot was installed on the river Batang Hari in 1854 for the stretch of water between the estuary and the capital.[122] Officials in Jambi had feared far worse—that the visit might herald higher import and export duties, the introduction of a salt monopoly, or even the occupation of the capital, measures that would not even cover the costs to the colonial government. But what mattered most to the Dutch was to put on a show of power and to improve communications with the capital. And although Gibson's name was not mentioned in the decision making, these events took place so soon

[119] Minuut, April 29, 1853, no. 180 secret, NA, Col., vb. April 29, 1853, no. 180 secret.

[120] See NA, Col., vb. October 29, 1852, no. 12 and October 22, 1852, no. 24. As recently as the beginning of July 1852, a hundred rifles (cheap ones of inferior quality, imported from Singapore) had been seized at Muara Kompeh. The Dutch East Indies Council declared itself opposed to the proposed ban on imports on political grounds: there were fears of complications with British trade. For had not Muara Kompeh been declared a free port? Implementing the measure would mean positioning a warship off the coast of Sumatra to enforce a blockade. But Duymaer van Twist paid no heed to this advice and promulgated the ban for one year, though it was extended annually until 1862. By then, the balance of power had changed dramatically. See E. de Waal, *Onze Indische financiën: Nieuwe reeks aanteekeningen,* 10 vols. (The Hague: Nijhoff, 1876–1907), 3: 227.

[121] "Onze betrekkingen tot Jambi worden voornamelijk geregeld door de wijze waarop wij de regten heffen"; Resident of Palembang to governor-general, December 16, 1852, NA, Col., vb. February 15, 1853, no. 26.

[122] Resident of Palembang to governor-general, December 16, 1852, NA, Col., vb. February 15, 1853, no. 26 and NA, Col., vb. July 14, 1854, no. 22.

after his escapade that the journey must have had something to do with the unwanted interest that had been aroused in this region. The impact of the journey is reflected in the explosive rise in the trade figures after 1852: in 1851 imports and exports were valued at 77,000 guilders; in 1852, at 104,000; then in 1853 they rose to 364,000; in 1854 they were back at 248,000, after which they gradually declined again until 1857.[123] A sudden rise of this kind undoubtedly derived from improved controls.

In the somewhat longer term, Gibson's actions proved to have more negative consequences for the sultan. In the appendices to his request of April 1853 for his government's support, Gibson had already stated that his guilt or innocence depended on the question of whether or not the Sultan of Jambi was subject to the authority of the Dutch colonial government.[124] Yet the American government did not have the 1834 contract, so it was unable to investigate this matter. Though the document had been sent to Britain in 1841, it had not been published. The Minister of Foreign Affairs sent it to the American ambassador in The Hague through "informal channels" in the summer of 1856, when the U.S. government had already abandoned its support for Gibson.[125]

In 1857, the news that the Americans were investigating the sovereign rights of the Netherlands in the archipelago reached Batavia from Washington, through The Hague.[126] It was passed on to Governor-General C. F. Pahud (1856–61), who had studied all the ins and outs of the Gibson case as Minister of Colonies. His successor at the Ministry, P. Mijer (1856–58), included in his report a worried question as to whether previous decisions to forgo expansion (on New Guinea, for instance) were not ripe for review. Was it not advisable to conclude new agreements where the existing ones were found wanting? Furthermore, shortly afterward the Dutch ambassador to Washington discovered that the 1834 contract with the Sultan of Jambi did not rule out foreign claims. It merely forbade the sultan to associate with the enemies of the Dutch, a category that could not be thought to include the United States. He advised tightening up the contract's terms. This too Mijer duly passed on to Pahud. He added that he himself thought it unwise to change the contract at that time, as it could bolster Gibson's claims.[127]

Batavia saw the matter differently, however. Indeed, to be one step ahead of the Americans, the Dutch officials there had conducted their own investigation of the rights of sovereignty in June 1857.[128] Precisely because the Americans planned to investigate the sovereignty question, the Dutch East Indies Council thought it

---

[123] Note of May 21, 1858, NA, Col., vb. June 3, 1858, no. 220 secret.

[124] See appendix no. 1810 to Gibson to Secretary of State, April 10, 1843, National Archives, State Department, Consular Reports Batavia, vol. 3.

[125] Minister of Colonies to Minister of Foreign Affairs, NA, Col., vb. September 23, 1856, no. 553 secret.

[126] Minister of Colonies to Minister of Foreign Affairs, March 7, 1857, NA, Col, vb. March 7, 1857, no. 122 secret; Minister of Colonies to governor-general, March 8, 1857, no. 151, NA, Col., semiofficial correspondence.

[127] Minister of Colonies to governor-general, July 20, 1857, NA, Col., vb. July 20, 1857, no. 356 a-b secret.

[128] Governor-general to Minister of Colonies, August 14, 1858, NA, Col., exh. October 16, 1858, no. 38. The report of the investigation, issued on June 2, 1857, to A. Prins, a member of the Dutch East Indies Council, was presented to the governor-general on March 18, 1858.

risky to postpone concluding a new contract with Jambi.[129] In the late 1850s the Dutch authorities succeeded in tightening up the terms of the contract.

This chapter has shown that Jambi was at the heart of two important diplomatic controversies in the period 1840–58. Both Britain and the United States sought trade advantages, not territorial expansion. And in both cases they gained concessions from the Dutch: the net result was the opening up of the East Indies. Britain persuaded the Dutch to limit its expansion on Sumatra and managed to open up the minor port of Muara Kompeh, though it still had a Dutch garrison. The United States acquired the right of consular representation to defend its trading interests in the East Indies. But although the Netherlands had been only a minor European power since 1839, the Dutch government retained a narrow margin in which to pursue its own independent policy. It did not bow to British demands for a new trade contract; it refused to compensate Gibson, and internally it redefined its own powers more precisely. Opening up to the outside world went hand in hand with closing off internally: "abstention" was combined with instructions to conclude new contracts and tighten up existing ones. In these decades, the fear of rival powers led to "preemption," the consolidation of the country's own contractually fixed rights to ward off all interested parties.

---

[129] Dutch East Indies Council June 19, 1857, no. XII, NA, Col., vb. June 3, 1858, no. 220 secret

CHAPTER FIVE

PREEMPTION IN PRACTICE: THE STRUGGLE FOR POWER IN 1858

In October 1855 a new sultan named Taha Safiuddin accepted authority over Jambi, following the death of Nazaruddin on August 18 that year.[1] With Taha a man ascended the throne who would prove to be the colonial government's prime antagonist in Jambi for almost forty years. A military expedition formally ended his rule in 1858, but behind the scenes he continued to act as the *dalang* of political life.

A NEW SULTAN: TAHA SAFIUDDIN

Described as "young," Taha was probably in his twenties at his accession. In 1900, Jambian sources gave his date of birth as 1833.[2] He was the son of Sultan Facharuddin, who had signed the contract of 1834. His mother was of Arab descent,[3] and she probably had an important influence on him, since unlike most Malay rulers Taha could read and write.[4] What is more, he understood the wider political stage of the Islamic world: in 1857 he would seek the diplomatic support of the sultan of Turkey, for which he probably drew on a knowledge of Arab networks learned from his mother.[5]

---

[1] *Gouvernementsbesluit* (resolution adopted by the colonial authorities) March 20, 1858, X secret, National Archives (NA), The Hague, Col., *verbaal* (file, hereafter "vb.") June 3, 1858, no. 220 secret.

[2] Advisory report of the Council of the Dutch East Indies, January 29, 1858, no. X, NA, Col., vb. June 3, 1858, no. 220 secret; *susuhunan* to Resident van Palembang, 18 sawal 1317 (February 19, 1900), translation, appended to Resident of Palembang to governor-general, March 20, 1900. NA, Col., *mailrapport* (postal report; hereafter "mr.") 1900/255, vb. August 19, 1901, no. 46. According to this source he would have been twenty-five in 1858. I have been unable to find any evidence to corroborate the date of birth generally assigned to him in Indonesia, which is 1816 (Kamajaya, *Delapan raja-raja Pahlawan Nasional, Buku I* [Yogya: U.P. Indonesia, 1981], p. 33); *Album 86 Pahlawan Nasional* (Jakarta: Bahtera Jaya, 1985), p. 18.

[3] Resident of Palembang to governor-general, December 8, 1882, NA, Col., mr. 1882/1215.

[4] J. M. Gullick, *Indigenous Political Systems of Western Malaya*, 2nd ed. (London: London School of Economics, 1965).

[5] See below. It is unlikely that Taha himself had undertaken the *haj*, as it would certainly have been recorded. In any case, Jambi was not represented with its own "house" at Mecca. For this, it was too insignificant, as few haji came from there. Jambi is not mentioned in Snouck Hurgronje's description of Mecca. C. Snouck Hurgronje, *Mekka*, 2 vols. (The Hague: Nijhoff, 1888–89), 1:352, 390.

Reconstructed portrait of Sultan Taha, *pahlawan nasional*
Kamajaya, *Delapan Raja-Raja Pahlawan Nasional, Buku I*
(Yogya: U. P. Indonesia, 1981).

Taha had not become *pangeran ratu* until 1854, having been recommended by the Residency's administration. Unfortunately there are no sources explaining the reasons for this choice. From the start it was clear, however, that the new *pangeran ratu* was a man to be reckoned with. He had declined to accept the insignia of his new office until Sultan Nazaruddin cast out a concubine who had great influence on the sultan.[6] In return, the sultan had refused to attend the inauguration ceremony. Raden Tabun, who by then had settled for the titles of *panembahan* and *susuhunan* (the sultan's senior honorary advisor) would hand Taha the insignia and try to persuade him to "bow to the sultan's wishes," according to the initial reports of the event from Palembang.[7] By the end of 1854, he had had a signal lack of success.[8]

European officials seldom recorded physical or psychological descriptions of local rulers. Thus we must try to reconstruct Taha's appearance and character from fragmentary accounts and his actual behavior. He clearly possessed a strong personality and was purposeful in his actions. In 1880 he was described as powerfully built, short-necked, and a little stout.[9] In 1881 the Resident of Palembang, P. F. Laging Tobias, characterized his political opponent—in epithets that were certainly not diluted by diplomacy—as vigorous and hot-tempered. Jambi's proverbial sluggishness was alien to him. But Laging Tobias also described Taha as sincere. While mistrustful of strangers, he vested great confidence in those who had proved their honesty. In enmity as in friendship, his commitment was absolute.[10] His demeanor to the Dutch authorities was firm, diplomatic, and above all consistent in his views and actions.

Taha simply notified the colonial government of his accession to the throne, as his predecessor had done before him.[11] While such notification had been acceptable in 1841, however, the situation was now very different. The form and wording of the contracts with local rulers had changed over the past fourteen years. For instance, in 1847 the Dutch authorities had received instructions to include in all contracts a clause forbidding local rulers to accept letters or gifts from foreign powers without Batavia's permission.[12] Contracts now always stated explicitly whether the sultan recognized the colonial government as a feudal overlord or as the sovereign power. Between 1850 and 1855 contracts with many local rulers in western Borneo and the South Celebes had been revised,[13] being

---

[6] Political report of the Palembang Residency 1854, ANRI, Palembang Residency Records 61.1. This source also makes it clear that a *pangeran ratu* could be appointed against the sultan's wishes.

[7] Resident of Palembang to governor-general, June 30, 1854, NA, Col., exh. September 2, 1854, no. 23.

[8] Political report of the Palembang Residency 1854, ANRI, Palembang Residency Records 61.1.

[9] Resident of Palembang to governor-general, January 29, 1880, NA, Col., vb. June 19, 1880, no. 6.

[10] Taha was described as *ten volle vijand* and *ten volle trouw*; Resident of Palembang to governor-general, December 8, 1881, NA, Col., mr. 1882/1215.

[11] *Gouvernementsbesluit*, March 20, 1858, no. X secret, NA, Col., vb. June 3, 1858, no. 220 secret.

[12] NA, Col., *gouvernementsbesluit*, April 19, 1847, no. V.

[13] J. H. Logemann, "Direct gebied met zelfbestuur," *Indisch Tijdschrift voor het Recht* 136 (1932): 1-49, esp. 36-44.

modeled on those with Sambas and Banjarmasin.[14] It was no longer acceptable for the Dutch claims to be surrounded by a haze of ambivalence.

NEGOTIATION OF A NEW CONTRACT

In this new constellation, the blunt notification of the accession that the Council of the Dutch East Indies received in March 1856 did not suffice. The Council demanded a new, revised contract and insisted on the sultan taking an oath of allegiance, as was now customary in other parts of the archipelago.[15] The Resident's proposals for a new contract were discussed in the Council in the summer of 1857 and sent to Palembang in September. Meanwhile, Palembang too had witnessed a change at the top in 1857. And since the new Resident P. T. Couperus was a little inexperienced, former Assistant Resident Storm van 's Gravesande who had headed the mission to Jambi in 1852, was asked to attend the talks in an advisory capacity. With all these preparations, the Dutch were not in a hurry to respond to Taha's message. What is more, negotiations could not begin until the unrest that had broken out a little earlier in the Komering Ulu (Palembang) had been quelled.[16] It was not until October 1857, when Taha had already been on the throne for two years, that a Dutch delegation headed by Resident Couperus set off for Jambi. By then the Americans were scrutinizing the Dutch rights of sovereignty, and everyone in Batavia was alive to the urgency of concluding a new contract.

Couperus presented a detailed draft with more than forty articles. Now the two newcomers confronted each other in the negotiations, although "confronted" is not an entirely accurate description, since Taha initially refused to meet the Resident, considering that he "lacked the necessary skills."[17] The new *pangeran ratu*, Marta Ningrat, the son of former sultan Nazaruddin and a cousin of Taha, who was believed to be more kindly disposed to the Dutch, was in Singapore during the Resident's visit.[18] Thus Taha immediately employed a tactic that would be his trademark until his death in 1904—that of elusiveness and avoiding contact.

Nonetheless, at the Resident's suggestion Taha appointed a Jambian committee that would identify for him the most contentious articles of the new contract. There were apparently quite a few: that Jambi would become part of the Dutch East Indies (art. 1), that it had to cooperate with the building of the fortress at Muara Kompeh and other Dutch fortifications (art. 4), that it could not maintain ties with other powers (art. 7, 8), that Europeans and Chinese would be subject to different judicial regimes (art. 12, 20), that cowpox vaccination would be permissible (art. 21), that hereditary succession would be subject to Dutch approval (art. 23, 24, 25), and that shipping, trade, and the internal administration of the

---

[14] They were also used as a model for Jambi (Council of the Dutch East Indies, June 19, 1857, no. XII, NA, Col., June 3, 1858, no. 220 secret).

[15] Council of the Dutch East Indies, March 15, 1856, no. XXI, NA, Col., vb. June 3, 1858, no. 220 secret.

[16] Council of the Dutch East Indies, June 19, 1858, no. XII, NA, Col., vb. June 3, 1858, no. 220 secret.

[17] Resident of Palembang to governor-general, October 26, 1857, NA, Col., exh. January 2, 1858, no. 5 secret; Council of the Dutch East Indies, January 29, 1858, no. X, NA, Col., vb. June 3, 1858, no. 220 secret.

[18] Council of the Dutch East Indies, January 29, 1858, no. X, NA, Col., vb. June 3, 1858, no. 220 secret.

territory would henceforth be supervised by the government of the Dutch East Indies (art. 29). In brief, Taha opposed all the articles that restricted the sultan's power (those recognizing the colonial government's sovereignty, and the articles providing for interference in hereditary succession, foreign policy, defense, trade, and the administration of justice). Clearly, he understood exactly—and indeed may not have needed any special committee to explain it to him—what the Dutch were aiming at, where he would be the loser, and which provisions were incompatible with his independence and prejudicial to the political interests of his realm.[19] Taha himself wanted to keep the old contract of 1834; after all, he argued, neither he nor any of his predecessors had ever violated it.

Unbeknown to the Dutch officials, Taha had already taken his own countermeasures, requesting the support of the sultan of Turkey. The *pangeran ratu's* departure for Singapore in October 1857 had not been to discuss trade but to undertake a diplomatic mission. Taha wanted to send a written request to the sultan, via Singapore, for a *cap* (seal) declaring that Jambi was Turkish territory to which outsiders had no rights. The *pangeran ratu* entrusted this letter to a Singaporese dignitary who was given thirty thousand Spanish dollars to take it to Constantinople.[20]

Here Taha demonstrated a keen awareness of the balance of power in the region. Throughout the archipelago the Ottoman Empire was seen as omnipotent, and many local rulers legitimized their power by tracing their genealogy back to Turkey.[21] Such attitudes harked back to the sixteenth century, when Turkey was indeed a power to be reckoned with by "infidel" countries. According to Acehnese tradition, Aceh had recognized Turkish suzerainty in those days and had sent a mission to Turkey. It was said that the rulers of Aceh and Pedir in northern Sumatra still possessed a seal and the right to protection that it conferred.[22] With the growing strength of reformist Islam and increased pressure from the Dutch colonial government on the Outer Islands, the old picture of Turkey's omnipotence acquired a new lease of life in the nineteenth century. It was in the Minangkabau that local resistance first rallied around the banners of Islam. Around the mid-nineteenth century, Islamic influence became stronger because of better travel links and growing numbers of hajis, people who had undertaken the pilgrimage to Mecca. Insurgent movements in Banten (western Java) and the Lampong region of southern Sumatra in 1850 and 1856 all had religious leaders. The uprising in Palembang

---

[19] Resident of Palembang to governor-general, October 26, 1857, NA, Col., exh. January 2, 1858, no. 5 secret.

[20] See *minuut*, October 18, 1864, H10/N1, NA, Col., vb. October 18, 1864, H 10/N1 secret. One Sharif Ali, also known as Said Ali al Jufri, was also involved. The reference was probably to the leader of the Arab community in Jambi, Pangeran Sharif Ali bin Alui Jufri. Various rumors circulated about him: one source related that in June 1858, that is, after the second round of negotiations with Couperus (see below), he went to Turkey, taking thirty thousand guilders with him; according to another rumor, he had received a sum of this order from the new sultan, Ahmad Nazaruddin (1858-1881), and left after the latter's accession in November 1858. In any case, from November 1860 onward he lived in Singapore (see *The Singapore Standard*, November 14, 1869, no. 100, NA, Col., exh. January 16, 1861, no. 38).

[21] This applied to Jambi and Buton, for instance, see chapter 2 and J. W. Schoorl, "Power, Ideology and Change in the Early State of Buton," in *State and Trade in the Indonesian Archipelago*, ed. G. J. Schutte (Leiden: KITLV Press, 1994), pp. 17-60.

[22] Resident of Palembang to governor-general, June 14, 1858, NA, Col., vb. October 6, 1858, no. 366 secret.

(1848–1859) also became more religious in nature as time went on. In 1857 the Mutiny, the rebellion of Islamic soldiers in India, would prove the power of Islam as a "countervailing force," striking fear into the hearts of the colonial rulers. Clearly, then, Taha was no exception, although he was one of the few rulers to ask directly for Turkey's political help. Later, in 1873, the sultan of Aceh would follow his example.[23]

Turkey itself did not pursue an active pan-Islamic policy. It had more to gain from forging good diplomatic relations with the Western powers at this time than from helping fellow Moslems in an obscure corner of the world. It therefore put international—that is, Western—rules of law before the ties of religion. Though the letter from Jambi reached the Turkish government in good order, the recipients acted as though it had not been written. "Since there are no relations whatsoever between the Ottoman Rulers and the sovereigns and inhabitants of these regions, [the letter] was considered nonexistent and treated as though it had not been received," the Turkish government informed the Dutch in response to an enquiry at the beginning of 1859.[24]

But we are moving ahead of the narrative. For now, Taha was ignorant of the Turkish response and hoped for an answer, and the Dutch delegates were equally ignorant of his demarche. They merely found themselves facing a recalcitrant sultan. Taha was implacable, and a week later the Resident returned to Palembang empty-handed, having formed a crudely stereotypical opinion of the sultan. Taha himself had not been responsible for the failure; he was an "insignificant person" who had little authority since he spent all his time hunting and fishing in the hinterland. No, it was his "profit-hungry and corrupt advisors" who were to blame. As they had "a poor understanding of political rights," they would not yield to "the power of reason and argument."[25] Convinced as he was of being in the right, Couperus obviously meant the power of *Dutch* reason and *Dutch* arguments.

Couperus did understand, however, that he, Couperus, had not understood much, and that his knowledge was altogether wanting. He suggested smoothing the path to a new contract by the peaceful means of further dialogue. To this end, the administrative officer (*civiel gezaghebber*) at Muara Kompeh, who he claimed had made no effort to get to know Jambi and to win the people's confidence, should be replaced by a civil servant.[26] The administrative officer was a military man and lacked diplomatic abilities, he maintained. Couperus also suggested that the sultan should be instructed to send a delegation to Batavia at the colonial

---

[23] A. Reid, "Nineteenth Century Pan-Islam in Indonesia and Malaysia," *Journal of Asian Studies* 26 (1967): 267-83.

[24] "Comme il n'existe aucune relation entre le Gouvernement Ottoman et les souverains et les habitans [*sic*] de ces contrées, elle a été considerée comme nulle et non avenue"; Minister-Resident in Constantinople to Minister of Foreign Affairs, February 2, 1859, NA, Col., vb. February 25, 1849, W. The Dutch ambassador thought the information reliable: "The matter was evidently an embarrassment." In an earlier interview, the Grand Vizier was not entirely sure whether or not Jambi was independent (Minister-Resident in Constantinople to Minister of Foreign Affairs, September 30, 1858, NA, Col., vb. October 19, 1858, E7 *kabinet*).

[25] Resident of Palembang to governor-general, October 26, 1857, NA, Col., exh. January 2, 1858, no. 5 secret.

[26] The administrative officer had already drawn attention to Taha's goodwill in April 1857. Taha had paid the 48-guilder reward for finding four exiles in hiding out of his own pocket, and had not wanted the colonial government to reimburse him (administrative officer to Resident of Palembang, April 7, 1857, no. 42, ANRI, Algemeene Secretarie, *ag.* 5444/57).

government's expense, apparently unaware that the Malay version of the contract of 1834 did not provide for such an order.[27] His report to Batavia echoed the old, familiar picture: weak ruler, sympathetic but powerless *pangeran ratu*, poor advisors, and hostile population. The strategy he proposed was equally familiar. However admirable it may have been to admit to a certain ignorance, it was naïve in the extreme to assume that becoming better acquainted (partly by way of an enforced visit to Batavia) would encourage the sultan to welcome the Dutch with open arms in Jambi. Thus ended the first phase of the negotiations.

SECOND ROUND

With the American investigation looming, the Council of the Dutch East Indies recommended in December 1857 that a second round of negotiations be undertaken. The draft contract was amended in places, incorporating suggestions made by Storm van 's Gravesande. While the Dutch were loath to change the articles on sovereignty, the fortresses, foreign relations, and jurisdiction involving Europeans, they were willing to tone down those relating to hereditary succession—enough to make them acceptable to the sultan, they hoped. The clause forbidding the sultan to erect fortifications without the government's permission could be scrapped, since the Jambian people had never built any fortifications of their own in the past, with the exception of some never-completed fortifications near the kraton. This being the case, the sultan would hardly start constructing them now, the Council of the Dutch East Indies reasoned optimistically. For the rest, Taha could continue to administer justice in cases involving Chinese and Arabs ("Vreemde Oosterlingen," Foreign Orientals) outside the area of Muara Kompeh, but he could not, of course, try Europeans. As for the supervision of shipping, trade, and internal administration, it would suffice to supervise trade alone, given that the Dutch lacked the staff needed for the rest. Cowpox inoculation, too, was negotiable. In short, the Dutch proposed a few insubstantial concessions: they were willing to water down some clauses and scrap one or two impracticable provisions. None of it affected the basic tenor of the contract.

Even so, Storm felt sure that Taha would sign the contract now, certainly when it was impressed upon him that all the local rulers in the archipelago were relinquishing the right to pursue an independent foreign policy with the conclusion of a contract. Jambians were simply a little slower than the other people in the archipelago. Besides, financial considerations would surely oil the machinery of goodwill: the sultan's annuity should be raised from 8,000 to 15,000 guilders. This would be a useful token of support for the more Dutch-minded *pangeran ratu*. Full of optimism and as unrealistic as ever, the officials expected that the sultan would soon acquiesce.

Earnestly the officials bent their heads over the procedure to be followed: they decided that the commander at Muara Kompeh and a Jambian envoy would present the sultan with a letter from the governor-general, using their sojourn at court to work out who stood where, politically speaking. After the obligatory salutations and fine words about the sultan's rights and the friendly intentions of the Dutch, the letter would make it clear that any further refusal to agree to the new terms

---

[27] Resident of Palembang to governor-general, October 26, 1857, NA, Col., exh. January 2, 1858, no. 5 secret.

would be construed as a sign of the sultan's hostile intent to the colonial government. The ensuing negotiations in Jambi would be led by a mission comprising Couperus and Storm van 's Gravesande.[28] The resolution of March 20, 1858, formally adopting this procedure did not include the observation made by the Council of the Dutch East Indies that since the Jambians were slow by nature, matters should not be pursued with too much haste.[29]

The advance party presented the letter from the governor-general in May 1858. Its members were accommodated in the Arab quarter on the left bank of the river, opposite the kraton. A steady stream of Arab visitors came to pay their respects, including the head of the Arab community in Jambi, Pangeran Sharif Ali bin Alui Jufri, whom the envoys found to be not ill-disposed toward them. No Jambians came to visit, however, and they saw little of Taha, who had referred them to the *pangeran ratu*. In the two sessions they had with the latter, he avoided actually discussing the matter of the new contract. First he asked to see a diplomatic note. When this was produced, he explained that he would have to wait until the end of *puasa* (Ramadan). Finally, he referred the envoys back to Sultan Taha, who told them in the presence of the *pangeran ratu* and a number of Jambian dignitaries that they could go. He gave them letters in which he expressed his hope that the contract of 1834 could be reaffirmed.[30]

In spite of this written rejection, Couperus and Storm set off to Jambi as planned in June 1858. Formally, they were treated with the greatest of respect. Again the leader of the Arab community played a prominent role. As for the purpose of their five-day mission (June 2-7), nothing was accomplished. Taha repeated his earlier responses. While he had no wish to live in enmity with the colonial government, he could not change the existing contract, which his father had concluded. In the event of a resort to arms, he would "submit to the dispensation of Providence." The *pangeran ratu* and other dignitaries, when sounded for their own position, supported the sultan. Outwardly, then, the court was united and Taha's power unquestioned. A Jambian committee reiterated the objections, which the Arab leader and another dignitary conveyed to the envoys. The message was brief and to the point. Taha saw no need for negotiations, and wished to adhere strictly to the terms of the 1834 contract. The envoys had no choice but to return to Muara Kompeh, smarting from the shock of a minor incident that occurred shortly before their departure. When they had undertaken a little rowing trip along the Batang Hari, women and children had thrown stones at the boat, denouncing its occupants as *kafir* (infidels). The envoys were incensed. Taha agreed to punish those concerned with a fine of five hundred reals and a term of imprisonment.[31]

Why had Taha not succumbed to the threats of force? Was he so full of religious faith as truly to believe that Providence would come to his aid? Or was he hoping that Turkey would respond to his plea for help, of which the mission

---

[28] Council of the Dutch East Indies, January 29, 1858, no. X, NA, Col., vb. June 3, 1858, no. 220 secret.

[29] *Gouvernementsbesluit*, March 20, 1858, X secret, NA, Col., vb. June 3, 1858, no. 220 secret.

[30] Sultan to governor-general, May 23, 1858 ("9 sawal te drie ure des jaars 1274") and Sultan to Resident of Palembang and Storm van 's Gravesande, May 24, 1858 ("10e van de maandstand sawal 1274"), translation, NA, Col., vb. October 6, 1858, no. 366 secret.

[31] Resident of Palembang to governor-general, June 14, 1858, NA, Col., vb. October 6, 1858, no. 366 secret.

had now been apprised? Was he "stubborn" and "stiff-necked," as the Dutch concluded?[32] The envoys were by now persuaded that they were not dealing with a man "of very limited powers of comprehension," as had been taken for granted hitherto. Taha, it was now clear, knew what he wanted and had proved a highly skilled negotiator, who had pulled the wool over the Dutchmen's eyes in a variety of ways. One of the myths that the delegation took home was that while Jambi was anticipating war and preparing for it, the ordinary people, the merchants, and a number of dignitaries inclined to Batavia. Furthermore, the Dutch had heard it said that the men who had been mustered to take up arms came from the uplands and that many had already deserted, proving that the Jambians had no taste for battle.[33]

THIRD PHASE AND MILITARY EXPEDITION

After this second refusal, the authorities in Batavia lost their patience. The Council of the Dutch East Indies called the rejection of the "gesture of indulgence" that Batavia had made in the second round of negotiations, and the manner in which it had been conveyed, "far from seemly, more than that, disrespectful . . ., indeed, completely disloyal."[34] The Council now acknowledged for the first time that the translation of the 1834 contract was flawed, but dismissed it as trivial. The gist was clear, after all. Swift action was now called for: a military campaign followed by the building of a fortress in the capital of Jambi itself. In July 1858 a formal decision was taken to dispatch troops, and The Hague was asked to consent to the posting of an Assistant Resident to Jambi. Taha would be given a forty-eight-hour ultimatum, demanding that he agree to a new contract and send envoys to Batavia. Refusal would lead to his replacement by a new sultan who would be given Jambi only in fief and would be required to sign a new contract.

It was a large expedition for its day that was dispatched to back up these demands. It comprised four companies of infantry, a detachment of artillery, a detachment of sappers twenty-five strong, and two hundred coolies, with four steamships and private vessels being used to transport the troops. The whole was a show of force calculated to make an impression. On September 2, 1858, Taha received the two envoys who came bearing the ultimatum. Within forty-eight hours he replied that he was willing to negotiate. The negotiators (the same delegation sent in May 1858) were barred from entering the kraton, however, nor were they granted an audience with the sultan. They were received at the residence of another *pangeran* (Surio Nata Krama), where the *pangeran ratu* met them and made it clear that Taha could accept only twelve articles of the draft contract, including five he had previously deemed unacceptable, such as the prohibition on concluding agreements with foreign powers (art. 7), the provisions governing the rights of European and Chinese groups in Jambi (art. 12, 20), the introduction of cowpox vaccination (art. 21) and the colonial authorities' supervision of shipping, trade, and internal administration (art. 29). Thus Taha

---

[32] Resident of Palembang to governor-general, June 14, 1858, NA, Col., vb. October 6, 1858, no. 366 secret.

[33] Ibid.

[34] Council of the Dutch East Indies, July 2, 1858, no. XXXIV, NA, Col., vb. October 6, 1858, no. 366 secret.

did make some significant concessions here. But the main bones of contention—acknowledgment of Dutch sovereignty and the regulation of hereditary succession—were not included. Interestingly, the content of these articles shows that the concessions that the Council had proposed in the second round in May/June 1858 had been scrapped again in the third round. Taha was presented with the strict terms of the original contract again. It is unclear what amount of money was proposed as an annuity. All in all, little effort had been made to arrive at an acceptable set of demands.

This was not the end of the dialogue, however. The next day, Taha sent a new delegation with the message that he could accept another article that had not been discussed before.[35] However, rather than concluding a new contract, as the governor-general wanted, he wanted the new articles incorporated into the contract of 1834. But Couperus would not stand for any more prevarication. On September 5, 1858, he decided to take action.[36]

At 3 A.M. on September 6 the troops disembarked in total silence.[37] Still, Taha was by no means caught unprepared, and mounted a far fiercer opposition than the Dutch had expected. Taha had set up a chain of *benteng*, fortified kampongs and houses, which had to be taken in single combat using the bayonet. Furthermore, the kraton was protected by marshland, so that an outflanking maneuver of the Dutch troops misfired. It took them almost three hours to brave a rain of spears to take the kraton, which was made even more impenetrable by the difficulty of climbing its two sheer fortifications. By then, their ammunition was almost gone. Had the enemy's "terrible fire" been aimed more accurately, the army would have suffered serious losses, according to the official report.[38] As it was, there were four dead and thirty-nine wounded. The losses on the other side were higher: at least fifty Jambian fighters were found dead at the end of the day.

When the Dutch had taken the kraton, they found it empty, as Taha and his retinue had fled to the upland marches. By late afternoon on September 6 the

---

[35] It is not clear which article was meant. In 1866-67 the new sultan's spokesman claimed that if the ultimatum had been extended by another twenty-four hours, there would have been no opposition. According to him the Dutch intentions had been misunderstood, and the article concerning compulsory vaccination, in particular, which had not been included in the old contract, had been viewed with suspicion because vaccination was seen as a brand (see above) (L. W. A. Kessler to Minister of Colonies, September 2, 1879, NA, Col., vb. September 6, 1879, no. 20). This retrospective Jambian explanation is not consistent with the official Dutch report, which states that the objections to the article about vaccination had been dispelled, but it does accord with the reservations raised about this same provision in the talks about the contract of November 1858; see below.

[36] Resident of Palembang to governor-general, September 8, 1858, NA, Col., vb. November 23, 1858, no. 6.

[37] The troopships had cast anchor two miles offshore near the capital, Jambi, on September 2. Before disembarkation, the noncommissioned officers and crew had been given a meal and a stiff drink. Each man received clothes, ammunition, and rations to take along ("een verschooning, de sprei, 30 patronen, . . . een paar harde beschuiten en een ration gekookt gezouten vleesch"), and each company received a further two or three rations of gin per head. Buglers and drummers took up a central position from which they provided musical fortification (Resident of Palembang to governor-general, September 8, 1858, and expedition commander to lieutenant-general, commander-in-chief of army, September 11, 1858, no. 19, NA, Col., vb. November 23, 1858, no. 6).

[38] Expedition commander to lieutenant-general, commander-in-chief of army, September 11, 1858, no. 19, NA, Col., vb. November 23, 1858, no. 6.

pangeran ratu's kraton too had been taken; shortly afterward followed the surrender of the people living on the opposite bank of the river, most of whom, unlike those on the right bank, had not taken flight.

With this unexpectedly fierce opposition, ended—officially, at any rate—the brief reign of a powerful Jambian sultan came to an end—officially, at any rate. But the Jambian court did not yield completely. Although it had suffered a military defeat, it could still do a great deal to determine the political form of the peace. Negotiations with the colonial government ensued, with the *pangeran ratu*, Marta Ningrat, acting as spokesman. This cousin of Taha declined to ascend the throne himself, preferring to retain his old title. However, Panembahan Prabu of the *suku* Kraton, a brother of Taha's father, Facharuddin, was an acceptable choice to him and to the dignitaries at court. More to the point, he was Taha's own choice. Prabu accepted the title of sultan as Ahmad Nazaruddin and signed a new contract in November 1858. Jambi was now a territory of the Dutch East Indies and as such under direct Dutch rule. Nazaruddin had his realm only in fief and would behave as a loyal vassal (art. 1). Predictably, he had been obliged to relinquish all rights to an autonomous foreign policy (art. 7, 8) as well as his independence regarding the succession. Each new sultan would have to legalize his title by obtaining a deed of recognition and confirmation from the governor-general (art. 25). In the event of a conflict or if the *pangeran ratu* had not yet reached the age of majority, the Resident and governor-general would resolve the issue (art. 23, 24). Although the sultan continued to bear sole responsibility for internal administration (art. 27), his wings were clipped by the Dutch supervision of shipping, trade, and government (art. 29). The provision on smallpox vaccination had again caused difficulties. Ahmad Nazaruddin acquiesced to it only after receiving assurances from Couperus that it would not be implemented in the near future and, if later, not before due consultation.[39] With his reservations, Nazaruddin was expressing his subjects' fear of vaccination with its permanent scar, that they saw as a *cap* branding them as Dutch property. He had also wanted clarification of the military support for the Dutch that the colonial government had incorporated into the contract. Would it be required in the event of war against France or Britain? The sultan's annuity had been increased, it should be added, but only to ten thousand guilders.[40]

Whether the Malay version of the contract was still ambiguous is impossible to say, as it has unfortunately not been preserved. In Dutch, it was now similar to those drafted for neighboring territories as well as those further afield. Those in force around 1860 all contained provisions, though worded differently, stating that the sultanate constituted part of the Dutch East Indies, that all contact with foreign countries must be conducted through Dutch mediation, that the succession was subject to the supervision of the colonial government, and that the latter possessed sole competence for the administration of justice in cases involving European nationals. Discrepancies from one contract to the next generally reflected local economic conditions.[41]

---

[39] Resident of Palembang to governor-general, November 13, 1858, NA, Col., vb. January 21, 1860, no. 16 secret.

[40] Contract, November 2, 1858, NA, Col., vb. January 21, 1869, no. 16 secret.

[41] Based on comparison with contracts in NA, Col., exh. October 16, 1858, no. 38 (Prins Memorandum) and vb. January 21, 1860, no. 16 secret. For instance, in the 1850s, a head tax was imposed instead of consignments of gold on North-Celebes, and Sumbawa was obligated to supply timber. The local rulers were certainly not always given compensation. This proved to

Now history repeated itself. Nazaruddin and Pangeran Ratu Marta Ningrat gratefully accepted the gifts that Batavia presented in honor of the sultan's inauguration, plus an additional gift of five thousand guilders. Like their predecessors, they suffered from a lack of revenue. The new sultan had always lived very modestly, and the former *pangeran ratu*'s home, his proas, and all his possessions had been destroyed by fire. Thus the new rulers did not have any independent resources to establish a court or to enforce their authority.[42]

After the contract was concluded on November 2, 1858, Couperus hastened to Palembang, since trouble had arisen in another part of his Residency, the Pematang Ulu.[43] This job was finished.

BATAVIA'S SUMATRA POLICY

The job had been finished at Batavia's instigation. Unlike the sequence of events in 1833, the initiative had come not from regional rulers but from the colonial capital. It was here that the hawks were to be found: the Council of the Dutch East Indies and governor-general Pahud himself. Pahud presented himself as such in the letter informing the Minister of Colonies of his decision to mount an expedition. He railed indignantly at the improper reception accorded the Dutch envoys, which Couperus himself had passed over without complaint, about the sultan's recalcitrance and his open preparations for battle.[44] Was Pahud aware of the need to "sell" the military action to The Hague?

In any case, the expedition was completely in line with Batavia's policy on Sumatra, a policy geared toward safeguarding Dutch interests against foreign claims. In 1856 the Englishman Wilson had crossed the Straits of Singapore with his own private army to intervene in the fight for the succession in Siak. When Wilson became too bold, the two claimants to the throne had made a pact and sought the support of the other regional power, the government in Batavia. A treaty of friendship signed in 1857 was followed by the renunciation of sovereignty in 1858. The Dutch expansion from western to eastern Sumatra, so rudely interrupted by Baud in 1841, had now been consummated. In a single contract the Netherlands had extended its authority over virtually the entire east coast to Aceh, with which it had signed a treaty of peace and friendship in 1857 shortly before concluding a contract with Siak. These measures were calculated to forestall

---

be a "privilege" applying to Sumatra (e.g., Jambi, Indragiri, Riau-Lingga). In 1858 all contracts with local rulers were again sent to London, since there was little point in concluding treaties if they were to be kept secret, according to a marginal note in the advice to the king. At the same time it was decided to notify the States-General of the treaties, although Minister Rochussen was averse to having them constantly discussed and deliberated in public. They would therefore be presented to Parliament only once a year (Minister of Colonies to king, June 2, 1860, NA, Col., vb. January 2, 1860, 2A secret).

[42] Resident of Palembang to governor-general, November 13, 1858, NA, Col., vb. January 21, 1860, no. 16 secret. Moreover, Jambi had suffered so much that sending a mission to the governor-general, as Batavia had ordered, was out of the question for the time being.

[43] Resident of Palembang to governor-general, November 2, 1858, NA, Col., exh. January 14, 1859, no. 32.

[44] Governor-general to Minister of Colonies, July 16, 1858, NA, Col., exh. September 16, 1858, no. 344.

any problems regarding the border sultanates.[45] The Dutch also concluded a new contract with the successor of the deposed sultan of Riau at the end of 1857 and another with the sultan of Indragiri in July 1858.[46] In November 1858 an expedition to North Reteh, north of Jambi, put an end to the pirates' haven presided over by the Panglima Besar Tengku Long, who had remained loyal to the deposed Sultan of Riau, Mahmud Muthlafar Shah.[47] Now that virtually the entire east coast of Sumatra had been placed under Dutch control, to have exempted Jambi would have seemed an anomaly.

The enforced contract was thus part of a policy of "preemption," the contractual formalization of colonial relations without incurring any significant immediate consequences for everyday governance. Fueled by fear of foreign adventurers, the policy was equally inspired by a desire for prestige. Economic arguments played no role. The contracts with Aceh and Siak were concluded before 1863, when Jacobus Nienhuys started up what would become his spectacularly successful tobacco business in Deli. For Jambi economic arguments were of even less importance than for the more richly endowed pepper regions in the northeast of the island. For although its imports and exports had grown by a multiple of eight between 1846 and 1857, Jambi still accounted for a tiny proportion of the total commerce in the archipelago.[48] The hoped-for income from the gold trade had never materialized.

Sumatra was not the only place where Batavia launched its expansionist drive under Pahud around 1858. The Prins Memorandum published in 1858 had reviewed the Netherlands' legal claims and identified weak spots. It was a sequel to a memorandum of 1855,[49] and paved the way for the Colijn Memorandum of the early twentieth century. In general the rapporteur took a fairly sanguine view of the situation. In his conclusions he made recommendations for tightening up Dutch claims to sovereignty where it was not wholly indisputable, ranging from securing local leaders' allegiance by distributing silver-tipped canes (in the remaining areas of Sumatra) and promoting trade (on Ampenan and Bali) to expanding Dutch territory (on Celebes) and defining the frontiers with Portugal (on Timor). In Jambi everything that needed to be done had been done, he observed. He ended on a triumphant note: "Any claims by the United States may now be safely awaited. None has yet been forthcoming."[50]

More than one-fourth of the Dutch East Indies army was on active duty in the late 1850s, the highest proportion in the entire period from 1840 to 1870. The army underwent its most rapid growth—by 40 percent—between 1854 and 1860.[51] In 1858 it

---

[45] P. van 't Veer, *De Atjeh-oorlog* (Amsterdam: Arbeiderspers, 1969), p. 24; A. Reid, *The Contest for North Sumatra: Atjeh, the Netherlands and Britain 1858-1898* (Singapore/London/New York: Oxford University Press; Kuala Lumpur: University of Malaya Press, 1969), pp. 25-27.

[46] *Surat-surat Perdjandjian antara Kesultanan Riau dengan Pemerintahan-Pemerintahan VOC dan Hindia-Belanda, 1784-1909* (Djakarta: Arsip Nasional Republik Indonesia, 1970), pp. 90-170; NA, Col., vb. January 6, 1860, 2A secret.

[47] "Reteh," in *Encyclopaedie van Nederlandsch-Indië* (The Hague/Leiden: Nijhoff;/ Leiden: Brill, 1917-1940), 3: 597.

[48] Note, May 21, 1858, NA, Col., vb. June 3, 1858, no. 220 secret.

[49] Logemann, "Direct gebied," p. 8.

[50] Prins Memorandum, NA, Col., exh. October 16, 1858, no. 38.

[51] C. Fasseur, "Een koloniale paradox: De Nederlandse expansie in de Indonesische archipel in het midden van de negentiende eeuw (1830–1870)," *Tijdschrift voor Geschiedenis* 92 (1979): 162-87, esp. pp. 177-82.

was also decided to undertake a punitive expedition to Bone (South Celebes), followed by another one in 1859 when it misfired. An expedition was also sent to Banjarmasin in southeast Borneo in 1859. Here it was not a fear of foreign rivals that provided the impetus but the behavior of new local rulers, which Batavia deemed an insult to Dutch authority and hence a threat to its power. The queen of Bone had ordered the Dutch flag to be flown upside down, for instance. In other parts of the East Indies too, contracts were signed to safeguard Dutch interests: new contracts were concluded with fourteen regions besides Jambi in 1858.[52] Policy in Jambi reflected what was happening throughout the archipelago on Batavia's instructions.

THE HAGUE AND THE POLICY OF ABSTENTION

How did The Hague respond to this apparent break with the official policy of abstention from interference? Was it truly a break? What Baud had ordered in 1841 amounted to abstention in deed plus expansion on paper. An overview of Dutch rights drawn up in 1845 had proved conclusively "how much uncertainty still exists regarding the correct delimitation of the territorial borders of our authority in the East Indies archipelago,"[53] and governor-general J. J. Rochussen (1845–51) had been sent to the East Indies to remedy the situation.[54] To consolidate the Dutch claims, grand new titles had been invented for regional leaders in the 1840s, such as governor of Borneo (1845–49), intended as a verbal thrust against Brooke, and governor of Celebes and Dependencies (1846–1949), intended to establish claims over that entire island in the eyes of the outside world.[55] The Prins Memorandum was part of this campaign.

Besides expansion on paper there was expansion by military force. In this sense, several decrees passed by Acting Governor-General J. C. Reynst in 1845 had already reversed the policy of abstention. If anything happened to jeopardize the authority of the colonial government or the balance of power between local rulers, military action was deemed admissible. Thus the principle of absolute abstention from interference had become one of "abstention in principle, barring. . . ."[56] A second decree provided that territorial expansion too was permissible. At his desk in The Hague, Baud did remark that these decrees effectively reversed the old regulations, but he did not write to Batavia about it. For Governor-General Rochussen, who has wrongly been credited with the authorship of these decrees and was consequently seen for many years as the first expansionist at Buitenzorg,[57] it was a simple matter to continue his predecessor's policy. He even deduced from

---

[52] NA, Col., vb. January 6, 1860, A secret and vb. January 21, 1860, no. 16 secret.

[53] The overview observed "hoeveel onzekerheid nog bestaat ten aanzien eener juiste afbakening der territoriale grenzen van ons gezag in den Indische archipel."

[54] Rapport omtrent den staatkundige toestand in Oost-Indië, March 12, 1845, NA, Col., 1814-49, no. 2955.

[55] Fasseur, "Een koloniale paradox," p. 169; NA, Col., vb. November 4, 1843, no. 459 M1 secret.

[56] NA, Col., *gouvernementsbesluit*, July 10, 1845, Y1 secret and September 26, 1845, P2 secret; H. van Beers, "Boni moet boeten: De Nederlandse gezagsuitbreiding op Zuidwest-Celebes ten tijde van het stelsel van onthouding 1838-1858" (MA thesis, Leiden University, 1986), pp. 6, 23; *Politiek beleid en bestuurszorg in de buitenbezittingen*, 4 vols. (Batavia: Landsdrukkerij, 1907-9), 1: 55-56.

[57] The governor-general's official residence, in present-day Bogor.

recent events that a "slow expansion of territory" had become official policy.[58] He was responsible for the three major expeditions to Bali in 1846 and 1849. However, his tentative decisions to expand the Dutch territory in Celebes in 1851 were disavowed by the Minister, Pahud, who insisted that retaining the abstention policy was "absolutely essential" for the time being.[59] Still, The Hague was never known for its consistency. Only one year later Duymaer van Twist obtained permission to annex territory along the coast of Celebes.[60] Later governors-general too would interpret the policy as they saw fit; those who had favored abstention while serving as Minister (e.g., Pahud) acted with no less aggression than the rest, while former governors-general returning to a ministerial post in The Hague (e.g., Rochussen) were suddenly imbued with the true meaning of abstention.

In May 1857 the Dutch Parliament too, which was more closely involved with colonial policy since the adoption of the new Constitution of 1848, had declared itself roundly in favor of expansion on Sumatra. From the lower house of the States-General had come the proposal to reoccupy the realms on the island's east coast that the Dutch had abandoned, since the ban on arms imports in Palembang that had been introduced in the 1840s had proved ineffective.[61] This suggestion arrived in Batavia from The Hague during the period when new contracts were being drafted with Siak and Jambi. The idea of reoccupation was discussed and eventually rejected in 1859, with the exception of Siak and Jambi.[62]

Thus no one in Batavia expected The Hague to raise any objections to the plans laid to resolve the Jambian question. Nonetheless, the Ministry proved decidedly unenthusiastic about the policy being pursued there. Just as in 1833, the Ministry found itself compelled to rubber-stamp existing policy. True, the opening of the overland route meant that letters now took only two or three months to arrive instead of eight. But this meant that Batavia still had to wait four to six months for an answer to a question. Peter Mijer, who as Minister of Colonies had warned against changing the contract in 1857, in the wake of the Gibson affair, heard about the first unsuccessful round of negotiations in January 1858. He therefore knew about the efforts to conclude a new contract but did not respond. By then, there was a new Minister.

On March 18, 1858, J. J. Rochussen (1858–61) had succeeded him, a man with considerable experience in the East Indies. The Minister and governor-general had known each other for years, though their roles were now reversed; Pahud had served as Minister for two years (1849–51) while Rochussen was governor-general. Now they would be working together again until Rochussen's departure in January

---

[58] Van Beers, *Boni moet boeten*, p. 34; NA, Col., vb. July 10, 1846, no. 206 secret; governor-general to Minister of Colonies, July 1, 1848, NA, Col., exh. October 5, 1848, no. 410 secret.

[59] NA, Col., vb. November 17, 1851, no. 295: see also *Politiek beleid en bestuurszorg*, 1: 72, quoted in Fasseur, "Een koloniale paradox," p. 171.

[60] *Politiek beleid*, vol. I, pp. 70-78.

[61] NA, Col., vb. June 4, 1857, A 1/722 and exh. February 11, 1859, no. 65 secret.

[62] The heads of the regional authorities of Sumatra's west coast and Riau and the former Resident of Riau favored reoccupation; the commander-in-chief of the army, the Council of the Dutch East Indies, and Governor-General Pahud were more cautious, although Pahud saw the reoccupation as a regrettable necessity and was convinced that it would eventually be unavoidable to use the government's "statutory rights" to bind the whole of Sumatra, with the exception of Aceh, to the Netherlands (governor-general to Minister of Colonies, December 22, 1858, NA, Col., February 11, 1859, no. 65 secret).

1861. In May 1858 the Minister heard that the contract's renewal would be enforced by military means if necessary.[63] Shortly afterward, he agreed to raising the annuity to fifteen thousand guilders; he could scarcely have refused, given that the negotiations about it were already in progress, as an aside noted dryly in the official advisory report.[64] Thus Rochussen too had known for some time about the imminent change of course. Yet it was not until September 1858, after the expedition had taken place, that he expressed his dissatisfaction about it in his semiofficial correspondence with Pahud. He thought the arguments that had been presented decidedly flimsy; to his mind, the sultan's actions did not justify the deployment of a military expedition to enforce the signing of a new contract. After all, he had always adhered to the terms of the existing one. The fortress at Muara Kompeh was sufficient to keep the river and the sultanate under Dutch control. A military expedition should be used only as a last resort; otherwise the resources might well be overstretched.[65] In October 1858 he responded officially to the request to post an Assistant Resident to Jambi. Since he had not yet been apprised of the outcome of the expedition, he deferred his decision. Once again his letter reflected reservations about the policy being pursued in the East Indies. His reservations were almost certainly inspired in part by personal animosity. The Minister, who has been described as "vain . . ., astonishingly quick-witted but indecisive," and the governor-general, reportedly "cold and calm by nature," disliked each other,[66] to which their semiofficial correspondence bore semi-silent witness.

More explicitly, the Minister's doubts arose from concern about the growth of the Dutch administrative apparatus in the archipelago. "How will the Netherlands find the staff and resources, in twenty-five years' time, to maintain all its establishments?" the secretary-general, the Ministry's most senior civil servant, demanded despairingly in his advisory report. He saw the expansion of Dutch authority on Celebes, Borneo, and Sumatra as an "alarming" development. In Jambi in particular, this expansion had not been forced upon the Dutch but had been deliberately "pursued" and "acquired not without injustice." Rochussen agreed. "Exactly, exactly," he had scribbled in the margin.[67] As usual, The Hague's objections were largely related to the concern that any further expansion in the archipelago would make Dutch control unaffordable. That the net credit balance from the territory peaked around this time around thirty-three million guilders, that is to say, more than half of the total national revenue, was either overlooked or actually compounded the fears: The Hague was now worried it could no longer manage on any less.[68]

---

[63] *Gouvernementsbesluit*, March 20, 1858, secret La.X and other documents in NA, Col., vb. June 3, 1858, no. 220 secret.

[64] Note, May 21, 1858, NA, Col., vb. June 3, 1858, no. 220 secret.

[65] NA, Col., semiofficial correspondence Minister of Colonies to governor-general, September 8, 1858, no. 184 and September 23, 1858, no. 185.

[66] The two men have been called "ijdel . . ., verbazend vlug van begrip maar wankelend van beslissing" and "van nature koud en kalm," respectively; see J. Loudon in C. Fasseur, *Kultuurstelsel en koloniale baten: De Nederlandse exploittie van Java 1840-1860* (Leiden: Universitaire Pers, 1975), pp. 261-62. In 1861, as a minister, Loudon would abolish the semiofficial correspondence.

[67] 1st Note September 17, 1858, NA, Col., vb. October 6, 1858, no. 366 secret.

[68] C. Fasseur, *The Politics of Colonial Exploitation: Java, the Dutch, and the Cultivation System*, trans. R. E. Elson and Ary Kraal (Ithaca, N.Y.: Southeast Asia Program Publications, 1992), pp.

The Minister agreed with Taha that he had been wrongly coerced into concluding a new contract. This did not mean, it should be said, that there were any doubts in The Hague about the Netherlands' rights of sovereignty in Jambi. Concluding a new contract was simply believed to be unnecessary, expensive, and hazardous. As to the ultimate goal, contractual recognition of Dutch sovereignty, The Hague and Batavia were in complete agreement. They differed only concerning the methods that should be used (whether or not to use military force) and how to consolidate this recognition of sovereignty (whether or not to establish an administrative post). In these respects, the Minister acted as the frugal guardian of the national coffers. Thus he was against installing an Assistant Resident in Jambi, preferring a political intermediary, with the rank—and salary—of controller. That was cheaper. Even so, the sheer distance meant that the Minister was once again faced with a fait accompli.

Summing up, the expedition of 1858 was an indirect consequence of the commotion surrounding Gibson and was part of a Dutch policy of expansion in the East Indies. This policy was aimed at safeguarding the territory against all threats, internal and external alike. Fear of a loss of power went hand in hand with a desire to be one step ahead of everyone else—"preemption"—in this early wave of expansion, which was certainly substantial enough to be called pre-imperialism. Batavia had taken the initiative, but the Ministry of Colonies had prepared the ground by calling for paper expansion and by raising the issue of the reoccupation of Sumatra in 1857. The Hague (in the person of Rochussen, the new Minister), worried about overreaching itself by taking on more territory than the treasury could cope with, was scarcely able to restrain the colonial authorities, however. Rochussen could do little more than moderate Batavia's demands for more money. Soon, however, Batavia's former indifference to Jambi would reassert itself. The sultanate was forgotten again for the next twenty years, until a new scientific expedition rekindled the interest of the Dutch authorities.

149-50; Janny de Jong, *Van batig slot naar ereschuld: De discussie over de financiële verhouding tussen Nederland en Indië en de hervorming van de Nederlandse koloniale politiek* (Groningen, 1989), p. 44 (published privately).

Map of the capital, Jambi, in 1878. The sultan's kraton previously stood on this site.
KITLV map collection D 3,2: no. 6

CHAPTER SIX

QUESTS FOR KNOWLEDGE AND POLITICAL CONSEQUENCES: THE 1860S AND 1870S

Over the next few decades, Dutch interest in the sultanate was confined to scholarly research. The Resident J. A. W. van Ophuijsen (1861–63 and 1867–70), the only Palembang official to visit Jambi in the 1860s, was driven by academic curiosity. From his visits in December 1861, in 1867, and in 1869, he built up a small collection of manuscripts concerning adat and popular culture, which he later bequeathed to the library of Leiden University. In the 1870s, Jambi was the destination of the first scientific expedition of the newly formed Dutch Geographical Society, an expedition that would impact on the Netherlands' empire building. Scholarship did not always go hand-in-hand with imperialism, however. In the 1860s the colonial government was mainly concerned to restore Jambi's confidence, which had been shattered by the military action. Couperus had already made an effort in this direction with a solemn inauguration of the new sultan. His successors continued in the same line.

BATAVIA'S GOAL: RESTORING CONFIDENCE

The Dutch presence in Jambi was now twice as large as before. Since 1858, the colonial government had possessed three clearly defined enclaves within the sultanate: the fortress at Jambi on the right bank of the river, Muara Kompeh, and Muara Saba. Then, in addition to the existing Arab quarter in the capital, the first reports were received of a Chinese settlement. These newcomers—who had followed in the footsteps of the Dutch and built raft-houses below the fortress at Jambi, which stood on a small elevation—were soon the largest group of non-European inhabitants under direct Dutch rule.[1]

There was now a political agent in the capital: a military commander who was responsible for enforcing compliance with the contract. The administrative officer stayed in Muara Kompeh. Garrisons were encamped at both places. The Jambian official from Muara Kompeh, the much-praised Tumenggung Haji Astra Wiguna

---

[1] Resident of Palembang to Director of Inland Administration, September 3, 1867, National Archive (NA), The Hague, Col., *verbaal* (file, hereafter "vb.") January 15, 1869, no. 21; memorandum A3, NA, Col., vb. November 2, 1878, no. 7; account of Van Ophuijsen's journey of 1869, NA, Col., vb. November 2, 1878, no. 7. The pattern of Chinese immigrants following in the wake of the Dutch colonials is similar to that in Java in the seventeenth and eighteenth centuries.

Hamza, moved to Jambi.[2] As a diplomat, he rubbed shoulders with Jambian dignitaries on an everyday basis, and since he was expected to receive them, his allowance was increased by twenty guilders a month. He was an important intermediary. His successor was even more so, judging by Dutch descriptions of him as a "mine of information and a mediator in diverse affairs" and "indispensable to the civil administration."[3]

Still, the ties between the colonial authorities and Jambi remained perfunctory, and depended heavily on the personal interest of the Residents of Palembang. Van Ophuijsen, in particular, had a passion for ethnography and linguistics. On one of his three visits (1867) he traveled to the Kubu region, which no Dutch official had visited before him. As the Kubu supplied forest products, they were "important to the country's treasury," an understandable justification for an unusual journey. All the measures taken in the 1860s to improve relations with Jambi and to clarify the terms of the contract originated with Van Ophuijsen.

As time went on, he concentrated the administrative presence in the capital. In 1868, the Muara Kompeh garrison was given up as part of a package of financial cutbacks; the Netherlands' military presence was confined to a garrison in Jambi itself, consisting of two officers (a captain and a lieutenant) and seventy men, sixteen of whom (11.5 percent) were Europeans.[4] A few years later, in 1871, the position of administrative officer at Muara Kompeh was abolished: only a tax receiver (who also acted as harbormaster, postmaster, warehouse supervisor, and manager of the coal depot) remained. At three other places—at Muara Saba, on the Tungkal, and on the Kuala or Berba, local investigating officers checked imports and exports,[5] and in 1872 the judicial powers of the political agent were therefore redefined. He was empowered to administer justice to native peoples and those of equivalent legal status within the Dutch settlements in the sultanate: that is to say, in Jambi itself, at Muara Kompeh, at Muara Saba, and on the Tungkal, and to Chinese settlers living outside these Dutch areas. This curtailment of the sultan's judicial powers basically derived from the general provisions of the contract of 1858, though formulated fourteen years later, and was a judicial consequence of Dutch sovereignty.[6]

---

[2] *Gouvernementsbesluit* (resolution adopted by the colonial authorities), August 5, 1859, no. 3, NA, Col., vb. October 13, 1859, no. 12; governor-general to Minister of Colonies, August 5, 1859, and Resident of Palembang to governor-general, November 24, 1858, both in NA, Col., vb. October 24, 1859, no. 2.

[3] In 1863 he would be replaced by Tumenggung Shech Abdul Rachman bin Ali Joban. This Arab agent too was praised at length. He had once lived in Jambi; he was "highly civilized, loyal, and meticulous"; and he had won the respect and affection of the sultan and leading dignitaries. What is more, he knew the uplands, and was familiar with Jambian laws and institutions (see Resident of Palembang to governor-general, May 16 1868, NA, Col., vb. December 16, 1868, no. 36).

[4] For the decision making on this matter, see NA, Col., vb. December 28, 1868, no. 12, and vb. January 15, 1869, no. 21. The battle between Van Ophuijsen and the Council of the Dutch East Indies about whether to give up the garrison in Jambi or Muara Kompeh had been won by Van Ophuijsen, who invoked the settlement's key function and the smaller risk of flooding. The military encampment in the Rawas, too, maintained in 1861 for fear of unrest among the Jambians, was abandoned in 1868.

[5] Resident of Palembang to Director of Finance, December 9, 1868, NA, Col., vb. December 15, 1871, no. 24.

[6] NA, Col., vb. December 15, 1871, no. 24 and vb. August 23, 1872, no. 15.

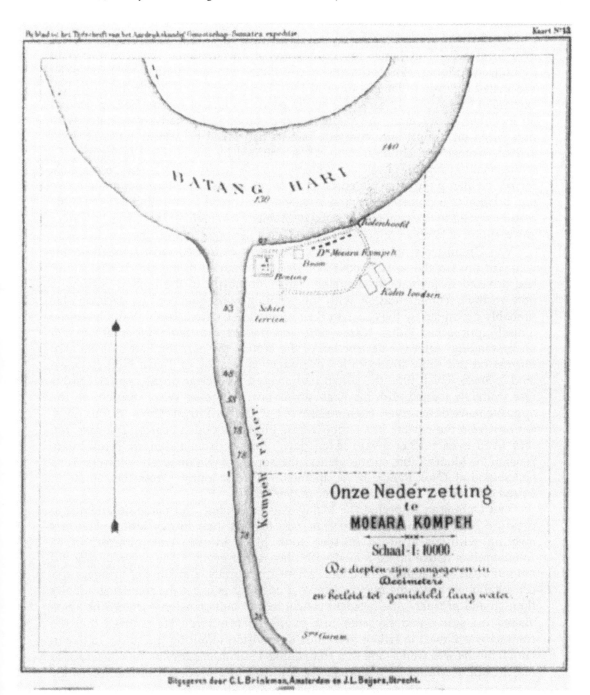

Plan of the settlement of Muara Kompeh after 1858
KITLV, Map collection D 3,2: no. 13

Another elaboration of the contract decided upon in 1870 was the appointment of a local official in Jambi to take charge of vaccinations. This too was Van Ophuijsen's doing. An enthusiastic supporter of vaccination, he had taken vaccinated children to Jambi—three in 1861, five in 1867, and two in 1869—as live carriers of the vaccine. In each case he did so after a lack of vaccine had suspended all inoculations for months. On his last trip, he had also had a vaccinator with him, hired on a short-term contract, and he had taken on a local assistant upon arrival. Women and children were rather daunted by the prospect of visiting the white, male European physician, who, as Jambi's health officer, was responsible for the civilian population's medical care. When a fresh smallpox epidemic broke out in Jambi in September 1869 and threatened to spread to Palembang, The Hague readily agreed to the appointment of a permanent vaccinator.[7] There was no longer any mention of Jambian opposition to the Dutch desire to "brand" them with a *cap*.

Van Ophuijsen's policy of reconciliation was expressed most strongly in his behavior toward the sultan's court. In 1861 the Council of the Dutch East Indies had advised in favor of recognizing Taha's authority in the upland regions, a noteworthy recommendation with far-reaching consequences.[8] Its decision was probably prompted by the constant flow of good news from Jambi. Van Ophuijsen himself approached Sultan Nazaruddin and the *pangeran ratu* with great tact and understanding. After the destruction of the kraton, the garrison had built its own fortress on this same strategically advantageous location of Tanah Pilih ("chosen land"), since which time the sultan had steered well clear of the capital. On his rare visits, he lodged with his Arab son-in-law, Pangeran Wiro Kesumo, on the opposite bank of the river. He himself lived at Dusun Tengah, three or four days' journey from the capital, in a simple house built of wooden boards. The *pangeran ratu* lived even further away, seven days' journey from Jambi, at Telok Puan, beneath the Muara Tabir, surrounded by the houses of two hundred followers. Taha had settled at Telok Renda in the uplands, ten days' journey from the capital, in fenced grounds not far from an Islamic prayer-house.[9]

Van Ophuijsen respected the Malay sense of shame and made no attempt to pressure Nazaruddin or the *pangeran ratu* to visit their former kraton. His first meeting with Nazaruddin in 1861 took place in the Arab quarter, in "a commonplace native house roofed with tiles, rather grimy." The *pangeran ratu* did not put in an appearance. "Tact, and, where appropriate, a mixture of firmness and consultation, is hence the rule to observe if one wishes to see the country gradually flourish and prosper," the Resident concluded on that occasion.[10] In 1867 he again visited the sultan and *pangeran ratu* in the Arab quarter. He realized that the contract was flawed in failing to include a provision requiring the sultan to live in Jambi. But he was well aware that compelling a sultan or *pangeran ratu* to return to his old kraton would be political folly. He therefore proposed instead that they

---

[7] Governor general to Minister of Colonies, NA, Col., vb. October 29, 1870, no. 26; vb. October 14, 1870, no. 36. See also the accounts of Van Ophuijsen's journeys of 1861, 1867, and 1869 in NA, Col., vb. November 2, 1878, no. 7.

[8] Governor-general to Minister of Colonies, April 15, 1861, NA, Col., exh. May 30, 1861, no. 3.

[9] Resident of Palembang to governor-general, November 21, 1860, NA, Col., exh. January 17, 1861, no. 1; account of Van Ophuijsen's journey of 1869, NA, Col., vb. November 2, 1878, no. 7.

[10] "Omzigtigheid en waar het te pas komt klem met overleg is dan ook de stelling die men zich als regel moet voorschrijven om gaandeweg het land in bloei en welvaart te kunnen zien toenemen"; account of Van Ophuijsen's journey of 1861, NA, Col., vb. November 2, 1878, no. 7.

build their own house in Jambi, and had the impression that his approach was bearing fruit: "I have won their confidence," he declared in 1867.[11]

The reception he received in 1869 appeared to confirm this. Pangeran Wiro Kesumo, Raden Hasan, another son-in-law of Nazaruddin, and the *pangeran ratu* all stood waiting to receive him in Muara Kompeh when he visited for a third time, in November 1869. He went to see Nazaruddin in the Arab quarter, and for the first time, the honor was reciprocated. The policy of withdrawal and avoiding contact had been abandoned, Van Ophuijsen noted cheerfully. Nazaruddin promised to build a house in accordance with the governor-general's wishes. Probably motivated by curiosity, the Resident then visited the sultan and *pangeran ratu* in their own homes at Dusun Tengah and Telok Puan, even steaming as far as Muara Tebo, which meant passing Taha's *dusun*. If a lack of coal had not forced him to turn back, he would certainly have continued his exploration of the Batang Hari.

Not until 1869 did Van Ophuijsen begin to comprehend the structure of the Jambian sultanate, thanks to a long report drawn up by the political agent. Previously, his curiosity had simply elicited the information that all records of native structures and borders had been destroyed by fire in 1858, and that the new sultan himself knew little about his realm. It was a reply characteristic of the Jambian policy of keeping the Dutch at a distance.

Given Van Ophuijsen's interest in the sultanate, it is striking that he failed to reply to Nazaruddin's letter of 1866 requesting forgiveness for Taha. The letter was addressed to the political agent, L. W. A. Kessler, who was replaced shortly afterward.[12] It was forwarded and filed away in the Residency's records in Palembang, where it was not rediscovered until 1879.[13] This request must have failed to reach Van Ophuijsen. After his term as Resident of Palembang in 1861, he had spent two years' sick leave in the Netherlands, after which he had served as Resident of Kedu on Java until his return to Palembang in 1867. He had not received the letter personally. In his Jambian travel journals of 1867 and 1869, however, he mentioned rumors of a request for forgiveness, which he thought an excellent idea: Taha could be a great help to the present sultan, since he was more intelligent and much respected. At this point, the situation was "static." Forgiveness would also bring Taha's large extended family "over to our side." Van Ophuijsen was apparently quite unaware that such a request had in fact been submitted, or he would certainly have supported it.

In the interim, Van Ophuijsen had changed his opinion of the Jambian leaders. On his first visit he had thought the sultan a weak figure, "a good man, though uneducated, not shrewd or forceful."[14] He knew little about his realm, noted the Resident, and he was often ill and seldom visited Jambi. Of the *pangeran ratu*, whom he had not yet met, he wrote that he was a man of great authority, whom others approached with veneration. It was an advantage that he lived in the interior, where he could help preserve peace and order. As for Taha, whom he had

---

[11] Account of Van Ophuijsen's journey of 1867, NA, Col., vb. November 2, 1878, no. 7.

[12] Resident of Palembang to governor-general, November 5, 1879, NA, Col., vb. January 30, 1880, no. 7. The request was dated 11 Rabieawal 1283 (July 24, 1866).

[13] Kessler to Minister of Colonies, September 2, 1879, NA, Col., vb. September 6, 1879, no. 20; anonymous memorandum, n.d., NA, Col., vb. July 9, 1903, no. 44.

[14] "Een goed mensch, en eer dom dan schrander en energique."

described in 1861 as "not highly regarded at all, but on the contrary hated," he completely revised his opinion of the former sultan after his second and third visits, writing that he was much loved by the local headmen and population of the hinterland.[15]

THE JAMBIAN RESPONSE

For the Dutch, a great deal had changed in 1858. Whether the same was true of Jambi is less obvious. The sultans of Jambi had not necessarily lived in the capital.[16] Malay sultans ruled over subjects, not territory. If ousted, they remained rajas and could continue to rule from elsewhere. They retained their regalia (*pusaka*), and their subjects were still under an obligation to obey them.[17] All this applied to Taha, who thus retained his formal position of power, and was quite free to exercise it under the new administrative regime. His cousin, the *pangeran ratu*, who had held office under him, was still there; thus, the actual power of government did not change hands. For this reason alone, Taha's finger was firmly embedded in the Jambian pie. As a popular ruler, he held sway over the uplands. Indirectly, he even continued to receive a share of the annuity from the colonial government, which Nazaruddin had promised him on his accession—something the Dutch did not discover until 1879.[18] Batavia confirmed Taha's position of power with its tacit acceptance, in 1861, that Taha was to be recognized as sultan in the uplands.

That is not to say that everything remained the same. Under the influence of the Dutch presence and the Dutch support to the "contract sultan" Nazaruddin, a rival center of power would develop in the capital around Nazaruddin and his son-in-law, Pangeran Wiro Kesumo. This too followed a Jambian tradition of rivalries within the *suku* Kraton.

All in all, in 1858–59 the Jambian leaders embarked on a policy vis-à-vis Batavia that would prove a successful formula for almost half a century. The *suku* Kraton withdrew from the danger zone, limiting the direct impact of Dutch rule. A combination of factors made this policy of withdrawal possible. In the first place, the colonial government was still largely ignorant of Jambian affairs. It was not until 1869 that the Dutch authorities started to grasp the consequences of allowing a division of power in Jambi, and even then they were slow to comprehend.[19] Geography was another important factor. Distances, the inaccessibility of the uplands, and the relative self-reliance of that region—which, as the main supplier of rice, could command the loyalty of the lowland peoples—created a natural division. Besides this, the Arab Said Idrus, alias Pangeran Wiro Kesumo, was a perfect middleman, acting as a front for the sultan's authority, disguising the true balance of power and cushioning the first blows of any confrontation.

---

[15] See the travel accounts in NA, Col., vb. November 2, 1878, no. 7.

[16] See chapter 2.

[17] J. M. Gullick, "'The Condition of Having a Raja': A Review of Kerajaan, by A. C. Milner," *Review of Indonesian and Malayan Affairs* 16,2 (1982): 109–29, esp. 113.

[18] Resident of Palembang to governor-general, November 5, 1879, NA, Col., vb. January 30, 1880, no. 7. He would cease making this payment in 1869, probably because by then he judged his strength sufficient to do so.

[19] Account of Van Ophuijsen's journey of 1869, NA, Col., vb. November 2, 1878, no. 7.

THE ARAB CONNECTION

The Arab connection in Jambi merits more attention than it has received. The Arab colony in Jambi had played a political role in the opposition to the sultan's authority since as far back as 1812. Whether the Al Jufri were already established in Jambi then is not known. They belonged to the *said*, one of nine families respected as religious nobles in the Hadhramaut (the south of the Arabian peninsula) because they could trace their lineage back to Muhammad's daughter and son-in-law. Literate and of high moral character—they bore no weapons and neither smoked nor gambled—they were universally venerated. They had retained their high status throughout the waves of economic migration from the Arabian peninsula from the late eighteenth century onward. To the local rulers in the archipelago, these descendants of the Prophet, with their knowledge of the holy language, were valuable assets, to whom they were happy to marry their daughters. Since Arab women did not emigrate, Arab men married local women or women of mixed descent, with a preference for the *said* daughters of royal houses. Thus the sultan of Siak had Arab forbears, as did the ruler of Kampar. On Borneo, the sultan of Pontianak and the lord of Kubu were of Arab descent. Their trade and marriage networks made Arabs, especially those belonging to the *said*, men of consequence throughout the East Indies. With their genteel manners and large vocabularies, they were destined, as it were, for lives as regional diplomats. They frequently mediated between local rulers and the Dutch colonial authorities throughout the nineteenth century.[20]

In Jambi, it was Said Idrus, a kinsman of Said Ali al Jufri, mentioned in chapter 5, who took this role upon himself. The Al Jufri emigrants to Sumatra, who came from the central Hadhramaut, had settled in Palembang, home of the island's richest and second-largest Arab colony (after Aceh), with a population of two thousand in 1885. Though fairly recent newcomers, they belonged to the wealthiest circles of this wealthy Palembang colony.[21] Their family had ties with neighboring regions: the *bendahara* of Patapahan in Siak was an Al Jufri (Said or Mohamad bin 'Aloui al-Juffri),[22] and their kinsmen were among the most influential groups in Singapore.[23]

The Al Jufri were well represented in Jambi. In the 1860s, Said Idrus—Pangeran Wiro Kesumo—became their spokesman, a man with "a more intelligent face than other dignitaries" and, in spite of his Arab attire, a decidedly non-Arab appearance.[24] In 1879 he was estimated to be about forty years old. He was probably rather older, since he had first served as Nazaruddin's official envoy to

---

[20] L. W .C . van den Berg, *Le Hadramouth et les colonies Arabes dans l'archipel Indien* (Batavia: Imprimerie du gouvernement, 1886).

[21] Ibid., p. 226.

[22] Ibid., p. 198.

[23] J. C. M. Peeters, "Kaum tua en kaum muda in de residentie Palembang: 1925–1934" (MA thesis, Leiden University, 1988), pp. 14, 31.

[24] Resident of Palembang to governor-general, July 18, 1879, NA, Col., vb. June 19, 1880, no. 10.

Batavia in 1861. His long political career spanned the period from 1860 to 1905, when he died of natural causes.[25]

Said Idrus's power was based on kinship, wealth, and knowledge. He was related to the *suku* Kraton in numerous ways. His grandfather, born as a full-blooded Arab in the Arabian peninsula, had migrated to the East Indies along with many of his compatriots at the end of the eighteenth century.[26] Said Idrus was part Jambian, as his father had taken a wife from the Jambian court; he himself later did the same. Said Idrus himself was related to the former sultan Taha, through a brother of Taha's mother, Abdulla bin Murah. Taha himself had close ties with Arabs, since both his mother and his first wife were of Arab descent.[27] Through his marriage to Sultan Nazaruddin's favorite daughter, Said Idrus had also acquired ties to the *suku* Kraton, becoming Taha's cousin by marriage.

Besides allowing him to marry his daughter, Sultan Nazaruddin had given him the title of Pangeran Wiro Kesumo. This title, which was also in use in 1853 for a member of the *suku* Kraton, signified then that its bearer was *pepati dalam,* a court dignitary whose task it was to act for the sultan in his absence and to supervise the royal household.[28] The powers vested in the new Pangeran Wiro Kesumo went further still. Nazaruddin had entrusted him with the management of all his affairs. Pangeran Wiro Kesumo had traveled widely, to Arabia, Egypt, Singapore, and Batavia, from which he was said to have acquired an ease of dealing with Europeans that made him the perfect intermediary.[29]

Pangeran Wiro Kesumo also had other, more tangible assets. His father-in-law had empowered him to administer the salt revenue, a monopoly of the sultan's that had not been introduced in Jambi until about 1865.[30] He also disposed of the opium monopoly until the treaty of 1880, under the terms of which it was relinquished to the Dutch colonial authorities. This meant he managed a substantial proportion of the income of the Jambian court. Furthermore, besides other trading relations he had an important appanage on the river Berba, a branch of the estuary of the Batang Hari, one hour by steamship from the estuary mouth. In 1875 he had a garden of sago palms there,[31] which made it easier for him to

---

[25] Account of Van Ophuijsen's journey of 1861, NA, Col., vb. November 2, 1878, no. 7; account of Van Ophuijsen's journey of 1867 in NA, Col., vb. November 2, 1878, no. 7; Resident of Palembang to governor-general, July 18, 1879, NA, Col., vb. June 19, 1880, no. 10; brief report for March 1905, *mailrapport* (postal report; hereafter "mr.") 1095/498, NA, Col., vb. April 28, 1906, no. 31.

[26] Resident of Palembang to governor-general, July 18, 1879, NA, Col., vb. June 19, 1880, no. 10.

[27] Resident of Palembang to governor-general, April 4, 1881, NA, Col., mr. 1881/563 secret.

[28] Account of Storm van 's Gravesande's journey of 1852, NA, Col., vb. February 15, 1853, no. 26.

[29] Resident of Palembang to governor-general, July 18, 1879, NA, Col., vb. June 19, 1880, no. 10.

[30] Account of Van Ophuijsen's journey of 1867, NA, Col., vb. November 2, 1878, no. 7. When Taha grew more powerful, Wiro Kesumo would later relinquish the revenue from the salt monopoly levied for and on behalf of Sultan Nazaruddin—the key moment, according to Snouck Hurgronje, being when the colonial government started explicitly taking Taha's power into account. After this, sales were concentrated in Muara Tembesi and Sungai Aroh in the uplands, which gave Taha a firmer hold on the trade. E. Gobée and C. Adriaanse, eds., *Ambtelijke adviezen van C. Snouck Hurgronje 1889–1936,* 3 vols. (The Hague: Nijhoff, 1957–65), 3: 2055.

[31] P. J. Veth, ed., *Midden-Sumatra: Reizen en onderzoekingen der Sumatra-expeditie, uitgerust door het Aardrijkskundig Genootschap 1877–1879,* 4 vols. (Leiden: Brill, 1881–92), vol. 1, pt. 2, p. 216.

smuggle opium. In 1880 the Chinese opium farmer in Palembang (not the most objective of informants) credited him with all the opium smuggling in the region.[32] He had also laid out a garden and some ladangs near Jambi; finally, in 1875 he was described as having control of the lower reaches of the Batang Hari and supervisory powers over the lower reaches of the Tungkal.[33] In short, he was a man of considerable power and resources.

Wiro Kesumo lived in Pecinan, the immigrant quarter across the river from the fortress. His wooden house, with the upper floor commonly found in Arab houses, survives to this day, although it is in a dilapidated state. The wide hall and wooden staircase still evoke the former glory of its princely entrance. This was where Nazaruddin stayed on his visits to Jambi.[34]

As the most important intermediary between the sultanate and the Dutch authorities, Wiro Kesumo immediately set out to convince Batavia of his good intentions. In 1861 he had two of his children inoculated against smallpox, probably also because he saw it as a salutary health measure. That year, Van Ophuijsen described him as "someone who wants to get ahead but who has to be kept on a fairly short leash."[35] Political agents of the 1860s were as little enamored of him as the dignitaries and the people of Jambi. They thought him "too independent . . ., arrogant and insolent."[36] Even so, he would remain an important, if not the most important, intermediary between the colonial government and the sultanate, even at the beginning of the 1870s, when a geographical expedition briefly reinvigorated relations between the two centers of power.

GEOGRAPHY AND IMPERIALISM

The connection between scholarship and colonial imperialism, both in general and in the case of the Dutch East Indies, is well documented.[37] Dutch academics researching the languages and cultures of the archipelago promoted the colonial government's cause and actively sought to cooperate with it. To what extent was the new discipline of geography, too, an imperialist, or empire-building, branch of learning? What role did the new Geographical Society play in this process? How did it affect Jambi? These questions can be answered by looking at the Society's first expedition to Central Sumatra (1877–79).

---

[32] Governor-general to Minister of Colonies, February 16, 1881, NA, Col., vb. November 24, 1881, no. 9. In 1885, too, a local informant described him as the main importer of clandestine opium (statement of Panglima Putih, June 13, 1885, NA, Col., mr. 1885/635).

[33] Veth, *Midden-Sumatra*, p. 223.

[34] Resident of Palembang to governor-general, July 10, 1879, NA, Col., vb. June 19, 1978, no. 10.

[35] Van Ophuijsen described him as "iemand die wel vooruit wil maar eenigszins kort gehouden dient te worden."

[36] They thought him "te zelfstandig . . ., arrogant en vrijpostig." Account of Van Ophuijsen's journey of 1861, NA, Col., vb. November 2, 1878, no. 7; Resident of Palembang to governor-general, July 10, 1869, NA, Col., vb. June 19, 1978, no. 10.

[37] W. F. Wertheim, "Counter-Insurgency Research at the Turn of the Century: Snouck Hurgronje and the Aceh War," *Sociologische Gids* 19 (1972): 320–28. A. A. J. Warmenhoven, "De opleiding van Nederlandse bestuursambtenaren in Indonesië," in *Besturen overzee. Herinneringen van oud-ambtenaren bij het binnenlands bestuur in Nederlandsch-Indië*, ed. S. L. van der Wal (Franeker: Wever, 1977), pp. 12–44.

The Geographical Society (which would acquire the official title of Royal Dutch Geographical Society in the 1880s) had been founded in 1873. In this respect the Netherlands was following in the footsteps of others—with characteristic sluggishness—as similar organizations had sprung up all over Europe in the 1820s. The Dutch initiative had come from secondary-school teachers, but it soon widened its support base in society. On its executive committee sat representatives from trade and industry, the army and navy, and academia. In 1874, the Society had 360 members, 25 percent of whom were civil servants or members of Parliament, 25 percent scholars or teachers, roughly 25 percent from trade and industry, and the rest from the armed forces.[38] Its first president was P. J. Veth, who was both a professor at the East Indies Institute in Leiden, which trained colonial officials, and editor-in-chief of the liberal periodical on the East Indies, *Tijdschrift voor Nederlandsch-Indië*. The patronage of Prince Hendrik, a brother of King William III, endowed the Society with a royal cachet.[39]

The Society was founded in the same year that saw the outbreak of the Aceh War in the far north of Sumatra. The two events were indisputably connected. They were two different expressions of Western expansionism, one in science and learning, the other in political power. Both focused on the East Indies, seeking to consolidate the Netherlands' existing colonial possessions. Both stemmed from the same desire, to gain a better grasp of the unknown reality of the colony. More importantly, however, the two endeavors were described in similar terms and shared a single national ideology. The Aceh War, it was hoped, would cleanse the Netherlands' escutcheon of the blot wrought by the insult to Dutch authority, since Aceh had violated the (imposed) treaty of trade, peace, and friendship.[40] The Geographical Society too sought greatness for the Netherlands, not only in scholarship, but also in economics and political influence. It was interested in not only acquiring, but also in disseminating knowledge, and exploiting it to benefit trade and industry. "Emulating and holding high our forefathers' glory" was one aim, and seeking "new ways and means for profitable relations" another.[41] When the decision was made in May 1874 to dispatch an expedition to Central Sumatra, one board member noted that the "preeminently Dutch enterprise" promised a great deal, such as "splendid results for both scholarship and trade," possible increases in "colonial agricultural production" and "new deposits of coal and metals" including tin.[42] Just how closely linked were expansion and scholarship at this time was clear from the Society's first meeting. The Society's president, Veth,

---

[38] "Verslag van de verrichtingen van het Aardrijkskundig Genootschap in 1873–1874," *Tijdschrift van het Aardrijkskundig Genootschap* 1 (1876): 37–39, esp. 37. The membership of the Geographical Society would remain more or less stable at around eight hundred throughout the nineteenth century, constituting a relatively large colonial lobby. The Indisch Genootschap (established in 1851), an organization of intellectuals and officials, was far smaller.

[39] Paul van der Velde, *Een Indische liefde: P. J. Veth (1814–1895) en de inburgering van Nederlands-Indië* (Amsterdam: Balans, 2000), p. 231.

[40] P. van 't Veer, *De Atjeh-oorlog* (Amsterdam: Arbeiderspers, 1969), pp. 52, 75.

[41] P. J. Veth, "Openingsrede van de eerste Algemeene Vergadering van het Aardrijkskundig Genootschap, gehouden te Amsterdam den 3 juni 1873," *Tijdschrift Aardrijkskundig Genootschap* 1 (1876): 13.

[42] Appendix, Executive Committee of Geographical Society to Minister of Colonies, p. 7, NA, Col., vb. November 18, 1874, no. 4. See also "Genootschappen," in *Encyclopaedie van Nederlandsch-Indië* (The Hague: Nijhoff; Leiden: Brill, 1918–40), 1: 773–75, esp. 774.

addressing the members, roundly advocated the continuation of the Aceh War that had broken out three months earlier, a position on which there was no consensus as yet in the Netherlands. Shortly after this inaugural meeting it was decided to ask the Minister of Colonies to add some researchers to the expedition bound for Aceh. The Geographical Society was happy to collaborate with an expansionist colonial government and to operate under its banner.[43] In its use of language, its objective (the East Indies), and its motives (boosting the Dutch economy through trade and industry, and fear of other countries), the Geographical Society was part and parcel of Dutch imperialism. To what extent it made an active contribution to it is a separate issue.

Batavia and the Society alike were able to profit from the technological advances that had narrowed the time lag of messages passing between the mother country and its colony to twenty-four hours. At the end of 1870, a telegraph line had been installed between Batavia and The Hague after the British Australian company had laid cables from Batavia to Singapore. This meant that Batavia was now linked up to the global telegraph network. Only now did it become possible for the Ministry of Colonies to exert direct influence on policy, if not to determine it. Telegrams from The Hague could be processed into decrees promulgated by the colonial government the very same day.[44] Since Palembang already possessed a telegraph connection with Batavia by then, and Aceh was connected up in 1873, Sumatra grew much closer to The Hague after 1870.

PLANS FOR A SCIENTIFIC EXPEDITION

A year after the founding of the Geographical Society, the executive committee decided to mount a major scientific expedition to the East Indies.[45] The goal was to explore Jambi and Kerinci, an enclosed valley adjoining Jambi in the Bukit Barisan. The researchers were attracted by the unknown. From the travels of Resident Van Ophuijsen they knew a little of the source and path of the Batang Hari, but less of other rivers, such as the Tabir and Merangin, and of Kerinci they were virtually ignorant. Their interest had probably been aroused by some comments in the 1872 issue of *Koloniaal Verslag*, the annual report to Parliament on the Dutch colonies.[46] The report noted the dearth of first-hand information about this fertile valley. It observed that its inhabitants were strict Muslims and that the region, formally part of Jambi, had now been independent for fifty years. However, the sultan of Jambi still counted it as part of his territory. It is certainly true that few Europeans had ever set foot in Kerinci—just a handful of private travelers had visited it in 1803, 1811, 1833, and 1838. In 1840 a treaty of friendship had been concluded between an envoy from Merkus, the government commissioner for Sumatra, and headmen from Kerinci, including promises of mutual trade advancement. But it was not until 1865 that Kerinci was mentioned in the *Koloniaal Verslag*, mainly because its traders had been offering coffee for sale at

---

[43] The Ministry rejected the proposal. Van der Velde, *Een Indische liefde*, p. 235.

[44] See e.g. NA, Col., *minuut vb.* April 22, 1879, no. 6 and *gouvernementsbesluit*, June 22, 1879, no. 6.

[45] Van der Velde, *Een Indische liefde*, pp. 236–37.

[46] *Koloniaal Verslag 1872, Bijlage C. van de Handelingen der Staten Generaal 1872–1873* (The Hague: Landsdrukkerij, 1872–73), app. 21.2.

the markets of Bengkulu. That good tobacco was grown here as well as coffee added to the area's attractions.[47]

Initially, then, the expedition was bound for Central Sumatra.[48] The organizers emphasized a variety of political motives for this choice: the good reports from Aceh "now that our moral position there is stronger perhaps than ever before" (it was still only the fall of 1874 when this was written) and the relations with the Jambian sultan and his circle, which were described at the time as "superb."[49]

By 1876, a mere two years later, the Society had fine-tuned its plans. Veth now described the aims of the expedition in far greater detail. National interests were still described as paramount (possibly in part to gain the Minister's support). The prime objective was to gain more knowledge by surveying virtually unknown areas, improving maps, testing the soil, and doing ethnological, linguistic, natural historical, and biological research, partly with a view to cultivating products for the European market. The secondary objective, now mentioned explicitly, was to find transportation routes for Ombilin coal, a factor that had played an important role in the choice of this area.[50] Clearly, the Society pursued a mix of scientific and economic goals, partly in order to gain wider support.

Coal had been a vexing issue for the colonial authorities since the mid-nineteenth century. With the advent of steamships, the Dutch had become convinced of the importance of having their own coal mines, if only to provide energy for their navy. Mining had started in 1846, at first only on Borneo. In 1868 a large coalfield had been discovered in the Padang uplands, at Ombilin. In terms of quantity and quality it held out great promise, but no one knew that this would prove to be the most important coalfield in the East Indies, with the best coal in the region.[51] One concrete problem impeded the rapid development of this new find—transportation. The coal fields were in the middle of the Central Bukit Barisan mountains. When the Geographical Society presented its plans for an expedition in 1874, the transportation debate was at its height.[52] In 1871, the leader of the mining survey, W. H. de Greve, had advocated using two separate lines of transportation, a railway line to Padang on Sumatra's west coast, and a river route to the east, on one of the three major rivers, the Siak, Kampar, or Indragiri.[53] His death in 1872 and the outbreak of the Aceh War in 1873 put an end to the river option for the time being, but the rail plans were set in motion. The first survey was conducted in 1875, but the hostility of the people of the independent Kwantan districts along the upper reaches of the Indragiri River and disruption

---

[47] C. W. Watson, *Kerinci: Two Historical Studies*, Occasional Paper 3 (Canterbury: Centre of South-East Asian Studies, University of Kent, 1984), pp. 10–13.

[48] President of Geographical Society to Minister of Colonies, NA, Col., vb. November 4, 1874, Y19.

[49] Veth to Minister of Colonies, NA, Col., vb. November 18, 1874, no. 4.

[50] W. F. Versteeg to Minister of Colonies, n.d., exh. February 28, 1876, NA, Col., vb. April 4, 1876, no. 40; see also C. M. van Kan, *De Nederlandsch expeditie naar Boven-Djambi en de Korintji-vallei* (Utrecht: Beijers, 1876), pp. 15–16.

[51] "Kolen," in *Encyclopaedie van Nederlandsch-Indië* (The Hague: Nijhoff; Leiden: Brill, 1918), 2: 400–08, esp. 400–01.

[52] Ibid., pp. 405–06.

[53] W. H. de Greve, *Het Ombiliën-kolenveld in de Padangsche Bovenlanden en het transportstelsel op Sumatra's Westkust* (The Hague: Landsdrukkerij, 1871).

from the Aceh War immediately torpedoed it. By then it had become clear that only the Indragiri was suitably navigable, and that the rail link was the main priority.[54] The Geographical Society's proposal to explore another transportation route for the Ombilin coal, over the Batang Hari, which had not been mentioned before, was therefore as topical as it was original.

The Ombilin fields lay, it was believed, at a walking distance of twenty hours from the *dusun* of Gassing on the Upper Batang Hari, which had already proved navigable for fairly large proas. The mountains in between were less impenetrable than those between the Ombilin fields and the west coast. Therefore, in February 1876 the Geographical Society suggested conducting a survey of the navigability of the Batang Hari from Gassing to the coast, and another survey of the terrain between the Ombilin fields and Gassing. According to the detailed plan presented at the end of March, the expedition would be divided into two parts: a river survey, focusing on the lower reaches of the Batang Hari, and a survey of the mountain regions in the south of the Padang uplands, the independent regions of Kerinci, Serampas, Sungei Tenang, and Pangkalan Jambi.[55] In retrospect we know that this would actually have bypassed the route between the Ombilin fields and the Batang Hari, but apparently the data that would have revealed the miscalculation were not available, as no objections were raised. The destination would be adjusted later on.

The railway option eventually carried the day, being the only rational solution. Quite aside from the fact that the east coast was further away, the freight that could be carried by train was many times larger than the cargo that could be accommodated in steam tugs traversing relatively shallow rivers through areas that were not yet under Dutch control. But these facts first had to be ascertained; this is what the Geographical Society wanted to do, and what it did.

The actual expedition of 1877–79 was preceded by a total of three years of deliberation and decision making. Even before the plans had been submitted in their final form, Batavia's consent and financial support had to be obtained, and a start was made on obtaining them in the fall of 1874. By May 1875 the Geographical Society was in receipt of the authorities' recommendations. All were moderately positive.[56] The Council of the Dutch East Indies thought it best to focus on the southern Padang uplands, where peace had reigned for thirty years and the population was "very benevolent." It felt that Batavia should give the expedition only moral, not material, support. Otherwise it would arouse suspicion, especially in the independent region of Kerinci, given the events in northern Sumatra. In 1875, in accordance with the recommendations, the governor-general (the newly appointed diplomat J. W. van Lansberge) advised the Minister (the likewise

---

[54] J. L. Cluysenaar, *Rapport over de aanleg van een spoorweg ter verbinding van de Ombilien-kolenvelden op Sumatra met de Indische Zee* (The Hague: Ministry of Colonies), pp. x, 112–16.

[55] Veth to Minister of Colonies, September 7, 1876, NA, Col., vb. October 5, 1876, no. 32.

[56] See the advisory reports in NA, Col., vb. May 24, 1875, no. 27. Only in the case of Kerinci did the advisors have some reservations, though not insuperable ones. For the people of this district were known for their determination to keep foreigners out of their territory, Europeans in particular, according to the Assistant Resident of Bengkulu (P. F. Laging Tobias, a name that we shall encounter again). The Resident of Palembang, A. Pruys van der Hoeven, emphasized the lawlessness of Jambi's uplands, adding that even the sultan's *jenang* did not dare to show themselves in Kerinci, which had once been subject to rule from Jambi. Still, like Laging Tobias he thought an expedition feasible, provided Sultan Nazaruddin cooperated.

newly appointed W. van Goltstein) to grant permission for the expedition. The necessary financial support should come from the Netherlands and not from Batavia and "the natives need not know anything about it."[57]

Thus, in May 1875, the Society received the green light for its plans. But permission did not guarantee funds. An expedition of this kind could not be financed purely from private capital; the government's support was essential, and it had to be applied for in several stages. Although the colonial authorities had initially ruled out material assistance, in 1876 they nonetheless made a steam launch available, and soon afterward they provided two hundred tons of coal, besides minor forms of help such as transportation to the infirmary for the sick and free nursing. Nor would the Society have to bear the expense of their members' board and lodging, except in Jambi itself. The authorities could not supply crews for the ships as they were short of manpower.[58] After some wrangling, however, they decided to place an expert official at the explorers' disposal, the controller A. L. van Hasselt, for the expedition to the uplands. The Minister (now F. Alting Mees) and Parliament agreed to award a special grant of twenty thousand guilders. Thus the "private" enterprise was in fact heavily subsidized by the government.

Meanwhile, private local committees from all over the Netherlands, from Middelburg to Sappemeer, had amassed thirty thousand guilders,[59] enough to finance the expedition for a year. The *Stoomvaartmaatschappij Nederland* transported the launch at a reduced rate. In contrast to the enthusiasm in the Netherlands, the expedition aroused little or no interest in the archipelago itself. Partly because of the negative reports in the local press, little money was raised here. Perhaps one had to live far away to respond to the appeal of this adventure.[60]

In January 1877, the expedition—led by Lieutenant J. Schouw Santvoort, who was in charge of the river survey, by D. D. Veth, the son of the Society's president, and by the zoologist J. F. Snelleman—was finally ready to depart.[61] Armed with a letter of recommendation to Nazaruddin from Van Ophuijsen the explorers set sail, with the Society's entire executive committee waving from the quayside.

Meanwhile, the purpose of the journey had been altered. In October 1876 the Society had scrapped Kerinci from the program "for the time being," at the urgent advice of the governor-general and the Minister. The plan was now to survey only those parts of the river Jambi that lay outside the range of the steam launch.[62] The reason for this curtailment, though it was not mentioned explicitly, was the Aceh

---

[57] See the recommendations in NA, Col., vb. May 24, 1875, no. 27.

[58] See NA, Col., vb. April 4, 1876, no. 40 (which refers to requests for support), June 1, 1876, no. 12 (Geographical Society's following questions), vb. June 24, 1876, no. 5 (offer of steamship); Minister of Colonies to President of Geographical Society, NA, Col., *minuut* vb. October 5, 1876, no. 32.

[59] Van Kan, *Nederlandsche expeditie*, pp. 15–16.

[60] Veth, *Midden-Sumatra*, 1: 9.

[61] "Veth was in Duitsland opgeleid als ingenieur en had twee jaar in Zwitserland gewerkt"; see Van der Velde, *Een Indische liefde*, p. 216.

[62] Governor-general to Minister of Colonies, August 6, 1876, NA, Col., vb. October 5, 1876, no. 32; Veth to Minister of Colonies, October 15, 1876, NA, Col., vb. October 18, 1876, no. 25. The explorers planned to visit the southern territory of the Padang uplands starting at Si Jujung opposite the border of Kerinci, Rankau di Baru, Pangkalan Jambi, Serampei, Sungei Tenang, Asei and Limun.

War, which was going badly for the Netherlands. Now that the Dutch were so unpopular in northern Sumatra, the people of Kerinci were unlikely to distinguish between private enterprise and the colonial government. To them, the expedition would appear nothing more or less than a reconnaissance mission.

REPERCUSSIONS IN THE EAST INDIES

Just the planning of an expedition had already had repercussions for Jambi, as it focused attention on this forgotten part of Sumatra. Once again, the response depended on one key individual, in this case A. Pruys van der Hoeven, Resident of Palembang since 1873. Pruys van der Hoeven was a man of action. The son of a Leiden professor, he had, after failing at school, worked his way up from cabin boy to Resident. When he secured this position in 1873 he already had a long career behind him as controller and Assistant Resident in various parts of western and southern Sumatra. He had distinguished himself in several military expeditions, including those to Rejang and Ampat Lawang (Palembang) in 1859. He had therefore been delighted with the appointment as Resident of Palembang, as it gave him an opportunity to complete "his work" in Bengkulu and the Lampongs, and to forge southern Sumatra into one whole. Combined with Jambi, Palembang would then make up the largest territory of the East Indies, larger in surface area even than Java.[63] From 1880 to 1883 Pruys would serve as governor of Aceh, after which he continued to help shape policy in the Outer Islands for ten years, as a member of the Council of the Dutch East Indies. One later governor-general described him as "thoroughly straightforward" but "unyielding and dogmatic" in his dedication to civil administration and to peace.[64] Doubts concerning the justification for the Dutch presence in the archipelago were alien to him; he ranked "a lack of faith in one's own power" among the colonial government's worst enemies.[65] These forceful opinions made him an enterprising administrator and an active empire builder.

With Van Ophuijsen it had been academic curiosity that drove him to visit Jambi; with Pruys van der Hoeven it was administrative zeal. The plans for the scientific expedition inspired him to undertake annual journeys to Jambi beginning in 1875, before which time no Dutch official had set foot in the region for six years. Other events too prompted the 1875 trip: a European soldier had been attacked, and Pangeran Wiro Kesumo was rumored to be trying to buy a steamship in Singapore. Since the outbreak of the Aceh War, Batavia was obsessed by the terrifying prospect of local dignitaries forging ties with Singapore. A year later, the rumor that Nazaruddin had ordered seven cannons in Singapore made Pruys decide to return to the region.[66]

---

[63] A. Pruys van der Hoeven, *Veertig jaren Indische dienst* (The Hague: Belinfante, 1894), pp. 211, 218.

[64] Maarten Kuitenbrouwer, *The Netherlands and the Rise of Modern Imperialism: Colonies and Foreign Policy 1870–1902* (New York: Berg, 1991), p. 165. "Pruys van der Hoeven," in *Encyclopaedie van Nederlandsch-Indië* (The Hague: Nijhoff; Leiden: Brill, 1921), 3: 516.

[65] "Pruys," p. 516.

[66] Resident of Palembang to governor-general, January 30, 1875, telegr., NA, Col., vb. May 24, 1875, no. 27; *minuut* vb. April 4, 1876, no. 40; Resident of Palembang to governor-general, March 31, 1875, NA, Col., vb. November 2, 1878, no. 7.

Residence of the sultan of Jambi at Dusun Tengah

from D. D. Veth, *Midden-Sumatra: Reizen en onderzoekingen der Sumatra-expeditie, uitgerust door het Aardrijkskundig Genootschap: Photographie-album* (Leiden: Brill, 1879); KITLV photograph collection 7142

Pruys was greatly relieved by his initial meetings. He had determined beforehand that he would not accept any excuse that the sultan was absent, nor would he agree to visit Nazaruddin rather than vice versa. To pay due respect to the Resident, as the representative of the highest authority, was the only way, he had decided, in which the Jambian court could meet its obligations. Nazaruddin responded affably to the admonitory hint in this direction. Although he had still not completed the house in Jambi that he had promised to build in 1869, he did at least come to the capital, where he met Pruys at the political agent's home in "a cordial if brief encounter." After this, Pruys returned the visit by meeting Nazaruddin first at Wiro Kesumo's home and later at Dusun Tengah. Like so many Dutch officials before him, he shook his head at the shabby surroundings in which he found himself. By European standards the sultan was poverty-stricken: he had asked to borrow chairs from the boat since he had no European furniture in his *pendopo*, an old bamboo shed thatched with atap. However, the talks had been conducted amicably enough. The sultan had promised to cooperate fully with the expedition, even offering the services of his son-in-law, Raden Hasan, as a guide. In addition, he had again pledged to comply with the contract's provisions on vaccination and slavery. This was something, although Pruys was not wholly satisfied. With the present indirect form of administration, matters would never be arranged as they should be. "Where the Dutch flag flies, a native ruler should not be entrusted with government. An Eastern ruler cannot comprehend such a combination; in his eyes, divided authority is no authority at all."[67]

Meanwhile, Nazaruddin could scarcely fail to notice a shift in Dutch policy. He had again been invited to settle in Jambi, and to make it more attractive for him to do so, he had been offered some European furniture for his new home. More important indications of the renewal of Dutch interest, however, were changes in the administrative structure and improved communication with Palembang. The garrison commander was relieved of his duties as political agent, which were given to a controller instead. This was because Pruys believed that a soldier would always be identified with the military expedition of 1858, and because as an officer, he could not leave the garrison. Controller C. A. Niesen was the first civilian administrator to be appointed political agent.

Furthermore, a steamship link had been opened up between Palembang and Jambi in 1877. "Given Singapore's attitude," Pruys thought it unfortunate that the connection between Jambi and Singapore was better than that between Jambi and Palembang. The steamboat belonging to the Dutch East Indies Steam Navigation Company (NISM) that would call at Jambi once a month brought it closer to Palembang.

All things considered, Pruys viewed his first journey as a success. True, the *pangeran ratu* had not put in an appearance, but on Pruys's second visit in March 1876, the sultan and *pangeran ratu* both met him in the capital. They prepared a warm reception for him in the sultan's still unfinished residence, for which their guest had brought some furniture. Sultan, *pangeran ratu*, and dignitaries signed the amended contract that had been discussed the previous year and talked about changes in the salt and opium monopolies.[68]

---

[67] Resident of Palembang to governor-general, March 31, 1876, NA, Col., vb. November 2, 1878, no. 7.

[68] Ibid.

Below the surface, however, political life in Jambi was anything but harmonious. Three months later (in June 1876) the *pangeran ratu*, Marta Ningrat, about whose obstructionist tactics Nazaruddin had complained the year before, suddenly tendered his resignation. According to Controller Niesen, he was regretting his decision of 1858 to forgo the sultan's title; besides, he no longer received his share of the government annuity of ten thousand guilders. Niesen advised against granting the request. An old sultan alongside a new one and an old *pangeran ratu* alongside a new one seemed to him too confusing.[69] Pruys saw the situation differently. He thought that Marta Ningrat, who had sunk in his esteem, had wanted to remain *pangeran ratu* in 1858 in order to preserve the status quo as much as possible. Only the Dutch flag flying at Jambi reminded the population of the change in the region's administration. Since Pruys's arrival at Palembang, however, the Dutch were insisting on closer adherence to the contract, generating friction between Nazaruddin and the *pangeran ratu*.[70]

This was certainly a more cogent analysis. Since Pruys was showing the face of the colonial government so clearly, and so often, he had become an attractive ally for Nazaruddin, who was gradually building up a power base rivaling that of Taha. That the sultan had the confidence to keep the entire ten thousand guilders he received from Batavia for himself reflected this increase in power.[71] Thus, the Dutch intervention had created two distinct centers in the Jambian power structure. Pruys's analysis, it should be said, relied heavily on the information he received from Nazaruddin. He said little about Wiro Kesumo, although in 1875 he had observed that the sultan and *pangeran ratu* left this powerful dignitary to manage all the affairs of the realm. Meanwhile, the *pangeran ratu's* request went unanswered. The expedition that got under way in 1877 would generate more than enough complications.

THE EXPEDITION

In April 1877, Schouw Santvoort embarked on a mission of his own: accompanied by a dignitary, four Malay servants, and a number of coolies, he traveled from Padang to the capital, Jambi. On his way he received a great deal of support from local village headmen. One headman protected him when he suddenly found himself menaced by an armed mob lining the river Jujuhan, a tributary of the Batang Hari he had to cross to reach the Jambian uplands. After that, Schouw Santvoort traveled as fast as possible and mainly at night in a

---

[69] Controller of Jambi to Resident of Palembang, June 16, 1876, and September 17, 1876, NA, Col., vb. November 2, 1878, no. 7. In September he reported that Pangeran Ratu Marta Ningrat had entered a reservation back in 1858 that had not been recorded. He had evidently repeated it in 1867. Now, he wanted to retire from worldly affairs and embark on a *haj*. His resignation was unrelated to salt or opium measures, according to the controller.

[70] Resident of Palembang to governor-general, June 30, 1876, NA, Col., vb. November 2, 1878, no. 7.

[71] Resident of Palembang to governor-general, July 18, 1879, NA, Col., vb. November 8, 1879, no. 18.

The Batang Hari outside Jambi with raft-houses and steamship in 1879
from D. D. Veth, *Midden-Sumatra: Reizen en onderzoekingen der Sumatra-expeditie, uitgerust door het Aardrijkskundig Genootschap: Photographie-album*; KITLV photograph collection 7128

Grave of Van Schouw Santvoort, Jambi
from D. D. Veth, *Midden-Sumatra: Reizen en onderzoekingen der Sumatra-expeditie, uitgerust door het Aardrijkskundig Genootschap: Photographie-album*; KITLV photograph collection 7131

covered proa, arriving in Jambi without encountering any further problems on April 18, 1877.[72] That he had managed to cross Sumatra safely, according to the wry congratulations of Controller Van Hasselt, was purely "thanks to the lack of interest you show in the land and the people of the areas you pass through."[73] Still, his journey yielded a rough map of Central Sumatra and delighted Governor-General Van Lansberge, who exclaimed that it had now been proven that such expeditions not only could benefit science but "above all could do a great deal to increase our political influence in the heart of Sumatra." He made available another twenty-thousand-guilder subsidy from the East Indies coffers for 1878.[74]

Still, Van Hasselt's skepticism was well founded. Schouw Santvoort's journey turned out to be counterproductive; it had precipitated the Jambian uplands into a state of alert. Tales spread all along the river about the *kapitan laut*, the sea captain. Nowhere was the explorer described as an honorable merchant, the disguise that the members of the expedition were to assume. The silver medal of merit given to the helpful village headman in token of Batavia's gratitude only served to confirm the direct link between the expedition and the Dutch authorities. Shortly afterward, rumors circulated that some of his party had been taken captive or even killed.[75]

Van Hasselt, Veth, and Snelleman found their hands were tied. The raja of independent Siguntur in the Padang uplands barred them from entering his territory. This made it impossible for them to ascertain whether the Batang Hari provided a suitable transportation route for the Ombilin coal. From another raja they heard that he would receive them only if they brought enough troops with them to guarantee their security. In August 1877 they therefore had to curtail their remaining travels to the Padang uplands. When Van Lansberge received reports in August and September 1877 about Taha having ordered barrages to be erected to block the progress of the Dutch, he issued instructions in October forbidding the travelers to continue their journey to Jambi.[76] They were not to cross the frontiers of the territory under Dutch control. The garrison at Jambi was brought up to full strength. In November, rumors spread of unrest in Jambi.

Meanwhile, Schouw Santvoort had started making preparations in Jambi for the river survey. However, it would not be until the rainy season, in December, that the waters of the Batang Hari would swell enough to permit a journey upstream. He explored the lower reaches of the Tungkal and Batang Hari and met with Nazaruddin. In the night of November 22, however, he suddenly fell ill; he died a few hours later and was buried in Jambi. There were no indications of foul play.[77]

Now the expedition came to a complete halt. In December, the three members of the land survey team returned to Padang from their trips in the region under direct Dutch control. Snelleman was recalled to the Netherlands in January 1878 in

---

[72] For an account of his journey, see *Tijdschrift Aardrijkskundig Genootschap* 3 (1879), supp. vol. 1, pt. 2, pp. 12–28; Veth, *Midden-Sumatra*, vol. 1, pt. 1, pp. 54–80; for a *syair* of his journey, see Museum Pusat Jakarta, collection Bataviaasch Genootschap CDLXVII 467.

[73] Veth, *Midden-Sumatra* vol. 1, pt. 2, p. 5.

[74] Governor-general to Minister of Colonies, July 14, 1877, NA, Col., vb. November 21, 1877, no. 21.

[75] Veth, *Midden-Sumatra*, vol. 1, pt. 2, pp. 8–9.

[76] NA, Col., *minuut* vb. November 21, 1877, no. 21.

[77] Veth, *Midden-Sumatra*, vol. 1, pt. 1, p. 266.

a round of financial cuts. Van Hasselt and Veth would find work to do in the Limun region bordering on the Rawas, the area between the Residency of Palembang and the Muara Tembesi.

THE RESIDENT TAKES ACTION

In December 1877, Pruys van der Hoeven resolved the impasse with an unexpected initiative. After Schouw Santvoort's death he had gone to Jambi, and then straight on to Dusun Tengah, where Sultan Nazaruddin had his residence. The sultan was out fishing at a nearby lake when the Resident arrived, but received him cordially upon returning home. He explained, "When the captains were in Jambi, I did not entirely understand the government's intentions. Since the controller gentleman has been here, however, all is clear, and we are in agreement. We shall deal with the business to be done together."[78]

Encouraged by these words, Pruys submitted to Governor-General Van Lansberge a surprising proposal that the latter warmly endorsed, and that would also be read with interest in The Hague. He wanted to sail up the Batang Hari in February 1878, together with Nazaruddin, and meet with Taha. Furthermore, he wished to "resolve the question of whether the Batang Hari can be used for the transportation of Ombilin coal."[79] Thus, Pruys basically took over the expedition himself, together with all the credit for it. For him, it was a stroke of good fortune that the competition had melted away. Schouw Santvoort's successor, C. F. Cornelissen, would not set sail from the Netherlands until February. Meanwhile, the instruments for the expedition and the navigating officer were at Pruys's disposal. "Anything the scientists can do, I can do better," he appears to have thought. Indeed, he could do better. For his journey would have three distinct goals: besides investigating the navigability of the Batang Hari and learning more about the situation in the interior, he would also be consolidating Dutch influence. No mere scientific expedition would have been able to extend its wings to such political and administrative breadths. Pruys blithely disregarded the earlier ban on operating outside the territory under direct Dutch rule. He wanted to see how far he could get, and possibly to sail beyond Jambi's borders.

For Pruys, his journey of February 1878 was an unqualified success. In the event he traveled without Nazaruddin, who had fallen out with Taha and stayed at home. So Pruys did not meet with the former sultan either. Still, for the first time, a Dutch steamship had penetrated to Jambi's borders at the *dusun* Tanjung Semelidu, a journey of thirty-six hours from the borders of western Sumatra and within cannon range of the turbulent Siguntur. He determined that the four- to five-foot-deep Batang Hari would accommodate cargoes of Ombilin coal transported in boats of one-foot draft, although a fresh survey needed to be done in the event of a drought. He had not seen any sign of Dutch sentiments on his travels. But because of the sultan's weakness, expanding the territory in Jambi and subjugating Taha by

---

[78] Resident of Palembang to governor-general, December 21, 1877, NA, Col., vb. November 2, 1878, no. 7.

[79] Ibid.

The bank of the Batang Hari outside Jambi, with the homes of Europeans and raft-houses in 1879 from D. D. Veth, *Midden-Sumatra: Reizen en onderzoekingen der Sumatra-expeditie, uitgerust door het Aardrijkskundig Genootschap: Photographie-album;* KITLV photograph collection 7129

establishing a base on the Tabir should now have top priority. In his view, the population yearned to shake off the yoke of this unloved former sultan. We shall look closely at his proposals in due course.[80]

Meanwhile, the Geographical Society's expedition had gained a new lease on life. The plan was that the "land survey group" (Van Hasselt and Veth) would set off from the Rawas and journey by way of the Limun to Sarolangun on the Tembesi, where they would meet the "river survey group" (Cornelissen, Jambi's political agent Niesen, and Raden Hasan). The river group had explored the Batang Hari beforehand, going beyond the Tebo estuary (June 19 to July 4, 1878); only upstream from Muara Tebo had the population appeared hostile.[81] The journey up the Tembesi, however, proved more of a challenge. A few miles before Sarolangun, in the area controlled by Pangeran Kusin, the entire male population of a *dusun* had turned out, ready to attack. Cornelissen and Niesen returned empty-handed to Jambi, where they learned that the land team too had failed to reach Sarolangun. The men had traveled by way of Batavia and Palembang, arriving in Surulangun, the capital of the Rawas, at the beginning of April. Here they had made contact with the headman Datuk Payung Putih ("*datuk* with the white parasol"), whom Nazaruddin had recently appointed to oversee the troika that was customary under adat (*datuk nan bertigo*). However, two of the three places in the troika were vacant, and the third, just appointed, was the headman's own son. Furthermore, Payung Putih had intervened successfully to persuade Nazaruddin to appoint his brother-in-law *demang*. Thus, with Nazaruddin's support, Payung Putih had expanded his power base. This usurpation of power, added to the fact that he had repudiated his wife, had given him many enemies. Thus, he was not the most reliable of allies. The headmen of the Limun objected to the *Blandas* (Dutch) undertaking this journey, and after several incidents, Van Hasselt and Veth decided to turn back.[82] So this part of the expedition, too, had miscarried. Shortly afterward the group disbanded. Over the next few years, the Society published its findings in four large volumes and many smaller ones, but its subsequent applications for permission for expeditions to Borneo (1882), New Guinea (1885), and the Aru and Obi Islands (1887) were all turned down. The only expeditions it was allowed to carry out were those to the Kei Islands (1887), Flores (1888), and New Guinea (1903)—unexplored regions that were either of little significance to the process of empire building (Kei Islands and Flores) or were already incorporated into it (New Guinea).[83] As a colonial lobby, the Society would exert limited influence on Dutch imperialism; at most, it expressed the existing ideology and propagated it in its own small circle.

---

[80] Resident of Palembang to governor-general, March 15, 1878, and report of the survey of the river Batang Hari as far as Jambi's western border near the *dusun* Tanjong, NA, Col., vb. November 2, 1878, no. 7.

[81] Veth, *Midden-Sumatra*, vol. 1, pt. 2, pp. 147–66.

[82] Ibid., pp. 167–244.

[83] Carla de Wildt, "Impulsen tot het moderne imperialisme. De invloed van het Koninklijk Nederlands Aardrijkskundig Genootschap op het Nederlandse koloniaal beleid, 1873–1903" (Department of History, Utrecht University, 1991, unpublished).

POLICY IN BATAVIA

Even an abortive expedition can have consequences. The unrest it had generated, in particular, had impressed upon the colonial authorities how little they knew about Jambi and how little power they could exert there. In response, they adopted a dual strategy. On the one hand, they renewed their efforts to contact Taha and to push through a reconciliation that would achieve his subjugation. On the other hand, they pursued a hard line, ranging from plans to expand the number of administrative posts to preparations for a military expedition. That these two approaches might be at variance with one another was at first unclear.

After his journey of February 1878, Pruys wrote a detailed analysis and made several concrete proposals encompassing both of these policies. He wanted to end Taha's power for good by arranging a "reconciliation," which basically meant compelling Taha to accept subjugation on mild terms. In addition, he advocated giving Nazaruddin more support and removing the *pangeran ratu* from office. The latter should be interned at Telok Puan, he proposed, and would have to obtain the political agent's permission to leave his home.

Pruys's second plan was to expand Dutch authority: this meant installing an Assistant Resident (Niesen) in the capital and a controller at a new post in the uplands, to be established near Pangeran Ratu Marta Ningrat at Telok Puan, near Taha, or near a representative of Nazaruddin. Third, Pruys wanted restrictions placed on debt slavery, the aim being to weaken the power of the elite. Although these debt slaves had been procured in a form of criminal procedure recognized under Jambian law, he considered their status incompatible with article 15 of the contract, which forbade the abduction of human beings.[84]

Pruys had been shocked to discover the powerlessness of the Jambian rulers and the autonomy of the population under the headmen of their own kampongs. The sultan had little control over them. Thus, in 1858, the battle had been fought solely by the sultans, their kinsmen, and their debt slaves. In itself, this analysis corresponds to what we now know of the Malay sultanate as an organizational structure. However, in his conclusions, Pruys went much too far. Reasoning from his own Western concept of power and the exercise of power, he found this loosely knit and fluid structure entirely alien. If the raja (Taha) had no direct control of the kampongs, and ruled only over his debt slaves, this meant, according to Pruys's logic, that he must be hated. That is what he wanted to hear, and what he was indeed told, against the grain of Van Ophuijsen's earlier reports. And so he described Taha as "feared for his stern appearance, his imposing height, and his ruthlessness" and reported that he imposed heavy taxes on products from the regions above the Tabir.[85]

Pruys's drastic proposals—to subjugate Taha, remove the *pangeran ratu* from office, expand Dutch authority, and clamp down on debt slavery—aroused mixed reactions in Batavia, provoking a conflict between the Council of the Dutch East Indies and Governor-General Van Lansberge. The Council's members were far from convinced that the population was "eagerly awaiting our arrival." The fact that Jambi was poorly governed did not pose an immediate threat to Dutch power on

---

[84] Resident of Palembang to governor-general, March 31, 1873, NA, Col., vb. November 2, 1878, no. 7.

[85] Ibid.

Sumatra. European interference, while it would certainly mean better government, would also mean greater expense and more expeditions. The Aceh War then raging made it impossible to commit forces elsewhere. As for abolishing debt slavery, the Council saw it as completely impossible, and even thought it unwise, given Batavia's limited sphere of influence. Who would actually have to count the debt slaves, determine their value, and discuss the appropriate reimbursement with their Jambian owners? The Council was more realistic than Pruys, and all it gave him was a riverboat to improve communications.[86] It rejected the plans to expand the responsibilities of the Dutch administration and to unseat the *pangeran ratu*, who would undoubtedly respond by joining forces with Taha.

In Van Lansberge, on the other hand, Pruys found a highly placed and enthusiastic ally. The governor-general had heard the Council and subsequently complied with his responsibilities under the Government Regulations of 1854, but he did not have to follow the Council's recommendations. He therefore presented Pruys's proposals, virtually unrevised, to the Minister. He also repeated the "colonial myth": "It is indisputable that the sultan and his people have no more ardent desire than to be freed from the oppression of unlawful authority," he assured his superior.[87]

The Hague's response was equivocal. In November 1878, the Minister of Colonies, P. P. van Bosse (1877–79), recommended that the plan be worked out in greater detail. It had "his full sympathy," although the *pangeran ratu*, who had been described in such glowing terms in previous reports, should be granted an annuity if removed from office.[88] At the end of April 1879, however, his successor, O. van Rees (March–August 1879) took a very different view. With one eye on the treasury, he stated his opposition to "any not completely unavoidable expansion of Dutch rule in the Outer Islands" until the Aceh War was over.[89] November 1879 brought another U-turn, as W. van Goltstein returned to serve a second term as Minister (1879–82). Given the failure to achieve a rapprochement with Taha and reports of unrest, he now favored an expansion of Dutch control in Jambi and asked for further information. Precisely because of the events in Aceh, he thought it wise to expand Dutch influence, by peaceful means, in the central region between the east and west coasts of Sumatra.[90] He was unquestionably influenced by favorable reports from the front in Aceh. The ministerial game of musical chairs was hardly conducive to consistency of policy in Batavia, Palembang, or Jambi. Meanwhile, the Dutch officials in the East Indies carried on forming their own views and devising their own policies.

A MILITARY EXPEDITION?

The geographical expedition had galvanized the sultanate. The Limun was still restless: a power struggle was going on there between Datuk Payung Putih, the headman supported by Nazaruddin, and Pangeran Kusin, a later son-in-law of Taha. In August 1878 there was an attack on the controller's residence in the

---

[86] Council of the Dutch East Indies, May 17, 1878, no. 8, NA, Col., vb. November 2, 1878, no. 7.

[87] Governor-general to Minister of Colonies, July 7, 1878, NA, Col., vb. November 2, 1878, no. 7.

[88] *Minuut* vb. November 2, 1878, no 7, NA, Col., vb. November 2, 1878, no. 7.

[89] *Minuut* vb. April 22, 1879, no. 6, NA, Col., vb. April 22, 1879, no. 6.

[90] *Minuut* vb. November 8, 1879, no. 18, NA, Col., vb. November 8, 1879, no. 18.

Rawas. In 1878–79 Nazaruddin asked for support to strengthen his position, invoking a pledge to this effect in the contract. Batavia refused to grant his request, even though Pruys defended it. The Resident also favored a plan to detach an entire company of soldiers (150 men) to the Tabir.[91]

At the same time, the first attempts were made to cajole Taha into accepting subjection to the Dutch authorities on mild terms. In March 1879, Pruys suggested pardoning him and giving him an annuity of three thousand guilders if he would agree to settle near the capital. The *pangeran ratu*, Taha's elder brother Pangeran Surio, and subsequently Pangeran Puspo Ali, head of the *suku* Perban of the Merangin, all visited Taha in the first half of 1879.[92] When even the last of these envoys had failed to achieve anything, it was the turn of an Arab from Palembang, Sheikh Abdullah bin Abubakar, whose daughter was married to a son of Taha's uncle, Abdulla bin Murah. This kinship by marriage gave him political access to Taha.[93] In December 1879 he visited Taha five times, though without explaining the purpose of his visits. He did attempt a veiled allusion to his real intentions, but this merely provoked a fierce response from Taha: Why should he accept a reconciliation? The governor-general had called him his child, but you do not beat your child or turn your great guns upon him. Now he was poor, but he was free. Were he to build a good house, one that kept out the rain, the Dutch would simply set fire to it the next time the occasion arose.[94] He wanted nothing to do with the colonial authorities. The whole of the Tabir region had prepared its defenses. Sheikh Abdullah reported that the trunks of all the highest trees had been notched to one-third of their thickness, so that they could be felled for defense at very short notice. Every steamboat that appeared on the Batang Hari was seen as proof of an impending military expedition. In short, these initial attempts to persuade Taha to adopt a milder position were a complete failure.

In Palembang as well as in The Hague, a change of the guard had ushered in a fresh approach. In the spring of 1879, Pruys van der Hoeven was appointed in Aceh, being succeeded in Palembang by P. F. Laging Tobias, former Assistant Resident of Bengkulu. At first, Laging Tobias reiterated his predecessor's demands for an expedition to quell the unrest and a reconciliation with Taha, although he considered Nazaruddin unreliable and saw the *pangeran ratu* as a more trustworthy intermediary. After all, he reasoned, the *pangeran ratu* was Taha's kinsman by marriage through two of his sons. Yet in February 1880 Laging Tobias expressed serious reservations to Van Goltstein's request for further information in light of a possible expansion of Dutch rule. He met with Van Lansberge specifically to discuss this issue and persuaded the governor-general that it was "too late" for the military option. True, all the attempts to placate Taha had failed to date, but the situation nonetheless seemed calmer than before. A Bengkulu

---

[91] Memorandum A3; Resident of Palembang to governor-general January 16, 1879, commander of army February 2, 1879, all in NA, Col., vb. April 22, 1879, no. 6. The commander rejected the latter plan in February 1879, because an isolated military base would be a permanent liability.

[92] See Resident of Palembang to governor-general March 8, 1879, March 23, 1879, and April 16, 1879; political agent to Resident of Palembang April 13, 1879, all in NA, Col., vb. November 8, 1879, no. 18.

[93] Resident of Palembang to governor-general, July 18, 1879, and January 30, 1880, NA, Col., vb. June 19, 1880, no. 10.

[94] Resident of Palembang to governor-general, January 29, 1880, NA, Col., vb. June 19, 1880, no. 10.

man long wanted by the authorities had been handed over, a son-in-law of Taha had recompensed the Dutch for the attack in the Rawas, and the headmen of Limun had agreed to accept the power of Payung Putih. Taha was not the hated despot of the uplands that Pruys had described, but on the contrary much loved by the people. There was by now plenty of evidence that he would not accept a Dutch post being established on the Tabir or in the upper reaches of the Batang Hari. He was busy strengthening his defenses through Indragiri. Even if he decided against attacking, the advent of a Dutch post would certainly trigger a form of guerrilla warfare in his territory. Ultimately, direct Dutch rule of Sumatra was the only solution, but for the time being Laging Tobias advocated abstention and reconciliation with Taha by peaceful means.[95]

This settled the matter. Van Lansberge was completely won over, and indeed went further still. No more overtures should be made to Taha. Taha might become afraid, or gain an exaggerated impression of his own importance. All this nagging was bad for the colonial government's prestige. After all, Taha was a rebel against Batavia's authority who had already been overthrown. If he truly wanted a rapprochement, he would doubtless say so. For the time being it was best to await further developments. It was this decision of April 28, 1880, that formalized the policy on Jambi that was to be followed for the time being.[96] Minister Van Goltstein resigned himself to it. He could scarcely oppose recommendations adopted unanimously by the Resident, the Council of the Dutch East Indies, and the governor-general.[97] From 1880 until the late 1890s, The Hague seemed to lose interest in Jambi, and decisions about the region were no longer taken at this high level.

In July 1880, Laging Tobias visited Jambi, and now advocated the use of force after all, provided the situation in Aceh did not prevent it, since the trouble in the Limun had still not been resolved. "Eventually we shall have to bring the whole of Sumatra under direct rule," he repeated.[98] But the Council of the Dutch East Indies urged moderation, as always, and Van Lansberge decided in August to "continue the existing policy while devoting most attention to Jambian affairs." He did want to be given the resources, however, to guarantee the success of any future show of force.[99] Thus, in December 1880, in the greatest of secrecy, an infantry captain was attached to the military staff in Palembang to explore the scope for an expedition.[100] His detailed report of December 1881 referred to an expedition as a remote possibility but stated that there was certainly no immediate need for one.

---

[95] The Arab envoy from Palembang reported that Taha exchanged the proceeds from forest products for gold from Kerinci via the Merangin (Pangeran Puspo Ali's territory) and then used the gold to purchase arms from Indragiri (Resident of Palembang to governor-general, January 29, 1880, NA, Col., vb. June 19, 1880, no. 10).

[96] *Gouvernementsbesluit*, April 28, 1880, no. 1, NA, Col., vb. June 19, 1880, no. 10.

[97] *Minuut* vb. June 19, 1880, no. 10, NA, Col.

[98] See the recommendations in NA, Col., vb. May 24, 1875, no. 27; NA, Col., mr. 1880/659 secret.

[99] See the recommendations in NA, Col., vb. May 24, 1875, no. 27; July 17, 1880, mr. 1880/615 secret; see the recommendations in NA, Col., vb. May 24,1875, no. 27; July 20, 1880; advisory report of Council of the Dutch East Indies, August 6, 1880, no. 10; *gouvernementsbesluit*, August 10, 1880, A IX top secret, all in mr. 1880/659 secret.

[100] General secretary to commander of army, December 2, 1880, NA, Col., vb. October 20, 1881, no. 10. This was prompted by an incident in which a *dusun* in the Rawas came under fire and by a theft of arms from the controller's house in Jambi.

He did, however, recommend "covert" preparations in the form of small fortresses at the estuaries of the Batang Hari's tributaries, to be manned by a total of 150 men. The commander of the army submitted the report along with a letter lavishing praise on it but at the same time made it clear that he himself could not spare so many men. And that, for the time being, was the very last word about a military expedition, as a sequel to the geographical survey of 1878.[101]

REPERCUSSIONS IN JAMBI

While in Batavia everything remained as before, the temporary upsurge of scientific and administrative interest left its mark on Jambi itself in numerous ways. Nazaruddin had consolidated his position. He had been able to appoint one of his protégés, Datuk Payung Putih, as headman in the Limun, Taha's territory, and he had stood up to the *pangeran ratu*, Marta Ningrat. But he had not been able to guarantee the expedition a safe passage. He had sensibly decided against antagonizing Taha and had therefore not accompanied Pruys on his journey. In 1877 and 1878 reports were received of frequent meetings at Taha's residence involving men close to Nazaruddin, who was also said to have sent Taha many weapons and other gifts.[102] Clearly, the sultan had not put all his eggs in the Batavian basket, and justifiably so. His requests of 1878 and 1879 for a show of force had not been granted; the most he had received was moral support. With the advent of a new Resident in June 1879, his prosperous days had come to an end.[103] In July 1880 he was deprived of his opium monopoly, which was clear evidence that the Dutch were willing to support neither him nor his deputy, Wiro Kesumo. The latter, too, had fallen on leaner times. Since the advent of Controller Niesen in 1875, the colonial authorities had tried to do business with the *pangeran ratu* or the sultan himself wherever possible, and Wiro Kesumo had been pushed into the background.[104]

The main beneficiary of these developments was Taha. This was underscored by the formal request of the *pangeran ratu*, Marta Ningrat, to be relieved of his duties in 1876, when Batavia came out openly in support of Nazaruddin. He remained loyal to Taha. In December 1877 he withdrew this request, but two months later he submitted it again to Pruys. The Resident was delighted, as it suited his policy perfectly. When Laging Tobias took over, however, Marta Ningrat changed his mind again; as the new cornerstone of Laging Tobias's reconciliation policy, he had every reason to stay. In 1879 Taha had arranged marriages—the traditional vehicle of political alliance—between his two daughters and Marta Ningrat's sons.[105]

Some of the Jambian elite who were loyal to Taha now made themselves heard for the first time: one was Taha's cousin Pangeran Kusin, a village headman in the

---

[101] Commander of army to governor-general, December 6, 1881, with appendices (Otken Report), NA, Col., mr. 1882/27.

[102] Otken Report, December 6, 1881, NA, Col., mr. 1881/27.

[103] Memorandum A3, NA, Col., vb. April 22, 1879, no. 6; Resident of Palembang to governor-general, telegr. August 25, 1879, NA, Col., vb. November 8, 1879, no. 18.

[104] Resident of Palembang to governor-general, July 18, 1879, NA, Col., July 19, 1880, no. 10.

[105] Resident of Palembang to governor-general, November 5, 1879, NA, Col., vb. January 30, 1880, no. 7. Only one son is mentioned in sources for the genealogy of the *suku* Kraton (appendix 1).

Tembesi, who was behind the attacks in the Rawas and the insurgency in the Limun. The report of December 1881 described him as "a very unpretentious man in his prime, neither an opium smoker nor a brutish fighter." He too had married one of Taha's daughters in 1881.[106] Interestingly, the report constantly referred to Batavia's opponents as men of high moral character and to the headmen clamoring for the Dutch to take control as unreliable.

Pangeran Puspo Ali, head of the *suku* Perban, who had made a seemingly serious attempt at mediation in 1879, also sided with Taha, a fact of which the Dutch were apparently unaware. He controlled the Merangin, one of the most important parts of the Jambian realm. Though no longer young, he was still vigorous and in good health, and he had played a major role in the defense of the capital in 1858. Taha regarded him as his right-hand man in these troubled years. Because he had taken over the sultan's supremacy in Kerinci, he wielded considerable influence. He possessed the sultan's power of arbitration, and could therefore mediate in important disputes in the region.[107] He was important to Taha not only because he possessed considerable wealth but also because his region controlled the access routes to Kerinci; through him Taha could obtain gold in exchange for forest products, gold that was indispensable to purchase weapons.[108] That the Dutch placed their hopes in this intermediary in 1879–80 shows on the one hand how little they understood of the situation in Jambi, and on the other hand the extent to which Taha could exploit their policy to his own advantage. All in all, the Residents found the balance of power in the region fairly inscrutable; the complexities of the existing constellation served as a perfect smoke screen.

The mounting Muslim opposition also reflected Taha's greater influence. The unrest created by the geographical expedition and the rumors of a military sequel led to a series of minor acts of revolt from 1878 onwards. Each of them proved to have arisen in Muslim circles, recalling the white-robed assailants who had been causing trouble sporadically since 1860.[109] The geographical expedition had also run into Muslim rebels: Cornelissen's river survey team, for instance, was held up on the Muara Tebo on Friday, June 8, 1878, by armed men wielding *klewang* who had followed the Dutchmen along the dry banks. The day of the week was not without significance, as mosques were often used for discussions of village affairs after Friday prayers. A little later, on the Tembesi, the entire male population had gathered at the mosque, bearing arms, and several hajis dressed in white assumed leadership.[110] The attack on the Controller's residence in the Rawas, in August 1878, had been led by an imam.[111] In November that year, a man from the Limun led an attack on members of the expedition, crying "la iláha ill'Allah." (None has the right to be worshiped but Allah). He later claimed to have been following Taha's orders.[112] Two days later came a second attack on two European sailors who had

---

[106] Otken Report, December 6, 1881, NA, Col., mr. 1882/27.

[107] Ibid.

[108] Resident of Palembang to governor-general, January 29, 1880, NA, Col., vb. June 19, 1880, no. 10.

[109] Once a year in 1860, 1861, 1872, 1873, and 1874 (see *Koloniaal Verslag* for these years).

[110] Veth, *Midden-Sumatra*, vol. 1, pt. 2, pp. 163, 193–94; see also J. M. Gullick, *Indigenous Political Systems of Western Malaya*, 2nd ed. (London: London School of Economics, 1965).

[111] Memorandum A3, NA, Col., vb. November 2, 1878, no. 7.

[112] Veth, *Midden-Sumatra*, vol. 1, pt. 2, pp. 230–33.

taken part in the expedition. This attack too was accompanied by the battle cry associated with holy war; the perpetrator confessed that Taha had given him white clothes and ordered him to kill as many Europeans as possible to redeem a debt.[113]

This Muslim resistance continued over the next few years. In July 1879 a rebel apprehended in Palembang stated that he had attended classes on *perang sabil*, or holy war, at Taha's own residence. Others too were preparing to kill Europeans, but they had not yet finished their training.[114] In November a white-garbed man from the Upper Tembesi was arrested. Armed with a klewang, a dagger, and prayer beads hidden in a bamboo case, he had drifted downstream in a leaky old sampan. He told his captors that more of his companions were on the way. It seems that Taha was still summoning headmen and people from the uplands and making them swear oaths and drink water that had been poured over a Koran. The content of these oaths was unknown.[115] In August 1880, Surulangun in the Rawas came under fire from eight Jambians who had a large number of Islamic objects with them. That same year, two hajis were sentenced to three or five years' forced labor for inciting the population to prepare for holy war, to be triggered if the Dutch made war on Jambi.[116] Later attacks in Jambi too were carried out by men in white garments shouting the Muslim battle cry. Although these were all small and separate incidents, they aroused considerable unease among the European administration and population about "Mohammedan fanaticism." This unease grew when an Arab-led plot was uncovered in Palembang in the summer of 1881, and family ties suggested a link with Singapore. There were rumors that all Europeans were to be murdered during Ramadan, the Muslim fasting period.[117] This conspiracy sowed great alarm and would often be mentioned in letters from Palembang in later years.

The confessions revealed that Taha, as the leader of the resistance, was using Islam as a countervailing force—as the banner under which to marshal and organize mass resistance against the Dutch. Whether he accomplished this Islamization by invoking the status within the faith that was traditionally associated with a raja[118] or simply by politicizing the existing opposition between Islam and Christianity is unclear for lack of evidence. The confessions reveal that he often ordered debt slaves or other debtors to carry out attacks in the name of Islam, which is suggestive of the latter explanation. Whatever the case may be, Islam certainly played a role in Taha's struggle against the colonial authorities. In this respect, Taha was no exception to a general rule in the archipelago; Islam played a similar part in Aceh and in the peasant revolts on Java.

---

[113] Kessler to Minister of Colonies, August 22, 1879, NA, Col., vb. August 28, 1879, no. 38. See also the recommendations in NA, Col., vb. May 24, 1875, no. 27.

[114] Resident of Palembang to governor-general, July 23, 1879, NA, Col., vb. June 19, 1880, no. 10.

[115] Political agent to Resident of Palembang, October 13, 1879, NA, Col., vb. June 19, 1880, no. 10.

[116] Resident of Palembang to governor-general, August 16, 1880, and August 20, 1880, mr. 1881/702 secret.

[117] Resident of Palembang to governor-general, September 23, 1881, NA, Col., mr. 1881/884.

[118] A. C. Milner, *Kerajaan: Malay Political Culture on the Eve of Colonial Rule* (Tucson: University of Arizona Press, 1982).

Not all protests were inspired by Islam, however. In November 1880, thirty rifles were stolen from the Dutch fortress in Jambi. The presumed culprit, Raden Anom, a member of the *suku* Kraton, escaped to the uplands in December 1880, after which the sultan's court refused to hand him over. Batavia was incensed, especially since Raden Anom was also suspected of having stolen money from Muara Kompeh and from evading import duties. Niesen, the political agent, dearly wanted to make an example of the miscreant, but it simply could not be done. Raden Anom should probably be seen as a maverick operator, an independent *anak raja* whose high birth gave him a certain immunity. In the eyes of the authorities, however, it was one of many incidents proving that the contract was not being duly observed.[119] The efforts to have Raden Anom taken into custody lingered on into the 1890s.

REVIEW AND CONCLUSIONS

Reviewing the entire period from 1860 to 1880, it is clear that Dutch policy in Jambi heavily depended on who held office as Resident of Palembang. Van Ophuijsen and Pruys van der Hoeven determined the course of events, and Laging Tobias virtually imposed the eventual policy of abstention. The distance between Batavia and The Hague and the resulting ignorance of politicians in the mother country continued to leave the colonial administrators considerable scope to shape policy.

Quests for knowledge could have very different political consequences, ranging from Van Ophuijsen's campaign to restore confidence to the tough approach launched later in the wake of the Geographical Society's expedition. The first expedition of the newly founded Society to Central Sumatra in 1877–79 proves, however, that in this case it was not scholarly interest as such that led to expansion but the political imbroglios surrounding it. True, the discourse of the Geographical Society's leaders resounded with nationalist and imperialist motifs, but its rhetoric was not what moved the colonial government to take action. Only when the Dutch officials sought closer ties with Jambi and digested the response did they start preparing for military intervention. The expedition had dispelled Batavia's illusions and shed light on the true balance of political power in the region. In this sense, quests for knowledge had a politicizing impact and were not so much a causative factor as a catalyst in the imperialist thrust.

Nonetheless, aside from improved communications with Palembang, the situation in Jambi remained fairly static. This was largely because of the Aceh War. On the one hand, the war can be seen as the beginning of the Netherlands' modern imperialism, since motives such as fear of foreign rivals and economic expectations (associated with the plantations in the south) that inspired imperialism elsewhere were also in evidence here.[120] On the other hand, the Aceh War was a "false start," in that it produced an immediate backlash that actually curtailed Dutch expansion.[121] The Aceh War hence had a Janus-like quality to it: it both represented imperialism and militated against it. From 1875 to 1877 this

---

[119] See documents in NA, Col., mr. 1881/33 and 1881/68.

[120] Kuitenbrouwer, *The Netherlands and Imperialism*, pp. 88–101. Van 't Veer, *Atjeh-oorlog*, pp. 70, 228–29.

[121] Kuitenbrouwer, *The Netherlands and Imperialism*, p. 333.

Sultan Achmad Nazaruddin (1858–1881) in 1879

from D. D. Veth, *Midden-Sumatra: Reizen en onderzoekingen der Sumatra-expeditie, uitgerust door het Aardrijkskundig Genootschap: Photographie-album;* KITLV photograph collection 7074

grueling conflict was such a drain on the Dutch treasury as to negate and reverse the profits from the archipelago. From then on, local officials seeking additional administrative resources or consent to expand the territory under Dutch control—in Borneo and New Guinea, for instance—generally found their requests turned down. A shortage of money and soldiers, added to a fear of fueling a second "Aceh" on Sumatra, made the colonial government decide, after prolonged deliberation, to abandon plans for military and administrative intervention in Jambi. As in previous years, this was simply part of general policy on the Outer Islands. Events in Jambi would continue to be determined by the war in Aceh.

It is interesting to reflect on what might have happened if the Dutch had been victorious in Aceh after, say, six months of fighting. Would Resident Pruys, seeking consent for expansion in the late 1870s, have found Batavia and The Hague more amenable? Yes, very probably, given the Ministry's constant volte-faces between 1878 and 1880. Two of the three Ministers who replaced one another in rapid succession were initially interested in plans for further expansion. Eventually, the colonial government's decision to embrace "abstention," as urged by Resident Laging Tobias and the Council of the Dutch East Indies, proved decisive. The Hague was a passive onlooker; it was Batavia, once again, that had determined policy.

Many of the reasons advanced—unsuccessfully, as it turned out—by those who wanted to expand Dutch control were the textbook arguments of imperialism: economic and administrative to begin with, and later "ethical" arguments citing the need to protect the population. For the first time, Jambi had attracted economic interest. The need to explore the navigability of the Batang Hari to transport Ombilin coal had been a key argument in the decision-making process, for Pruys as well as for the organizers of the expedition. However, it had gradually vanished into the background (partly because other transportation routes were found, and partly because Jambi turned out to be less peaceable than anticipated), to be replaced by an administrative argument: it was important to strengthen Batavia's authority in the unstable region of Jambi, and to expand its influence throughout Sumatra. Economic and scientific arguments alike had been politicized, creating political problems that only political, administrative, or military decisions could resolve. On the administrative argument, Resident Pruys, Governor-General Van Lansberge, and two of the three Ministers in The Hague were in agreement. To reinforce his plea for military action, Pruys had added the "ethical" argument, according to which the population yearned to be rid of Taha, of whom they were terrified; only then would they be open to development. Van Lansberge had imbibed and transmitted this colonial ethical myth, though The Hague had not elaborated it further. Was it too soon, or would this myth be raised only as a means of justifying military action, as happened later on? Whatever the case may be, if action had been taken in Jambi on the basis of these three arguments, it would certainly have been a prime example of modern imperialism. That this did not happen was wholly attributable to the war in Aceh.

For the people of Jambi, the main result of the geographical expedition was unrest in the sultanate, generated by rumors of an imminent military expedition.[122]

---

[122] Thus the soldier Otken, ordered to investigate Jambi at the end of 1880 in preparation for a possible expedition, was nicknamed "tukan teken Jambi" (Jambi's cartographer). The purpose of his visit leaked out in spite of orders urging secrecy (Otken Report, December 6, 1881, NA, Col., mr. 1882/27).

The rumors put Jambi on the defensive. As long as the expedition failed to materialize, Taha could retain and consolidate his influence. What did he have to gain from a reconciliation with the colonial government that would simply mean accepting subjugation? Not much. The terms he was being asked to consider were hardly attractive—to quit the uplands in return for an annuity. Undoubtedly, it was in his interests to maintain the status quo. Batavia appeared not to notice Taha's growing power base. The colonial archives contain no analyses pointing at this conclusion; all we find are brief fragments that can be construed, retrospectively, as a pattern. For the colonial authorities it was simply "business as usual" after 1880, as if there was not a cloud in the sky; they continued to hope for a reconciliation and Taha's subjugation. For the Jambian sultanate this meant that nothing changed: Batavia's long policy of seeking a rapprochement with Taha—which it had tried to accomplish in diverse ways since 1860 without ever achieving the desired result, Taha's subjection—continued to dominate relations between the colonial government and the sultanate for decades.

CHAPTER SEVEN

RITUAL DANCES (1882–1895)

Relations between the colonial authorities and the sultan's administration changed little in the 1880s and early 1890s. They can best be illustrated, in this period of the Netherlands' "reluctant imperialism," by looking at the rituals that surrounded the installation of a new sultan and high-level meetings. Meanwhile, successive Residents' petitions for a military expedition gradually acquired a ritualistic quality of their own. Batavia's policy vis-à-vis Jambi, a mix of reconciliation and abstention, created ample scope for a kind of ritualistic dance expressing perceived or hoped-for relations of power.

INAUGURAL CEREMONY AND RITUAL (1882)

Rituals can be seen as nonverbal expressions of an existing or willed reality. Any definition of them, whether largely in terms of ceremony[1] or their emotional significance, or their recurrent nature,[2] will invariably include their symbolic quality. This holds good for political rituals as well as for any other. In the Dutch East Indies, with its strict hierarchical order, political rituals enacted a real or imagined balance of power. And when it came to the self-governing sultans, there was a wealth of etiquette to be observed. There must have been something approximating a Debrett Guide to Etiquette with rules for the reception of envoys and rulers. For instance, when a letter arrived from the sultan of Jambi, the governor-general received it "with the traditional signs of respect."[3] These signs were nowhere specified, but the point is clear enough. Every ritual and symbol was geared towards demonstrating Dutch hegemony and magnifying Dutch honor and glory.

The use of language was likewise symbolic. In 1878, for instance, the Ministry of Colonies had ordered a break with the custom in the East Indies of according local rulers "a higher rank than that to which they were entitled." Words such as "sovereign," "realm," and "heir to the throne" were to be abandoned in favor of

---

[1] J. Tennekes, *Symbolen en hun boodschap* (Assen: Van Gorcum, 1982), p. 89.

[2] S. Lukes, ("Political Ritual and Social Integration," *Sociology* 9 [(1975)]: 289–308, esp. 291) defines ritual as: "rule-governed activity of a symbolic character, which draws the attention of the participants to objects of thought and feeling, which they hold to be of special significance"; I. D. Kertzer, (*Ritual, Politics and Power* [(New Haven: Yale University Press, 1988], p. 9) defines it as "symbolic behavior that is standardized and repetitive and wrapped in a web of symbolism."

[3] See the following provisions of contracts with Jambi: 1858 art. 26, 1882 art. 28, 1888 art. 21, in NA, Col., *verbaal* (file, hereafter "vb.") January 21, 1860, no.16, *Handelingen Staten-Generaal 1883–1884* (The Hague: Staatsdrukkerij, 1883–84), app. 133.4; *Handelingen Staten-Generaal 1889–1890* (The Hague: Staatsdrukkerij, 1889–90), app. 76.7 respectively.

Sungai Asam and kampong near the capital of Jambi, Jambi
from D. D. Veth, *Midden-Sumatra: Reizen en onderzoekingen der Sumatra-expeditie, uitgerust door het Aardrijkskundig Genootschap: Photographie-album* (Leiden: Brill, 1879); KITLV photograph collection 7133

neutral terms such as "native administrator," "region," and "successor in the administration."[4] This linguistic downgrading was intended to convey the balance of power as the Dutch saw and wanted it.

While the Dutch enacted their political rituals, the Jambians—rivals not easily cowed—responded with rituals of their own. In the 1880s and early 1890s, the sultanate parried the Dutch maneuvers with new or revamped conventions by "inventing tradition."[5] Such rituals were enacted along the fault lines of the two parties' interaction. As is so often the case, the political confrontation, basically an undeclared power struggle, was expressed in terms of competitive rituals. Rituals surrounding meetings were, of course, nothing new, but in this period they were staged more carefully, described in more detail, and determined more heavily by implicit competition.

The Ministry in The Hague took no part in all this; its interest in Jambi had waned by then. This is reflected by the way in which reports and letters concerning the sultanate were filed away at the Ministry of Colonies from July 1880 onwards. Instead of being collected as before in subject files (*verbalen*), they were stored as separate postal reports (*mailrapporten*), indicating that the Ministry merely took note of them. The Hague would not concern itself with Jambian affairs for twenty years, aside from issuing its obligatory annual reports to the lower house of Parliament in the *Koloniaal Verslag*. In this indifference the policy of "abstention" found its clearest expression.

Act One of the ritual dance was played out at the new sultan's inauguration ceremony in 1882. Nazaruddin's death in July 1881 had come at rather an opportune moment for Laging Tobias, whose reconciliation policy relied heavily on the *pangeran ratu*, Marta Ningrat. To his great satisfaction, the latter was now willing to become sultan, a dignity he had refused in 1858. The new sultan was supported by Taha's elder brother Pangeran Surio, who was appointed *pangeran ratu* (Cakra Negara) and by his son, who was married to one of Taha's daughters. These appointments were thus instruments of reconciliation, paving the way to Taha and appearing to bring a peaceful solution within reach. The opposition of Pangeran Wiro Kesumo, who had wanted the sultanate to go to his wife's brother, one of Nazaruddin's sons, made little impact. His credentials were tarnished by then. Far more important was the consent of the Taha clan, the other members of the sultan's family, and the dignitaries.[6]

With a view to securing a reconciliation, Laging Tobias had obtained the consent of Governor-General F. s'Jacob (1881–84) for the grandest possible inauguration ceremony, an occasion "that the people of Jambi would talk about for years to come."[7] Since the new sultan, who was taking the name "Mohildin," had told him that he would be accompanied by numerous village headmen and other subjects from the uplands, Laging Tobias took pains to ensure that the Dutch

---

[4] *Politiek beleid en bestuurszorg in de buitenbezittingen*, 4 vols. (Batavia: Landsdrukkerij, 1907–9), 2b: 22–23.

[5] E. Hobsbawm and T. Ranger, *The Invention of Tradition* (Cambridge: Cambridge University Press, 1983).

[6] Political agent to Resident of Palembang, July 16, 1881; Resident of Palembang to governor-general, October 14, 1881, National Archives (NA), Col., *mailrapport* (postal report; hereafter "mr.") 1881/707 secret and mr. 1881/925 secret.

[7] See Laging Tobias's report of May 27, 1882, NA, Col., mr. 1882/903.

contingent was just as large and magnificent, decked out in full ceremonial dress. With the buglers of the Palembang garrison and eleven Palembang dignitaries,[8] together with another nine kampong headmen who had volunteered to bear ceremonial lances, Laging Tobias set off for Jambi towards the end of April 1882. The old custom of regional administrators carrying ceremonial lances when visiting other parts of the realm had passed into disuse in Palembang in the 1860s, but Laging Tobias thought this an ideal opportunity to reinstate all the trappings of a "real Oriental pageant."

The Dutch contingent found the capital awash with festive decorations. The political agent, following instructions, had arranged for a vast covered structure to be erected to accommodate the inauguration. It had festive lighting and was festooned with greenery and flags, as was the road leading from the jetty to the *pendopo*.

For a brief moment, the whole event hung in the balance when Cakra Negara, who was to be appointed *pangeran ratu*, turned out to be too ill to attend the parade. His presence was deemed indispensable, and Mohildin hastily dispatched a proa to fetch him. Quinine and sleeping drafts saw him through the signing of the new contract, though he stayed in his proa for the rest of the ceremony, partly for fear of some act of treachery. As Taha's brother, he was evidently feeling not just unwell but also rather unsafe.

In line with the old protocol established by Pruys, the sultan designate paid the first visit to Laging Tobias. Two reception committees, each composed of four dignitaries, stood waiting for him at the pier and at the entrance to the controller's compound. Mohildin himself was attended by a large retinue of dignitaries and headmen and a multitude of ordinary people. As *pangeran ratu*, he had on occasion met with Pruys and even Laging Tobias barefoot, sometimes clad in "indecorously dirty apparel."[9] Now, in contrast, he was sumptuously dressed. He bore the yellow *pangeran ratu*'s *payong* (parasol) that the colonial government had presented to him, because—as enquiries revealed—the children of the deceased sultan wanted the white sultan's *payong* to be buried along with their father. They later relented and lent Mohildin the white *payong* upon receiving a pledge that he would shortly be presented with a new one.

Many other innovations became apparent when the Dutch officials made their return visit, in the Pecinan quarter. On this bank of the river, too, the ceremony had been prepared with the utmost care. The sultan's residence had acquired a new upper story and a fresh coat of paint, its once bare interior transformed beyond recognition. The Resident too was welcomed by two reception committees, each one composed of not four but six dignitaries. This numerical detail was not lost on Laging Tobias, who saw it as signifying recognition of his superiority. A band from Singapore played the "Wilhelmus"—the Dutch national anthem—to greet the officials, who were also treated (much to their surprise, given the early hour) to a glass of champagne. In the evening, a thousand lanterns illuminated the visitors' departure. That these lanterns, also from Singapore, were left over from the New Year's celebrations of the sons of the Prince of Wales, to which inscriptions proclaiming "A happy new year" and "Merry Christmas" bore witness, was not

---

[8] They included a cousin of Taha's Arab mother and the Chinese neighborhood officer (*wijkmeester*), who, as a merchant, was a close friend of Pangeran Wiro Kesumo.

[9] Resident of Palembang to governor-general, July 17, 1880, NA, Col., mr. 1880/615 secret.

taken amiss. In all respects the event made a sharp contrast with previous Dutch visits to sultans of Jambi, which had invariably been marked by the extreme simplicity, or indeed poverty, of the reception, and by complaints of a lack of cash. This time the sultan's court unmistakably did its best to make an impression and succeeded beyond measure.

The grand signing of the contract, a few days later, followed a similar protocol. The ceremony took place on the grounds of the former kraton. The sultan's arrival was heralded by a thirteen-gun salute and by the strains of the "Wilhelmus" played by the military buglers. A naval guard of honor posted in front of the ceremonial shelter presented arms to Mohildin to the accompaniment of a roll of drums. This time he was even more ornately dressed than before. However, residual fears evidently persisted that the colonial government might suddenly abduct the sultan and *pangeran ratu*. Not all Jambians, many of whom bore arms, could be accommodated within the controller's compound. When the gate was shut as a precautionary measure, voices were immediately raised in alarm and panic broke out. However, the leader of the Arab community and several dignitaries immediately restored order with a mixture of force and calm reassurance. At one point Pangeran Wiro Kesumo actually seized a broken post from the smashed fence and started thrashing about in the crowd to subdue the people.

When Cakra Negara too had arrived, and was received according to the same ritual, the time had come to sign the contract. The text was read out, and the sultan, *pangeran ratu*, and seven dignitaries all swore an oath on the Koran pledging to adhere to it. Then the contract was signed and sealed, while the Dutch flag was first lowered and then hoisted again. To mark the ceremony, a twenty-one-gun salute was fired, and the buglers again played the "Wilhelmus," this time accompanied by the gamelan. In his speech, Laging Tobias congratulated the new sultan and spoke with satisfaction of the auspicious circumstances of his accession. Was not the new *pangeran ratu* a brother of Taha? Was not this the first time for many years that so many headmen from the uplands had appeared "in our midst," men who had not been seen in Jambi since 1858? He hoped there would soon be peace. But first, on behalf of the colonial government, he invited all the dignitaries to attend a party that same evening. Mohildin replied, promising his cooperation, after which the Jambian dignitaries kissed his hand, and the lower-ranking headmen kissed his foot. According to Laging Tobias, when the Dutch delegation left, accompanied by the same ritual as before, Mohildin was genuinely moved, all vestiges of mistrust dispelled. Together with the dignitaries he returned in the evening to attend the party, at which the refreshments were enlivened by a Chinese wayang and a display of fireworks from Batavia.[10]

This inauguration was a "mixed" act—one in which Dutch and Jambian ceremonies were combined and vied with one another. The following day, on the other hand, centered on the observance of a Jambian tradition. It was the day of the *raja sehari*—"sultan for a day"—an old custom that Resident Boers had described

---

[10] As a frugal Dutchman, Laging Tobias presented the budget for all this to his governor-general, explaining that the total (including the building of the temporary shelter and the festive lighting) would cost the colonial government 1,373 guilders, but that he had been able to persuade Jambi's military commander to buy the wood used to build the structure, reducing the total by 100 guilders (see his report of May 27, 1882, NA, Col., mr. 1884/903).

back in 1840.[11] The senior elder from the *dusun* Jebus from the Kompeh region of Lower Jambi took on the role of sultan for one day. Mohildin had not yet called for the enactment of the ritual. The contract stipulated that he should succeed to the sultanate immediately following his predecessor's decease, which he had thought incompatible with staging the *raja sehari*. Now, however, the custom was reinstated, with Dutchmen attending it for the first time. As the Resident was ill, the political agent acted as his deputy.

It is reasonable to assume that both sides judged the inauguration of 1882 a great success, although the Jambian reactions are not documented. Laging Tobias, in any case, was very pleased with all the festivities. Both sides had gone to considerable trouble and expense. Even if the Jambians had merely sought to convey a desire for rapprochement and peace, this goal had been fully accomplished. The inauguration must also have had a salutary effect on the balance of power in Jambi: the Jambians had met the Dutch on an equal basis, on their own territory, in a sparkling ritual that was partly new (champagne and lanterns) and partly based on adat (the *raja sehari*).

On May 8, 1882, Laging Tobias returned to Palembang. To his astonishment, he found the quays lined with huge crowds. The rumor that he would be assassinated in Jambi had sown widespread alarm. That he had noticed nothing at all indicative of base plots gratified Laging Tobias immensely: peace seemed at last to be within his grasp.[12]

CONTRACT

The inauguration had been accompanied by the signing of a new contract, as required under the terms laid down in 1858. Meanwhile, Batavia's efforts to forge a consistent standard in this connection had borne fruit in 1875, in the form of a standard model contract. The General Secretariat had all too often discovered omissions in the drafts. Regional governors frequently proved to be ignorant of the regulations or forgot to take account of changed requirements when drafting new contracts. The standard model would take care of these problems.[13]

The Jambian contract of 1882, however, had not been based on these guidelines. In itself this was not surprising. It had been impressed upon officials that the new standard contracts should be introduced with tact, and only when a good opportunity presented itself. Tinkering with the contracts would undermine respect for them; it was hard enough to persuade local rulers to negotiate new terms. Basically, the model served merely to jog the memory when amendments were being made. It would not be adopted as the basis for all new contracts until later in the 1880s. Even them, noticeable discrepancies would remain between different parts of the archipelago, leading to "regional" model contracts.[14]

Even so, Batavia had in fact wanted to apply the new standard contract in Jambi in 1882. The omission to do so was attributable in part to a communication breakdown and in part to Laging Tobias's policy of reconciliation. He had no

---

[11] J. W. Boers, "Oud volksgebruik in het Rijk van Jambi," *Tijdschrift van Neêrland's Indië* 3, 1 (1840): 372–84.

[12] Resident of Palembang to governor-general, May 27, 1882, NA, Col., mr. 1882/903 secret.

[13] For the events leading to the standard model contract, see NA, Col., vb. January 17, 1876, E1.

[14] *Politiek beleid*, 2b: 1–24, 155–85.

experience with standard guidelines from earlier postings, and when he was informed about them shortly before leaving for Jambi in April 1882, he found that the records in Palembang did not contain a copy of the standard model contract. So he could not take it with him. And in any case, he wanted at all costs to avoid sowing mistrust. He would have preferred to use the old contract, but when the sultan himself had asked for his annuity to be increased, he too had proposed a few changes.[15] Once more, it was the policy of reconciliation that dictated the form of the contract.

To avoid intimidating the new sultan Mohildin (1881–85), he was given permission, at his own request, to live not in Jambi but at Telok Puan on the Batang Hari, near the Tabir, provided he put in an appearance once every three months. The *pangeran ratu*, Cakra Negara, *was* expected to live in Jambi's capital, but he too could have a dignitary act on his behalf if need be.[16] Pruys van der Hoeven would have shaken his head at such laxity, but the colonial government was willing to go to great lengths to accomplish a reconciliation with Taha.

Some changes were uncontroversial, such as raising the annuity from ten thousand to twelve thousand guilders and granting free admission to Jambian ports for merchants.[17] More contentious was a provision that "andere Vreemde Oosterlingen"—which basically meant Arabs—were henceforth to have the same status as Chinese. It meant that prominent Arabs such as Pangeran Wiro Kesumo and Taha's mother would be subject to Batavia's authority and barred from owning land; they would have to apply for residence permits and would be subject to European justice—truly a peculiar and unworkable construction. This problem was resolved by an additional clause that the provision would apply only to new immigrants and would have no retroactive force. While transfers of land and the issue of residence permits would require Batavia's formal consent, decisions on such matters would be left to the sultan. These clauses reassured dignitaries of Arab origin.

Another amendment that met with objections concerned the colonial government's mining operations—coal mines, in the main. Mining was one of the matters that had consistently been overlooked in the contracts, prompting the decision to draft a standard model contract. Because of the gold deposits in the Limun, this had caused some consternation. The objections were defused by an assurance that mining did not include panning for gold.[18]

RENEWED EFFORTS AT RECONCILIATION

In December 1882, fresh terms were formulated for negotiations with Taha: the former sultan must accept subject status and recognize the colonial government's sovereignty. He must recognize the present sultan as such and pledge to uphold the contract. Essentially, he had to relinquish his power. In exchange he would be permitted to retain the titular rank of sultan. After all, reasoned Laging Tobias, everyone always called him sultan anyway. He would also receive an appanage

---

[15] Resident of Palembang to governor-general, May 27, 1882, NA, Col., mr. 1882/903 secret.

[16] Resident of Palembang to governor-general, copy telegr. 245 secret n.d., NA, Col., mr. 1881/760.

[17] *Politiek beleid*, 2b: 9.

[18] Resident of Palembang to governor-general, May 27, 1882, NA, Col., mr. 1882/903 secret.

and an annuity of no more than six thousand guilders (five hundred guilders a month), on the condition that he came to get it himself.[19] Behind the reconciliation policy, there was still a glimmer of hope of economic benefit. "Later travelers, discovering Jambi open, will probably soon establish the best route to the Ombilin coalfields" suggested Laging Tobias, in an effort to make his proposal sound attractive.[20]

Reports received from Jambi suggested that Taha was willing to accept subject status. According to the *pangeran ratu*, Cakra Negara, Taha had confessed to feelings of fear and shame that disinclined him to have any dealings with the Dutch ("tidak mahoe tjampoer sama belanda sebab akoe takoet dan maloe"), partly because of the treacherous deception practiced upon his ancestors by the Dutch, and partly because of his aggrieved sense of honor.[21] Furthermore, he had been urged not to accept subject status by Pangeran Kusin—a man "greatly esteemed among the population for his clear perceptions and remarkable gift for prophecy," and who had ordered a raid in Palembang as recently as June 1882.[22] The constant stream of rumors concerning the prospects for reconciliation gathered steam when a mission of six Jambian *pangeran* and dignitaries led by Wiro Kesumo came to attend the formal departure of Laging Tobias as Resident of Palembang in February 1883.[23] All it meant, however, was a considerable expense of time.

In November 1883, Taha had still not been notified of the terms that had been communicated to the sultan. He was informed of them in February, and in April 1884 a reply was finally received. Taha had taken the terms into consideration and would send his son Raden Mohamad to meet with the authorities. The "taciturn and diffident boy" aged eighteen or twenty, who seemed ill at ease with Europeans, duly arrived to convey Taha's greetings at the beginning of May 1884.[24] Sultan Mohildin saw the visit as an encouraging sign of rapprochement.

The new Resident, G. J. du Cloux (1883–87) saw things differently. He suspected that Taha was pursuing a policy of "perseverance with neither rapprochement nor hostility."[25] His analysis was correct. In 1885 one of Taha's supporters was arrested, and when questioned he confirmed the Resident's suspicions. Back in 1882, at a meeting between Sultan Mohildin, Pangeran Ratu Cakra Negara, and several dignitaries,[26] Taha had sworn that he would never accept subject status, but would flee to Kerinci in the event of an attack. Mohildin had persuaded him of the usefulness of a policy of pretense, as otherwise the annuity might be forfeited. It

---

[19] Resident of Palembang to governor-general, December 8, 1882; Council of Dutch East Indies, December 18, 1882, no. 1I, both in NA, Col., mr. 1882/1215. As a pure formality, the colonial government maintained that these conditions could not be laid down in a contract, since they concerned a vassal who had been in revolt for twenty-five years. The only admissible form was a document that the *pangeran ratu* and dignitaries too would have to sign.

[20] Resident of Palembang to governor-general, December 8, 1882, NA, Col., mr. 1882/1215.

[21] Resident of Palembang to governor-general, December 18, 1882, NA, Col., mr. 1882/1227.

[22] Commander of army to governor-general, June 1, 1885, NA, Col., mr. 1885/332.

[23] Resident of Palembang to governor-general, February 7, 1883, and February 14, 1883, NA, Col., mr. 1883/141 and mr. 1883/183.

[24] Resident of Palembang to governor-general, May 14, 1884, NA, Col., mr. 1884/358.

[25] Ibid.

[26] They were the following *pangeran*: Mangku Negara, Kesumo di Laga, Puspa Ali of the Merangin, Singa di Laga (a brother of Taha, the later Dipo Negoro), and Lemong (Muara Kilis, a young uncle of Taha), most of them notorious opponents of the colonial government later on.

had therefore been decided to delude the authorities into believing that Taha was considering capitulation. That was why Raden Mohamad had come to Jambi. The same informant told his captors that the people of Jambi, who lived in their own settlements with their own headmen, were utterly indifferent to the sultan's authority. The only officials with any influence were Taha, Pangeran Puspo Ali, and Pangeran Kusin.[27]

Taha's policy of dogged resistance consisted of arousing expectations, intimating a change of policy, and meanwhile marking time and watching vigilantly for any movement on the part of his opponent. By suggesting to the colonial authorities that he was ready to accept a rapprochement, he kept them at bay while assuring himself of their unflagging interest. Even so, he feared a Dutch attack. In 1882 or 1883 he had withdrawn to *dusun* Pematang, where he lived in a wooden house roofed with tiles. He had fortified his compound well and accumulated a fine arsenal. Fortifications had also been built on the river Merangin in Puspo Ali's region, and on the river Tabir near the residence of Pangeran Dipo Negoro, Taha's eldest brother and a fierce opponent of the colonial government. Thus, Taha's policy was wholly defensive, although for a brief period in 1885 it seemed otherwise.

INTERNAL POWER STRUGGLE IN JAMBI

In February 1885, quite unexpectedly, Sultan Mohildin died. Following customary practice, an interim authority was installed under the *pangeran ratu*'s leadership. However, Cakra Negara proved reluctant to accept the sultanship, and rumors spread that Taha wanted to reclaim his throne. The *pangeran ratu*, now in his sixties, was in fact not really eligible for the throne, as his mother was of low birth. His father, Sultan Facharuddin, had traded with Palembang merchants in the 1820s, before becoming sultan, and he had married a "common" Palembang woman. The *pangeran ratu* had been born there, only journeying to Jambi later on;[28] when Taha was born (in the 1830s) he had already been married for a few years. According to Jambian tradition, it was unacceptable for someone of low birth to ascend the throne; it would anger the gods and upset the cosmic balance. Moreover, the *pangeran ratu* was in poor health. He had required heavy sedation to attend the inauguration ceremony in 1882, and twelve months later he had been too ill to receive the Resident for his annual visit.[29]

The reason underlying Cakra Negara's appointment as *pangeran ratu* in 1882, in spite of tradition, was probably that his presence would enhance Taha's influence at the sultan's court. His low birth meant that Cakra Negara was obliged to obey his brother. The appointment illustrated Taha's political pragmatism. He used the position of *pangeran ratu* as a means of wielding power, in defiance of

---

[27] Resident of Palembang to governor-general, May 27, 1882, and September 29, 1885, NA, Col., mr. 1882/903 and 1885/653.

[28] See Resident of Palembang to governor-general, May 27, 1882, NA, Col., mr. 1882/903 secret. The observation in this letter, that the *pangeran ratu* had already been married for several years when Taha was born, is scarcely compatible with the estimated year of Taha's birth, around 1830 or a few years later. This would mean Cakra Negara was married by about ten years of age.

[29] Resident of Palembang to governor-general, May 14, 1884, NA, Col., mr. 1884/358.

tradition—perhaps, indeed, even in defiance of the cosmic powers.[30] Intentionally or not, the appointment had in any case boosted the confidence of the Dutch and strengthened their belief in Taha's speedy capitulation.

In May 1885, Cakra Negara declared his willingness to accept the throne. The ceremony was delayed, however, because the choice of *pangeran ratu* proved a thorny problem. Six months went by with the sultanate in this uneasy interim status—six months full of unrest and incidents, ensuing from an internal power struggle in which the ever rebellious Raden Anom repeatedly challenged Batavia's authority, possibly with the approval of the sultan's court and Taha. It started in May 1885, with a murderous attack on seven Dutch officers and officials at the Social Club just outside the fortress. Two Jambians dressed as hajis forced their way into the building, and although the Dutch put up a stout resistance with billiard cues, they managed to kill one man and wound another seriously with their *klewang*.

Suspicions initially focused on Taha. But since he cooperated in the rapid arrest and extradition of the murderers, the authorities' attention shifted, at the beginning of June, to Raden Anom. He had been passed over in recent *pangeran* appointments, and the *pangeran ratu* had thwarted his marriage to the widow of the dignitary Pangeran Mangku Negara. Perhaps he was motivated by resentment and sought to discredit the sultan's administration.[31]

He very nearly succeeded. Du Cloux's initial response was to call for military fortifications and an expedition.[32] He had misgivings about the *pangeran ratu*.[33] But in August 1885 the latter proved his good faith by warning the political agent about an imminent attack, again by Raden Anom. The maverick nobleman and his army, three hundred strong, were converging on the capital, where the European residents had taken refuge in the fortress; a week later he attacked. About this, too, the *pangeran ratu* had given advance notice. The Dutch had responded by fortifying the garrison in May—it now numbered 174 men—and by summoning to Jambi the European officials from Simpang and Tungkal in charge of collecting duties. They had also demolished the kampongs surrounding the fortress, creating a no-man's-land between the fortress and the Jambian settlements.[34]

The unrest persisted into December 1885. Almost every day saw exchanges of gunfire between Jambians and the ensconced Dutch soldiers. In October reports were received of hostile groups massing in the Rawas. At the beginning of October, someone set fire to the colonial government's coal supply shed in the capital. The fire was impossible to extinguish, and 262 tons of coal went up in the blaze, creating what was undoubtedly a magnificent spectacle. Then, at the end of October, a

---

[30] He was also said to have designated the next *pangeran ratu* in 1883, namely his son-in-law Pangeran Prabu, the eldest son of Sultan Mohildin, an appointment that as ruling sultan he was entitled to make, according to *adat*. Taha put forward Prabu's name as his preferred candidate again in 1899, this time for the sultan's throne (Resident of Palembang to governor-general, January 17, 1883, NA, Col., mr. 1883/73).

[31] Resident of Palembang to governor-general, June 16, 1885, NA, Col., mr. 1885/383.

[32] Resident of Palembang to governor-general, May 27, 1885, NA, Col., mr. 1885/323.

[33] Resident of Palembang to governor-general, July 29, 1885, NA, Col., mr. 1885/475.

[34] Resident of Palembang to governor-general, August 27, 1885, and September 7, 1885, NA, Col., mr. 1885/526a and 1885/566; acting commander to commander of army, January 3, 1885, NA, Col., mr. 1885/548.

cruiser was attacked off the shore of the kampong Saba.[35] In November the Dutch authorities heard alarming rumors of impending war between Taha's supporters and his enemies in the Rawas border territory and sent a company of soldiers to the Rawas. In short, Jambi was throbbing with agitation. The constant rumors of planned or imminent attacks by Jambian fighters generated unrelenting tension.

On the Jambian side, persistent rumors circulated that the dreaded forces of Batavia were coming to take control. Understandably so. Did not the reinforcement of the garrison at Jambi, Du Cloux's calls for an expedition, and the arrival of an additional company in the Rawas all point in that direction? Batavia was said to favor war and was preparing to invade Jambi. Taha found the population's fear of Batavia a useful recruitment vehicle, and he again used the Muslim/Christian opposition to mobilize support.[36]

Closer analysis of these rumors and reports shows that Taha was beset by internal opposition at this time, from Raden Anom and his father-in-law Pangeran Singa di Laga (Dipo Negoro) and from Puspo Ali, who all thought Taha was not pursuing a sufficiently hard line against the Dutch. For instance, Taha had strongly condemned Raden Anom's attack on Jambi at the end of August and punished him for it.[37] Possibly his strategy was to leave his three critics to pull the chestnuts out of the fire while supporting them from the wings; there is too little evidence to say for sure. One thing is clear, however—he was defensive and ever vigilant.

While Taha encouraged certain acts of aggression, he never did so outside Jambian territory, or even in the border areas. In this time of heightened tension, he explicitly forbade an attack on the Rawas.[38] Perhaps he did so in part because it would impede trade with the Rawas, which was indispensable at the time because of a rice shortage in the uplands. In February 1886, however, he would repeat his prohibition.

Was Taha looking to Aceh as his example? The incidental and unsystematic nature of Jambian resistance militates against such an interpretation: a raid in May, another in August, a fire in a supply shed, a seized cruiser, rumors of insurgency in the Rawas mingling with rumors denying it, the fortress regularly coming under fire, though largely by way of symbolic resistance as no more than five shots were ever fired in a day: this was no Aceh War. At most, it was a sign that many people in Jambi were unhappy about the Dutch presence. And this was scarcely news to the colonial government.

The part that the sultan's court played in all this was elusive. In spite of repeated invitations and summonses, the *pangeran ratu* stayed well away from Jambi's capital. He sent word that he was ill, probably for fear of being

---

[35] Resident of Palembang to governor-general, October 9, 1885, October 16, 1885, October 18, 1885, and November 2, 1885, NA, Col., mr. 1885/649, mr. 1885/667, mr. 1885/667 and mr. 1885/687.

[36] Resident of Palembang to governor-general, October 28, 1885, and December 29, 1885, NA, Col., mr. 1885/687 and mr. 1886/12.

[37] Resident of Palembang to governor-general, October 16, 1885, and October 18, 1885, NA, Col., mr. 667; military commander at Jambi to commander of the army, September 9, 1885, NA, Col., mr. 1885/590. Jambians said that a dream had foretold that all Raden Anom's undertakings against the Dutch would succeed. They also asserted that he could make himself invisible.

[38] Resident of Palembang to governor-general, October 9, 1885, and October 18, 1885, NA, Col., mr. 1885/649 and mr. 1885/667.

apprehended and held responsible for the attacks and for the failure to hand over Raden Anom.[39] Because of this, the colonial authorities knew very little about the internal situation in Jambi. As Du Cloux wrote in September 1885, "It is unfortunate, indeed lamentable, that the politics and internal affairs of Jambi are such a closed book to us."[40] Still, however imperfect the colonial government's grasp of the situation may have been, one thing was clear: the vacant sultan's throne was the fount of all evil.

POLITICAL PLANS

Rituals tend to repeat themselves; indeed it is one of their defining features. The unrest led to what was by then itself an almost ritualistic demand from Palembang for an expedition. Du Cloux initially beat about the bush in intolerably long, tortuous, vacillating, and obsequious letters to his superiors. Maybe the *pangeran ratu* should be appointed, or maybe not; maybe a rapid expedition should be mounted, or maybe not; maybe a reconciliation should be effected with Taha, or maybe not; maybe Taha should even be asked to ascend to the throne.[41] Du Cloux broached every conceivable issue. The Council of the Dutch East Indies responded brusquely that he could have omitted all mention of launching an expedition "since this measure is certainly receiving less consideration than ever before."[42]

Undeterred, in October 1885 Du Cloux put forward a proposal for an expedition. He wanted Jambi annexed to the colonial government's territory under its own Resident; to his mind, it was the only solution. At the very least, the Dutch should "dig their heels in" by declaring the power of the *pangeran ratu* and the dignitaries in Jambi null and void, canceling the annuities, fortifying the fortress at Jambi, and biding their time until funds permitted decisive action. The vulnerable control posts outside Jambi should be abandoned, cruisers sent to patrol the Batang Hari estuary, and Surulangun fortified.[43]

Batavia was distinctly unenthusiastic. Although the army commander asserted that only vigorous action could accomplish the desired result in Jambi, his letter also made clear that the commitment of his forces in Aceh ruled out a major offensive for the time being. And a limited punitive raid he thought pointless, since it would not foster a lasting solution. He therefore favored adopting a purely defensive approach and awaiting further developments. Besides, the Council of the Dutch East Indies was convinced that Du Cloux's idea of appointing Taha would have adverse repercussions throughout the East Indies, especially in Aceh. The Council wanted to maintain its ties with the *pangeran ratu*. An expedition would not serve any definite short-term purpose, since imposing direct Dutch rule was out of the question. Summarized, the Council's recommendations were to play for time while maintaining the current position, to protect Dutch citizens, and to make sure that the river provided free passage from the estuary to the fortress.[44]

---

[39] Resident of Palembang to governor-general, October 16, 1885, NA, Col., mr. 1885/667.

[40] Resident of Palembang to governor-general, September 7, 1885, NA, Col., mr. 1885/635.

[41] Resident of Palembang to governor-general, August 27, 1885, August 29, 1885, August 29, 1885, NA, Col., mr. 1885/526a, mr. 1885/548 and mr. 1885/635.

[42] Council of the Dutch East Indies, September 18, 1885, no. 2, NA, Col., mr. 1885/635.

[43] Resident of Palembang to governor-general, October 16, 1885, NA, Col., mr. 1885/667.

[44] Council of the Dutch East Indies, November 9, 1885, no. 1, NA, Col., mr. 1885/622.

Peace did not return to Jambi until December 1885, when reports reached Batavia from various sources, from Jambi, neighboring Bengkulu, and Singapore, that the insurgents had laid down their arms.[45] After December 8, all reports of gunfire and ominous crowds had ceased. In January, word came that the *pangeran ratu* was coming to Jambi and that Raden Anom was disgraced. Since patrolling the borders of the Rawas antagonized the population and prompted angry gatherings, the Resident decided to abandon these patrols, which had been stepped up in August.[46] He was therefore furious when a jittery controller at Surulangun (in the Rawas) responded to rumors of an impending attack by expelling Jambians and closing the border. There went his cautious wait-and-see policy. Sure enough, within a month Taha was urging village headmen in the uplands to take up arms in readiness to repulse a Dutch raid. Once again, his letters expressly prohibited any occupation of territory under Dutch control.[47]

Although Du Cloux was worried and did not entirely trust Taha ("in appraising this prohibition, the Sumatran's characteristic disloyalty and penchant for deception must be borne in mind"[48]), he nonetheless believed that this content was indicative of a calmer mood and even of a rapid rapprochement. In May 1886, the 250-kilometer-long road connecting Jambi and Palembang—little more than a footpath, which was partly submerged in the monsoon season—was opened up again, and in June virtually all the special military regulations in force in the Rawas were canceled. Only those in Jambi itself were maintained until the general atmosphere of rebellion finally ebbed away, in September—October 1886.[49]

SECOND INAUGURAL RITUAL (1886)

Cakra Negara finally arrived in Jambi in July 1886. His journey may well have been prompted by a lack of cash, his allowance having been stopped in July 1885. The *pangeran ratu* took care not to arrive until the postal steamship had put out to sea; his fear of being abducted was deeply entrenched. The meeting took place at the beginning of August.[50] Finally, in September 1886, it was time for a ritual reconciliation and a sober inauguration ceremony. Cakra Negara had first obtained assurances that he would not be held accountable for the unrest, and made it plain—an equally fervent desire—that he wanted the ceremony performed in

---

[45] Resident of Palembang to governor-general, December 9, 1885, January 13, 1886, and January 26, 1886, NA, Col., mr. 1885/764, mr. 1886/40, and mr. 1886/41; Resident of Bengkulu to governor-general, January 22, 1886, NA, Col., mr. 1886/95; consul at Singapore to governor-general, January 18, 1887, NA, Col., mr. 1887/97.

[46] Resident of Palembang to governor-general, January 13, 1886, and January 26, 1886, NA, Col., mr. 1886/40 and mr. 1886/40; consul at Singapore to governor-general, January 28, 1886, mr. 1886/97.

[47] Resident of Palembang to governor-general, February 28, 1886, and March 17, 1886, NA, Col., mr. 1886/149 and mr. 1886/196.

[48] Resident of Palembang to governor-general, March 17, 1886, NA, Col., mr. 1886/196.

[49] Resident of Palembang to governor-general, March 17, 1886, and April 9, 1886, NA, Col., mr. 1886/196 and mr. 1886/255; *Gouvernementsbesluit* (resolution adopted by the colonial authorities), June 20 1886, no. 4c, NA, Col., mr. 1886/410.

[50] Resident of Palembang to governor-general, July 19, 1886, and July 26, 1886, NA, Col., mr. 1886/490 and mr. 1886/519; see also the correspondence between the political agent and *pangeran ratu* in NA, Col., mr. 1886/579.

Pecinan, on Jambian soil.[51] Sultan Mohildin's inauguration had been celebrated in the fortress, which was why, in the *pangeran ratu's* view, he had died after reigning for only three years; in any case it made a sharp contrast with the twenty-three-year reign of his predecessor, Nazaruddin, whose inauguration had taken place on Jambian soil. Batavia's compromise solution was found acceptable: a meeting to discuss the *pangeran ratu's* pardon would be held on Dutch-ruled territory, followed by another one on Jambian soil. Interestingly, Batavia did not explicitly rule out the idea of appointing Taha at this time. After all, his only crime had been to announce his accession instead of formally renewing the sultanate's recognition of Dutch rule. If he was now prepared to do this and to sign a new contract, the colonial government had no objection to his appointment. The only condition was that he should openly take the initiative in this respect, to impress clearly upon the population that he was bowing to the colonial government's authority. Once again he was promised additional funds. For the rest, the negotiations were left to the Resident.[52] Thus, the colonial government was willing to go to considerable lengths to procure a reconciliation.

In September 1886 the formalities were concluded and Cakra Negara finally became Sultan Zainuddin. After the first visit of the ever timid *pangeran ratu* (the report describes him as edging further and further away from the Resident "until the sofa permitted no more edging"),[53] the Resident and political agent visited him again in Pecinan.[54] Here, the *pangeran ratu* defended his actions during the troubles of 1885 with sufficient credibility to be considered worthy of acceding to the throne. To end the eighteen-month-old interim administration as fast as possible, and to restore clarity, his inauguration was celebrated on Jambian soil shortly afterwards. Because of the months of tension preceding the ceremony, there were no festivities this time; neither the Dutch nor the Jambians felt any need for them. The Jambian reception committee consisted of only three men.

Raden Abdul Rachman, Sultan Mohildin's son (and the later Pangeran Adipati), was Du Cloux's preference for the new *pangeran ratu*.[55] However, the Jambian dignitaries nominated Taha's son Pangeran Anom Kesumo Judo, who was eligible for this position because his mother was of noble birth. The drawback of his youth—he was only seven years old—could be overcome by appointing regents. The Resident, just as sanguine as his predecessors, decided that Taha would be gratified by this appointment and soon fall into line.

The new draft contract was very different from past versions, as it was now based on the standard model contract of 1875. Like his predecessor, Sultan Zainuddin was to be permitted to live in his own settlement, in this case Muara

[51] *Pangeran ratu* to political agent, 19 sawal 1303 (July 21, 1886), NA, Col., mr. 1886/579. For the procedure and the account of the inauguration, see Resident of Palembang to governor-general, October 18, 1886, NA, Col., mr. 1886/686.

[52] General secretary to Resident of Palembang, August 25, 1886, NA, Col., mr. 1886/579.

[53] For an account of the ceremony, see Resident of Palembang to governor-general, October 18, 1886, NA, Col., mr. 1886/686.

[54] The previous day ritual gifts had been exchanged: on the Jambian side four elephant's teeth and an ox, which was slaughtered immediately according to custom and divided between the Europeans and Jambians; on the Dutch side an unnamed gift of the same value.

[55] By 1890 he would already bear the title of *pangeran depati* (see Resident of Palembang to governor-general, August 29, 1890, NA, Col., mr. 1890/878). And like his half-brother, Pangeran Prabu Negara, he would temporarily occupy a more prominent position in 1899.

Ketalo on the Batang Hari, on the condition that he visited Pecinan once every three months and that the *pangeran ratu's* regents or their representatives would live there. Dutch territory in Jambi was expanded, making life more difficult for potential aggressors. The contract stipulated expressly that the compensation of twelve thousand guilders (plus another four thousand for the opium farm) would only be paid if the terms of the contract were adhered to. This amounted to formalizing the de facto state of affairs, since the money had not been paid for more than a year. The contract did not include a provision requiring the Dutch to hand over escaped debt slaves, as the Jambians had requested. This would have been too flagrantly at odds with the Dutch desire to abolish the phenomenon altogether, as a veiled form of slavery. In fact the contract stated that the sultan, *pangeran ratu*, and dignitaries would work together to gradually eliminate debt slavery. Batavia would only extradite criminals to the Jambian authorities if the charges against them also constituted an offense under the law of the Dutch East Indies. This certainly did not include a debt slave absconding from servitude.[56] With the adoption of this draft contract, all the troubles of 1885 appeared to have come to an end.

The contract was not actually signed until June 1888, when the sultan was installed according to "ancient adat", and the regents who were to act for the young *pangeran ratu* (a cousin and a son-in-law of Taha) were appointed.[57] The documents recording this ceremony are among the few that are missing from the National Archives in The Hague.[58] For the first time, the sultan was presented with the gilded and diamond-studded royal kris called Si Genjei, which had remained in Taha's custody until then. Legend had it that the kris came from Java. Paduka Berhalo, the founder of the dynasty that had freed Jambi from the Mataram empire, was said to have taken it from his overlord and used it to legitimize his power.[59] Nazaruddin and Mohildin had possessed only the *pusaka* of the *pangeran ratu*, the rather less lavishly decorated kris Senja Merjaya.[60] This ceremony too was interpreted by the Dutch authorities as betokening Taha's imminent

---

[56] Resident of Palembang to governor-general, October 18, 1886, NA, Col., mr. 1886/686. Contract with Jambi 1888, in *Handelingen Staten-Generaal 1890–1891*, app. 76.7.

[57] For an account of this, see *Koloniaal Verslag 1889, Bijlage C van de Handelingen der Staten-Generaal 1889–1890* (The Hague: Staatsdrukkerij, 1889–90), p. 11. In January rumors circulated that a new *pangeran ratu* had been elected in the uplands. Shortly afterwards, Pangeran Ratu Anom Kesumo Judo sent word that a second *pangeran ratu* was in fact to be chosen to act on his behalf, on account of his youth; he sent this information in response to the request (or order) to journey to the capital for a meeting with the Resident. He failed to attend the signing of the contract in 1888. Meanwhile, the usual rumors were circulating: people in the uplands were preparing to repulse a Dutch attack. The only reason the Dutch wanted Pangeran Ratu Anom Kesumo Judo to come to the capital, it was said, was to use him as a hostage for his father (see documents in NA, Col., mr. 1888/70).

[58] Resident of Palembang to governor-general, June 7, 1888, NA, Col., mr. 1888/424 (posted June 18, 1888), not found either in NA, Col., file 6468 or elsewhere.

[59] C. van den Hamer, "Beschrijving van de twee krissen, als rijkssieraad verbonden aan het Sultansgezag over Djambi en het Pangeran Ratoeschap aldaar," *Tijdschrift voor Indische Taal-, Land- en Volkenkunde* 48 (1906): 106–12; R. C. Van der Bor, "Vertaling; Over het rijkssieraad van Djambi, genaamd Si Gendjé," *Tijdschrift voor Indische Taal-, Land- en Volkenkunde* 48 (1906): 142–60.

[60] *Koloniaal Verslag 1889*, p. 11. For a description of the two krisses, which are exhibited at Museum Pusat in Jakarta, see Van den Hamer, "Beschrijving van de twee krissen."

capitulation. In these circumstances, it was, of course, quite impossible to grant the requests submitted simultaneously by two *marga* (districts) on the Batang Asei for subjection to Dutch authority, which would release them from the obligation to pay tax to Pangeran Puspo Ali. Overtures from western Kerinci were likewise rejected.[61] The reconciliation policy was incompatible with any such expansion of power.

It is possible to construe the ritual ceremony of 1888, however, as yet another successful stratagem to delude the colonial government. The sultan's administration affected a warm and peace-loving disposition, while in reality its resurrection of old traditions was in part calculated to impress the local population. The rituals of 1886 and 1888, like those of 1882, represented the rivalry between the two centers of power, and as a trial of strength it did not exactly turn out to the advantage of the Dutch: the inauguration of 1886 took place within Jambian territory, and the Jambian crown jewels were brought into the ceremony of 1888, also harking back to ancient custom. Furthermore, the protagonists included one of Taha's sons (the *pangeran ratu*) and one of his brothers (the sultan), with a cousin and a son-in-law (the regents) having substantial supporting parts.

MEETING THE PANGERAN RATU

The symbolic power struggle was most marked in the rituals surrounding the first meeting between the political agent H. J. A. Raedt van Oldenbarnevelt and the *pangeran ratu* Anom Kesumo Judo in 1894.[62] In 1888, only the regents had been present at the ceremony; the *pangeran ratu* had excused himself.[63] Now the time had come to make the acquaintance of Taha's son. The long postponement of this meeting was undoubtedly attributable to the *pangeran ratu*'s youth; he turned out to have been born not in 1879, as stated in 1886, but in 1883, "the year of the eruption of the Krakatau." In other words, he was only three years old at the time of his appointment, and the dignitaries had had good reason to keep him away from the Dutch officials.

The meeting again took place within Jambian territory, at the residence of Sultan Zainuddin, who now lived at Dusun Tengah. This meeting is better documented than the previous one. Raedt van Oldenbarnevelt himself was greatly impressed by the reception, to which he testified in a long and detailed report. Once more, the sultan's entourage had gone to considerable trouble and expense to make this impression. To start with, they had drummed up a large crowd. Thousands of people came to witness the ceremony—no mean figure in a total population estimated at 75,000 and in a region where each *dusun* had no more than 50 to 500 inhabitants. Furthermore, all the Jambian dignitaries from the uplands had gathered at Dusun Tengah, with the exception of Taha and his brother Singa

---

[61] See documents in NA, Col., mr. 1888/298, 1888/469 and 1888/471. Kerinci had more cordial relations with Taha than with the contract sultan, as further investigation revealed.

[62] Political agent to Resident of Palembang, February 21, 1894, NA, Col., mr. 225. By then one of the regents, Pangeran Jaya Kesuma, had been replaced (in 1890) by Pangeran Nata Menggala, son of Pangeran Krama di Laga and a sister of the former Sultan Nazaruddin. Reports received in the intervening years of Taha's death or Zainuddin's resignation always proved to have been unfounded (see Resident of Palembang to governor-general, December 31, 1889, and April 19, 1890, NA, Col., mr. 1890/5 and mr. 1890/292).

[63] *Koloniaal Verslag 1889*, p. 11.

(Dipo Negoro), one of the fiercest opponents of Dutch rule. It was rumored that they were following the ceremony from the seclusion of a private room, however, and that they were responsible for the event's excellent organization.

Preceding the actual meeting between the political agent and the *pangeran ratu*, there was a grand procession honoring the sultan and *pangeran ratu*, which the political agent watched from his ship. Sultan Zainuddin was borne aloft by forty men in an oval-shaped palanquin draped with white cloth, in accordance with Jambian adat. Two hundred lance-bearers marched in twos ahead of him in close formation. A few Jambian dignitaries had also seated themselves in the palanquin, holding a white sultan's *payong* over his head—a gift from the former Resident Du Cloux. On either side of the palanquin marched dignitaries and others wearing the insignia of the realm. Their sabers and lances were all sheathed in white cloth.

Then came the *pangeran ratu*'s lance-bearers, also numbering a few hundred. Just in front of the *pangeran ratu*'s yellow palanquin marched twelve lance-bearers whose long jackets and turbans were bright crimson. These men, who were conspicuously darker in complexion than the rest, constituted the *pangeran ratu*'s special bodyguard, and never let him out of their sight. The *pangeran ratu*'s palanquin was square and surmounted by a canopy. Above it appeared the yellow *payong* that went with his office, borne by one of his *mantri*. Jambian dignitaries from the uplands, some wearing insignia, thronged around the palanquin. Bringing up the rear were the many councilors belonging to the sultan's large family.

When the *pangeran ratu* and sultan had entered the reception hall, the political agent himself, in "grand dress," was rowed ashore, where he was received by a committee of Jambian dignitaries. He made his way between two rows of lance-bearers to the reception hall, where Sultan Zainuddin greeted him and immediately introduced him to the *pangeran ratu*, Anom Kesumo Judo. He was then invited to take the seat of honor at the table, to the sultan's right, while the *pangeran ratu* sat to his left. Besides dignitaries from the capital, including Pangeran Wiro Kesumo, the company included some close relatives of Taha—two sons, a brother-in-law, and a son-in-law—and a son-in-law of Dipo Negoro. The political agent had the impression that the company included many more of Taha's kinsmen.

Raedt van Oldenbarnevelt was very favorably impressed by the *pangeran ratu*, even though the boy had been ill for the past few days and his face still bore the signs of fever. He wore yellow silk robes stitched with gold thread, a gift from Pangeran Wiro Kesumo. Though he looked no more than eleven years old, the *pangeran ratu* was far from timid and took clear pleasure in his gift, a saloon rifle.

After a friendly exchange of pleasantries, the political agent announced that he would say farewell. Cordially escorted by the dignitaries he set off back to his ship, after which the sultan and *pangeran ratu* also left in the same way they had come. To mark their departure, Raedt fired an eleven-gun salute and lowered and raised the Dutch flag three times.

Immediately after this reception, as Raedt learned through hearsay, Taha assembled all the dignitaries and had them sign a document swearing unconditional obedience to his son. The authorities in Batavia would also be sent a copy, after the dignitaries from the lowland areas had signed. Raedt interpreted this, although he did not write it down explicitly, as meaning that all the dignitaries would henceforth obey the lawful representative of Dutch authority.

Furthermore, plans were afoot for Taha and Dipo Negoro to journey to the Tembesi to resolve all the issues involving Dutch citizens. Pangeran Wiro Kesumo and other dignitaries would accompany them. This plan too held out the prospect of cooperation. Brimming with pleasure, the political agent wrote of his confidence in the future. It would not be long now before "we can start thinking of a peaceful annexation of the Jambian realm."[64] The old dream was still very much alive.

This Jambian ritual is susceptible to an entirely different explanation, however—as a grand pageant to legitimize the young *pangeran ratu*'s power in the population's eyes. It is clear that Taha had gone to great trouble and expense to create an impressive spectacle. Pangeran Wiro Kesumo too had played a role, by paying for the *pangeran ratu*'s splendid costume. He had unmistakably chosen sides now; he had repudiated his wife, Nazaruddin's daughter, and married his son to one of Taha's daughters, making his wealth available to Taha. Just as in 1882, there was not a sign of shabbiness or the legendary Jambian poverty. On the contrary, the Dutch observer had been impressed by the pomp and ceremony, and the smooth organization of the event.

Taha had undoubtedly strengthened his position vis-à-vis the colonial authorities. All those in positions of power in Taha's immediate circle had received the official representative from Batavia, and they had done so on Jambian soil. To the outside world, it might therefore appear that the colonial government had taken a step towards Taha, had possibly even accepted his position as ruler. The oath of allegiance to his son confirmed this; the dignitaries had sworn allegiance not to the actual ruler, who was bound contractually to Batavia, but to the young son of the only man who had real authority in the realm. And in doing so, they pledged themselves to Taha. He appeared almost to have accomplished his purpose. Within a few years his son would be sultan of Jambi, whether or not under the Dutch flag. How Taha saw this situation is unknown. While the Resident too acknowledged the identification between *pangeran ratu* and Taha, he saw it as advantageous for the colonial government, as a sign of rapprochement. The ritual was not recognized as that of a rival.

SECOND MEETING

The *pangeran ratu* also had to make the acquaintance of the Resident, at that time J. P. de Vries (1889–96). This meeting was planned for April 1895. However, one afternoon earlier that month, while the military commander and the controller were drinking tea on the verandah of the controller's residence, a Jambian dressed in white had launched himself upon them, to the shriek of holy war. This attack, which the sultan's court blamed on Raden Anom, delayed the meeting until February 1896.[65]

This time the meeting took place within Dutch territory, in the political agent's home.[66] The formalities were discussed with the Resident at a preparatory

---

[64] Political agent to Resident of Palembang, February 21, 1894, NA, Col., mr. 1894/225.

[65] Resident of Palembang to governor-general, April 21, 1895, and April 27, 1895, NA, Col., vb. January 2, 1895, no. 27. In this first *verbaal* since July 1880 the documents had merely been deposited; they had not yet led to a ministerial decision.

[66] For the report, see Resident of Palembang to governor-general, February 29, 1896, NA, Col., vb. November 2, 1896, no. 27.

meeting. On the appointed day, a committee of only four men stood waiting for the sultan on the landing stage. The provisions of the contract, calling for thirteen- and eleven-gun salutes, were followed to the letter. The sultan and *pangeran ratu* walked past a guard of honor, which greeted them with a military salute, and then reached the political agent, who stood waiting for them at the entrance. After the *pangeran ratu* had been introduced by Sultan Zainuddin, Raedt van Oldenbarnevelt addressed them in "excellent Malay" on the Resident's behalf. He then entertained his two guests. In spite of De Vries's disappointment with the *pangeran ratu*'s youth, he was favorably impressed by his appearance, although he was said to have a "hot temper." This time too, the Dutch carefully scrutinized the Jambian retinue: it contained no fewer than five of Taha's sons. Their father was absent, however, as De Vries remarked with some regret. But he too was satisfied. Of course it would have been better still if Taha had joined the gathering, but it was unreasonable to expect it of that "proud old man." And like the chorus of an old song, the Dutch decided that there was every reason to be pleased, since Taha had "tired of resistance" and chosen Batavia's side.[67] Like so many of his predecessors, De Vries was confident that the rapprochement was just around the corner.

REVIEW AND CONCLUSIONS

Rituals illustrate policy and views on both sides. In this case they constituted symbolic allusions to real or hoped-for relations of power: the colonial government chose to construe them as evidence of its own hegemony and Taha's desire for subject status on peaceful terms, while Taha saw them as a way of cementing his power within his own area and of maintaining a distance. Far from having a monolithic and shared significance, the rituals were polyinterpretable, as indeed are all symbols and symbolic actions. The message of the other, the opponent, was not understood as such—certainly not by the Dutch, at any rate. And the rituals thus expressed the ongoing power struggle.

Psychologists view symbols as the gateway to the subconscious, as clues to the knowledge that is stored there. The same can be said of rituals with their symbolic messages, such as the ritualistic meetings between the authorities in Batavia and the Jambian sultan's court. They expressed matters of which the parties themselves were as yet not fully aware, or that the Dutch, at any rate, doggedly refused to understand. A good psychoanalyst would probably have been able to construe them into a clearly defined picture of the power structure. Dutch policymakers, in contrast, were signally lacking in this facility. For fifteen years they reenacted the same routine with little variation in their approach to Jambi, countless times afresh.

Throughout this period, the two parties circled around each other in a ritual dance; the Dutch fully expected the Jambians to yield at any moment, and the Jambians were happy to foster that impression, while zealously guarding their terrain. The colonial government went to great lengths to win Taha over: putting his relatives on the throne (1882, 1886); allowing the sultan to live outside Jambi; giving parties and receptions in honor of inaugurations and new acquaintances

---

[67] Resident of Palembang to governor-general, February 29, 1896, NA, Col., vb. November 2, 1896, no. 27.

(1882, 1894); delaying the introduction of the standard contract (1882); dangling the prospect of concessions before Taha, if only he would accept subject status (1883); even intimating a readiness to reappoint him (1886). None of it to any effect.

These major concessions were a direct consequence of the abstention policy dictated by the Aceh War. As long as the military operation, which Batavia too saw as the only ultimate solution, had to be deferred, ways had to be found of placating the other side. "Honey works better than vinegar" appeared to be the motto.

The actions taken at the three levels of government displayed what has by now become a familiar pattern: the Resident made proposals and urged action, Batavia made decisions, and The Hague looked on. The rapid succession of appointments at the local level enhanced this pattern. Every political agent and every Resident was confident that Taha would eventually (and probably very soon) abandon his resistance, and every political agent and every Resident hoped and expected that he would be the one to accomplish a peaceful resolution of the Jambian problem.

These rituals accord with a relationship under international law as described by Resink.[68] They were part of the machinery of diplomacy between the colonial government and the self-governing sultanates, and served a definite political purpose. However, they also marked the limits of that relationship. For Batavia, Dutch sovereignty in the face of the outside world was a given, which constrained the sultan's right of governance and made his own sovereignty a purely internal matter.[69]

Finally, one of the most important reasons for this long ritual dance was the lack of a compelling reason for a showdown. In these two decades there was no need

---

[68] G. J. Resink, *Indonesia's History between the Myths: Essays in Legal History and Historical Theory* (The Hague: Van Hoeve, 1968).

[69] Just how much it took its own sovereign rights for granted is apparent from a legal case that was heard in 1880. A young Arab ship's captain from Palembang, who had refused to pay the duties on his cargo at Muara Saba, had his conviction overturned by the Court of Justice and the highest court of appeal, the Supreme Court of the Dutch East Indies. According to the judgment, the special rates set for Jambi in 1847 could be levied only in Muara Kompeh and not in Muara Saba. This was because Jambi, although part of the territory of the Dutch East Indies, did not belong to the territory liable to pay duties under the terms of the 1873 Tariffs Act. The sultanate of Jambi did not come under the authority of the Residency of Palembang. This meant that the said captain did not have to pay duties at Muara Saba. The colonial government hastened to nullify the adverse consequences of this ruling; of the over 41,000 guilders it received in revenue, only a tiny percentage came from duties levied at Muara Kompeh, the rest coming from Jambi's other ports. For in 1847, in designating Muara Kompeh as the place where duties were to be levied, the legislature had intended the tax to apply throughout Jambi. An ordinance was therefore promulgated that thenceforth goods did not have to be declared in Muara Kompeh: they could also be declared at Tungkal, Simpang, Muara Saba, or Jambi. With this provision the colonial government safeguarded its specific trading rights in Jambi. The effect was immediate. Since then, payments had been regular. See *gouvernementsbesluit*, December 2, 1880, no. 1, NA, Col., exh. January 13, 1981, no. 1. See also Resink (*Indonesia's History between the Myths*, p. 129), who regards the judgments of the Court of Justice in Batavia and the Supreme Court of the Dutch East Indies as evidence of relations under international law between the colonial government and Jambi. He did not know about the colonial government's response. It shows that the relationship under international law was recognized only at the legal level; Batavia saw itself as possessing exclusive competence. It therefore seems to me that the rulings of the Court of Justice and the Supreme Court can be construed as narrow juridical interpretations of regulations that lagged behind administrative practice

to consolidate Dutch trading interests on Sumatra as in the 1830s; there were no pirates menacing the Jambian coast as in the 1840s and 1850s; there was no reluctant sultan as in 1858, nor any threat to Dutch explorers as in 1877–79. It was not until a new factor drew attention to Jambi that a more direct approach suddenly became a matter of urgency. That new factor was oil.

CHAPTER EIGHT

OIL: 1890–1900

The 1890s brought a permanent change in Batavia's relations with Jambi, as with other self-governing regions in the Outer Islands. The colonial government's growing need for income, an increase in private enterprise, and the revival of colonial self-confidence produced a new Dutch assertiveness vis-à-vis local rulers. When oil was discovered in the waning years of the century, the colonial government started insisting on cooperation and eventually proved willing to enforce it by military means. The Jambians found themselves unable to sustain their traditional policy of evasiveness. In this new situation, the Dutch saw the real nature of the local rulers' attitude far more clearly than before. By looking at the decision-making procedures in the East Indies, we can analyze the Dutch motives for taking action and place them in the context of the imperialism debate. These procedures shed light on the way the Dutch administered their colony and what they sought to achieve.

NEW POLICY ON THE OUTER ISLANDS

The traditional policy of "abstention," renewed in the 1870s under the influence of the Aceh War, had limited Dutch territorial expansion but never stopped it entirely: the pattern established before 1870 remained intact.[1] This policy dictated by The Hague was often breached, whether to head off foreign rivals or from a desire to avenge a failed expedition. For instance, in 1877 the sultan of Brunei gave a private British company, the North Borneo Company, sovereign rights over an area that the Netherlands regarded as Dutch territory. Batavia responded by sending a warship and establishing an administrative post there to defend the Dutch flag at Batu Tinagat, the "official" border. The ensuing diplomatic protests and negotiations led in 1891 to the signing of a British-Dutch convention regulating the borders. Batu Tinagat was ceded to Britain. Meanwhile, Batavia had strengthened its relations with local sultans in East Borneo and was now visiting the area more frequently.[2]

In 1890, Governor-General Cornelis Pijnacker Hordijk (1888–93) had given the go-ahead for a punitive raid against tribes on Flores that had obstructed a tin

---

[1] C. Fasseur, "Een koloniale paradox: De Nederlandse expansie in de Indonesische archipel in het midden van de negentiende eeuw (1830–1870)," *Tijdschrift voor Geschiedenis* 92 (1979): 162–87; Maarten Kuitenbrouwer, *The Netherlands and the Rise of Modern Imperialism: Colonies and Foreign Policy 1870–1902* (New York: Berg, 1991), p. 260.

[2] G. Irwin, *Nineteenth-Century Borneo: A Study in Diplomatic Rivalry* (The Hague: Nijhoff, 1955); I. Black, "The 'Lastposten': Eastern Kalimantan and the Dutch in the Nineteenth and Early Twentieth Centuries," *Journal of Southeast Asian Studies* 16 (1985): 286–91; Kuitenbrouwer, *The Netherlands and Imperialism*, pp. 119–23, 177–81.

expedition. Designed for prestige rather than profit, the operation was wholly unsuccessful. This military debacle, attributable to a mix of overconfidence, ignorance, and poor organization, had made Pijnacker Hordijk more cautious about allowing military action in the Outer Islands.[3] Meanwhile, a new flow of rhetoric was issuing from The Hague. In 1891 Aeneas Mackay, Minister of Colonies (1890–91), thought expanding Dutch control of the independent Batak regions feasible "when the time is ripe."[4] This remark effectively drew a line through the policy of abstention, although Parliament and public opinion still favored it. The 1870s and 1880s are therefore best described as a transitional period, a long stretch between the stricter policy of abstention pursued until 1870—though never rigidly even then—and the decisive expansion of Dutch rule that started in the 1890s.[5] This process ran parallel to economic trends in the Netherlands, which experienced a transitional period of twenty-odd years in the industrialization process at the same time.

The Lombok expedition in 1894 provided the first trumpet call for a new direction. Initially hesitant, the colonial government had decided in 1893, under a new governor-general, Carel H. A. van der Wijck (1893–99), to order military intervention in the civil war raging in Lombok. Van der Wijck, the son of a member of the Council of the Dutch East Indies, himself a highly successful East Indies official, was a far more forceful and experienced administrator than his predecessor. Though possessed neither of a brilliant mind nor a broad outlook, he was a bold decision maker and had an eye for the twin motors needed to drive the East Indies' development—government and industry.[6] Administrative and "ethical" aims, notably to strengthen Dutch prestige and protect the vulnerable Sasak, the Islamic population group in Lombok, from the yoke of Balinese domination, underpinned his decision. He anticipated a simple victory, but a night raid on the East Indies garrison in August 1894 shattered this illusion. Never before had so many Dutch soldiers—around a hundred—been killed at once. The punitive expedition sent in response was fierce and vengeful, and coincided with a wave of Dutch nationalism in colony and mother country alike. The "popularization of the colonial argument" in the Netherlands over the previous three decades now became manifest in a virulent strain of national self-awareness.[7] Action committees and support groups sprang up everywhere. The second expedition succeeded in its

---

[3] P. Jobse, *De tin-expedities naar Flores 1887–1891: Een episode uit de geschiedenis van Nederlands-Indië in het tijdperk van het moderne imperialisme,* Utrechtse Historische Cahiers 3 (Utrecht: Utrecht University, 1981).

[4] *Politiek beleid en bestuurszorg in de buitenbezittingen,* 4 vols. (Batavia: Landsdrukkerij, 1907–9), 1: 168.

[5] Kuitenbrouwer, *The Netherlands and Imperialism;* J. Th. Lindblad, "Economic Aspects of the Dutch Expansion in Indonesia, 1870–1914," *Modern Asian Studies* 23 (1989): 1–23.

[6] J. van Goor, "De plaats van de biografie in de koloniale geschiedenis: Van der Wijk bijvoorbeeld . . . ," in *Between People and Statistics: Essays on Modern Indonesian History Presented to P. Creutzberg,* ed. Francien van Anrooij et al. (The Hague: Nijhoff, 1979), pp. 283–90; C. Fasseur, "C. H. A. van der Wijck," in *Biografisch woordenboek van Nederland,* ed. J. Charité, 5 vols. (The Hague: Nijhoff, 1979–2001), 1: 664–66.

[7] Leonard Blussé and Elsbeth Locher-Scholten, "'Buitenste binnen': De buiten-Europese wereld in de Europese cultuur," *Tijdschrift voor Geschiedenis* 105 (1992): 341–45; Paul van der Velde, *Een Indische Liefde: P. J. Veth (1814–1895) en de inburgering van Nedelands-Indië* (Amsterdam: Balans, 2000).

purpose, though not without claiming large numbers of Balinese casualties. The sultan was banished and direct Dutch rule imposed. This military triumph, the first after an endless series of failures and defeats in Aceh and Flores, filled the Dutch with a new colonial pride. Soon, scores of towns in the Netherlands boasted their own "Lombok street."[8]

The abandonment of the principle of abstention was also reflected in the policy on New Guinea. For years, The Hague had rejected any plans for greater involvement in this island's affairs. But in 1896 it gave serious consideration to Batavia's proposals for expanding Dutch control in New Guinea—not motivated by visions of fat profits, it should be said, but largely to introduce administrative order. The monthly visits of the newly founded Royal Dutch Steam Packet Company (KPM), which had launched a line to the island in 1891, had brought it closer to Batavia, boosting trade but also multiplying indignant complaints about the uncivilized inhabitants. Headhunting Papuans from the south of the island, who had expanded their operations to British territory, were soon at the center of an international controversy. Although a border treaty was signed with the British government in 1896, there was nothing to indicate that the local population would respect these fictional Western lines, thus resolving the international imbroglio.[9] Two controllers were therefore posted to Fak-Fak and Manokwari in 1898, and four years later an official was sent to Merauke to forestall problems with the British neighbors and to offer the post a measure of protection. Given the vastness of New Guinea, these officials faced a Herculean task. In fact their role was symbolic, and as such they were primarily part of the colonial ritual that enacted effective control (or the effort to achieve it), as required by the Berlin Conference of 1884–85.

However, the main change of policy took place in Aceh. In 1896 Tengku Umar, an Acehnese dignitary long trusted by the Dutch, chose the side of the rebels. The Dutch response, the successful punitive raid masterminded by the Lombok veteran General J. A. Vetter, persuaded opponents of an active policy of expansion to drop their resistance. One success led to another. Even before 1896, commentators had prepared the ground for a shift in colonial thinking about Aceh. The official report on Aceh by Christiaan Snouck Hurgronje, an expert on Islam,[10] and a pamphlet that Johannes van Heutsz (at the time captain-adjutant) produced on his own authority about the subjection of Aceh[11] confirmed the view of those who felt a change of policy in Aceh was long overdue. Snouck and Van Heutsz—not the first critics but the most influential—urged the necessity of a strong military campaign and an unequivocal show of force. The "concentrated line" of troop positions, from which the Dutch soldiers occasionally launched their raids and then scurried back again,

---

[8] J. van Goor, "De Lombokexpeditie en het Nederlands nationalisme," in *Imperialisme in de marge: De afronding van Nederlands-Indië*, ed. J. van Goor (Utrecht: Hes, 1986), pp. 19–70, esp. 64.

[9] P. W. Van der Veur, *Search for New Guinea's Boundaries: From Torres Strait to the Pacific* (Canberra: ANU Press, 1966), pp. 61–70; Historische Nota, National Archives (NA), The Hague, Col., file (*verbaal;* hereafter vb.) December 18, 1897, no. 32.

[10] C. Snouck Hurgronje, *De Atjehers*, 2 vols. (Batavia: Landsdrukkerij; Leiden: Brill, 1893–95).

[11] J. B. van Heutsz, *De onderwerping van Atjeh* (The Hague: Van Cleeff; Batavia: Kolff, 1893).

like monkeys on a leash being teased,[12] was abandoned in 1896. Then, in 1898, Snouck Hurgronje and Van Heutsz were given the powers they needed to put their ideas into practice. The mobile brigade, which had been founded in 1890, was placed at their disposal. The 1898 expedition to Pedir, the center of the Aceh resistance, was their initiative and was conducted under their authority. Their success reflected well on the new policy, which consequently spread from Aceh throughout the archipelago.[13] In numerous places throughout the East Indies, The Hague and Batavia no longer insisted on abstention.

At the same time, the economy of the East Indies showed signs of revival. The Netherlands had not received any profits from the colony since 1877, and Batavia's budget had come under increasing pressure. The only way to finance the Aceh War and the new railway tracks was by increasing taxation in the East Indies. Between 1867 and 1897 taxes rose from 33 percent to 58 percent of the total revenue from the colony, while sales of tropical produce, which had once accounted for 50 percent of the total, sank to a mere 11 percent.[14] Both the Minister and the colonial authorities therefore vested their hopes more and more in revenue from the Outer Islands.[15] Initially an attempt was made to achieve this by raising taxes and the price of opium and other concessions. But Batavia was also interested in raw materials; the desire for more tax revenue served as an impetus for economic development. Although the colonial government had in general eschewed state-run enterprises since the abolition of the Cultivation System, it nonetheless had a finger on the pulse of the economy, on the lookout for fiscal benefit. To gain a hold on mining operations, it tried wherever possible in the 1890s to acquire the exploration and mining rights for mineral resources where it did not already possess them.

With the growing demand on the world market for lamp oil, the colonial authorities' hopes focused on oil. Successful prospecting in the 1880s had led to the establishment of several oil companies, notably the Dordtsche Petroleum Company (1887) and the Royal Dutch Company for the Exploration of Petroleum Sources in the Dutch East Indies, usually known in short as the Koninklijke (1890). Pioneering engineers secured the concessions, with European banks putting up the capital. The Koninklijke piped its first crude oil from northern Sumatra in 1890, the same year that petroleum was first mentioned separately under the heading of mining in the *Koloniaal Verslag*.[16]

The fresh interest also led to new legislation in the Netherlands. The old ordinance of 1873 was finally replaced by a new Mineral Extraction Act in 1899, which had taken a full fourteen years to draft. It did not enter into force until 1907,

---

[12] The image is Snouck Hurgronje's; F. Schröder, "Oriëntalistische retoriek: Van Koningsveld over de vuile handen van Snouck Hurgronje," *De Gids* 143 (1980): 785–806.

[13] Kuitenbrouwer, *The Netherlands and Imperialism*, pp. 266–69; J. Somer, *De Korte Verklaring* (Breda: Corona, 1934), pp. 239–50; P. van 't Veer, *De Atjeh-oorlog* (Amsterdam: Arbeiderspers, 1969), pp. 186–259.

[14] Lindblad, "Economic Aspects," pp. 13–14.

[15] First government secretary to Resident of Palembang, April 24, 1894, with appendixes, NA, Col., postal report (*mailrapport*; hereafter "mr.") 1894/425.

[16] *Koloniaal Verslag 1890, Bijlage C van de Handelingen der Staten-Generaal 1890–1891* (The Hague: Staatsdrukkerij, 1890–91), p. 235.

by way of an implementing ordinance promulgated in Batavia.[17] While according greater freedom to private enterprise, the Act gave a modest benefit to the state, in the form of a standing charge plus a 4 percent tax on gross earnings. The colonial government took the view that a growth in private enterprise would automatically bring prosperity to the region. Although the Dutch Parliament was in principle not averse to a state-run enterprise, given the good experience gained with Bangka tin and Ombilin coal, the idea was rejected under the influence of Minister J. T. Cremer (1897–1901), himself a former entrepreneur. However, the government retained the right to exclude private companies from specified areas in the public interest. Finally, the new Mineral Extraction Act introduced a sharper contrast between above and below ground, restricting the rights of indigenous landowners to the minerals extracted from their land. Although provisions of this kind also occurred in similar European legislation, they strengthened the colonial power to the detriment of the local population, and in this sense the Mineral Extraction Act was a piece of colonial legislation that belonged to the process of imperialism.[18] This is the backdrop against which we should view developments in Jambi, since it was oil that placed Jambi at the center of Batavia's attention.

JAMBI AND THE PROFIT--MAKING FACTOR

Jambi had never been likely to make the colonial government's fortune. In the period 1880 to 1900, 99 percent of its exports, which seldom exceeded a value of 500,000 guilders annually, still consisted of forest products (mainly India rubber, gutta-percha, and rattan), while imports of a similar value consisted of cloth, rice, and consumer goods. Income from import and export duties provided on average only a tiny proportion of the total revenue from the Outer Islands.[19] To increase the revenue from the Outer Islands, taxes had been introduced in 1892 throughout Palembang— hence also in the Jambian capital and Muara Saba—on the slaughter of pigs, on Chinese dice games, and on strong liquor. Given the millions of guilders that were needed, however, the few hundred guilders raised in this way were a drop in the ocean. Thus the tax on Chinese dice games was estimated to bring in 360

---

[17] "Mijnwetgeving," in *Encyclopaedie van Nederlandsch-Indië* (The Hague: Nijhoff; Leiden: Brill,1918), 2: 847–52, esp. 849.

[18] E. P. Wellenstein, *Het Indische mijnbouwvraagstuk* (The Hague: Nijhoff, 1918), pp. 48–85; H. A. Idema, *Parlementaire geschiedenis van Nederlandsch-Indië 1891–1918* (The Hague: Nijhoff, 1924), pp. 123–27.

[19] Figures for Jambi's share in revenue from import and export duties and warehouse rental costs from the Outer Islands: 1880, 2.9 percent; 1885, 4.5 percent; 1890, 2.7 percent; 1895, 2.9 percent. See *Koloniaal Verslag 1881*, app. OO; *Koloniaal Verslag 1886*, app. PP; *Koloniaal Verslag 1891*, app. OO; *Koloniaal Verslag 1896*, app. SS. This statistical survey does not appear in earlier or later issues of *Koloniaale Verslag*. Interestingly, Jambi's share of the revenue gained from imports and experts is far larger, according to these figures, than the percentages of Jambi's real imports and exports in 1900 (less than 1 percent) (see statistics in the Netherlands-Indies Trade Statistics, 1870–1938; History of European Expansion Data Bank; Nederlands Historisch Data Archief (which, in spite of its title, does not begin for Jambi until 1900; *Statistiek van den handel, de scheepvaart en de in- en uitvoerrechten in Nederlandsch-Indië over het jaar 1880* (Batavia: Landsdrukkerij,1884).

guilders a year.[20] Jambi remained "a burden on the budget," as the director of internal administration put it in 1898.[21]

The first signs of interest in Jambi's oil arose in the late 1880s. That Palembang had petroleum had been known as far back as 1865: local people used it to caulk their proas.[22] Prospectors had set off to the region in the 1880s. Jean Baptiste August Kessler, director of the Koninklijke, started collecting as many exploration licenses as possible in the early 1890s, generally using agents to act as a front. He listed them under the name of the Dutch East Indies Exploration Company, which, in 1896, started exploring the jungle in northern Palembang along the border with Lower Jambi. Palembang was the most popular part of the archipelago for oil prospecting in the late 1890s.[23] After the first successful test drilling, the recently established Sumatra-Palembang Petroleum Company (SUMPAL), which was linked to the Koninklijke, started its operations in 1897. That same year the company Muara Enim started drilling for oil further south in Palembang. In 1901 they were joined by the company Musi Ilir. Within the following five years, the Koninklijke gained control of these three companies.[24]

Jambi was soon drawn into this oil boom. The marshy coastal regions of Palembang and Jambi formed a single geological unit, and oil is unlikely to be troubled by human borders. In 1891 Taha's son-in-law Pangeran Prabu Negara, who had been entrusted by Taha (as an appanage holder in the lowlands) with all oil-related business, had issued an exploration license.[25] The same year, however, the colonial government rejected an initial exploration application. More were to follow. In May 1893 Governor-General Pijnacker Hordijk therefore urged Resident De Vries to conclude a supplementary contract, whereby the sultan's administration would relinquish the right to award mining concessions in the safe lowlands of Jambi.[26] Formally speaking, oil prospectors were entitled to conclude contracts with local self-governing administrations according to the 1888 contract with Jambi, but the same contract required them to obtain the colonial government's approval.[27] This was partly related to security considerations. Only if security

---

[20] NA, Col., vb. January 16, 1892, no. 52; director of finance to governor-general, November 7, 1893, NA, Col., mr. 1893/181.

[21] Director of internal administration to governor-general, September 1, 1898, NA, Col., vb. March 26, 1900, M4.

[22] W. H. de Greve, "Petroleum en aardolie en haar voorkomen in Nederlandsch-Indië," *Tijdschrift voor Nijverheid en Landbouw in Nederlandsch-Indië* 9 (1865): 281–356, esp. 343, 346.

[23] *Koloniaal Verslag 1899*, app. EEE, p. 5.

[24] "Petroleum," in *Encyclopaedie van Nederlandsch-Indië* (The Hague: Nijhoff; Leiden: Brill, 1919), 3: 394–401, esp. 397; F. C. Gerretson, *Geschiedenis der "Koninklijke,"* 5 vols. (Baarn: Bosch and Keuning, 1971–73), 2: 48–53.

[25] Memorandum of April 7, 1903, from the head of the Department of Mineral Extraction, NA, Col., vb. January 8, 1904, no. 20. Gerretson notes that some contracts had already been concluded with the local rulers for petroleum exploration in 1888, though none of them actually led to drilling (Gerretson, *Geschiedenis der "Koninklijke,"* 2: 295). I have been unable to find these contracts in the records. In 1890 an Englishman whose interest in oil prospecting had led him to Upper Jambi had paid for this curiosity with his life. As he had been denied permission to undertake this journey, there were no political repercussions (*Koloniaal Verslag 1891*, p. 10).

[26] First government secretary to Resident of Palembang, December 24, 1897, NA, Col., vb. January 8, 1904, no. 20.

[27] *Koloniaal Verslag 1889*, pp. 248, 257; see also NA, Col., *minuut* of vb. January 8, 1904, no. 20.

could be guaranteed was the colonial government willing to approve an application; otherwise it judged the risk of incidents and military or diplomatic complications to be unacceptably high. It was therefore simpler for the authorities in Batavia to omit the intermediate stage of the local rulers and to claim the exclusive right of decision for itself—certainly in Jambi, where political relations had always been rather unclear. Acquiring this sole right was Batavia's primary aim in Jambi as in other parts of the Outer Islands in the 1890s.

Resident De Vries did nothing to further this goal, however, and for four years the instructions were left unheeded. After the colonial government repeated them in July 1897, however, a draft was prepared, and by December it was ready for use.[28] Thus, the initiative clearly came from Batavia. Meanwhile, the colonial government continued to reject all applications for exploratory operations in Jambi—turning down fifteen in December 1897—including several from SUMPAL.[29]

ADMINISTRATIVE TANGLES

The instructions issued in July 1897 stirred the new Resident—Henri Jules Monod de Froideville had taken over in March—to take action. Monod had served as controller in Palembang in the early 1870s, subsequently serving in other parts of the Outer Islands (including a stretch as Resident in Bangka). There he had gotten a close look at the advantages of mineral extraction for the colonial authorities. In his new post, consequently, he warmly advocated the expansion of such activities. He immediately protested against the rejection of the applications in December 1897, since the supplementary contract was almost ready for use.[30] Urged by Batavia, he visited Jambi in June 1898, taking the draft contract with him.

He was to return empty-handed, although the political agent R. L. A. Hellwig had already informed him in December 1897 that the sultan's administration had no objections to relinquishing its rights. Neither Sultan Zainuddin nor Pangeran Ratu Anom Kesumo Judo, both of whose signatures were required, turned up to sign the contract. The sultan sent word that he was indisposed, while the *pangeran ratu* was supposedly afraid to leave the uplands because of a smallpox epidemic.[31] This failure to appear was a familiar tactic. Taha did not want a supplementary contract and was not prepared to sign one. Opening up Jambi for European private enterprise would inevitably lead to more Dutch intervention.

Taha had demonstrated yet again who really held the strings in Jambi. Over the past two decades he had expanded his influence further by conferring titles, granting appanages, and pursuing a vigorous form of marriage politics.[32] By Malay standards he was indeed a great and good ruler; his fertility proved it. According to genealogical lists he had at least eighteen children in 1901, whereas his brother

---

[28] First government secretary to Resident of Palembang, February 16, 1898, NA, Col., vb. January 8, 1904, no. 20.

[29] First government secretary to Resident of Palembang, December 24, 1897, NA, Col., vb. January 8, 1904, no. 20; *Gouvernementsbesluit*, December 24, 1897, no. 19.

[30] First government secretary to Resident of Palembang, February 16, 1898, NA, Col., vb. January 8, 1904, no. 20.

[31] Resident of Palembang to governor-general, July 15, 1898, NA, Col., mr. 1898/648, vb. March 26, 1900, M4.

[32] E. B. Kielstra, "Onze verhouding tot Djambi," *Onze Eeuw* 1 (1901): 1176–94.

Dipo Negoro had twelve and the former sultans Nazaruddin, Mohildin, and Zainuddin had six, eight, and four.[33] Almost all his children he had placed with—that is, married to—enemies of the Dutch authorities, thus building up an impressive political network. Through his children's marriages (i.e., as *bhisan*) he was related to Batavia's three fiercest opponents: Pangeran Dipo Negoro; his eldest brother by a non-noble mother, Pangeran Kusin of Sekamis; and Pangeran Puspo Ali of the Merangin, the head of the Kedipan family of nobles. Only Raden Anom did not belong to his close circle, but as Pangeran Dipo Negoro's favorite son-in-law he was not far from it. Furthermore, some of Taha's sons-in-law were leading dignitaries: among them were Pangeran Prabu Negara, son of former sultan Mohildin, and the second regent, Pangeran Surio Nata Menggala. Taha was also related to Pangeran Wiro Kesumo, since one of his daughters was married to one of the *pangeran*'s sons. Furthermore, since this son-in-law was one of the few dignitaries who lived in Taha's own village of Sungai Aroh, he was under his direct influence.[34] Indirectly Taha also controlled the lowlands, since the main appanage holders here were Pangeran Prabu Negara (Bulian catchment basin), the two regents (Bahar and Limun catchment basins in the Kompeh), Pangeran Wiro Kesumo, and Raden Anom, who had a small appanage in the Kompeh.[35] In the uplands, another son-in-law, Pangeran Anjang, was appanage holder of the VII and IX Kota and *jenang* of the Upper Batang Hari, while the *pangeran ratu* was appanage holder of the Tembesi and Tebo.[36] With these instruments of power, Taha not only controlled the entire region but heavily determined Jambian policy.

Taha also had a shrewd grasp of the relationship between the Jambian administration and the colonial government. In 1898 Batavia learned that the political agent had been corresponding for years directly with the *pangeran ratu* instead of with the regents—behind their backs, in fact. "The letters were given to the captain of the *Yusuf* who delivered them into Taha's hands on his trade journeys to the uplands."[37] The regents had no influence whatsoever, were terrified of Taha, and sometimes stayed in their appanages from one year to the next. They seldom journeyed to Jambi, any more than did Sultan Zainuddin or Pangeran Ratu Anom Kesumo Judo, all of which was in flagrant defiance of the 1888 contract. It meant that Taha could keep to his old policy—defenses at the ready in case the Dutch launched an action aimed at expansion, and otherwise avoiding contact with them. The refusal of the sultan and *pangeran ratu* to attend the meeting planned for the summer of 1898 was entirely in line with this.

For the colonial government, however, none of this was clear. Unschooled in appanages and genealogies, it necessarily acted in blind faith. For Resident Monod, Pangeran Wiro Kesumo was therefore the most important intermediary; and he followed him blindly, partly because he thought that Wiro Kesumo's position and appanage meant it was greatly in his interest to help the colonial government take

---

[33] KITLV, coll. Wellan, 590a.

[34] Data from list n.d., KITLV, coll. Wellan, 590a.

[35] Register of nobles, KITLV, coll. Wellan, 590 c; G. J. Velds, "De onderwerping van Djambi, 1901–1907: Beknopte geschiedenis naar officiëele gegevens," *Indisch Militair Tijdschrift*, Extra-bijlage 24 (1909): 37.

[36] Register of nobles, KITLV, coll. Wellan, 590 c; Velds, "De onderwerping van Djambi," p. 37.

[37] Resident of Palembang to governor-general, December 23, 1898, NA, Col., mr. 1899/100, vb. March 26, 1904, M4.

the right action.[38] Monod would prepare all his plans in consultation with Wiro Kesumo to the exclusion of all other Jambian dignitaries, never acting without seeking his advice. Wiro Kesumo thus provided the Resident with his only picture of Jambian reality, and it was a colored one.

Monod was disgusted with this insult to Dutch authority in Jambi. In his report of July 15, 1898, he presented a long list of grievances demonstrating its worthlessness. Mineral extraction operations were impossible to arrange, internal disputes were allowed to fester, the population was exploited, and criminals were not extradited. He then made the following proposal: Sultan Zainuddin, who was old, frail, and in ill health, should be persuaded to abdicate for an annuity of four thousand guilders. He had already discussed the matter at his meeting with the dignitaries in Jambi. Pangeran Ratu Anom Kesumo Judo, fifteen years old by them, should be crowned sultan, supervised by two powerful regents who were well disposed toward the Dutch. For the latter posts he took Wiro Kesumo's advice and suggested the names of two of Taha's great-nephews—Pangeran Adipati and Pangeran Prabu Negara, sons of the former sultan Mohildin. With these men in prominent positions, Wiro Kesumo believed that Taha's cooperation would be "assured." The old demand about accepting subject status had silently been dropped. Monod himself wanted to undertake a journey along the Tembesi and Limun to study the prospects for mining exploration. He was still in buoyant mood: "If my combination [of regents] creates a better situation, the ample riches slumbering in Jambi's soil will soon be laid bare, generating a rich source of income for the government of the Dutch East Indies that will compensate tenfold or hundredfold for today's minor sacrifices," he enthused to his superiors.[39]

Governor-General Van der Wijck, though known as a strong administrator, took six months to respond to this letter. Having consulted the Council of the Dutch East Indies, which was highly critical of Monod's plans, he urged restraint. He referred to Sultan Zainuddin's abdication in a meeting of local dignitaries as premature, and he demanded a meeting of the nominated candidate regents before they were appointed. He also vetoed Monod's planned journey, suggesting this should be left to a controller and a mining engineer. From then on, the Resident must not visit Jambi unless he had received guarantees of the sultan's presence. Batavia was clearly responding to the significant blow that had been dealt to the prestige of the Resident and the Dutch authorities. However, Van der Wijck had no objection in principle to the former sultan receiving an annuity of 3,600 guilders.[40]

Toward the end of 1898, further misunderstandings seemed to be brewing between the colonial government and the Resident, and in April 1899 Monod was summoned to Batavia for a discussion of policy. In May he finally received written permission to arrange Sultan Zainuddin's abdication, provided the matter could be concluded successfully. A meeting would have to be held to discuss grievances

---

[38] Resident of Palembang to governor-general, July 15, 1898, NA, Col., vb. March 26, 1900, M4.

[39] "Wordt door mijne combinatie een betere toestand geboren, dan zullen over een betrekkelijk korte tijd de groote rijkdommen, die in den bodem van Jambi sluimeren aan den dag gebracht kunnen worden en rijke bronnen van inkomsten ook voor het Nederlandsch-Indische gouvernement kunnen vloeien, die in de naaste toekomst tien- en honderdvoudig de kleine opofferingen van het heden zullen kunnen vergoeden"; Resident of Palembang to governor-general, July 15, 1898, NA, Col., vb. March 26, 1900, M4.

[40] First government secretary to Resident of Palembang, December 2, 1898, NA, Col., vb. March 26, 1900, M4.

concerning the avoidance of meetings with Dutch officials, the failure to hand over criminals (notably Raden Anom), and the regulation of a border dispute with the Rawas, an important issue in connection with any future oil drilling. If the *pangeran* did not show up, the annuity could be withheld.[41] Later that month Monod presented his next plan, a variation on an old theme. By compelling the sultan to abdicate and replacing him with the *pangeran ratu*, he sought to persuade Taha and Dipo Negoro to agree to a rapprochement. Referring to the conditions set in the early 1880s, he proposed giving Taha the title of sultan plus an annuity of four thousand guilders and to grant Dipo Negoro an annuity of two thousand guilders in exchange for both men's recognition of Dutch sovereignty. In June, Batavia gave the go-ahead for this proposal.[42]

Two years had now elapsed since the first instructions to conclude a supplementary contract. It was time to convene a meeting with Jambi's dignitaries. At the end of June 1899, Monod paid a week-long visit to Jambi to arrange it. Tension had been growing over the previous months: would Sultan Zainuddin show up? The reports varied from one day to the next: he was coming; no, he was too ill to come. A spy reported that the sultan and *pangeran ratu* were taking laxatives to feign illness.[43] Taha was said to have threatened in May to murder the first man who came looking for oil.[44] How the relevant lowlands appanage holders, such as Pangeran Wiro Kesumo, Pangeran Prabu Negara, the regent Pangeran Ario Jaya Kesumo, and Raden Anom, thought about the matter is not known.

Monod's visit to Jambi at the end of June proved a pointless exercise. Neither the sultan nor the *pangeran ratu* turned up. They were presented with a twenty-day ultimatum, "in full consultation with Pangeran Wiro Kesumo."[45] Not until August 12, twelve days after the expiry of a second ultimatum, did Sultan Zainuddin finally appear in the capital—and even then he came not at 10 A.M., as the Resident had demanded, but two and a half hours later. It was yet another successful effort to keep the initiative and to uphold his dignity. His excuse was that the men staffing the ferryboat that was to have transported him had gone on strike. Meanwhile, Resident Monod had visited Jambi twice more, from July 18–21 and from August 8–14, sending back regular reports. These were largely full of rumors and counter-rumors about who was on which side, and what Taha was alleged to have said and to have ordered. Wiro Kesumo was again the primary informant. The tenor of these reports conveyed the rising tension in the capital during these summer months. After Monod's fruitless journey at the end of June the population lived in fear of war.[46]

When Zainuddin finally turned up, he came alone; nothing was said about the *pangeran ratu*. Pangeran Prabu and Pangeran Adipati were also absent, though for

[41] First government secretary to Resident of Palembang, May 6, 1899, NA, Col., vb. March 26, 1900, M4.

[42] Resident of Palembang to governor-general, May 31, 1899, and First government secretary to Resident of Palembang, June 13, 1899, NA, Col., vb. March 26, 1900, M4.

[43] Political agent to Resident of Palembang, May 12, 1899, May 17, 1899, May 23, 1899, and May 25, 1899, NA, Col., vb. March 26, 1900, M4.

[44] Political agent to Resident of Palembang, May 25, 1899, NA, Col., vb. March 26, 1900, M4.

[45] Resident of Palembang to governor-general, July 10, 1899, NA, Col., vb. March 26, 1900, M4.

[46] Resident of Palembang to governor-general, August 18, 1899, NA, Col., vb. March 26, 1900, M4.

legitimate reasons. Thus, the governor-general's condition of a meeting with the candidate regents could not be met. Nor had the sultan decided as yet on the proposals to be put to Taha; he wanted to arrange his affairs first. He did submit a request to abdicate but sent it only by word of mouth. When pressured, he said that he expected Taha to agree to the conditions.

The events of July had prompted Monod to submit a fresh proposal. It was now clear to him that Taha would not agree to the sultan's title passing to his son. He therefore modified his plan in one small though essential respect. While still requiring Zainuddin to step down, he now stipulated that Pangeran Ratu Anom Kesumo Judo could not succeed to the throne until Taha and his brother Dipo Negoro accepted subject status. Otherwise, Anom Kesumo Judo would stay on as *pangeran ratu* and the sultan's title would go to either Pangeran Adipati or Prabu Negara. The accession was also to be conditional on the signing of a supplementary contract ceding mineral extraction rights. Monod now openly repeated another argument as proof of Jambian misgovernment: the exploitation of the population by local headmen, "a swarm of bloodsuckers and vampires" that had dealt a deathblow to Jambi's trade. "Jambi's princes and their offspring had attached themselves to the population in the manner of parasites."[47]

Van der Wijck agreed that Taha and Dipo Negoro should first accept subject status, but he rejected the idea of making Anom Kesumo Judo's accession conditional on a supplementary contract. If Taha balked at this, it would delay matters yet again, and putting a government in place was paramount. For Van der Wijck, administrative matters outweighed economic interests for the present. He would even accept a continuation of "the old situation," which would mean that not one of the oil concessions previously approved by the sultan's administration would be recognized until the succession and Jambi's internal administration were settled. This was of overriding importance before economic affairs could be dealt with.[48] In October 1899 Zainuddin's formal abdication request was granted, and the *pangeran ratu*'s elevation to sultan was made conditional upon Taha and Dipo Negoro's notification to the Resident of their acceptance of subject status.[49] For the Jambian sultanate, this meant that the autonomy to which it had clung so long and with such tenacity now hung by a thread.

A NEW ADVISOR: SNOUCK HURGRONJE

Though the Dutch had finally accomplished Zainuddin's abdication, they had effectively created a gaping power vacuum. The sultan's administration did not respond to the conditions that had been set. Formally left without a government, Jambi was now de facto ruled by Taha. Monod now played a familiar card—his last, in the circumstances. He proposed a military expedition or—his own personal preference—the establishment of an administrative post in the uplands to gain more control of the region and its ruler.[50] This proposal, his fourth

---

[47] Resident of Palembang to governor-general, July 10, 1899, NA, Col., vb. March 26, 1900, M4.

[48] First government secretary to Resident of Palembang, September 29, 1899, NA, Col., mr. 1899/668, vb. March 26, 1900, M4.

[49] *Gouvernementsbesluit* October 22, 1899, no. 1, NA, Col., vb. March 26, 1900, M4.

[50] Resident of Palembang to governor-general, December 11, 1899, NA, Col., vb. March 26, 1900, M4.

to date, prompted the new governor-general, the military man Willem Rooseboom (1899–1904), to consult a new advisor. In his military career he had learned to value the qualities of Christiaan Snouck Hurgronje, advisor on Islamic and Native Affairs, from his recommendations on Aceh. Now Rooseboom asked his opinion on Jambi. Since Snouck Hurgronje may be regarded as one of the spiritual fathers of Dutch imperialism, it is worth considering both the man himself and his advice at some length.

Christiaan Snouck Hurgronje (1857–1936) was born from the second marriage of an unfrocked clergyman.[51] This biographical detail alone may help to clarify his departure from the theology faculty in favor of oriental studies. But to some extent his choice also reflected the *Zeitgeist:* many of his contemporaries at the modernizing university of Leiden abandoned their Calvinist faith at this time. "Where naturalism has taken root, the realm of revealed truths is at an end," he proclaimed in his first article in *De Gids* (1886). An ardent supporter of the Enlightenment ideal of progress, Snouck naturally gravitated to politics. In his age, and with his particular scientific bent, this meant colonial politics and relations with Islam. As an academic, Snouck placed his knowledge and later his network at the disposal of the colonial rulers. His first teaching post, at the municipal institute in Leiden that trained colonial officials, was indicative of this course. To gain a better understanding of the role of Islam in Aceh, he journeyed to the Arab port of Jeddah in 1884, and he was even allowed to visit Mecca. Five years later he asked the Minister of Colonies to let him do research in Aceh and to use his contacts in Mecca to study the social and political conditions in the region. The opposition of the military commander prevented him from putting this plan into action until 1891. His 1892 report, as we have seen, ushered in a new hard line in Aceh. That this approach was fashioned by a nonmilitary man with an impressive fund of knowledge gave it added credibility, as its author evidently had no ax to grind.

For Aceh, Snouck Hurgronje detailed a five-point objective: military subjection, the introduction of direct Dutch rule, rapprochement with local headmen, the prosecution of religious leaders, and an overall improvement in prosperity. On Islam, especially in relation to the *ulama* (spiritual leaders) in Aceh, he pronounced the negative verdict that characterized many of his contemporaries: it could never become the force for modernization that he considered essential for the East Indies. If progress were to be achieved, it would have to come from an enlightened Western administration. He therefore saw it as Europe's responsibility to destroy the "political" power of Islam and to foster free thinking. It was a responsibility he placed squarely on the shoulders of the colonial rulers. It was this goal that underlay his insistence on forging ties with local headmen and his subsequent pleas to school the local administrative elite. His emphasis on education and modernization was entirely in tune with the evolutionary thinking that dominated anthropology in the late nineteenth century. Native peoples were

---

[51] On Snouck Hurgronje, see Schröder, "Oriëntalistische retoriek"; P. S. van Koningsveld, "Snouck Hurgronje zoals hij was," *De Gids* 143 (1980): 785–806; E. Gobée and C. Adriaanse, eds., *Ambtelijke adviezen van C. Snouck Hurgronje 1889–1936*, 3 vols (The Hague: Nijhoff, 1957–65), 1: i, ix–xxi; 3: 1908–2175; Elsbeth Locher-Scholten, "Association in Theory and Practice: The Composition of the Regency Council (ca. 1910–1920)," in *Between People and Statistics: Essays on Modern Indonesian History Presented to P. Creutzberg*, ed. Francien van Anrooij et al. (The Hague: Nijhoff, 1979), pp. 209–11.

seen as children, lacking development, not inferior to Western peoples but lower down the ladder of civilization. This is how Snouck looked upon the indigenous peoples of the archipelago.

But education and development must be preceded by obedience and well-ordered government, that is, by "pacification" and clear contractual relations with the Dutch overlords. For this reason, Snouck and Van Heutsz drafted a simple formula in 1898 consisting of three articles, which became known as the Brief Declaration (Korte Verklaring). Under the proposed terms, the local ruler declared that his land was part of the Dutch East Indies and subject to Dutch rule, that he would refrain from all foreign contacts, and that he would adhere to all regulations laid down by the colonial government. This contract, almost simplistic in its straightforwardness, forestalled any tedious tug-of-war about the content of articles. It also allowed the self-governing administrations perhaps to cherish for a little longer the illusion that everything was still open while giving the colonial authorities scope to restrict their power. When the General Secretariat raised legal objections to the Brief Declaration, Snouck parried them with political and administrative arguments. The succinct declaration became one of the primary instruments of Dutch imperialism.

Six years elapsed between Snouck's first report on Aceh and his appointment as advisor on East Indies and Native Affairs in 1898. Only then did the colonial government recognize his abilities and take advantage of them.[52] But once he was installed in this position, his views were taken very seriously. Jambi was his first major assignment in the expansionist project after Aceh, and it brought him more rapid success. One month after his appointment, at the end of January 1900, he submitted recommendations that were adopted in their entirety. He went to work differently here than in Aceh. Instead of conducting lengthy interviews in the region, he betook himself to the General Secretariat to sift through the records.[53] He did not actually visit Jambi until the autumn of 1900. Moreover, he probably had few contacts in Jambi; there was no separate "lodge" for Jambians, as only Pangeran Wiro Kesumo and a few other dignitaries from the region had undertaken the *haj*.[54] But the letters and reports from Palembang told him enough, and he drew freely on his experience in Aceh to interpret them.

Snouck Hurgronje identified two main causes of the impasse in Jambi. First was the colonial government's mistake in allowing Taha to retain his influence after his deposition in 1858. He had been left with much of his income intact, and a situation had been created in which the "sham sultans" (i.e., contract sultans) "would never agree to anything without first obtaining his approval." The second key reason was the policy of abstention itself, as a result of which the Dutch had been left wholly in the dark concerning Taha's power. This second root cause bore

---

[52] Schröder, "Oriëntalistische retoriek."

[53] His mode of information gathering had a morality of its own. He did not shrink from contacting informers from Aceh through acquaintances in Mecca, nor from learning about Javanese society through a marriage with the daughter of a Javanese chief *penghulu* (1890–95) and later with the daughter of an assistant judge (189?– 1906, when he left the East Indies) (Van Koningsveld, "Snouck Hurgronje"), but in 1896 he rejected a request to enlist the aid of Acehnese spies for the government (Schröder, "Oriëntalistische retoriek").

[54] Pangeran Kusin of the Merangin canceled his plans to undertake a *haj* in 1900 at the request of Taha, who probably did not want to be without him at this tense juncture (see Resident of Palembang to governor-general, March 15, 1900, NA, Col., vb. August 19, 1901, no. 46).

the brunt of Snouck's vitriol, since he thought the abstention policy an abomination. "The lack of any contact whatsoever with a Native realm would be preferable, leaving aside the international balance of power perhaps, to maintaining the kind of relations such as those maintained with Jambi these past forty years. It has not even meant stagnation, but constant regression." The sham sultan "at no time exerted any authority that was of benefit to us."[55]

Snouck Hurgronje was acquainted with the policy of appointing ineffectual lowly relatives as intermediaries, having encountered it in a variety of situations in Aceh. His denunciation of the contract was also informed by his Acehnese days. He preferred a Brief Declaration, seeing the contract as a useless vehicle of hollow rhetoric. Snouck did not express a preference for direct or indirect rule, which he thought dependent on the vigor of the self-governing authorities. But the goal should be the same: "a constant effort must be made to reform internal misadministration to accord with our principles of government; we do not advance the cause of progress in a Native country, nor do we gain a jot of influence, if we leave the Native leaders to practice extortion and tyranny with impunity."[56] And acquiring more influence was impossible with this contract, certainly since the Dutch had undertaken not to interfere in Jambian affairs. What was needed here was as succinct an agreement as possible.

Snouck emphasized the adverse consequences of abstention, namely a total lack of firsthand information coupled with conflicting reports—it was impossible to build policy on such foundations. Only now, with the abdication of Sultan Zainuddin, had the real situation become clear. Unfortunately this clarity was of little benefit, since there was no successor. To find a reliable candidate, talks should be convened under Dutch leadership, but this was something that the most influential Jambians were studiously avoiding. Snouck's conclusion was clear: a closer liaison would have to be enforced by calling a meeting between the leading members of the sultan's family, to be chaired by the Resident. Until this meeting had taken place, the annuity should be withheld, except for the money promised in exchange for the sultan's abdication and a few small sums that the political agent paid directly to minor intermediaries. The latter category presumably included Pangeran Wiro Kesumo, although Snouck did not mention any names. Snouck was confident that this procedure would yield a candidate willing to accept the sultan's title.

But what about the next stage? Snouck rejected Resident Monod's plans: he opposed the establishment of a few trading posts in the unknown Jambian hinterland, and was equally dismissive of the idea of conducting a military expedition, which would secure only a temporary advantage without any permanent political results. Again he argued, from his own experience in Aceh, that only a mobile column of soldiers could produce results in the Jambian interior. Snouck was no believer in the colonial myth of a population yearning for the Dutch to come and rule them. "The population certainly does not as yet have any such clear understanding of what is in its best interests."[57] Reports to the contrary were merely the false promises of sycophants. But the people would certainly resign

---

[55] Gobée and Adriaanse, *Ambtelijke adviezen*, 3: 2032–3.

[56] Ibid., p. 2034.

[57] Ibid., p. 2040.

Encampment during the Pedir expedition in Aceh, with Snouck Hurgronje at far left, wearing a white jacket, Van Heutsz the diminutive figure seated at the table at far left, and Van Rijn van Alkemade seated, wearing a white administrator's uniform

from P. van 't Veer, *De Atjeh-oorlog* (Amsterdam: Arbeiderspers, 1969)

themselves to the change—their "main desire being to pursue their normal activities without hindrance"—once the local headmen had accepted subject status or been stripped of their influence. This was where the mobile column came in. First, Taha's village must be occupied, as nothing was more likely to hasten the capitulation of a local ruler than homelessness. Besides, this operation would acquaint the forces with the terrain and help them decide on the next area to be occupied. Given the knowledge and experience gained in the far more warlike Aceh, the mission could not fail.

To sum up, Snouck's advice contained four elements: (1) consider the sultan to have been deposed and pay him an annuity; (2) suspend the annuity to the sultan's administration; (3) call a meeting of all designated Jambian dignitaries for a discussion of Jambian affairs with a representative of the colonial government and for the election of a sultan; and (4) build up as much information as possible about the Jambian interior, with a view to possible armed intervention with mobile units like those used in Aceh.[58] His advice was entirely in line with his ideas on Aceh: abolish the policy of abstention, strengthen Dutch control, conclude a concise contract, and undermine the position of hostile local headmen by deploying a mobile column.

For Snouck too, it was the administrative arguments that weighed most heavily. He was not inspired by visions of rich oil returns. Oil did not even figure in his first recommendations of January 1900. Nor did he mention it in a memorandum of May 1901 about the local administration or in his recommendations of June 1901 about taking action against Taha. Finally, when asked in December 1901 for his views on the idea of opening up the Jambian lowlands for mineral extraction, he responded favorably—but on the basis of administrative considerations. He thought it should be pursued as a matter of urgency, "as one of the main peaceful means of firmly establishing our influence in that region." The advent of such industry would also have the effect of improving communications, making the region easier to control. He wanted the exploration rights sold to the highest bidder. A state-run enterprise seemed to him a bad idea, given the state of the treasury. The best way to serve the state's interests was to "leave mining operations to private individuals, while securing the best possible terms for the state."[59] In short, oil should serve the country's wider interests; the country should not be serving the interests of the oil companies. Like Van der Wijck, Snouck always put administrative considerations first.

Snouck placed his own stamp on Dutch activities in Jambi for years to come. His advice was adopted in its entirety, although not straightaway. Much of 1900 was taken up with measures intended to pave the way for its implementation. The army commander's opposition to deploying a mobile unit was gradually overcome by the district military commander of Palembang, while Monod was promoted away to Riau in October 1900. He was the first Resident for thirty years for whom Palembang was not the final chapter in his career. His lack of confidence in Snouck's plan, especially in the proposed meeting, his inconsistent policy with its succession of fresh plans, and his unshakable confidence in his informant, Pangeran Wiro Kesumo, were ample reason to replace him. Monod's final claim, that reliable sources informed him that Taha was truly on the point of accepting subject

---

[58] Ibid., pp. 2042–3.

[59] Ibid., pp. 2078, 2081.

status and had already set aside some elephant's teeth as a fit to the governor-general, did not avert his fate.[60]

His successor was a man who had served in Aceh, I. A. van Rijn van Alkemade, forty-two years of age. He had been junior controller for a year in Palembang, and had subsequently served on Sumatra's east coast. He had then performed well as acting Assistant Resident in Aceh and its dependencies. He had been knighted in the Order of the Dutch Lion for displaying special merit during the Pedir expedition. It was on that expedition that he had met Snouck. His Jambi period exemplified his unflagging energy. Together with Snouck Hurgronje, who had by then been appointed his adviser, he determined the policy pursued in Jambi from November 1900 onward.

THE JAMBIAN ADMINISTRATION

The Jambian administration had also made changes. In February 1900, Taha had sent a letter stating explicitly, for the first time, by way of former Sultan Zainuddin, that he had sworn on the Koran in 1858, at twenty-five, together with his brother Dipo Negoro, never again to meet with a representative of "their father the Governor-General." The rejection, all those years ago, of their request to leave the contract unchanged, as they had sworn to their father, and the ensuing military expedition, had been "unjust," for they had still been "young and rash." Even so, they bore no grudge against the colonial government and had supported the sultans as far as possible for forty-two years. Taha had even parted with his own son "in proof of [his] sincerity."[61] Though rhetoric probably accounted for much of this letter, it was Taha's first explicit statement of his position, which was indeed entirely consistent with his behavior since 1858.[62] Clearly, he would not be attending any meeting.

In March 1900 reliable sources reported that Taha had offered the sultanate to his nephew Pangeran Adipati, the son of the former Sultan Mohildin, who was, however, willing to accept only if Taha promised strict compliance with all the terms of the contract with the colonial government. Otherwise, he would gladly let the honor pass to his half-brother Pangeran Prabu. Neither man seemed eager to assume the role of buffer; since Taha still wielded the real power in Jambi, any trouble with the Dutch would originate with him.[63] In September the festivities held to mark the circumcision of the *pangeran ratu* produced a crop of fresh titles and status for young dignitaries, the sons of Dipo Negoro, and Pangeran Puspo Ali; political consultations were also held on this occasion.[64] At the beginning of November 1900, Pangeran Adipati was reported to have finally been appointed

---

[60] Resident of Palembang to governor-general, October 30, 1900, NA, Col., vb. August 19, 1901, no. 46.

[61] Translation, *susuhunan* to Resident of Palembang, 18 sawal 1317 (February 19, 1900), enclosed with Resident of Palembang to governor-general, March 1900, NA, Col., mr. 1900/255, vb. August 19, 1901, no. 46.

[62] How this can be reconciled with his request for pardon in 1867 is unclear. Perhaps he considered the oath less compelling at that time, for pragmatic reasons.

[63] Resident of Palembang to governor-general, March 15, 1900, NA, Col., vb. August 19, 1901, no. 46.

[64] Extract of the journal of the political agent in Jambi, October 30, 1900, NA, Col., vb. August 19, 1901, no. 46.

sultan. Raedt van Oldenbarnevelt, who had been reelected political agent on the basis of his earlier experience, described the fifty-year-old Adipati in glowing terms: "civilized manners . . . pleasing demeanor, cheerful, unaffected and approachable, . . . a keen sense of justice, godly, and devoid of all fanaticism." He went so far as to call him Jambi's most popular leader. Pangeran Wiro Kesumo too had praised him as virtuous, cultivated, and influential.[65] By the beginning of December, however, his appointment turned out to have misfired: Adipati had refused to accept the throne. The election had taken place in his absence. And Taha had a higher opinion of his own son-in-law and nephew Pangeran Prabu Negara, whom he treated with unparalleled deference. For these reasons Adipati had decided to turn the honor down.[66] If free elections had been held, the headmen would in all probability have chosen Taha. They would also have been content to accept the *pangeran ratu*, but Dipo Negoro had made any such appointment conditional on his own son becoming the next *pangeran ratu*. And this would be a double breach of adat, since the latter was neither the son of a former sultan nor born of a noble mother. According to Malay views of the sultan as the link between microcosm and macrocosm, his accession would spell disaster for Jambi. The people had not forgotten Zainuddin's reign, with its failed harvests and its epidemics.[67]

In November, consultations were held on an almost everyday basis between representatives of the colonial government (the political agent Raedt van Oldenbarnevelt and Snouck Hurgronje) and Jambian dignitaries (Wiro Kesumo, the former sultan, the *pangeran ratu*, envoys from Taha, Prabu Negara, and Adipati) At the beginning of December, Pangeran Prabu Negara, described as "abrupt, somewhat haughty and hot-tempered, . . . a man of few words . . . and hard of hearing,"[68] was elected sultan, and accepted the title. Taha, whose name, it should be said, was never mentioned to a Dutchman by a Jambian—even Pangeran Wiro Kesumo referred to him circuitously as the *pangeran ratu's* father[69]—remained the real ruler. But his authority had been dented, as all the entanglements surrounding the choice of sultan made clear. And his political ideal (remaining on good terms with the colonial government without accepting subject status) was becoming increasingly difficult to sustain.

For Batavia, Prabu's accession without a meeting of all the dignitaries entitled to vote (including Taha and Dipo Negoro) led by the Resident was unacceptable. Although it was already clear by May 1900 that this meeting would not materialize, the ceremony was nonetheless scheduled for February 6, 1901. It was a last-ditch effort without any hope of success. In January, Resident Van Rijn van Alkemade received another request from Taha and Pangeran Dipo Negoro, asking

---

[65] Political agent to Resident of Palembang, November 7, 1900, NA, Col., vb. August 19, 1901, no. 46; Resident of Palembang to governor-general, July 15, 1898, NA, Col., vb. March 26, 1900, M4.

[66] Resident of Palembang to governor-general, May 1, 1900, NA, Col., vb. August 19, 1901, no. 46; Resident of Palembang to governor-general, July 15, 1898, NA, Col., vb. March 26, 1900, M4; Resident of Palembang to governor-general, December 3, 1900, NA, Col., vb. August 19, 1901, no. 46.

[67] Resident of Palembang to governor-general, December 14, 1900, NA, Col., vb. August 19, 1901, no. 46.

[68] Political agent to Resident of Palembang, November 7, 1900, NA, Col., vb. August 19, 1901, no. 46.

[69] Resident of Palembang to governor-general, May 1, 1900, NA, Col., vb. August 19, 1901, no. 46.

to be excused in exchange for a promise that all the remaining dignitaries would meet in the capital. This request was rejected.[70] February 6, 1901, was a quiet day in the capital. Of the thirty-three people invited to attend, most of them members of the *suku* Kraton, Kedipan, and Perban, even those the Dutch had hoped would come did not show up.[71]

As a result, Van Rijn decided to adopt the role of sultan himself. As long as there was no sultan, he would adopt the responsibilities that went with this position. Appanage holders and local headmen were placed under an obligation to follow his orders. Van Rijn's patience had been exhausted. He brushed aside a few vague suggestions from Pangeran Wiro Kesumo for a meeting with Taha in the uplands: the initiative for any meeting would now have to come from the other side.[72] To force some kind of a response from the headmen in the uplands, it had been decided on February 10, 1901, to send two hundred infantrymen to occupy Muara Tembesi. In May 1901 an administrative post was set up there.[73] The location had been chosen for its strategic value: Muara Tembesi was the key to the uplands; the colonial authorities now had control of both ends of the Tembesi, Jambi's southern flank, the Rawas of Palembang, and Muara Tembesi. Van Rijn continued to hope that his differences with the Jambians could be resolved peacefully. He thought a military expedition neither necessary nor desirable in a realm in which only the leaders were uncooperative and the population displayed no hostility. As we shall see in the next chapter, events would not go as he had planned. Before discussing this, however, we should look at the role of the mother country in this process of imperial expansion.

POLICYMAKING (OR NOT) IN THE HAGUE

Up to this point, all key decisions had been made by the officials in the East Indies, while the Minister looked on and gave tacit consent. This suggests that The Hague endorsed Batavia's actions as wholly in accordance with the gradual relinquishing of the nineteenth-century policy of abstention, as exemplified in

---

[70] Resident of Palembang to governor-general, January 22, 1901, NA, Col., vb. August 19, 1901, no. 46.

[71] According to a list of the thirty-three guests invited in May 1900, nine dignitaries were definitely expected (those of the lowlands, the two regents, a brother of one of them, and Pangeran Wiro Kesumo). Eleven were certain to stay away: the sick *susuhunan* Zainuddin, Taha, Pangeran Dipo Negoro, Pangeran Adipati, Pangeran Prabu Negara, Pangeran Tumenggung Puspo Ali of the Merangin (chief of the suku Kedipan) and his younger brother Pangeran Surio, Pangeran Depati of Muara Tebo, Pangeran Cito Kesumo of the Tungkal, Pangeran Jaya Kesumo, and Pangeran Cakra of Muara Kilis. Of the rest, six would go to Jambi only on Taha's orders. Seven were thought likely to attend: Pangeran Surio (Zainuddin's son), Pangeran Puspo Jaya Ningrat (Zainuddin's son-in-law), Pangeran Marta Jaya Kesumo of the Merangin, Pangeran Haji Umar (Pangeran Puspo Ali's son-in-law), Pangeran Nata Kesumo (the son of Pangeran Depati of Muara Tebo), Pangeran Putra, and Raden Mesuut (both half-brothers of Pangeran Prabu Negara). Why these men were expected to come is not clear (see list appended to Resident of Palembang to governor-general, May 15, 1900, NA, Col., vb August 19, 1901, no. 46).

[72] Resident of Palembang to governor-general, April 7, 1901, NA, Col., vb. August 19, 1901, no. 46.

[73] *Gouvernementsbesluit*, February 10, 1901, no. 1; it was also decided to connect Jambi and Palembang by telephone; *gouvernementsbesluit* of February 10, 1901, no. 4, NA, Col., vb. August 19, 1901, no. 46.

Lombok and Aceh a few years earlier. At any rate, not a word of admonition or protest issued from the Dutch government. The Minister followed the events in Jambi and reported them in 1899, 1900, and 1901 to the young queen, Wilhelmina, who took a great interest in the administrative affairs of the East Indies.[74] The government approved budgetary increases and defended spiritedly the policy pursued in Jambi in the lower house of Parliament in November 1901. By then, the military operation had already been launched.

The Minister of Colonies who defended the policy to the assembly during the debate on the East Indies budget, was T. A. J. van Asch van Wijck (1901–2). Since he died in September 1902 after only one year as Minister, he has rather been overlooked in the annals of colonial history. Wrongly so, for this former burgomaster of Amersfoort and ex-governor of Suriname was the mouthpiece of the new "ethical" dimension of colonial politics.[75] It was under his responsibility that the speech from the throne was given in 1901, with its much-quoted passage, "As a Christian power, the Netherlands has an obligation . . . to suffuse every part of government policy with the consciousness that the Netherlands has a moral obligation to the population of that region." His "ethical" approach is also apparent from the position he adopted on mineral extraction and his motives for it. At the beginning of 1902 he declared his support, in principle, for a state-run enterprise, citing the fraudulent practices that were often associated with private companies and their disgraceful ill-treatment of coolies. He based this information on initial reports of coolie atrocities that had reached him in 1901. Furthermore, the state could accept a narrower profit margin than a private company, avoiding any semblance of a conflict of interests among officials.[76] The strength of Van Asch van Wijck's "ethical" convictions was apparent in the parliamentary debate on Jambi that took place in November 1901.

The questions that were asked in this debate on the East Indies budget give a good picture of the colonial ideology that held sway in the Netherlands at the time. The Minister had his officials prepare a memorandum giving a "broad outline" of the historical background, and emphasizing points that showed that the Dutch actions were intended "to protect the population from the extortionate practices of their own leaders."[77] Interestingly, this historical account contains not a word about oil or the failure to conclude a supplementary contract. Much was made of the abuses: the lack of a fair administration of justice or of measures to raise the general level of prosperity, the uncooperative attitude of the local rulers,

---

[74] See NA, Col., *minuut* of the *verbalen* July 24, 1899, no. 49, April 26, 1900, M4; August 19, 1901, no. 46.

[75] "T. A. J. van Asch van Wijck," in *Nieuw Nederlandsch Biografisch Woordenboek* (Leiden: Sijthoff, 1911–37), 1: 1591. However, it has since been demonstrated that Van Asch van Wijck's "ethical" position did not apply across the board. Where education was concerned, for instance, he was heavily influenced by his officials and showed little initiative (H. van Miert, *Bevlogenheid en onvermogen: Mr. J. H. Abendanon en de Ethische Richting in het Nederlands kolonialisme* [Leiden: KITLV Uitgeverij, 1991], pp. 56–64). In mitigation it may be noted that the hugely expensive plans of the enthusiastic director of education in Batavia were scarcely practicable.

[76] See note by Van Asch van Wijck in NA, Col., vb. March 12, 1902, no. 41; Jan Breman, *Taming the Coolie Beast: Plantation Society and the Colonial Order in Southeast Asia* (Delhi: Oxford University Press, 1989).

[77] See note by Van Asch van Wijck in NA, Col., vb. July 9, 1903, no. 44.

the ruthless exploitation of the population, and the "sheer anarchy" that prevailed; but how such matters had come to light was not explained.[78]

Parliament had never concerned itself with Jambi before, merely acknowledging contractual amendments of which it received formal notification. It had been kept informed of events through the annual reports in the *Koloniaal Verslag*. Now a wide-ranging exchange of views arose about Jambi amid a debate on numerous other topics such as the Aceh War, missionary work, and the development of industry in the East Indies. The lower house was inclined to see military action as unnecessary in the absence of any foreign threat or international problems; furthermore, the expedition had been poorly prepared. The socialist H. H. van Kol, a fierce and very well informed critic of Dutch imperialism, spoke at length. Praising the Minister and appreciative of the "completely honest explanation" of the reasons for the expedition—"as one would indeed expect from this Minister"—he proceed to give his own rather free account of Jambian history. The Minister had proceeded on the false premise that Jambi was "our lawful territory." Van Kol dwelt at length on the colonial government's mistakes, describing the imprecise formulations of the contracts of 1833–34 as "international contract fraud."[79] He discussed the attempt of 1866 to procure a rapprochement with Taha, blaming its failure on the Dutch officials' incompetence, and stated that Taha had a right to rebel, despite his personal reservations about this "haughty Malay."[80] He warned the Minister in general terms to beware the "imperialist proclivities of our times" and the "capitalist motives" that were driving colonial politics. But he too was silent on the subject of a supplementary contract, and only in passing did he mention "influential people . . . who had an interest in the rapid annexation of the region," some hundreds of applications for concessions that were already lying ready in Jambi, and "an out-and-out speculators' club in the Netherlands."[81] In his eyes, the war could have been prevented.

Idenburg, speaking as a new member of Parliament, dwelt at length on the term "imperialism," a much-used word that needed to be properly defined. He endeavored to fill the gap:

> If one means that the Netherlands, driven by ambition and a lust for profit, . . .
> by murderousness and bloodlust, is adding one region after another to its
> territory, that an unbridled hunger for more power and influence is impelling it
> to secure more and more territory, then I have no hesitation in refuting the

---

[78] *Handelingen Staten-Generaal 1901–1902* (The Hague: Staatsdrukkerij, 1901–2), *Bylagen* B4.43, pp. 43–45.

[79] In this connection, Van Asch van Wijck asked the authorities in Batavia in January 1902 for the Malay translation of these contracts (NA, Col., vb. January 21, 1902, K1). For the reply, see NA, Col., vb. October 17, 1903, D16. It acknowledged that the "contract concerned had indeed been rendered in a sloppy translation, which only one who was of good will would be willing to accept." Its publication, however, was deemed inadvisable for political reasons, as was the idea of consulting a linguist to obtain an accurate translation. After all, the thrust of the two versions was the same; furthermore, rectification would be of little practical usefulness after seventy years. Idenburg, who had since been appointed Minister, added the marginal note that the lower house of Parliament was unlikely to change this point of view. In other words, the matter was best forgotten.

[80] *Handelingen de Staten Generaal: Tweede Kamer, 1901–1902* (The Hague: Staatsdrukkerij, 1901–2), p. 103.

[81] Ibid., p. 136

accusation . . . as a general qualification as unjust. . . .. If one means, however, that the moral cause we have embraced in the East Indies, as a Western and superior Power, constantly brings us into conflict with those who have an interest in preserving unjust, frequently inhuman, conditions; if one wishes to indicate that the rule of law we have established and pledged to observe in our region is under constant threat along the borders and must be defended; if one wishes to convey that European law cannot ultimately tolerate situations that offend our sense of justice, and if one observes that in consequence . . . conflict is unavoidable, and that this conflict often leads, and cannot but lead, to the decision to seize direct power, in other words to annexation; . . . that the responsibility for what happens in what we call our territory, also in the face of the outside world, will more than once necessitate violent action—if one refers to all this as imperialism, then the word no longer jars on my ear."[82]

Thus, Idenburg distinguished between imperialism born of a sheer love of power, which he called "imperialism in the evil sense," and imperialism to fulfill a moral mission. The desire to end inhumane conditions, and to uphold a European legal order that he believed to be of a higher level than its indigenous equivalent, justified this mission, his belief in which was utterly sincere.

The Minister replied by assuring the house that what was at issue was indeed the "ethical" argument, as defined by Idenburg. The point in Jambi was not to expand the Netherlands' overseas possessions; the aim was to "stand up for the people who languished under the yoke of their rulers," that is to say, in Van Kol's terms, to protect "the rights of the little man."[83] For his reply, he had jotted down all the relevant passages from Monod's letters since July 1899 on a scrap of paper that he used to jog his memory.[84] Jambi's internal administration was in "severe decline": exploitation, the shielding of felons, the imposition of tolls, and debt slavery were the serious abuses that the colonial government would eradicate. He correctly observed that Taha had sworn, not in 1866 but as far back as 1858, never again to meet with a Dutchman. He scarcely mentioned oil, reporting merely that the Resident planned to open up Lower Jambi for entrepreneurs.

Was it naiveté, ignorance, or a willful manipulation of the facts that underlay this blind spot in Van Asch van Wijck's argument? It is hard to say. He had only recently joined the government, and the economic argument—the conclusion of a supplementary contract for the benefit of mineral extraction—was only one of the factors mentioned in the general report, and one on which the Ministry had placed little emphasis. For this Minister, oil had not yet become a hot issue. With Van Asch van Wijck, in the Netherlands the "ethical" argument started to lead a life of its own, detached from colonial reality in general and Jambian reality in particular.

The next Minister, A. W. F. Idenburg (1902–5), was again called to account when the budget was debated in 1902 and 1903 and was again warned against the pursuit of imperialism.[85] Van Kol reminded Parliament of the influence of Dutch capitalism, recalling that the editor-in-chief of the *Soerabaja Courant*, W. F.

---

[82] Ibid., p. 109.

[83] Ibid., pp. 117, 143.

[84] On the debate in the lower house of Parliament, see NA, Col., vb. July 9, 1903, no. 44.

[85] *Handelingen Tweede Kamer*, 1902–1903, pp. 128–29; 1903–1904, pp. 384–86.

Schimmel, had been sued at the end of 1901 over an article alleging that oil companies had offered bribes to high-ranking officials and army officers "if a military victory was achieved and concessions granted."[86] But neither the Minister nor the lower house of Parliament took up this point. In the upper house, Idenburg again referred briefly to the campaign in Jambi as "an inevitable consequence of our sovereign duties" before returning to the main political topics of the day.[87] The oil

---

[86] *Soerabaja Courant*, November 23, 1901, NA, Col., vb. March 12, 1902, no. 41. Schimmel, who opposed the expedition for fear of provoking a second Aceh, had written that the advocates of war had set their sights on gold and petroleum and had deliberately allowed the situation to escalate against the advice of peace-minded advisors like Snouck Hurgronje. He also claimed that the European population believed the rumors that were circulating of large sums of money having been offered to the authorities. The official report of December 3, 1901, revealed that these "authorities" referred to the military commander W. G. A. C. Christan and Van Rijn van Alkemade, each of whom was said to have been promised a hundred thousand guilders. The rumor had originated with officers in Jambi. Minister Van Asch van Wijck had been persuaded by the documents that Van Rijn van Alkemade had an interest in the Koninklijke, although he believed that "this will not have influenced his advice" (note n.d. NA, Col., vb. March 12, 1902, no. 41). I have been unable to discover the outcome of the legal proceedings. No judgment had been given by November 1902 (*Handelingen Tweede Kamer*, 1902–1903, p. 151). See also *Java-Bode*, November 26, 1901, which called "in muted tones" for an investigation in response to this report, though it deemed the charge as such as improbable, partly because the report contained factual errors. That Van Rijn himself favored allowing the extraction of oil in Jambi is clear from the account given below. Whether and to what extent he had an interest in the Koninklijke is unclear. At the registration for the lottery at the beginning of January 1903, it transpired that the two brothers J. and E. Deen, both of whom were actively seeking to acquire concessions and therefore had regular contact with the Koninklijke, were lodging in his house (*Bataviaasch Nieuwsblad*, February 29, 1903). The former, who was editor-in-chief of the *Deli-Courant* in 1890, had followed the example of A. J. Zijlker, the first franchise holder for oil drilling in northern Sumatra, and had first acquired a concession in 1891 of 60,000 *bouw* in Langkat, which he transferred to the Koninklijke in 1893, after an offer to the American Standard Oil Company had failed. This secured for the Koninklijke a permanent monopoly position in northern Sumatra. After this success, Deen became one of the most active license hunters; he secured *inter alia* oilfields in Perlak, which he transferred to the Koninklijke at the end of the 1890s. His brothers, E. and H. Deen, were also in the oil business; they founded the Eastern Exploration and Development Company in 1895. E. Deen and H. W. A. Deterding were still corresponding regularly in 1901 (Gerretson, *Geschiedenis van de "Koninklijke,"* 2: 127–29, 236). Van Rijn van Alkemade probably knew J. Deen from his period as an administrative official on Sumatra's east coast and from his term in Aceh. The applications for concessions in Jambi that the Deen brothers submitted in 1903 were alleged to be among the inadmissible practices described above. In January 1903, the Deen brothers submitted six hundred applications for prospecting in fifteen oilfields, employing the device that failure to obtain the first oilfield would automatically secure the second, or if this one had already been allocated, the third (*Bataviaasch Nieuwsblad*, February 26, 1903). Between 1900 and 1910, the Deen brothers would be at the heart of a second group of parties interested in petroleum in The Hague alongside the Koninklijke; meanwhile they were also setting up branches of their companies in the United States. Since these enterprises never managed to establish independent oil extraction operations of their own, they continued to rely on the Koninklijke or other foreign companies (Gerretson, *Geschiedenis van de "Koninklijke,* 3: 512–16). The Deen brothers were also involved in the debate about the development of Jambi's oil in the period 1910–20. Here they overplayed their hand in the public tendering procedure and their company, Zuid-Perlak, was forced to withdraw (Gerretson, *Geschiedenis van de "Koninklijke,"* 5: 171–91); on the financial and physical demise of these oil speculators, see S. F. van Oss, *Van Oss' effectenboek voor 1930*, vol. 1, *Binnenland* (The Hague: Van Oss, 1931), pp. 1096–7.

[87] *Handelingen der Staten-Generaal: Eerste Kamer*, 1902–1903 (The Hague: Staatsdrukkerij 1902–3), p. 82.

issue would not be debated at length in Parliament until 1903 and the following years, and even then the debate had no impact on policy.

Parliament continued to favor the tradition of abstention from interference in the East Indies for longer than the Minister or the colonial government. Still, its criticism was not accompanied by deeds; it did not insist on a change of policy. The Hague was content to let Batavia make its decisions and act accordingly. Only in the matter of mineral extraction did the Minister (Idenburg) utter a mildly dissenting opinion in 1903 and 1904; where administration was concerned, he fully endorsed the colonial authorities' actions. For Jambi, imperialism came from Batavia.

MINERAL EXTRACTION

It was oil, then, that prompted the Dutch to become more closely involved with Jambi and to strengthen Dutch control, although Van der Wijck and Snouck, administrators to the core, emphasized the exercise of authority, and Minister Van Asch van Wijck, far away in the Netherlands, stressed the moral imperative of protecting the population. That administrative matters overshadowed all economic considerations is clear from a closer look at what may be called Jambi's "oil drama."

The first applications for exploration licenses were submitted in 1891. By 1896 another fifteen had been received, all relating to Lower Jambi. Only seven fulfilled the set criteria, however, as the others had asked for more than the statutory limit of 35,000 *bouw*.[88] March 1898 saw the rejection of another nine exploration agreements that had been concluded with internal administrators in June 1897. All subsequent applications met the same fate.[89]

While these events were taking place, the new Mineral Extraction Act was being debated in The Hague; it was passed in 1899. However, this legislation had no impact on any oil extraction in Jambi, as what it provided was largely a legislative framework, and the debate focused on matters other than specific regions or companies. The fact that the Mineral Extraction Act's passage through Parliament coincided with the Jambian oil controversy primarily reflected the interest that existed around 1900 in the legal, technological, and political problems posed by oil.

So long as the administrative crisis in Jambi persisted, nothing could be done. It was not until February 1901, when the Resident firmly seized control, that new avenues opened up for action on the oil front. Even then, oil prospecting remained a slippery business. In May 1901, Resident Van Rijn van Alkemade took the initiative, proposing that Lower Jambi be opened up for private mineral extraction companies as soon as possible. The previous insistence on a supplementary contract was no longer relevant, since there was no sultan to sign one. The next sultan would have to abide by the government measures that would have been put in place by then. Safety would be no problem; and in any case, this was also a matter for entrepreneurs themselves. In addition, the local headmen favored opening up the region, certainly if they were soon to receive remuneration. Van Rijn therefore

---

[88] A *bouw* was a unit of surface area measuring 7,096.5 m².

[89] Official memorandum from the head of the Department of Mineral Extraction, April 7, 1903, NA, Col., vb. January 8, 1904, no. 20.

wanted the colonial government to have the exclusive right to grant concessions, after consultation with the local rulers and an investigation of the rights of third-party landowners. He hoped to promulgate this decision as of July 1, 1901.[90]

The colony's machinery of government did not, however, move so fast. In September 1901 the Council of the Dutch East Indies, more legalistic than Van Rijn, rejected his proposal on the grounds that the contract was still legally valid, and that security was far from guaranteed. If the region were opened up for mining and drilling operations, the population of the uplands would doubtless react. Governor-General Rooseboom tempered this advice; while rejecting the legal argument, he agreed with the security concerns, and asked the Resident to reconsider his decision. He also asked him to comment on the scope for gold mining and on the idea of setting up a state-run oil company. In December 1901 Van Rijn reviewed the options, and with Snouck Hurgronje's backing he managed this time to persuade the Council of the Dutch East Indies to endorse his plan. All those concerned opposed the idea of a state-run enterprise, on account of the fierce competition and the lack of proper machinery.[91]

So this problem, at least, had been resolved by the beginning of 1902. The next step was to gain ministerial approval for opening up the region. In March, Van Asch van Wijck gave the plan his blessing, though not without reservations, since the concept of a state-run enterprise was more in line with his ethical convictions.[92] It was another six months before the decision to allow private oil companies into the region was finally made official; for it seemed at first that the existing mining regulations did not provide for the opening up of an area for a single product (petroleum). In August 1902 the Minister finally authorized the opening up of Lower Jambi without restriction, one year later than Van Rijn had expected. Where the uplands were concerned, the idea of a state-run enterprise had not yet been completely abandoned. Upper Jambi was thought to harbor gold, and was to be reserved for state exploration for the time being.[93] On September 5, 1902, the *Javasche Courant* reported that Lower Jambi was opened up as from January 2, 1903, noting that all previous contracts and applications were now null and void. In 1897 the colonial government had decreed that all applications submitted to the Residency's premises in office hours on a particular day would be regarded as having arrived simultaneously. All interested parties, old and new, could submit their applications in Palembang on January 2, 1903. Previous applications submitted by the Sumatra-Palembang Company, the Koninklijke, De Lange, the Muara Enim, and the Musi Ilir—all these major oil companies had joined the race for Jambian oil before 1903—had already been, or were now, rejected.[94]

---

[90] Resident of Palembang to governor-general, May 18, 1901, NA, Col., vb. March 12, 1902, no. 41.

[91] See NA, Col., vb. March 12, 1902, no. 41.

[92] Cf. the note in NA, Col., vb. March 12, 1902, no. 41. Regarding the coolie scandals, Van Asch van Wijck had written in February that a state-run enterprise should receive more attention, even if it required a large initial outlay of capital. This would undoubtedly be the best solution for the population, he maintained (NA, Col., *minuut* vb. February 4, 1902, no. 16).

[93] NA, Col., vb. August 7, 1902, no. 61, and vb. December 31, 1902, no. 24.

[94] See note from the head of the Department of Mineral Extraction to April 7, 1903, NA, Col., vb. January 8, 1904, no. 20.

The new procedure gave these companies no advantage whatsoever. Not only could they derive no claims from having the oldest rights, but the solution was a bureaucratic concoction that betrayed ignorance of oil operations as well as of Jambian geography. The authorities had divided Lower Jambi into equal portions that were to be distributed by means of a lottery. This meant that companies could end up with non-adjacent pieces of land, which would be a great hindrance to their operations, as the directors of SUMPAL pointed out.[95]

When January 2, 1903, arrived, the applications flooded in. As many as 1,660 were submitted at 8 A.M., followed by another 374 between 8 and 11 A.M. and 58 more later on, making 2,092 in total. The East Indies press described colorful scenes of concession hunters with bulging briefcases, some of them half a meter thick, marching to the Resident's office at 8 A.M.[96]

The result was total chaos, partly because of the way Van Rijn went about it. The notional order in which the applications had been received was to be decided by a lottery, which Van Rijn held on January 3 without giving either the government or the director of the Department of Education, Religion, and Industry prior notification. This was in violation of the rules. Furthermore, his methods were peculiar, as emerged when the Ministry's Department of Mineral Extraction in Batavia performed its obligatory examination of the applications. Van Rijn had included in the lottery only the 1,660 applications that had been submitted at 8 A.M.; contrary to the regulations, he had disregarded the 374 applications submitted between 8 A.M. and 11 A.M. Worse still, many of those first 1,660 applications did not comply with the statutory regulations concerning clearly defined limits and maximum surface area. On top of this, applications had been submitted in duplicate—in some cases up to six hundred copies!—with all copies being included in the lottery. Thus, 860 lots might represent an actual number of twelve applications.

At the end of February 1903, Godefroy, head of the Department of Mineral Extraction in Batavia, having completed his examination of the applications, proposed that 1,150 of the 2,034 applications be rejected out of hand as not compliant with the statutory requirements.[97] A fresh lottery should be held among the remaining 884. In the ensuing conflict between Resident and Godefroy, Governor-General Rooseboom threw his weight behind Godefroy.

But all this reopened the controversy surrounding the principle of the lottery. On January 20, 1903, Idenburg, the new Minister of Colonies, had sent Rooseboom a telegram urging that entrepreneurs who had submitted applications before the procedure started be given priority, as they had already incurred costs. He had evidently been put under pressure by oil companies in the Netherlands, which had already asked the East Indies authorities to grant preferential treatment for

---

[95] See NA, Col., vb. October 31, 1901, no. 58.

[96] *Bataviaasch Nieuwsblad*, January 16, 1903, and February 26, 1903, ook in NA, Col., vb. October 31, 1903, no. 58.

[97] Viz., those applications that failed to comply with the requirement of precise definition, those that had been submitted in duplicate, those submitted by the same individuals (where this meant that the persons concerned had exceeded the maximum), and those submitted in the name of deceased persons or fugitive brokers, and those that were unsigned (official memorandum from the head of the Department of Mineral Extraction, February 28, 1903, NA, Col., vb. January 8, 1904, no. 20).

previous applicants in 1902 and been denied.[98] Now Idenburg broached the issue again. And although some senior officials in the East Indies, such as Godefroy, thought it wiser to restrict prospecting and drilling in an extensive oil field to a few big Dutch companies, or—better still—to a joint venture, now that the principle of a lottery had been adopted, the authorities saw the decision as irreversible. All those involved had incurred costs.[99]

This decision-making process took another six months. It was not until September 1903 that Rooseboom decided to reject the protests of earlier applicants. He also dismissed the idea of restricting the allocation to a few large companies: a trust agreement that had recently been concluded restricted the quantity of oil they could supply. This meant that new oil fields would primarily be kept in reserve. Besides, he saw no reason for the government to give precedence to companies that strove to keep prices high. The decision to retain the lottery reflected his mistrust of the oil companies. Like other senior officials, he thought they made huge profits without the state receiving its fair share.[100] Though by no means an enthusiastic supporter of the lottery, Rooseboom considered that his predecessor's actions had made it inevitable.[101] In October 1903, the *Javasche Courant* published a notification declaring the lottery held in Palembang on January 3 invalid and announcing another one to be held in Batavia on November 10, 1903.

This decision ignited a fresh offensive on the part of the oil companies, led by SUMPAL, which bombarded the Minister in The Hague with protests against the procedure. And once again Idenburg decided to intervene in this issue. At the end of October he sent Batavia a telegram which, though phrased in diplomatic language, ordered the lottery's postponement pending written instructions that would follow in due course. Rooseboom immediately replied by telegram that postponing a lottery that had already been announced would make "a very bad impression." Formally speaking he was entitled to go ahead, since under the terms of the Mineral Extraction Act a lottery of this kind was a matter for the East Indies authorities alone to decide, as he pointedly reminded the Minister.[102] The private correspondence between these men reveals that this disagreement was not as sharp as the official documents suggest.[103]

In the event, a fresh lottery was held among 993 applicants on November 10, 1903. Thanks to a leak at the Department in Batavia—an official had copied and sold the relevant documents—the entire episode was by then public knowledge in

---

[98] See official memorandum from head of the Department of Mineral Extraction, April 7, 1903, NA, Col., vb. January 8, 1904, no. 20; vb. November 20, 1901, no. 4; vb. September 8, 1902, no. 33; vb. December 31, 1902, no. 24, containing questions on the opening up of Jambi.

[99] Official memorandum from the head of the Department of Mineral Extraction, March 14, 1903, and April 7, 1903, NA, Col., vb. January 8, 1904, no. 20.

[100] First government secretary to the director of Education, Religion, and Industry, October 9, 1903, NA, Col., vb. January 8, 1904, no. 20. Rooseboom to Idenburg, November 30, 1903, Free University (VU), Documentatiecentrum voor het Nederlandse Protestantisme (Doc. Ned. Prot.), coll. Idenburg.

[101] Governor-general to Minister of Colonies, November 4, 1903, NA Col., vb. January 8, 1904, no. 20.

[102] NA, Kol, Cf. vb. October 31, 1903, no. 58, and vb. November 10, 1903, no. 21.

[103] See Idenburg to Rooseboom, January 11, 1904, VU, Doc. Ned. Prot., coll. Idenburg.

the East Indies.[104] On the day of the lottery Idenburg avowed his distaste for the whole procedure, declaring that the oil companies had been in the right.[105] In January 1904 he reiterated his position in response to Rooseboom's lengthy account in justification of his actions. True to his Calvinist convictions, he thought the lottery a despicable instrument, which "should not be encouraged in my view, any more than any other form of gambling or betting."[106] He reiterated legal arguments that had already been mentioned, but did not ask for the lottery to be declared invalid. This seemed to be the final word on the matter.

Yet the lottery winners were still not to be allowed to enjoy their prizes in peace. While initially the head of the Department of Mineral Extraction had criticized the lottery held by the Resident of Palembang, the latter now took revenge. Van Rijn conducted a virtual repeat of the investigation conducted after the first lottery and stated in May 1904 that the following were inadmissible as border definitions: rivers whose courses were unknown and lines of longitude and latitude passing through the homes of the headmen of kampongs that did not exist or through places whose locations were misrepresented on the makeshift map.[107] Months of official wrangling ensued. The conflict was eventually resolved in July 1904 by J. H. Abendanon, Director of the responsible Department of Education, Religion, and Industry. He decided to adopt the borders proposed by the head of Mineral Extraction, with the proviso that the license holder must pay in advance all the costs associated with any border dispute and call upon the administrative authorities to settle the matter. This created a financial safety net to resolve the anticipated conflicts.

However, when the conflict in the East Indies appeared to have been virtually resolved by the consistent decision of the authorities in Batavia to side with their own officials, The Hague called a temporary halt to the operations, this time for financial reasons. In July 1904 Idenburg and Rooseboom's designated successor, General Johannes van Heutsz, held consultations. Two memoranda, one drafted by Idenburg and one by Van Heutsz in response, together constituted their "government agreement," a unique phenomenon in colonial history. While Idenburg stressed the duty of a Christian government to protect the spiritual and physical well-being of the indigenous population, Van Heutsz proposed a range of concrete financial measures. On the importance of balancing the East Indies budget better than before, the two men were in complete agreement. The revenue from mineral extraction would, hopefully, help to achieve this. Van Heutsz, who had eyed the profits being earned by the oil companies when he had served in Aceh, thought that the Dutch authorities should be taking a far greater share.[108] Rooseboom had agreed and asked Van Heutsz to prepare a paper on the subject at the end of 1903.[109] Thus

---

[104] "De beslissing in zake Djambi," *Tijdschrift voor Nijverheid en Landbouw in Nederlandsch-Indië* 69 (1904): 494–505, esp. 501–2.

[105] NA, Col., *minuut* vb. November 10, 1903, no. 21.

[106] NA, Col., *minuut* vb. January 8, 1904, no. 20. Their private correspondence, however, reveals a far friendlier tone and more mutual understanding (Idenburg to Rooseboom, January 11, 1904, VU, Doc. Ned. Prot., coll. Idenburg).

[107] Nota A1, NA, Col., vb. June 20, 1906, no. 29; see also NA, Col., vb. July 5, 1906, no. 20.

[108] See Van Heutsz to Idenburg, December 7, 1903, VU, Doc. Ned. Prot., coll. Idenburg.

[109] Rooseboom to Idenburg, November 30, 1903; Van Heutsz to Idenburg, December 7, 1903, VU, Doc. Ned. Prot., coll. Idenburg.

there was no difference of opinion between the authorities in Batavia and those in The Hague when it came to oil. Idenburg proposed that the colonial government consider conducting exploratory investigations of its own, and possibly even embarking on its own drilling operations. Van Heutsz was in full agreement and listed three possible avenues. The first was to secure for the state a larger share in the profits from oil than it had before (or than it would have after the introduction of the Mineral Extraction Act), and the second was to have a state-run business explore the best areas and then to sell the mining rights to third parties under favorable terms, as was provided for by the new Act. The third option was to enact separate legislation for the transfer of exploration and mining rights. These suggestions revived the debate on a state-run oil industry. "My personal preference is for a state-run enterprise with *skilled* staff to conduct the exploratory operations: the extraction itself can be tendered out or regulated by contract," said Idenburg.[110] The tide was thus turning in favor of a state mining enterprise (at least for exploration), the "ethical" hobbyhorse of Van Asch van Wijck that had previously been rejected for reasons of technology.

At the end of July 1904, D. J. A. Kessler, director of the Koninklijke (SUMPAL), gave Idenburg another trump card, when he claimed that the lottery winners included straw men acting on behalf of the American-based Standard Oil Company. Standard Oil's negotiations with the Muara Enim Company had already prompted the Minister of Colonies to intervene back in 1898. Now Kessler asked for the lottery to be declared invalid again—this time for the noble objective of excluding foreigners—and at the same time to recognize the agreements concluded earlier between the oil companies and local headmen. For Idenburg, Kessler's information was the last straw. He had already told Rooseboom to postpone the granting of any concessions pending the outcome of talks with Van Heutsz. Now he sent a terse message that granting concessions at this time was inopportune, and that the matter should be resolved by Rooseboom's successor Van Heutsz,[111] who was due to take over on October 1. The Dutch government was more deferential to the wishes of the oil industry than the authorities in Batavia. Still, it was not tied to their apron strings. On the contrary, the postponement gave the Dutch and colonial authorities time to look into the idea of state-run exploration or extraction; they retained the initiative, without revealing their hand to the oil companies.

The advent of Van Heutsz ushered in the penultimate chapter in the history of Jambi. The new governor-general arrived in the colony at the beginning of October and immediately immersed himself in the material on Jambi. Using the maps at his disposal he tried to chart the oil fields for which applications had been submitted, the aim being to compare Van Rijn's method to that of Godefroy. Given the complexity of this material, it is not surprising that the task defeated him. On November 16, 1904, he rejected all 2,092 applications, declaring that they failed to meet the requirement of denoting "accurately specified pieces of land." At the same time he provisionally revoked the opening up of Jambi for private enterprise. The

---

[110] Written exchange of views on points of government policy, "Nota bevattende punten ter sprake gebracht door den Minister of Colonies en Nota bevattende de punten ter sprake gebracht door den luitenant-generaal J. B. van Heutsz"; July 20, 1904, VU, Doc. Ned. Prot., coll. Idenburg. Idenburg later reiterated his preference for state-run oil extraction in a personal letter of December 11, 1904 to Van Heutsz (NA, coll. Van Heutsz).

[111] Cf. NA, Col., *minuut* vb. July 26, 1904, L16.

primary reason was ostensibly a fear of endless border disputes—in short, of administrative chaos. This was the official reason cited in an anonymous article in the December 1904 edition of *Tijdschrift voor Nijverheid en Landbouw in Nederlandsch-Indië*, which sided with the government and was probably written at its instigation. The article made no mention of plans for a state-run enterprise or foreign intervention, but merely emphasized the concern to preserve administrative order and peace.[112] Van Heutsz took advantage of the dispute between the Resident of Palembang and Godefroy to further his own aims.[113]

The view presented to the outside world was that administrative considerations were paramount. Internally, discussions centered on the desire to increase the state's share of the proceeds from oil and the fear of foreign interference. Now as before, the debate involved a mix of economic and administrative arguments. Given the net result, it is fair to say that in practice, administrative considerations gained the upper hand. For despite the backtracking, the region was not rapidly opened up for a state-run operation. Jambi's oil remained where it was—underground—for years to come. Oil companies and government alike had to do without the projected profits. Hoping ultimately to secure a larger share for the state, the Minister and governor-general took their time. Oil extraction in Jambi eventually got under way after a protracted procedure in the 1920s, via a public-private partnership: the Dutch East Indies Petroleum Company (see chapter 11). The first pipelines carrying oil from Jambi to Palembang were opened in 1923.

MOTIVES: POWER, PROFIT, OR PRINCIPLES

This long account of the oil issue brings us to an assessment of the underlying motives. Was it power, profit, or principles that provided the driving force for Dutch expansion in Sumatra, in this case Jambi? It was certainly a quest for profit that aroused interest in an area previously deemed unworthy of attention. Obstacles to the start of oil exploration led in 1898 and 1899 to the resumption of Dutch involvement with the internal administration, resulting in its apparent dissolution. Still, far from meekly heeding the demands of the oil industry, the colonial government kept the industry dangling until 1904. Then it closed Jambi, hoping to procure a larger share of the oil profits for the state. In line with some theories of imperialism, hopes of profiting from Jambian riches provided the thrust for Dutch expansion. But when we look more closely at the overall decision making in relation to Jambi, we see that these hopes were closely interwoven with administrative aims. The economic motif—the expectation of an oil industry that would yield revenue for the state—was soon politicized, and became part of a more general political problem. Monod pointed this out back in 1898. It was not only oil that made the lack of fruitful liaison with the Jambian administration a burning issue. In the eyes of the Dutch, the failure to extradite criminals, the exploitation of the population by the *anak raja*, and the recurrence of internal disputes all constituted evidence of misrule. It was not oil that mattered most to men like Governor-General Van der Wijck and Snouck Hurgronje. Their primary aim was to

---

[112] "Beslissing in zake Djambi"; *Handelingen Tweede Kamer*, 1907–1908, Bijlagen 319.

[113] Cf. NA, Col., vb. June 20, 1906, no. 29, including the exchange of views on this topic within the Ministry of Colonies.

establish a permanent administrative structure and to enforce the colonial government's authority. Oil was at most a useful instrument of pacification; "authority" was paramount. As time went on, this emphasis became more palpable, and the significance of oil faded. We shall return to this topic in the description of the Jambi War (1901–7). Thus in terms of the politicization of the economic motif, the actions taken by the Dutch correspond to Fieldhouse's model of imperialism.

Meanwhile, in the Netherlands, Van Asch van Wijck placed great emphasis on the ethical argument: the need to protect the local population from exploitation by their own leaders. In justification of Dutch policy in its remote colony, he emphasized matters of principle, reflecting his religious convictions. This Minister was in some ways a textbook example of the "ethical school of colonial politics." The passage for which he bore responsibility in the famous speech from the throne of 1901, his preference for a state-run enterprise to prevent the abuse of coolies by entrepreneurs, his mistrust of corrupt oil companies, and his warm defense of the policy on Jambi to Parliament—all exemplify these concerns. As for Parliament and the general public, who knew little of the administrative situation in Jambi and were rather suspicious of oil companies, this "ethical" approach represented the soundest and most recognizable line of argument. It also accorded with the Netherlands' foreign policy, which had placed more emphasis on international law and ethical considerations since 1870, an argument to which the Dutch public readily responded. In short, the Netherlands presented its policy on Jambi as an imperialism underpinned by an ethical rationale.

The actual business of imperialism was pursued entirely by the colonial authorities in Batavia and the Residents in Palembang. The Hague merely followed Batavia, as before. Still, it had previously given the go-ahead for expansion in other parts of the archipelago. In this respect it had supplied the context for expansion and state formation, not only by sanctioning it but also by enacting general legislation that supported the Netherlands' national interests. Especially where the treasury and mineral extraction were concerned, The Hague kept a close watch on developments. Here too, however, Idenburg, for instance, acted in close consultation with Van Heutsz. The latter's ideas on mineral extraction contracts were much the same as those of his predecessor, Rooseboom. Every concrete proposal for action arose in the colony itself, from the demand for a supplementary contract to the actions of Monod, which led to the joint initiative of Van Rijn and Snouck. The role of the press, whether in the Netherlands or in the East Indies, was almost negligible. Parliament too had little impact on the course of events. The debates on Jambi took place after the fact and did not cause a change of policy. All decisions originated with the officials in Batavia; the role of the Ministry in The Hague was to watch events unfold with interest and to staunchly defend whatever action had been taken. The policy that was pursued in relation to Jambi remained an example of "peripheral" imperialism, albeit in line with the wider-ranging policy of increased control sanctioned by The Hague. The events discussed in this chapter clearly demonstrate that imperialism was a "linked" process, a chain of events, each element of which was furnished with its own arguments and motives.

AVOIDANCE BEHAVIOR AS A DELIBERATE STRATEGY

To what extent was this peripheral imperialism on the government's part induced by the "periphery of the periphery," the internal administration of Jambi? To answer this, let us first review the policy pursued by Taha. In psychological terms, it can be classified as avoidance behavior. He avoided contact with the more powerful colonial government in order to preserve his independence and autonomy in his own space. Avoidance behavior is always chosen by the weaker party in relation to the stronger, or at any rate the party judged·to be stronger; it is the "weapon of the weak."[114] Open, organized political activity is the prerogative of the strong. Taha hence resorted to what James C. Scott describes as the everyday mode of resistance by peasants in Southeast Asia in relation to their superiors: "foot dragging, dissimulation, desertion, false compliance, pilfering, feigned ignorance, slander, arson, sabotage and so on."[115] Such resistance has certain advantages: it requires little coordination or planning, avails itself of informal networks, constitutes a form of individual self-help, and justifies the avoidance of contact with authorities. "Low-profile" techniques of this kind were ideally suited to Jambi's political and administrative structure: the sparsely populated land, limited communication channels, and the lack of a formal national organization. Overall, Taha's policy exhibits a striking similarity to the modes of resistance adopted by the dispossessed, from medieval peasants to African-American slaves or *tani* in Southeast Asia.

Avoidance behavior is primarily based on a fear of confrontation and of the consequences of conflict. Taha was *takoet dan maloe*, "fearful and ashamed," as was reported at the beginning of the 1880s. At the same time, avoidance behavior implies heightened vigilance in relation to those with whom one seeks to avoid contact. This too was characteristic of Taha. He remained on the defensive and took care to protect his "borders" from any Dutch incursion.

His evasive response to the Westerners was characteristic of colonial relations in general; such a response may range from abstention to adaptation or even assimilation on the outside, combined with an "inner resistance," the development or preservation of a separate identity.[116] To the Westerners, the result was a diffuse and elusive Other. Or, as the Council of the Dutch East Indies put it in 1885, mulling over the possibility that Pangeran Ratu Cakra Negara, the later Sultan Zainuddin, had been playing a double role: "The character of the native has so many baffling facets that it is virtually unfathomable."[117] For the colonial rulers, this ambivalence, which they found unintelligible, was also a source of profound irritation. It was translated into the image of the ever unreliable non-Westerner, an image repeated in relation to Jambians too, from as early as 1833 onward.

Taha's chosen mode of resistance was effective for a long time. His evasiveness made a clash impossible, even when the colonial government gained an appetite for one. The Dutch found themselves pummeling a cushion raised by way of

---

[114] James C. Scott, *Weapons of the Weak: Everyday Forms of Peasant Resistance* (New Haven: Yale University Press, 1985).

[115] Scott, *Weapons of the Weak*, p. xvi.

[116] Ashis Nandy, *The Intimate Self: Loss and Recovery of Self under Colonialism*, 2nd ed. (Oxford: Oxford University Press, 1988); James Clifford, *The Predicament of Culture: Twentieth-Century Ethnography, Literature, and Art* (Cambridge: Harvard University Press, 1988).

[117] Council of the Dutch East Indies, September 18, 1885, no. 2, NA, Col., mr. 1885/635.

protective shield, as it were, without ever reaching Taha himself. Until 1901, relations with Jambi could be classified as what organizational sociologists call a "cold conflict," which could not erupt since one of the two parties evaded the heat of battle—to the opponent's growing fury. This form of resistance could be sustained until the colonial government raised the stakes, penetrated Taha's isolation and transformed the relationship into open conflict. Then the Dutch were drawn into the periphery—or as Fieldhouse puts it, "pulled into imperialism by the magnetic force of the periphery."[118] We shall explore the causes of this transformation in chapter 10. But let us first see how the conflict ended.

---

[118] D. K. Fieldhouse, *Economics and Empire 1830–1914*, 2nd ed. (London: Macmillan, 1894), p. 463.

Advancing artillery, posing for photograph in the *dusun* Rantau Kapas Muda
from *Eigen Haard*, August 30, 1902, no. 35

CHAPTER NINE

STATE FORMATION AND GUERRILLA WAR (1901–1907)

Imperialism, as argued in the introduction, can be equated with colonial state formation.[1] From 1870 onward there was a growing trend for the imperialist powers to export their polity to their colonies, emphasizing the features that suited them best. European ethnocentrism was translated into political structures, with the Western state figuring as the model for the organization or reorganization of overseas possessions. The main concerns of the colonial rulers were to define their borders and shape a uniform territorial entity, to secure a monopoly of violence (army and police), and to achieve a central administration and standardized taxation system—all features of the "modern state."[2] The high ratio of ruled to rulers, the colonial power's fear of any erosion of its supremacy, and the lack of education among the colonized meant that some of the other features of the modern state, such as general social provision and grassroots political participation, were often left behind.[3]

In the East Indies of the turn of the century, the two phases of this process overlapped. In Java, which had long been under Dutch control, the authorities made a modest start, after 1900, on the second phase by introducing various measures: administrative decentralization, some forms of local participation in decision making, limited social provision (health care and education) initiatives to boost the local economy by providing information on agriculture and credit and encouraging migration to more sparsely populated areas, and tentative trials with representative assemblies. It was this package of measures that was meant by the term "ethical policy" used in the Netherlands.[4] In Jambi and the remaining Outer Islands, the process of state formation had not yet progressed beyond the first phase, that of establishing power followed by the centralization and standardization of administrative regulations.

---

[1] J. van Baal, "Tussen kolonie en nationale staat: De koloniale staat," in *Dekolonisatie en vrijheid*, ed. H. J. M. Claessen et al. (Assen: Van Gorcum, 1976), pp. 92–108; J. à Campo, "Politieke integratie en staatsvorming Nederlands-Indië 1870–1920" (unpublished lecture to the Politicologen Etmaal Amersfoort, 1983); J. à Campo, *Koninklijke Paketvaart Maatschappij: Stoomvaart en staatsvorming in de Indonesische archipel 1888–1914* (Hilversum: Verloren, 1992).

[2] C. Tilly, "Western State Making and Theories of Political Transformation," in *The Formation of National States*, ed. C. Tilly (Princeton, N.J.: Princeton University Press, 1975), pp. 601–38.

[3] À Campo, *Koninklijke Paketvaart Maatschappij*, p. 27.

[4] Elsbeth Locher-Scholten, *Ethiek in fragmenten: Vijf studies over koloniaal denken en doen van Nederlanders in de Indonesische archipel 1877–1942* (Utrecht: HES, 1981).

Once it had been decided, at the beginning of 1900, to liaise more actively with the sultan's administration, the object, here as elsewhere, was to bring the entire area under Dutch control, to secure a monopoly on the use of force and on taxation, and to introduce central government—none of which, understandably enough, was accepted without protest. Although the colonial authorities had more frequent contact with the sultan's administration in this period, it is not easy to read between the lines and reconstruct Jambian perceptions of events. The former sultan's administration had become the enemy; the old diplomatic approach, which required knowledge of local power structures, had made way for military and administrative tactics. The change was reflected in the Dutch reports on Jambi, which were now full of military and administrative information.

MILITARY EXPANSION

Right at the beginning of 1900—that is, almost immediately after Snouck Hurgronje's first advisory report—the Dutch started preparing for armed conflict, although they continued to express a preference for peaceful expansion. They began by gathering information about the Jambian hinterland. In September 1900, a reconnaissance mission spent some hours studying the situation at Muara Tembesi. Two months later, armed steamships were deployed to explore the basin of the Batang Hari, up to the mouth of the Jujuhan, its northernmost tributary. At the same time, a telephone and telegraph line was laid between Jambi and Palembang to safeguard good communications in an emergency.[5]

These preparations were not lost on Taha. His response, however, was cautiously cooperative. He himself authorized the Dutch reconnaissance mission at Muara Tembesi, and the documents show that he forbade any interference with the Dutch steamships on the Batang Hari. In this period, before February 6, 1901, he clearly wanted to avoid risks of any kind. Conversely, Dutch officers were under orders to refrain from provoking the Jambians. Meanwhile, reports and rumors of arms smuggling were rife, but boats sent to patrol Jambi's coastline between September and November 1900 produced no results.[6] In March 1901 Muara Tembesi was occupied without incident, and in May 1901 Van Rijn and Snouck even traveled to Muara Tebo with one of Taha's sons as their guide. The expansion of Dutch control appears to have got off to an auspicious start.

At the end of May, however, the climate changed. There were two immediate causes of the outbreak of hostilities: an investigation to track down fugitive thieves from Palembang, who were hiding in Jambi, and an incident around the same time in which a reconnaissance patrol came under fire on the banks of the Upper Tembesi. Then, at the beginning of June, a group of Jambians attacked Surulangun in the Rawas. These latter two actions were said to have been part of a plan originating long ago with one of the sultans, who had instructed the headmen of the Upper Tembesi to prevent the Dutch from passing beyond the Rawas.[7] Patience was now in short supply in Batavia, which dispatched a company almost immediately. Van Rijn had asked for a military force before; after the smooth

---

[5] G. J. Velds, "De onderwerping van Djambi, 1901–1907: Beknopte geschiedenis naar officiëele gegevens," *Indisch Militair Tijdschrift*, Extra-bijlage 24 (1909): 28–33.

[6] Ibid., pp. 29–33.

[7] Ibid., p. 47.

occupation of Muara Tembesi, he had wanted to advance on Taha and Dipo Negoro on the Tabir. This plan was deferred, however, as there was other business in hand: in August, Dutch troops started to advance on Jambi from the Rawas, signaling the beginning of war.

Like most colonial conflicts, this was a guerrilla war; small units of the Jambian population, which had the advantage of an intimate knowledge of the land, pitted themselves against a trained professional army.[8] The Aceh War cast a long shadow over this struggle, and comparisons were frequently drawn. But Aceh had been so traumatic that it was the differences that were emphasized: here the Dutch were dealing with a larger and far more sparsely populated area, and since there was no clash between *ulama* and adat headmen in Jambi, popular resistance was far less organized. Although Islam was always a significant factor, the sources do not mention any Islamic leaders as having played a prominent role in the resistance.

The fluid structure of the Jambian state meant that resistance tended to be local, concentrated around a handful of Jambian dignitaries. In colonial discourse the conflict was described as one with local leaders, not with the population. As the war progressed, these leaders lost many of their followers and their lives became less settled. They often journeyed from one district to another with their wives, children, and closest supporters. Women occasionally participated in the resistance: four men and two women dressed as men carried out a raid in 1903, for instance, and dignitaries' wives were sometimes found to have been involved in conspiracies against the Dutch.[9]

These itinerant leaders resorted to tactics varying from a summons to "holy war" to rank intimidation to recruit fighters as they moved from one district to the next.[10] Resistance groups fought with rifles, mainly easy-maintenance breech-loaders, *lila* (a type of cannon), lances, and *klewang*. They laid ambushes and built fortifications: earthworks protected by wooden palisades or by spiky bamboo stems angled forward *(ranju)*. The ensuing battle generally claimed casualties on both sides, but since the Dutch had better weapons and were better trained as marksmen, their losses generally numbered no more than one or two in each encounter, as against ten to twenty on the other side. Adding up Veld's meticulous figures for the

---

[8] See H. L. Wesseling, "Colonial Wars: An Introduction," in *Imperialism and War: Essays on Colonial Wars in Asia and Africa*, ed J. A. de Moor and H. L. Wesseling (Leiden: Brill/Universitaire Pers Leiden, 1989), pp. 1–11. The information on the way this war was waged derives from Velds, "De onderwerping van Djambi," and Jang Aisjah Muttalib, "Jambi 1900–1916: From War to Rebellion" (Ph. D. diss., Columbia University, 1977), both of which adopt a more chronological than thematic approach. Velds, who served in the war as a captain, based his study on sources from the archives in Batavia (both Department of War and General Secretariat), while Muttalib, working almost three-quarters of a century later, used the National Archives in The Hague. Even so, their findings are very similar, many of them deriving from monthly military reports.

[9] Muttalib, "Jambi 1900–1916," pp. 57–58; Velds, "De onderwerping van Djambi," p. 110; Brief Report, December 1903, National Archives (NA), Col., *verbaal* (hereafter vb.) August 24, 1904, no. 36. This is one of the few things known about women as a factor in Jambian history. We have discussed them earlier in the context of political marriages (on the economic significance of women at the sultan's court in the seventeenth and eighteenth centuries, see B. Watson Andaya, "The Cloth Trade in Jambi and Palembang Society during the Seventeenth and Eighteenth Centuries," *Indonesia* 47 [1989]: 26–46).

[10] Muttalib, "Jambi 1900–1916," pp. 42, 88–89.

Royal Dutch East Indies Army (KNIL) soldiers killed in the six-year conflict in Jambi, we arrive at only forty-one, as opposed to five hundred on the Jambian side. This paints a very different picture from the Aceh War, which claimed 60,000 to 70,000 Acehnese lives and another 37,500 among the KNIL in thirty years of conflict.[11] The reliability of the Jambian figures is not unassailable, however.[12]

After Aceh, the KNIL was well prepared for—and practiced in—counterguerilla operations. Small units, varying in size from 100 to 250 men, smaller still later on, moved across Jambi from one bivouac to the next. Until 1904 these men were not from the Mobile Brigade, as Snouck had wanted, but detachments from the Second Infantry Battalion and the garrison in Palembang.[13] They were always accompanied by an equally large or larger number of carriers, as supplying the troops was one of the biggest problems in this conflict. How could supply lines be maintained in a sparsely populated region in which many of the villagers had deserted their *dusun* in terror and were hiding in the jungle? At the beginning, the troops headed north through the jungle. When they came to one of the Batang Hari's west-east tributaries they either followed it upstream or carried on to the next one.

To reach the local population and bring it under Dutch control, the Dutch troops turned some of their strategically placed bivouacs into permanent encampments. By the end of 1902 there were eight of these scattered along the major rivers in addition to the base in the capital.[14] Local headmen were summoned to bivouacs to formally accept subject status, after which the people were registered and issued with identity cards. This was an instrument designed to break the resistance, since regular checks soon made it clear who had joined the enemy. Arms too were registered. Furthermore, people were forbidden to travel from one part of Jambi to another without obtaining prior permission from a Dutch official. *Dusun* suspected of supporting the resistance were fined sums ranging from 200 to 1,500 Singapore dollars and compelled to supply the Dutch troops or to build roads. Their headmen were stripped of their positions and all weapons were confiscated or destroyed. After 1904, when the Dutch were zeroing in on the last pockets of resistance, heavier fines were imposed, patrols were introduced at the expense of suspect *dusun*, and people were forbidden to go looking for forest products. Appanage

---

[11] P. van 't Veer, *De Atjeh-oorlog* (Amsterdam: Arbeiderspers, 1969), pp. 211, 311.

[12] Six KNIL soldiers would later be killed in the conflict in Kerinci (see below), while three hundred men, women, and children of Kerinci perished in a single battle; no figures are available for the total number of casualties among the population of Kerinci (H. J. van der Tholen, "De expeditie naar Korintji in 1902–1903: Imperialisme of ethische politiek," *Mededelingen van de Sectie Militaire Geschiedenis Landmachtstaf* 10 (1987): 70–89, esp. 82).

[13] At that time the garrison battalion consisted of a staff of 14, plus 35 European officers commanding 224 European soldiers and 750 local fighters. The second infantry battalion was composed of one European and three Ambonese companies, a mountain artillery platoon, 500 bearers (prisoners), and auxiliary services (Velds, "De onderwerping van Djambi," p. 49). This included a platoon of military engineers. At the beginning of 1903, one of the Ambonese companies was replaced by Sundanese, as no Ambonese reserves were available (ibid., p. 121).

[14] They were Muara Tembesi, Sarolangun, and Muara Enom on the Tembesi, Limbur on the Merangin, Rantau Panjang on the Tabir, Bangko on the Mesumai, Muara Tebo on the Tebo, and Sekaladi near the source of the Batang Asei (ibid., pp. 98–99). How many soldiers were encamped at each place is not known, except in the case of Muara Tembesi, where there were 200 men (p. 34). By the end of 1903 there were thirteen permanent encampments (pp. 120–21). Those on the Tungkal, on the border with Kerinci, and along the northern border were new.

holders too were soon instructed to exert themselves to maintain law and order in their area, on pain of losing their appanage.[15]

The area surrounding each bivouac and permanent encampment was patrolled. At the beginning, this was very strenuous work. The inhospitable terrain had been made even harder to explore by high water levels after months of heavy rain, besides which beriberi, cholera, and malaria all took their toll among the troops. This first battalion was therefore relieved in its entirety after six months, by which time it was already serving under its third commanding officer. In 1904, when the last vestiges of resistance were being eradicated, a company of European soldiers was replaced by Ambonese soldiers, who were thought better suited to the many long patrols, as they not only were supposedly blessed with a keen nose and agility but had "little need of food."[16] Besides this, a mobile unit of forty very well trained Ambonese and Sundanese soldiers was mustered and armed with bayonets and *klewang,* followed by another one a few months later. But when the government commissioner for the Outer Islands, Hendricus Colijn (Van Heutsz's former aide-de-camp in Aceh) visited Jambi in 1905, he was not yet satisfied. By then Colijn had been appointed advisor for the Outer Islands, supplanting Snouck Hurgronje.[17] In response to his recommendations, the entire second battalion was sent home, leaving behind only a company of Ambonese and Sundanese troops, which was converted into a Mobile Brigade under the command of the Aceh veteran Captain Darlang. This must certainly have pleased Van Rijn, who had asked for an Aceh officer before. Darlang's orders were to hunt down the remaining few resistance leaders with unstinting zeal, especially Raden Mat Tahir, the son of Pangeran Kusin of Sekamis, who had surrounded himself with "an aura of extreme bravery and invulnerability."[18] All this exemplifies the way in which military strategy was influenced by the experience gained in the Aceh War.

The second element of the "Aceh method," bringing civil and military administration under a single authority, was not applied here; the shifting and more diffuse nature of the resistance encountered in Jambi made it impossible. Furthermore, when Van Heutsz, who started to apply this approach in Southeast Borneo and South Celebes in 1905, urged its introduction in Jambi toward the end of that year, the civil administration was already so finely tuned, and the population so accustomed to it, that a radical upheaval of this kind would have

---

[15] See below; see also Brief Report, December 1903, NA, Col., vb. August 24, 1904, no. 36.

[16] Velds, "De onderwerping van Djambi," p. 121.

[17] After Van Heutsz's arrival, Snouck Hurgronje issued only one more recommendation, relating to Bone (E. Gobée and C. Adriaanse, eds., *Ambtelijke adviezen van C. Snouck Hurgronje 1889–1936*, 3 vols. [The Hague: Nijhoff, 1957–65], 3: 2106–14). After this the governor-general made no further use of his services for the Outer Islands. The gap between the two men who had once worked together in Aceh had become unbridgeable, partly because they disagreed about the agreement concluded in 1903 with the claimant to the throne of Aceh. Still, it is debatable whether the change of advisor made much difference to those concerned at the time. Neither Snouck nor Colijn were in any doubt about the correctness of the East Indies borders. Where they differed was on the polity of the state within these borders. Colijn was more of a tax specialist and therefore placed more emphasis on moneyed interests than Snouck Hurgronje, whose concerns centered on education and the formation of an elite.

[18] See Resident of Palembang to governor-general, May 16, 1905, and August 29, 1905, NA, Col., vb. March 26, 1907, no. 15. Velds, "De onderwerping van Djambi," p. 136.

been an administrative and military folly.[19] Colijn reiterated that the Jambian resistance was not a popular uprising but was confined to the insubordination of a few dignitaries who only reacted under provocation.

Unlike Aceh, Jambi has not handed down histories of major military scandals.[20] The war fought here was merely, true to Clausewitz's famous dictum, the continuation of politics by other means. The political objective was the *conquête d'âmes* of the Jambian people, their voluntary acceptance of subject status under Dutch rule. Given the low profile of the resistance, this goal was to be pursued wherever possible by peaceful means. From 1901 onward, the army therefore received orders to refrain from provoking the population. Sporadic cases of overzealous prosecution resulted in official reprimands.[21]

This military mixture of hard and soft measures proved effective. One of the most striking features of this colonial war as revealed by the sources is the cooperation of the local population. And this is not just a distortion shaped by a colonial ideology that defined the conflict as one fought solely by and against the local leaders. The cases of collaboration were too numerous for this explanation to hold water. A host of Jambians offered their services as guides, obligingly leading Dutch patrols to the resistance leaders' hideouts. Besides this, the Jambians set up their own patrols to maintain law and order and willingly handed over the insurgents to the Dutch, as happened in the case of Pangeran Tumenggung Puspo Ali of the Merangin in 1903 and virtually all the other resistance leaders, even Taha. The success of the Dutch troops was to a large extent the result of the local population's support. Part of the explanation for their attitude lies in the structure of the Jambian state: the autonomy of the *dusun* under their own headmen and the symbolic significance of the sultan created a fragmented sense of nationhood. Another factor was the attitude, common in the archipelago, that any ruler who made his power felt was to be obeyed. The successful exercise of power was seen as legitimizing the ruler. And the Dutch were asserting their authority more and more forcefully. On a more banal note: rewards of 1,000 to 1,500 dollars were not to be spurned, even if the money came from the fines imposed on *dusun* and individuals for supporting the resistance.[22] Besides, the resistance leaders did their cause no good by committing acts of vengeance, including violence and arson.

---

[19] See documents with Colijn's memorandum of December 11, 1905, no. 324, NA, Col., vb. March 26, 1907, no. 15; see also the appendixes to the *Memorie van Overgave* (Memorandum on leaving office) Resident O. L. Helfrich 1908, NA, Col., MvO 216.

[20] One incident has been recorded, however, involving the execution of a prisoner-of-war. Redactie, "Mededeelingen van de redactie: Indische militaire rechtspleging," *Militair Rechtelijk Tijdschrift* 2 (1906): 215–16; C. J. M. Stuivenga, "Op de grens van twee werelden: De expeditie naar Djambi, 1901–1907" (Department of History, Leiden University, 1999), p. 18.

[21] Muttalib, "Jambi 1900–1916," pp. 94–95. This happened in January 1906, for instance, in response to the report on Lieutenant Craendijk, who had ill-treated the people of a *dusun* in the Sumai district north of the Tebo in August 1905 and killed an informant. First government secretary to commander-in-chief of the army, January 20, 1906, NA, Col., *mailrapport* (postal report; hereafter "mr.") 1906/119, vb. March 26, 1907, no. 15.

[22] Velds, "De Onderwerping van Djambi," p. 125.

KERINCI AND THE OTHER DEPENDENT REGIONS

The operation to bring the entire territory under Dutch rule meant extending the war beyond Jambi's borders. In 1902 Kerinci became involved. Snouck had already said in 1900 that the independent regions bordering on Jambi could not be left out of the conflict, since Jambian resistance leaders would seek refuge there. It was a shrewd prediction. At the end of 1901, the headmen of Kerinci supplied 300 to 400 troops with arms and ammunition at Taha's request.[23] Van Rijn van Alkemade and Snouck Hurgronje both saw this as clear justification for intervention. The same men who had been responsible for the expansion of territory in Jambi now advocated expansion in Kerinci.

The Jambian pattern was repeated in Kerinci, though the immediate cause was different. It was not oil that drew the colonial government into the periphery, nor indeed Kerinci's gold, as some were saying in the Netherlands. It was the region's role as a safe haven for Jambian insurgents. The underlying rationale, however, was the same—establishing authority was paramount. Or, as Snouck wrote in his advisory report, "The truth of the matter is that anyone who is not for us is against us; countenancing a neutral Native territory in our midst is a practical impossibility."[24] The strategy, too, was very similar: again the Dutch endeavored to use peaceful means, but soon resorted to force.[25]

Rooseboom, by nature a more cautious man, adopted the recommendations of Van Rijn and Snouck, but he defined the political objective more narrowly. Since Kerinci had stopped helping the Jambian resistance in the spring of 1902, he ordered negotiations in May of that year, though with the sole aim of preventing any resumption. But when the two local emissaries bearing the letter proposing negotiations were murdered in August 1902, the process was accelerated. At the end of October 1902, Rooseboom ordered an economic blockade of Kerinci and a military expedition in retaliation, without consulting Minister Idenburg beforehand. In September 1903 he informed the Minister that Kerinci had been annexed after a brief period of resistance and that his troops had withdrawn.

So here was another case of Batavia launching its own expansionist project without seeking any mandate from The Hague. Initially it looked as though Idenburg was going to protest, given the danger of burdening the treasury. But Rooseboom's ninety-two-page justification assuaged his doubts, since the governor-general evidently agreed that military force was only to be used as a last resort. Rooseboom had taken offense at Idenburg's criticism, especially the suggestion "that I am not averse to pursuing what some would call an imperialist endeavor, whereas I have in fact always opposed such aims."[26] He knew that the Dutch were overstretched in the East Indies and thought it best to focus on a few specific regions, one being Sumatra. "Sooner or later Sumatra must become like today's Java."[27] Though not opposed to expansion, he wanted it to be carefully directed and not unduly expensive. His ethical arguments—gaining control of Kerinci was about strengthening the rule of law and protecting the weak—also appealed to the

---

[23] Van der Tholen, "De expeditie naar Korintji," p. 74.

[24] Gobée and Adriaanse, *Ambtelijke adviezen*, 3: 2017.

[25] Van der Tholen, "De expeditie naar Korintji," pp. 75–76.

[26] Governor-general to Minister of Colonies, February 15, 1903, NA, Col., vb. March 28, 1903, H5.

[27] Van der Tholen, "De expeditie naar Korintji," p. 84.

Minister. Both men justified the policy on Kerinci by emphasizing the factors of "power" and "principle." As in Jambi, Dutch imperialism here was cloaked in an ethical discourse that proved particularly effective in stilling criticism in The Hague.[28]

In 1905 attention turned to the independent regions north of Jambi—Kota Besar, Si Guntur, and the Kwantan districts and uplands of Indragiri. Van Rijn had urged the annexation of these regions too in 1903. But again he had found himself opposed by Rooseboom, who would not consider annexation unless the rulers voluntarily accepted subject status. In 1905, however, Van Rijn gave Van Heutsz, the new governor-general, little choice. Members of the Jambian resistance had taken refuge in these regions; they must be pursued. Reversing the sequence of events this time, an expedition was sent first, and as expected, the headmen then asked for their territory to be placed under direct Dutch control. As before, this policy was justified by invoking the need to establish administrative authority. There was little likelihood of economic gain in these territories, nor did this ever figure as an argument. Van Rijn did make one financial proposal, though: mindful of the need to alleviate the budgetary distress of the administrators in Batavia and The Hague, he advocated the introduction of a poll tax that would help balance the budget in these newly conquered parts of Sumatra.[29] In this case, it was not Batavia but an even lower echelon of administration, at district level, that initiated expansion. And once this operation had been completed, the whole of southern Sumatra was under Dutch control.

THE JAMBIAN *ANAK RAJA*

The attitude of the Jambian *anak raja* to the Dutch authorities was as varied as that of the population. As we have seen, Taha did not initially set himself up against the colonial government. It was not until 1902 that the Dutch gained possession of documents originating from him, inciting Jambians to revolt. However, Pangeran Ratu Anom Kesumo Judo and many other appanage holders had already complied with a Dutch summons to report to the authorities in 1901. As a result, Lower Jambi had effortlessly fallen to the Dutch. In May 1901 the *pangeran ratu* reached the age of majority (eighteen) and the guardianship ceased to apply. As an independent crown prince, next in line to head Jambi's internal administration, he assumed the title of Pangeran Ratu Marta Ningrat.[30] And in Dutch eyes he was doing a reasonable job. He came when summoned and complied with the orders he was given.[31] He briefly seemed to be inclining toward the resistance in February 1903, when he visited Taha and refused to meet with Dutch officials. But his mother intervened, and a month later he was toeing the Dutch line again. A Jambian advisor was placed at his disposal to "educate" him, a man who stayed with him for eight months and gained his confidence, but who also reported back to

---

[28] Ibid., pp. 84–85.

[29] Resident of Palembang to governor-general, May 16, June 26, and August 2, 1905, NA, Col., vb. March 26, 1907, no. 15.

[30] This is how he was known afterward, though he was generally referred to only by his title.

[31] Velds, "De onderwerping van Djambi," p. 78.

the Dutch authorities on his master's relations with the guerrilla fighters.[32] In the summer of 1903, the *pangeran ratu* even went along on the military expedition to the Tebo and warned of the possible dangers. Thus, the Dutch saw him as wholly reliable, an impression that was reinforced in December 1903, when he transferred his appanage to the colonial government and allowed himself to be moved to Jambi along with his family and several kinsmen. He said he no longer felt safe in his own territory.[33]

His actions were prompted in part by the ambiguities and difficulties now surrounding his position as *pangeran ratu*. On the one hand, it was his duty to represent the sultan's administration and to defend Jambian interests. On the other hand, from the outset he had always sought to cooperate with the Dutch authorities and had opted for the middle road. It is possible that Taha himself had encouraged him to do so, in order to assure himself of a reliable intermediary with the Dutch authorities. But Resident Van Rijn had insisted to Pangeran Ratu Marta Ningrat in ever stronger terms that he take responsibility for upholding law and order in his appanage, the stretch of the Batang Hari between Muara Tembesi and Muara Tebo. This was a near-impossible task, as there were always resistance fighters to be found in this key area of the Jambian sultanate. Other Jambian dignitaries who had been found wanting in rigor by the district authorities had been deprived of their appanages. So perhaps Marta Ningrat's "advisor" suggested this solution of relinquishing his appanage voluntarily. Since Jambi had been placed under the authority of an Assistant Resident of Palembang in the summer of 1903, direct rule was getting closer anyway. What is more, Taha himself appeared to have washed his hands of Marta Ningrat, as he appointed a new *pangeran ratu* in December 1903—Raden Mat Tahir, the most important resistance leader.[34] This appointment, which was contrary to adat—Mat Tahir was not the son of a former sultan—made it clear that Pangeran Ratu Marta Ningrat could expect few favors from Taha.

In March 1904, Pangeran Prabu Negara followed his example. He too had received a reprimand for supporting Mat Tahir (several *dusun* had been removed from his control) and had been served for a short time by an "advisor." Like Marta Ningrat, he probably surrendered his power because he recognized that he would be incapable of complying with the colonial authorities' ever more stringent demands to maintain law and order in his territory. Possibly he had also taken offense at the appointment of Mat Tahir. Besides his appanage, he also surrendered the Si Genjei (Siginjei) kris that he had received from Taha at the beginning of 1901, while the *pangeran ratu* relinquished the Sendya Merjaya kris.

---

[32] Resident of Palembang to governor-general, January 4, 1904, NA, Col., vb. August 14, 1904, no. 36. The advisor was the retired Abdul Sukur, *datuk* of Bengkalis, with whom Van Rijn had had dealings when serving as an official on the east coast of Sumatra (see also Muttalib, "Jambi 1900–1916," p. 65).

[33] Resident of Palembang to governor-general, December 28, 1903, telegram and Brief Report, December 1903, NA, Col., vb. August 24, 1904, no. 36. The relatives who accompanied him without protest were his mother, the *ratu*, five lower-ranking wives, a son, two daughters, and two sons-in-law.

[34] Muttalib, "Jambi 1900–1916," p. 60; cf. Brief Report, November 1903; political report, December 1903, NA, Col., vb. August 24, 1904, no. 36. Alternatively, it is possible that Taha did not appoint Raden Mat Tahir as his successor until after the transfer of the *pangeran ratu*'s appanage. The rumor of it reached the Dutch authorities in the same month.

The Dutch administration was jubilant about what it regarded as a great political victory.[35] The surrender of the royal insignia *(pusaka)* was a ritualistic enactment of the transition from self-government to colonial rule. Recent research confirms that the royal insignia in the archipelago (in Luwu and Bali, for example) were far more than outward symbols of power.[36] They actually embodied power. Thus, their surrender is open to conflicting interpretations: either as a sign of the deep rift among the *anak raja,* whereby the *pangeran ratu* and Pangeran Prabu Negara were willing to relinquish their national symbols and hence to challenge Taha, or as evidence that these *pusaka* were imbued with less significance in Jambian culture. Given Taha's previous transfer of the regalia in 1888 (to the contract sultan, Zainuddin), his pragmatic policy on adat, and the fact that the *pangeran ratu* later briefly inclined toward rebellion, the latter seems the likeliest explanation.

Once the *pusaka* had changed hands, the lowland appanages rapidly came under Dutch control. The Kompeh had already been taken from the former regent Pangeran Nata Menggala in March 1904, as the *pangeran* was a proven fellow conspirator of Raden Mat Tahir. Lowland appanage holders such as Pangeran Wiro Kesumo and the other former regent, Pangeran Ario Jaya Kesumo, surrendered their territories of their own free will a month later. In exchange, Pangeran Wiro Kesumo again became the intermediary between the Dutch and local Jambian administrations, this time as a *demang* (administrative official), until his death in 1905.[37]

By this time, the *suku* Kedipan in the Merangin had also abandoned their opposition. At the beginning of 1902 Controller O. L. Helfrich had taken advantage of a factional dispute in this *suku* to win over Pangeran Kerto Negara, the son of Pangeran Tumenggung Puspo Ali. A few months later Kerto Negara formally took over from his eighty-year-old father, who had opposed the colonial government ever since 1858. In February 1903, Puspo Ali presented himself to the Dutch authorities, but one month later he fled, taking with him his sons Pangeran Kerto Negara and Pangeran Haji Umar. The *suku* Kedipan then briefly reverted to its traditional resistance, but in May 1903 Puspo Ali was taken captive by a local patrol and banished to Ambon. Pangeran Kerto Negara died from gunshot wounds in January 1904.[38]

The year 1904 witnessed the near-complete elimination of the sultan's administration. In April 1904, Taha himself was betrayed. On April 21, the location of his refuge on the Sungai Besar, a tributary of the Batang Hari, was discovered. Two days later a patrol set off to take him captive. After alternately marching and lying in ambush for three days, one group, composed of an officer and nine men, found tracks leading to a hiding place. The Jambian guide seems to have had a crisis of conscience, as he tried to distract the group's attention at the last

---

[35] Brief Report, February 1904; Resident of Palembang to governor-general, April 16, 1904, NA, Col., vb. August 24, 1904, no. 36.

[36] S. Errington, "The Place of Regalia in Luwu," in *Centers, Symbols and Hierarchies: Essays on the Classical State of Southeast Asia,* ed. L. Gesick (New Haven: Yale University Press, 1983), pp. 124–214; H. Schulte Nordholt, *The Spell of Power: A History of Balinese Politics, 1600–1940* (Leiden: KITLV Press).

[37] Brief Report, April 1904; Brief Report, March 1905, NA, Col., in vb. August 24, 1904, no. 36 and vb. April 28, 1906, no 31 respectively.

[38] Velds, "De onderwerping van Djambi," p. 114; Muttalib, "Jambi 1900–1916," pp. 49, 56.

Surrender of the royal insignia (*pusaka*) on March 26, 1904. Probably shows Pangeran Ratu Marta Ningrat (third from left), Assistant Resident O. L. Helfrich (second from right), Pangeran Prabu Negara (far right)
KITLV photograph collection 26,644

moment, but it was too late. On the morning of April 26, a local police officer—a non-Jambian who had donned Jambian disguise for a solo reconnaissance mission—discovered the hiding place. The patrol attacked from two sides, and the ensuing gun battle with the few inhabitants claimed three lives. Taha was one of them.[39] He was identified by a committee of local headmen and buried at Muara Tebo.[40]

Dipo Negoro and Raden Anom also died in April 1904, though of natural causes. Former sultan Zainuddin had already died in May 1903. Following the deaths of these key figures, all the kinsmen of Taha and Dipo Negoro in turn gradually yielded to the Dutch authorities. Of the *suku* Kraton, only Pangeran Singo, whom his father, Dipo Negoro, had nominated as *pangeran ratu* in 1900, refused to give in. Most of the other remaining resistance leaders belonged to the *suku* Kedipan.[41]

All the dignitaries who had yielded to the authorities were instructed to take up residence in the Pecinan quarter of the capital, where they would be subject to a *demang*'s supervision. Controls were tightened up in August 1904 in response to an unexpected development. An outsider, Abdullah Yusuf of Turkey, arrived in Jambi, ostensibly to help the resistance. In fact, his intervention would have the opposite effect.

ABDULLAH YUSUF

Taha had always taken an interest in Turkey, but he had not succeeded in establishing relations with the Ottoman rulers.[42] Toward the end of the nineteenth century, however, Turkey seemed to be following the pan-Islamic movement in the Malay archipelago more closely. In 1901 the new Turkish consul, Haji Attaullah Effendi (whose appointment had been blocked for a very long time by the British, partly under pressure from the Dutch government) arrived in Singapore. Taha contacted him almost immediately.[43] Reports state that the consul promised to place two Turkish warships at Taha's disposal in 1902. But the messenger whom Taha then dispatched to Singapore did little more than flaunt the money he had been given, after which he failed to return home. That same year, Taha also sent envoys to Constantinople. After being received by the Grand Vizier, they set off to Mecca to undertake the haj. In 1903 a member of the Al Juffri family in Constantinople—possibly a distant relative of Pangeran Wiro Kesumo, although this is not mentioned in the sources—received the vast sum of thirteen thousand guilders to muster support for the Jambian resistance. However, he used the money to fund a journey to Mecca, where the earlier haji took legal action against him for

---

[39] Velds, "De onderwerping van Djambi," p. 127.

[40] Resident of Palembang to governor-general, April 29, 1904, and Brief Report, April 1904, both in NA, Col., vb. August 24, 1904, no. 36; Brief Report, May 1904, NA, Col., vb. April 28, 1906, no. 31; Muttalib, "Jambi 1900–1916," p. 67. According to the *pahlawan* literature, Taha escaped when the Dutch attacked; he died of natural causes a few days later (though this version too gives April 26, 1904, as the date of his death). See Kamajaya, *Delapan Raja-Raja Pahlawan Nasional, Buku I* (Yogya: U.P. Indonesia, 1981), p. 40; see also *Album 86 Pahlawan Nasional* (Jakarta: Bahtera Jaya, 1985), p. 18.

[41] Velds, "De onderwerping van Djambi," p. 128.

[42] See chapter 5.

[43] Resident of Palembang to governor-general, June 2, 1903, NA, Col., mr. 1903/578, vb. August 24, 1904, no. 36.

misuse of funds and he ended up in jail.[44] In 1903 Taha made one more attempt, and this time his letter finally reached Sultan Abdul Hamid of Turkey. The sultan did exactly the same as his predecessor had done in 1857—he showed the letter to the Dutch envoy.[45] Thus far, the Turkish connection had not been much help to Taha.[46]

In April 1904, however, things started to look more promising when a Turkish visitor calling himself Abdullah Yusuf came to Jambi. The authorities noted the stranger's arrival and permitted him to lodge with the receiver of import and export duties, who diligently watched his movements as instructed. Yusuf's interest in Pecinan was duly reported and he was forbidden to go there. The authorities in Batavia made inquiries in Singapore and discovered that their visitor was in fact not Turkish at all, but a Hungarian doctor in his thirties named Karl Hirsch who had served in the Turkish army. From May until August the stranger stayed in Batavia, where he called himself a special representative of the sultan of Turkey and went about in Turkish uniform with decorations, as a result of which he soon made contact with the Arab community. Here too the authorities kept a close eye on him, using spies who even recorded his visits to a prostitute. He proved to be a short-tempered man with little respect for the local population; at one point he struck a Javanese railway official, for which he was sentenced to three days in jail. The colonial government discovered that this "Abdullah Yusuf" had also traveled around China and Japan. In Shanghai he had boasted that the headmen of Palembang and Jambi had offered him five thousand guilders for procuring Turkey's assistance in their fight against the Dutch. At the same time he let slip that, as a Turkish envoy, he hoped to extract money from gullible princes.[47]

The spies' reports described the stranger as a highly intelligent man who spoke fluent German, French, and Italian. His behavior scarcely bore witness to great intelligence, however.[48] On September 7, 1904, he returned to Jambi at 3 A.M., this time in the company of a Turk and two Jambians, one of whom acted as interpreter. Considering what he was planning, he did not exercise much prudence: when the captain of the steamship told him he could not disembark at such an hour, he pulled out a revolver. Upon arrival in Jambi, he and his companions went to call on an acquaintance of the interpreter, who went off—though it was still nighttime—to fetch the *pangeran ratu*. Yusuf, a tall, dark man who wore a fez with a red tassel, kissed him on both cheeks upon his arrival, introduced himself as an envoy from the sultan of Turkey, and personally set about dressing the twenty-one year-old Marta Ningrat in a Turkish uniform. After this the group went to the *pangeran ratu*'s home, where Yusuf/Hirsch gave orders to call all Jambi's dignitaries to arms. Some failed to appear on account of illness or because they had been away from home; Pangeran Wiro Kesumo said he would come only if the gathering was taking place with the authorities' knowledge. Presently one hundred men had

---

[44] See NA, Col., vb. July 11, 1905, no. 4.

[45] A. Reid, "Nineteenth-Century Pan-Islam in Indonesia and Malaysia," *Journal of Asian Studies* 26 (1967): 267–83, esp. 282.

[46] Taha was not alone in pinning his hopes on Turkey, the resistance in Bone also hoped for Turkish assistance (Muttalib, "Jambi 1900–1916," p. 74; see also B. Watson Andaya, "From Rüm to Tokyo: The Search for Anti-Colonial Allies by the Rulers of Riau, 1899–1914," *Indonesia* 22 [1977]: 123–56).

[47] See the documents about him in NA, Col., vb. August 15, 1906, no. 52.

[48] For the most detailed report on these events, see NA, Col., exh. March 6, 1905, no. 80.

assembled in and around the house, and Yusuf/Hirsch again introduced himself as an envoy from the sultan of Turkey, brandishing a wad of telegrams by way of proof. He told his audience, through the interpreter, that he had to send a telegram to Constantinople asking for the warships to be sent. The telegram would cost eight hundred guilders, he explained. The money was produced (and Dutch officials later found it on the impostor), after which the leading dignitaries all swore on the Koran "to die together, to live together" (*sama sama mati/sama sama hidup*). When Yusuf asked where he could lodge, he was given the use of the school building, with furniture supplied by the *pangeran ratu*.

The local Dutch officials had failed to notice this nocturnal escapade. But the controller of Jambi heard about it at 7.30 A.M. that same day, and immediately gave orders for Yusuf and the *pangeran ratu* to be summoned. Shortly afterward, Assistant Resident O. L. Helfrich, evidently considering a summons inadequate, ordered some soldiers to fetch the two Turks and two Jambians. They were just about to leave when the kampong chief returned with Pangeran Wiro Kesumo, saying that the men refused to come. Instead they had sent a note in French in which Yusuf explained that he had come to do business with an Arab who had been living in Pecinan for three years. At this, the controller, the local military commanders, the Assistant Resident, and Pangeran Wiro Kesumo all crossed to the other side of the river, accompanied by a patrol. Having been dropped off the patrol opposite the fort to continue on foot, the ship carried the officials to the *pangeran ratu*'s house, which was next to that of Pangeran Wiro Kesumo.

Abdullah Yusuf was out of luck. When the ship arrived, he had just stepped off the landing stage in front of Wiro Kesumo's house, where he had been relieving himself, as the military commander noted, and was now "arranging his clothes in an indecorous manner."[49] He tried to escape, but the patrol had him surrounded. Piles of krisses, knives, lances, and swords were discovered in the school. A lone Jambian who ran amok was disarmed by Pangeran Adipati and a group of soldiers. All those present were arrested, with the exception of the *pangeran ratu* and a small group of companions, who fled from the scene. The key role played by Turkish uniform captures the spirit of this enterprise, which was more like a farce than a serious attempt to stage a rebellion. The main point of Yusuf/Hirsch's plan was a swindle. But the colonial government, fearful of any expression of pan-Islamic sentiments, was not amused, and viewed the episode as out-and-out sedition. The attempted swindle was not even mentioned in the official reports.

This incident bears eloquent testimony to the dignitaries' beliefs and their gullibility. Pangeran Prabu and Adipati themselves, by no means uneducated men, conceded as much during their interrogation. When asked why they had heeded the summons and sworn the oath, both replied that they would not have done so of their own accord, but that they had been driven "by fear of the sultan of Turkey, whose envoy Abdullah Yusuf was."[50] The episode can be viewed in the context of the supernatural/religious ideas that were circulating in Jambi at the time. The *pangeran ratu*, Marta Ningrat, had recently heard a rumor that Taha was not

---

[49] Report of commander-in-chief of the army of September 13, 1904, NA, Col., exh. March 6, 1905, no. 80.

[50] Official report, Pangeran Prabu and Adipati, October 5, 1904, NA, Col., exh. March 6, 1905, no. 80.

dead.[51] And now an envoy from Turkey came bearing promises of help in the struggle against the infidels. Their actions were comparable to the protests of Javanese peasants in the pre-nationalist era, who often attacked well-armed soldiers in small groups armed only with sticks and *jimat* (amulets believed to confer invulnerability). As an adventurer, Hirsch was more of a mid-nineteenth-century figure, though it is doubtful whether he would have had much success even then. He was in any case wholly out of step with the twentieth century. Modern states had no patience with antics of this kind.

Hirsch had a marked adverse effect on the Jambian cause. Seventeen Jambian dignitaries, most of them from the *suku* Kraton, including the *pangeran* Prabu and Adipati, were banished to Madiun.[52] Van Rijn had wanted to banish forty-three, including many dignitaries who had not even attended the gathering, but the director of the Justice Department in Batavia intervened. He did stop their allowances, however. For the next six months they would be given ten or fifteen guilders a month to live on, after which they would have to fend for themselves.[53] Those permitted to remain in Jambi found their freedom of movement curtailed; besides being required to live in the Pecinan quarter, they were forbidden to travel further afield than Muara Tembesi or Muara Saba. Self-government was now definitively consigned to the past. Its main representatives were all dead or banished. Pangeran Wiro Kesumo died in March 1905.[54]

Hirsch himself was sentenced to ten years' imprisonment. The Turkish consul-general in Batavia had distanced himself from the miscreant. Although it is not impossible that Hirsch may have been encouraged in his plans by senior Turkish representatives in Singapore and Batavia, no one would accept responsibility at an official level.[55] International pan-Islamism, it seemed, had little to offer the Jambian resistance. Nor indeed did Islam in Jambi itself. True, a few individual hajis were involved in the resistance. Mosques—every *dusun* had one—were often used as refuges or political meeting places,[56] but this was not enough to mobilize the masses.

After this, "gangs" numbering thirty to forty men clustered around key resistance leaders such as Raden Mat Tahir, Pangeran Singo, the *pangeran ratu*, and others scattered around Jambi. Hopes of assistance no longer centered on Turkey but on a rising star in the political firmament—Japan, which had triumphed against Russia in 1905. The victory imbued many local rulers in the archipelago with visions of salvation, and they made overtures to the Japanese government.[57] Jambi's resistance leaders were the first to pursue this avenue.[58] But these hopes too came to nothing. They had been fueled by reports from Singapore, by now home to a

---

[51] Muttalib, "Jambi 1900–1916," p. 81.

[52] "Djambi," in *Encyclopaedie van Nederlandsch-Indië* (The Hague: Nijhoff; Leiden: Brill, 1917–40), 1: 612; see NA, Col., vb. July 16, 1908, no. 56.

[53] NA, Col., exh. March 6, 1905, no. 80.

[54] Brief Report, March 1905, NA, Col., vb. April 28, 1906, no. 31.

[55] Gobée and Adriaanse, *Ambtelijke adviezen*, 3: 1741–44.

[56] Muttalib, "Jambi 1900–1916," p. 73.

[57] Watson Andaya, "From Rüm to Tokyo," pp. 123–56.

[58] Brief Report, July 1907, NA, Col., vb. June 16, 1908, no. 56.

large community of Jambian refugees, who had easier access to newspapers and were well informed about international relations and the balance of power.[59]

The resistance soon came more and more to resemble a pattern familiar from the days in which a loose agglomerate of rebel headmen and gangs had defied the sultan's authority. Such an opposition could not last long. Pangeran Singo was killed in December 1906, as was a grandson of Taha, Raden Hamzah, who had been active in the north. April 1907 witnessed the death of Pangeran Haji Umar, the last member of the *suku* Kedipan. On September 12, 1907, Pangeran Ratu Marta Ningrat gave himself up to the local authorities along with his one remaining supporter. He was banished to Menado.[60] Finally, Raden Mat Tahir, the most important leader of the resistance, was killed while attempting to flee to Singapore at the end of September 1907. His death brought to an end the war in Jambi, although a few gangs continued to operate here and there.[61]

Colonial wars often ended without any peace treaty being signed, and this is what happened in Jambi. War gradually made way for peace. For this period had not only obliterated Jambian self-government and the influence of Jambian dignitaries in general. It had also given the colonial authorities the tools to introduce a uniform centralized administration.

UNIFORM ADMINISTRATION

The first step toward uniformity, in 1901, was a package of financial measures, including the introduction of excise duties on petroleum and matches and the abolition of the salt monopoly and the "special rate" of import and export duties that had applied since 1847. The reasons for this were obvious: with self-administration temporarily out of the picture, Jambi was an easy target for tax specialists seeking to increase the state's revenue. Having said this, the measures taken were perfectly logical: under the 1873 Tariffs Act, which had introduced free trade and from which Jambi had previously been excluded, it was not possible to exempt certain products from the rate applicable in Jambi.

With one eye on the treasury, Batavia had already urged Resident Monod to introduce excise duties on petroleum and matches back in 1898. He demurred at making any decisions in the absence of a sultan, however, since the contract stipulated that the sultan's administration must be consulted. Monod's successor, the pragmatic Van Rijn, had fewer scruples. He regarded the contract as having expired; more to the point, he calculated that the duties on petroleum and matches would bring in 14,000 guilders and import duties on salt another 15,000 each year. The salt monopoly, which still belonged to the sultan's administration, could be withdrawn in exchange for 5,000 guilders of compensation. Encouraging though these figures were, a legal framework was indispensable. Administrative officials couched their arguments in legalistic terms even in times of military and

---

[59] Velds, "De onderwerping van Djambi," p. 138.

[60] *Gouvernementsbesluit*, November 15, 1907, no. 25, NA, Col., vb. June 16, 1908, no. 56. The *pangeran ratu* had also surrendered in May 1906 but had fled a month later. Jambian dignitaries were interned all around the archipelago in 1908: in Madiun, in Lumajang, on Ternate, in the Moluccas, and in Menado. By 1930 some had returned to Jambi, including Pangeran Prabu Negara (see "Nota over de vorstentelgen van Djambi," *Memorie van Overgave*, 1930, NA, Col., MvO 879).

[61] Velds, "De onderwerping van Djambi," pp. 131–42.

administrative uncertainty, but they manipulated the legal arguments to suit their purpose. In October 1901, Minister Van Asch van Wijck approved the abolition of the "special rate" in Jambi and the introduction of uniform import and export duties.[62] This put an end to Jambi's special fiscal status, which had been devised in 1847 under British influence and had lasted for more than half a century. Britain did not react. Given Jambi's relative economic insignificance and its status as a Dutch colonial possession, there was indeed little reason for it to do so.

The Dutch wanted administrative as well as economic uniformity, and they soon followed up their military expansion by consolidating the machinery of government. In December 1901, the political agent in Jambi was promoted to the rank of Assistant Resident. The man in question was O. L. Helfrich, an energetic administrator who traveled all over Jambi and who would live on in local folklore as the legendary *orang pendek* (small man).[63] In August and December 1902, controllers' posts were established in the Merangin and Mesumai regions, followed by another in the Tembesi. In the districts in which appanages had been surrendered, local *demang* became the intermediaries between these controllers and *dusun* headmen. They started off as the controllers' "assistants." Most had been trained at the special school for the sons of the administrative elite and did not come from Jambi. Pangeran Wiro Kesumo was an exception to the rule.

In August 1903, Jambi was formally annexed to the Residency of Palembang as a district or sub-Residency, although it was still to be administered indirectly. Eight controllers were installed in places that the army had made safe, each one thus administering an area larger than the average province in the Netherlands.[64] A police force was set up at the same time. Even now, however, the sultan's administration continued to exist in name. A Residency with direct rule enclosing a self-governing sub-Residency was not an uncommon construction in the archipelago.

It was not until the departure, in 1906, of Van Rijn van Alkemade—who had assumed the duties of sultan for five years as Resident of Palembang—that the de facto demise of Jambian self-administration was formalized. At Van Rijn's repeated insistence, the former sultanate of Jambi became a separate Residency that year. Kerinci, which had been annexed to the west coast of Sumatra in 1903, became part of this new Residency. Economically, politically, and in terms of communications, Kerinci and Jambi belonged together, as Snouck Hurgronje and the Council of the Dutch East Indies had emphasized.[65] Moreover, the resistance of the Kedipan nobles of the Merangin could be broken only if their port of refuge, Kerinci, came within the administrative ambit of Jambi.

The new Residency seemed capable of becoming financially self-sufficient—indeed, this was one of the criteria for its formation. Harboring great expectations of this "prosperous region," the Dutch had not thought the plan unduly expensive. Van Rijn had written in 1904, "The fertile soil, the wealth of minerals and forest products, the many waterways accessible to steamships, the convenient location in

---

[62] See NA, Col., vb. October 15, 1901, no. 3.

[63] *Memorie van Overgave*, Resident H. E. K. Ezerman, 1928, p. 42, NA, MvO 222.

[64] Viz., the following districts: Jambi, Lower Tembesi, Upper Tembesi, Merangin and Upper Tabir, Upper Batang Hari and Tungkal; "Djambi," p. 612; Velds, "De onderwerping van Djambi," pp. 119–20.

[65] In 1922 it was annexed to Sumatra's west coast again (J. Tideman and P. L. F. Sigar, *Djambi* (Amsterdam: Koloniaal Instituut, 1938), p. 251).

relation to Singapore, and the rather industrious and docile population, who, in spite of the gross misrule of past sultans nonetheless enjoy a measure of prosperity, prove that all the conditions needed for substantial and lasting economic development are present."[66]

These were the usual lyrical outpourings of a colonial official about the golden future of his region. Van Rijn was not the only person urging Batavia onward at this time; such rhetoric was part of the administrative discourse of the period.[67] Besides, it was wholly in line with the financial views of a hard-liner like Colijn, who believed that development work should be undertaken only if it could be paid for, and with those of Idenburg in The Hague, who was always mindful of the need to balance the budget.[68] The formal introduction of direct rule was really nothing more than a confirmation of the existing situation. The assumption of the sultan's role, the surrender of appanages, the relinquishment of the *pusaka*, the internment and subsequent banishment of the *anak raja*, and the establishment of a colonial administrative structure had led inexorably to this decision. Direct rule also meant the formal end of almost a century of relations between the colonial government and the sultan's administration.

THE EAST INDIES CONTEXT

Jambi was no exception to the general pattern of the East Indies in this period. It was an early example of the expansion of Dutch control; war, generally known euphemistically as "pacification," was soon a common feature of the Outer Islands. The East Indies army was active in all parts of the archipelago around the turn of the century. In Ceram, patrols were stepped up from 1898 onward; military action to "pacify" the island started in 1903.[69] And expansion was significantly boosted when the circumspect Governor-General Rooseboom was replaced by Van Heutsz. The new governor-general launched a quick succession of expeditions using the "Aceh method": to the Dusun districts of Southeast Borneo in 1904; to Bone, Luwu, and the Toraja regions of Celebes in 1905; and to Tambanan on Bali in 1906. As we have seen, the Aceh method meant a temporary concentration of civil and military

---

[66] Resident of Palembang to governor-general, June 25, 1904, NA, Col., vb. January 21, 1906, no. 22.

[67] See, e.g., P. M. H. Groen, "'Soldaat' en 'bestuursman': Het Indische leger en de Nederlandse gezagsvestiging op Ceram: Een case study," *Mededelingen van de Sectie Militaire Geschiedenis Landmachtstaf* 5 (1982): 203–44, esp. 212; W. Manuhutu, "Pacificatie in practijk, de expansie van het Nederlands gezag op Ceram, 1900–1942," in *Imperialisme in de marge: De afronding van Nederlands-Indië,* ed. J. van Goor (Utrecht: HES, 1986), pp. 267–316, esp. 295, on Ceram.

[68] Like Idenburg, Colijn saw cost as the main criterion for retaining self-government. The finances of the self-governing authority, the *landschapskassen,* in which the compensation for surrendered rights as well as taxes should be deposited, should be placed under strict Dutch control. Where improving the welfare of the local population was concerned, too, nothing should be done beyond "what finances will permit," the emphasis being on developing natural resources and stepping up production under the leadership of European capital and entrepreneurship. As for education for the masses, this they should largely fund themselves. The policy that Colijn advocated was wholly based on rational considerations. Expansion pursued thus would not disrupt the financial balance but consolidate it. For a survey of Colijn's ideas, see M. Koning, "De Nederlandse expansie en ethische politiek in de visie van Colijn" (M.A. thesis, Leiden University, 1983).

[69] Groen, "'Soldaat' en 'bestuursman.'"

Grave of Taha at Muara Tebo in 1985
Photograph by Elsbeth Locher-Scholten

Grave of Pangeran Wiro Kesumo at Jambi in 1985
Photograph by Elsbeth Locher-Scholten

authority in the hands of one man, who was usually an officer who had served in Aceh. When all opposition had been overcome, however, civil administration was reinstated. The fact that military rule was always temporary—in contrast to practice in the French colonies—reflects the civil nature of Dutch society. Though himself a military man, Van Heutsz himself restored civil administration; he thought soldiers made poor administrators.[70] Summing up, the military action taken in Jambi and the steps taken to introduce a uniform administrative structure provide an early example of the way in which the Dutch consolidated their territorial gains. As such, they are wholly representative of the Netherlands' approach to the East Indies in this period, and illustrative of the process of colonial state formation.[71]

---

[70] Van Heutsz to Van der Wijck, February 22, 1906, NA, coll. Van Heutsz 2. At the lowest level, the military official continued to serve in an administrative capacity, but for purely financial reasons; it was the cheapest type of administration (H. W. van den Doel, "De ontwikkeling van het militaire bestuur in Nederlands-Indië: De officier-civiel gezaghebber, 1880–1942," *Mededelingen van de Sectie Krijgsgeschiedenis Landmachtstaf* 12 [1989]: 27–50).

[71] For other administrative measures, see chapter 11 and Tideman and Sigar, *Djambi*.

Governor-General J. B. van Heutsz, August 31, 1909
KITLV photograph collection 28,703

JAMBIAN ISOLATION AND DUTCH IMPERIALISM

Using the material set forth in the previous chapters, we are now ready to provide a more detailed description of the two strands in the relationship between Batavia and Jambi—Dutch imperialism and Jambian strategies. These descriptions will enable us to answer the questions posed in the first chapter.

TAHA'S POLICY

Taha's policy was characterized in chapter 8 as avoidance behavior, the "weapon of the weak." But it is important not to see this in purely linear terms, and to bear in mind what James Clifford has called "a history of hesitations."[1] There is ample evidence of demurral and deliberation among the Jambian leadership, both in reports of consultations in the early 1880s and in Raden Anom's opposition around the same time. All in all, it is fair to say that the "hesitations" all culminated in the policy of avoidance that was tenaciously maintained for forty years.

The question that arises is whether this avoidance behavior and isolation was the sole option for Jambian foreign policy—foreign policy being the appropriate term, from Jambi's perspective, for its relations with the colonial government. Isolation is a common position in international relations, a position generally chosen when four conditions or determinants are satisfied: a weak central government, economic self-sufficiency, the availability of resources to ward off a threat, and natural borders.[2] The first of these, weak central authority, was typical of the Malay *kerajaan* in general and the structure of the Jambian state in particular, with its *dusun* autonomy, its diverse population, and its independent appanage holders. Though economic self-sufficiency was never entirely accomplished, this condition was not essential, since the colonial authorities never posed a threat to trade with Singapore. The resources to ward off outside threat consisted of intermediaries, whom we shall discuss in a moment. As for the fourth and last condition, natural borders, Jambian geography and the contrast between *ulu* and *ilir* provided Taha with ideal conditions. In this situation, withdrawal

---

[1] James Clifford, *The Predicament of Culture: Twentieth-Century Ethnography, Literature, and Art* (Cambridge, MA: Harvard University Press, 1988), p. 343.

[2] K. J. Holsti, *International Politics: A Framework for Analysis*, 4th ed. (Englewood Cliffs, N.J.: Prentice-Hall, 1983), p. 99.

into self-elected isolation was a rational choice to make. It was the strategy of a ruler who could exercise only tenuous central authority.[3]

Taha had the benefit of three mediators who could avert danger: the contract sultan, the *pangeran ratu*, and Pangeran Wiro Kesumo. They acted as effective shields between the Dutch authorities and Taha, and it was between these three men and Batavia that the game was played out. Each Dutch administrator tended to single out one of the three as his favorite, viewing the others with varying degrees of suspicion. Thus Resident Pruys van der Hoeven placed his faith in Sultan Nazaruddin, his successor Laging Tobias inclined toward the *pangeran ratu* Cakra Negara, and Resident Monod de Froideville, ten years later, trusted in Wiro Kesumo.

Wiro Kesumo's role as middleman merits closer attention. As the narrative has shown, Wiro Kesumo had a genius for sheltering with the strongest party. In the years 1858–81, when Sultan Nazaruddin exercised formal power, he managed to make himself indispensable by becoming the sultan's representative *(wakil)* in the capital. He owned the largest lowland appanage and was married to one of Nazaruddin's daughters. When Taha expanded his influence in the last two decades of the century, Wiro Kesumo ingratiated himself with him. He made Taha's son, Pangeran Ratu Anom Kesumo Judo, the gift of a gold-embroidered festive costume for his public appearance in 1894, and even managed to become *bhisan* to Taha (i.e., a relative by marriage) by marrying his son to Taha's daughter. Since this son then settled in his father-in-law's *dusun*, the ties became even closer.

Still, a middleman can exist only by virtue of a gap between two parties that one of them seeks to bridge.[4] Once Batavia no longer accepted the gap and forced the other side to engage in direct contact, Wiro Kesumo's mediation became superfluous. Through his trade with Singapore he was well informed about recent developments in the archipelago, and living in the lowlands, within Batavia's immediate area of control, he knew that it was in his best interests to side with the Dutch. He was not open to charges of siding with the resistance, as he voluntarily relinquished his appanages in 1904. Even then he remained active; as district headman he kept his intermediate position between the Dutch and the local administration, a middleman until his death in 1905. Taha had reason to be grateful to him, however, since it was Wiro Kesumo who enabled him to sustain the avoidance behavior that made him a national hero of the Republic of Indonesia, presaging the nationalist noncooperation of the 1920s and 1930s.

After war broke out in Aceh in 1873, Jambi's history was overshadowed by events in this area of northern Sumatra. It therefore makes sense to look for parallels between the two regions. First, here as in Aceh, the resistance (modest though it may have been) was inspired by Islam. The almost annual attacks of the 1870s and those of 1885 and 1895 were all perpetrated by men dressed in white. The opposition that had beleaguered the Geographical Society was also rooted in Islam. Some orthodox Muslim *dusun* with a large number of hajis, such as Lubuk

---

[3] This is also the view of Taufik Abdullah ("Responses to Colonial Powers: The Jambi Experience in Comparative Perspective," *Prisma: The Indonesian Indicator* 33 [1984]: 13–29, esp. 13).

[4] S. van Bemmelen et al., "Introduction," *Women and Mediation in Indonesia*, KITLV Verhandelingen 152 (Leiden: KITLV Press, 1992;), pp. 1–12.

Resam on the Tembesi, had a long tradition of resistance (1878, 1901). In 1904 the Hungarian charlatan Hirsch had to disguise himself as Yusuf of Turkey to gain an audience. But in Jambi this Muslim protest was as fragmented as the power of the state itself. There were no foundations on which to build the kind of resistance that the *ulama* had set up in Aceh.

Withdrawal into isolation was the logical choice, the way to turn weakness into strength. There was no indigenous culture strong enough to weather a confrontation with the West and indeed to be regenerated by it, as happened in Aceh. The Jambian response resembled that of many local rulers in the nineteenth century (on Sumatra, in the *Vorstenlanden* of Java, on Bali, and elsewhere): it amounted to withdrawal behind a semblance of cooperation that created or preserved scope for independent action. Taha's complete isolation was the most extreme example: when it became impossible for him to sustain the illusion of cooperation, his scope for action was eliminated. His contemporary, Sultan Mohamad Soleiman of Kutai (1845–99) on Borneo's east coast, pursued the same objective by a different avenue, that of collaboration.

Since Mohamad Soleiman operated in roughly the same period, and like Taha wielded power for half a century, it is illuminating to compare their policies. The two regions also had certain similarities: both were coastal regions with marshlands, wide rivers, impenetrable jungles, and poor communications. Kutai too had attracted the interest of European mineral extraction companies, albeit for coal rather than oil and a decade earlier, in the 1880s. And in Kutai too a contract (that of 1844) had resulted from the misadventures of a buccaneer, in this case the Scot Erskine Murray, who, emulating James Brooke, had attempted to establish himself in Kutai in 1843.[5] In 1846 Kutai came under the control of an Assistant Resident, a title not so much indicative of active supervision as it was symbolic of Dutch claims in the region. In the Dutch struggle against the sultan of Banjarmasin in 1860, Sultan Soleiman remained neutral; he subsequently purged his court of all anti-Dutch elements. He was not fearful of change. Unlike Taha, Soleiman agreed to surrender his mineral extraction rights—something that did him no harm whatsoever financially. He became a close friend of the Dutch entrepreneur J. H. Menten. In 1888 the first coal was extracted from the soil of Kutai in his presence, and in 1897 oil prospecting produced astonishing results.[6] Soleiman also allowed the Europeans to set up large plantations: trials with the cultivation of coffee and other crops were carried out in the 1890s. By then he had already set up a school at his own expense (in 1890), which was run by a teacher trained in Makassar. He sent his two sons to Europe in 1898 to attend the festivities surrounding the inauguration of Queen Wilhelmina, he himself attending the ceremonies staged in the capital of the Residency of Banjarmasin.[7] Outwardly, the policy of this "modern" sultan, a man of the world, was quite the opposite of that pursued by Taha. While the

---

[5] "Koetei," *Encyclopaedie van Nederlandsch-Indië* (The Hague: Nijhoff; Leiden: Brill, 1918), 2: 374–77, esp. 376.

[6] J. T. Lindblad, *Between Dayak and Dutch: The Economic History of Southeast Kalimantan 1880–1942*, KITLV Verhandelingen 134 (Dordrecht: Foris, 1988), p. 32.

[7] *Koloniaal Verslag 1890, Bijlage C van de Handelingen der Staten-Generaal 1890–1891* (The Hague: Staatsdrukkerij, 1890–91), p. 16; *Koloniaal Verslag 1899, Bijlage C van de Handelingen der Staten-Generaal 1900–1901* (The Hague: Staatsdrukkerij 1900–1901), p. 34.

latter withdrew into taciturn seclusion, Soleiman apparently obliged the Dutch at every turn.

Yet it was purely a difference of strategy—in both cases the aim was to preserve some independence, some room to maneuver. Soleiman saw the colonial government as a useful counterbalance to Buginese and Banjarese competition; he needed it. His strategy enabled him to achieve absolute supremacy within Kutai for himself and his family. He pushed up taxes and managed to enrich himself. And in spite of his openness, he succeeded in keeping the Dutch at a distance. When a new Assistant Resident arrived in the sultanate in 1884, he was appalled to see the ramshackle premises, an hour and a half from the kraton by boat, that were to house his administrative post. Soleiman used the Dutch just as they used him.[8] Ultimately, Soleiman's cooperation was more successful than Taha's policy of noncooperation; Kutai retained self-government until many years after his death— until 1942, in fact—although under the policy on the Outer Islands that came into force after 1900, it was subject to stricter constraints.

Thus, to achieve the same goal of retaining a degree of autonomy, local rulers could choose a strategy ranging from cooperation to its complete opposite. But Taha could only afford to sustain his policy of noncooperation as long as the Dutch government kept at a distance and believed in the "collaboration" of the sultan's administration. After that, this strategy proved to be a far more dangerous option than cooperation.

DUTCH IMPERIALISM

This brings us to the issue of Dutch expansion. We can now return to the questions asked in chapter 1:

- What do the relations between Batavia and Jambi in the period 1830–1907 tell us about the theme of continuity versus discontinuity?
- How can we define the relationship between the center and the periphery? Where did the initiative lie? What role did the sultan's administration play?
- What were the motives underlying the decisions taken by the government of the East Indies in this period?

We can also compare Batavia's actions in Jambi to those elsewhere in the archipelago, to test their consistency with general policy in the Outer Islands. Only then will it be possible to formulate some conclusions about Dutch imperialism.

FIELDHOUSE'S MODEL OF IMPERIALISM AND JAMBIAN HISTORY

Comparison of the history of relations between Batavia and Jambi and Fieldhouse's model of imperialism, with its emphasis on continuity, peripheral imperialism, and the politicization of economic arguments, reveals a very close fit. There was certainly continuity. These relations dated from the early nineteenth century. Whether they were regarded as relations in the sphere of international

---

[8] I. Black, "The 'Lastposten': Eastern Kalimantan and the Dutch in the Nineteenth and Early Twentieth Centuries," *Journal of Southeast Asian Studies* 16 (1985): 281–91, esp. 288–89.

law, which was a possible interpretation from the Jambian perspective, or as a formal constitutional relationship with a dependency, which is how Batavia saw it, a relationship of sorts certainly existed. In Batavia's view, Jambi had belonged to the territory of the Netherlands since 1833. This was indeed no "informal" but a "formal" empire—at least on paper.[9] The 1858 contract simply constituted a written record of this relationship, as interpreted by the colonial government. Besides continuity there was also "contiguity." The protection of existing Dutch interests in adjacent regions, namely Palembang and Sumatra's west coast, constituted a significant motive for the Netherlands' actions in 1833. Thus, Jambi fits the model developed by Betts and Kuitenbrouwer (contiguity) as well as those of Fieldhouse and Wesseling, both of which stress continuity.

In 1901 the Dutch abandoned their policy of abstention from interference: it was "the end of an old story," the end of relations with the sultan's line, the *kerajaan*. This was certainly how the Jambians viewed the abolition of the sultanate. For it put an end to the internal exercise of sovereign rights by the sultanate, the sovereignty "within its own sphere" it had enjoyed until then.[10] Even though this sphere had shrunk in the course of the nineteenth century, with the surrender of trading rights, opium trade, and some jurisdiction, and though it had surrendered its external sovereignty—that is, in international relations—in 1858, the sultanate had managed to hold on to its internal autonomy until 1901.

Every end is also a beginning. In this case it was the beginning of Jambi's integration into the colonial state through a series of administrative and financial measures. The intensification of administrative intervention after 1900 entailed a qualitative change, not just for previous Jambian administrators but also for the government of the Dutch East Indies. The appearance of a relationship under international law, which both parties had preserved with rituals in the 1880s, though for different reasons, had become unsustainable. The colonial government was happy to abandon this ambivalence.

Throughout the nineteenth century, Dutch actions in Jambi provided a textbook example of peripheral imperialism. Every initiative was taken in the periphery. It was the men bearing direct responsibility in the region, the Residents of Palembang (Praetorius, Boers, Couperus, Pruys van der Hoeven, Laging Tobias, Monod de Froideville, and Van Rijn van Alkemade) who favored vigorous action. Each one in turn urged that Jambi be brought under Dutch control or administered more directly. Batavia often watered down their proposals, which consequently reached The Hague either in a radically altered form or not at all. However, in 1833, 1858, 1879, and 1900 the colonial authorities adopted them. So it was Batavia that determined the course of action.

The Hague scarcely figured in the picture. In 1833–34 the Minister of Colonies did not receive the reports of a military expedition until months after it had taken place; the events of 1858, too, unfolded without any direction from the Netherlands. Even around the turn of the century, The Hague did not take any initiative. When the Minister did prescribe policy, as in 1841, it was not to urge

---

[9] Gallagher and R. Robinson, "The Imperialism of Free Trade," *Economic History Review*, 2nd ser., 6, 1 (1953), 1–15.

[10] This is the origin of the concept of sovereignty; see P. H. D. Leupen, "De ontwikkeling van het middeleeuwse souvereiniteitsbegrip: Teloorgang van een relationele conceptie," *Theoretische Geschiedenis* 18 (1991): 387–98.

expansion but quite the contrary, to insist on abstention from interference and the decommissioning of posts. It was only when the colonial policy of expansion jeopardized Dutch interests in the international arena (in Sumatra around 1840), when foreign interests (in the form of an American adventurer in 1852 and the Standard Oil Company in 1904) appeared to constitute a threat to Dutch interests in the colony, or when the coffers of the Dutch East Indies were in danger of running dry (in 1841 and 1904, for instance) that directives were issued from the Netherlands. Only in the period 1879–80 was there a Minister more expansion-minded than his governor-general, but his term of office was too brief to make an impression. Policy was made in Batavia and reported to The Hague, where the Minister defended it—after 1900 on the basis of "ethical" considerations.

Initiatives were born in the region itself because that was where the Dutch officials encountered acute administrative problems. As Fieldhouse puts it, in general terms, "positive action normally began as a response to existing peripheral problems or opportunities rather than as the product of calculated imperialist policy."[11] This certainly applied to Jambi, where the sultan's administration succeeded in presenting an appearance of collaboration for many years. But the roots of these peripheral problems lay in the demands imposed by the Dutch. The colonial government aroused expectations and made false promises in 1833; later on, in 1858, stricter requirements were attached to the contract, and in the 1890s to the local administration. The local elite had no desire to comply, and were in any case poorly equipped to meet the growing Dutch demands for cooperation within a colonial state. An analysis of the problems in the periphery and their causes shows that the colonial authorities created their own problems. Thus Fieldhouse's proposition that "Europe was pulled into imperialism by the magnetic force of the periphery" is not wholly valid here.[12] The root cause, the disruption of the balance of power between Europe and the non-Western world, can be traced to European developments and the way in which they were translated by the Europeans living in the archipelago. And this defines imperialism, after all, as a primarily Western phenomenon.

The motives underlying decisions to act have been discussed at length above. They can be briefly summarized in relation to three critical points in time: 1833, 1858, and the turn of the century. In 1833 these motives were largely political and economic, consisting of Van den Bosch's plans for Sumatra and Sumatran trade plus measures to protect existing interests in the neighboring regions. In 1858, fear of foreign rivals and the use of contracts to ward off adventurers played a key role. In 1901, plans for mineral extraction underlay the efforts to seek closer contact, efforts that exposed a range of administrative abuses. Except for the events of 1858, Dutch expansion in Jambi was not a response to foreign imperialism or a "function of international politics."[13] By the time the fear of foreign rivals came to the fore— here especially in relation to Standard Oil in 1904—the plans had already been made. Although these plans were based on hopes of profit, before long the main focus was on the need to establish firm authority, to create tranquility and order.

---

[11] D. K. Fieldhouse, *Economics and Empire 1830–1914*, 2nd ed. (London: Macmillan, 1984), p. 462.

[12] Ibid., p. 463.

[13] H. L. Wesseling, "The Giant That Was a Dwarf or the Strange History of Dutch Imperialism," *Journal of Imperial and Commonwealth History* 16 (1988): 58–70, esp. 66.

This is entirely in accordance with the politicization of arguments described in Fieldhouse's model. Economic motives led to, and were gradually reformulated in terms of, an administrative and political problem.

The Dutch expansion in Jambi more than demonstrates the existence of a Dutch imperialism. Not only do the actions there fit Fieldhouse's model, they highlight certain matters to which Fieldhouse has paid relatively little attention, such as the renewed thrust toward state formation and the European nature of modern imperialism. Still, it remains to determine whether they were representative of Dutch policy in the Outer Islands as a whole.

JAMBI AND DUTCH POLICY ON THE OUTER ISLANDS

At each critical stage of the nineteenth century, Dutch behavior in Jambi bore all the signs of general colonial behavioral patterns. The enforcement of the new contract of 1833 was part of Van den Bosch's overall policy for Sumatra. And the conclusion of the 1858 contract was in line with a larger wave of expansion in Sumatra and beyond in the 1850s. Pruys van der Hoeven's more vigorous approach in the 1870s reflected the new imperialism of which the Aceh War, which started in 1873, was the military embodiment. The expansion in the first few years of the twentieth century, on the other hand, was bound up with the "ethical imperialism" that would culminate in the final consolidation of the Dutch East Indies.

Still, it would be nonsense to suggest that any of this was indicative of a uniform, carefully devised policy. The reality was simply that local officials requested intervention when some incident occurred—a murder here, some headhunters there, a Dutch flag flown upside down or a raid—and Batavia responded. The haphazardness of this policy is clear from the way the standard model contract came into existence. The model was finally ready in 1875, after which it ended up being frequently applied in numerous variations, rather defeating the purpose. But although the motives prompting requests for assistance varied, the responses became more and more similar as time went on. The mind-set of the administrative center evidently dictated identical reactions to a range of situations.

This pattern—different motives, similar responses—emerges clearly when we compare examples of Dutch expansion, using Fieldhouse's model, and look more closely at the details of these motives. Was it fear (of foreign rivals), power, profit, or principle that underlay this expansionist drive? A comparative overview, singling out these points, of recent critical studies of Dutch expansion in the archipelago between 1873 and 1906—that is, in the age of modern imperialism—can clarify the general pattern of this expansion and the diversity that it embraced. It also sheds light on the specific features of Dutch expansion as compared to that of other colonial powers. The twelve critical studies included in the accompanying table focus on Aceh (1873), at the outbreak of the Aceh War; Northeast Borneo (1878), where Batavia tried to enforce its rights after a British company established itself there; Flores (1890), where a punitive raid was launched and miscarried after the local Rokka population attacked a Dutch tin prospecting expedition; Lombok (1894), where Dutch intervention in a civil war

Schematic Overview of Twelve Military Expeditions
in the Indonesian Archipelago

	Region	Continuity	Crisis periphery	Initiative	Fear of foreign rivals	Money	Principle	Power
1	Aceh 1873	+/-	+	The Hague/ Batavia	+	+	-	+
2	NE Borneo 1881	-	+	The Hague/ Batavia	+	-	-	-
3	Flores 1890	-	+	Batavia	-	+	-	+
4	Lombok 1894	+	+	Batavia	-	-	+	+
5	New Guinea 1898	-	+	Batavia/ The Hague	+	-	+	+
6	Aceh 1896	+	+	Batavia	-	-	-	+
7	Jambi 1901	+	+	Batavia	-	+	+	+
8	Kerinci 1902	-	+	Batavia	-	-	+	+
9	Ceram 1904	+	+	Batavia	-	-	-	+
10	Banjarmasin 1904	+	+	Batavia	-	-	-	+
11	Bone 1906	+	+	Batavia	-	+	+	+
12	Badung/ Bali 1906	+	+	Batavia	-	-	+	+

between Muslim Sasaks and Hindu Balinese provoked a surprise nighttime attack on the East Indies troops, followed by occupation and annexation by way of reprisal; Aceh (1896), where a new, more aggressive approach was developed in response to the defection of Tengku Umar; New Guinea (1898), where the first two administrative officials were stationed that year; Jambi (1901) and Kerinci (1902); Ceram (1904), one of the Moluccan Islands in which the insurgent Alfur, an indigenous mountain tribe, were subdued by force; Banjarmasin (Southeast Borneo, 1904), which witnessed the "settling of accounts" with the sultan's administration, ousted in the 1860s; Bone (South Sulawesi, 1905), where the local ruler was deposed when he refused to surrender his trading rights; and Badung (1906), one of the last independent principalities on Bali, which refused to pay compensation for the plundering of a trading vessel and was punished by a military expedition.[14]

CONTINUITY

If continuity is understood to refer to preexisting diplomatic or administrative relations between the colonial government and local principalities, it existed in the form of a contract in seven out of the twelve regions. Of the remaining five, three (Northeast Borneo, Flores, and New Guinea) were subject to Dutch authority, as they belonged to the territories of local rulers with whom the colonial government had concluded contracts. Only Aceh and Kerinci were still completely independent when the Dutch took action there.[15]

When we review the series of expeditions, it appears that while contracts did exist in most cases, they did not provide watertight guarantees for Dutch claims. Northeast Borneo fell outside Batavia's direct sphere of action and influence until the late 1870s, although the Dutch did lay claim to sovereignty on paper. Flores had belonged constitutionally to the territory of the Dutch East Indies since 1859, when Portugal had relinquished its claims. It was part of the Residency of Timor and dependencies, with the exception of Western Flores, which came under the colonial authorities of Celebes. But Batavia had never concluded a contract of any kind with the Rokka village headmen of the central highlands, against whom the expedition of 1890 had been launched. They too could hence be classified as independent.

In the case of Lombok a contract had existed since 1843, but its ambiguous translation (like the early Jambian contracts) gave rise to conflicting interpretations. It was unclear whether its ruler, the Balinese sultan of

---

[14] For Aceh in 1873 see M. Kuitenbrouwer, *The Netherlands and the Rise of Modern Imperialism: Colonies and Foreign Policy 1850–1902* (New York: Berg, 1991), and A. Reid, *The Contest for North Sumatra: Atjeh, the Netherlands and Britain 1858–1898* (Singapore: Oxford University Press: Kuala Lumpur: University of Malaya Press, 1969); for Northeast Borneo see Kuitenbrouwer, *The Netherlands and Imperialism*, and G. Irwin, *Nineteenth-Century Borneo: A Study in Diplomatic Rivalry*, KITLV Verhandelingen 15 (The Hague: Nijhoff, 1955;); for Flores see P. Jobse, *De tin-expedities naar Flores 1887–1891: Een episode uit de geschiedenis van Nederlands-Indië in het tijdperk van het moderne imperialisme*, Utrechtse Historische Cahiers 3 (Utrecht: Department of History, Utrecht University, 1980); for Lombok see J. van Goor, *Kooplieden, predikanten en bestuurders overzee: Beeldvorming en plaatsbepaling in een andere wereld* (Utrecht: HES, 1982), and van Goor, "De Lombokexpeditie en het Nederlands nationalisme," in *Imperialisme in de marge: De afronding van Nederlands-Indië*, ed. J. van Goor (Utrecht: HES, 1986), pp. 19–70; for Aceh in 1896 see Kuitenbrouwer, *The Netherlands and Imperialism*; for Jambi see this volume; for Kerinci see H. J. van der Tholen, "De expeditie naar Korintji in 1902–1903: Imperialisme of ethische politiek," *Mededelingen van de Sectie Militaire Geschiedenis Landmachtstaf* 10 (1987): 70–89; for Banjarmasin see E. van Breukelen, "De Nederlandse gezagsuitbreiding in de Zuider- en Oosterafdeling van Borneo 1900–1906" (MA thesis, Utrecht University, 1991); for Bone see Elsbeth Locher-Scholten, "'Een gebiedende noodzakelijkheid': Besluitvorming rond de Boni-expeditie 1903–1905," in *Excursies in Celebes: Een bundel bijdragen bij het afscheid van J. Noorduyn als directeur-secretaris van het Koninklijk Instituut voor Taal-, Land- en Volkenkunde*, ed. H. A. Poeze and P. Schoorl, KITLV Verhandelingen 147 (Leiden: KITLV Uitgeverij, 1991;), pp. 143–64; for Bali see H. Schulte Nordholt, *The Spell of Power: A History of Balinese Politics, 1650–1940* (Leiden: KITLV Press, 1966), pp. 191–217.

[15] In the case of Aceh a peace and friendship treaty existed, which had been forced on the sultanate in 1857.

Karangasem, had surrendered his independence. New Guinea was nominally subject to the sultan of Tidore, on which grounds the colonial government had laid claim to the right of possession at the beginning of the nineteenth century, specified more precisely in 1849 up to the 141st parallel. However, consolidation had not gone beyond low-level administrative posts (1828–36, 1893). The action taken in Aceh in 1896–98 after Tengku Umar switched sides was part of the Aceh War, and as such furnish the clearest example of continuity. The continuous relations with Jambi have already been discussed at length. The only ties with independent Kerinci consisted of a forgotten friendship treaty dating from 1840.

Ceram, Banjarmasin, Bone, and Badung provide clearer examples of continuity. Ceram, as part of the Moluccas, had been formally under Dutch authority since 1814; in fact, however, this authority was only exercised over the coastal region. Banjarmasin had been under direct rule since the 1860–66 war; as in Jambi, the sultan's administration had retreated to the uplands. Bone had been a self-governing fief of the colonial government since the Bone War of 1860. Contracts had existed with the Balinese sultanates since 1849.

Regardless of the degree of continuity that existed in the form of contracts, contiguity and a shifting frontier were present in all cases, "new" independent regions as well as those where ties were well established. The three clearest examples are Aceh (1873), Lombok, and New Guinea. Siak had surrendered its independence in 1858 and Deli had been brought under Dutch rule in 1863; the colonial government was gradually advancing northward. Lombok too was drawn into the Dutch sphere of influence with the formation of the Residency of Bali and Lombok in 1882, because of the problems with opium smuggling in the region and improved shipping and telegraph connections; the question was no longer *whether* but *when* this part of the archipelago would come under stricter control.[16] New Guinea, a center of controversy among Dutch administrators ever since the 1870s, was drawn in when the Royal Mail Steam Packet Company (KPM) opened up a quarterly service to this island in 1891, a service with a purely administrative character.[17] For all other regions the same thing applied, mutatis mutandis: the Dutch came closer through administrative expansion (e.g., in Kerinci) and Western technology, were better informed as a result, and felt challenged by local reactions to consolidate their presence. Contacts, "informal if possible, formal if necessary," became formal by virtue of (Dutch) necessity in this period.[18]

This fairly matter-of-course process of pushing back frontiers was recognized and emphasized by contemporaries. Thus in 1901 Idenburg stated that "the legal order that has been established and consolidated in our territory is constantly being threatened and assailed along the borders and must therefore be defended."[19] Expansion was hence an "unavoidable consequence of our sovereign rights."[20] Or as

---

[16] Van Goor, *Kooplieden, predikanten en bestuurders overzee*, pp. 72–76; Van Goor, "De Lombokexpeditie," p. 21.

[17] J. á Campo, *Koninklijke Paketvaart Maatschappij: Stoomvaart en staatsvorming in de Indonesische archipel 1888–1914* (Hilversum: Verloren, 1992), p. 191.

[18] Gallagher and Robinson, *Imperialism of Free Trade.*

[19] Handelingen van de Staten-Generaal: *Tweede Kamer 1901–1902* (The Hague: Staatsdrukkerij, 1901–2), p. 109.

[20] Idenburg, memorandum in reply, Handelingen der Staten Generaal: *Eerste Kamer 1902–1903* (The Hague: Staatsdrukkerij, 1902–3), p. 82.

Governor C. A. Kroesen of Celebes put it before the Bone expedition, almost with a long-suffering sigh, "It is simply the curse resting on every colonial power that it is constantly compelled by circumstances to expand the area over which it exerts direct rule."[21]

Thus, Fieldhouse, Betts, Wesseling, and Kuitenbrouwer all confirm what contemporaries already knew: whether you call it modern imperialism, expansion, or even (to use the contemporary term) "pacification," its basic features—inside and outside the Indonesian archipelago—were established interests, more or less direct relations, and shifting frontiers. Or, to quote Fieldhouse again, "Clearly the novelty of late nineteenth-century imperialism is to be looked for in the speed and universality of the European advance and not in the mere fact that it happened."[22] What applied to Jambi applied to all other territories: with the end of the old story came a renewal of constitutional structures and the strengthening of the colonial state.

THE PERIPHERY: CENTER OF CRISIS, CENTER OF INITIATIVE

The initiative for the twelve examples of expansion mentioned was taken almost without exception by the "periphery," not by the "center"—that is, by the colonial government in Batavia, not by The Hague. Batavia invariably set the pace. Often diluting the proposals of the local European administrators, it always went beyond what the Minister thought advisable, given budgetary constraints. Only in a handful of cases, involving Aceh, Lombok, and New Guinea, did The Hague play a role. Kuitenbrouwer has pointed out that the thrust toward a more forceful approach against Aceh had come mostly from The Hague until 1872. This changed with the advent of the assertive Governor-General James Loudon. The new governor-general sent warships to Aceh to break the blockade of renegade vassals; Aceh responded by dispatching envoys to Singapore and Constantinople, which exacerbated Dutch fears of foreign intervention. The panicky telegram from the Dutch consul-general in Singapore about Acehnese intrigues with foreign powers then provided a fuse that the indecisive Minister Isaac D. Fransen van de Putte failed to extinguish. This made the Aceh War a joint Hague-Batavian enterprise.

In the case of other expeditions this is less clear. Flores, for example, was an initiative taken wholly in Batavia to which the Minister eventually called halt at the insistence of the lower house of Parliament. Lombok was a more complicated case. Minister Willem Karel van Dedem had urged support for the Muslim Sasaks in their civil war against the Hindu Balinese even before 1894, a position echoed in the contemporary Dutch press. Governor-General Cornelis Pijnacker Hordijk refused permission, the debacle of Flores still painfully fresh in his memory. After his departure, the new governor-general, Carel van der Wijck, immediately sent a relief expedition. It was also Van der Wijck who took the first initiative to send troops after the Dutch garrison there had been attacked. The Minister swiftly endorsed this decision.

In New Guinea, the Minister adopted Batavia's proposals in 1896 to install two controllers (at Fak-Fak and Manokwari), about which agreement had already been

---

[21] Governor of Celebes to governor-general, March 21, 1903, National Archives (NA), The Hague, Col., vb. July 16, 1904, lt X 15.

[22] Fieldhouse, *Economics and Empire*, p. 460

reached at the senior level in Batavia in 1892; as we have seen, on this vast island, such decisions were merely symbolic tokens of Dutch power. For the rest, The Hague was often notified of events late in the day, sometimes too late altogether (as in the case of Kerinci). It either rubber-stamped Batavia's decisions or criticized them after the fact. As time went on, however, The Hague seems to have sought more influence. In his consultations with Van Heutsz in 1904, Idenburg stated that funds were running too low to support military action, and that in no case could the territory under direct rule be expanded "unless this has been shown to be absolutely essential and the consent of the government obtained." Any such expansion should immediately be accompanied by a quest for resources to cover the fresh administrative expenses. In Jambi—by then at an advanced stage of "pacification"—Idenburg allowed the operations to go ahead, but in the case of Southeast Borneo, Bone, and Bali he called for further talks.[23] He inclined against the expedition to Bone until Van Heutsz had convinced him of the "compelling need" for it. Financial restrictions and the obligation to keep the Dutch government informed imposed constraints on Batavia's scope for imperialism, at least in theory, as in practice they never counted for much. Where Ceram was concerned, for instance, no talks were held at all.

Although the decisions were taken in Batavia, in all twelve cases they were in line with the new policy in The Hague—that of abandoning the strategy of abstention from interference. This is clear from the Ministry's limited criticism. The policy of abstention was never formally abolished, although a comment that Aeneas Mackay, Minister of Colonies, made in 1890 about the Batak regions suggests that it had been nuanced; the lower house of Parliament adhered to abstention for rather longer.[24] The new policy was part and parcel of the expansion of the government's influence in numerous areas of society and the gradual interlacing of state and society. Acts of Parliament were passed for a national steam packet service in 1888 and for the formation of a customs union in the eastern archipelago in 1899 (an indirect cause of the expedition sent against Bone, because of the abolition of free trade in Makassar), and the Mineral Extraction Act was also passed in 1899. All this legislation was geared toward standardizing regulations and securing monopolies for the colonial government. In this sense we can classify the expansion as orchestrated jointly by The Hague and Batavia, though the colonial authorities continued to provide the decisive momentum.

The initiative lay with the periphery because of the crises that occurred there—or rather, those that occurred in "the periphery of the periphery," the still ragged edges of the Netherlands' colonial possessions. Every instance of expansion was provoked by such a crisis: in Aceh (1873) there were complaints about piracy and the slave trade, political disintegration under a youthful sultan, and rumors of foreign aid; in Flores, the local population attacked a tin-prospecting expedition; in Lombok, Batavia intervened in a civil war and its troops were attacked as a result; in Aceh (1896), the trigger was Tengku Umar's decision to change allegiance. In New Guinea, there was the dislocation of the social structure after the KPM opened up the region for trade in bird skins and other goods, just as the Papuans' headhunting raids compelled the British to establish administrative posts in

---

[23] Written exchange of views concerning points of government policy. "Nota bevattende punten ter sprake gebracht door den minister van koloniën," VU, Doc. Centr. Ned. Prot., coll. Idenburg.

[24] Kuitenbrouwer, *The Netherlands and Imperialism*, p. 260.

their colonial territory. In Jambi, the crisis consisted of the impossibility of finding a suitable candidate for the position of sultan; in Kerinci, it was the region's function as a safe haven for the Jambian resistance. In Banjarmasin, the followers of the sultan who had retreated to the hinterland after his deposition in 1860 had opposed the advent of Dutch rule back in 1899. In Bone, the local ruler refused to surrender his import and export duties, a change necessitated by the abolition of free trade in Makassar. In Badung, expansion was prompted by the refusal of the sultan's administration to pay compensation for a freight ship that had been plundered after running aground. Thus in each case, a crisis in the periphery triggered expansion. And in each case, the crisis consisted of the avoidance or rejection of collaboration by the local elite.

This refusal to cooperate was not a consequence of changes in local power structures, although in some cases, such as in Aceh and Badung, experienced rulers had recently been succeeded by new and inexperienced ones. As noted above, the refusal was a reaction to the more pressing demands of the Dutch, whether these had to do with abolishing piracy and the slave trade (Aceh), accepting the sudden and unexpected presence of a company of white tin prospectors (Flores), ending a civil war (Lombok), or surrendering the right to collect import and export duties (Jambi, Bone). The balance of power swung toward Europe as a result of the expansion of European activities in the non-Western world. So the imperialism practiced here was a European phenomenon after all, although of a less conspiratorial nature than is sometimes claimed. The Hague had no detailed master plan for the expansion of Dutch influence in the colony. But ever since the 1840s the Dutch had been imbued with an awareness of the outer borders of the archipelago to which their influence might extend, a vague sense of an "imagined community" that did not take on concrete form until foreigners "intruded." Several decades down the line, the Europeans responded in a far more uniform fashion, though not in any sense by orchestrated design, to the failure of local rulers to meet their demands.

FEAR OF FOREIGN RIVALS

Precisely because the Netherlands expanded its overseas possessions later than other colonial powers, the "fear of foreign rivals" factor has always attracted ample attention in the literature, and the Dutch are said to have been primarily reactive, responding to the initiatives of others.[25] But the significance of international competition, which Betts and Kuitenbrouwer discuss in terms of "preemption," is confined to three cases: Aceh, Northeast Borneo, and New Guinea. These were regions that adjoined other European colonies and whose borders—in the latter two cases at any rate—had not yet been precisely determined. The Aceh War broke out after rumors reached the Dutch that the sultanate was seeking to obtain American and Italian support. An ultimatum was presented to which the Acehnese refused to respond, and the already tense situation erupted into open conflict. That the rumors later proved to be false does not detract from the fears that the Dutch felt at the time.

In the other two cases, however, fear of British influence did not immediately lead to expansion. In Northeast Borneo, the territorial claims of a private British

---

[25] For example, in the writings of Wesseling.

company, which had acquired rights of sovereignty over a large territory from the sultan of Brunei in 1877, prompted a belated show of force with a warship. The aim was to protect the Dutch flag in the newly established administrative post of Batu Tinagat on the "official" border. But neither military display nor diplomatic protest had the slightest effect in London. It was decided not to try more vigorous measures. In 1888 the Dutch government was forced to concede its weakness in the international arena and set up a committee of inquiry, which led in 1891 to the signing of an Anglo-Dutch convention.[26] The issue thus centered on defining frontiers rather than crossing them or pushing them back. The only response to the British presence was a rather more active supervision in the mid-1880s, which, it should be added, was fairly ineffectual. For instance, the findings of an investigation of the situation in the interior were not followed up by action, as the Aceh War absorbed all available resources.[27]

The same initially applied in the case of New Guinea. The debate about whether or not to extend Dutch rule there, which flared up again in the 1880s, was not reinvigorated by the arrival of new neighbors, the Germans having established a presence in the north (1883) and the Australians in the south (1884). It was deemed pointless to set up an administrative post, in view of the nomadism of the population and the vastness of the territory; besides, it was too expensive so long as the Aceh War continued to drain the treasury. However, an Australian's application for a concession of "a million acres" in 1889 showed up the weakness of Dutch control; there was no form whatsoever of "effective occupation," an international requirement since the Berlin Conference (1884–85).[28] It is fair to say that annual visits of the fleet and escutcheons hanging in the mangroves, whose "slim and delicate aerial roots provide an apt symbol of the firm foundations of our authority in New Guinea,"[29] had little effect. But for the Minister who took over the East Indies portfolio in 1896, ethical motives—protecting missionary work and advancing the development of the population—were more important than keeping foreign rivals at bay. Furthermore, when the Dutch did finally establish an administrative presence, they did so against the backdrop of growing popular unrest as a result of the more aggressive trading practices of both European and local merchants—competition made possible by the KPM, which provided regular shipments of goods for trade. Thus, the fear of foreign competition was mingled with ethical and administrative motives, which in turn grew out of changing economic processes.

"Preemption," a significant factor in Jambi fifty years earlier, was therefore not so relevant in the Dutch imperialism of around 1900 as Kuitenbrouwer suggests. Nor did the example of international imperialism serve as an explicit stimulus for a variety of expeditions, as Wesseling believes. The most we can say, perhaps, is that the actions of the West elsewhere in Africa and Asia had created an international climate of expansion that was so much taken for granted that it was no longer written about, having passed the stage of words, so to speak.

---

[26] Kuitenbrouwer, *The Netherlands and Imperialism*, pp. 178–80.

[27] Black, "The 'Lastposten,'" p. 287.

[28] "Historische nota betreffende de plaatsing van bestuursambtenaren op Nederlandsch New Guinea," NA, Col., vb. December 8, 1897, no. 33.

[29] The quotation comes from H. van Kol, member of the lower house of Parliament, Handelingen der Staten-Generaal: *Tweede Kamer 1897–1898* (The Hague: Staatsdrukkerij, 1897–98), p. 172.

There is nothing surprising about this lack of comment. The outer frontiers of the Netherlands' overseas possessions had gradually been determined in the course of the nineteenth century. Agreements with Britain, the most powerful rival and protector in the region, dated from 1871 (the Sumatra Treaty), 1891 (North Borneo), and 1896 (New Guinea). Portugal was too small to pose a threat to Dutch territory: Lisbon recognized the borders with Timor in a gradual process in treaties signed in 1893, 1897, and 1916. While other countries such as the United States, Germany, and Italy were close by, through their trading links, Germany confined itself to northern New Guinea and recognized the borders with Dutch New Guinea; Italy is scarcely mentioned except in relation to the Aceh panic of 1873, and the United States, whose only interest was in trade relations, was satisfied by the introduction of free trade in 1873. Even the American presence in the Philippines after 1898 failed to provoke any panic reactions from the Dutch.[30] We may therefore conclude that the borders of the Dutch possessions had been secured before the heyday of Dutch imperialism. Fear of foreign rivals had influenced decisions regarding expansion only prior to 1900, and then only in a few border areas. The Dutch expeditions took place within the Netherlands' own territorial borders, which were internationally recognized as such. Each one was presented in the administrative discourse as a purely internal affair, a view of the Indonesian archipelago that would even outlive the Second World War.

This is not to say that fear of foreign rivals played no part in the colonial politics of the day, still less that decisions were made in an international vacuum. The Netherlands' colonial policies and foreign policies were as intimately connected as before. It was to its reputation of European "dwarf" and colonial "giant" that the Netherlands owed its status of "middle power"—or its presumption as such.[31] The consolidation of the colonial state and the rise of new powers in the region, such as Japan, brought an added sense of vulnerability and sent the Dutch looking for international cooperative structures to protect their position of power—for instance, in the failed attempt to conclude a South Seas Convention with the United States and others.[32] Still, as far as the expansion within the archipelago was concerned, the international situation was not the decisive factor.

THE PROFIT MOTIVE

The profit motive is generally absent from mainstream interpretations or else distorted, as we saw in connection with Jambi. Lindblad recently showed in relation

---

[30] N. A. Bootsma, *Buren in de koloniale tijd: De Philippijnen onder Amerikaanse bewind en de Nederlandsche, Indische en Indonesische reacties daarop, 1898–1942* (Dordrecht: Foris, 1986), p. 19.

[31] Another aspect foreign and colonial policy had in common was the pattern of using the contract as a political lever. As a small country, the Netherlands sought after 1870 to safeguard its position in the world through international agreements. It should be added that respect for agreements was very strong in the East Indies—so much so that discrepancies in the form of the written contract were overlooked (L. Y. Andaya, "Treaty Conceptions and Misconceptions: A Case Study from South Sulawesi," *Bijdragen tot de Taal-, Land- en Volkenkunde* 134 (1978): 275–95; Locher-Scholten, "Een gebiedende noodzakelijkheid").

[32] N. A. Bootsma, "Nederland op de conferentie van Washington, 1921–1922," *Bijdragen en Mededelingen betreffende de Geschiedenis der Nederlanden* 93 (1978): 101–26, esp. 109–15.

to peaceful and military forms of expansion that private as well as fiscal interests underlay administrative expansion around 1900, although official documents often fail to mention them explicitly.[33] Even so, he too rejects the notion that "Dutch rule was extended or consolidated with . . . overall economic expansion in mind."[34] Where military expansion is concerned, hopes of financial gain can be clearly demonstrated only in respect of Aceh, Flores, Jambi, and Bone. Economic prospects generated by the rapid development of the adjoining region of Deli helped firm Dutch resolve to lock horns with the Acehnese sultanate in 1873. The first expedition to Flores had been dispatched to look for tin, but the second expedition was a military operation, and the object was not tin but punishment.

That the action in Lombok too was about hopes of enrichment, as claimed by Alfons van der Kraan, has previously been refuted by Jurriën van Goor. It has recently become apparent that the Dutch did rather well out of the establishment of direct rule on this island, but that this was not their primary motive.[35] Jambi provides a perfect illustration of the way profit went hand in hand with administrative considerations, and was eventually overshadowed by them. The same applied to Bone. Here too, it was economic interests—Sultan La Pawawoi's refusal to relinquish the rights to import and export duties—that focused attention on this region. Since Makassar would lose its status as a free port in 1905 to be incorporated into a customs union with the eastern archipelago, the sultan's decision was of decisive importance to government finances. Furthermore, the sultan of Bone actively encouraged many other rulers of South Celebes to follow his lead. Yet here too, an initial economic impulse resulted in the exposure of misrule. Here too, in other words, the profit motive became "politicized." In other cases (Kerinci, Ceram, Southeast Borneo, and Bali) the profit motive was never mentioned. As for New Guinea, all the administrative officials in the region conceded roundly that the island had little to offer.

Although profit was not the *immediate reason* for expansion, it was often the *result* of the introduction of direct rule, as the Outer Islands became connected to the world market through new products such as oil, rubber, and copra. However, À Campo has shown that it was not so much the Netherlands that reaped the benefit—on the contrary, its share in trade actually declined—but international trade and the global market.[36]

AN ETHICAL IMPERIALISM?

In the historiography, it is common to find the assertion that the Netherlands' actions cannot be classified as imperialism pure and simple because they were based on ethical motives. I have defined the ethical policy and imperialism elsewhere as two manifestations of the same revival of interest in the colony, a

---

[33] J. T. Lindblad, "Economische aspecten van de Nederlandse expansie in de Indonesische archipel, 1870–1914," in *Imperialisme in de marge: De afronding van Nederlands-Indië*, ed. J. van Goor (Utrecht: HES, 1985), pp. 227–66.

[34] J. T. Lindblad, "Economic Aspects of the Dutch Expansion in Indonesia, 1870–1914," *Modern Asian Studies* 23 (1989): 1–23, esp. 16.

[35] À Campo, *Koninklijke Paketvaart Maatschappij*, pp. 172–85.

[36] J. à Campo, "Orde, rust en welvaart: Over de Nederlandse expansie in de Indische Archipel omstreeks 1900," *Acta Politica* 15 (1980): 145–89.

consequence of what may now be called the "popularization of the colonial discourse" in the latter half of the nineteenth century.[37] Whereas in Java, a region long under Dutch control, this renewed interest focused on efforts to advance the population, in the Outer Islands it took the form of expansion. When we peruse the list of twelve expeditions, ethical motives in fact seem thin on the ground. In Aceh they played no role whatsoever. The same applies to Flores, where the Rokka people were treated with striking contempt—the Dutch called them "much like apes."[38] On Lombok, Minister Van Dedem in The Hague did in fact want to protect the Sasaks; the Dutch press made similar noises. In the East Indies, however, Van der Wijck maintained that the main point was that a focus of unrest within Dutch territory and the open defiance of Dutch authority could not be tolerated.

The ethical argument weighed more heavily in the Netherlands than among the Dutch administrators of the colony. Where Dutch New Guinea was concerned, too, it was the Minister in The Hague, Jacob T. Cremer, who emphasized ethical motives. "We are simply going to perform a civilizing task here," he told the lower house of Parliament in 1897.[39] That this same pattern applied to Jambi has by now become clear. Where Kerinci was concerned, Rooseboom managed to convince Minister Idenburg of the legitimacy of the expedition with a mix of ethical and administrative arguments. For Bone, officials at the Ministry of Colonies drafted a memorandum a few years later reversing the order of the objections raised by the East Indies authorities, highlighting La Pawawoi's exploitative practices. Here too, it was said that the aim was to protect the population. Ethical motives were used to justify military expansion, especially when arguing the case in the mother country.

For Bali, the roles appear initially to have been reversed. Commenting on the abuses there, Rooseboom wrote in 1903 that the Dutch, wherever there was injustice, would "not be able to remain inactive in the protection of the weak and the oppressed. This is in complete accord with the ethical direction of colonial politics."[40] He had wanted to take action in response to a case of widow-burning, but was restrained by Minister Idenburg, who was known as a fervent ethicist. In response to Rooseboom's letter he had commented, "Yes, but allowing ourselves to be guided by these ethical considerations brings us into conflict everywhere, making self-restraint essential." To Van Heutsz, the sultan of Badung's defiance of the colonial government's authority in 1905 was a severe and hence punishable offense, constituting grounds for military action sanctioned by The Hague. Of the many reasons used to justify launching an expedition, protecting the population was never the first or primary one. It was a motive formulated later on to back up other grievances.

The success of the ethical motive can be explained by a variety of factors. The suspicion of local rulers was deeply ingrained among the Dutch. Sultans who left the business of government to the crown prince and spent their days hunting and fishing, who maintained large harems of wives and concubines, and who had little authority over their unruly subjects, as the above account has made plain,

---

[37] Elsbeth Locher-Scholten, *Ethiek in fragmenten: Vijf studies over koloniaal denken en doen van Nederlanders in de Indonesische archipel 1877–1942* (Utrecht: HES, 1981), pp. 196–208.

[38] Jobse, *De tin-expedities naar Flores*, p. 38.

[39] Handelingen Tweede Kamer 1897–1898, p. 175.

[40] Schulte Nordholt, *Spell of Power*, p. 210.

commanded little respect. Besides, the idea of an ethical obligation was something to which the general public of the late nineteenth century could relate. It helped them comprehend an otherwise unfamiliar and remote terrain of foreign policy and overseas administration, with which they were suddenly grappling for the first time, having only recently acquired more democratic influence.

Ethical arguments were indeed part and parcel of the general fin-de-siècle discourse.[41] They expressed the tradition of Dutch foreign policy as preached in Protestant churches, a tradition that had been heightened by the policy of neutrality pursued since 1839. In a country with little experience of power, the evergreen appeal was to ways in which "a small country can became great."[42] It expressed the Dutch nationalism that existed around 1900.[43] It was in sound colonial administration benefiting the local population that the Netherlands would fulfill its historic mission in the world. Or as Idenburg assured Queen Wilhelmina in 1904, "It is my firm belief that the best way to safeguard the lasting and ever-respected possession of our colonies is a peaceful, just, and enlightened administration that teaches Your Majesty's millions of subjects to know and appreciate the blessings of our rule, and that this is the only way in which we can fulfill the great calling that the possession of those extensive territories has placed upon our shoulders."[44]

ADMINISTRATIVE MOTIVES: POWER AND ORDER

One motif dominates the decision making for many expeditions: the administrative imperative. This was the common denominator that ultimately provided decisive and in many cases directly led to action.

The fear of a loss of prestige and the desire to boost Dutch authority became stronger as time went on. In Aceh this authority had been dealt a grievous insult, and finally the only solution was to seek definitive redress. The showing of the flag in Northeast Borneo was largely a matter of prestige. The expedition against the Rokka on Flores in 1890 was equipped "to enforce Dutch rule in the Timor archipelago" and to counter "intolerable offenses against the authorities."[45] Van der Wijck believed, as we have seen, that the Dutch had to intervene in the civil war raging in Lombok because the colonial government could not afford to allow the continued existence of such a hotbed of unrest and open defiance of Dutch authority; the ultimate "revenge" for the "treason" there had been purely a question of an injured sense of honor and an insult to Dutch nationalism. The Director of the

---

[41] Locher-Scholten, *Ethiek in fragmenten*, pp. 177–81.

[42] C. B. Wels, *Aloofness and Neutrality: Studies on Dutch Foreign Relations and Policy-Making Institutions* (Utrecht: HES, 1982); J. J. C. Voorhoeve, *Peace, Profits and Principles: A Study of Dutch Foreign Policy* (Leiden: Nijhoff, 1985).

[43] Kuitenbrouwer, *The Netherlands and Imperialism*; M. Kuitenbrouwer, "Het imperialisme van een kleine mogendheid: De overzeese expansie van Nederland 1870–1914," in *De kracht van Nederland: Internationale positie en buitenlands beleid*, ed. N. C. F. van Sas (Haarlem: Becht, 1991), pp. 42–71; L. Blussé and E. Locher-Scholten, "'Buitenste binnen': De buiten-Europese wereld in de Europese cultuur," *Tijdschrift voor Geschiedenis* 105 (1992): 341–45, esp. 344; Henk te Velde, *Gemeenschapszin en plichtsbesef: Liberalisme en nationalisme in Nederland 1870–1918* (The Hague: SDU Uitgeverij, 1992).

[44] Memorandum in NA, Col., vb. July 16, 1904, X15.

[45] Jobse, *De tin-expedities naar Flores*, p. 37.

Department of Internal Administration in New Guinea asserted, in a statement reflecting a marvelous mix of administrative and ethical motives, "that the prestige of our nation in respect of foreign peoples cannot suffer the population of New Guinea to be left any longer in its present wretched and depraved condition."[46] Where Jambi is concerned, of course, the administrative motive has already been discussed at length. Snouck Hurgronje's official recommendations on Jambi, Kerinci, Banjarmasin, and Bone, which were adopted by the colonial government and therefore acquired more than personal significance, were identical in this respect. In 1904 he considered any postponement of firm action in Bone to be justifiable only on grounds "that are of more consequence than the enforcement of Dutch authority in the colonial government of Celebes."[47] Or as he had said before, more pointedly, "Those who are not for us are against us," the "us" in this case standing for the colonial administration.[48] In the case of Badung, injured prestige was both the immediate and underlying reason to take action.

Advances in technology gave the power motif a strong additional thrust. The military historian Petra Groen holds that the nineteenth-century policy of abstention was a direct derivative of the technological capacity of the armed forces. A simple cost-benefit analysis taught that military operations in impenetrable jungles were seldom worthwhile. This simple calculation, which The Hague never failed to make, limited the scope for expansion.[49] À Campo arrives at the same conclusion: it was not until the availability of regular steamship connections that the archipelago became more accessible, making expansion a real possibility if not an inevitability.[50] The desire to consolidate Dutch control, never entirely absent, was reinforced after 1890 by technological progress, which led to innovations ranging from more highly trained mobile brigades and better steamships to more nutritious army rations such as tinned vegetables.

There is nothing surprising, of course, about the emphasis in official documents—which are the most important sources for all the studies quoted here— on the importance of consolidating Dutch authority. Just as the ethical motif was common currency in the Dutch idiom of the day, the administrative motif was embedded in the mind-set of officialdom. This raises the question of the value of these sources. In a study of imperialism, is it valid to rely on official documents (rather than company reports, newspaper editorials, and suchlike), which obviously focus on administrative concerns? Is it fair to take the "official mind" as a gauge for such an analysis? I believe it is. They reflect the mentality of the colonial elite. What strikes us most about them is their myopic quality.

After the mid-1890s, the focus, as asserted by Kuitenbrouwer, was roundly on the systematic expansion of Dutch control. At first sight this may seem to be begging the question, a line of reasoning that interprets imperialism as a need to

---

[46] Director of Internal Administration to governor-general, February 6, 1892, included in "Historische nota," NA, Col., vb. December 8, 1897, no. 33.

[47] E. Gobée and C. Adriaanse, eds., *Ambtelijke adviezen van C. Snouck Hurgronje 1889–1936*, 3 vols. (The Hague: Nijhoff, 1957–65), 3:, p. 2106.

[48] Ibid., p. 2017.

[49] P. M. H. Groen, "'Soldaat' en 'bestuursman': Het Indische leger en de Nederlandse gezagsvestiging op Ceram: Een case study," *Mededelingen van de Sectie Militaire Geschiedenis Landmachtstaf* 5 (1982): 203–44, esp. 208.

[50] À Campo, *Koninklijke Paketvaart Maatschappij*.

expand Dutch territory without analyzing the objective.[51] Officials in the East Indies (and elsewhere) did not, it is true, formulate grand visions for the future or long-term objectives. The analysis points to a narrow administrative mentality, a tendency to respond ad hoc according to an ever more consistent pattern. In the new colonial mentality of stronger self-awareness generated by the successes of 1894 and 1896–98, the expansion of Dutch control—which technological advances had brought within reach—became an end in itself, sometimes in response to economic problems, sometimes only to administrative problems, and occasionally to fears of foreign rivals. This new colonial ideology had its own idealized image of itself as a nation, what Anderson has called its "imagined community,"[52] which was that of a powerful colonial state encompassing the entire archipelago. Just as nationalism is defined in psychological terms as a state of mind, a *désir de vivre ensemble*, we might say that the Dutch nationalists in the colony had their *désir du pouvoir*.[53] And although contemporaries believed that it was not about imperialism, as soon as the elite within the colony's borders refused to cooperate, it was coerced and intimidated into toeing the line. Local rulers had to know their place and be left in no doubt as to where the seat of power lay. Only then could the colonial state be developed and administered. That is the very essence of modern imperialism.

THE NETHERLANDS AND MODERN IMPERIALISM

Several conclusions can be distilled from the above account. First, Jambi was no exception to the general approach to the Outer Islands in the pattern of decision making and motives. Second, Dutch expansion fits very well into the more general phenomenon of modern imperialism as classified by Fieldhouse and others. In other words, Dutch imperialism did indeed exist. It should be said that Fieldhouse appears to provide a more workable model than Betts, because of his cogent analysis of the imperial dynamics in the periphery.

The third conclusion relates to the view that the Netherlands was an exceptional case as a colonial power. Three points are sometimes cited in the literature in support of this contention: its "ethical" justification of expansion, its late arrival upon the colonial scene, and the fact that Dutch expansion took place within preexisting borders. The latter distinction proves to be the only one that was of abiding significance.[54]

Where the ethical rationale is concerned, it was largely developed in the mother country, by way of retrospective justification or rationalization.[55] Besides, the suggestion that the Dutch had a monopoly on this "ethical" brand of imperialism is highly questionable. Americans advanced the same argument in

---

[51] H. L. Wesseling, *Indië verloren, rampspoed geboren en andere opstellen over de geschiedenis van de Europese expansie* (Amsterdam: Bert Bakker, 1988), p. 190.

[52] Benedict Anderson, *Imagined Communities: Reflections on the Origin and Spread of Nationalism*, 2nd ed. (London: Verso, 1991).

[53] These definitions, coined by Ernest Renan and Lothrop Stoddard and still in use today, which Anderson provided with a new content, can be found in J. T. Petrus Blumberger, *De nationalistische beweging in Nederlandsch-Indië* (Haarlem: Tjeenk Willink, 1931), p. 3.

[54] Kuitenbrouwer, *The Netherlands and Imperialism*, pp. 354, 364.

[55] This term derives from G. J. Resink (communicated personally).

connection with their attack on the colonial forces of Spain in 1898.[56] French colonial rulers had their *mission civilisatrice,* and new concepts of colonial administration arose elsewhere too around the turn of the century.[57] The indispensability of the "moralizing rhetoric" for domestic and foreign consumption in international politics has recently been stressed yet again. The U.S. diplomat George Kennan, an eminent expert in this field, has called it "the histrionics of morality."[58] It is a fallacy to appropriate ethical motives for imperialism as a Dutch prerogative. At most, we could say that as a small nation, the Netherlands avoided or had become unaccustomed to the "discourse of power," and felt more comfortable with an ethical justification for the expansion of colonial power.

The second argument for the Netherlands' uniqueness is similarly untenable. Both Japan and the United States embarked upon their expansion in this region in the same decade, in China (1894–95) and the Philippines (1898), respectively. Furthermore, it was precisely the Netherlands' relatively early tussle with imperialism, the "false start" in Aceh, that impeded all other expansionist projects in the 1870s and 1880s, not just in Jambi but also in Borneo and New Guinea, to name but a few examples. Had the Aceh War proceeded rapidly and successfully as a traditional punitive assault, would not Dutch imperialism have taken major strides forward in the 1880s? It seems very likely, especially given the assumption that the dynamics of the periphery determined this process of imperialism. Technological and military capabilities were still in development at that stage, however. What is more, many key factors that would play a role in the 1890s were not yet present in the Netherlands. In terms of industrialization and nationalism, the years 1870–90 served as a transitional period. For instance, shipping companies received little government support, and then rather grudgingly, from national motives.[59] The orientation toward colonial possessions and the rapid rise of the German hinterland boosted the trade function of the Dutch economy beyond its industrial function.[60] It was not until the end of the 1880s that the national consciousness had developed—in shipping circles at any rate—such as to generate the will and the capacity to exclude foreign rivals. A popular mood of nationalism had also been bred by feelings of kinship with South Africa, as Kuitenbrouwer has shown. Erupting in Dutch fury about "the treachery of Lombok" in 1894, the turning point in Dutch imperialism, it crystallized into a sense of ethical superiority.

Although two of the three supposedly characteristic features of Dutch imperialism can thus be dismissed, the third—that Dutch expansion took place within preexisting borders—is perfectly valid. This was how imperialism manifested itself in a small country, opting for expansion within the borders of its largest colony, after 1871, when it relinquished its last colonial possession in Africa. Cautious contemporaries thought even the East Indies too large an area; in

---

[56] In February 1899 Rudyard Kipling published *The White Man's Burden* to help dispel the Americans' hesitation regarding the Philippines (Bootsma, *Buren in de koloniale tijd,* p. 8; see also R. E. M. van Vuurde, "'Koloniale gerustheid' (1898)," in *Geschiedenis en cultuur: Achttien opstellen,* ed. E. Jonker and M. van Rossem (The Hague: SDU, 1990), pp. 107–18, esp. 107.

[57] Locher-Scholten, *Ethiek in fragmenten,* p. 196.

[58] F. E. Oppenheim, *The Place of Morality in Foreign Policy* (Lexington: Lexington Books, 1991), p. 47.

[59] À Campo, *Koninklijke Paketvaart Maatschappij,* pp. 93–103.

[60] À Campo, "Orde, rust en welvaart," pp. 163–64.

1902, for instance, Van Kol published plans for the sale of part of the Outer Islands. And Rooseboom had been stung by Idenburg's criticism of his Kerinci expedition: "No one is more aware than myself that our territory here in the East Indies is too large. . .. I would therefore think it very much in the interest of both the Netherlands and this colony if we could devote our energies wholly to part of our so extensive possessions."[61]

For others such as Van Heutsz, the borders of the archipelago defined the borders of Dutch imperialism. That he was willing to "confine" himself to this region was a consequence of earlier power and claims acquired since 1824—a consequence, in other words, of the historical heritage. Unlike other small powers such as Belgium, the Netherlands had no cause, in the era of modern imperialism, to look beyond those frontiers.[62] It had quite enough blank spaces on the map within its own territory.

THE PRIMARY CAUSE?

All that remains is to make the transition from motives to factors, from participants to underlying processes, from "subjective views" to the "objective causes"[63] that prompted the systematic filling in of those blank spaces. Here we can be brief. It is precisely the "subjective views" in the form of administrative discourse or the "official mind"—the lion's share of the source material used here—that reveal that the process was driven by discrepancies between the traditional sultanate and the modern Western state. The local elite could no longer comply with the new demands in the realm of leadership and constitutional and economic cooperation, whether these demands had to do with opening up the region for the global market, legal protection and social care for their subjects, or the management of the police. In his book on the carving up of Africa by the Western powers, Wesseling traces the causes back to the Industrial Revolution.[64] He also suggests that it makes little sense to distinguish between economic and administrative elements, since this distinction was gradually eroded in the modern state as it evolved in the course of the nineteenth century.[65] The history of Jambi suggests that the key factor was the development of the modern Western state. The "result" of modern imperialism, the formation of colonial and national states, points in the same direction. Yet, modern states too were formed under the influence of the Industrial Revolution. Perhaps the historical development is therefore best described in terms of two simultaneous processes in the Western world—economic development and state formation—that fueled and influenced one another and became increasingly entwined.[66] And a plaited cord will always be stronger. The result, the modern imperialism of the Netherlands and of other colonial powers, has made its mark on today's world.

---

[61] Quoted in Van der Tholen, "De expeditie naar Korintji," p. 84.

[62] Kuitenbrouwer, *The Netherlands and Imperialism*, p. 363.

[63] H. L. Wesseling, *Verdeel en heers: De deling van Afrika 1880–1914* (Amsterdam: Bert Bakker, 1991), p. 455.

[64] Ibid., p. 459.

[65] Ibid., p. 458.

[66] For the synchronicity of the industrial revolution and the awareness of national statehood, see Anderson, *Imagined Communities*.

CONTINUING LINES AND CHANGING PATTERNS (1907–1949)

Given that this book deals with Batavia-Jambi relations and Dutch imperialism, both narrative and analysis could conclude here. But history does not end with a historical reconstruction, any more than the actors' lives end when the curtain has fallen. Three questions that follow logically from the above account need to be answered: questions about the further integration of Jambi into the colonial state, into the hoped-for economic boom in this region (whether or not generated by oil), and into the idealized or real place of the sultan's administration in the subsequent history of Jambi. The 1916 uprising makes clear, for instance, that the introduction of colonial rule in this region did not proceed entirely smoothly, that Jambi's economy did not immediately flourish as anticipated, and that the sultanate lived on as an idea in the minds of the people.

THE 1916 UPRISING

On August 26, 1916, the president of the nationalist party Sarekat Islam (Islamic Association) in Muara Tembesi, Haji Agus, contacted the Malay government clerk Abel gelar Baginda Marah to confirm earlier rumors of an impending rebellion.[1] The clerk was the most senior colonial official there at the time, since both the controller and the *demang* had gone to monitor the situation in the region two days before in response to the rumors. Abel made a record of the reports for his superiors. That same day, Haji Agus begged for assistance after being threatened by a group of armed men. The clerk set off, and soon found himself facing a large crowd of people from two nearby *dusun*. He heard that the Imam Mahdi (the Messiah) had come, and when the people threatened him he fled to the local police barracks. He subsequently tried again to calm the crowd, using a mix of carefully chosen words and a police guard, but found the task impossible. An attack on the police left several officers dead. The mob then set fire to the barracks, forced open the jail and freed the prisoners, destroyed the post office, and plundered the

---

[1] For the following account I used the doctoral dissertation by Muttalib (Jang Aisjah Muttalib, "Jambi 1900–1916: From War to Rebellion" [PhD dissertation, Columbia University, 1977]) and the master's thesis by Van Wijk (E. M. H. G. van Wijk, "Opstand in Djambi: De geschiedenis van een millenaristische verzetsbeweging tegen het Nederlandse gouvernement in Indonesië aan het begin van deze eeuw" [Amsterdam: University of Amsterdam, 1979]), both of which deal with the rebellion. Their accounts are consistent and complement each other in narrative and analysis. Both have been published in abridged form: Jang Aisjah Muttalib, "Suatu Tinjauan Mengenai Beberapa Gerakan Sosial Di Jambi Pada Perempatan Pertama Abad Ke 20," *Prisma* 8 (1980): 26–37; and E. M. H. G. van Wijk, "De Djambi-opstand: Millenaristisch verzet in Indonesië," *Skript* 2 (1980): 38–52.

homes of Chinese and officials. By the end of the day, the Javanese health official, a member of the *demang*'s household, and all the police officers lay dead. Other officials were forced, together with the population of Muara Tembesi, to join the Sarekat Islam, and Haji Agus was compelled to swear them in.[2]

This meant that the rebels, who by now numbered some two thousand men, controlled Muara Tembesi. It was not until September 2 that the colonial troops retook this settlement with the aid of reinforcements from Palembang. Meanwhile, the riot had spread, partly because the district commander had too few men and was waiting for more to arrive from other districts. With the exception of Muara Bungo, the capital Jambi, and Kerinci, all the main settlements became embroiled in the revolt, which also spread to the Rawas. Mobs numbering hundreds (at Muara Tebo) or thousands (at Sarolangun in Jambi, Bangko, and Surulangun in the Rawas) attacked posts defended by only a few dozen police officers. Confident of their invincibility, they assailed the government buildings armed only with knives. In numerous places, local administrators accused of collaborating with the "infidels" were killed, and telegraph and telephone lines were destroyed. But when the requested reinforcements finally arrived from the surrounding regions and from Java in mid-September, the resistance was completely suppressed within a few months. From late September onward, the population started handing rebels over to the Dutch authorities, a pattern familiar from the Jambi War. And by December 1916, life was back to normal in all districts. Only the long sentences handed down recalled the revolt, which ranked alongside the Communist uprising of January 1927 as one of the largest in twentieth-century colonial Sumatra. Jambian rebel losses numbered 390. The sentences were very harsh: 1,387 ten- to twenty-year terms of imprisonment and a further 1,465 shorter ones, in addition to 62 death sentences, three of which were carried out, the rest being commuted into life imprisonment or long sentences in chains.[3] The losses of the colonial authorities included sixty-three armed police officers, nine local administrators, and a European controller, while five Chinese and forty-nine Jambians also lost their lives.[4]

All the official reports of the uprising identify the distance between administrators and population as one of the main causes of the violence. There was widespread resentment about the way the region had been governed since 1906. Integration had not progressed as well as the first Resident of Jambi, Helfrich, had hoped. Between 1906 and 1916, Jambi had seen no fewer than five Residents and many more controllers come and go. At the beginning of their careers, young and inexperienced, they never had the opportunity to gain a thorough knowledge of this newly subjected region.

Furthermore, in the ten intervening years, two consecutive rounds of administrative reform had sidelined the traditional adat leaders. The old governing nobles had been stripped of their influence as well as their income from appanages in 1904, and the limitations imposed on their freedom of movement reduced them to the status of ordinary citizens. In 1906, Resident Helfrich had divided Jambi rationally into eighty-three districts based on adat communities, each one under a Jambian district headman *(pasirah)*. These leaders were no longer elected by and from the population, but appointed by Batavia, and they were

---

[2] Muttalib, "Jambi 1900–1916," pp. 262–66, Van Wijk, "Opstand in Djambi," pp. 10–12.

[3] Jang Aisjah Muttalib, "Suatu tinjauan mengenai beberapa gerakan sosial di Jambi," p. 35.

[4] Van Wijk, "Opstand in Djambi," p. 18.

hence closer to the Dutch authorities, their *demang* superiors liaising between them and the colonial administration. The *demang* had to meet certain educational standards and therefore came from outside Jambi, which widened the gap between administration and population.

In 1912 followed a second reorganization: the eighty-three districts were combined on paper to make twenty-five, while in practice there were only seventeen. The intermediate position of *demang* was abolished, although the title itself was retained for the new district headmen, who derived their power not from adat but from government appointment. This operation was intended to eliminate the non-Jambian influence of the *demang*. Yet it had the opposite effect. While the original intention had been to allow these positions to be filled naturally whenever a post became vacant, dismissals soon followed instead. The higher demands of the new position again disqualified most Jambians, so that the administrators were once more drawn from other parts of Sumatra, in particular from the Minangkabau. They used their power to advance their relatives' careers and to demand more forced labor than was permissible by law. The reforms therefore created a large group of frustrated, sidetracked adat headmen.[5] But the authorities made light of the complaints about the new administrative measures and took no action.

Economic factors too were causing unease. Under the influence of the Dutch administration there was a new wave of immigration from the neighboring regions. People from Padang and Palembang along with Chinese and other outsiders profited from the "pacification" of Jambi. Although the opening up of the territory had not yet resulted in an oil industry, it had yielded rubber, which was a very lucrative product on the global market around the turn of the century. The first rubber plants had been imported from Singapore in 1904, and Jambian farmers laid out rubber plantations, encouraged by the authorities, in the beginning largely in *dusun* around Jambi, Muara Tembesi, and Muara Bungo. Although the plantations themselves were in Jambian hands, the rubber trade was soon taken over by faster operators like Chinese and Minangkabau entrepreneurs.[6]

Besides boosting export profits, rubber supplanted rice growing, so that more and more of this staple food had to be imported. The failure of the rice harvest in 1914 and the following years drove up prices, forcing people into debt and impeding the payment of taxes. A second problem was a fall in the export price of rattan, another important export product, which was more than halved in 1915–16. The year 1914 ushered in a period of economic malaise for the majority of the Jambian population.

In this situation, taxes and forced labor were more of a burden than before, and most popular resentment focused on these grievances. In the district of Tembesi, where many complaints about forced labor had been received, the maximum number of days had been increased shortly before the uprising from twenty-one to thirty-eight. But non-Jambian headmen regularly exceeded even this maximum, making it harder for the people to produce their own food. Furthermore, in 1914 the head money had been replaced by a corporation and income tax, which was sharply increased in 1916. Once again, scant attention was paid to complaints received about this charge, the collection of which was as relentless as its calculation was

---

[5] Muttalib, "Jambi 1900–1916," pp. 119–33; Wijk, "Opstand in Djambi," pp. 26–27.

[6] Muttalib, "Jambi 1900–1916," pp. 175–87.

haphazard. Thus, in the Rawas it was the custom in 1915 to have defaulters sit bare-chested in the sun for hours at a stretch—sometimes for days. One Indonesian spokesman denounced the "sometimes highly offensive manner" in which taxes were collected.[7]

This accumulation of administrative and economic problems hardened people's hearts against Western rule; nor did they feel much gratitude for "ethical" measures such as education and vaccination. Education was the special concern of administrative officials, who rightly saw it as the only way to produce a corpus of Jambian administrators. Thus, in 1915, thirty-eight new public schools were founded in the Residency.[8] But how could "kafir" education ever become popular if a special school tax was imposed, even on people who had no school-age children, and on those who had no school in their area? What is more, teachers—like so many of the new elite groups—were non-Jambians. This made Jambians fearful: perhaps their children too would be sent elsewhere when they finished their schooling. Because of this, the percentage of absenteeism in Jambi was so high (reaching 50 percent in places) that in some cases the *demang* set off with police support to take the children to school, to bring absenteeism down to below the legal limit of 5 percent.[9] Islamic education too had been placed under supervision, partly under the influence of the government's Islamic policy as formulated by Snouck Hurgronje. The policy was to refrain from interfering in the religious aspects of Islam and Islamic organizations while monitoring the imams' secular duties and the education they provided.

The local population was equally lukewarm about the boons of modern health care. Every major population center acquired its own local physician—another non-Jambian. Enforced vaccination and measures taken in the cholera epidemic of 1909–10, like quarantine and the burning of clothes, jarred with Jambian concepts of disease as a manifestation of angry spirits who needed to be placated in rituals by the *dukun*.[10] Restrictions imposed on Jambian customs included a ban on the sale of *jimat*, talismans used to fend off disease and confer invulnerability. Taken together, these cultural changes made the sultan's administration look ever more like a paradise, compared to the heavy-handed colonial regime. The abolition of debt slavery and increased legal certainty could not compensate for the burden of taxation and the loss of the traditional administrative structure. Unwittingly, the colonial government had itself sowed the seeds of protest among the weak.

The leaders of the rebellion capitalized shrewdly on this mood. Discontented former adat headmen and Islamic leaders channeled the general dissatisfaction that existed in 1916 into a focus on Islamic symbols and expectations. They mobilized the masses by promising to abolish taxes and forced labor and to drive the foreign overlords from their land with Turkish support, and by holding out a vision of the Messiah who would come and restore an Islamic kingdom. Like most of the pre-nationalist protest movements in the archipelago before 1920—Yusuf's

---

[7] Van Wijk, "De Djambi-opstand," p. 41.

[8] Muttalib, "Jambi 1900–1916," p. 196.

[9] Ibid., p. 197.

[10] Ibid., p. 200.

actions of 1904, for instance—this rebellion too had a millenarian quality about it.[11]

That the rebellion proved more enduring than most had to do with the beginnings of nationalist organization. In 1912, a mystical Islamic doctrine had spread across Jambi in spite of government controls, the *ilmu abang* ("red secret learning").[12] Its followers were said to acquire invulnerability by using magical practices, a special combat technique, and *jimat*. The rapid growth of this *ilmu abang* was partly attributable to the Sarekat Islam, the first Islamic nationalist movement (also launched in 1912), which reached Jambi and Palembang in 1914. The *ilmu* adopted its organizational structure, becoming a *sarekat*, an association.[13] Furthermore, Sarekat Abang adherents soon discovered that recruiting new members for Sarekat Islam could generate funds. They could also exploit the intensification of Islamic religious life—another consequence of the rise of Sarekat Islam. This explains why the people were so willing to believe in the advent of the Imam Mahdi and in imminent Turkish assistance.[14] The convergence of the two movements strengthened the Sarekat Abang in Jambi.

The Central Sarekat Islam on Java was not apprised of the rebellion, although it is quite possible that Raden Gunawan, president of the Western Java branch, had been informed of the secret plans during his visit to Jambi earlier in 1916.[15] The events were masterminded wholly by the Sarekat Abang, however, which used the Sarekat Islam's organization to boost its support and funds. In Jambi the rebellion is still referred to as the "Perang Sarekat Abang."[16]

Although conceived on a larger scale than most millenarian movements—initially indeed mobilizing more men than the Jambi War—the uprising collapsed as soon as the government launched a counteroffensive with modern arms. The problem was a lack of leadership: the rebels had only Raden Gunawan, their figurehead, who had been venerated as a Messiah when he visited Jambi in 1916.

---

[11] Sartono Kartodirdjo, *Protest Movements in Rural Java: A Study of Agrarian Unrest in the Nineteenth and Early Twentieth Century* (Singapore: Oxford University Press, 1973).

[12] *Ilmu* is a method of acquiring supernatural knowledge.

[13] Although the new Sarekat Abang had an unshakable superiority complex, there were parts of Jambi—Sarolangun, for instance—where it was identical to the Sarekat Islam. In most of the territory, however, Sarekat Islam remained true to its middle-class, law-abiding roots, earning it the derisory epithet "Sarekat Kompeni." ["Kompeni" (Company) was a term left over from the days of the Dutch East India Company, and hence referred to the Dutch—transl.]

[14] Administrative officials in Muara Tembesi were required to drink water in which the Imam Mahdi's feet had been washed. The officials who were killed had to be buried in the Christian graveyard since they were regarded as *kafir* (infidels). Muttalib, "Jambi 1900–1916," pp. 265–66.

[15] Muttalib, "Jambi 1900–1916," pp. 207–12, 227–57; Van Wijk, "Opstand in Djambi," pp. 57–60, 64–72. See the reports of G. A. J. Hazeu, J. H. Liefrinck, and Snouck Hurgronje: Hazeu to governor-general, July 21, 1917, no. 320, National Archives (NA), The Hague, Col., *verbaal* (file, hereafter "vb.") January 17, 1918, no. 1; J. H. Liefrinck, *Onderzoek naar de heffing van de belastingenen de vordering van heerendiensten in eenige deelen der Buitenbezittingen* (Batavia: Landsdrukkerij, 1917); report by Snouck Hurgronje in *Ambtelijke adviezen van C. Snouck Hurgronje 1889–1936*, ed. E. Gobée and C. Adriaanse, 3 vols. (The Hague: Nijhoff, 1957–65), 3: 2081–105.

[16] R. Zainuddin, M. Yuhadi, and Bachtiar As, *Sejarah Kebangkitan Nasional Daerah Jambi 1900–1942* (Jakarta: Proyek Penelitian dan Pencatatan Kebudayaan Daerah, Pusat Penelitian Sejarah dan Budaya, Departemen Pendidikan dan Kebudayaan, 1981).

Many rebel commanders legitimized their authority by putting themselves forward as Gunawan, something that Muttalib takes as proof of a power struggle among them.[17] The people lived in the confident expectation that their savior would descend in an airplane as a deus ex machina. One rebel leader in the Rawas explained under interrogation that while attacking the enemy he had been scanning the skies for signs of Gunawan. When no plane appeared, he had fled to the forest in disappointment.[18] In Muara Tebo, Raden Gunawan was described as the son of "the Raja Stambul," the Turkish sultan.

The former sultan's administration figured only indirectly in the uprising. The millenarian protest included nativist elements, in the form of a nostalgic desire to reinstate the old sultanate. One man attending an assembly of two thousand people in Muara Tembesi spoke out, "Let it be known that we delivered our land from the hands of the Company, and that we shall now restore the rule of our own former princes."[19] These princes were named quite explicitly: Pangeran Ratu Ningrat, Raden Mat Tahir gelar Sri Maharaja Batu, and Raden Gunawan. True, the first two were already deceased, but they had risen again and would be returning home from Turkey, having received medals from the sultan in Istanbul. Gunawan was deputizing for them.

The rebel leader Basar, a former police officer, identified himself at the beginning of the rebellion as the resurrected Sultan Taha, after which he handed over the administration to the fugitive prisoner Duhawid, whom he called—displaying a mythical construction of history—his "son, Raden Gunawan or Raden Mat Tahir," and on whom he conferred the title of Sri Maharaja Batu, the name of the first sultan of Jambi. The new appointee in turn appointed a *dukun* as Raden Gunawan or *pangeran ratu*. A scar on Duhawid's throat was displayed in public by way of identification, the real Mat Tahir having been killed by a knife thrust to the throat. Later on, rebels drank soup made with one of Mat Tahir's jackets as a magic potion. Other rebel leaders too adopted the names of deceased or banished *anak raja*, such as Pangeran Prabu.[20] Some did so from habitual identification with the sultan's administration, as in the case of one key rebel in Muara Tembesi whose father had been sentenced to five years' forced labor for his part in the Jambi War.

The old sultanate was chiefly invoked, however, to legitimize the uprising. There is no evidence whatsoever that the rebels ever had any specific member of the *suku* Kraton in mind as a potential ruler. On the contrary, the fact that they placed themselves in the genealogical tradition of this *suku* rather suggests that they wanted power for themselves. Only five *raden* from Jambi, members of the local aristocracy, were involved in the rebellion. Nothing in the sources suggests that the *suku* Kraton played an active role.[21] The tradition of the sultanate lived on in Jambi, but only in the form of a myth.

It is clear from the above account that the integration of Jambi into the colonial state of the Dutch East Indies provoked a fierce, initially underground response on the part of the population. In the name of the "elevation" of the population, the

---

[17] Muttalib, "Jambi 1900–1916," pp. 262, 266–67, 272, 274, 289.

[18] Van Wijk, "Opstand in Djambi," p. 91.

[19] Note 1 from Kiagus Mohamad Amin of December 10, 1916, NA, Col., *mailrapport* (postal report: hereafter "mr.") 1917/543, vb. January 17, 1918, no. 1.

[20] Van Wijk, "Opstand in Djambi," p. 58; Muttalib, "Jambi 1900–1916," pp. 263, 267, 270–71.

[21] Van Wijk, "Opstand in Djambi," p. 75; Muttalib, "Jambi 1900–1916," p. 271.

burden of taxation and forced labor had been increased, a new non-Jambian middle class had been inserted into society, along with "kafir" education and modern vaccination programs that offended local views of sickness and health. In the protest against this enforced acculturation, however, the sultanate played only a token role. It was Islam—or a mystical, heretical branch of it—through which the protests were expressed, with clerics leading the way. This reflected the syncretic expansion of Islam in these regions. The revolutionary ideology that legitimized the rebellion was a weird and wonderful concoction of symbols derived from the sultan's tradition and from traditional and modern Islam. Its main ingredients were a belief in invulnerability, support from Turkey, flying Gunawans and rulers rising from the dead. This heady mix of mythical elements could be exploited by rebel leaders, who were themselves probably true believers, to woo a gullible population.

Once again, it was Snouck Hurgronje who pronounced judgment on the administration of Jambi in 1917, which he had formerly helped to bring about. He had left the region in 1906 to accept a professorship in Leiden, while remaining in office as advisor to the Minister of Colonies. This new report was based on written accounts of the uprising received from the East Indies. His verdict was damning. He started by commenting on the Jambians' poor level of development and consequent superstitious nature, factors he attributed to geographical isolation, and observed that the burden of taxes and forced labor imposed by the colonial government was at least as heavy as under the former local dignitaries: "In both respects, one encounters an excess that is a primary failing of our colonial administration."[22] Worse still, far from creating any organs through which the population could express their views, the administration had actually frustrated those that had arisen from the people themselves, such as the Sarekat Islam. The resulting discontent had been allowed to ferment, since the initial efforts to crush the resistance had been "so extraordinarily feeble." Prompter and more vigorous action could certainly have nipped it in the bud, as in 1904 following the intrigues of Yusuf/Hirsch. The events strengthened Snouck in his conviction that education was the main weapon in the fight against superstition, a cornerstone of his vision of colonial policy. He also inveighed against what he saw as the chronically inefficient manning of Jambi's administrative posts. "This lax and inconsistent administration in Jambi over the past several years, with incompetent management and largely inexperienced staff, is beyond all doubt the primary cause underlying the unrest."[23]

His report ended by criticizing the constant changes in police regulations. "Our administration in the East Indies is more than paternalistic, it is exceedingly meddlesome." Indeed, it would not have surprised him to learn "that the indigenous population had been instructed to relieve nature at certain set times and places, on penalty of a number of days' forced labor."[24] As a rule the local people did what the Dutch authorities prescribed without complaining, but there were certain "chronic exceptions" such as in Jambi.

---

[22] Gobée and Adriaanse, *Ambtelijke adviezen*, 3: 2087.

[23] Ibid., 3: 2100.

[24] Ibid., 3: 2101.

Anchorage place for Chinese paddle-steamer and
rattan spread out to dry outside Jambi
KITLV photograph collection 18,821

Road in Jambi around 1920
KITLV photograph collection 26,340

Besides his emphasis on education and competent administration, Snouck Hurgronje therefore urged above all the need for officials "who understand how important it is to encourage the population to speak out, even if disharmonious voices predominate at the outset, scarcely gratifying the complacency of those who believe themselves to be doing a splendid job. For this reason, the Sarekat Islam in Java, for all its grave shortcomings, promises greatly to improve relations between rulers and ruled."[25] The Sarekat Islam could not be seen as the cause of the unrest, and the *ilmu abang*, the importance of which he downplayed, was no different from magical practices believed throughout the archipelago to confer certain qualities, for good or for ill.[26] Whether or not this Ilmu Abang had used the organizational techniques of the Sarekat Islam was something he thought of little relevance to understanding the Jambian movement.

In short, Snouck's analysis differed in certain respects from the findings of recent investigations of the events leading up to the uprising in Jambi. He saw the Sarekat Abang as trivial and identified the Dutch administrative situation as wholly responsible for what had happened. He left Jambi's economic situation in 1916 out of consideration. His positive attitude to the Sarekat Islam is particularly noteworthy. Snouck Hurgronje, the man who had placed Jambi under Dutch administration and had curbed the influence of Islam, now advocated encouraging an Islamic nationalist movement. For the rest, his recommendations reflected his views about Western-style education and the need for development, not just for the local elite but also for the population at large. And his report embodied his pragmatic administrative outlook, his awareness that seeking to rule a people and promote their self-advancement by applying pressure will not work.

He therefore recommended more education for headmen and the general population, creating bodies through which the population could channel their grievances, fair practices in respect of forced labor and taxes, improved selection procedures for administrative officials in Jambi, and fewer regulations: these were the measures he urged should be introduced in Jambi and elsewhere "with the greatest of speed." His report was forwarded by the "ethical-minded" governor-general Johan Paul, Count van Limburg Stirum (1916–21) to all heads of district administrative authorities. How much they appreciated it is not known.

Nor do the sources reveal whether all these proposals were rapidly acted on. Several Residents complained in the 1920s about the quality and lethargy of administrative officials.[27] Little schooling was available until the late 1920s, and what there was attracted only limited interest from the Jambians themselves. Forced labor was indeed imposed far more cautiously than before, but it resulted in the total neglect of the road system. That Jambi took no part in the second serious revolt on Sumatra, the Communist uprising in the Minangkabau in January 1927, was attributable not to better administration but to the influence of new ideas after 1916, to strict government controls, and a marked increase in prosperity. Rubber production boosted Jambi's economy in the 1920s, and Van Rijn's one-time vision of the region's "golden future" seemed to be coming true.

---

[25] Ibid., 3: 2103.

[26] Ibid., 3: 2105.

[27] *Memorie van Overgave* (Memorandum on Leaving Office), Resident G. J. van Dongen 1927, NA, MvO 221.

RUBBER

It was not oil but rubber that would keep Jambi afloat. As noted several times, Jambi's economy had never been very significant. Throughout the nineteenth century, its exports consisted of forest products, most notably rattan, gutta-percha, and India rubber. In 1900 forest products accounted for 94 percent of exports, at a total value of 653,000 guilders.[28] Jambian trade was also of negligible importance (less than 1 percent) in relation to total trade in the other Outer Islands.[29] Only Bengkulu and the Lampongs had comparably low export figures.[30] Imports too were low: in 1900 they consisted of textiles (38 percent), rice (16 percent), and hardware (6 percent), valued in total at 516,000 guilders.[31] Jambi was still one of the most sparsely populated regions of the archipelago, and its capital of the same name, the only town of any size, had a population of only 8,800 in 1905, including 38 Europeans (as compared to 61,000 in Palembang, for instance). By 1917 Jambi's population had grown to 37,000, including 88 Europeans.[32]

The Hevea plants from which rubber was extracted grew in the wild in Jambian soil, so it was in itself unremarkable that they flourished when cultivated there. The people of Melaka had started growing rubber in the 1890s using plants smuggled in from Brazil, and Chinese merchants imported seedlings from these plants to Sumatra and Borneo. Jambi was in the vanguard of this new business; its first rubber plantation was mentioned in reports as early as 1904. Resident Helfrich provided some encouragement by distributing new trees from the district gardens maintained in Jambi and Muara Tembesi free of charge. But the most significant impulse for growth came from the high rubber prices in 1910–12. Hevea was planted on a massive scale, and gardens could be found everywhere except in the few highland regions. They were laid out in strips at most four kilometers in width, winding along the banks of the major rivers, because transport was assured there. By 1918, rubber cultivation was commonplace, and small family holdings predominated.[33]

Rubber cultivation was ideally suited to Jambi's ecological and economic conditions. It required a great deal of land but little capital, and there was no need for labor-intensive care. In the eyes of Western entrepreneurs, the local rubber plantations exuded an air of neglect. New little trees were planted in young woodland areas or among the rice, where they were abandoned to their fate for six

---

[28] *Statistiek van den handel, de scheepvaart en de in- en uitvoerrechten in Nederlandsch-Indië over het jaar 1900* (Batavia: Landsdrukkerij, 1901), pp. 206–10.

[29] "Trade between Palembang and Jambi in relation to all the Outer Islands, imports and exports," Netherlands Indies Trade Statistics 1870–1938, computer data in History of European Expansion Data Bank, Nederlands Historisch Data Archief. I am grateful to L. J. Touwen for printing out these data for me.

[30] L. J. Touwen, "Voordeel van veelzijdigheid: De economische ontwikkeling van Palembang en Djambi tussen 1900 en 1938," *Economisch en Sociaal-Historisch Jaarboek* 54 (1991): 134–82, esp. 153.

[31] *Statistiek van den handel*, pp. 206–10.

[32] Touwen, "Voordeel van veelzijdigheid," p. 157.

[33] A. H. P. Clemens, "De inheemse rubbercultuur in Jambi en Palembang tijdens het Interbellum," in *Het belang van de Buitengewesten; Economische expansie en koloniale staatsvorming in de Buitengewesten van Nederlands-Indië 1870–1942*, ed. A. H. P. Clemens and J. T. Lindblad (Amsterdam: NEHA, 1989), pp. 214–19; *Memorie van Overgave*, P. J. van der Meulen 1936, p. 78, NA, Col., MvO 225.

years until the time came to start tapping the milk. The tapping itself was a more intensive business than on Western plantations: the owners did not allow their trees much rest. There was no coolie class in Jambi, and the professional tapping on the large local rubber plantations was done by Javanese workers. In smaller businesses the owner and his family would do everything themselves.

The heyday of Jambi's rubber cultivation was in the 1920s, after which it plunged during the Great Depression and revived in the late 1930s. International rubber prices started to rally in 1922 after a brief collapse, peaking in 1925. Jambi's income from rubber exports attained the dizzying heights of 46 million guilders that year, a wholly unrepeatable statistic.[34] Together with Borneo's two regions, Jambi took first place in the East Indies' exports in 1925, followed by Palembang and Sumatra's east coast. Rubber accounted for 90 percent of Jambi's exports at this time. The rubber trade was in the hands of Chinese and Jambian merchants, who generally transported their wares in the form of rafts towed by proas. The advent of the KPM in 1926 temporarily dislodged the Chinese from their ascendancy in this sector.[35]

But besides boosting production, the price rises also had the effect of corrupting the product; people took to using sand, stones, bits of iron, old soles, and on occasion even dead monkeys to increase weight, and since it was actually transported *in* the river, 46 percent of the rubber sold was water. In 1926 one consignment was found to contain only 48 percent rubber.[36] Small wonder, then, that Jambian rubber had a poor reputation in Singapore. In 1928 a supervisory system came into effect, imposing stricter requirements on the production process and the product itself, limiting raft transport, and promoting the production of dry rubber. This, together with the fall in prices and the Depression, sealed the fate of the Jambian "waterborne" rubber merchants.[37] In 1934 a public information officer started a campaign to encourage people to produce a cleaner, drier, and thinner form of rubber to improve overall production. His progress was slow but sure. "Any over-hasty measures, any pressure to quickly abandon the tried and tested methods of the past, would only lead to passive resistance."[38]

In spite of the poor quality of the product, the rubber boom of the 1920s brought the Jambians an unprecedented degree of wealth, which they called a *hujan emas*, or golden rain.[39] The earnings were converted into houses and journeys to Mecca and created a new elite. It was this new prosperity—in addition to the strict controls on nationalist activity that had been imposed since 1916—that made the region less accessible to Communist propaganda. Because of the predominance of family businesses and the absence of professional coolies, the new wealth did not lead to a dramatic erosion of traditional social structures.

The fall in rubber prices that started in 1928 benefited small businesses. By the end of the 1920s, almost everyone in the rubber region had one or more rubber

---

[34] Touwen, "Voordeel van veelzijdigheid," p. 175.

[35] Clemens, "De inheemse rubbercultuur in Djambi," p. 218.

[36] J. Tideman and P. L. F. Sigar, *Djambi* (Amsterdam: Koloniaal Instituut, 1938), p. 192; Clemens, "De inheemse rubbercultuur in Djambi," p. 218.

[37] Clemens, "De inheemse rubbercultuur in Djambi," pp. 218–19.

[38] *Memorie van Overgave*, P. J. van der Meulen 1936, p. 78, NA, Col., MvO 225.

[39] Zainuddin, Yuhadi, and As, *Sejarah Kebangkitan Nasional*, p. 87; Clemens, "De inheemse rubbercultuur in Djambi," pp. 221–22.

plantations. But the Jambian monoculture also entailed risks. This became all too clear in the Depression, when rubber prices collapsed from 1.08 guilder per kilo of "standard sheet" in 1929 to 12.5 cents a kilo in 1932.[40] The Jambian rubber farmer accustomed to receiving 40 guilders for every 100 kilos of rubber was now getting a mere 2 guilders for them.[41] While the population in nearby Palembang could switch to other products like coffee, which had fallen less dramatically in price, Jambian rubber producers had no alternative crop. All they could do was export rattan, step up rubber production, and accept the drop in profits. Between 1928 and 1936, rubber exports grew from just under 20,000 tons to about 26,000 tons in 1936. In 1932, almost one-third of the rubber produced by small holdings in the Dutch East Indies came from Jambi. The value of these exports plummeted, however, from 16.5 million to about 2 million guilders.[42]

Government measures were powerless to curb this production growth. As early as 1925, the government had claimed its share of the growing prosperity by imposing export duties of 5 percent of the value. In 1934 international rubber quotas were adopted, by which all rubber-producing countries, including the Dutch East Indies, agreed to be bound. The government of the Dutch East Indies tried to keep to its quota and limit production by imposing a "special export duty" on rubber from small holdings. The rationale was that the tax would bring prices down further and hence reduce exports. This special export duty, introduced in 1934, had to be constantly increased over the next few years: from 16 cents per kilo (1934) to 59 cents (1936). The determination of local people to continue at the higher production levels had been underestimated.[43] It was not until 1936 that the rubber production in the East Indies was driven back within the permissible limits. Since the special export duty had not been introduced primarily for fiscal purposes, the proceeds were deposited in a fund for the rubber-producing regions, providing Jambi's public sector with a substantial injection of income.

In 1937 there was a shift to individual quotas, each producer compelled to keep to a specific quota by a system of coupons. This system had been made possible by the recent introduction of a registration system for rubber plantations. Comparison with other rubber-producing regions (Palembang, Western Borneo, and Southeast Borneo) again brings out the intensity with which this crop was cultivated in Jambi. Although in absolute terms the number of plantation owners was smallest here, at a little over 43,000, it was very high relative to the total number of farmers, which stood at 77,000.[44] Furthermore, the number of trees tapped here per plantation owner was twice as high as elsewhere.[45]

With prices rising again, the introduction of individual quotas meant that rubber producers once again received the entire proceeds of their rubber themselves,

---

[40] Clemens, "De inheemse rubbercultuur in Djambi," 222.

[41] Zainuddin, Yuhadi, and As, *Sejarah Kebangkitan Nasional*, p. 118

[42] Clemens, "De inheemse rubbercultuur in Djambi," p. 235; Touwen "Voordeel van veelzijdigheid," pp. 160–62, 175.

[43] Clemens, "De inheemse rubbercultuur in Djambi," pp. 227–28.

[44] Tideman and Sigar, *Djambi*, p. 53.

[45] See the table in Clemens, "De inheemse rubbercultuur in Djambi," p. 229. Clemens rightly points out that the figures supplied by the rubber producers were far too low. In 1942, for instance, it appeared that Jambi had three times as much land under rubber cultivation as registered.

which in some cases multiplied their income by a factor of five or six. Another golden age dawned, this one being referred to as the *zaman koepon* (the coupon period), since besides the rubber itself there was also a brisk trade in coupons, which served as licenses to harvest the crop.[46] In 1937 Jambi experienced its second rubber boom: exports rose from over 2 million to more than 21 million guilders, only to fall again in 1938 to just below 9 million, the level of 1930.[47] Under the influence of the growing wartime demand for rubber in 1940 and 1941, production figures grew to 37,000 tons in 1940 and 45,000 tons in 1941, but by then Jambi had been ousted from first place by Palembang.[48]

To sum up, exports of rubber produced by small holdings in Jambi from the early 1920s onward greatly boosted the income of individual rubber producers (Jambians), merchants (Chinese), and the region as a whole, a growth that was only temporarily interrupted by the Great Depression.[49] Unlike the situation on Sumatra's east coast, rubber production was almost entirely in the hands of the local people here. There were no Western rubber companies.[50] Oil, on the other hand, was a Western monopoly.

OIL

The pipelines sending the first Jambian oil to the refinery in Palembang did not become operational until the 1920s—in 1923, to be precise. This was more than a quarter of a century after the first failed attempt at exploration. In 1921, after tortuous negotiations between the Dutch government and the Batavian Petroleum Company (BPM, launched in 1907 as a joint daughter of the Koninklijke and Shell), the Dutch East Indies Petroleum Company (NIAM) was established, with each of the two companies taking 50 percent ownership. In accordance with the plans of Van Heutsz and Idenburg, the government had commissioned its own exploration in the first decade of the century. The small quantities of oil made the Dutch government decide, following Batavia's advice, to leave its extraction to private

---

[46] Clemens, "De inheemse rubbercultuur," p. 230; Zainuddin, Yuhadi, and As, *Sejarah Kebangkitan Nasional*, p. 120.

[47] Touwen, "Voordeel van veelzijdigheid," p. 175.

[48] I do not have any figures for the value of the goods involved. See Economisch verslag Jambi over maart 1949:18, NA, Algemene Secretarie 3137; for Jambi's rubber exports in the period 1918–40, see Clemens, "De inheemse rubbercultuur in Djambi," p. 235.

[49] The following numbers of hajis reflect trends in prosperity:

Year	N	Year	N
1926	1,940	1931	13
1927	2,522	1932	6
1928	228	1933	18
1929	no figures found	1934	8
1930	76	1935	21

See *Memorie van Overgave*, H. E. K. Ezerman 1928, p. 4; *Memorie van Overgave*, W. Steinbuch 1933, p. 56; and *Memorie van Overgave*, P. J. van der Meulen 1936, p. 23, NA, Col., MvO 222, 224 and 225.

[50] Between 1927 and 1931 there were two European and three Chinese companies processing rubber in Jambi (*Memorie van Overgave*, G. J. van Dongen 1927, p. 18; H. E. K. Ezerman 1928, p. 50; NA, Col., MvO 221 and 222).

companies. But in 1915 the lower house of Parliament, which had been responsible for approving concessions for oil extraction since 1911, rejected the bill that was to make this possible, instructing the government to set up a public company instead. In 1917 a second bill also foundered, this one proposing a public-private partnership, because the BPM, one of the proposed partners, had not been consulted when it was drafted. The long, drawn-out debate on the proper structure for extracting Jambian oil was concluded in 1921, when the lower house finally agreed to the economic novelty of a public-private partnership by a small majority of forty-five votes to thirty-seven. Even this was a close call, as the U.S. government had protested through diplomatic channels at the exclusion of American oil companies. For the United States, which was afraid that its own oil would run dry by the late 1930s, by which time the colonial rulers would have closed their borders, Jambi was "the most valuable of the remaining prospective petroleum territories in the Netherlands East Indies."[51] If the lower house had been informed of this American "oil scare" and its diplomatic consequences before, the bill might well have foundered.[52] Just as in the Gibson case, however, the United States missed out because of the determination of Dutch diplomacy and the preservation of confidentiality.

Oil drilling began in Jambi in 1922, first east and then west of the capital. The best oil fields proved to be Bajubang and Tempino, joined in the 1930s by Kenali Assam, to the southwest of the capital. In the Great Depression, Jambi was the only place where the BPM expanded its oil wells.[53] The oil did not prove much of a boon for the population or for Jambi itself. It did bring in half a million guilders between 1923 and 1930 in the form of wages for the local population, and it provided work for 2,400 people in 1929. But the companies were Western enclaves, and most of their workers were non-Jambians, primarily Javanese. Jambians preferred to remain masters of their own rubber production than to hire themselves out to oil.[54] What is more, the oil was not refined in Jambi itself; it was piped some 270 kilometers from the three oil wells to Plaju in Palembang. Around 1930, Resident Verschoor van Nisse suggested basing a Jambian oil company in Muara Sabah, but the NIAM and BPM rejected the idea.[55]

So Jambian oil was not counted in the regional export figures, but was included in those of Palembang. Until 1937 it accounted for only a tiny proportion of the total oil production in the East Indies: 0.4 percent in 1925, 3.4 percent in 1930, and 6.1 percent in 1935. It was not until 1938 that Jambi began to make a more significant contribution to the economy of the East Indies, at 14 percent of the total oil production.[56] Jambi was never a very profitable part of the colony. From 1905 to 1919 its exports ranged from 0.5 to 1.5 percent of the total exports from the Outer Islands, whereas between 1919 and 1938 it averaged 2 to 3 percent, peaking at 5 percent in

---

[51] Quoted in M. Zevenbergen, "De Djambi-affaire: Een Nederlands-Amerikaans conflict over de Nederlands-Indische aardolie 1920–1921" (MA thesis, Catholic University of Nijmegen, 1983), p. 75.

[52] Zevenbergen, "De Djambi-affaire."

[53] *Memorie van Overgave*, J. R. F. Verschoor van Nisse 1931:169, NA, Col., MvO 223.

[54] Touwen, "Voordeel van veelzijdigheid," p. 158.

[55] *Memorie van Overgave*, J. R. F. Verschoor van Nisse 1931, p. 169, NA, Col., MvO 223.

[56] Touwen, "Voordeel van veelzijdigheid," pp. 154–55, 177.

1925. Jambi's imports accounted for an even smaller share (though only marginally) of total imports to the Outer Islands.[57]

What impact did rubber and oil have on Jambi's socioeconomic development? Oil yielded nothing beyond the enclave already mentioned and NIAM's limited support for the building of some roads and an airport. In 1936, Resident V. E. Korn complained that not one cent of the two million guilders' profits made by oil companies in 1935 had gone to the region.[58] Where rubber is concerned, Touwen has pointed out that while rubber supplied considerable momentum for development, the one-sidedness of Jambi's economy was a handicap in times of economic malaise.[59] As late as 1931, Resident J. R. F. Verschoor van Nisse complained, "It is appalling that this region is an absolute terra incognita not only to the general public but to central government agencies as well."[60] Jambi did not acquire its first paved road until 1930, covering the ninety-two kilometers between Jambi and Muara Tembesi (about three-quarters of which was financed by NIAM). This contrasts sharply with Palembang, for instance, which had paved roads connecting it to all the towns in the interior by then. The colonial government's five-year plan for paved roads in South Sumatra did not even mention Jambi. And it was not until the 1930s that a railroad was built linking Jambi and Sumatra's west coast.[61]

However, the region profited greatly from the revenue generated by the rubber duties, which were deposited in a special fund in the years 1934–36. The effect was to add millions of guilders to Jambi's budget, which did not as a rule exceed 500,000 guilders.[62] It was thanks to this cash boost that Jambi's road system finally underwent major expansion, one of the administration's priorities in the 1930s. By 1936 there was a road linking Palembang to Padang by way of Jambi, and the district capitals too were almost all connected. In 1933 an airport was opened near Jambi, partly with NIAM's support.[63] So Jambi's isolation was largely a thing of the past by the late 1930s. The rubber duties fund was also used to buy off forced labor and lower taxes, to pay for exemptions from contributions to education, to build roads and buildings, and to pay for a few smaller services such as information campaigns for local rubber farmers.[64]

Even so, Jambi was still an underdeveloped region, and with 5.5 inhabitants—that is, just one family per square kilometer, it was one of the most sparsely populated areas of Sumatra. Non-Jambians controlled the economy. Chinese businessmen monopolized rubber exports; European countries had withdrawn, and

---

[57] These figures on the trade between Palembang and Jambi in relation to all the Outer Islands, imports and exports, derive from Netherlands Indies Trade Statistics, Nederlands Historisch Data Archief.

[58] *Memorie van Overgave*, V. E. Korn 1936, p. 65, NA, Col., MvO 226.

[59] Touwen "Voordeel van veelzijdigheid."

[60] *Memorie van Overgave*, J. R. F. Verschoor van Nisse 1931, p. 1, NA, Col., MvO 223.

[61] Touwen, "Voordeel van veelzijdigheid," pp. 156–57.

[62] Namely, 1,434,700 guilders in 1934 and 3,699,350 guilders in 1935, out of a total budget of 2,028,995 and 4,171,155 guilders (*Memorie van Overgave*, P. J. van der Meulen 1936, p. 136, NA, Col., MvO 225, appendix).

[63] *Memorie van Overgave*, P. J. van der Meulen 1936, pp. 103, 110–11, and *Memorie van Overgave*, V. E. Korn 1936, p. 65, both in NA, Col., MvO 225 and 226; Clemens, "De inheemse rubbercultuur in Djambi," p. 228.

[64] *Memorie van Overgave*, P. J. van der Meulen 1936, pp. 110–11, and appendix, NA, Col., MvO 225.

European and local administrators of the sub-district of Jambi outside the
controller's office on the Queen's Birthday (then August 31), 1936
Photograph from collection Cees Fasseur

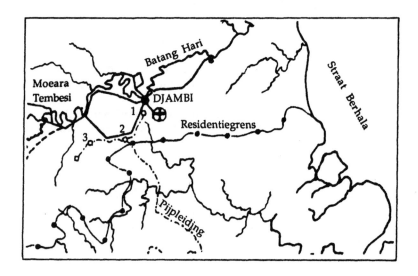

Rough map of the surroundings of Jambi with oilfields
J. J. Nortier, "Orde en rustverstoring in het Djambisch, februari 1942,"
Militaire Spectator 152 (1983)

the coolies were Javanese. There was little love lost between these different groups. The Javanese, who accounted for 6 percent of the population in 1930, were tolerated, but they did not integrate into Jambian society. The Minangkabau (3 percent) were regarded as foreigners, while people from Palembang (2 percent) were treated as kinsmen. So when the subject of the region's administrative future was raised, the Jambians always expressed a clear preference for incorporation into South Sumatra rather than into West or Central Sumatra, which were Minangkabau.[65] The Chinese inhabitants were strongly oriented toward Singapore, and their only ties with the Jambians were economic.[66]

The main official positions too were held by non-Jambians. In 1936 only two of the seven *demang* and three of the ten assistant *demang* were of local origin.[67] There was little interest in Western-style education, even in the 1930s: only twenty-three of the 160 pupils (14 percent) of the "Dutch Native School" in Jambi were Jambian. The headmen had shown no interest in the establishment of a boarding school for their sons.[68] The Dutch objective of creating a line of well-trained and loyal administrators to replace the adat headmen would not be realized. Most adat headmen could neither read nor write.[69] Illiteracy was still almost universal in 1930, with literacy levels standing at a mere 7.3 percent. Yet when cuts were made during the Depression it was in public education, which the people by then had ceased to see as a veiled form of forced labor: seventeen schools were closed down in 1932.[70] There was no local newspaper.[71]

To the Jambian Residents, the political situation between the wars was therefore "wholly favorable," which basically meant that nothing happened. Jambi was "an island amid an ocean of turbulent political currents."[72] The Residents attributed this serenity not to pro-Western attitudes but to the aftermath of the traumatic events of 1916, to the Jambians' "natural aversion to foreign interference," and to the fact that adat permitted them to keep outsiders out of

---

[65] *Memorie van Overgave,* J. R. F. Verschoor van Nisse 1931, p. 36, NA, Col., MvO 223. The region's population included Minangkabau and a number of groups that can be classed collectively as "Jambians," including Pengulu and Kerinci (22 percent). In 1930 Jambi also had a 6 percent minority of Banjarese, who cultivated coconuts in Lower Jambi. "Jambians" accounted for only 58 percent of the total population (see Tideman and Sigar, *Djambi,* p. 46).

[66] *Memorie van Overgave,* G. J van Dongen 1927, p. 18 and *Memorie van Overgave,* V.E. Korn 1936, p. 32, NA, Col., MvO 221 and 226. Just how much Chinese profited from Jambi's economic development is clear from the 1920 and 1930 censuses. While Jambi had almost 2,800 Chinese in 1920, ten years later their numbers had risen to almost 8,800, while the total population had grown from 161,000 to 235,000. By 1934 their numbers had increased further. Europeans were counted to the nearest hundred in these censuses: just under 200 and just under 500, respectively (*Memorie van Overgave,* P. J. van der Meulen 1936, p. 11, NA, Col., MvO 225; Tideman and Sigar, *Djambi,* pp. 43–47).

[67] *Memorie van Overgave,* V. E. Korn 1936, p. 5, NA, MvO 226.

[68] *Memorie van Overgave,* J. R. F. Verschoor van Nisse 1931, p. 101, and *Memorie van Overgave,* W. Steinbuch 1933, p. 80, NA, Col., MvO 223 and 224.

[69] *Memorie van Overgave,* H. E. K. Ezerman 1928, p. 4, and *Memorie van Overgave,* V. E. Korn 1936, p. 18, NA, Col., MvO 222 and 226.

[70] Tideman and Sigar, *Djambi,* p. 121.

[71] *Volkstelling van Nederlandsch-Indië/Census of the Netherlands East Indies 1930,* vol. 4, *Inheemsche bevolking van Sumatra* (Batavia: Landsdrukkerij, 1933), p. 73; Zainuddin, Yuhadi, and As, *Sejarah Kebangkitan Nasional,* p. 93.

[72] *Memorie van Overgave,* W. Steinbuch 1933, p. 67, NA, Col., MvO 224.

their districts *(marga)*.[73] Nationalist organizations did not arise until shortly before the Second World War. Even the socioeconomically oriented Muhammadiyah had only two schools in the entire region in the 1930s. It was not until 1939 that the Sarekat Islam, which had by then become the Partai Sarekat Islam Indonesia, opened up a branch in Jambi, followed in 1940 by other parties: the Partai Muslimin Jambi and the Partai Arab Indonesia. The Parindra too opened up a branch, as a result of which the population learned, on the eve of the war, of the political federation Gapi and its efforts to gain a parliament.[74] The region itself had no form of participation in decision making: there were no local authorities or committees of elders. Though the sultan's descendants were still treated with a certain reverence, they lived in poverty in *dusun* outside the capital. In matters of morality, the chief *penghulu*, an appointee of the Dutch authorities, had a conservative religious influence through his administration of Islamic justice.[75]

If Jambi entered the war as a depressed region, the Japanese invasion at the end of February 1942 made things far worse. The oil wells at Kenali Assam, Tempino, and Bajubang were destroyed by the KNIL, along with three of the four rubber factories. The guerrilla warfare that had been planned to prevent them reopening never materialized, because the KNIL withdrew from Lower Jambi in disarray before the Japanese army's arrival.[76] The old hope that "rich resources" would transform the land into a "flourishing region, a new pearl on Insulinde's crown," had become a hollow boast from the past.[77]

REVOLUTION IN JAMBI

By an irony of history, the revolution that elsewhere ousted sultans from their thrones briefly invested the pro-sultanate party in Jambi with political power. More ironically still, it was the pro-sultanate party that turned to Lieutenant Governor-General H. J. van Mook in 1946 for help against the Republic of Indonesia,

---

[73] *Memorie van Overgave*, P. J. van der Meulen 1935, p. 35, NA, Col., MvO 225.

[74] Zainuddin, Yuhadi, and As, *Sejarah Kebangkitan Nasional*, pp. 103–15.

[75] *Memorie van Overgave*, V. E. Korn 1936, p. 4, NA, MvO 226.

[76] On this controversial military operation, see J. J. Nortier, "Orde en rustverstoring in het Djambische, februari 1942," *Militaire Spectator* 152 (1983): 565–77, esp. 568, and the "Verslag over vernielingen Djambi," by J. F. A. van de Wall, captain of the former KNIL 1980, and Wall to A. G. Vromans, April 15, 1954, Netherlands Institute of War Documentation (NIOD), Amsterdam, Indische coll. 081268 and 048043. For the period 1942–45, see report by Lieutenant-Colonel/Assistant Resident C. Monod de Froideville, October 28, 1945, NA, Algemene Secretarie 3133; Economisch verslag Jambi 1949, NA, Algemene Secretarie 3137. According to Monod's report of 1945, the advent of the Japanese had proceeded without incident. The thirty-odd Europeans were interned, the men being transferred out a few months later while the women and children were not removed for another two years. The local administration continued as before under a Japanese Resident. But since trade gradually ground to a standstill—even in rubber—and salt imports too were halted, living conditions were very harsh. J. R. Glaubitz, who served as controller at Muara Bungo in 1941, gives a different account of the European males, writing that they were interned in Jambi for eighteen months and then transferred to Muntok, where conditions were worse still; in February 1945 they were transferred to Lubuk Linggau, a camp in Palembang (see J. R. Glaubitz 1940–46, NIOD, Indische Collectie 030289).

[77] G. J. Velds, "De onderwerping van Djambi, 1901–1907: Beknopte geschiedenis naar officiëele gegevens," *Indisch Militair Tijdschrift*, Extra-bijlage 24 (1909): 142.

proclaimed on August 17, 1945. In other words, the Dutch authorities that had ended the sultan's authority in 1901 were now being asked—in Jambi as elsewhere in the archipelago—to help restore the sultanate.

This would not have seemed a likely turn of events in 1945. The Minangkabau physician Sagaf Jahja had started the Jambian branch of the Parindra before the war. Because the region had suffered grievously under the Japanese occupation, he decided almost immediately after the declaration of independence of August 17 that Jambi should side with the Republic.[78] There was no need, at this time, to take any account of the Dutch authorities. As on Java, the British troops that liberated the Dutch East Indies occupied only a few large towns as bridgeheads on Sumatra: Medan, Padang, and Palembang. They left Jambi alone altogether. The oil fields were placed under the temporary protection of the Japanese and were transferred to the Republic's administration in November 1945.[79] The leadership was in the hands of "foreigners" like Menadonese, Bataks, and Javanese, and even the workers still included only a minority of Jambians.[80]

Political activity increased in November 1945, and Sumatra's Republican administration appointed Raden Inoue Kertopati, the assistant *wedana* in Jambi, as Resident. Kertopati was by then a man in his sixties; he belonged to the *suku* Kraton, and as Taha's son was its most prominent member. Kertopati had surrendered during the Jambi War back in July 1904. After attending the lower colonial government school in West Java, he joined the civil service in 1911, serving on the opium control board. He spent a time working with the police before his appointment as assistant *demang* in Jambi, a position he held from 1919 to 1942. Although his Dutch superiors had never held a very high opinion of his abilities, he had a reputation for honesty and reliability.[81] He owed his appointment to the considerable support he enjoyed among the people as Taha's son. They believed that he possessed magical powers.[82]

He chiefly defended Jambi's interests within the Republic, pressing for a "Jambi for the Jambians." In the spring of 1946 he protested against the recent incorporation of his Residency into the Minangkabau province of Central Sumatra, and shortly afterward he also complained about the power of the Republican army in Jambi, which controlled the civil administration. This seemed to signal his demise, since during the peaceful "social revolution" in September 1946 he found himself joined by an "acting" Resident, the Javanese R. M. Utoyo, vice-president of Palembang council of representatives. The "foreigners" were in the ascendancy at

---

[78] NEFIS publication July 9, 1947, no. 68, NA, Algemene secretarie 3974; Zainuddin, Yuhadi, and As, *Sejarah Kebangkitan Nasional*, p. 109. The stop on rubber exports and rice imports had compelled the population to concentrate on growing food crops in *ladang* (report from L. I. Graf to the director of the office of the governor-general, July 4, 1949, NA, Algemene Secretarie 3136).

[79] *Officiële bescheiden betreffende de Nederlands-Indonesische betrekkingen 1945–1950*. Ed. S. L. van der Wal, P. J. Drooglever, and M. J. B. Schouten, 20 vols. (The Hague: Nijhoff, 1971–96), 2: 378, 532, 5: 121.

[80] Report from L. I. Graf to the director of the office of the governor-general, July 4, 1949, NA, Algemene Secretarie 3136. According to this same report, when the Japanese army withdrew from Jambi in the summer of 1946, the oilfields came under the control of the Republican army, which also appropriated the oil.

[81] *Officiële bescheiden*, 11: 666.

[82] Assistant Resident to Resident of Riau, October 25, 1946, NA, Algemene Secretarie 3134; J. J. van de Velde, *Brieven uit Sumatra, 1928–1949* (Franeker: Wever, 1982), p. 202.

this time. A number of Jambian officials were removed from their positions during the "social revolution."[83] Before long, Kertopati stepped down as president of the military council and the council of representatives in favor of Utoyo.[84] This had the effect of increasing both Republican influence and anti-Republican feeling among the Jambian population.

Kertopati remained in office as Resident, and from early 1947 onward he became even more strongly identified with the cause of Jambian nationalism. This local movement was directed against the appointment of especially the Padangese, but also the Bataks, Palembangese, and Javanese, to the most important positions. It was almost traditional for the Minangkabau of Sumatra's west coast to view Jambi as their "area of colonization" *(merantau)*. According to a Dutch political analysis they needed Jambi and Indragiri, since without them the regional government of Central Sumatra, enclosed behind the Bukit Barisan, would be confined to the tribal land of the Minangkabau, and hence scarcely capable of counterbalancing North and South Sumatra.[85]

Meanwhile, the tensions in Jambi prompted repeated visits by Republican dignitaries from Java, who tried to defuse the situation. In June 1947, Kertopati's request for the appointment of eleven Jambian officers to replace non-Jambians was finally granted.[86] After this victory, political parties brought charges of corruption against seven non-Jambian officials, including Utoyo. By then the lack of enthusiasm for the Republican cause had become clear in Yogya. Mohammed Hatta visited Jambi shortly before the first Dutch military assault or so-called Police Action at the beginning of July 1947, stating publicly that he had heard in Batavia that Jambi did not wish to be part of the Republic.[87]

It is true that a representative of Kertopati and his pro-sultanate party had asked the government of the Dutch East Indies through the consulate-general in Singapore in the fall of 1946 (repeating the request several times in 1947) to support the restoration of an independent sultanate.[88] The Dutch had initially demurred, partly because cooperation seemed too dangerous for the population itself and partly because they hoped that the Linggajati Agreement (November 1946) would present a diplomatic solution for the problem of regional separatism.[89]

---

[83] Politiek verslag Sumatra, August and September 1946:21, October 1946:14–15, both in NA, Minog, Rapportage Indonesië 1945–1949, 454.

[84] *Officiële bescheiden*, 6: 52, 7: 610.

[85] Ibid., 12: 58–59.

[86] Ibid., 9: 458, 560.

[87] Consul-general in Singapore (Vigeveno) to the lieutenant governor-general, July 8, 1947, NA, Algemene Secretarie 3134.

[88] *Officiële bescheiden*, 12: 59; consul-general in Singapore (Vigeveno) to the lieutenant governor-general October 8, 1946, and May 1, 1947, NA, Algemene Secretarie 3134. The representative, the son of one of Taha's former assistants, who would control all the trade that was conducted between Jambi and Singapore, requested military assistance on four conditions: a separate flag to be flown below the Dutch flag, Kertopati's appointment as sultan, nonintervention in religious affairs as before 1942, and a form of government comparable to that in the Malay states of Melaka. Similar requests for Dutch support were received from Indragiri and the Batak leaders of Siantar and Tapanuli.

[89] Note by director of the office of the governor-general (Remark by P. J. Koets) on a letter from the consul-general in Singapore to the lieutenant governor-general, February 21, 1947; id. on note from the lieutenant governor-general to the director of the office of the governor-general, March 3, 1947; government advisor on political affairs for Sumatra to the lieutenant governor-

It was not until the summer of 1947 that the Dutch made a gesture of support toward the independence movement. In the plans for the Police Action involving Palembang, Medan, and Padang, it was decided after some hesitation to include Jambi, partly because Van Mook and others were interested in its oil fields.[90] The second-phase occupation was scheduled for August 7–10, 1947. Jambians interested in taking part could present themselves in Batavia on August 5.

The Security Council resolution and the Dutch government's instructions to Van Mook to halt the action on August 4 meant that this plan had to be abandoned, however,[91] to the great satisfaction of BPM-NIAM's agent in Batavia, who had unexpectedly opposed the plans. He thought military action unwise because the large distances involved made the oil fields particularly vulnerable. Moreover, if the Republican troops destroyed the installations he was worried that the high petroleum content of the oil would intensify the resulting fire and hence cause immense damage to the oil fields themselves.[92] He was also worried about the activities of Japanese industrial saboteurs who might have remained behind. Still, the agent agreed to supply financial support to compensate disappointed separatists and to bribe saboteurs. A NEFIS (Dutch Military Intelligence) report later confirmed the deployment of well-paid Jambian security units (each one twenty-five strong) protecting all of Jambi's oil installations, which employed a total of fifteen hundred workers at the time.[93]

After August 1947, the pro-sultanate party received only verbal and financial support, despite the continuing pleas for military assistance, including requests from Kerinci. Kertopati was given ten thousand Singapore dollars through indirect channels as a token of support.[94] Now that the Republic had strengthened its grip on the region, however, Jambi had to learn to accept the Padangese presence. Although the Republic was aware of the population's lack of enthusiasm for its cause, Kertopati did not find himself discredited among the Republicans after July 1947; on the contrary, he acquired a military title.

By now, Jambi's economy was doing better. Since Palembang had been placed under mixed Dutch-Republican authority in November 1946, following the

---

general, March 25, 1947, all in NA, Algemene Secretarie 3134. J. J. van de Velde, government advisor on political affairs for Sumatra, consulted the sultan's representative in Singapore on several occasions in March and the following months of 1947.

[90] Lieutenant governor-general to the director of the office of the governor-general, March 3, 1947, NA, Algemene Secretarie 3134; memorandum J. J. van de Velde for discussion in Batavia July 2, 1947, NA, Algemene Secretarie 2319. C. O. van der Plas, as acting director of Internal Administration, had urged the rapid occupation of Jambi in 1945, partly because of the oil fields (*Officiële bescheiden*, 2: 116–17).

[91] *Officiële bescheiden*, 10: 73, 214.

[92] Director of the office of the governor-general to the lieutenant governor-general, August 2, 1947, NA, Algemene Secretarie 3505.

[93] Report by the commissioner of general police in Palembang, August 28, 1947; "Recomba" (government commissioner for administrative affairs) for South Sumatra to the lieutenant governor-general, October 22, 1947, both in NA, Algemene Secretarie 3505. In March 1948, the BPM transferred five thousand dollars to Jambi "for the designation known to you," according to Van de Velde to the commissioner of special services in Singapore, March 10, 1948, NA, Algemene Secretarie 3136.

[94] Government advisor on political affairs for Sumatra to the lieutenant governor-general, February 7, 1949, NA, Algemene Secretarie 3134.

departure of the British, Jambi had taken its place as the Republicans' port.[95] In fact, after the First Police Action it was the only remaining port on Sumatra's east coast. Gone were the days of famine and burlap clothes. Jambi became the exporter of products from the Republican part of Palembang and Sumatra's west coast, including rubber. More rubber was exported this year than in the prewar record year of 1941.[96] The town itself came to resemble "a miniature Singapore," with fine *toko* (grocery stores) and a lively street trade.[97] Still, the new wealth reached only a small proportion of the population; income from the trade with Singapore largely filled the Republic's coffers and the pockets of the administrative and military elite.[98]

In 1948, however, Van Mook and his advisors seriously considered intervening in Jambi. This was partly because Washington had indirectly suggested to the Republic, in the new Cold War climate, that it should curb the Communist activity around the oil fields, and partly because private American companies were making moves to buy up Jambian oil.[99] Talks were held in May 1948 about the BPM-NIAM and other companies returning to their sites, with the BPM assuming operational leadership and the Republic remaining in charge.[100] An immediate takeover was impossible at the time because Jambi was in the throes of a smallpox epidemic.[101]

In Jambi itself, Republican sentiments had not vanished altogether: Sukarno and Hatta got a warm reception when they visited Sumatra in July and November 1948. But on the whole Jambians tended to be conservative in their politics. They gravitated largely toward the Islamic party, Masyumi, although the left-wing Pesindo Partai achieved a respectable second place in August 1948 (that is, before the Communist coup in Madiun). Pesindo, like Sukarno's Partai Nasional Indonesia (PNI) and the small but well-organized PKI, attracted primarily Minangkabau and Javanese voters.[102] The allegiance of the pro-sultanate party was less obvious in 1948. UN observers from the Committee of Good Offices, which mediated between the opposing sides after the First Police Action, did not see any sign of an independence movement when they visited the region.[103] But Kertopati persisted in trying to get the Netherlands' support for his plans. In November 1948 the Dutch Resident of Riau received a Jambian delegation that came to present a letter from

---

[95] Mestika Zed, "Kepialangan, Politik dan Revolusi: Palembang 1900–1950" (PhD diss., Free University, Amsterdam, 1991), pp. 349, 389.

[96] Rubber exports rose to 5,000 tons a month, as compared to 3,760 a month in 1941. See *Economisch verslag van Jambi over maart 1949*, NA, Algemene Secretarie 3137.

[97] *Officiële bescheiden*, 11: 664.

[98] *Politiek verslag Sumatra voor juni 1948*:14, NA, Minog, Rapportage Indonesië 1945–1949, 456.

[99] *Officiële bescheiden*, 13: 63–64, 553, 15: 205.

[100] See the source documents, esp. Basisovereenkomst met de Republiek over terugkeer NIAM in NA, Algemene Secretarie 3509.

[101] *Officiële bescheiden*, 13: 733.

[102] *Politiek verslag Sumatra over juni 1948*, p. 14, over augustus 1948, p. 13, and oktober 1948, p. 20, NA, Minog, Rapportage Indonesië 1945–49, 456.

[103] Memorandum from the director of the office of the governor-general to the High Representative of the Crown, December 2, 1948, NA, Algemene Secretarie 3134. See also *Politiek verslag Sumatra over maart 1948*, p. 11, NA, Minog, Rapportage Indonesië 1945–1949, 456.

the Republican Resident, written five months earlier, asking for Dutch military intervention.[104]

It was the second Police Action of December 1948 that turned the long-planned campaign in Jambi into a reality, granting the wishes of the pro-sultanate party and bringing Jambian oil within the reach of the Dutch. Jambi's "very significant oil fields" had certainly played a role in the plans. All operations in South Sumatra were postponed until these, "the most important objects in South Sumatra," could be occupied.[105] On December 30, 1948, for the first time since their departure in 1942, the Dutch set foot in the by then fire-ravaged capital of the region. Low-lying clouds had ruled out any possibility of a surprise attack. The drone of airplane engines and pamphlets distributed from the air had alerted the Republican troops in the morning of December 29 and given them plenty of time to plunder and destroy the entire Chinese quarter. The Chinese suffered most from the Indonesian fury, in which two-thirds of the town was laid waste. The oil fields—where the occupation began, on the afternoon of December 29—suffered only minor damage, however. Only Kenali Assam was set ablaze, and this fire was quickly extinguished.[106] The Dutch paratroopers, it should be said, were guilty of severe misconduct: the authorities received numerous complaints of plunder and of civilians being shot and killed for no reason.[107]

J. J. van de Velde, who had written numerous reports about Resident Kertopati while serving as government advisor on political affairs, now actually met the man for the first time. The initial impression was disappointing. The Resident struck him as an "ornament" who had immense influence with the kampong population but not with the intelligentsia. Kertopati had weathered all conditions because he was completely harmless, while Republican leaders had been able to impose their will by ensuring that Javanese, Minangkabau, and Bataks infiltrated into every area of officialdom and every service branch. His affability and integrity too had made Kertopati acceptable to all parties. He was never obstructive. Van de Velde repeated once again that the sultan's movement was a reaction on the part of the indigenous population led by a few old feudal leaders to the advent of foreigners who had secured the main positions in politics, administration, and trade—a miniature anticolonial struggle. The movement also expressed the Jambians' institutionalized inferiority complex in relation to more highly developed groups in the archipelago. Their own weakness—their *kurang dynamis* (undynamic) nature,[108] according to one Republican verdict—had led them to seek Dutch support. So Van de Velde did not think it wise to back this particular horse, effectively fueling Sumatran federalism—since it was the weaker groups in Sumatra, such as the Jambians, who favored a federalist solution.[109]

---

[104] *Officiële bescheiden*, 15: 748.

[105] Ibid., 16: 539, 550.

[106] Ibid., pp. 442, 475, 482. Seventy kilos of opium were discovered in the Bank Negara, which had yet to be traded for the Republican cause.

[107] J. Bank, ed., *De Excessennota: Nota betreffende het archiefonderzoek naar de gegevens omtrent in Indonesië begaan door Nederlandse militairen in de periode 1945–1950* (The Hague; SDU, 1995), pp. 35–36.

[108] This epithet comes from a Republican report (see Graf to the director of the office of the governor-general, July 4, 1949, NA, Algemene Secretarie 3136).

[109] Van de Velde, *Brieven uit Sumatra*, pp. 208–24.

The weakness of the pro-sultanate party also made the senior representative of the Crown, L. J. M. Beel, decide not to inform the UN's Committee of Good Offices that was mediating between the parties about the "independence movement" in Jambi, which was as yet scarcely worthy of the name.[110] In March 1949, the Dutch East Indies government again adopted the position that the forming of a *daerah istimewa,* or autonomous region, was inopportune, partly because barely one-third of Jambi was under Dutch control.[111] The Dutch authorities certainly did not encourage Jambi's aspirations, which may partly explain why so little has been written about the Jambian regionalism of this era.

Still, Van de Velde and the Dutch East Indies government soon saw that they could not do without Kertopati. "As far as I know, Kertopati is the only example in recent political history of a simple man, known for his uprightness, who has to be accepted by both the Republic and the Netherlands, solely on account of the great influence he has among his people."[112] Aging, sincere, and much loved, he was venerated almost as a saint. He was therefore chosen as a matter of course as the new Resident. And in the territory under Dutch control, his aspirations for a Jambi with a separate identity, a *Jambi asli,* became a mass movement. Besides the simple *dusun* population, his support included all traditional headmen *(pasirah)* and religious officials, a portion of the merchant class, and some of the clergy, led by the chief *penghulu.*[113]

In March 1949 the Provisional Jambi Council (Dewan Jambi Sementara) was installed and recognized by the Dutch East Indies government. It promptly ruled out any return to Republican authority and sought membership of the Assembly for Federal Consultation (BFO). Since the Council did not yet represent the whole of Jambi, its delegation was admitted to the BFO with observer status only.[114] There too it expressed the desire to form a *daerah istimewa.* But as a constitutional formula it was decidedly vague: Jambi wanted an independent place in the United States of Indonesia instead of being incorporated into Central Sumatra. In May 1949 it joined other Sumatran delegations in protesting against the Van Royen–Roem Agreement, which left too little room for such a solution.[115] Jambi also delegated its own representative to the Round Table Conference but was unable to exert any further influence there.

Meanwhile, in the "liberated" areas, which by August 1949 included all the main regional towns such as Muara Bungo and Bangko, a start was made on setting up an administration largely carried by Indonesians. The Dewan Jambi Sementara held its first plenary session in August; in its new composition there was the same consensus as before on regional autonomy, but no progress was made. In September a

---

[110] Note by the director of the office of the governor-general on territorial administrative official of Jambi to the High Representative of the Crown, January 15, 1949, NA, Algemene Secretarie 3136.

[111] "Regvind" (government of Dutch East Indies) to "TBA" (Territorial administrative official), coded telegram of March 3, 1949, NA, Algemene Secretarie 2457.

[112] Van de Velde to the director of the office of the governor-general, July 8, 1949, NA, Algemene Secretarie 3136.

[113] Kort overzicht nopens de politieke situatie in het bevrijde deel van Djambi, March 1, 1949, app. IIb to state secretary to High Representative of the Crown, March 25, 1949, NA, Algemene Secretarie 2457.

[114] Politiek-politioneel verslag van Djambi over april 1949, NA, Algemene Secretarie 3137.

[115] Stukken Eerste en Tweede Sumatra-conferentie April–May 1949, NA, Minog, 460.

local cease-fire agreement was concluded with last remaining Republican army units, and lines of demarcation were established. Implementation went smoothly. The transfer of administrative authority was accomplished in December 1949.[116]

Closer analysis of the Indonesian revolution in Jambi reveals the repetition of certain historical patterns. The *ulu-ilir* contrast (that is, between Upper and Lower Jambi) had remained significant in this postwar period, for instance. Kertopati drew most of his support from the kampong people of the lowlands, while the people of the upland regions, together with the intelligentsia, favored the Republic. In this sense Kertopati had more in common with the contract sultans than with his father, Taha. And in an echo of the events around 1700 and 1900, the colonial government had taken its cue from the lowlands. The *ulu-ilir* dichotomy was also acknowledged in Republican circles: in 1949 there were even plans to divide the region into two autonomous districts, the *kabupaten* Batang Hari Ilir and the *kabupaten* Merangin. The rationale was that this would effectively do away with the name of Jambi, and hence with Jambian nationalism.[117]

Another pattern that repeated itself was the weakness of the Jambian pro-sultanate party. Like Sultan Facharuddin in 1830, Sultan Abdulrachman Nazaruddin in 1841, and the contract sultans later in the nineteenth century, the party had sought the support of a powerful neighbor, the Dutch authorities, because it did not believe itself strong enough to compete alone in the game of power politics.

Still, contradictory connections and new patterns muddied these historical lines. Kertopati's natural authority among the people was something he shared with his father. And unlike the past, there was now a differentiation on the basis of ethnic origin. The Javanese, Minangkabau, and Jambians each had their own leaders,[118] a trend that had developed only recently, after the abolition of the sultan's administration. Another new factor was a generation conflict: the older people inclined to Kertopati, while the young supported the Republic. This was particularly clear when Kertopati toured Jambi in 1949. In reaction to the treatment they received during the Republican period, the older generation now threatened to impose their will on the young during debates. They sometimes urged the restoration of the sultanate. But Dutch officials made it clear that restoring the structures of the past was impossible, and that if a sultan were reinstated in some form, he would automatically be subject to the authority of Parliament. In that sense, a new-style sultanate would not necessarily be undemocratic. Kertopati himself was not a contender for this hereditary position and did not become sultan; however, he was elected *kepala daerah*, or regional head.[119]

---

[116] Politiek-politioneel verslag van Djambi over augustus 1949, over september 1949, NA, Algemene Secretarie 3137.

[117] Politiek-politioneel verslag over augustus 1949, NA, Algemene Secretarie 3137; Kort overzicht nopens de politieke situatie in het bevrijde deel van Djambi, March 1, 1939, app. IIb to state secretary to High Representative of the Crown, March 25, 1949, NA, Algemene Secretarie 2457, March 25, 1949, NA, Algemene Secretarie 2457.

[118] *Officiële bescheiden*, 16: 568.

[119] Kort overzicht nopens de politieke situatie in het bevrijde deel van Djambi, March 1, 1949, app. IIb to state secretary to High Representative of the Crown, March 25, 1949, NA, Algemene Secretarie 2457. It is striking that the debate on the reinstatement of the sultanate was waged most passionately—by advocates and opponents alike—in Lubuk Rusam, which had a long

Thus in Jambi as in other parts of the archipelago, the regional dynamics of the revolution turned out to consist of a battle of old against young, and of the uneducated against the intelligentsia.[120] There was also the same contrast between the traditional nobles and secular Republicans that existed in Aceh, Palembang, and other regions of Sumatra.[121] And here too, Islam played a role. But in Jambi the representatives of Islam supported an anti-Republican independence movement and sought the support of the one-time colonial rulers. It should be added that Jambi did not witness a social revolution that rounded on the former nobles as collaborators with the colonial regime and destroyed them, as happened in Aceh and in parts of Java. The "social revolution" of September 1946 was only a weak echo of powerful movements elsewhere. The feudal overlords had scarcely been corrupted by any prewar cooperation with the colonial regime. So there were no local peasant riots as on Java, nor was there a violent counterrevolution as in Ambon. More than anything else, Jambi's revolution was characterized by an absence of revolutionary violence and the peaceful coexistence of the various parties and groups. This reflects a variety of factors: the initial strength of the Republican administrative organization in Jambi (which was able immediately to assume authority from the Japanese and to remain in power until 1948), the weakness here of the anticolonial tradition that in other regions spurred the primary revolutionary groups to take action, the relative absence of social tension, and a low level of political awareness.[122]

The course of events in the Jambian revolution illustrates once again the significance of local factors and the decisive influence of historical patterns in the local reaction to the national revolution. The Jambian revolution was one of the many regional episodes in the archipelago. The ideal it pursued was not in the first place independence from the Netherlands, but the concept of a reformed sultanate, an "imagined community" of limited size and with traditional features, that would take its place within a United States of Indonesia while preserving the existing ties with the Netherlands. Its supporters identified the revolutionary Republic with a Minangkabau and to a lesser extent a Javanese "imperialism." And that was something to which the Jambians were firmly opposed.

With the advent of independence in 1949, relations between the colonial government and the royal house, the *suku* Kraton, were consigned to history. By then Jambian oil was being piped to Palembang; the prewar level of production had rapidly been restored in 1949.[123] The movement to restore a Jambian sultanate had lost the battle. Jambi became part of the province of Central Sumatra, one of the states of the United States of Indonesia—in 1950 the Republic of Indonesia. It was not until 1957 that "Jambi for the Jambians" took shape in the form of an autonomous province. Capitalizing on the general unrest outside Java, it seceded from Central Sumatra in January of that year. As the province of Jambi, Taha's old

---

history of anti-Dutch feeling (see also Politiek-politioneel verslag over augustus 1949, NA, Algemene Secretarie 3137).

[120] Kahin, Audrey, ed., *Regional Dynamics of the Indonesian Revolution: Unity from Diversity* (Honolulu: University of Hawaii Press, 1985), p. 279.

[121] Ibid.; Zed, "Kepialangan, Politik dan Revolusi," pp. 358–60.

[122] Kahin, *Regional Dynamics*, pp. 267–69, 277.

[123] Economisch verslag over mei 1949, NA, Algemene Secretarie 3137

kingdom in modernized form, it would continue its development within the Republic of Indonesia.

GENEALOGY OF THE *SUKU* KRATON

1. Sultan Mohildin (c.1811)

2. Sultan Facharuddin (between 1821 and 1829–41)—Sultan Abdulrahman Nazaruddin (1841–55)—Sultan Ahmad Nazaruddin (1858–81)

3a. Children of Sultan Facharuddin
Sultan Taha (1855–1904)
Anak Palembang=Pangeran Ratu Cakra Negara (1881–85)=Sultan Zainuddin (1886–99)
Pangeran Dipo Negoro/Singa di Laga

3b. Children of Sultan Abdulrahman Nazaruddin
Pangeran Ratu Marta Ningrat (1855–81)=Sultan Mohildin (1882–85)

3c. Children of Sultan Ahmad Nazaruddin
daughter Haji Mariam (m. Pangeran Wiro Kesumo)
daughter Kemudo (m. Raden Taha, son of Pangeran Prabu)
daughter Ketut (m. Raden Taha, son of Sultan Mohildin)
Pangeran Ario Jaya Kesuma (regent in 1901)

4. Children of Taha:
daughter (m. Pangeran Prabu Negara (son of Sultan Mohildin)
daughter (m. Pangeran Kusin of the Sekamis, died March 1901,=grandson of Facharuddin, cousin to Taha)
daughter (m. Pangeran Surio Nata Mengala, regent in 1901)
daughter (m. Wiro Nata Krama/Pangeran Anjang)
daughter Mas Intan (m. Suta Jaya Kesuma, son of Pangeran Wiro Kesumo)
daughter (m. Raden Mupati, son of Pangeran Dipo Negoro)
daughter (m. Raden Suut, son of Sultan Nazaruddin)
daughter (m. Raden Ma-aji, son of Pangeran Tumenggung Puspo Ali of the Merangin)
Pangeran Adi Kesuma (m. daughter of Pangeran Dipo Negoro)
Pangeran Ratu Anom Kesumo Judo/Marta Ningrat (1888–1907)

5. Children of Mohildin:
Prabu Negara (m. daughter of Taha)
Adipati Marta di Ningrat

Source: Derived from J. W. Palm's "Stamboom familieleden sultan Djambie," August 1881, and anonymous "Adelslijst na 1901," KITLV, coll. Wellan, 590.

Note: Confined to persons mentioned in the text.

ADMINISTRATIVE OFFICERS (*CIVIELE GEZAGHEBBERS*)/COLLECTORS OF IMPORT AND EXPORT DUTIES AT MUARA KOMPEH AND POLITICAL AGENTS IN JAMBI

Year in almanac	Name	Years in office
Administrative officers		
1834[a]	Keyner	
1835[b]	Eveneron	
1837	W. F. Blancken	2 years
1839	J. K. D. Lammleth	9 years
1848	J. W. Piper	2 years
1850	H. G. Dielwart	2 years
1852	—	
1853	L. A. de Klerck (1st lt., acting)	3 years
1856	J. T. Backerus (1st lt., acting)	3 years
1859	J. J. M. Offerman (1st lt., acting)	3 years
1862	F. A. J. Perié	1 year
1863	—	
1864	F. P. J. Rochell	2 years
1866	J. H. P. Kroesbeek	4 years
1871	—	
1872	C. A. Willems	
1874	no more references to this post in the Almanac	
Political agents in Jambi		
1860	J. G. G. H. Strengaerts	1 year
1861	K. F. Schultze	4 years
1865	R. T. van Rhijn	1 year
December 24, 1865	L. W. A. Kessler	2.5 years
May 27, 1868	L. de Paauw	3.5 years
January 30, 1871	E. D. C. Middelaer	2 years
April 21, 1873	J. H. van der Schalk	1.5 year
September 30, 1874	F. H. Borderwijk	5 months
January 28, 1875	C. A. Niesen	6 years
1881	J. W. Palm	4 years
August 4, 1885	C. A. Niesen (Ass. Res., acting political agent ad interim)	2.5 years

March 8, 1887	A. G. Valette	4 years
1891	H. J. A. Raedt van Oldenbarnevelt	4 years
1895	R. L. A. Hellwig	4 years
1899	L. Knappert	2 years
1901	H. J. A. Raedt van Oldenbarnevelt	

post abolished in 1901

Source: Regeeringsalmanak voor Nederlandsch-Indië 1837–1902 (Batavia: Landsdrukkerij, 1838–1903).

[a] J. W. Boers, "Bezoek ter hoofdplaatse van het Djambische rijk op Sumatra in 1834, door den toenmaligen resident van Palembang," *Tijdschrift van.Nederlandsch-Indië* 12, 2 (1850): 463–70.

[b] Report Darpa Wiguna, n.d., NA, coll. A. H. W. de Kock, VROA 1891, 11.2.

RESIDENTS OF PALEMBANG AND JAMBI

Date of appointment	Name	Years in office
Residents of Palembang		
1823	J. J. van Sevenhove, Comm.	1 year
1824	J. C. Reijnst	3 years
1827	H. S. van Son, Acting Res.	2 years
1829	C. F. E. Praetorius	5 years
1834	J. W. Boers	6 years
1840	H. F. Buschkens, lt. col., Acting Res.	2 years
1842	A. H. W. de Kock, lt. col., Acting Res.	7 years
1849	C. P. C. Steinmetz	2 years
1851	C. A. de Brauw, lt. col.	5 years
1856	A. van der Ven	1 year
1857	—	
1858	P. T. Couperus	3 years
1861	W. E. Kroesen	1 year
1862 (December 1861)	J. A. W. van Ophuijsen	1 year
1863	P. L. van Bloemen Waanders	4 years
February 19, 1867	J. A. W. van Ophuijsen	3.5 years
September 5, 1870	F. E. P. van den Bossche	2 years
November 24, 1872	M. H. W. Nieuwenhuijs	0.5 years
May 11, 1873	A. Pruijs van der Hoeven	6 years
March 23, 1879	P. F. Laging Tobias	4 years
February 6, 1883	G. J. du Cloux	4 years
March 8, 1887	C. A. Niesen	2 years
February 22, 1889	J. P. de Vries	8 years
April 15, 1897	H. J. Monod de Froideville	3.5 years
October 23, 1900	I. A. van Rijn van Alkemade	5.5 years
May 9, 1906	F. L. K. Storm van 's Gravesande	
Residents of Jambi		
July 2, 1906	O. L. Helfrich	2 years
December 2, 1908	A. J. N. Engelenburg	2 years
July 15, 1910	T. A. L. Heyting	3 years
September 24, 1913	A. L. Kamerling	2 years
December 3, 1915	H. C. E. Quast	2.5 years
February 3, 1918	H. L. C. Petri	5 years
March 7, 1923	C. Poortman	2 years
April 1, 1925	G. J. van Dongen	3.5 years
November 8, 1928	J. R. F. Verschoor van Nisse	3 years

November 2, 1931	W. Steinbuch	2 years
June 10, 1933	P. J. van der Meulen	3 years
September 26, 1936	M. J. Ruychaver	3.5 years
March 31, 1940	J. Reuvers	2 years

Source: Regeeringsalmanak voor Nederlandsch-Indië 1823–1942 (Batavia: Landsdrukkerij, 1823-1942).

GOVERNORS-GENERAL

January 1830–June 1833	J. Graaf van den Bosch
June 1833–February 1836	J. C. Baud
February 1836–May 1840	D. J. de Eerens
June 1840–January 1841	C. S. W. Graaf van Hogendorp
January 1841–August 1844	P. Merkus
August 1844–February 1845	J. C. Reijnst
February 1845–May 1851	J. J. Rochussen
May 1851–May 1856	A. J. Duymaer van Twist
May 1856–September 1861	C. F. Pahud
October 1861–October 1866	L. A. J. W. Baron Sloet van de Beele
December 1866–January 1872	P. Mijer
January 1872–March 1875	J. Loudon
March 1875 –April 1881	J. W. van Lansberge
April 1881 –April 1884	F. s' Jacob
April 1884–June 1888	O. van Rees
September 1888–October 1893	C. Pijnacker Hordijk
October 1893–October 1899	C. H. A. van der Wijck
October 1899–October 1904	W. Rooseboom
October 1904–December 1909	J. B. van Heutsz
December 1909–March 1916	A. W. F. Idenburg
March 1916–March 1921	J. P. Graaf van Limburg Stirum
March 1921–September 1926	D. Fock
September 1926–September 1931	A. C. D. de Graeff
September 1931–September 1936	B. C. de Jonge
September 1936–September 1945	A. W. L. Tjarda van Starkenborgh Stachouwer
September 1945–November 1948	H. J. van Mook (lt. gov.-gen.)
November 1948–May 1949	L. J. M. Beel (High Representative of the Crown)
May 1949–December 1949	A. H. J. Lovink (High Representative of the Crown)

MINISTERS OF COLONIES

May 1834–December 1839	J. Graaf van den Bosch
January 1840–March 1848	J. C. Baud
March 1848–November 1849	J. C. Rijk (ad interim)
November 1848–June 1849	G. L. Baud
June 1849–November 1849	E. B. van den Bosch
November 1849–January 1856	C. F. Pahud
January 1856–March 1858	P. Mijer
March 1858–January 1861	J. J. Rochussen
January 1861–March 1861	J. P. Cornets de Groot van Kraaijenburg
March 1861–February 1862	J. Loudon
February 1862–January 1863	G. H. Uhlenbeck
January 1863–February 1863	G. G. Betz (ad interim)
February 1863–May 1866	I. D. Fransen van der Putte
May 1866–September 1866	P. Mijer
September 1866–July 1867	N. Trakranen
July 1867–June 1868	J. J. Hasselman
June 1868–November 1870	E. de Waal
November 1870–January 1871	L. G. Brocx (ad interim)
January 1871–July 1872	P. P. van Bosse
June 1872–August 1874	I. D. Fransen van der Putte
August 1874–September 1876	W. Baron van Goltstein
September 1876–November 1877	F. Alting Mees
November 1877–February 1879	P. P. van Bosse
February 1879 –March 1879	H. O. Wichers (ad interim)
March 1879–August 1879	O. van Rees
August 1879–September 1882	W. Baron van Goltstein
September 1882–February 1883	W. M. de Brauw
February 1883–April 1883	W. F. van Erp Taalman Kip (ad interim)
April 1883–November 1883	F. G. van Bloemen Waanders
November 1883–February 1884	A. W. P. Weitzel (ad interim)
February 1884–April 1888	J. P. Sprenger van Eyk
April 1888–February 1890	L. W. C. Keuchenius
February 1890–August 1891	A. Baron Mackay
August 1891–May 1894	W. K. Baron van Dedem van Vosbergen
May 1894–July 1897	J. H. Bergsma
July 1897–August 1901	J. T. Cremer
August 1901–September 1902	T. A. J. van Asch van Wijck
September 1902–September 1902	J. W. Bergansius (ad interim)
September 1902–August 1905	A. W. F. Idenburg
August 1905–February 1908	D. Fock

February 1908–May 1908	T. Heemskerk (ad interim)
May 1908–August 1909	A. W. F. Idenburg
August 1909–August 1913	J. H. de Waal Malefijt
August 1913–September 1918	T. B. Pleijte
September 1918–November 1919	A. W. F. Idenburg
November 1919–August 1925	S. de Graaff
August 1925–September 1925	H. Colijn (ad interim)
September 1925–March 1926	C. J. I. M. Welter
March 1926–August 1929	J. C. Koningsberger
August 1929–May 1933	S. de Graaff
May 1933–June 1937	H. Colijn
June 1937–July 1939	C. J. I. M. Welter
July 1939–August 1939	C. van den Bussche
August 1939–November 1941	C. J. I. M. Welter
November 1941–May 1942	P. Gerbrandy
May 1942–February 1945	H .J. van Mook
February 1945–July 1946	J. H. A. Logemann[a]
July 1946–August 1948	J. A. Jonkman
August 1948–February 1949	E. M. J. A. Sassen
February 1949–March 1951	J. H. van Maarseveen

[a] In February 1945 the title was changed to Minister of Overseas Territories.

GLOSSARY

adat	customary law
anak raja	Jambian nobility
babad	chronicle
bangsa	tribe
Bangsa XII	twelve tribes
batin	adat title: head, also name of ethnic group (see chap. 2, note 13)
bendahara	title of nobleman; treasurer
benteng	fortress, stronghold
bhisan	relatives of son-in-law or daughter-in-law
Blandas	Dutch
cap	seal
Cultuurstelsel	Cultivation System, whereby the Dutch made it compulsory to grow specific export crops.
daerah	district
daerah istimewa	district with special status
dalang	puppeteer in wayang, classical Javanese puppet drama
datuk	headman
datuk nan bertigo	title: district headman; overseer of troika that was customary under adat
demang	local administrative official
depati	title for official
dewan	council
Dewan Jambi Sementara	Provisional Jambi Council
dukun	healer
dusun	hamlet
gelar	title
haj	pilgrimage to Mecca
haji	someone who has undertaken the pilgrimage to Mecca
ilir	downstream; lower part of territory (e.g. Lower Jambi)
ilmu	secret learning, science
ilmu abang	"red secret learning"
jajah	taxation
jenang	tax collector (see chap. 2, note 73)
jimat	talisman
juragan	captain
kabupaten	sultan's residence, administrative unit
kafir	non-Muslim
kapitan laut	sea-captain
kepala daerah	head of an administrative region
kerajaan	sultanate

klewang	large knife
koyang	unit of weight equivalent to about 30 piculs
kraton	palace
ladang	dry-land plantation
langgar	mosque
laut	sea
lila	type of cannon
mailrapport	postal report
mantri	official
marga	district
merantau	to migrate
muara	estuary
onthoudingspolitiek	policy of abstention from interference in the "Outer Islands"
orang	people
orang laut	name of an ethnic group
orang pendek	small man
orang timur	name of an ethnic group
panembahan	royal title
pahlawan nasional	national hero
pangeran	title of dignitary, nobleman
pangeran ratu	crown prince
panglima besar	title of nobleman, supreme commander
pasirah	district headman
payong	parasol
pendopo	reception hall
penghulu	adat title: spiritual head; also name of ethnic group (see chap. 2, note 13)
penghulu-pindah	name of ethnic group
pepati dalam	court dignitary; minister for the interior
perang sabil	holy war
perdirian	self-reliance, independence
piagem	letter of appointment
puasa	Ramadan, the Muslim fasting month
pusaka	the sultan's regalia
raden	title of nobleman
raja	sultan, ruler
ranju	pointed bamboo rod
rapat	council
ratu agung	sultan's wife; title of high-ranking woman
rio	adat title; headman
sahabat	friend
said	descendant of Muhammad
sarekat	association
sawah	flooded paddy field
serah	gift signifying liability to pay taxes (see chap. 2, note 74)
shariah	Muslim law
suku	noble family, clan
suku pindah	name of ethnic group, nomadic clan
susuhunan	title, sultan's oldest honorary adviser

syair	Malay narrative poem
takut	afraid
tanah pilih	chosen land
tani	peasant
tiku	deputy
ulama	spiritual leader
ulu	upstream; upper part of territory (e.g. Upper Jambi)
undang-undang	laws
verbaal	subject file
wakil	representative, deputy
wedana	district headman
zaman	time
zaman kupon	time of the rubber coupons

BIBLIOGRAPHY

ARCHIVES CONSULTED FOR THIS BOOK

National Archives (NA), The Hague

Archives of the General Secretariat (Algemene Secretarie) for 1945–49
Archives of the Ministry of Foreign Affairs
Archives of the Ministry of Colonies (Col.) 1814–49; 1850–99; 1900–1963
Coll. J. C. Baud
Coll. J., Graaf van den Bosch
Coll. J. B. van Heutsz
Coll. A. H. W. de Kock
Memoranda on Leaving Office (Memories van Overgave; MvO)
Report on Indonesia (Rapportage Indonesië) 1945–49

Arsip Nasional Republik Indonesia (ANRI), Jakarta

Archives of the General Secretariat (Algemeene Secretarie)
Archives of the Residency of Palembang

Dutch Protestantism Documentation Center (Documentatiecentrum voor het Nederlands Protestantisme), Free University, Amsterdam

Coll. A. W. F. Idenburg

Royal Institute of Anthropology (KITLV), Leiden

Coll. O. L. Helfrich
Coll. A. H. W. de Kock
Coll. J. W. J. Wellan
Coll. Oriental Manuscripts

National Archives, Washington

State Department, Consular Reports Batavia, vol. 3.

Dutch Historical Data Archives (Nederlands Historisch Data Archief), Amsterdam

History of European Expansion Data Bank; Netherlands Indies Trade Statistics 1870–1930 (computer data set)

Netherlands Institute for War Documentation (Nederlands Instituut voor Oorlogsdocumentatie; NIOD), Amsterdam

    East Indies Collection

Leiden University Library

    Coll. Oriental manuscripts

LITERATURE

Abdullah, Taufik. "Responses to Colonial Powers: The Jambi Experience in Comparative Perspective." *Prisma: The Indonesian Indicator* 33 (1984): 13–29.

Adas, M. "From Avoidance to Confrontation: Peasant Protest in Precolonial and Colonial Southeast Asia." *Comparative Studies in Society and History* 32 (1981): 217–47.

"Adatrechtgegevens uit Sarolangoen (1905)." *Adatrechtbundel* 30 (1932): 262–97.

"De adel van Benkoelen en Djambi." *Adatrechtbundel* 22 (1923): 309–40.

Adler, J., and G. Barrett, eds. *The Diaries of Walter Murray Gibson 1886, 1887.* Honolulu: University of Hawaii Press, 1973.

Album 86 Pahlawan Nasional. Jakarta: Bahtera Jaya, 1985.

Andaya, L. Y. "Treaty Conceptions and Misconceptions: A Case Study from South Sulawesi." *Bijdragen tot de Taal-, Land- en Volkenkunde* 134 (1978): 275–95.

Anderson, Benedict. "The Idea of Power in Javanese Culture." In *Culture and Politics in Indonesia*, ed. C. Holt, pp. 1–69. Ithaca, N.Y.: Cornell University Press, 1972.

———. *Imagined Communities: Reflections on the Origin and Spread of Nationalism.* 2nd ed. London: Verso, 1991.

Anderson, John. *Acheen and the Ports on the North and East Coast of Sumatra.* London: Allen, 1840.

———. *Mission to the East Coast of Sumatra in 1823.* With an introduction by N. Tarling. 1826. Reprint, Kuala Lumpur: Oxford University Press, 1971.

Andriesen, S. K. "De affaire-Gibson." *Spiegel Historiael* 15 (1980): 42–48.

"Asch van Wijck, T. A. J. van." In *Nieuw Nederlandsch Biografisch Woordenboek*, 1:1591. Leiden: Sijthoff, 1911–37.

Baal, J. van. "Tussen kolonie en nationale staat: De koloniale staat." In *Dekolonisatie en vrijheid*, ed. H. J. M. Claessen et al., pp. 92–108. Assen: Van Gorcum, 1976.

Bank, J. ed. *De Excessennota: Nota betreffende het archiefonderzoek naar de gegevens omtrent in Indonesië begaan door Nederlandse militairen in de periode 1945–1950.* The Hague: Sdu, 1995.

Bastin, John. "Introduction." In W. Marsden, *The History of Sumatra*, pp. v–x. 1783. Reprint, Kuala Lumpur: Longman. 1966.

Baud, W. A. ed. *De semi-officiële particuliere briefwisseling tussen J. C851 en enige daarop betrekking hebbende andere stukken.* 3 vols. Assen: Van Gorcum, 1983.

Baumgart, W. *Der Imperialismus: Idee und Wirklichkeit der englischen und französischen Kolonialexpansion 1880–1914.* Wiesbaden: Steiner, 1975.

Beers, H. van. "Boni moet boeten; De Nederlandse gezagsuitbreiding op Zuidwest-Celebes ten tijde van het stelsel van onthouding 1838–1858." MA thesis, Leiden University, 1986.

Bemmelen, Sita van, M. Djajadiningrat-Nieuwenhuis, E. Locher-Scholten, and E. Touwen-Bouwsma. "Introduction." In *Women and Mediation in Indonesia,* pp. 1–12. KITLV Verhandelingen 152. Leiden: KITLV Press, 1992.

Berg, L. W. C. van den. *Le Hadhramout et les colonies arabes dans l'archipel indien.* Batavia: Imprimerie du Gouvernement, 1886.

———. "Rechtsbronnen van Zuid-Sumatra, uitgegeven, vertaald en toegelicht door L. W. C. van den Berg." *Bijdragen tot de Taal-, Land- en Volkenkunde* 43 (1894): 123–96.

"De beslissing in zake Djambi." *Tijdschrift voor Nijverheid en Landbouw in Nederlandsch-Indië* 69 (1904): 494–505.

Betts, R. F. *The False Dawn: European Imperialism in the Nineteenth Century.* Minneapolis: University of Minnesota Press, 1975.

Black, I. "The 'Lastposten': Eastern Kalimantan and the Dutch in the Nineteenth and Early Twentieth Centuries." *Journal of Southeast Asian Studies* 16 (1985): 281–91.

Blussé, Leonard. "Labour Takes Root: Mobilization and Immobilization of Javanese Rural Society under the Cultivation System." *Itinerario* 8,1 (1984): 77–117.

Blussé, Leonard, and Elsbeth Locher-Scholten. "'Buitenste binnen': De buiten-Europese wereld in de Europese cultuur." *Tijdschrift voor Geschiedenis* 105 (1992): 341–45.

Boers, J. W. "Oud volksgebruik in het Rijk van Jambi." *Tijdschrift van Neêrland's Indië* 3, 1 (1840): 372–84.

———. "Bezoek ter hoofdplaatse van het Djambische rijk op Sumatra in 1834, door den toenmaligen resident van Palembang." *Tijdschrift van Nederlandsch-Indië* 12, 2 (1850): 463–70.

Bootsma, N. A. "Nederland op de conferentie van Washington, 1921–1922." *Bijdragen en Mededelingen betreffende de Geschiedenis der Nederlanden* 93 (1978): 101–26.

———. *Buren in de koloniale tijd: De Philippijnen onder Amerikaans bewind en de Nederlandsche, Indische en Indonesische reacties daarop, 1898–1942.* Dordrecht: Foris, 1986.

Bor, R. C. van der. "Aanteekeningen betreffende bestuursvorm en rechtspraak in de Boven-Tembesi tijdens het sultanaat van Djambi." *Tijdschrift voor het Binnenlandsch Bestuur* 30 (1906): 431–63.

———. "Aanteekeningen betreffende het grondbezit in de Boven-Tembesi." *Tijdschrift voor het Binnenlandsch Bestuur* 30 (1906): 179–90.

———. "Een en ander betreffende het ressort van den controlleur te Sarolangoen, onderafdeeling Boven-Tembesi, der afdeling Djambi." *Tijdschrift voor het Binnenlandsch Bestuur* 30 (1906): 1–13.

———. "Vertaling: Over het rijkssieraad van Djambi, genaamd Si Gendjé." *Tijdschrift voor Indische Taal-, Land- en Volkenkunde* 48 (1906): 142–60.

Breman, J. *Taming the Coolie Beast: Plantation Society and the Colonial Order in Southeast Asia* (Delhi: Oxford University Press, 1989).

———. *The Shattered Image: Construction and Deconstruction of the Village in Colonial Asia.* Dordrecht: Foris, 1988.

Breukelen, E. van. "De Nederlandse gezagsuitbreiding in de Zuider- en Oosterafdeling van Borneo 1900–1906." MA thesis, Utrecht University, 1991.

Brunschwig, H. *Mythes et réalités de l'impérialisme colonial français, 1870–1914.* Paris: Colin, 1960.

Burger, D. H. *Sociologisch-economische geschiedenis van Indonesië,* met een historiografische introductie door J. S. Wigboldus. 2 vols. Wageningen: Landbouwhogeschool/KIT/KITLV, 1975.

Cain, P. J., and A. G. Hopkins. "Gentlemanly Capitalism and British Expansion Overseas: I. The Old Colonial System, 1688–1850." *Economic History Review,* 2nd ser., 39 (1986): 501–25.

———. "Gentlemanly Capitalism and British Expansion Overseas: II. New Imperialism, 1850–1945." *Economic History Review,* 2nd ser., 40 (1987): 1–26.

Campo, J. à. "Orde, rust en welvaart; Over de Nederlandse expansie in de Indische Archipel omstreeks 1900." *Acta Politica* 15 (1980): 145–89.

———. "Politieke integratie en staatsvorming: Nederlands-Indië 1870–1920." Unpublished lecture to the "Politicologen Etmaal Amersfoort," 1983.

———. *Koninklijke Paketvaart Maatschappij: Stoomvaart en staatsvorming in de Indonesische archipel 1888–1914.* Hilversum: Verloren, 1992.

Clemens, A. H. P. "De inheemse rubbercultuur in Jambi en Palembang tijdens het Interbellum." In *Het belang van de Buitengewesten: Economische expansie en koloniale staatsvorming in de Buitengewesten van Nederlands-Indië 1870–1942,* ed. A. H. P. Clemens and J. T. Lindblad, pp. 213–41. Amsterdam: NEHA, 1989.

Clifford, James. *The Predicament of Culture: Twentieth-Century Ethnography, Literature, and Art.* Cambridge: Harvard University Press, 1988.

Cluysenaar, J. L. *Rapport over de aanleg van een spoorweg ter verbinding van de Ombilien-kolenvelden op Sumatra met de Indische Zee.* The Hague: Departement van Koloniën, 1876.

———. *Nota over spoorweg-aanleg in Midden-Sumatra.* The Hague: Departement van Koloniën, 1884.

Colenbrander, H. T., ed. *Dagh-register gehouden int Casteel Batavia vant passerende daer ter plaetse als over geheel Nederlandts-India, anno 1636.* The Hague: Nijhoff, 1899.

Cornets de Groot van Kraaijenburg, J. P. "Notices historiques sur les pirateries commises dans l'archipel Indien-Oriental, et sur les mesures prises pour les réprimer par le gouvernement néerlandais, dans les trente dernières années." *Le Moniteur des Indes-Orientales et Occidentales* 1 (1847): 158–63, 194–204, 230–41, 267–76, 319–30.

———. "Dirk Hendrik Kolff jr., kapitein ter zee." *Handelingen en Geschriften van het Indisch Genootschap* 5 (1858): 180–200.

Creutzberg, P., ed. *Public Finance 1816–1939.* Changing Economy in Indonesia: A Selection of Statistical Source Material from the Early 19th Century up to 1940, vol. 2. The Hague: Nijhoff, 1976.

Davis, L., and R. Huttenback. *Mammon and the Pursuit of Empire: The Political Economy of British Imperialism, 1860–1917.* Cambridge: Cambridge University Press, 1986.

"De denkbeelden van den generaal Van den Bosch over het Nederlandsch gezag op Sumatra." *Tijdschrift voor Nederlandsch Indië,* 3rd ser., 1, 1 (1867): 385–414.

Descamps, Baron, Louis Renault, and Jules Basdevant, eds. *Recueil international des traité's du XIXe siècle contenant l'ensemble du droit conventionnel entre les états et les sentences arbitrales (tetxtes originaux avec traduction française).* Paris: Rousseau, 1914.

"Djambi." In *Encyclopaedie van Nederlandsch-Indië,* 1:108–14. The Hague: Nijhoff; Leiden: Brill, 1917–40.

Dobbin, C. *Islamic Revivalism in a Changing Peasant Economy in Central Sumatra 1784–1847.* London: Curzon Press, 1883.

Doel, H. W. van den. "De ontwikkeling van het militaire bestuur in Nederlands-Indië: De officier-civiel gezaghebber, 1880–1942." *Mededelingen van de Sectie Krijgsgeschiedenis Landmachtstaf* 12 (1989): 27–50.

Eltink, T. "Wat doet Amerika? Een onderzoek naar Amerikaans imperialisme in de Indische archipel in de negentiende eeuw, de vrees daarvoor bij Nederlandse bestuurders en waar die toe leidde." MA thesis, Catholic University Nijmegen, 1985.

Engelenberg, A. J. N. "Opmerkingen over en naar aanleiding van ons bestuur in Djambi." *Verslagen der Algemeene Vergaderingen van het Indisch Genootschap 1911–1912* (1912): 81–112.

Errington, S. "The Place of Regalia in Luwu." In *Centers, Symbols and Hierarchies: Essays on the Classical State of Southeast Asia,* ed. L. Gesick, pp. 194–214. New Haven: Yale University Press, 1983.

Fasseur, C. *Kultuurstelsel en koloniale baten: De Nederlandse exploittie van Java 1840–1860.* Leiden: Universitaire Pers, 1975.

———. "Een koloniale paradox: De Nederlandse expansie in de Indonesische archipel in het midden van de negentiende eeuw (1830–1870)." *Tijdschrift voor Geschiedenis* 92 (1979): 162–87.

———. *The Politics of Colonial Exploitation: Java, the Dutch and the Cultivation System,* trans. R. E. Elson and Ary Kraal. Ithaca, N.Y.: Southeast Asia Program Publications, 1992.

———. "C. H. A. van der Wijck." In *Biografisch woordenboek van Nederland,* ed. J. Charité, 1:664–66. 5 vols. The Hague: Nijhoff, 1979–2002.

Fieldhouse, D. K. "'Imperialism': A Historiographical Revision." *Economic History Review,* 2nd ser., 14 (1961): 187–209.

———. *Economics and Empire 1830–1914.* 2nd ed. London: Macmillan, 1984.

Galbraith, J. S. "The 'Turbulent Frontier' as a Factor in British Expansion." *Comparative Studies in Society and History* 2 (1960): 150–68.

Gallagher, J., and R. Robinson. "The Imperialism of Free Trade." *Economic History Review,* 2nd ser., 6,1 (1953): 1–15.

Geertz, C. *Negara: The Theatre State in Nineteenth-Century Bali.* Princeton, N.J.: Princeton University Press, 1980.

———. "Introduction." In *Centers, Symbols and Hierarchies: Essays on the Classical State of Southeast Asia,* ed. L. Gesick, pp. viii–x. New Haven: Yale University Press, 1983.

"Genootschappen." In *Encyclopaedie van Nederlandsch-Indië,* 1:773–75. The Hague: Nijhoff; Leiden: Brill, 1917–40.

Gerretson, F. C. *Geschiedenis der "Koninklijke."* 5 vols. Baarn: Bosch and Keuning, 1971–73.

Gerretson, F. C., and W. P. Coolhaas, eds. *Particuliere briefwisseling tussen J. van den Bosch en D. J. de Eerens 1830–1840 en eenige daarop betrekking hebbende andere stukken.* Groningen: Wolters, 1960.

Gibson, W. M. *The Prison of Weltevreden and a Glance at the East Indian Archipelago, Illustrated from Original Sketches.* London: Sampson Low, Son, and Co.; New York: Riker, 1856.

Gobée, E., and C. Adriaanse, eds. *Ambtelijke adviezen van C. Snouck Hurgronje 1889–1936.* 3 vols. The Hague: Nijhoff, 1957–65.

Goedemans, A. J. M. *Indië in de branding: Een diplomatiek steekspel 1840–1843.* Utrecht: Oosthoek, 1953.

Goor, J. van. "De plaats van de biografie in de koloniale geschiedenis: Van der Wijk bijvoorbeeld. . . ." In *Between People and Statistics: Essays on Modern Indonesian History Presented to P. Creutzberg,* ed. Francien van Anrooij et al., pp. 283–90. The Hague: Nijhoff, 1979.

———. *Kooplieden, predikanten en bestuurders overzee: Beeldvorming en plaatsbepaling in een andere wereld.* Utrecht: HES, 1982.

———. "Imperialisme in de marge?" In *Imperialisme in de marge: De afronding van Nederlands-Indië,* ed. J. van Goor, pp. 9–18. Utrecht: HES, 1986.

———. "De Lombokexpeditie en het Nederlands nationalisme." In *Imperialisme in de marge: De afronding van Nederlands-Indië,* pp. 19–70. Utrecht: HES, 1986.

———. "Seapower, Trade and State-Formation: Pontianak and the Dutch." In *Trading Companies in Asia 1600–1830,* ed. J. van Goor, pp. 83–106. Utrecht: HES, 1986.

Gould, J. W. "The Filibuster of Walter Murray Gibson." *Report for the Hawaiian Historical Society* (1960): 7–32.

Greve, W. H. de. "Petroleum en aardolie en haar voorkomen in Nederlandsch-Indië." *Tijdschrift voor Nijverheid en Landbouw in Nederlandsch-Indië* 9 (1865): 281–356.

———. *Het Ombiliën-kolenveld in de Padangsche Bovenlanden en het transportstelsel op Sumatra's Westkust.* The Hague: Landsdrukkerij, 1871.

Groen, P. M. H. "'Soldaat' en 'bestuursman': Het Indische leger en de Nederlandse gezagsvestiging op Ceram. Een case study." *Mededelingen van de Sectie Militaire Geschiedenis Landmachtstaf* 5 (1982): 203–44.

Gullick , J. M. *Indigenous Political Systems of Western Malaya.* 2nd ed. London: London School of Economics, 1965.

———. "The Condition of Having a Raja: A Review of *Kerajaan,* by A. C. Milner." *Review of Indonesian and Malayan Affairs* 16 (1982): 109–29.

Haga, B. J. "Eenige opmerkingen over het adatstaatsrecht van Djambi." In *Feestbundel uitgegeven door het Koninklijk Bataviaasch Genootschap van Kunsten en Wetenschappen bij gelegenheid van zijn 150 jarig bestaan 1778–1928*, 1:233–50. Weltevreden: Kolff, 1929.

Hall, K. R. "The Coming of Islam to the Archipelago: A Re-assessment." In *Economic Exchange and Social Interaction in Southeast Asia: Perspectives from Prehistory, History and Ethnography*, ed. K. L. Hutterer, pp. 213–32. Michigan Papers on South and Southeast Asia 13. Ann Arbor: Center for South and Southeast Asian Studies, University of Michigan, 1977.

Hamer, C. van den. "Beschrijving van de twee krissen, als rijkssierraad verbonden aan het Sultansgezag over Djambi en het Pangeran Ratoeschap aldaar." *Tijdschrift voor Indische Taal-, Land- en Volkenkunde* 48 (1906): 106–12.

Handelingen der Staten-Generaal: Eerste Kamer, 1901–1906. The Hague: Staatsdrukkerij, 1901–1906.

Handelingen der Staten-Generaal: Tweede Kamer 1856-1857; 1901-1906. The Hague: Staatsdrukkerij, 1857; 1901-1906.

Handelingen der Staten-Generaal: Bijlagen 1901-1902. The Hague: Staatsdrukkerij, 1901-1902.

Hargreaves, J. D. "Towards a History of the Partition of Africa." *Journal of African History* 1 (1960): 96–109.

Helfrich, O. L. "Nota omtrent het stroomgebied der Boelian Djeba en Djangga." *Tijdschrift van het Bataviaasch Genootschap* 45 (1902): 530–40.

Heutsz, J. B. van. *De onderwerping van Atjeh*. The Hague: Van Cleef; Batavia: Kolff, 1893.

Hilferding, Rudolf. *Finance Capital: A Study of the Latest Phase of Capitalist Development*. Ed. Tom Bottomore. Trans. Morris Watnick and Sam Gordon. London: Routledge Kegan Paul, 1981.

Hobsbawm, E., and T. Ranger. *The Invention of Tradition*. Cambridge: Cambridge University Press, 1983.

Hobson, J. A. *Imperialism: A Study*. London: Allen and Unwin, 1902.

Holsti, K. J. *International Politics: A Framework for Analysis*. 4th ed. Englewood Cliffs, N.J.: Prentice-Hall, 1983.

Hooyer, G. B. *De krijgsgeschiedenis van Nederlandsch-Indië van 1811 tot 1894*. 3 vols. with atlas. The Hague: Van Cleef' Batavia: Kolff, 1895–97.

Idema, H. A. *Parlementaire geschiedenis van Nederlandsch-Indië 1891–1918*. The Hague: Nijhoff, 1924.

IJzereef, W. De Zuid Celebes affaire: Kapitein Westerling en de standrechtlijke executies. Dieren: Bataafsche Leeuw, 1984.

Ikhtisar Keadaan Politik Hindia-Belanda Tahun 1839–1848. Jakarta: Arsip Nasional Republik Indonesia, 1973.

Irwin, G. *Nineteenth-Century Borneo: A Study in Diplomatic Rivalry*. KITLV Verhandelingen 15. The Hague: Nijhoff, 1955.

Jacobs, Els M. *Koopman in Azië: De handel van de Verenigde Oost-Indische Compagnie tijdens de 18de eeuw*. Zutphen: Walburg Pers, 2000.

Jobse, P. *De tin-expedities naar Flores 1887–1891: Een episode uit de geschiedenis van Nederlands-Indië in het tijdperk van het moderne imperialisme.* Utrechtse Historische Cahiers 3. Utrecht: Department of History, Utrecht University, 1980.

Jong, Janny de. *Van batig slot naar ereschuld: De discussie over de financiële verhouding tussen Nederland en Indië en de hervorming van de Nederlandse koloniale politiek.* Groningen, 1989. Published privately.

Juynboll, H. H. *Catalogus van de Maleische en Soendaneesche handschriften der Leidsche Universiteits Bibliotheek.* Leiden: Brill, 1899.

Kahin, Audrey, ed. *Regional Dynamics of the Indonesian Revolution: Unity from Diversity.* Honolulu: University of Hawaii Press, 1985.

Kamajaya. *Delapan Raja-Raja Pahlawan Nasional, Buku I.* Yogya: U.P. Indonesia, 1981.

Kan, C. M. van. *De Nederlandsch expeditie naar Boven-Djambi en de Korintji-vallei.* Utrecht: Beijers, 1876.

Kemp, P. H. van der. *Handboek tot de kennis van 's Lands zoutmiddel in Nederlandsch-Indië: Eene economisch-historische studie.* Batavia: Kolff, 1894.

———. "Palembang en Banka in 1816–1920." *Bijdragen tot de Taal-, Land- en Volkenkunde* 51 (1900): 331–764.

———. "De geschiedenis van het Londensch Tractaat van 17 Maart 1824." *Bijdragen tot de Taal-, Land- en Volkenkunde* 56 (1904):1–245.

Kemp, T. "The Marxist Theory of Imperialism." In *Studies in the Theory of Imperialism,* ed. R. Owen and B. Sutcliffe, pp. 15–35. London: Longman, 1972.

Kertzer, I. D. *Ritual, Politics and Power.* New Haven: Yale University Press, 1988.

Kielstra, E. B. "De uitbreiding van het Nederlandsch gezag op Sumatra." *De Gids* 51, 4 (1887): 256–96.

———. "Onze verhouding tot Djambi." *Onze Eeuw* 1 (1901): 1176–94.

———. *Indisch Nederland.* Haarlem: Bohn, 1910.

———. *De vestiging van het Nederlandsche gezag in den Indischen archipel.* Haarlem: Bohn, 1920.

Kleintjes, P. *Staatsinstellingen van Nederlandsch-Indië.* 2 vols. Amsterdam: De Bussy, 1927–29.

Klerck, E. S. de. *History of the Netherlands East Indies.* 2 vols. Rotterdam: Brusse, 1938.

Klooster, H. A. J. *Indonesiërs schrijven hun geschiedenis: De ontwikkeling van de Indonesische geschiedbeoefening in theorie en praktijk, 1900–1980.* Dordrecht: Foris, 1986.

Kniphorst, J. H. P. E. "Historische schets van den zeeroof in den Oost-Indischen archipel." *Tijdschrift voor het Zeewezen,* 1875–1881.

Koebner, R., and H. D. Schmid. *Imperialism: The Story and Significance of a Political Word, 1840–1960.* Cambridge: Cambridge University Press, 1960.

"Koetei." In *Encyclopaedie van Nederlandsch-Indië,* 2:374–77. The Hague: Nijhoff; Leiden: Brill, 1917–40.

"Kolen." In *Encyclopaedie van Nederlandsch-Indië,* 2:374–77. The Hague: Nijhoff; Leiden: Brill, 1917–40.

"Kolff, Dirk H. Jr." In *Biographisch woordenboek der Nederlanden*, ed. A. J. van der Aa, 4:93–94. 7 vols. Haarlem: Van Brederode, 1852–78.

Koloniaal Verslag, Bijlage C van de Handelingen der Staten-Generaal 1880–1906. The Hague: Staatsdrukkerij, 1880–1906.

Koning, M. "De Nederlandse expansie en ethische politiek in de visie van Colijn." MA thesis, Leiden University, 1983.

Koningsveld, P. S. van. "Snouck Hurgronje zoals hij was." *De Gids* 143 (1980): 785–806.

Kuitenbrouwer, Maarten. "Het imperialisme van een kleine mogendheid: De overzeese expansie van Nederland 1870–1914." In *De kracht van Nederland: Internationale positie en buitenlands beleid*, ed. N. C. F. van Sas, pp. 42–71. Haarlem: Becht, 1991.

———. *The Netherlands and the Rise of Modern Imperialism: Colonies and Foreign Policy 1870–1902.* Translated by Hugh Beyer. New York: Berg, 1991.

Langer, W. L. *The Diplomacy of Imperialism, 1890–1902.* 2nd ed. New York: Knopf, 1972.

Laporan Politik Tahun 1837/Staatkundig overzicht van Nederlandsch-Indië 1837. Jakarta: Arsip Nasional Republik Indonesia, 1971.

Lenin, V. I. *Imperialism: The Highest Stage of Capitalism. A Popular Outline.* New York: International Publishers, 1977.

"Legenden van Djambi." *Tijdschrift voor Neêrland's Indië* 8, 4 (1846): 33–56.

Leupen, P. H. D. "De ontwikkeling van het middeleeuwse souvereiniteitsbegrip: Teloorgang van een relationele conceptie." *Theoretische Geschiedenis* 18 (1991): 387–98.

Liefrinck, J. H. *Onderzoek naar de heffing van de belastingen en de vordering van heerendiensten in eenige deelen der Buitenbezittingen.* Batavia: Landsdrukkerij, 1917.

Lindblad, J. Thomas. "Economische aspecten van de Nederlandse expansie in de Indonesische archipel, 1870–1914." In *Imperialisme in de marge: De afronding van Nederlands-Indië*, ed. J. van Goor, pp. 227–66. Utrecht: HES, 1985.

———. *Between Dayak and Dutch: The Economic History of Southeast Kalimantan, 1880–1942.* KITLV Verhandelingen 134. Dordrecht: Foris, 1988.

———. "Economic Aspects of the Dutch Expansion in Indonesia, 1870–1914." *Modern Asian Studies* 23 (1989): 1–23.

Locher-Scholten, Elsbeth. "Association in Theory and Practice: The Composition of the Regency Council (ca. 1910–20)." In *Between People and Statistics: Essays on Modern Indonesian History*, ed. Francien van Anrooij et al, pp. 207–18. The Hague: Nijhoff, 1979.

———. *Ethiek in fragmenten: Vijf studies over koloniaal denken en doen van Nederlanders in de Indonesische archipel 1877–1942.* Utrecht: HES, 1981.

———. "'Een gebiedende noodzakelijkheid': Besluitvorming rond de Boni-expeditie 1903–1905." In *Excursies in Celebes: Een bundel bijdragen bij het afscheid van J. Noorduyn als directeur-secretaris van het Koninklijk Instituut voor Taal-, Land- en Volkenkunde*, ed. H. A. Poeze and P. Schoorl, pp. 143–64. KITLV Verhandelingen 147. Leiden: KITLV Uitgeverij, 1991.

————. "Rivals and Rituals in Jambi, South Sumatra (1858–1901)." *Modern Asian Studies* 27 (1993): 573–92.

————. "Dutch Expansion in the Indonesian Archipelago around 1900 and the Imperialism Debate." *Journal of Southeast Asian Studies* 25 (1994): 91–111. Reprinted in *South East Asia: Colonial History*, vol. 2, *Empire-Building during the Nineteenth Century* , ed. Paul H. Kratoska, pp. 107–31, London and New York: Routledge, 2001.

Logemann, J. H. A. "Direct gebied met zelfbestuur." *Indisch Tijdschrift voor het Recht* 136 (1932): 1–49.

Lukes, S. "Political Ritual and Social Integration." *Sociology* 9 (1975): 289–308.

Maarseveen, J. G. S. J. van, ed. *Briefwisseling van Nicolaas Gerard Pierson 1839–1909*, vol. 1, *1851–1884*. Amsterdam: Nederlandsche Bank, 1991.

Manuhutu, W. "Pacificatie in practijk: De expansie van het Nederlands gezag op Ceram, 1900–1942." In *Imperialisme in de marge: De afronding van Nederlands-Indië*, ed. J. van Goor, pp. 267–316. Utrecht: HES, 1986.

Marsden, W. *The History of Sumatra, Containing an Account of the Government, Laws, Customs and Manners of the Native Inhabitants with a Description of the Natural Productions and a Relation of the Ancient Political State of that Island*. 1811. Reprint, Kuala Lumpur: Longman, 1966.

Mennes, H. M. M. "Eenige aanteekeningen omtrent Djambi." *Koloniaal Tijdschrift* 21 (1932): 36–39.

"Merkus." In *Encyclopaedie van Nederlandsch-Indië*, 2:713–14. The Hague: Nijhoff; Leiden: Brill.

Meulen, W. C. van der. "Aantekeningen betreffende de bestuursinrichting in de onderafdeeling Tebo en de daarmede samenhangende volksinstellingen en gebruiken." *Tijdschrift voor het Binnenlandsch Bestuur* 36 (1911): 1–37.

"Michiels (Andreas Victor)." In *Encyclopaedie van Nederlandsch-Indië*, 2:724. The Hague: Nijhoff; Leiden: Brill.

Miert, H. van. *Bevlogenheid en onvermogen: Mr. J. H. Abendanon en de Ethische Richting in het Nederlands kolonialisme*. Leiden: KITLV Uitgeverij, 1991.

Mills, L. A. "British Malaya, 1824–1867." *Journal of the Malaysian Branch of the Royal Asiatic Society* 33, 3 (1960): 5–424.

Milner, A. C. *Kerajaan: Malay Political Culture on the Eve of Colonial Rule*. Tucson: University of Arizona Press, 1982.

————. "Islam and the Muslim state." In *Islam in South-East Asia*, ed. M. B. Hooker, pp. 23–49. Leiden: Brill, 1983.

Moertono, Soemarsaid. *State and Statecraft in Old Java: A Study of the Later Mataram Period, 16th to 19th Century*. Ithaca, N.Y.: Cornell University Press, 1972.

Mommsen, W. J. *Der europäische Imperialismus: Aufsätze und Abhandlungen*. Göttingen: Vandenhoeck und Ruprecht, 1979.

————. *Imperialismustheorien: Ein Ueberblick über die neueren Imperialismusinterpretationen*. 2nd ed. Göttingen: Vandenhoeck und Ruprecht, 1980.

Moor, J. A. de. "Warmakers in the Archipelago: Dutch Expeditions in Nineteenth Century Indonesia." In *Imperialism and War: Essays on Colonial Wars in Asia and Africa*, pp. 50–71. Leiden: Brill, 1989.

Mr. C. van Vollenhoven's verspreide geschriften. 3 vols. Haarlem: Tjeenk Willink; The Hague: Nijhoff, 1935.

Muttalib, Jang Aisjah. "Jambi 1900–1916: From War to Rebellion." PhD diss., Columbia University, 1977.

———. "Suatu Tinjauan Mengenai Beberapa Gerakan Sosial di Jambi pada Perempatan Pertama Abad ke 20." *Prisma* 8 (1980): 26–37.

"Mijnwetgeving." In *Encyclopaedie van Nederlandsch-Indië*, 2:847–52. The Hague: Nijhoff; Leiden: Brill.

Nagtegaal, L. "Rijden op een Hollandse tijger: De Noordkust van Java en de V.O.C. 1680–1743." PhD diss., Utrecht University, 1988.

———. *Riding the Dutch Tiger: The Dutch East Indies Company and the Northeast Coast of Java, 1680–1743.* Translated by Beverley Jackson. Leiden: KITLV Press, 1996.

Nandy, Ashis. *The Intimate Self: Loss and Recovery of Self under Colonialism.* 2nd ed. Oxford: Oxford University Press, 1988.

"De Nederlandse expansie in Indonesië in de tijd van het moderne imperialisme." *Bijdragen en Mededelingen betreffende de Geschiedenis der Nederlanden* 86 (1971): 1–89.

Nortier, J. J. "Orde en rustverstoring in het Djambische, februari 1942." *Militaire Spectator* 152 (1983): 565–77.

Ophuijsen, C. A. van. "Eenige opmerkingen naar aanleiding van de door prof. mr. L. W. C. van den Berg bezorgde uitgave van de oendang-oendang Djambi." *Bijdragen tot de Taal-, Land- en Volkenkunde* 46 (1896): 153–213.

Oppenheim, F. E. *The Place of Morality in Foreign Policy.* Lexington, Mass.: Lexington Books, 1991.

Oss, S. F. van. *Van Oss' effectenboek voor 1930*, vol. 1, *Binnenland.* The Hague: Van Oss, 1931.

Owen, R., and B. Sutcliffe, eds. *Studies in the Theory of Imperialism.* London: Longman, 1972.

Peeters, J. C. M. "Kaum tua en kaum muda in de residentie Palembang: 1925–1934." MA thesis, Leiden University, 1988.

"Petroleum." In *Encyclopaedie van Nederlandsch-Indië*, 3:394–401. The Hague: Nijhoff; Leiden: Brill.

Petrus Blumberger, J. T. *De nationalistische beweging in Nederlandsch-Indië.* Haarlem: Tjeenk Willink, 1931.

Politiek beleid en bestuurszorg in de buitenbezittingen. 4 vols. Batavia: Landsdrukkerij, 1907–9.

"Pruys van der Hoeven." In *Encyclopaedie van Nederlandsch-Indië*, 3:516. The Hague: Nijhoff; Leiden: Brill.

Pruys van der Hoeven, A. *Veertig jaren Indische dienst.* The Hague: Belinfante, 1894.

Redactie. "Mededeelingen van de redactie: Indische militaire rechtspleging." *Militair- Rechtelijk Tijdschrift* 2 (1906) 215–16.

Regeeringsalmanak voor Nederlandsch-Indie 1823–1942. Batavia: Landsdrukkerij, 1823–1942.

Reid, A. "Nineteenth Century Pan-Islam in Indonesia and Malaysia." *Journal of Asian Studies* 26 (1967): 267–83.

———. *The Contest for North Sumatra: Atjeh, the Netherlands and Britain 1858–1898.* Singapore: Oxford University Press; Kuala Lumpur: University of Malaya Press, 1969.

———. *Europe and Southeast Asia: The Military Balance.* Occasional Papers 16. Townsville, Queensland: Centre for Southeast Asian Studies, 1982.

———. "Introduction." In *Slavery, Bondage and Dependency in Southeast Asia.*, ed. A. Reid and J. Brewster, pp. 1–43. St Lucia: University of Queensland Press, 1983.

Reinsma, R. "De cultuurprocenten in de praktijk en in de ogen der tijdgenoten." In *Geld en geweten: Een bundel opstellen over anderhalve eeuw Nederlands bestuur in de Indonesische archipel*, ed. C. Fasseur, 1:59–90. 2 vols. The Hague: Nijhoff, 1980.

Resink, G. J. *Indonesia's History between the Myths: Essays in Legal History and Historical Theory.* The Hague: Van Hoeve, 1968.

"Reteh." In *Encyclopaedie van Nederlandsch-Indië*, 3:596–98. The Hague: Nijhoff; Leiden: Brill.

Ricklefs, M. C. *Jogjakarta under Sultan Mangkubumi 1749–1792: A History of the Division of Java.* London: Oxford University Press, 1974.

Robinson, R. "Non-European Foundations of European Imperialism: Sketch for a Theory of Collaboration." In *Studies in the Theory of Imperialism*, ed. R. Owen and B. Sutcliffe, pp. 117–42. London: Longman, 1972.

Ronkel, P. S. van. "De Maleische handschriften van Nederlandsch-Indië van het Koninklijk Instituut voor Taal-, Land- en Volkenkunde." *Bijdragen tot de Taal-, Land- en Volkenkunde* 60 (1908): 181–248.

———. *Supplement-catalogus der Maleische en Minangkabausche handschriften in de Leidsche Universiteitsbibliotheek.* Leiden: Brill, 1921.

Sahlins, Marshall. *Islands of History.* Chicago: University of Chicago Press, 1985.

Said, E. W. *Orientalism.* 3rd ed. London: Penguin Books, 1987.

Sartono Kartodirdjo. *Protest Movements in Rural Java: A Study of Agrarian Unrest in the Nineteenth and Early Twentieth century.* Singapore: Oxford University Press, 1973.

Sas, N. C. F. van. "Fin-de-siècle als nieuw begin: Nationalisme in Nederland rond 1900." *Bijdragen en Mededelingen betreffende de Geschiedenis der Nederlanden* 106 (1991): 595–609.

Schöffer, I. "Dutch 'Expansion' and Indonesian Reactions: Some Dilemmas of Modern Colonial Rule (1900–1942)." In *Expansion and Reaction: Essays on European Expansion and Reaction in Asia and Africa*, ed. H. L. Wesseling. Leiden, pp. 78–99: Leiden University Press, 1978.

Schoorl, J. W. "Power, Ideology and Change in the Early State of Buton." In *State and Trade in the Indonesian Archipelago*, ed. G. J. Schutte, pp. 17–60. Leiden: KITLV Press, 1994.

Schröder, F. "Oriëntalistische retoriek: Van Koningsveld over de vuile handen van Snouck Hurgronje." *De Gids* 143 (1980): 785–806.

Schulte Nordholt, Henk. *The Spell of Power: A History of Balinese Politics 1650–1940.* Leiden: KITLV Press, 1996.

Scott, James C. *Weapons of the Weak: Everyday Forms of Peasant Resistance.* New Haven: Yale University Press, 1985.

Semmel, B. *Imperialism and Social Reform: English Social-Imperialist Thought 1895–1914.* London: Allen and Unwin, 1960.

Smail, J. R. W. "On the Possibility of an Autonomous History of Modern Southeast Asia." *Journal of Southeast Asian History* 2, 2 (1961): 72–102.

Smulders, C. M. *Geschiedenis en verklaring van het tractaat van 17 maart 1824 te Londen gesloten tusschen Nederland en Groot-Brittannië ter regeling van wederzijdsche belangen en rechten in Oost-Indië.* Utrecht: Siddré, 1856.

Snouck Hurgronje, C. *Mekka.* 2 vols. The Hague: Nijhoff, 1888–89.

———. *De Atjehers.* 2 vols.; Batavia: Landsdrukkerij; Leiden: Brill, 1893–95.

Somer, J. *De Korte Verklaring.* Breda: Corona, 1934.

Statistiek van den handel, de scheepvaart en de in- en uitvoerrechten in Nederlandsch-Indië over het jaar 1880. Batavia: Landsdrukkerij, 1884.

Statistiek van den handel, de scheepvaart en de in- en uitvoerrechten in Nederlandsch-Indië over het jaar 1900. Batavia: Landsdrukkerij, 1901.

"Stoomvaart." In *Encyclopaedie van Nederlandsch-Indië,* 3:111–19. The Hague: Nijhoff; Leiden: Brill.

Stuivenga, C. J. M. "Op de grens van twee werelden: De expeditie naar Djambi, 1901–1907." Department of History, Leiden University, 1999. Unpublished.

Surat-Surat Perdjandjian antara Kesultanan Riau dengan Pemerintahan-Pemerintahan VOC dan Hindia-Belanda, 1784–1909. Jakarta: Arsip Nasional Republik Indonesia, 1970.

Sutherland, Heather. "The Taming of the Trengganu Elite." In *Southeast Asian Transitions: Approaches through Social History,* ed. Ruth McVey, pp. 32–58. New Haven: Yale University Press, 1978.

Tambiah, S. J. *Culture, Thought and Social Action: An Anthropological Perspective.* Cambridge: Harvard University Press, 1985.

Tarling, N. "British Policy in the Malay Peninsula and Archipelago 1824–1871." *Journal of the Malayan Branch of the Royal Asiatic Society* 30, 3 (1957): 5–228.

———. *Anglo-Dutch rivalry in the Malay World 1780–1824.* Cambridge: Cambridge University Press; Sydney: University of Queensland Press, 1962.

———. *Imperial Britain in South-East Asia.* Kuala Lumpur: Oxford University Press, 1975.

Tennekes, J. *Symbolen en hun boodschap.* Assen: Van Gorcum, 1982.

Tholen, H. J. van der. "De expeditie naar Korintji in 1902–1903: Imperialisme of ethische politiek." *Mededelingen van de Sectie Militaire Geschiedenis Landmachtstaf* 10 (1987): 70–89.

Tideman, J., and P. L. F. Sigar. *Djambi.* Amsterdam: Koloniaal Instituut, 1938

Tilly, C. "Reflections on the History of European State Making." In *The Formation of National States,* ed. C. Tilly, pp. 3–83. Princeton, N.J.: Princeton University Press, 1975.

Touwen, L. J. "Voordeel van veelzijdigheid: De economische ontwikkeling van Palembang en Djambi tussen 1900 en 1938." *Economisch en Sociaal-Historisch Jaarboek* 54 (1991): 134–82.

Van der Kroef, J. M. "On the Writing of Indonesian History." *Pacific Affairs* 31 (1958): 352–71.

———. "On the Sovereignty of Indonesian States: A Rejoinder." *Bijdragen tot de Taal-, Land- en Volkenkunde* 117 (1961): 238–66.

Van der Veur, P. W. J. *Search for New Guinea's Boundaries: From Torres Strait to the Pacific.* Canberra: ANU Press, 1966.

Veer, P. van 't. *De Atjeh-oorlog.* Amsterdam: Arbeiderspers, 1969.

Velde, Henk te. *Gemeenschapszin en plichtsbesef: Liberalisme en nationalisme in Nederland 1870–1918.* The Hague: SDU, 1992.

Velde, J. J. van de. *Brieven uit Sumatra, 1928–1949.* Franeker: Wever, 1982.

Velde, Paul van der. *Een Indische liefde: P. J. Veth (1814–1895) en de inburgering van Nederlands-Indië.* Amsterdam: Balans, 2000.

Velds, G. J. "De onderwerping van Djambi, 1901–1907: Beknopte geschiedenis naar officiëele gegevens." *Indisch Militair Tijdschrift,* Extra-bijlage 24 (1909).

Versnel, H. S. "Geef de keizer wat des keizers is en Gode wat Gods is: Een essay over een utopisch conflict." *Lampas* 21 (1988): 233–56.

Veth, D. D. *Midden-Sumatra: Reizen en onderzoekingen der Sumatra-expeditie, uitgerust door het Aardrijkskundig Genootschap. Photographie-album.* Leiden: Brill, 1879.

Veth, P. J., ed., *Midden-Sumatra: Reizen en onderzoekingen der Sumatra-Expeditie, uitgerust door het Aardrijkskundig Genootschap 1877–1879.* 4 vols. Leiden: Brill, 1881–92.

Volkstelling van Nederlandsch-Indië/Census of the Netherlands East Indies 1930, vol. 4, *Inheemsche bevolking van Sumatra.* Batavia: Landsdrukkerij, 1933.

Voorhoeve, J. J. C. *Peace, Profits and Principles: A Study of Dutch Foreign Policy.* Leiden: Nijhoff, 1985.

Vos, Reinout. *Gentle Janus, Merchant Prince: The VOC and theTightrope of Diplomacy in the Malay World, 1740–800.* Trans. Beverley Jackson. Leiden: KITLV Press, 1993.

Vuurde, R. E. M. Van. "'Koloniale gerustheid' (1898)." In *Geschiedenis en cultuur: Achttien opstellen,* ed. E. Jonker and M. van Rossem, pp. 107–18. The Hague: SDU, 1990.

Wal, S. L. van der, P. J. Drooglever, and M. J. B. Schouten, eds. *Officiële bescheiden betreffende de Nederlands-Indonesische betrekkingen 1945–1950.* 20 vols. The Hague: Nijhoff, 1971–96. [P. J. Drooglever and M. J. B. Schouten, eds. vols. x–xx]

Waal, E. de. *Onze Indische financiën: Nieuwe reeks aanteekeningen.* 10 vols. The Hague: Nijhoff, 1876–1907.

Warmenhoven, A. A. J. "De opleiding van Nederlandse bestuursambtenaren in Indonesië." In *Besturen overzee: Herinneringen van oud-ambtenaren bij het binnenlands bestuur in Nederlandsch-Indië,* ed. S. L. van der Wal, pp. 12–44. Franeker: Wever, 1977.

Watson, C. W. *Kerinci:Two Historical Studies.* Occasional Paper 3. Canterbury: Centre of South-East Asian Studies, University of Kent, 1984.

Watson Andaya, B. "From Rüm to Tokyo: The Search for Anti-Colonial Allies by the Rulers of Riau, 1899–1914." *Indonesia* 22 (1977): 123–56.

———. "The Cloth Trade in Jambi and Palembang Society during the Seventeenth and Eighteenth Centuries." *Indonesia* 47 (1989): 26–46.

———. "Cash Cropping and Upstream-Downstream Tensions: The Case of Jambi in the Seventeenth and Eighteenth Centuries." In *Southeast Asia in the Early Modern Era: Trade, Power and Belief*, ed. A. Reid, pp. 91–122. Ithaca, N.Y.: Cornell University Press, 1993.

———. *To Live as Brothers: Southeast Sumatra in the Seventeenth and Eighteenth Centuries*. Honolulu: University of Hawaii Press, 1993.

Watson Andaya, B., and L. Y. Andaya. *A History of Malaysia*. London: Macmillan, 1982.

Wehler, H. U. *Bismarck und der Imperialismus*. Cologne: Kiepenhauer und Witsch, 1969.

Wellan, J. W. J. and O. L. Helfrich *Zuid-Sumatra: Overzicht van de literatuur der gewesten Bengkoelen, Djambi, de Lampongsche districten en Palembang*. 2 vols. The Hague: Smits, 1923–28.

Wellenstein, E. P. *Het Indische mijnbouwvraagstuk*. The Hague: Nijhoff, 1918.

Wels, C. B. *Aloofness and Neutrality: Studies on Dutch Foreign Relations and Policy-Making Institutions*. Utrecht: HES, 1982.

Wertheim, W. F. "Counter-Insurgency Research at the Turn of the Century: Snouck Hurgronje and the Aceh War." *Sociologische Gids* 19 (1972): 320–28.

Wesseling, H. L. "Nederland en de Conferentie van Berlijn, 1884–1885." *Tijdschrift voor Geschiedenis* 93 (1980): 559–77.

———. "Bestond er een Nederlands imperialisme?" *Tijdschrift voor Geschiedenis* 99 (1986): 214–25.

———. "The Giant That Was a Dwarf or the Strange History of Dutch Imperialism." In *Theory and Practice in the History of European Expansion: Essays in Honour of Ronald Robinson*, ed. A. Porter and R. Holland. Special issue of *Journal of Imperial and Commonwealth History* 16 (1987–88): 58–70.

———. *Indië verloren, rampspoed geboren en andere opstellen over de geschiedenis van de Europese expansie*. Amsterdam: Bert Bakker, 1988.

———. "Colonial Wars: An Introduction." In *Imperialism and War: Essays on Colonial Wars in Asia and Africa*, ed. J. A. de Moor and H. L. Wesseling, pp. 1–11. Leiden: Brill/Universitaire Pers Leiden, 1989.

———. *Verdeel en heers: De deling van Afrika 1880–1914*. Amsterdam: Bert Bakker, 1991.

Westendorp Boerma, J. J. *Een geestdriftig Nederlander: Johannes van den Bosch*. Amsterdam: Querido, 1950.

———, ed. *Briefwisseling tussen J. van den Bosch en J. C. Baud, 1829–1832 en 1834–1836*. 2 vols. Utrecht: Kemink, 1956.

White, Benjamin. *"Agricultural Involution" and Its Critics: Twenty Years after Clifford Geertz*. Working Papers Series 6. The Hague: Institute of Social Studies, 1983.

Wijk, E. M. H. G. Van. "Opstand in Djambi: De geschiedenis van een millenaristische verzetsbeweging tegen het Nederlandse gouvernement in Indonesië aan het begin van deze eeuw." MA thesis, University of Amsterdam, 1979.

———. "De Djambi-opstand: Millenaristisch verzet in Indonesië." *Skript* 2 (1980): 38–52.

———. *De Zuid-Celebes affaire: Kapitein Westerling en de standrechtelijke executies*. Dieren: Bataafsche Leeuw, 1984.

Wildt, Carla de. "Impulsen tot het moderne imperialisme: De invloed van het Koninklijk Nederlands Aardrijkskundig Genootschap op het Nederlandse koloniaal beleid, 1873–1903." Department of History, Utrecht University, 1991. Unpublished.

Wisseman Christie, J. *Theatre States and Oriental Despotisms: Early Southeast Asia in the Eyes of the West*. Occasional Papers 10. Hull: Centre for South-East Asian Studies, University of Hull, 1985.

Woelders, M. O. *Het sultanaat Palembang 1811–1925*. KITLV verhandelingen 72. The Hague: Nijhoff, 1975.

Wong Lin Ken. "The Trade of Singapore 1819–69." *Journal of the Malaysian Branch of the Royal Asiatic Society* 33, 4 (1960): 1–315.

Zainuddin, R., M. Yuhadi, and Bachtiar As. *Sejarah Kebangkitan Nasional Daerah Jambi 1900–1942*. Jakarta: Proyek Penelitian dan Pencatatan Kebudayaan Daerah, Pusat Penelitian Sejarah dan Budaya, Departemen Pendidikan dan Kebudayaan, 1981.

Zed, Mestika. "Kepialangan, Politik dan Revolusi: Palembang 1900–1950." PhD diss., Free University, Amsterdam, 1991.

Zevenbergen, M. "De Djambi-affaire: Een Nederlands-Amerikaans conflict over de Nederlands-Indische aardolie 1920–1921." MA thesis, University Njmegen, 1983.

INDEX

SOUTHEAST ASIA PROGRAM PUBLICATIONS
Cornell University

Studies on Southeast Asia

Number 36   *Southeast Asia over Three Generations: Essays Presented to Benedict R. O'G. Anderson*, ed. James T. Siegel and Audrey R. Kahin. 2003. 398 pp. ISBN 0-87727-735-4

Number 35   *Nationalism and Revolution in Indonesia*, George McTurnan Kahin, intro. Benedict R. O'G. Anderson (reprinted from 1952 edition, Cornell University Press, with permission). 2003. 530 pp. ISBN 0-87727-734-6.

Number 34   *Golddiggers, Farmers, and Traders in the "Chinese Districts" of West Kalimantan, Indonesia*, Mary Somers Heidhues. 2003. 316 pp. ISBN 0-87727-733-8

Number 33   *Opusculum de Sectis apud Sinenses et Tunkinenses (A Small Treatise on the Sects among the Chinese and Tonkinese): A Study of Religion in China and North Vietnam in the Eighteenth Century*, Father Adriano de St. Thecla, trans. Olga Dror, with Mariya Berezovska. 2002. 363 pp. ISBN 0-87727-732-X.

Number 32   *Fear and Sanctuary: Burmese Refugees in Thailand*, Hazel J. Lang. 2002. 204 pp. ISBN 0-87727-731-1.

Number 31   *Modern Dreams: An Inquiry into Power, Cultural Production, and the Cityscape in Contemporary Urban Penang, Malaysia*, Beng-Lan Goh. 2002. 225 pp. ISBN 0-87727-730-3.

Number 30   *Violence and the State in Suharto's Indonesia*, ed. Benedict R. O'G. Anderson. 2001. Second printing, 2002. 247 pp. ISBN 0-87727-729-X.

Number 29   *Studies in Southeast Asian Art: Essays in Honor of Stanley J. O'Connor*, ed. Nora A. Taylor. 2000. 243 pp. Illustrations. ISBN 0-87727-728-1.

Number 28   *The Hadrami Awakening: Community and Identity in the Netherlands East Indies, 1900-1942*, Natalie Mobini-Kesheh. 1999. 174 pp. ISBN 0-87727-727-3.

Number 27   *Tales from Djakarta: Caricatures of Circumstances and their Human Beings*, Pramoedya Ananta Toer. 1999. 145 pp. ISBN 0-87727-726-5.

Number 26   *History, Culture, and Region in Southeast Asian Perspectives*, rev. ed., O. W. Wolters. 1999. 275 pp. ISBN 0-87727-725-7.

Number 25   *Figures of Criminality in Indonesia, the Philippines, and Colonial Vietnam*, ed. Vicente L. Rafael. 1999. 259 pp. ISBN 0-87727-724-9.

Number 24   *Paths to Conflagration: Fifty Years of Diplomacy and Warfare in Laos, Thailand, and Vietnam, 1778-1828*, Mayoury Ngaosyvathn and Pheuiphanh Ngaosyvathn. 1998. 268 pp. ISBN 0-87727-723-0.

Number 23   *Nguyễn Cochinchina: Southern Vietnam in the Seventeenth and Eighteenth Centuries*, Li Tana. 1998. Second printing, 2002. 194 pp. ISBN 0-87727-722-2.

Number 22   *Young Heroes: The Indonesian Family in Politics*, Saya S. Shiraishi. 1997. 183 pp. ISBN 0-87727-721-4.

Number 21   *Interpreting Development: Capitalism, Democracy, and the Middle Class in Thailand*, John Girling. 1996. 95 pp. ISBN 0-87727-720-6.

Number 20   *Making Indonesia,* ed. Daniel S. Lev, Ruth McVey. 1996. 201 pp.
ISBN 0-87727-719-2.

Number 19   *Essays into Vietnamese Pasts,* ed. K. W. Taylor, John K. Whitmore. 1995.
288 pp. ISBN 0-87727-718-4.

Number 18   *In the Land of Lady White Blood: Southern Thailand and the Meaning of
History,* Lorraine M. Gesick. 1995. 106 pp. ISBN 0-87727-717-6.

Number 17   *The Vernacular Press and the Emergence of Modern Indonesian
Consciousness,* Ahmat Adam. 1995. 220 pp. ISBN 0-87727-716-8.

Number 16   *The Nan Chronicle,* trans., ed. David K. Wyatt. 1994. 158 pp.
ISBN 0-87727-715-X.

Number 15   *Selective Judicial Competence: The Cirebon-Priangan Legal Administration,
1680–1792,* Mason C. Hoadley. 1994. 185 pp. ISBN 0-87727-714-1.

Number 14   *Sjahrir: Politics and Exile in Indonesia,* Rudolf Mrázek. 1994. 536 pp.
ISBN 0-87727-713-3.

Number 13   *Fair Land Sarawak: Some Recollections of an Expatriate Officer,* Alastair
Morrison. 1993. 196 pp. ISBN 0-87727-712-5.

Number 12   *Fields from the Sea: Chinese Junk Trade with Siam during the Late
Eighteenth and Early Nineteenth Centuries,* Jennifer Cushman. 1993.
206 pp. ISBN 0-87727-711-7.

Number 11   *Money, Markets, and Trade in Early Southeast Asia: The Development of
Indigenous Monetary Systems to AD 1400,* Robert S. Wicks. 1992. 2nd
printing 1996. 354 pp., 78 tables, illus., maps. ISBN 0-87727-710-9.

Number 10   *Tai Ahoms and the Stars: Three Ritual Texts to Ward Off Danger,* trans., ed.
B. J. Terwiel, Ranoo Wichasin. 1992. 170 pp. ISBN 0-87727-709-5.

Number 9   *Southeast Asian Capitalists,* ed. Ruth McVey. 1992. 2nd printing 1993.
220 pp. ISBN 0-87727-708-7.

Number 8   *The Politics of Colonial Exploitation: Java, the Dutch, and the Cultivation
System,* Cornelis Fasseur, ed. R. E. Elson, trans. R. E. Elson, Ary Kraal.
1992. 2nd printing 1994. 266 pp. ISBN 0-87727-707-9.

Number 7   *A Malay Frontier: Unity and Duality in a Sumatran Kingdom,* Jane
Drakard. 1990. 215 pp. ISBN 0-87727-706-0.

Number 6   *Trends in Khmer Art,* Jean Boisselier, ed. Natasha Eilenberg, trans.
Natasha Eilenberg, Melvin Elliott. 1989. 124 pp., 24 plates.
ISBN 0-87727-705-2.

Number 5   *Southeast Asian Ephemeris: Solar and Planetary Positions, A.D. 638–2000,*
J. C. Eade. 1989. 175 pp. ISBN 0-87727-704-4.

Number 3   *Thai Radical Discourse: The Real Face of Thai Feudalism Today,* Craig J.
Reynolds. 1987. 2nd printing 1994. 186 pp. ISBN 0-87727-702-8.

Number 1   *The Symbolism of the Stupa,* Adrian Snodgrass. 1985. Revised with
index, 1988. 3rd printing 1998. 469 pp. ISBN 0-87727-700-1.

SEAP Series

Number 19   *Gender, Household, State: Đổi Mới in Việt Nam,* ed. Jayne Werner and
Danièle Bélanger. 2002. 151 pp. ISBN 0-87727-137-2.

Number 18 *Culture and Power in Traditional Siamese Government*, Neil A. Englehart. 2001. 130 pp. ISBN 0-87727-135-6.

Number 17 *Gangsters, Democracy, and the State*, ed. Carl A. Trocki. 1998. Second printing, 2002. 94 pp. ISBN 0-87727-134-8.

Number 16 *Cutting across the Lands: An Annotated Bibliography on Natural Resource Management and Community Development in Indonesia, the Philippines, and Malaysia*, ed. Eveline Ferretti. 1997. 329 pp. ISBN 0-87727-133-X.

Number 15 *The Revolution Falters: The Left in Philippine Politics after 1986*, ed. Patricio N. Abinales. 1996. Second printing, 2002. 182 pp. ISBN 0-87727-132-1.

Number 14 *Being Kammu: My Village, My Life*, Damrong Tayanin. 1994. 138 pp., 22 tables, illus., maps. ISBN 0-87727-130-5.

Number 13 *The American War in Vietnam*, ed. Jayne Werner, David Hunt. 1993. 132 pp. ISBN 0-87727-131-3.

Number 12 *The Political Legacy of Aung San*, ed. Josef Silverstein. Revised edition 1993. 169 pp. ISBN 0-87727-128-3.

Number 10 *Studies on Vietnamese Language and Literature: A Preliminary Bibliography*, Nguyen Dinh Tham. 1992. 227 pp. ISBN 0-87727-127-5.

Number 9 *A Secret Past*, Dokmaisot, trans. Ted Strehlow. 1992. 2nd printing 1997. 72 pp. ISBN 0-87727-126-7.

Number 8 *From PKI to the Comintern, 1924–1941: The Apprenticeship of the Malayan Communist Party*, Cheah Boon Kheng. 1992. 147 pp. ISBN 0-87727-125-9.

Number 7 *Intellectual Property and US Relations with Indonesia, Malaysia, Singapore, and Thailand*, Elisabeth Uphoff. 1991. 67 pp. ISBN 0-87727-124-0.

Number 6 *The Rise and Fall of the Communist Party of Burma (CPB)*, Bertil Lintner. 1990. 124 pp. 26 illus., 14 maps. ISBN 0-87727-123-2.

Number 5 *Japanese Relations with Vietnam: 1951–1987*, Masaya Shiraishi. 1990. 174 pp. ISBN 0-87727-122-4.

Number 3 *Postwar Vietnam: Dilemmas in Socialist Development*, ed. Christine White, David Marr. 1988. 2nd printing 1993. 260 pp. ISBN 0-87727-120-8.

Number 2 *The Dobama Movement in Burma (1930–1938)*, Khin Yi. 1988. 160 pp. ISBN 0-87727-118-6.

Cornell Modern Indonesia Project Publications

Number 75 *A Tour of Duty: Changing Patterns of Military Politics in Indonesia in the 1990s*. Douglas Kammen and Siddharth Chandra. 1999. 99 pp. ISBN 0-87763-049-6.

Number 74 *The Roots of Acehnese Rebellion 1989–1992*, Tim Kell. 1995. 103 pp. ISBN 0-87763-040-2.

Number 73 *"White Book" on the 1992 General Election in Indonesia*, trans. Dwight King. 1994. 72 pp. ISBN 0-87763-039-9.

Number 72 *Popular Indonesian Literature of the Qur'an*, Howard M. Federspiel. 1994. 170 pp. ISBN 0-87763-038-0.

Number 71 *A Javanese Memoir of Sumatra, 1945–1946: Love and Hatred in the Liberation War*, Takao Fusayama. 1993. 150 pp. ISBN 0-87763-037-2.

Number 70   *East Kalimantan: The Decline of a Commercial Aristocracy*, Burhan Magenda. 1991. 120 pp. ISBN 0-87763-036-4.

Number 69   *The Road to Madiun: The Indonesian Communist Uprising of 1948*, Elizabeth Ann Swift. 1989. 120 pp. ISBN 0-87763-035-6.

Number 68   *Intellectuals and Nationalism in Indonesia: A Study of the Following Recruited by Sutan Sjahrir in Occupation Jakarta*, J. D. Legge. 1988. 159 pp. ISBN 0-87763-034-8.

Number 67   *Indonesia Free: A Biography of Mohammad Hatta*, Mavis Rose. 1987. 252 pp. ISBN 0-87763-033-X.

Number 66   *Prisoners at Kota Cane*, Leon Salim, trans. Audrey Kahin. 1986. 112 pp. ISBN 0-87763-032-1.

Number 65   *The Kenpeitai in Java and Sumatra*, trans. Barbara G. Shimer, Guy Hobbs, intro. Theodore Friend. 1986. 80 pp. ISBN 0-87763-031-3.

Number 64   *Suharto and His Generals: Indonesia's Military Politics, 1975–1983*, David Jenkins. 1984. 4th printing 1997. 300 pp. ISBN 0-87763-030-5.

Number 62   *Interpreting Indonesian Politics: Thirteen Contributions to the Debate, 1964–1981*, ed. Benedict Anderson, Audrey Kahin, intro. Daniel S. Lev. 1982. 3rd printing 1991. 172 pp. ISBN 0-87763-028-3.

Number 60   *The Minangkabau Response to Dutch Colonial Rule in the Nineteenth Century*, Elizabeth E. Graves. 1981. 157 pp. ISBN 0-87763-000-3.

Number 59   *Breaking the Chains of Oppression of the Indonesian People: Defense Statement at His Trial on Charges of Insulting the Head of State, Bandung, June 7–10, 1979*, Heri Akhmadi. 1981. 201 pp. ISBN 0-87763-001-1.

Number 57   *Permesta: Half a Rebellion*, Barbara S. Harvey. 1977. 174 pp. ISBN 0-87763-003-8.

Number 55   *Report from Banaran: The Story of the Experiences of a Soldier during the War of Independence*, Maj. Gen. T. B. Simatupang. 1972. 186 pp. ISBN 0-87763-005-4.

Number 52   *A Preliminary Analysis of the October 1 1965, Coup in Indonesia (Prepared in January 1966)*, Benedict R. Anderson, Ruth T. McVey, assist. Frederick P. Bunnell. 1971. 3rd printing 1990. 174 pp. ISBN 0-87763-008-9.

Number 51   *The Putera Reports: Problems in Indonesian-Japanese War-Time Cooperation*, Mohammad Hatta, trans., intro. William H. Frederick. 1971. 114 pp. ISBN 0-87763-009-7.

Number 50   *Schools and Politics: The Kaum Muda Movement in West Sumatra (1927–1933)*, Taufik Abdullah. 1971. 257 pp. ISBN 0-87763-010-0.

Number 49   *The Foundation of the Partai Muslimin Indonesia*, K. E. Ward. 1970. 75 pp. ISBN 0-87763-011-9.

Number 48   *Nationalism, Islam and Marxism*, Soekarno, intro. Ruth T. McVey. 1970. 2nd printing 1984. 62 pp. ISBN 0-87763-012-7.

Number 43   *State and Statecraft in Old Java: A Study of the Later Mataram Period, 16th to 19th Century*, Soemarsaid Moertono. Revised edition 1981. 180 pp. ISBN 0-87763-017-8.

Number 39   Preliminary Checklist of Indonesian Imprints (1945-1949), John M. Echols. 186 pp. ISBN 0-87763-025-9.

Number 37   *Mythology and the Tolerance of the Javanese*, Benedict R. O'G. Anderson. 2nd edition, 1996. 104 pp., 65 illus. ISBN 0-87763-041-0.

Number 25   *The Communist Uprisings of 1926–1927 in Indonesia: Key Documents*, ed., intro. Harry J. Benda, Ruth T. McVey. 1960. 2nd printing 1969. 177 pp. ISBN 0-87763-024-0.

Number 7   *The Soviet View of the Indonesian Revolution*, Ruth T. McVey. 1957. 3rd printing 1969. 90 pp. ISBN 0-87763-018-6.

Number 6   *The Indonesian Elections of 1955*, Herbert Feith. 1957. 2nd printing 1971. 91 pp. ISBN 0-87763-020-8.

Translation Series

Volume 4   *Approaching Suharto's Indonesia from the Margins*, ed. Takashi Shiraishi. 1994. 153 pp. ISBN 0-87727-403-7.

Volume 3   *The Japanese in Colonial Southeast Asia*, ed. Saya Shiraishi, Takashi Shiraishi. 1993. 172 pp. ISBN 0-87727-402-9.

Volume 2   *Indochina in the 1940s and 1950s*, ed. Takashi Shiraishi, Motoo Furuta. 1992. 196 pp. ISBN 0-87727-401-0.

Volume 1   *Reading Southeast Asia*, ed. Takashi Shiraishi. 1990. 188 pp.
ISBN 0-87727-400-2.

Language Texts

INDONESIAN

Beginning Indonesian through Self-Instruction, John U. Wolff, Dédé Oetomo, Daniel Fietkiewicz. 3rd revised edition 1992. Vol. 1. 115 pp. ISBN 0-87727-529-7. Vol. 2. 434 pp. ISBN 0-87727-530-0. Vol. 3. 473 pp. ISBN 0-87727-531-9.

Indonesian Readings, John U. Wolff. 1978. 4th printing 1992. 480 pp. ISBN 0-87727-517-3

Indonesian Conversations, John U. Wolff. 1978. 3rd printing 1991. 297 pp. ISBN 0-87727-516-5

Formal Indonesian, John U. Wolff. 2nd revised edition 1986. 446 pp. ISBN 0-87727-515-7

TAGALOG

Pilipino through Self-Instruction, John U. Wolff, Maria Theresa C. Centeno, Der-Hwa V. Rau. 1991. Vol. 1. 342 pp. ISBN 0-87727—525-4. Vol. 2. 378 pp. ISBN 0-87727-526-2. Vol 3. 431 pp. ISBN 0-87727-527-0. Vol. 4. 306 pp. ISBN 0-87727-528-9.

THAI

A. U. A. Language Center Thai Course, J. Marvin Brown. Originally published by the American University Alumni Association Language Center, 1974. Reissued by Cornell Southeast Asia Program, 1991, 1992. Book 1. 267 pp. ISBN 0-87727-506-8. Book 2. 288 pp. ISBN 0-87727-507-6. Book 3. 247 pp. ISBN 0-87727-508-4.

A. U. A. Language Center Thai Course, Reading and Writing Text (mostly reading), 1979. Reissued 1997. 164 pp. ISBN 0-87727-511-4.

A. U. A. Language Center Thai Course, Reading and Writing Workbook (mostly writing), 1979. Reissued 1997. 99 pp. ISBN 0-87727-512-2.

KHMER

Cambodian System of Writing and Beginning Reader, Franklin E. Huffman. Originally
published by Yale University Press, 1970. Reissued by Cornell Southeast Asia
Program, 4th printing 2002. 365 pp. ISBN 0-300-01314-0.

Modern Spoken Cambodian, Franklin E. Huffman, assist. Charan Promchan, Chhom-
Rak Thong Lambert. Originally published by Yale University Press, 1970.
Reissued by Cornell Southeast Asia Program, 3rd printing 1991. 451 pp. ISBN
0-300-01316-7.

Intermediate Cambodian Reader, ed. Franklin E. Huffman, assist. Im Proum. Originally
published by Yale University Press, 1972. Reissued by Cornell Southeast Asia
Program, 1988. 499 pp. ISBN 0-300-01552-6.

Cambodian Literary Reader and Glossary, Franklin E. Huffman, Im Proum. Originally
published by Yale University Press, 1977. Reissued by Cornell Southeast Asia
Program, 1988. 494 pp. ISBN 0-300-02069-4.

HMONG

White Hmong-English Dictionary, Ernest E. Heimbach. 1969. 8th printing, 2002. 523 pp.
ISBN 0-87727-075-9.

VIETNAMESE

Intermediate Spoken Vietnamese, Franklin E. Huffman, Tran Trong Hai. 1980. 3rd
printing 1994. ISBN 0-87727-500-9.

* * *

Southeast Asian Studies: Reorientations. Craig J. Reynolds and Ruth McVey. Frank H.
Golay Lectures 2 & 3. 70 pp. ISBN 0-87727-301-4.

Javanese Literature in Surakarta Manuscripts, Nancy K. Florida. Vol. 1, *Introduction and
Manuscripts of the Karaton Surakarta*. 1993. 410 pp. Frontispiece, illustrations.
Hard cover, ISBN 0-87727-602-1, Paperback, ISBN 0-87727-603-X. Vol. 2,
Manuscripts of the Mangkunagaran Palace. 2000. 576 pp. Frontispiece,
illustrations. Paperback, ISBN 0-87727-604-8.

Sbek Thom: Khmer Shadow Theater. Pech Tum Kravel, trans. Sos Kem, ed. Thavro
Phim, Sos Kem, Martin Hatch. 1996. 363 pp., 153 photographs. ISBN 0-87727-
620-X.

In the Mirror: Literature and Politics in Siam in the American Era, ed. Benedict R. O'G.
Anderson, trans. Benedict R. O'G. Anderson, Ruchira Mendiones. 1985. 2nd
printing 1991. 303 pp. Paperback. ISBN 974-210-380-1.

To order, please contact:

Cornell University
SEAP Distribution Center
369 Pine Tree Rd.
Ithaca, NY 14850-2819 USA

Online: http://www.einaudi.cornell.edu/southeastasia/publications/
Tel: 1-877-865-2432 (Toll free – U.S.)
Fax: (607) 255-7534

E-mail: SEAP-Pubs@cornell.edu
Orders must be prepaid by check or credit card (VISA, MasterCard, Discover).